S. SWEET LAW BOOKSELLER No
3, CHANCERY LANE
IN 1799

Ex Libris

ELEMENTS OF ROMAN LAW

AUSTRALIA
The Law Book Company Ltd.
Sydney: Melbourne: Brisbane: Perth

CANADA
The Carswell Company Ltd.
Toronto: Calgary: Vancouver: Ottawa

INDIA
N. M. Tripathi Private Ltd.
Bombay
and
Eastern Law House Private Ltd.
Calcutta

M.P.P. House
Bangalore

ISRAEL
Steimatzky's Agency Ltd.
Tel Aviv

PAKISTAN
Pakistan Law House
Karachi

CUPIDAE LEGUM JUVENTUTI

THE
ELEMENTS OF ROMAN LAW

with a translation
of the

INSTITUTES OF JUSTINIAN

By

R. W. LEE, D.C.L., F.B.A.
Reader in Roman Law of the Inns of Court

FOURTH EDITION

LONDON
SWEET & MAXWELL LIMITED
11 NEW FETTER LANE
1956

First Edition 1944
Reprinted 1945
Reprinted 1946
Reprinted with corrections 1946
Second Edition 1949
Third Edition 1952
Fourth Edition 1956
Second Impression 1960
Third Impression 1986
Fourth Impression 1987
Fifth Impression 1990
Sixth Impression 1993

Printed in Great Britain

ISBN 0 421 01780 5

PREFACE

THIS book was published in 1944 and met with a very gratifying reception, Professor Beinaart reviewing the third edition spoke of " this delightful textbook." The sales have been continuous and have been extended to every part of the world. Evidently the book supplied what students wanted. But did it, perhaps, supply some of them with more than they wanted ? The author has felt a very active sympathy with students who came to Roman Law for the first time and were cast adrift on an uncharted sea. To meet this case, in imitation of other textbooks, the author has attempted to distinguish between what is essential and what is unessential, or, at least, between what a student may, at first, safely regard as the one or the other. Obviously the line is arbitrary, no two persons would agree as to it. But it is offered as an aid. There is no difference of type except that the less essential passages are more closely packed.

But there is more than this in the new edition. To avoid raising the price of the book the publishers had in previous reissues set the narrowest limits to the permissible amount of the alterations of the text. As in this edition the book has been completely reset the author has been free to rewrite his book as he pleases. He has exercised his freedom with restraint. There have been additions, rearrangements and so forth with the principal object of making the subject reasonably plain to the intelligent reader. But the general character of the book remains unchanged.

For the purpose of this edition the reader is assumed to have a competent knowledge of Latin. A Vocabulary explaining the meaning of Latin words and phrases is provided for those not so fortunately placed.

The author is indebted to Mr. A. D. Hughes, B.A., of Brasenose College for valuable help in proof-correcting.

R. W. L.

ALL SOULS COLLEGE,
OXFORD,
October, 1955.

EXTRACT FROM
PREFACE TO FIRST EDITION

MANY books have been written in English on Roman Law. Most of them have been soon forgotten. This might serve as a warning to anyone who proposes to add to their number. But the circumstances of the time and the convenience of students may justify the venture. In the Inns of Court and in our Universities law students are required to submit to an examination in Roman Law. Sometimes this implies knowledge of a Latin text, sometimes not. Since Latin today, unfortunately, no longer holds its former place in a general education, few will go to the original sources unless they are required to do so, and even then the study of the text is too often reluctant and perfunctory. To me at least it seems lamentable that anyone should be credited with a knowledge of Roman Law who has not read Justinian's Institutes. If students cannot or will not read the original, they may, perhaps, be induced to read a translation. The study of the Institutes demands an Introduction and a Commentary. The works of Moyle and Sandars are available. but are not calculated to attract students who know little Latin and who do not intend to devote much of their life to the study of Roman Law. William Murray (afterwards Lord Mansfield) did well when he advised the young Duke of Portland to " read and study Justinian's Institutes without any other comment than the short one of Vinnius." [1] This is a little duodecimo volume containing the text with Latin notes. But even this goes beyond what is required today. In this book I have tried to combine commentary and text so that the first will supply what is wanted to make the second intelligible and to place it in a right perspective. I have put in the margin of the commentary references to the text and in the margin of the text references to the commentary. It is hoped that students will make it their practice to go from one to the other. The next step will be to refer to the passages cited in the margin or at the foot of the page from the Institutes of Gaius. Some will perhaps go further and turn up a passage in the Digest or the Code.

Much has been written on the existing crisis in the study of Roman Law. The trouble is that for the first time in its history an unbridgeable gulf separates the expert scholar from the docile student who is not concerned with critical dissection of Latin texts and who looks to scholars to communicate their conclusions, if and when they reach them. With this reservation the study of Roman Law remains what it always has been and carries on its secular tradition.

---

[1] Fifoot, *Lord Mansfield*, p. 29.

The reasons which justify it, particularly for students who breathe a Common Law atmosphere, are principally these:—

1. Roman Law is one of the great things which have happened in the world. It is part of a liberal education to know something about it.

2. Roman Law is an introduction to the study of the Science of Law, or, as we call it, Jurisprudence. For many centuries the Science of Law *was* Roman Law. If in modern times it has widened its outlook and improved its methods its debt to Roman Law remains unquestioned.

3. Roman Law is a key to the terminology and, to a great extent, to the substance of foreign systems.

4. Roman Law enlarges the mind. Burke has well said that " the science of law does more to strengthen the mind than to liberalise it." The study of Roman Law liberalises the mind by expanding the range of vision.

To return to the subject of this book. The whole of the Institutes is not of equal interest. The parts which seem to me of less importance are printed in smaller type. The text is sometimes verbose. I have not hesitated upon occasion to trim the feathers of the imperial eagle. But the whole has been translated with a few trifling omissions. The sequence of the Titles has been changed to accommodate it to the order of treatment in the commentary. I have included some translated extracts from Gaius, in particular his account of the formula. The few remarks on the modern law interspersed through the book are intended not to furnish precise information so much as to direct attention to some features in the landscape. It may be that many of my readers will read no other book on Roman Law than this. If they retain in their memories something worth having I shall have achieved my purpose.

June, 1944.

CONTENTS

SUMMARY OF TEXT

BOOK I

THE LAW OF PERSONS

BOOK II

THE LAW OF PROPERTY

BOOK III

THE LAW OF SUCCESSION

THE INSTITUTES OF JUSTINIAN

CONTENTS

BOOK III

BOOK IV

CHRONOLOGY

THE EMPIRE

FIRST IMPERIAL PERIOD—THE DIARCHY

AUGUSTUS ...	B.C. 27–A.D. 14	
TIBERIUS	... 14–37	
GAIUS (CALIGULA) ...	... 37–41	
CLAUDIUS	... 41–54	
NERO	... 54–68	

GALBA	68–69	
OTHO	69	
VITELLIUS	69	
VESPASIAN	69–79	
TITUS	78–81	
DOMITIAN	81–96	
NERVA	96–98	
TRAJAN	98–117	
HADRIAN	117–138	
ANTONINUS PIUS ...	138–161	
MARCUS AURELIUS ...	161–180	
COMMODUS	180–192	

SECOND IMPERIAL PERIOD—ABSOLUTE MONARCHY

THE DIVIDED EMPIRE

West

East

Legislation of Theodosius II

CITATIONS AND ABBREVIATIONS

Arangio-Ruiz, Istituzioni del Diritto Romano.
——, Storia del Diritto Romano.
Bruns, Fontes Juris Romani Antiqui.
Buckland, Manual of Roman Private Law, 2nd ed. 1939.
——, Text-Book of Roman Law from Augustus to Justinian, 2nd ed. 1932.
Buckland and McNair, Roman Law and Common Law.
Bürgerliches Gesetzbuch für das Deutsche Reich [B.G.B.]·
Code Civil (français) [C.C.].
Code Civil Suisse [Swiss C.C.].
Codex Juris Canonici.
Collatio Legum Mosaicarum et Romanarum [Coll.].
Corbett, The Roman Law of Marriage.
Girard, Manuel élémentaire de Droit Romain (éd. 8).
——, Textes de Droit Romain (éd. 5).
Greenidge, Roman Public Life.
Halsbury-Hailsham, Laws of England.
Holdsworth, A History of English Law.
Hunter, A Systematic and Historical Exposition of Roman Law.
Jolowicz, Historical Introduction to the Study of Roman Law.
——, Digest 47.2, De Furtis, edited with translation and commentary.
Jörs-Kunkel, Römisches Privatrecht, Berlin, 1935.
Lawson, Negligence in the Civil Law.
Lee, An Introduction to Roman-Dutch Law, 5th ed.
Monro, The Digest of Justinian translated (to Book XV, Title IV).
——, Digest XLI. 1, edited with translation and notes.
Moyle, The Institutes of Justinian; text commentary and translation.
Novels of the Emperor Theodosius II [Nov. Theod.].
Pauli Sententiae [Paul. Sent.].
Planiol Ripert-Boulanger, Traité élémentaire de Droit Civil.
Roby, Roman Private Law in the times of Cicero and of the Antonines.
Sandars, The Institutes of Justinian with English Introduction, Translation
          and Notes.
Schulz, History of Roman Legal Science.
——, Classical Roman Law [Schulz].
Sohm-Mitteis-Wenger, Institutionen des Römischen Rechts (1933).
Sohm's Institutes of Roman Law, translated by Ledlie, 3rd ed., 1907.
Ulpian, Liber Singularis Regularum [Ulp.].
Vaticana Fragmenta [Vat.].
Walker, Dig. XLI. 1 and 2, translated and annotated.
Windscheid, Lehrbuch des Pandektenrechts, 9te aufl. Th. Kipp, 1906.
Zulueta, de, Digest 41. 1 and 2, Translation and Commentary.
——, The Roman Law of Sale.
——, The Institutes of Gaius, Part I, Text and Translation;
                              Part II, Commentary.

ELEMENTS OF ROMAN LAW

INTRODUCTION

I. HISTORICAL SKETCH

1. THE REGAL PERIOD.—According to the traditional story Rome was founded in B.C. 753, and from that date until B.C. 509 was ruled by kings. This is the earliest or regal period of Roman history. But since most ancient monuments and records must have perished when Rome was burnt by the Gauls,[1] *circ.* B.C. 390, and what passes for the history of this time was largely a fabrication of later ages, or at best a vague tradition, adorned with stories of gods and heroes, we cannot have any exact knowledge of the course of events. We may, however, form some picture of the state of society. The law was customary, not enacted, and when we find rules or institutions attributed to Romulus or another of the early kings all that we can conclude is that they were of a high antiquity, or, at least, were thought to be so in later ages. The social unit was the patriarchal family, in which the highest living ascendant was sole proprietor[2] and at the same time judge and priest. Kinship was agnatic, that is, reckoned exclusively through males. The family consisted of a group subject to the power of a living male ascendant (paterfamilias). The agnates comprised these and all others known to be descended through males from a common ancestor no longer living. Outside these was the gens or clan, whose members had a common name and a common worship, and supposed themselves related to one another by descent from a common ancestor, though the relationship was imaginary or too remote to be traced.

2. KING—SENATE—PEOPLE.—The organisation of the community was of a type which is not uncommon in primitive societies, and is familiar to readers of Homer's Iliad. It consisted of three elements—King, Council or Senate, and People. The king held office for life, chosen by the people, or nominated

---

[1] Liv. 6. 1.
[2] Or " visible steward of the family possessions." Maine, *Ancient Law.* p. 248. *Cf.* Inst. 2. 19. 2.

by his predecessor.[3] He was leader in war, chief judge and
chief priest. The Senate was an advisory body, chosen by, or
imposed upon, the king. The popular element was the Comitia
or Assembly of the People. The People was distributed into
thirty lesser units, called curiae, and the assembly was similarly
constituted, each curia casting one vote. What the curia was is
a question on which there is no general agreement. It may have
been based on kinship. It may have been a local division, as we
speak of a parish or ward ; it may have been both. This body
—the comitia curiata—is represented as giving its assent to
measures proposed to it by the king (§ 6) ; but it is more
probable that it rarely, if ever, passed laws of general application ; its function was rather, as in later times, to authorise
particular departures from settled custom, e.g., to allow a citizen
to adopt into his family, and therefore into his potestas (§ 86),
another citizen of independent status (adrogatio: § 107), or to
sanction a disposition of property by will (testamentum comitiis
calatis, § 278), contrary to the usual rule of intestacy, or to give
effect to other processes intimately connected with the
constitution of the Roman family.

3. PATRICIANS—PLEBEIANS—CLIENTS.—Many doubts exist as
to the composition of the citizen body in this early period. We
read of patricians, plebeians, and clients, but the nature and
origin of these distinctions are obscure. It was formerly thought
that the patricians constituted the original citizen body, and that
the plebeians consisted of a rabble of fugitive aliens or manumitted slaves without civic rights or duties. But this view has
not remained unquestioned. It is said that the distinction
between patricians and plebeians " appears as far back in Roman
history as we can go, and in all times of which we know anything for certain, the plebeians were citizens—unprivileged
citizens, no doubt, but not mere resident foreigners." [4] The
clients may be regarded as occupying an intermediate position.
They enjoyed the protection of the patrician houses at the
expense of personal dependence. Every client had his patron.
The bond which united them was held to be sacred. The Law
of the Twelve Tables declared accursed the patron who wronged
a client and Virgil in the Aeneid assigns to him a special place
in hell.[5] The institution of clientage was not peculiar to Rome ;
it occurs also in Latium generally, and other parts of Italy, and

---

[3] Jolowicz, *Historical Introduction to the Study of Roman Law*, p. 17.
[4] Jolowicz, p. 8.
[5] Aeneid, vi. 609.

in Greece. Indeed, such a relation easily arises wherever economic and social conditions weigh heavily upon a section of the community.

4. THE SERVIAN CONSTITUTION.—Servius Tullius, the last but one of the seven kings of Rome, is credited with the creation of a new popular assembly, part of the so-called Servian constitution, which may, however, belong to a later date. The Roman army was made up of companies of a hundred men called "centuries," and the Assembly, which was only the army under another name, was similarly organised under the name of Comitia Centuriata (Assembly of the Centuries). It consisted of ten centuries of cavalry (equites), rich patricians, and of the main body of infantry, distributed in five Classes progressively diminishing in wealth, subdivided into centuries (in the first 80, in the second, third and fourth 20, in the fifth 30). The whole scheme depended upon the ownership of land, later of property in general.[6] Voting was by centuries and began with the equites. If they and the centuries of the first class were of one mind, as they usually would be, this secured an absolute majority of votes and the lower classes were not asked to express their opinions. It is plain that the system was nicely calculated to give a preponderating influence to the comfortable citizens of the first class, particularly if we consider that the impressive number of centuries assigned to them may have consisted largely of *cadres* which were never brought up to strength. But, however that may be, the Comitia Centuriata was always the army and as such met outside the City, usually in the Campus Martius. This condition attached to it until it expired in the first century of the Empire.

5. ECLIPSE OF COMITIA CURIATA.—The new assembly pushed the comitia curiata into the background. This lost any legislative functions it may have had, but continued to be convoked to give formal authority to the higher magistrates at the beginning of their term of office (lex curiata de imperio), and under the name of comitia calata so late as the time of Gaius (§ 48) still met to give formal sanction to adrogations and wills,[7] and for other purposes affecting the family religion or otherwise of religious significance.[7a] These proceedings were controlled by the college of pontiffs, but the fiction of an assembly of the

---

[6] Jolowicz, p. 19.
[7] G. 1. 99; 2. 101.
[7a] According to Livy (v. 46) Camillus was recalled from exile in 399 B.C. by a resolution of the comitia curiata. This is the last recorded instance of its concern with public affairs.

curiae was maintained by the attendance of thirty lictors, one from each curia. Cicero refers to this practice in connection with a meeting of the comitia curiata held for the purpose of taking the auspices.[8] The farce was carried still further when it was possible to suggest that three augurs had been asked to swear to a meeting of the comitia which in fact had never taken place.[9]

6. LEGES REGIAE.—We have observed above that it is unlikely that there was anything that could be called legislation in the period of the kings. However, Pomponius, a jurist of the time of Hadrian, who, in a long passage cited in the Digest is our principal source of information as to this early period of legal history, tells us that Romulus and the later kings laid projects of law before the comitia curiata. " All of these," he says, " are extant in the book of Sextus Papirius," whom he describes as contemporary with the last king of Rome, and who may be the same as a Papirius elsewhere mentioned as first pontifex maximus of the Republic. " This book," he continues, " is called the jus civile Papirianum ; not that Papirius introduced into it anything of his own, but because he reduced to order statutes which had been passed without system." [10] If this is true, enacted law goes back to the time of the kings ; but the story is generally discredited, and it is thought that the collection in question was made in a much later age. In any event, it was probably of a religious character or belonged to " the borderland between law and religion." [11]

7. THE ROMAN REPUBLIC.—The monarchy came to an end—so the story goes—with the expulsion in B.C. 509 of Tarquinius Superbus, the last of the kings. The single ruler with a life tenure was replaced by two annual officers called at first praetors, later consuls. A phantom king was retained for religious purposes. " In order that the national gods might not refuse to the kingless city the protection which they gave to the royal city the so-called rex sacrorum was left in the ancient royal residence called the regia." [12] But all other functions of kingship passed to the new officers. An important consequence of the substitution of two annual magistrates for the single magistrate holding office for life was the increased power of the

[8] Cic. de leg. agr. II. 12. 31.
[9] Cic. Epist. ad Attic IV. 17 (18). 2
[10] Dig. 1. 2. 2, 2.
[11] Jolowicz, p. 84.
[12] Girard, p. 22, also called rex sacrificulus, Liv. 2. 2.

Senate, which was the most permanent element in the constitution. Its members were nominated by the consuls, later by the censors (§ 23). In practice it came to consist, for the most part, of ex-magistrates. Originally a purely patrician body, it changed its character as plebeians, in the course of a long struggle between the two " orders," obtained access to the higher magistracies. It was the practice for the magistrates to consult the Senate on all matters of importance, so that it became the permanent executive of the Roman State. This body, or, more precisely, its patrician nucleus, gave a formal sanction to laws passed by the assembly. This was called the auctoritas patrum. By the lex Publilia Philonis of B.C. 339 it had to be given before, not after, a measure had been submitted to the people. It is commonly said that this law reduced the privilege of the patrician members of the Senate to a mere formality. Whether it did so or not, the rapidly increasing preponderance of plebeians in the Senate soon had this effect.[13]

8. LEX-PLEBISCITUM.—Another consequence of the abolition of the monarchy was the increased importance of the popular assembly. Its functions were electoral, legislative and judicial. It elected the consuls. It passed laws of general application. By a measure under the name of lex Valeria de provocatione attributed to the first year of the Republic, but probably of later date, it entertained appeals from capital sentences passed upon a citizen. Early in the Republic a new body came into existence called the comitia tributa, an assembly of the people organised on a basis of tribes or local divisions. Distinct from this, again, was a body called the meeting of the plebs (concilium plebis), which consisted exclusively of plebeians. It chose the tribunes (§ 25), and passed resolutions called plebiscita, which originally bound the plebeians only, but by the lex Hortensia of B.C. 287 were made binding upon the whole people and so acquired the force of law.[14] The same effect is attributed to two earlier statutes (one more instance of the uncertainty which attaches to all this period of Roman history). We get the surprising result that part of the community asserted and secured power to legislate for the whole, and that there were four types of assembly in theory or in fact competent to make laws for the whole people, viz., 1, comitia curiata ; 2, comitia centuriata ; 3, comitia tributa ; 4, concilium plebis. But the first, as we have seen, was a legislative body in form only, while the second and

---

[13] Greenidge, p. 125.
[14] Inst. 1. 2. 4.

third were the popular assembly variously organised. In the second half of the third century B.C. a measure of reform, of which the details are obscure, reorganised the comitia centuriata so as to bring it into conformity with the distribution of the people in tribes with a consequent increase in the influence upon the vote of the inferior classes in the Servian constitution.[15] Before Mommsen (§ 36), the distinction between the comitia tributa populi and the concilium plebis had escaped the attention of historians, and with the constant diminution in the number of the patrician families was, in fact, ultimately of little importance. But these bodies were formally distinct, and continued to be so until they ceased to function in the early days of the Empire.[16] The comitia centuriata was convoked (usually) by a consul (§ 20), the comitia tributa by a consul or praetor (§ 21), the concilium plebis by a tribune (§ 25). In the later Republic the concilium plebis was the normal vehicle of legislation, and its enactments were termed leges (no longer plebiscita). The comitia centuriata was summoned to vote upon questions of peace or war, or otherwise of constitutional importance, and once in every four or five years passed the law which invested the censors with their functions (lex de censoria potestate).

9. SENATUSCONSULTA.—In addition to the above-mentioned modes of legislation, the Senate by virtue of its authority as the motive power of the executive, passed resolutions called senatusconsulta, which were directed to suspending the law in case of urgency or dispensing with it in favour of individuals,[17] or assumed the form of advice, practically instruction, to a magistrate. In particular, the Praetor, if desired to do so, would incorporate such a recommendation in his Edict (§ 14). This was, in effect, legislation promoted by the Senate. Under the early Empire senatusconsulta came to have an independent validity as a source of civil law (§ 26). But to conservative sentiment this seemed an encroachment upon the legislative prerogative of the Roman People, and so Gaius wrote: " A senatusconsultum is what is ordered and established by the Senate, and it has the force of a statute, though this was formerly called in question." [18] During the Republic in times of crisis the Senate on several occasions passed a resolution known as the senatusconsultum ultimum directing the consuls and other magistrates " to look to it that the commonwealth takes no harm." It

---

15 Girard, p. 26 ; Jolowicz, p. 20.
16 Greenidge, Appendix I.
17 Girard, p. 37.
18 G. 1. 4.

was in reliance upon such a resolution that Cicero, as consul, put to death without trial Catiline's principal associates in the conspiracy of B.C. 63. His enemies had their revenge five years later when they procured his banishment on the ground that he had exceeded his constitutional powers.[19]

10. THE TWELVE TABLES.—The first certain landmark in the history of Roman Law is the Law of the Twelve Tables. The plebeians complained that knowledge of the law was withheld from them, and that its administration by patrician consuls was arbitrary and tyrannical. In the year B.C. 462 Gaius Terentilius Arsa, one of the tribunes, proposed measures of reform. After ten years of fierce controversy and civil commotion an agreement was come to. Commissioners were to be appointed to draw up a code of laws. But first three delegates were sent to Greece to inquire into the laws and institutions of the Greek States and particularly to investigate the famous code of laws which Solon had given to Athens.[20] Such, at least, is Livy's account of the matter; how far historically correct is questioned. After the return of the commission ten men, all patricians, were appointed to hold office during the following year. There was to be no appeal to the people from their decisions, and the functions of the other magistrates were to be in suspense. The ten men— decem viri—commonly known as the " Decemvirs," drew up ten tables of laws which were submitted to and approved by the comitia centuriata (B.C. 451). But their task was incomplete. A new commission of ten, this time including some plebeians, was appointed for the following year. They produced two additional tables, which Cicero describes as of an inequitable character.[21] When their term of office was over, they continued to exercise a usurped authority during another year, until a popular rising overthrew them and re-established the old constitution (B.C. 449). Nevertheless, the newly elected consuls submitted to the comitia the two last Tables, which, together with the first ten, constituted " The Law of the Twelve Tables." This was looked upon by the Romans of later ages as the starting point of their legal history, " the fountain," Livy calls it, " of all public and private law." [22] When Cicero was young schoolboys learnt it by heart,[23] and it was commented upon by jurists of the late Republic and early Empire, including Labeo (§ 30) and

[19] Jolowicz, p. 34.
[20] Liv. 3. 31.
[21] Cic. de Rep. 11. 61. In particular, marriage between patricians and plebeians was prohibited. This was ended by the lex Canuleia (B.C. 445).
[22] Liv. 3. 34.
[23] Cic. De Leg. 2. 23. 59.

Gaius (§ 48). It remained formally in force until superseded by Justinian's legislation, nearly ten centuries later.

11. The Law of the Twelve Tables is usually spoken of as a code, but it was far from being a codification of the whole law. Perhaps it dealt with matters of current controversy and left untouched principles which had not been called in question. But as to this we have no certain knowledge, and we cannot say what changes the Tables made in the law. Our knowledge of their contents is derived from fragmentary citations, references and descriptions, to be found in legal literature, or in the works of Cicero and other ancient writers. Though, therefore, we have not enough material to reconstruct the Tables in their original form, and though we know little as to their order and arrangement, nevertheless the fragments which in one form or another have come down to us convey an impression which we can rely upon as tolerably complete and accurate. It is a picture of a primitive agricultural society, in which government has scarcely emerged from the stage of regulated self-help, in which law has not yet been disentangled from religion, in which the sinister exercise of magic is a thing to be guarded against and visited with religious sanctions. On the other hand, the provisions forbidding excessive expenditure on funerals, said to be derived from the laws of Solon, seem to point to increasing wealth and inequality in its distribution. Modern editors, beginning with Jacques Godefroy (Gothofredus) early in the seventeenth century, have attempted to assign the fragments to their appropriate Table and by so doing have, if nothing else, reduced them to system. They are found to relate to: Civil Procedure and Execution (Tables 1, 2 and 3); Patria potestas (Table 4); Tutelage, Inheritance and Property (Tables 5, 6 and 7); Crimes (Table 8); Public Law (Table 9); Sacred Law (Table 10); with two further Tables described as an appendix. But this reconstruction is wholly artificial, and is useful merely as a general indication of the scope of the decemviral legislation, so far as we have knowledge of its contents.

[The problem of the Twelve Tables raises many difficulties. Besides questions of date, text and interpretation there is the question of social and economic background. The late Professor Tenney Frank, who concluded from the evidence of archaeology that " at the close of the regal period Rome was a large and busy commmercial city," wrote " We must ask the students of law to modernise their ideas of what Rome was like in B.C. 450 and to interpret their fragments in the light of this new knowledge." (*Social Behaviour in Ancient Rome* (Harvard University Press, 1932, pp. 128, 125).) Mr.

A. S. Diamond in his challenging book *Primitive Law* (Longmans, Green & Co., 1935) reduces the Twelve Tables to "a school-book used by the priestly order," compiled from earlier materials about the year B.C. 190 (p. 142).]

12. INTERPRETATIO.—Law of whatever kind calls for interpretation, and those who are accepted as interpreters of the law necessarily influence its development. For about a century after the enactment of the Twelve Tables the interpretation of the law and of the actions founded upon it was in the hands of the college of pontiffs.[24] To this period may be referred a development of the law by legal fictions, that is, contrivances by which a legal rule or institution is diverted from its original purpose to accomplish indirectly some other object, as we shall see in the case of adoption (§ 113), emancipation (§ 118), and in jure cessio (§ 165).[25] The ascendancy of the pontiffs came to an end in B.C. 304 when, according to the story, one Gnaeus Flavius, secretary of Appius Claudius (censor in 312), stole his master's manuscript and made public the forms of action appropriate to each state of circumstances,[26] a secret up till then jealously guarded by the priesthood. Perhaps his master was privy to the "theft." This completed the process begun by the Twelve Tables. The law and above all its use in practice was no longer hidden in the bosom of the priests. From having been religious, it became secular, and public property. It is perhaps not unreasonable to see some connection between the publication of this so-called jus Flavianum and the lex Ogulnia of B.C. 300 which for the first time admitted plebeians to the pontifical college.[27] A further step in the same direction was taken by Tiberius Coruncanius, consul, B.C. 280, first plebeian pontifex maximus, B.C. 253, who, as Pomponius (§ 48) tells us, was the first to profess law publicly,[28] which seems to mean that he held himself out to give consultations accompanied by instruction to students of law, a sort of legal hospital practice. A second publication enlarging the work of Gnaeus Flavius, to which Pomponius gives the name of jus Aelianum,[29] is attributed to Sextus Aelius, consul B.C. 198. He was also (or is it another name for the same thing?) the author of a work called *Tripertita*,[30] which expounded the civil law under three heads,

---

[24] Dig. 1. 2. 2, 6.
[25] Girard, p. 49.
[26] Dig. 1. 2. 2, 7.
[27] Jolowicz, p. 88.
[28] Dig. 1. 2. 2, 35, 38.
[29] Dig. 1. 2. 2, 7.
[30] Dig. 1. 2. 2, 38.

1. The Law of the Twelve Tables ; 2. the interpretation of the same ; 3. statute actions (legis actiones, § 669). This was the earliest systematic treatise on the civil law, containing, as Pomponius says, " a cradle of the law." From this time forward lay jurists, unhampered by pontifical control, continued to influence the development of the civil law. It is significant that Pomponius describes the civil law as " that which consists without writing entirely in the interpretation of learned men." [31] There were in fact in these early days but two principal sources of law, custom and the Twelve Tables and of both the lawyers were the skilled interpreters. The contribution of the law-making bodies to the development of the law was relatively unimportant.

13. THE JURISTS AT WORK.—The jurists of this early period, who are referred to in later writings as the veteres, or ancients, engaged in activities which are described in semi-technical language as respondere, cavere, scribere, agere. They advised clients, or the magistrates, or judges (respondere). They saw that legal forms were properly employed and drafted legal instruments (cavere—scribere). They undertook the general conduct of litigation (agere).[32] But the task of argument in court was reserved to another class of men, known as advocates, who, as will appear from a story to be related below, were not always conspicuous for their knowledge of law. The earliest legal literature, as is always the case, consisted in books of practice, such as the Tripertita. Works of a scientific character belong to a later date. The family of the Mucii Scaevolae produced many distinguished lawyers. Publius Mucius Scaevola (consul B.C. 133, later pontifex maximus) and with him Brutus and Manilius, are named as " founders of the civil law." [33] But it was his son Quintus Mucius Scaevola, consul B.C. 95, and, like his father, pontifex maximus, who first made a digest of the civil law, which he arranged under heads in eighteen books.[34] This was the basis of most of the later works on the jus civile.[35] It is frequently cited by the writers of the classical period in the excerpts preserved in Justinian's Digest (§ 41).

14. MAGISTRATUUM EDICTA.—In the year 367 the measures of reform known as the Licinian Laws or Rogations proposed by the tribunes Sextius and Licinius had provided inter alia that

[31] Dig. 1. 2. 2, 12.
[32] Girard, p. 50 ; Buckl. M. p. 15.
[33] Dig. 1. 2. 2, 39.
[34] Dig. 1, 2, 2, 41.
[35] Jolowicz, p. 90.

one consul must always be a plebeian. Sextius himself was the first plebeian consul. The patricians sought to mitigate the effect of this enactment by creating new offices, the curule aedileship (of which we shall speak below) and the praetorship, reviving for this the name anciently borne by the consuls. The praetor was to be a colleague of the consuls, but specifically for the administration of justice.[36] This took effect in 366, or some years later. About 242 a second praetor was instituted to administer justice in cases in which one or both parties were aliens. The first came to be known as the praetor urbanus, the second as the praetor peregrinus. All the higher magistrates of the Roman People had authority to issue edicts or administrative orders dealing with matters within their competence, and the praetors, in particular after the lex Aebutia (§ 689), and perhaps before, at the beginning of their term of office issued an edict in which they stated the rules of procedure by which they intended to be governed in the coming year. These were inscribed on wooden tables in black letters with a white background (whence the description of the document as the praetor's album) with red captions (rubricae) and posted in the forum. This edict, being intended to remain in force during the praetor's year of office, was known as the perpetual edict (edictum perpetuum) by way of contrast with edicts of a merely occasional nature. As was natural, a praetor would adopt, in the main, the edict of his predecessor, modifying or enlarging it as seemed desirable. Thus the great mass of the edict went on unaltered from year to year and became a perpetual edict in a larger sense. In this connection it is called the edictum tralaticium, or the edict " handed on," while any new matter was known as edictum novum. But it happened from time to time that magistrates arbitrarily departed from the terms of their edict. Verres in Sicily had been particularly outrageous in this as in countless other matters. Accordingly a lex Cornelia of B.C. 67 required that praetors should abide by their edict during their term of office. This assured to the edict a stability which it was in danger of losing. The praetor could not, properly speaking, make law, because he had no legislative authority, but owing to his control of procedure he was able to make fundamental changes in the legal system, as, for instance, in the matter of intestate succession, and the praetor's edict became the source of a system of equity which existed side by side with the civil law without being absorbed in it, just as the equity of the English

---

[36] Praetorem jura reddentem et collegam consulibus. Liv. 7. 1.

Chancellor existed side by side with the common law. It was due to this influence more than to any other that the law of Rome was transformed from a narrow technical system into a system fit to meet the demands of a growing civilisation and an expanding empire. But the praetor in framing his edict did not exercise an arbitrary discretion. Though, like every educated Roman, he would have some knowledge of law, he was not necessarily a highly skilled lawyer. He was expected, therefore, to consult his consilium, a body of expert advisers, and he was, of course, controlled by public and professional opinion.[37]

15. The praetor's control of procedure was one aspect of the imperium or residuary sovereignty vested in the higher magistrates of the Roman People, a legacy, it is said, of the paramount authority of the kings. It assumed several forms. In particular, since the administration of justice was placed in his hands, it was within his competence to give or refuse an action (edere actionem—denegare actionem). If he said in his Edict judicium dabo or agere permittam he made law, not civil law but praetorian law. If he said potestatem agendi non faciam he did not indeed repeal the civil law, but checked its effect.

16. There were many other contrivances by which the praetor re-formed or developed the law. Such were the adaptation of civil law actions (§§ 698–9), the use of exceptions in the formula, particularly the exceptio doli and the exceptio pacti (§ 741), and a number of praetorian creations, particulars of which will be given in later pages—the interdict procedure, restitutio in integrum, missio in possessionem, praetorian stipulations (§§ 763 et seq.).

17. The outcome of the activities of successive generations of praetors was to bring into existence a supplementary body of law which came to be known as the jus honorarium or jus praetorium. It neither absorbed the civil law, nor was absorbed into it. Rather the two systems continued to exist side by side like two streams which pursue a common course without mingling their waters. This continued until, and even after, the Roman State had lost its identity in the Roman Empire. It is significant that the great jurists of the golden age, in particular Ulpian and Paul, are still found to be writing separate treatises on the Civil Law (libri ad Sabinum)) and on the Edict (libri ad Edictum). In precisely the same way we in England expect from our contemporary writers separate treatises on Common Law

---

[37] Maine, *Ancient Law*, p. 66.

and Equity. It is unnecessary at this stage to accumulate instances of this " dualism," as Professor Biondi calls it.[38] They will crowd upon the observation of the reader as he pursues his way through our pages.

18. Besides the edicts of the two praetors and a provincial edict which varied in detail in the several provinces,[39] there was the edict of the curule aediles (§ 22). These were officers charged with the police of the city and the control of the markets. Rules introduced by them in the law of sale have left their impress on those modern systems of law which have inherited the Roman tradition (§ 480). The law (for such in effect it was) [40] contained in the edicts was known as the jus 1. 2. 7. honorarium, because it proceeded from the holders of offices (honores). " The Edict," when the term is used without qualification, means the edict of the urban praetor.

19. The Edict, like the civil law, was the subject of systematic comment. The earliest treatise of the kind was the work of Servius Sulpicius Rufus, consul in B.C. 51, who " left two very short books bearing the title ' On the Edict ' " ; but he wrote much besides, for he is said to have left about one hundred and eighty books.[41] As an orator he enjoyed a reputation second, if to anyone, only to Cicero. He is said to have taken up the study of law in consequence of a reproach of Quintus Mucius, who said that it was a disgrace that a patrician, a noble and an advocate should be unacquainted with the law which was his daily concern. During the early Empire commentaries on the Edict occupied an important place in legal literature. It is sufficient to refer to that of Ulpian in 81, and that of Paul in 78, books, both of which were extensively drawn upon to supply the material of Justinian's Digest (§ 42). Gaius was the author of a treatise on the provincial edict in thirty books and of another in two books on the edict of the curule aediles. He also commented upon the Edict of the urban praetor in numerous separate titles. There is no record of a commentary upon the edict of the peregrine praetor, and, indeed, with regard to this surprisingly little is known.[42]

---

[38] See Biondi, *Istituzioni*, p. 66, to which I express my acknowledgments.

[39] Jolowicz, p. 368.

[40] Some claimed for the Edict that is was a lex annua. Cic. *in Verr.* 2. 1. 42 (109). But in *de Invent.* 2. 22. 67 Cicero ascribes the rules of the Edict to custom (consuetudo). Justinian includes magistratuum edicta under jus scriptum (§ 63).

[41] Dig. 1. 2. 2, 43, 44. " Books " means parchment rolls.

[42] Girard, p. 59, n. 3.

20. THE MAGISTRATES OF THE REPUBLIC.—Before passing from the Republic to the Empire, occasion may be taken to say a few words about the magistracies of the Republic, most of which have been incidentally mentioned already.[43] The principal inheritors of the royal authority and dignity were the two consuls elected by the comitia centuriata. They enjoyed equal powers. In the calendar the year was distinguished by their names. They convoked and initiated legislation in either comitia. In special emergencies, particularly in times of grave crisis, either consul might appoint a dictator who exercised supreme authority, but not beyond six months, unless re-appointed. This was, in effect, a temporary reversion to monarchy. Under the Empire the consulship became a dignified sinecure. The emperors made appointments to the office and frequently held it themselves. It was abolished by Justinian in A.D. 541, though later emperors continued to assume the title.

21. PRAETORS.—The praetors are described as colleagues, but minor colleagues, of the consuls. Like the consuls they were competent to command armies, to initiate legislation in either comitia, to summon, and transact business with, the Senate. But while the consuls exercised an unlimited imperium derived from the monarchy, the praetors, apart from these general powers, were confined to the special sphere of action assigned to them by lot after their election to office, and they were subject to the consular veto.[44] Mention has been made above of the two praetors who administered justice. Later, the number was increased to four (B.C. 227), to six (B.C. 198), and by Sulla (B.C. 81) to eight. It became the practice to retain them in Rome during their year of office to exercise civil and criminal jurisdiction. When their year of office was over they were, like ex-consuls, available to govern provinces or for other service abroad. Under the Empire a numerous body of praetors exercised judicial functions in the capital,[45] and we hear of special praetors appointed to deal with particular departments, such as the praetor tutelaris and the praetor fideicommissarius

---

[43] For further detail, see Greenidge, *Roman Public Life*, and Jolowicz, *Historical Introduction to Roman Law*.

[44] An amazing feature of the Roman constitution was the power of magistrates to forbid by anticipation or to annul *ex post facto* the acts of other magistrates of subordinate and in the second case also of equal authority. The first is coercitio, the second intercessio, but the term intercessio or " veto " is commonly applied to both. For particulars see Greenidge, pp. 173 *et seq*. The tribunician " veto " (§ 25) is a conspicuous instance.

[45] Jolowicz, p. 340.

(§ 758), charged respectively with jurisdiction in matters of guardianship and of fideicommissa (§ 360).

22. CURULE AEDILES.—The aediles were originally plebeian officers. From B.C. 366, the year which saw the institution of the praetorship, two other aediles were appointed with a superior status. They were magistrates of the Roman People and were distinguished by the name of "curule aediles" because, like the other higher magistrates, they sat in a chair of state (sella curulis). Reference has already been made to their control of the markets (§ 18).

23. CENSORS.—The censorship, instituted in B.C. 443, was an office of great dignity. The censors (two in number) were chosen every four or five years for the purpose of the census or roll of citizens. They assessed each person's means for purposes of taxation and assigned his place in century and tribe. They placed government contracts and let to farm the sources of revenue (§ 507). About a century after the institution of the office they acquired the important function of determining the composition of the Senate. This gave them the power of expulsion from, or refusal of admission to, that body, one aspect of the general control which they exercised over public morals.

24. QUAESTORS.—The office of quaestor goes back at least to the beginning of the Republic. Each year two quaestors were nominated by the consuls, later elected by the comitia tributa, to assist the consuls in matters of finance. This continued to be their principal concern, but they enlarged their functions as their numbers increased.[46] The quaestorship was not held in such high esteem as the other magistracies of the Roman People. Custom or law prescribed a regular succession of offices through which a Roman ambitious of public distinction rose to the high dignity of consul. This was known as the cursus honorum. The quaestorship ranked below the curule aedileship and praetorship, which with the consulship made up the "tergemini honores" of Horace.[47] The censorship and the office of pontifex maximus were usually the reward of elder statesmen, though Julius Caesar procured his election to the latter dignity at the early age of thirty-six (B.C. 63).

25. TRIBUNES.—The tribunate was a plebeian office, instituted, so we are told, on the occasion of the first "secession" of the plebs in the year B.C. 494 to protect the plebeians from the

---

[46] Jolowicz, p. 49.
[47] Odes. 1. 1. 8.

arbitrary authority of patrician consuls. The plebeians set up
for themselves on the " Sacred Mount," thus forcing the patricians to come to terms. The manoeuvre was repeated in 449
B.C. (second secession of the plebs). The tribunes were at first
two, or, as some say, five, later ten. Their person was sacrosanct
and consequently immune from arrest. From this seemingly
modest beginning they attained a position of formidable pre-
dominance and by their power to veto and annul the acts of
other magistrates (intercessio) found it only too easy to hold the
State to ransom in the interest of party. They acquired the
right to sit in the Senate [48] and (ultimately) to convoke it. They
convoked and initiated legislation in the concilium plebis. It is
significant of the importance attached to the office that Augustus
and succeeding emperors caused themselves to be invested for
life with tribunician authority. From the tribunes of the people
must be distinguished military tribunes with consular power
(tribuni militares consulari potestate). Though the consulship
is said to have been re-established after the expulsion of the
Decemvirs, it was in fact in abeyance more often than not
during the next eighty years.[49] In this period the two consuls
were frequently replaced by three or four or six military
tribunes. This contrivance provided more magistrates competent
to exercise supreme authority at home and in the field. Plebeians
were eligible, so that they gained access to consular power,
though not to consular office.[50]

26. TRANSITION TO EMPIRE—THE PRINCIPATE.—The Roman
Empire may be said to date from B.C. 27 when Octavian,[51]
great-nephew of C. Julius Caesar (murdered B.C. 44), who by his
will adopted him as his son and made him his heir, after crushing
the last of his rivals, Marcus Antonius (Mark Antony) in the
naval battle of Actium (B.C. 31), laid down the extraordinary
powers assumed during the civil wars and " restored the
Republic." [52] This (paradoxically) marks the beginning of the
Empire. The change was at first disguised. Octavian, better
known as Augustus (a title with religious associations which has
passed into a personal name), carefully retained the forms of
republican government, and by concentrating numerous offices in
his own hands gave a formal validity to his usurpation of

---

[48] By a plebiscitum Atinianum of the second century B.C.
[49] Jolowicz, p. 13.
[50] Livy, 4. 6 and 7.
[51] He was the son of C. Octavius. After adoption, in accordance with
the usual practice, he became Julius Octavianus.
[52] Jolowicz, p. 333 ; *Cambridge Ancient History*, vol. x, pp. 127 *et seq.*

power. This inaugurated the first imperial period, which lasted until the end of the third century. It was in form a joint rule of emperor and senate, to which the name has been given of diarchy or principate.

27. THE LEGAL SYSTEM UNDER THE EMPIRE.—In the first century of the Empire the old forms of legislation passed out of use (if we except the formal survival of the comitia curiata). Lex and plebiscitum ceased to be living sources of law, though Gaius, with a lawyer's conservatism, in the middle of the second century still speaks of them as such. They were replaced by senatusconsulta, but it was some time before these were recognised as definitely legislative in character, and not, as they had been under the Republic, directions to the magistrates. The earliest case of direct legislation by the Senate is said to be the S. C. Tertullianum of the reign of Hadrian (A.D. 117–38).[53] But 3. 3. 2. the senatusconsultum was in fact merely the expression of the Emperor's will. Indeed, the assent of the Senate became so completely a matter of form that the speech (oratio) in which the Emperor introduced a project of law to the Senate was regarded as having in itself binding force. Thus an important restriction on the administrative powers of tutors (§ 135) is attributed to an oratio of the Emperor Severus of A.D. 195.[54] The senatusconsultum persisted through the third century,[55] but was finally superseded by other forms of imperial legislation. The edicts of the praetors and the curule aediles continued to be issued year by year in the early Empire, and may have effected some small changes in the law, but even this ceased when the jurist Salvius Julianus at the instance of the Emperor Hadrian consolidated the edicts (circ. A.D. 130) and gave them a permanent form (edictum perpetuum or Salvianum). From this time the Edict ceased to be a living source of law. But commentaries on the Edict continued for some hundred years longer to develop the principles of Roman equity.

28. IMPERIAL CONSTITUTIONS.—It has been already remarked that senatusconsulta were, in effect, dictated by the Emperor. The direct expression of the imperial will assumed different forms, viz., judgments (decreta) ; answers to questions submitted (rescripta), which might be answers to magistrates sent by post (epistolae) or to private citizens (subscriptiones—so-called because the Emperor's reply was written at the foot of the

---

[53] Girard, p. 62 ; Jolowicz, p. 373.
[54] Dig. 27. 9. 1.
[55] Buckl. *T.* p. 15 ; *M.* p. 12.

petition); instructions to officials (mandata); and orders issued
in his capacity of chief magistrate (edicta). All these are known
collectively as constitutiones, and Gaius shortly describes constitutio as " that which the emperor ordains by decree, by edict
or by letter." It is remarkable that none of these processes was
exclusively legislative in character.[56] Whether in any case it
was intended to lay down a general rule had to be gathered from
the tenor of the constitution and the interpretation put upon it.
In the later Empire the different types of constitutio were merged
in the absolute power of the Emperor to legislate as he pleased.
The commonest forms were general laws (leges edictales or
generales) and rescripta.[57]

G. 1. 5.

29. RESPONSA PRUDENTIUM.—One more source of law
remains to mention, viz., responsa prudentium. After the
emancipation of the law from pontifical control a class of
professional jurists came into existence who held themselves out
to give opinions on points of law to all who sought their advice.
These opinions were called responsa. They were sometimes
collected by their author and published. Under the Empire this
came to be a frequent type of legal literature.[58] During the
Republic such opinions were unauthoritative. But the Emperor
Augustus introduced the practice that jurists should give their
answers by the Emperor's authority and under seal.[59] The
effect seems to have been to give special weight to the responsa
of a limited number of privileged jurists, who enjoyed what was
called the jus (publice) respondendi, i.e., the right of giving legal
opinions to all comers. Masurius Sabinus is said to have been
the first jurist to receive such a patent of precedence, not from
Augustus, however, but from his successor Tiberius. The
account of the matter given by Pomponius leaves much
unexplained. By the time of Gaius the replies of the jurists
(responsa prudentium) had attained such high authority that he
enumerates them amongst the sources of written law and
describes them as " the decisions and opinions of persons authorised to lay down the law " (sententiae et opiniones eorum quibus
permissum est jura condere). The practice of giving authorised
responsa faded out in the third century.[60]

G. 1. 7.

30. THE JURISTS—THE LAW OF CITATIONS.—To what extent
these opinions were authoritative is difficult to say. Gaius

---

[56] Jolowicz, p. 382.
[57] Jolowicz, p. 478.
[58] Girard, p. 71.
[59] Dig. 1. 2. 2, 49.
[60] Jolowicz, p. 372.

continues: " If they are unanimous they have the force of law ; if they disagree the judge may follow whichever opinion he chooses, as is ruled by a rescript of the Emperor Hadrian." Evidently, difficulty had arisen from the fact that the opinions of the jurists were frequently conflicting. But the question remains what opinions were counted. Perhaps, the rule meant that the judge was to take account of the opinions of living jurists who enjoyed the jus respondendi produced by the parties with regard to the matter in hand.[61] Later, the authority allowed to living jurists was extended to jurists who were no longer living, perhaps not necessarily only to such as had had the jus respondendi, and not only to responsa properly so-called, but to any of their published works. The result was that the law had to be extracted from a mass of legal literature, which, as we shall see, served as the foundation of Justinian's Digest (§ 42). These works of jurisprudence belong principally to the first 200 or 250 years of the Christian era. The rival schools of the Sabinians and Proculians, founded, it is said, by Capito and Labeo in the time of Augustus and carried on by Sabinus under Tiberius and Proculus under Nero, from whom they took their names, divided between them most or many of the jurists of the first century and a half of the Empire.[62] Gaius (§ 48) whose Institutes was written about A.D. 161, was one of the latest of the Sabinians. The greatest names in Roman jurisprudence gather round the end of the second and the beginning of the third century—Papinian, put to death in 212 by the Emperor Caracalla for refusing to justify the Emperor's murder of his brother Geta ; Ulpian, assassinated by the Praetorian Guard in 228 ; Paulus, a contemporary of Ulpian ; Modestinus, a pupil of Ulpian alive as late as 244, who passes for the last of the great classical jurists. In the late Empire the works of these and of other jurists were cited as authoritative in courts of law with the result that the ascertainment of the law from so incoherent a mass of material was matter of great difficulty, particularly in an age in which legal science was suffering a rapid decline. Various attempts were made to meet the situation. Thus, Constantine forbade the use of Ulpian's and Paul's notes on Papinian. Finally, in 426 the Emperors Theodosius II and Valentinian III attempted a comprehensive reform by the so-called Law of Citations.[63] This enacted in effect as follows :—(a) All writings of Papinian, Paul, Gaius, Ulpian and

---

[61] Girard, p. 77.
[62] Jolowicz, p. 388.
[63] Cod. Theod. 1. 4. 3 ; Sohm, translated by Ledlie, p. 119.

Modestinus are confirmed. Gaius is to have the same authority
as the others; (b) Citations made by any of the above from
earlier writers are also admitted, for example from Scaevola,
Sabinus, Julian and Marcellus, provided that, to overcome the
uncertainty which attaches to ancient writings, they are confirmed by a comparison of manuscripts; (c) If conflicting
opinions are produced, the majority is to prevail. If the
numbers on each side are equal, preference is to be given to the
view favoured by Papinian. If Papinian is silent, the judge may
choose for himself; (d) The notes of Ulpian and Paul on
Papinian are again declared inadmissible. Paul's *Sentences*
(§ 47) are to have authority. These provisions, by which
opinions are to be numbered not weighed, " mark probably,"
says Buckland, " the lowest point reached by Roman jurisprudence." [64]   But there was a lower point yet to come in the
age which followed the destruction of the Western Empire.

31. ABSOLUTE MONARCHY—THE DIVIDED EMPIRE.—More
and more, as time went on, the dual sovereignty of Senate and
Emperor, to which the name has been given of " diarchy " or
" principate," was transformed into an absolute monarchy. The
process was complete by the reign of Diocletian (284–305) or of
his successor Constantine. Diocletian divided the Empire into
four territories for the purpose of administration, and devised a
too ingenious scheme, designed to secure a peaceful succession to
the imperial throne. There were to be two Augusti and two
Caesars, each with his own sphere of government. When an
Augustus died or retired (for this also was part of the .cheme)
he was to be replaced by a Caesar, a new Caesar being appointed
to supply the vacancy. Diocletian, who abdicated the throne in
305 and died in 313, lived to see the failure of his plan. After
many years of war or insecure peace Constantine (called the
Great) reigned as sole Emperor from 324 to 337. By the " Edict
of Milan " (313) [65] Christianity was tolerated, though it was only
in the last twenty years of the century that pagan rites were
formally proscribed. In 330 Constantine transferred the capital
of the Empire to Byzantium (Constantinople). Diocletian's
abortive scheme foreshadowed the division of the Empire into
the Empires of East and West. The first formal partition took
place in 364 when Valentinian shared the Empire with his

---

[64] Buckl. *T.* p. 34.
[65] " When early in 313 Constantine met his ally Licinius at Milan a
policy of complete religious freedom was agreed upon. Technically there
was no Edict of Milan." It is " a symbolic representation of historical
truth," *Cambridge Ancient History*, xii, 686.

brother Valens. Theodosius I was, in effect, sole emperor from 392 to 395, but on his death the Empire was divided (this time finally) between his sons Arcadius and Honorius, who had been formally associated with their father during the last years of his life. In theory, however, the Empire remained one and indivisible. For some time legislation ran in the name of both emperors, and was promulgated and binding in both parts of the Empire. Later, as the separation became more complete, the legislation of one part of the Empire was not current in the other unless expressly adopted.

32. DECLINE AND FALL OF THE WESTERN EMPIRE.—In 410 Rome was taken and plundered by Alaric the Goth. About the same time Britain was left exposed to the ravages of Picts and Scots from the North and of Saxons from the East, as one adventurer after another, in making a bid for the imperial throne, denuded her of the defending legions. In 455 Rome was again sacked by the Vandals. The Western Empire was falling to pieces. The year 476, in which Romulus Augustulus was compelled to resign the throne to the barbarian Odoacer, is arbitrarily assigned as the date of its overthrow, though Zeno (474–91) and Justinian for a time reasserted the authority of the Empire in the West. But this was of no long duration. The Western Empire broke up into the barbarian kingdoms built upon its ruins. The Eastern Empire continued to exist until Constantinople was taken by the Turks in 1453.

33. ROMAN LAW IN WESTERN EUROPE.—The conquerors of the Western Empire had acquired a tincture of civilisation during centuries of intercourse with the Romans. They had their own customary laws, of which various collections have come down to us, generally described as the *Leges Barbarorum*. In most of these Roman influences are apparent. They also made compilations of Roman Law. Of these we have three, all dating from about 500. Far the most important is the *Lex Romana Visigothorum* or *Breviarium Alarici* (Breviary of Alaric), issued by Alaric II, King of the Visigoths, in 506. It contains in abbreviated form a large part of the Theodosian Code (§ 40), and many post-Theodosian Novels,[66] an epitome in two books of the first three Books of the Institutes of Gaius, an abbreviated version of the *Sententiae* of Paul and a single extract from the *Responsa* of Papinian. The so-called *Lex Romana Burgundionum* was issued probably about the same time by King

---

[66] *i.e.*, new laws (§ 43).

Gundobad, who had previously drawn up a code of law for his Burgundian subjects. He died in 516. The Edict of Theoderic, King of the Ostrogoths, of about the same date, unlike the other two compilations, was to govern Goths and Romans alike. The reason of the difference was that Theoderic claimed to rule, not as conqueror, but as delegate of Zeno, Emperor of the East.

34. THE BREVIARY OF ALARIC.—The Law of the Burgundians and the Edict of Theodoric are of limited scope and inferior interest. They had no abiding effect. Far different was the future of the Breviary. When it was promulgated the West-Gothic Kingdom included Spain and a great part of southern Gaul. But only a year later Alaric met with defeat and death at the hands of Clovis, King of the Franks. After this the law of the Visigoths had little validity north of the Pyrenees. In Spain it remained in force until replaced by another code in 654. But it retained a *de facto* authority, which extended far beyond its original bounds, and through abbreviations and abbreviations of abbreviations was the principal means of keeping some tradition of Roman Law alive in western Europe during the darkest period of the Middle Ages.

35. THE DARK AGES.—How far, if at all, the Roman Law continued to exist during these centuries was long uncertain. Savigny (*infra*) demonstrated its continuance, but much of the story remains obscure. Speaking generally, it may be said that it continued to exist in a state of solution, and with an admixture of barbarian and, later, of feudal law. "The life of Roman Law in the barbaric states," says Vinogradoff, "was upheld by the continuance of fragmentary and garbled rules, derived more or less directly from the system formed during the prosperous periods of Roman civilisation." [67] In Italy (or parts of it) the degeneration was not so complete. But knowledge of the sources was limited to the Institutes, the Code and the Novels (§§ 40, 43). The Digest had disappeared from sight.

36. THE REBIRTH OF ROMAN LAW.—The revived study of Roman Law was the work of the law schools of northern Italy, Ravenna, Pavia (the University of Lanfranc, the first Norman Archbishop of Canterbury) and, particularly, Bologna, in the eleventh and twelfth centuries. This is the age of the jurists who are known as the glossators, because their activity took the form of inserting glosses or notes in the margin and between the lines of the texts of the Roman Law. This treatment of legal

[67] *Roman Law in Medieval Europe*, p. 36.

texts had been employed by the Lombard lawyers in northern Italy. It was first applied to the texts of the Roman Law by Irnerius, a grammarian of Bologna, towards the end of the eleventh century. According to the story, he was consulted by a teacher of theology as to the meaning of the text—" Nonne duo passeres asse veneunt "—" Are not two sparrows sold for a farthing? " [68]—and his research as to the meaning of the Roman word *as* was the beginning of a profound study of Roman Law. The last of the glossators was Accursius, who died in the year 1260. Next came the post-glossators, who are reproached with having paid more attention to the gloss than to the text, but must have the credit of adapting the Roman Law to practical application in the courts. The best known of these is Bartolus (1314–57). The revival of letters in the sixteenth century gave a fresh impulse to the study of Roman Law. The scholars of this age known as " humanists," notably Jean Cujas (Cujacius, 1522–90) and Hugues Doneau (Donellus, 1527–91), professors at the University of Bourges in France, did not limit themselves to the study of the text, but called in aid whatever could be learnt from ancient literature and history. Doneau, who was a protestant, found it prudent to withdraw from France and for a time taught law in the University of Leiden in Holland, founded in 1574. In the seventeenth and eighteenth centuries the study of Roman Law was pursued in Holland by a number of eminent jurists, amongst who John Voet, in particular, was widely known for his Commentary on the Pandects [69] (1698–1704) still in use in the Union of South Africa. In France the most famous names of this period are in the seventeenth century Domat (1625–96) and in the eighteenth Pothier (1699–1772), whose works were largely drawn upon for the compilation of Napoleon's *Code Civil* published in 1804. In the nineteenth century Roman Law studies were prosecuted with most effect in Germany by Savigny (1779–1861), Ihering (1818–92) and Mommsen (1817–1903), and by a host of writers who systematised the Roman Law for use in the courts.

37. THE " RECEPTION " OF ROMAN LAW.—Leaving the history of the study of Roman Law to consider its influence upon the administration of justice, we must take note of an event of cardinal importance in European legal history, namely, the " reception " of Roman Law in Germany and the Netherlands in the fifteenth and sixteenth centuries. It had been for centuries a

---

[68] Matth. x. 29.
[69] § 40.

pose of the German Emperors to regard themselves as successors of the rulers of the Roman Empire. But this was a flourish and a maxim of statecraft rather than an influence in forming the private law. Doubtless, for centuries, through different channels, there had been an infiltration of Roman Law into the systems of northern Europe, but this was incommensurate in scale and consequence with the general reception which now took place. A number of circumstances combined to bring it about. At the end of the Middle Ages, when the revival of letters and the discovery of the world had effected a revolution in every aspect of life, the old customary law, which was primitive in character and varied from province to province and from town to town, was quite inadequate to meet the needs of the time; and, if the law was unequal to the occasion, so were the courts of the local magistrates who administered it. There was a general movement towards the creation of new courts, or the reform of old ones, exercising a wider and appellate jurisdiction. These were constituted in increasing measure of judges who were highly trained in the system which was the universal subject of University study, the Roman Law. Notable instances of such new courts were the Imperial Chamber (Reichskammergericht) created for the German Empire by Maximilian I in 1495, and the Great Council established at Mechlin by Charles the Bold, Duke of Burgundy, in 1473, with an appellate jurisdiction for the provinces of the Netherlands included in his dominions.[70] These courts, and ultimately the local courts as well, administered as the law of the land the Roman Law, in the form in which it had been transmitted by the glossators and post-glossators. It became the common law of Germany, and so remained, except where it had been replaced by codes, until the German civil code came into operation on January 1, 1900. The Roman Law was similarly " received," though in unequal measure, in the different provinces of the Netherlands.

38. In Italy there was no " reception " of Roman Law. Rather it emerged, so to say, from the soil. It was the task of the glossators and post-glossators to adapt it to practical application in the courts. In France as early as the eleventh century[71] a distinction was drawn between the southern provinces, in which the Roman Law in some form or another had continued to exist and which were known as the countries of the written law (les pays du droit écrit), and the northern

---

[70] Lee, p. 4.
[71] Vinogradoff, pp. 44, 47.

provinces, where customary law existed with numerous local variations, which were known as the countries of the customary law (les pays du droit coutumier). But here, too, as government became more centralised, the Roman Law asserted its authority, and wherever the customary law was silent, was admitted in subsidium as law or at least as " written reason " (ratio scripta). This meant, in effect, that the Roman Law occupied the whole field of Obligations. The great variety of customary law, which made Voltaire say that in France a traveller changed his law as often as he changed his horses, though to some extent mitigated by Royal Ordinances, continued to exist until the promulgation of the *Code Civil* in 1804.

39. ROMAN LAW IN THE BRITISH EMPIRE.—In what used to be called the British Empire a number of systems exist which have to some extent at least a Roman Law foundation. This may be said of :—1, the customary laws of the Channel Islands ; 2, the law of Scotland ; 3, the pre-Napoleonic law codified in the Province of Quebec and St. Lucia in the West Indies ; 4, the law of the *Code Civil* in the colonies of Mauritius and Seychelles ; 5, the Roman-Dutch Law in force in South Africa and Ceylon, but from 1917 no longer in British Guiana ; 6, the law of Malta. There has, of course, been infiltration of Roman Law into the law of England, both common law and equity.[72]

40. ROMAN LAW IN THE EASTERN EMPIRE—JUSTINIAN'S LEGISLATION.—We must now revert to the Eastern Empire, where the Roman Law remained in vigour, though, doubtless, much influenced by the legal institutions of Greece and the East. By the sixth century the legislation of the Republic had receded far into the background. For centuries the imperial constitutions had been the only source of new law. This was known as lex. The old law still in force was to be found in the writings of the jurists, known as jus. Lex and jus together with custom—consuetudo—covered the whole field of existing law. The material both of lex and of jus was immense and unwieldy. We have seen how Valentinian and Theodosius dealt with the jus in the Law of Citations (§ 30). Various attempts had been made to bring order into the statute law, first by private effort in the *Codex Gregorianus* and the *Codex Hermogenianus* (both *circ.* A.D. 300), called after the names of their compilers Gregorius and Hermogenianus ; later, in the official code of Theodosius II (*Codex Theodosianus*), issued in 438. We have

---

[72] See Plucknett, *A Concise History of the Common Law*, p. 260; Potter, *Historical Introduction to English Law* (2nd ed. 1943) Appendiᵛ

fragments of the first two of these and a very considerable part of the third.

41. JUSTINIAN'S LEGISLATION—CODE—INSTITUTES—DIGEST. —Such was the situation when Justinian came to the throne of the Eastern Empire in 527. Inspired, perhaps, by the example of the barbarian kings (§ 33), he conceived a comprehensive project of legal reform.[73] To do this it was necessary to introduce order into the existing chaos. He first (528) directed attention to the lex, entrusting the task to a commission of ten persons, one of whom was Tribonian, at that time a member of the imperial civil service. There were to make use of the earlier codes and of subsequent legislation, reducing the whole to a systematic form with necessary amendments. The result was the first edition of Justinian's Code, afterwards called the codex vetus, issued in 529. After this the jus was taken in hand. At the end of 530 a commission was issued to Tribonian, and others to be named by him (he named sixteen), ordering them " to read and revise the books on Roman Law of the ancient jurists to whom the emperors gave authority to write and interpret the laws," selecting and arranging matter of living interest and importance, rejecting all that was obsolete or unfit to be perpetuated.[74] In order to clear the ground a series of ordinances was issued in the years 529–31 settling questions which had been matter of controversy between the jurists, and abolishing many obsolete technicalities. The most important of these enactments were collected and issued under the name of the Fifty Decisions [75] (*Quinquaginta Decisiones*), but the text has not been transmitted to us. The labours of the commission resulted in a work known as the Digest or Pandects (a Greek word meaning " collection "),[76] published December 16, 533. It had been preceded a few weeks earlier by the *Institutiones*, commonly called the Institutes, an elementary work designed for the use of students, the composition of which, as Justinian's preface (Proem) informs us, had been entrusted to Tribonian and the law professors Theophilus and Dorotheus. It was based upon the institutional works of earlier writers, particularly Gaius, and

---

[73] See *Proem* to the Institutes, *infra*, p. 42.

[74] The commission to Tribonian is contained in a constitution known from its opening words as the constitutio *Deo auctore*, which together with two other introductory constitutions c. *Omnem* and c. *Tanta* is printed in editions of the Digest. For particulars, see Jolowicz, p. 490. These constitutions will repay study—English versions in Monro's translation of the Digest (Cambridge University Press).

[75] There is a reference to this work in Inst. 1. 5. 3.

[76] Cicero's freedman Tiro wrote a book of miscellanea thus entitled. Aul. Gell. 13. 9.

another work of (or attributed to) the same author styled *Res Cottidianae* or *Aurea* (Law in Daily Life or Golden Sayings). The Digest, and, strangely, the Institutes as well, received the force of law from December 30, 533.

42. THE COMPOSITION OF THE DIGEST.—Some forty jurists supplied the material for the Digest, but in very unequal degree. About one-third of the whole is taken from Ulpian, one-half from Ulpian and Paul together, two-thirds from the five jurists who occupy the place of honour in the Law of Citations. The great majority belong to what is called the classical age of Roman jurisprudence, which may be taken to extend from the beginning of the Empire to the middle of the third century. Contrary to their apparent instructions the compilers included a few jurists who had not had the jus respondendi.[77] Much attention has been given to the method of arrangement of the texts of the Digest. A young German of the name of Bluhme early in the last century advanced a theory which has been generally accepted.[78] According to this, the works of the jurists were distributed among three committees. One dealt with the commentaries of Ulpian and others on Sabinus and other works on the civil law, another with commentaries, principally Ulpian's commentary on the Edict, a third with the *Quaestiones* and *Responsa* of Papinian and other miscellaneous matter. There resulted three " masses " which are distinguished as the Sabinian mass, the Edictal mass, and the Papinian mass. The committees compared their results and in each Title the longest mass was (usually) placed first, then the other two according to their size. To these was sometimes added a Supplement or Appendix.

43. THE SECOND CODE—NOVELS.—In the year 534 a new edition of the Code was issued called the code of the second edition—codex repetitae praelectionis—which superseded the codex vetus of 529. It is made up of a great number of rescripts of earlier date than Constantine (one only as old as Hadrian), and of later constitutions, mostly abbreviated (thus we have only a sketchy version of Leo's important legislation on the stipulation (§ 448)), the whole interpolated (§ 45), though perhaps not so heavily as the Digest. This completed the consolidating legislation of Justinian. He supplemented his reform of the law by reorganising legal education in the Law Schools of Berytus,

---

[77] In particular, three Republican jurists and Gaius (§ 48), but perhaps the compilers understood their instructions to include any authors admitted by the Law of Citations (§ 30). Buckl. *T.* p. 40; Jolowicz, p. 492.

[78] Jolowicz, p. 494; Buckland, *M.* p. 23.

Rome and Constantinople. Subsequent laws known as new constitutions—novellae constitutiones or Novels—continued to be issued, principally in Greek, during the remainder of Justinian's reign, which lasted until 565, but few after Tribonian's death in 546. These have come down to us in three versions:—
1. The *Epitome Juliani* in Latin consisting of 122 novels; 2. The *Authenticum*, a fuller Latin version, so-called because in the age of the glossators it enjoyed authority in the courts and was thought by some to be an official collection made by Justinian's order for promulgation in Italy; 3. A Greek version of 168 novels, some later than Justinian.

The glossators used to note in their texts of the code changes made by subsequent legislation. Any such note is cited as authentica (constitutio) ad codicem, or, merely, authentica, and later writers frequently refer to these summaries instead of to the full text. An instance familiar in South Africa is Nov. 134 c. 8, which forbade married women to bind themselves as sureties for their husbands (§ 583). A summary of this was inserted after Cod. 4. 29. 22, and is commonly cited as authentica siqua mulier; that is, the summary which begins with the words siqua mulier (" if any woman ").[79]

44. The Digest is divided into fifty books, each of them (except Books XXX, XXXI, and XXXII, which relate all three to the single topic of Legacies and Fideicommissa) subdivided into chapters or Titles, each having at its head a rubric shortly describing its contents. Each Title consists of extracts from the works of the jurists. In every case the source of the citation is given, *e.g.*, " Ulpian in Book X on the Edict," " Florentinus in Book VI of the Institutes." These extracts are described as " fragments " or, since the whole of the Digest had statutory authority, as leges (laws). In modern editions the " fragments " for convenience of reference are subdivided, if of considerable length, into numbered sections or paragraphs; but the initial section or paragraph is not numbered, and is cited as pr.= principium. Thus (to take an example) Dig. 41. 1. 10 pr. means the first (unnumbered) section or paragraph of the tenth fragment or lex of the first Title (de adquirendo rerum dominio) of Book XLI of the Digest. The paragraph next following is cited as Dig. 41. 1. 10, 1, and so on. The Institutes consist of four Books, subdivided into Titles, but, since the subject-matter is presented in narrative form and not as a collection of extracts, there is no further subdivision except into sections or paragraphs. Thus, " Inst. 2. 1 pr." means the opening (unnumbered) section or paragraph of the first Title (de rerum divisione) of Book II of the Institutes. The next section or paragraph is Inst. 2. 1. 1, and so on. The Code consists of twelve Books divided like the

---

[79] Lee, p. 315.

Digest and Institutes into Titles, which are subdivided as in the Digest into laws (leges) and sections or paragraphs. The Novels are usually divided into chapters and sections.

45. Before leaving the subject of Justinian's legislation a few words may be devoted to its general character. In the first sentence of his *Ancient Law* Maine declares that " the most celebrated system of jurisprudence known to the world begins, as it ends, with a code." When he says that it ends with a code he means that Justinian's legislation as a whole may be described as a work of codification. Plainly, it bears no resemblance to a code in the modern sense. The Institutes is an elementary textbook for students, for the most part compiled from earlier sources. The Novels are statutes, called for by the exigencies of the occasion or the reforming zeal of the Emperor. The Code and the Digest are compiled from earlier codes and statutes and from a vast juristic literature. They do not pretend to reproduce the original texts, but have brought them up to date so as to accommodate them, more or less successfully, to the existing state of the law. This has been effected by additions, omissions and alterations which are comprehensively described as inter-polations. The older writers called them emblemata Triboniani —Tribonian's " interjections." Much effort has been directed, particularly in recent years, to the detection of these changes with a view to reconstructing the original text of the laws and authors cited and the ascertainment of the law of the classical period. The problem is complicated by the fact, now generally admitted, that the work of interpolation did not begin with Justinian. This would naturally be so in the case of the Code, the earlier constitutions of which had already passed through two or three editions. But there is reason to suppose that the texts of the Digest too suffered changes in the course of transmission, accidental certainly, perhaps also designed. Some of the works cited are thought to carry a false attribution. Thus, it is said that the so-called *Opiniones* of Ulpian, and, perhaps, the *Res Cottidianae* or *Aurea*, ascribed to Gaius (§ 48), were not the work of these' authors, but belong to the post-classical period. Intimately connected with the question of interpolation are two others ; first, as to the course of development of the Roman Law from the end of the classical period until the age of Justinian ; secondly, as to the general character of Justinian's codification and of the Digest in particular. The interval of some three centuries which separates Modestinus from Justinian is, so far, at least, as our knowledge goes, a dark age in the history of Roman

Law, not indeed for want of material, for the Theodosian code and other documents fall within the period, but because the material does not afford an answer to our questions. In the west it was a time of decline and decay. In the east there was considerable activity in the Law Schools, particularly of Constantinople and Berytus. The law—how could it be otherwise? —was very different in the time of Justinian from what it was in the time of the great jurists. What was the nature of the change? On one view the Roman Law underwent a natural process of development principally in the west, incorporating new elements, but continuing to be " a legitimate descendant of the classical law." [80] On another view, Justinian's Corpus Juris [81] not only registered the absorption in the system of rules and institutions of Hellenic and Eastern origin, but was conditioned by a moral and intellectual atmosphere, prevailing in the Law Schools and outside them, wholly alien from the spirit of the classical law. This is what is meant when we are told that Justinian's legislation was " Byzantine " in character. But as regards the Digest, in particular, though the commissioners made innumerable alterations in matters of detail, it cannot be believed that they gave an entirely new complexion to the ancient texts. Such a thing would under any circumstances scarcely have been possible. It was certainly impossible in the few years in which the commissioners completed their task ; nor is it proved that any such revolutionary revision of the texts had been made at an earlier date. We are justified, therefore, in concluding in favour of the fundamentally Roman character of the law which has been preserved in the Digest. It is true that in many respects it is far removed from the classical law, but neither is it completely harmonised with the law of Justinian's own time. Justinian offered it to the world as a coherent whole, free of inconsistencies and too clear to require commentary. The medieval and modern lawyers who had to make the system work in practice displayed an inexhaustible ingenuity in reconciling conflicting texts. For the scholar of today these discrepancies— " antinomies " as they are called—are provocative and alluring. They help him to see the Roman Law not as a static system, but as a dynamic force, changing through the centuries, adapting itself to changing social and moral ideas and a changed environment. It is easy to point out the imperfections in the Digest,

---

[80] Buckl. *Harvard Law Journal* (1941), vol. liv, p. 1273.
[81] This term describes the whole of Justinian's legislation, Institutes, Digest, Code, Novels. The texts are, or should be, accessible to everybody in what is called the Berlin stereotype edition.

but without it we should know little indeed of Roman Law, and we must be grateful to Justinian for having given us a work " which has influenced European life more than it has been affected by any other work except the Bible." [82]

[It lies outside our scope to enter upon the subject of interpolations. Reference may be made to Buckl. *T.*, p. 42; Jolowicz, p. 497. The following may serve as examples. In Dig. 13. 7. 8, 3., as the text stands, a feminine pronoun eam refers back to a neuter noun pignus (eam in place of id). It is plain that pignus has been substituted for fiducia (§ 259). Similarly, traditio is substituted for mancipatio, fidejussio for fidepromissio, etc. In a text attributed to Ulpian (Dig. 30. 1. 1.) it is said that legacies have been in all respects assimilated to fideicommissa. This was not so until Justinian. In Dig. 18. 6. 19 (18), 1. by substituting nisi for tametsi, which, as appears from the *Vatican Fragments* (§ 47) was the original text, the compilers attribute to Papinian the opposite of what he really said. In all this there is no question of " passing off." Justinian (fortunately for Roman Law studies) indicates the sources from which his material is drawn; as he says himself (c. *Tanta* 10), he did this out of respect for ancient authority, " so that the names of men learned in the law should not be consigned to oblivion."]

46. ROMAN LAW IN THE EASTERN EMPIRE.—In the Eastern Empire, where the Digest seemed most secure, it was, in defiance of Justinian's order, even during his lifetime, made the subject of commentaries and later of abridgments.[83] These were written in Greek, the common language of the east. Overlaid by such literature, as well as by statute and new customary law, Justinian's legislation was already in process of dissolution when it was recalled to life at the beginning of the tenth century by the *Basilica*, a restatement of the Roman Law, in which the whole of the Corpus Juris was fused into a single compilation in sixty books. This was projected by the Emperor Basil I, known as the Macedonian (867–86), and promulgated by his son Leo the Philosopher (886–911).[84] It has been described as " an authoritative and official rendering for the first time of the Latin treatises of Justinian into Greek." [85] In Italy, the Digest had an authority which lasted only so long as Justinian's short-lived triumph over the barbarians. It passed out of sight until it re-emerged to be converted by glossators and post-glossators into a common law for western Europe, which as a *modernus usus Pandectarum* retained its authority in many parts of Germany

[82] Buckl. *ubi sup.*
[83] Jolowicz, p. 491.
[84] Jolowicz, p. 514.
[85] Sheldon Amos, *The History and Principles of the Civil Law of Rome*, p. 400.

until the end of the last century, and still does so in the Union of South Africa.

47. OTHER ROMAN LAW SOURCES.—The Corpus Juris of Justinian is the principal source of our knowledge of Roman Law. But there is a considerable mass of material of earlier date. The *Codex Theodosianus* has been already mentioned (§ 40). Of the Institutes of Gaius we shall speak below. Here mention may be made of a few other sources. The *Vatican Fragments* is particularly valuable as containing citations from Papinian, Paul and Ulpian unaffected by the interpolations of Justinian's compilers. The work dates from before the Theodosian Code. The *Collatio legum Mosaicarum et Romanarum*, commonly called the *Collatio*, is a comparison of the law of Moses and the Roman Law mainly in the matter of criminal law, made, apparently, with the design of showing the superiority of the former. It dates from the fourth century and contains extracts from the old writers, but is of less value than the *Vatican Fragments*, for it is not the work of a lawyer. The short work described as *Tituli ex corpore Ulpiani* and identified with a book attributed to Ulpian under the name *Liber singularis regularum* is an abridgment of a work by Ulpian or some other classical author. The so-called *Sententiae* of Paul, for the most part preserved in the Breviary of Alaric, is an abridgment of a work by Paul together with post-classical elements.[86]

48. GAIUS NOSTER.—Gaius deserves a section to himself, though, indeed, we know little about him. He emerges from obscurity in the later Empire. He does not seem to have had the jus respondendi,[87] but the Law of Citations promoted him to the first rank. Justinian calls him " our Gaius " (Gaius noster). Of the man personally next to nothing is known. He flourished (so much appears from his Institutes) in the reigns of Antoninus Pius (138–61) and Marcus Aurelius (161–80). He was still alive in 178, for he wrote a monograph on the S. C. Orfitianum of that year. There are some indications in his book that he was a provincial, not resident in Rome, but opinion on this point is divided. Besides the Institutes (more correctly *Institutiones*) he is credited with the authorship of the *Res Cottidianae* or *Aurea* (§ 41). His other works include commentaries on the Twelve Tables (§ 10), on Quintus Mucius Scaevola (§ 13), and on the urban and provincial Edicts (§ 19). Occasion may be

G. 1. 188.

---

[86] Jolowicz, p. 476.
[87] Most of the jurists cited in the Digest must have had it. But, by chance, our sources mention only Masurius Sabinus (§ 29) and, perhaps, an otherwise unknown Innocentius in the reign of Diocletian.

taken to mention Sextus Pomponius, a contemporary of Gaius, a prolific writer, like Gaius a teacher of law, but unlike him frequently cited by later writers. Alone of the Roman jurists he took an interest in legal history. A long extract from an elementary work entitled Enchiridion incorporated in the Digest makes us wish that the whole work had been preserved to us, and free from the blemishes too apparent in the Digest fragment.

49. The Institutes of Gaius is the only work of the classical age of Roman Law which has survived substantially in the form which the author gave it. It was known only from extracts in the Digest and from the epitome included in the Breviary of Alaric (§ 33) until in 1816 the historian Niebuhr discovered an original text, erased (as the practice was) to make the parchment available for other matter, but not incapable of being to a great extent deciphered. This is what is known as the Verona palimpsest from the place of its discovery, where it still is, the chapter library at Verona. Recently, fragments forthcoming in Egypt have confirmed and supplemented the text. Some fragments of a paraphrase of Gaius discovered at Autun in 1898 (the Autun Gaius) have little value, but make an interesting contribution on one matter in the law of delict (§ 641).

50. Niebuhr's discovery made an epoch in the study of Roman Law. The manuscript supplied in a compendious form a picture of the law as it was in the second century, and since Justinian took the Institutes of Gaius for the model of his own Institutes, it has been possible to print the two books in parallel columns, as in Gneist's *Syntagma*, thus affording the student the opportunity of noting the changes in the law which had taken place in the course of four centuries, or were effected by Justinian himself. Above all, the fourth book of Gaius (omitted from the epitome) threw a flood of light on the subject of civil procedure. It is our primary source of knowledge of the nature of the formula (§ 689) and its various practical applications.

II. The Institutes—Preliminary Definitions

51. JUSTICE—JURISPRUDENCE.—The Institutes begins with definitions borrowed from Ulpian.[88] " Justice is a set and 1. 1 pr. constant purpose, giving to everyone his due. . . ." " Jurisprudence is the knowledge of things divine and human ; the

---

[88] Dig. 1. 1. 10.

science of the just and the unjust." The first was a commonplace of the schools of philosophy. The second, if it is to be
regarded as anything more than a rhetorical flourish, may be
a tradition from a time when the sanctions of law and religion
were not sharply distinguished. The definition of justice given
in the text is a definition of a moral virtue, an attribute of
human character. To the lawyer of today the words—" just "—
" justice "—suggest rather the quality of an act estimated with
reference to some standard of conduct. This may be (a) a moral
standard, or (b) a legal standard.

52. (a) When we apply a moral standard we find it outside
the limits of any given system, *e.g.*, if one ventured to say that
an Act of Parliament or a decision of the House of Lords was
" unjust." Our standard here is external to the law. It is one
by which a rule of law may be criticised and perhaps condemned. To fix this standard is the business not of law, but of
ethics, or moral philosophy.

(b) When we apply a legal standard we mean by " justice,"
right or wrong as determined by the law of our country. In
this sense we speak of the " administration of justice."

53. Jurisprudence is the science of justice in the legal sense
of the word. Ulpian's definition is too comprehensive, for it
seems to merge into a single formula, law, morality and religion.
This may be attributed partly to the historical connection of
Roman Law with Roman religion, partly to the ambiguity of the
word jus, which includes both morality and law. However, it
serves to correct the too narrow definition of jurisprudence
adopted by some English writers. Thus Holland defines jurisprudence as " the formal science of positive law." This will do
well enough so far as relates to what is called specifically
" analytical jurisprudence," which consists in the analysis and
classification of legal institutions and terms, but is inadequate
as an account of legal science in general, because it fails to take
account either of historical jurisprudence, that is the study of the
way in which law has grown up, or of critical (or, as Bentham
calls it, censorial) jurisprudence, that is the theory of what law
ought to be. We must be content to define jurisprudence as
" the science of law," distinguishing its three departments,
analytical, historical and critical. Any one of these may employ
the comparative method of study. This is the meaning of the
elusive term " comparative law."

54. JUS PUBLICUM—JUS PRIVATUM.—Justinian goes on to say
that the study of law comprises two branches, Public Law and

Private Law. This is the division which the Roman lawyers take as the primary line of cleavage in the legal system. " Public Law has regard to the constitution of the Roman State. Private Law is concerned with the interest of individuals." The classification is intelligible and convenient, though there are points at which the two overlap. The first includes constitutional law, administrative law, criminal law and procedure and the jus sacrum. The second comprises those branches of law which regulate the relations of citizens to one another, family law, property, obligations and succession. The Institutes is mainly concerned with private law. It ends with one Title on criminal law, which belongs to the jus publicum.

55. JUS NATURALE—JUS GENTIUM—JUS CIVILE.—The jus privatum, we are told, is threefold. " It is derived from natural precepts, or from the precepts of universal law,[89] or from the precepts of the civil law." This is taken from the Institutes of Ulpian,[90] and, combining passages taken from Ulpian and Gaius, Justinian goes on to develop the subject in the following passage: " The law of nature is the law which nature has taught all animals. . . . This is the source of the union of male and female, which we call matrimony, as well as of the procreation and rearing of children. . . . The civil law is distinguished from universal law as follows. Every people which is governed by laws and customs uses partly a law peculiar to itself, partly a law common to all mankind. For the law which each people makes for itself is peculiar to itself and is called the civil law, as being the law peculiar to the community in question. But the law which natural reason has prescribed for all mankind is held in equal observance amongst all peoples, and is called universal law, as being the law which all peoples use. Thus the Roman People uses a law partly peculiar to itself, partly common to all mankind."

56. Such is the threefold division of the Roman private law, which has been the source of endless commentary. The difficulty is that each of the three terms—jus naturale—jus civile—jus gentium—is used in various senses and the meanings which have most value for the legal historian are not the meanings which are given to them in the above passage. It is necessary, therefore, to examine each of them in turn and it will be convenient to begin with the jus civile.

The marginal references read: 1. 1. 4. / 1. 1. 4. / 1. 2 pr. / 1. 2. 1.

---

[89] I take occasion to say that this is my translation of jus gentium. " Law of nations " is misleading, " Law of peoples " obscure. But for the most part I shall leave the words untranslated.
[90] Dig. 1. 1. 1, 2.

57. JUS CIVILE.—Nations (we use the word to include any independent community of men), particularly in the early stages of their history, are generally satisfied with their own institutions, and do not concern themselves much with the institutions of their neighbours. Each has its own system of law which is its peculiar and cherished possession. It is the law of the civitas or State and may be described as the jus civile of the State in question. The Romans had their system of customary law, partly embodied in the Law of the Twelve Tables. This was their jus civile, and this, therefore, is the original meaning of the term. It is the whole body of the law of Rome, and particularly this body of law as expounded and interpreted by the jurists.[91] Sometimes the term is used in a narrower sense to point a contrast. Thus, within the body of the Roman Law the jus civile may be distinguished from the jus gentium (as in this passage) or from the praetor's equity, the jus honorarium. In much the same way English lawyers use the term " common law " now in a wider, now in a narrower sense.

58. JUS GENTIUM.—The term jus gentium has two meanings, which we may distinguish as the practical and the theoretical. In primitive communities the law may seem stationary, but insensibly it changes by development from within. When it is exposed to external influences the pace is accelerated. This was the experience of Rome. The emancipation of the law from priestly influence opened the way to a wider outlook. Simultaneously, the need was felt of a law which could be applied to unprivileged alien residents, who from the third century B.C. formed an increasingly numerous section of the population. They were outside the pale of the civil law, but it was impossible to treat them as outside the pale of all law whatever. The Romans found a solution in developing a subsidiary or secondary civil law, which they applied both to aliens and to their own people. It came to be known as jus gentium or the law of peoples, that is, of peoples in general ; for jus gentium is Latin for " the law of the world " just as " ubi gentium? " is Latin for " where in the world? " The consequence was that the whole body of the Roman Law, that is of the jus civile in the wider sense, came to consist of two parts, a nucleus which was the peculiar birthright of Roman citizens, including the formal and ceremonial part of the law such as dominium ex jure Quiritium (§ 152), mancipatio (§ 158), in jure cessio (§ 165), sponsio (§ 445), and a circumference which was free from these technicalities,

---

[91] Dig. 1. 2. 2, 5.

and was available to citizen and foreigner alike.[92]   It provided
for the ordinary exigencies of commercial life, buying and
selling, letting and hiring and the transfer of property in
movables by transfer of possession.   Besides this, the peculiarly
Roman institution of the verbal contract was made available
to a wider circle, though the use of the solemn form " spondesne "?   " spondeo " (§ 446) continued to be restricted to
citizens.

59. THE ORIGIN OF THE JUS GENTIUM.—The process by
which the jus gentium was evolved has been much discussed.
There can be little doubt that it was the work of the courts and
of lay jurists, using material partly inherent in the original
system, partly introduced from outside.   We may be sure that
there was no conscious search for uniformities in the laws of
Rome and her neighbours, nor is there evidence for the existence
of a mercantile law common to the trading nations of antiquity
like the Rhodian Sea Law of a later age (§ 504).   The cradle
of the jus gentium was the court of the (Urban) Praetor.   When
his work became too heavy for him he was given a colleague to
relieve him of the burden of alien litigants.   It was an adjustment of functions comparable to what had taken place a
hundred years earlier when the office of praetor was carved out
of the consulship.   The view, commonly asserted that the jus
gentium crept into the Roman Law by way of the edict of the
Peregrine Praetor must be rejected.[93]

60. GREEK PHILOSOPHY.—It was a commonplace of Greek
philosophy, particularly of Stoic philosophy, to distinguish in a
legal system the part which was peculiar to it, and the part
which it had in common with other systems.   The first seemed
to be arbitrary and accidental, the second was thought of as
rational and universal and, therefore, of a higher validity.   It
was natural justice.   When in the last century and a half of the
Republic Rome came under the influence of Greek ideas, her
own empirical rules were brought within the framework of
Greek speculation with the result that the jus gentium and the
jus naturale were for most purposes identified.   Thus on the one
hand concrete principles of Roman Law, as in the matter of
the acquisition of ownership, are attributed indifferently to jus

---

[92] Whether this " circumference " was known to the Romans as jus
gentium has been questioned.   It is common experience that terms assume
in retrospect a precision which did not belong to them at first (if ever).
[93] Cf. Pomponius, Dig. 1. 2. 2, 28 ; post aliquot deinde annos non
sufficiente eo praetore, quod multa turba etiam peregrinorum in civitatem
veniret, creatus est et alius praetor qui peregrinus appellatus est ab eo
quod plerumque inter peregrinos ius dicebat.

gentium and to jus naturale, and on the other hand, abstract principles which commend themselves by their reasonableness are said to be prescribed by the jus gentium.[94] In theory the identification is complete. But the theory retains many inconsistencies. The jus gentium, we are told, is common to all mankind, because " peoples have established certain laws for themselves as occasion and the necessities of human life required." But the law of nature was " established by nature at the origin of mankind," [95] and " the laws of nature which are observed amongst all peoples alike, being established by a divine providence, remain ever fixed and immutable." Plainly facts and theory cannot be brought into perfect harmony, and there is the question of slavery to which we refer below.

61. JUS NATURALE.—The subject of jus naturale has necessarily been anticipated in the foregoing section. Ulpian describes it as " the law which nature has taught all animals." [96] But this is to speak of law in a sense quite different from that in which we commonly speak of human beings as being subject to law. The description belongs to the order of ideas which represent law as the plan of the universe, and lies outside the field of jurisprudence.[97] We may ignore it, as it was in fact generally ignored by the Roman jurists.[98] The common usage was to limit the term natural law or law of nature to rules of human conduct, supposed to be rational and universal, and scarcely distinguishable from the jus gentium, which also is represented as established by natural reason. But there is one point at which the two conceptions draw apart, namely, in connection with slavery, which, though universally recognised and therefore permitted by the jus gentium, was considered by later speculation (not by Aristotle) to be repugnant to natural reason and therefore to the jus naturale. So that we arrive, finally, at a conception of the jus naturale which distinguishes it from the jus gentium, namely, " an ideal to which it is desirable that law should conform " [99]; not that we must think of this as an ideal code, but as an abstract principle by which institutions

(margin references: 2. 1. 11.   1. 2. 2.   1. 2. 11.   1. 2. 1.   1. 3. 2.)

---

[94] *e.g.*, prohibition of marriage between ascendants and descendants, Dig. 23. 2. 68—condictio ex injusta causa, Dig. 25. 2. 25.

[95] Cum ipso genere humano proditum, Dig. 41. 1. 1; quod cum ipso genere humano rerum natura prodidit, Inst. 2. 1. 11.

[96] Dig. 1. 1. 1, 3; Inst. 1. 2 pr.

[97] Holland (*Jurisprudence*, pp. 19 *et seq.*) distinguishes and illustrates the two principal meanings of Law; *viz.*, 1. Law as the order of the Universe; 2. Law as a rule of action. The distinction is often blurred by Religion, Poetry and Metaphor. Some readers may recall Hooker's magnificently rhetorical description of Law in the *Ecclesiastical Polity*.

[98] Goudy, *Trichotomy in Roman Law*, p. 26.

[99] Buckl. *M.* p. 29.

are to be assessed. Thus we revert to a triple division of law, though not in the sense intended by Ulpian. Medieval writers usually distinguish jus gentium and jus naturale, and in later political literature the doctrine of a social contract opens out a further field of speculation. Starting from the assumption that civil societies somehow or other originated in contract, the writers of the sixteenth and following centuries suppose an original state of nature antecedent to the contract, governed actually or potentially by laws of nature. Since this state of nature is merely imaginary, it was open to each writer to frame the laws of nature according to the dictates of his own fancy. Generally, they are found to coincide more or less with the fundamental principles of morality, and this is the sense in which the term "laws of nature" is still sometimes employed. As interpreted by Grotius the Law of Nature was one of the principal elements in the formation of the modern system of International Law.

62. CONCLUSION.—To revert to the Roman Law, the conclusion to be drawn is that the distinction between jus civile and jus gentium is a question of history, but this, unfortunately, is precisely the point on which the texts of the Roman Law leave us uninformed. The distinction between jus gentium, used now in a vaguer abstract sense, and the jus naturale, so far as they are distinguished, is a matter of theoretical speculation. Gaius and Justinian reflect in a blurred and confused picture the doctrine of Greek philosophy. They would have done us a better service if they had given us some account of the way in which the Roman jus gentium grew up and was or became part of the law of Rome.

63. JUS SCRIPTUM—JUS NON SCRIPTUM.—Justinian goes on to distinguish written law and unwritten law. The Romans use the term jus scriptum in a sense which is wide enough to include any authoritative statement or exposition of the law which is expressed in writing. English usage limits the term "written law" to statute law, that is "an express precept which not only declares or contains, but in its very words constitutes the law." [1] Unwritten law is law which is created by custom or usage, which as Justinian quaintly observes imitates a statute. This recalls the equally strange idea once current that the English common law was statute law ground small.

---

[1] Pollock, *A First Book of Jurisprudence*, p. 219.

1. 2. 3.

64. THE SOURCES OF THE JUS SCRIPTUM.—Justinian enumerates lex—plebiscitum—senatusconsultum—magistratuum edicta—responsa prudentium—principum placita. We have traced above the historical development of these several institutions. Long before Justinian the first five had ceased to be living sources .of law. All fresh law proceeded from the

1. 2. 11.

Emperor. It must be noticed that according to the Institutes (and in the Digest Julian is quoted to the same effect) [2] written laws may be abrogated not only by express enactment but also by desuetude and tacit consent. On the other hand, a constitution of Constantine is inserted in the Code to the effect that custom is not to override reason or statute,[3] but this may mean that local customs are not to be allowed to abrogate a general statute. It has been questioned whether Justinian really contemplated as possible the abrogation of imperial legislation by mere disuse.[4]

65. THE LAW OF PERSONS.—" The whole of our law," says

1. 2. 12.

Justinian, repeating the language of Gaius, " relates either to persons or to things or to actions." What is the meaning of this arrangement? The two latter terms are clearer than the first. " The law of actions " means legal remedies and procedure. " The law of things " means the law of property, understood in a sense wide enough to include obligations and succession. But doubt has prevailed as to the meaning and scope of the law relating to persons. This is due partly to the desultory way in which the subject is treated both by Gaius and by Justinian, but still more to the common tendency of writers to interpret the text in accordance with a preconceived system. It is to Gaius rather than to Justinian that we must look ·for a solution, for Justinian merely follows the arrangement of the older writer, while introducing fresh matter which seems to confuse the issue. It may safely be said that the law relating to

1. 3.

persons (or, as it is also called, " the law of persons ") is not " family law " in any of the senses which may be given to that phrase, nor the law of status, if this is to be taken to include the consequences of variations of status in the departments of property and obligations. But in a more limited sense the law of persons may be identified with the law of status. Differences of status give colour to every legal relation. Before going further we should at least know what these differences are. It

---

[2] Dig. 1. 3. 32, 1 (*in fine*).
[3] Cod. 8. 52. 2.
[4] Buckl. *M.* p. 26.

is the business of the law of persons to tell us what they are.
" Let us speak first of persons," says Justinian, " for it is of little
use to know the law if we do not know the persons for whom
the law is made." Thus understood, the law of persons will be 1. 2. 12.
" concerned with a description only of the principal among those
different classes of persons whose distinctive characteristics are
legally important " and an explanation in each case of the ways
in which the status in question is acquired and lost.[5] It should
be remembered that, until, at least, the end of the Republic,
there was little place for a law of " domestic relations." The
Roman family was an autonomous institution, very much older
than the State, not at all inclined to invite or accept the intro-
mission in its affairs of an extraneous authority.

66. SUMMARY OF THE INSTITUTES.—We are now in a position
to summarise the contents of the Institutes of Gaius and
Justinian. The first Book will tell us what are the principal
classes of persons known to Roman Law. This is the Law
relating to Persons. The next section, comprising in Gaius
Books II and III and in Justinian Books II and III and Titles I
to V of Book IV, will deal with the substance of the Law. This
is the Law relating to Things. The last section, comprising in
Gaius the whole and in Justinian the remainder of Book IV, is
concerned principally with procedure. This is the Law relating
to Actions. But this distinction of topics is by no means rigidly
maintained.

[5] Buckl. *Elementary Principles*, p. 8 ; *Textbook*, p. 59 :

THE INSTITUTES OF JUSTINIAN

Proem

In the name of our Lord Jesus Christ

THE EMPEROR CAESAR FLAVIUS JUSTINIANUS; CONQUEROR OF THE ALAMANNI, GOTHS, FRANKS, GERMANS, ANTAE, ALANI, VANDALS, AFRICANS; PIOUS; PROSPEROUS; RENOWNED; VICTORIOUS; TRIUMPHANT; EVER AUGUST; TO YOUNG MEN DESIROUS OF THE LAW:—

The imperial Majesty should be not only made glorious by arms, but also arméd with laws, that war and peace alike may be well directed, and that the Roman Emperor may not only be triumphant in battle, but also by pursuing the paths of law overcome the wicked designs of unprincipled men and be seen to be as much a scrupulous upholder of justice as victorious over conquered foes.

1. Both ends with untiring effort and unfailing foresight by God's blessing we have attained. The valour of our arms barbarian nations made subject to our sway have learnt to know. Africa and innumerable other provinces, after so long an interval by the victories which God has given us restored to our rule and Empire, bear witness to it. All nations now are ruled by laws which we have issued or compiled.

§ 40.

2. For when we had reduced to splendid harmony the unordered mass of imperial constitutions, we next extended our care to the immense material of the ancient jurisprudence, and adventuring, so to say, into mid ocean, by Heaven's favour completed a task, which might well have been deemed hopeless.

3. This too by God's blessing accomplished, to the most eminent Tribonian, master and ex-quaestor of our Sacred Palace together with the illustrious Theophilus and Dorotheus, professors of law, who have given many proofs of their ability, legal knowledge, and faithful discharge of our orders, we have issued special directions by our authority and at our instance to compile a book of Institutes, that so you may get your first notions of law not from ancient fables, but from the bright light of the imperial throne, and may hear and apprehend nothing useless, nothing out of place, but only what rests upon a solid basis of fact; thus, a thing to which former students attained only after four years' application—the reading of the imperial constitutions—you may now enter upon from the very beginning, being found worthy of the honour and the happiness of receiving your law from first to last from the mouth of the Emperor. 4. Accordingly, after the completion of the fifty books of the Digest or Pandects, in which with the help of the eminent Tribonian and other illustrious and learned men the whole of the old jurisprudence has been compiled, we have ordered the composition in four Books of these Institutes, destined to contain the elements of the whole science of law. 5. In these a short account is given of the law of former days as well as of law which having been obscured by disuse has been brought into the light by our reforming hand. 6. These four Books, compiled from all the institutional works of ancient

§§ 40, 48.

authors and in particular from the Institutions of our Gaius and from his book on " Daily Affairs " and many other commentaries, the three eminent men aforesaid have submitted for our approval. We have read and examined them, and have given them the force and effect of one of our constitutions.

7. Receive therefore earnestly and with eager attention these our laws and show yourselves so far advanced in your studies that you may be encouraged by the noble ambition of being able, when your training is complete, to undertake such functions of government as may be assigned to you in the different departments of our Empire.

Given at Constantinople on the eleventh day before the Kalends of December in the third consulate of the Emperor Justinian, Ever August (November 21, A.D. 533).

BOOK I

TITLE I

Of Justice and Law

Justice is a set and constant purpose giving to every man his due. § 51.

1. Jurisprudence is the knowledge of things divine and human, the science of the just and the unjust.

2. So much being premised, since we are to explain what are the laws of the Roman People, it seems that the most convenient method will be to treat each subject in an easy simple way before proceeding to a careful and elaborate exposition. Otherwise, if from the very beginning we overload the mind of the student, still untrained and unequal to the burden, with a mass of various detail, one of two things will happen, either we shall deter him from the study of law, or, at the cost of much toil and self-distrust, which so often discourages young men, we shall at last bring him to a point of attainment, which, led by an easier road, he might have reached more quickly, without great toil and want of confidence in his own powers.

3. The precepts of the law are these—to live honestly, not to § 54. harm another, to give every man his due. 4. The study of law has two branches, public and private. Public Law has regard to the constitution of the Roman State: Private Law is concerned with the interest of individuals. We are to speak of Private Law, which is of three kinds, being derived from natural precepts or from the § 55. precepts of universal law or from the precepts of the civil law.

TITLE II

Of the Law of Nature, Universal Law and the Civil Law

The law of nature is the law which nature has taught all animals. § 61. This law is not peculiar to the human race, but belongs to all living creatures, birds, beasts and fishes. This is the source of the union of male and female, which we called matrimony, as well as of the procreation and rearing of children; which things are characteristic of the whole animal creation.

1. The civil law is distinguished from universal law as follows. Every people which is governed by laws and customs uses partly a law peculiar to itself, partly a law common to all mankind. For

§§ 55, 57.

the law which each people makes for itself is peculiar to itself, and is called the civil law, as being the law peculiar to the community in question. But the law which natural reason has prescribed for all mankind is held in equal observance amongst all peoples and is called universal law, as being the law which all peoples use. Thus the Roman People uses a law partly peculiar to itself, partly common to all mankind. What those laws are, we shall explain severally in proper sequence.

2. The civil law takes its name from the country to which it belongs. Thus the laws of Solon or of Draco may properly be described as the civil law of the Athenians. In the same way we describe the law which the Roman People uses as the civil law of the Romans, or as the law of the Quirites (jus Quiritium), because the Romans are called Quirites after Quirinus.[6] But when we use the term jus civile without specifying any State in particular we mean our own law, just as " the Poet " without mention of any name in particular means for the Greeks Homer, for us Virgil. But universal law is common to the whole human race. For under the pressure of use and necessity the peoples of mankind have created for themselves certain rules. Thus, wars arose and captivity and slavery, which is contrary to natural law, for by natural law from the beginning all men were born free. From this universal law almost all contracts are derived, such as sale, hire, partnership, deposit, loan and countless others.

3. All our law is written or unwritten, according to the distinction made by the Greeks. The written law consists of statute (lex), plebiscita, senatusconsulta, enactments of the Emperors, the edicts of magistrates, the answers of men learned in the law. 4. A lex is that which the Roman People used to enact on the proposition of a senatorial magistrate,[7] such as a consul. A plebiscitum is that which the plebs used to enact on the proposition of a plebeian magistrate, namely,[8] a tribune. The plebs differs from the People as species from genus. For the word People signifies the whole citizen body, patricians and senators included.[9] The word plebs means the citizens exclusive of patricians and senators. After the enactment of the lex Hortensia plebiscita began to have the same force as statutes. 5. A senatusconsultum is that which the senate orders and enacts. For when the Roman People had become so greatly enlarged that it was difficult for it to be called together for the purpose of enacting a law, it seemed right that the Senate should be consulted instead of the People. 6. Further, what the Emperor has been pleased to command has the force of law since by the lex

§ 8.

§ 9.

§ 28.

---

[6] Quirinus was the name given to the deified Romulus.

[7] The phrase is inexact. The tribunes, too, in the later Republic, were senators (§ 25). The proper term is " curule magistrate," i.e., a magistrate of the Roman People.

[8] The tribunes alone (not the plebeian aediles) had the right of initiating legislation in the concilium plebis.

[9] Justinian has departed from the text of Gaius by adding the words " and senators." This is a mere blunder. In the later Empire patricius and senator were titles of nobility. This had nothing to do with the ancient division of the community into patricians and plebeians, which scarcely survived the Republic.

regia [10] passed about his sovereignty the People has made over to him all its own sovereignty and power. Whatever, therefore, the Emperor has settled by letter or decided judicially or ordained by edict certainly has the force of a statute. All such expressions of the imperial will are called constitutions. Clearly some of these are personal and do not create a precedent to be followed, such not being the Emperor's intention. For example, a special instance of reward or punishment or of relief not intended to create a precedent does not go beyond the person concerned. Other constitutions, being general in character, are undoubtedly binding on everyone. 7. The edicts of the praetors too have considerable legal authority. We commonly call them the jus honorarium, because holders of offices (honores), that is to say magistrates, have given authority to this branch of law. The curule aediles also used to publish an edict dealing with certain matters, and this forms part of the jus honorarium. 8. The answers of men learned in the law (responsa prudentium) are the decisions and opinions of those who were authorised to state the law. For in ancient times there were men charged with the function of public interpretation of the laws, on whom the Emperor had conferred the right of giving responses (jus respondendi). They were called jurisconsults. The decisions and opinions of them all had so much authority, that the judge was not allowed to depart from their responses,[11] as was ordained by imperial constitutions. 9. Unwritten law consists of rules approved by usage; for long-continued custom approved by the consent of those who use it imitates a statute. 10. So the civil law seems to be neatly distinguished as of two kinds. The distinction may be said to be derived from the institutions of two States, Athens and Lacedaemon. The Lacedaemonians maintained an oral tradition of the rules which they observed as laws, while the Athenians were the custodians of what they found written in their statute law.

§§ 14–18.

§ 29.

§ 63.

11. The laws of nature which are observed amongst all peoples alike, being established by a divine providence, remain ever fixed and immutable, but the laws which each State makes for itself are frequently changed either by tacit consent of the people, or by a later statute.

§ 60.

§ 64.

12. The whole of our law relates either to persons, or to things, or to actions. Let us first consider persons; for it is of little use to know the law if we do not know the persons for whom the law was established.

§ 65.

---

[10] This passage is taken from Ulpian's Institutes (Dig. 1. 4. 1, where the word " regia " is interpolated). In the early Empire specific powers were conferred upon a new Emperor, as by the so-called lex de imperio Vespasiani, the text of which is only in part preserved (Girard, *Textes*, p. 106), but there is no proof of a general delegation of legislative power. Cf. *Cambridge Ancient History*, xi, 404.

[11] The translation reflects the vagueness of the text. The words " of them all " (quorum omnium) are a reminiscence of Gaius, since the Law of Citations (§ 30) no longer applicable.

BOOK I

THE LAW OF PERSONS

67. "Three things are ours," says Paulus, "freedom, citizenship, family." [12] These are what the commentators have described as the momenta, or determining factors, of status. [13] We meet with them particularly in connection with the subject of capitis deminutio. Gaius might conveniently have made them the foundation of his exposition of the Law of Persons. But he has not done so. Perhaps he felt that citizenship belonged rather to the sphere of public law, or it may be said that Roman Law is not much concerned with free persons who are not citizens. Citizenship is assumed to be the normal condition. [14] Consequently, there is no attempt to define it, or to say, except incidentally, how it is acquired and lost. The topics of freedom and family remain, but it cannot be said that these, any more than citizenship, are made the basis of a systematic treatment. The whole law of persons resolves itself into an explanation of the different " divisions " of persons, that is the different principles of classification. Persons are free or unfree. Persons are sui juris or alieni juris. Of persons sui juris some have a tutor or curator, others not. These divisions constitute for Gaius and Justinian the framework of the first Book of the Institutes. Justinian has brought Gaius up to date by omissions and additions. In many cases he introduces into the text definitions of the term used. Thus we have definitions of servitus, libertas, manumissio, nuptiae, tutela. The general tone of Justinian tends to be diffuse, while Gaius is succinct. This and, in particular, the unity of the earlier work, contrasted with the composite character of Justinian's Institutes, makes the former more agreeable reading. But it is to Justinian that we owe the transmission of the Roman Law to the modern world, and Justinian, not Gaius, will principally be our guide in the following pages.

§ 120.

I. The First Division of Persons

(Free Men and Slaves)

1. 3 pr.

68. The first division of persons is into Free Men and Slaves. Slaves are born so or become so; they become so either

---

[12] Dig. 4. 5. 11.
[13] Moyle, p. 86.
[14] Buckl. T. p. 60.

jure gentium, that is by being taken captive, or by civil law. 1. 3. 4.
We may distinguish the so-called investitive facts of slavery
as: 1, unfree birth; 2, hostile capture; 3, rules of the civil law.

69 (1). UNFREE BIRTH.—The general rule of the jus gentium
was that children followed the status which the mother had at
the time of birth, contrary to the rule of the civil law that
where the parties had conubium (§ 92) and were lawfully
married the issue followed the status of the father at the time
of conception.[15] In principle, therefore, children born of a slave
mother were slaves. But in favour of freedom they were held
to be born free if the mother was free at the time of conception 1. 4 pr.
or at any subsequent time during pregnancy. There were some
statutory exceptions from the general rule but they were repealed
by Hadrian and Vespasian.[16]

70 (2). HOSTILE CAPTURE.—This continued to be a source 1. 3. 4.
of slavery through the whole course of Roman Law. It applied
not only to declared enemies, but in principle to any foreigner,
who was found within the Empire unprotected by treaty or
other amicable arrangement.[17]

71 (3). RULES OF THE CIVIL LAW.—In the old law a father
might sell his children into slavery, but within the limits of
Rome only in the modified form of mancipium (§ 124). By the
Twelve Tables insolvent debtors might be sold trans Tiberim
(across the Tiber), i.e., into Etruria (§ 683). Enslavement was
the fate of persons who evaded inscription on the census, and,
perhaps, of the " manifest " thief [18] (§ 606). Under the Empire,
slavery might come into existence in any of the following ways—
(a) when a free man upwards of twenty years of age fraudulently 1. 3. 4.
allowed himself to be sold with a view to sharing the price;
(b) by the S. C. Claudianum (A.D. 52) a woman who persisted in
cohabiting with a slave in spite of denunciations from the slave's
master might by judicial decree be herself declared his slave [19];
(c) condemnation to death or to labour in the mines entailed
loss of freedom (Persons so condemned were said to be slaves of
punishment—servi poenae. They had no dominus); (d) freed-
men who were guilty of serious ingratitude to their patrons might 1. 16. 1.
be reduced to slavery; (e) under stress of poverty parents were
allowed to sell their new-born children into slavery with a right
of redemption (§ 88). Of the above methods of enslavement

---

[15] G. 1. 78; Ulp. V. 8.
[16] G. 1. 83-6.
[17] Dig. 49. 15. 5, 2.
[18] G. 1. 160; 3. 189.
[19] G. 1. 91, 160; Inst. 3. 12. 1

Justinian abolished (b) and (c),[20] retaining the others, none of them of frequent occurrence.

72. RIGHTS OF MASTERS OVER SLAVES.—Slaves were in the power of their masters (§ 86). This implied complete disability, personal and proprietary. The master had "the right of life and death" (jus vitae necisque), and everything acquired by the
1. 8. 1. slave was acquired for the master (a rule only formally qualified if the slave was held in usufruct (§ 232)). Under the Empire there was legislation designed to protect the slave from the most heinous kinds of cruelty. A lex Petronia, which dates from before A.D. 79 (a record of it having been found in Pompeii, destroyed in that year by the eruption of Vesuvius), forbade masters to expose their slaves to fight with beasts in the arena without authority from the magistrate. The Emperor Antonius Pius (138–61) protected the slave's life even as regards his master by enacting that a master who killed his own slave without cause
1. 8. 2. was to be punished as if he had killed another man's slave.
4. 18. 5. This meant that he incurred the capital penalty of the lex Cornelia de sicariis (B.C. 81). The same Emperor by a rescript addressed to Aelius Marcianus in the case of certain slaves who had fled for protection to the statue of the Emperor, gave orders that if they had been too badly treated, they should be sold on
1. 8. 2. the terms that they should not revert to the master's power. This was understood to lay down a general rule. The practice of holding an inquiry in such cases, as Buckland says, "in a roundabout way gives the slave access to the courts."[21] Later, it seems, the access was more direct. It is significant that the jurist cited in the Digest[22] to this effect is Hermogenianus, who is thought to be the latest of the jurists made use of by the compilers.

73. So much of the slave's condition *de jure*. His position *de facto* is a different matter. We are speaking of an institution which existed through the whole course of Roman history and over the whole extent of the Empire. Volumes have been written on the subject. The matter may be very briefly stated as follows. In the earliest times there were few slaves and the slave was a member of the household. Plutarch in his Life of Coriolanus tells us that in those days (5th cent. B.C.) the Romans treated their slaves with much consideration, for they worked and lived with them on equal terms. When Rome began to

---

20 Inst. 3. 12. 1; Cod. 7. 24; Nov. 22. 8; Buckl. *T.* p. 70.
21 *Main Institutions of Roman Private Law*, p. 41.
22 Dig. 5. 1. 53.

extend her conquests outside Italy and to engage in distant wars
there was a vast increase in the slave population. Julius Caesar
(to give a single instance) is said to have taken captive a million
Gauls. In town and country alike slave labour replaced free
labour, and the great Italian estates were cultivated by immense
slave-gangs, whose condition was pitiable. In the towns slavery
was on the whole more tolerable. It was the practice to allow
slaves to deal with their peculium as their own and to purchase
their freedom.[23] They were sometimes highly educated men
who held important positions in the business world, or made
their mark in literature, art or science. In the later Empire
things changed for the worse. The deterioration of economic
conditions and the development of a system of hereditary castes
excluded slaves from employments previously open to them.
On the other hand, the philosophic ideal of the jus naturale and
the influence of Christianity encouraged manumission, and there
is evidence that as time went on slavery declined in importance.[24]
On the land it gave place to colonatus (§ 75), which anticipated
the villenage of the Middle Ages.

74. Was the Roman slave a thing or a person? The answer
is he was both. He could be owned and as such was a res.
But he was a human being and as such a person, for the idea
that personality implies " a being or group capable of legal
rights and duties " [25] developed slowly and took shape only in
the Byzantine period under the influence, it is said, of ideas
derived from theology. The moral claim of the slave to be
regarded as a human being was recognised in many ways apart
from the legislation above referred to. Thus, to mention only
two examples, the burial of a slave made the ground locus
religiosus (§ 146) and, though slaves could not contract a legal
marriage, natural kinship was recognised as defining the degrees   1. 10. 10.
within which marriage was not permitted after manumission.
Slaves were subject to the criminal law. They were bound by
delict, but during slavery the liability attached to the master,
absolutely or to the extent of noxal surrender (§ 638). After
manumission they were personally answerable. Their contracts
created a natural obligation (§ 406) available after manumission
not as a ground of action but as a defence by, or against them.[26]

---

[23] Through an intermediary, who had to manumit. Dig. 40. 1. 4 pr.
The peculium was a fund of which a slave had *de facto* control.
[24] Arangio-Ruiz, *Istituzioni*, p. 45.
[25] Buckl. *M.* p. 34.
[26] In particular it might be pleaded as a set-off (p. 466) and excluded
the condictio indebiti (§ 591).

All of this is contained in the following passage of Ulpian :
" Slaves are bound by delict and remain bound after manumission. By contract they are not bound by civil law, but by
natural law they are bound themselves and bind others to
them." [27]

1. 3. 5.

75. QUASI-SERVILE CONDITIONS.—Justinian says that all
slaves are of one pattern. This requires some qualification.
Some slaves of the Roman People were in a privileged position
(§ 302). A slave manumitted conditionally (statuliber) [28] was,
pending the condition, guaranteed by the praetor against abusive
exercise of the master's rights and so were slaves manumitted
informally or by a bonitary owner (§ 81) before the lex Junia
gave them a special status.[29] A freeman in good faith treated
as a slave (liber homo bona fide serviens) [30] was in an anomalous
position, which gave rise to special rules ; and there were a few
other cases of qualified or restricted freedom.[31] In the later law
the coloni formed a class apart. They were personally free, but
bound to the soil.[32] Their *de facto* position was not far
removed from slavery.

1. 4 pr.

76. If a man was not a slave he was free, either born free
(ingenuus) or made free (libertinus).[33] A free-born man was

1. 5 pr.

one born of free parents (free-born or free-made) or of a free
mother. A free-made person (freedman) was one who had been
manumitted from civil law slavery, that is not merely from
slavery *de facto* or from slavery *jure gentium* resulting from
hostile capture ; for one who returned from foreign slavery
recovered his former status by postliminium (§ 117).

77. MANUMISSION.—The status of slavery might be brought
to an end by manumission, when the slave's master took the
appropriate steps to make him free. There were various modes
of manumission, which may be distinguished as regular and
irregular, or formal and informal. The regular or formal modes
of manumission were—(a) vindicta, by a fictitious law-suit.[34]
The process took its name from the wand (vindicta) with which
the plaintiff (adsertor libertatis) touched the slave, alleging that

---

[27] Dig. 44. 7. 14.
[28] Perhaps for statuto liber a man made free on terms. Dig. 40. 7. 1.
[29] G. 3. 56.
[30] The phrase is misleading. It was the bona fides of the master
which was relevant, not of the slave.
[31] Moyle, p. 112.
[32] Cod. 11. 52. 1 ; Buckl. *M.* p. 53.
[33] In relation to his patron a libertinus was termed libertus, *e.g.*,
Caesaris libertus—Ceasar's freedman.
[34] Or not fictitious? Buckl. *M.* p. 43 ; Roby I, p. 26 ; Schulz, p. 53.

he was free (§§ 672, 690). Long before Justinian this had become a mere formality. Hermogenianus (third or fourth century) says " today manumission is effected by means of the lictors," [35] and ultimately manumission might take place on any day (not necessarily a Court day) and anywhere the magistrate was to be found, as for example when he was on his way to the bath or the theatre; (b) censu—by enrolment on the census; (c) testamento—by will. Testamentary manumission might be direct—Stichus servus meus liber esto—" be my slave Stichus free," or fideicomissary—fidei committo heredis mei ut Stichum servum manumittat [36]—" I charge my heir with a trust to manumit my slave Stichus " (§ 360). In the first case he was said to be the dead man's freedman (libertus orcinus).[36] He had no living patron, but the rights of patronage passed to the family of the testator.[37] In the second case the fiduciary manu-mitter was his patron. The irregular or informal modes of manumission were inter amicos—by declaring the man free amongst friends; per epistolam—by sending him a letter importing a gift of freedom; and, in the later Empire, convivii adhibitione—by asking him to dinner.[38] Manumission before the Bishop in Church, as regulated by Constantine, may be regarded as formal, for it conferred citizenship on the manu-mitted slave, if other conditions were satisfied.[39] To these modes of manumission Justinian added some more, e.g., appointing a slave your heir, even unaccompanied by an express gift of freedom, adopting him as your son, appointing him by will tutor to your son. All these modes of manumission were voluntary acts of the master. There were, besides, cases in which manu-mission took place independently of his wishes or in which a slave became free independently of manumission. These were cases in which the law converted the slave into a free man, either to reward the slave or to punish the master.[40] Instances of the latter kind were frequent in the later Empire. Thus the slaves of pagans, heretics and Jews became free on adopting Christianity. In some cases the magistrates manumitted or com-pelled the master to do so; in others freedom was acquired

1. 5. 2.

2. 24. 2.

1. 5. 1.

1. 6. 2.
1. 11. 12.
1. 14. 1.

---

[35] Dig. 40. 2. 23. The lictors were a body of police, of whom a certain number were attached to each magistrate, twelve to a consul, two to the praetor urbanus.
[36] Ulp. II. 7 & 8
[37] Dig. 26. 4. 3, 3 ; Cod. 7. 6. 1, 7.
[38] The phrase is taken from the Epitome of Gaius (§ 33). Theophilus in his Greek paraphrase of the Institutes (Jolowicz, p. 512) speaks of manumissio per mensam.
[39] Cod. 1. 13. 2 ; Buckl., The Roman Law of Slavery, p. 450.
[40] Buckl. p. 598.

automatically. The history and consequences of manumission will be considered below. But first it will be convenient to say something about the legal condition of freedmen.

78. STATUS OF FREEDMEN.—A freedman was in an inferior position relatively to an ingenuus in the sphere both of public and of private law.[41] In the first, he was excluded from the Senate and from magistracies. In the second, marriage with freeborn persons was perhaps forbidden before the lex Julia of B.C. 18,[42] which restricted the prohibition to senators and their children, and further descendants for two generations in the male line.[43] This and later statutes remained in force until abrogated by Justinian.[44]

79. A freedman's relation to his patron is summed up in the words—obsequium, operae, bona—respect, services, property.

(a) Obsequium. He owed respect to his patron, and might not bring an action against him except by permission of the magistrate. There was a reciprocal duty of support in case of need.

(b) Operae. The freedman was usually required to render services to his patron, by no means of a nominal character. The Digest contains many details as to what might, and might not, be demanded.[45] The obligation to render the services was usually secured by oath (§ 443).

3. 7. pr.

(c) Bona. By the Law of the Twelve Tables the patron succeeded to the libertus, if the latter died intestate without leaving a suus heres (§ 336), and together with this had the right or duty of tutelage. By the later law, he was entitled in certain events to take a share of the estate if the freedman had made a will, but by Justinian's legislation, if the freedman had children, he need not leave anything to his patron (§ 401).

1. 17.

The status of freedman might be ended by imperial grant. By restitutio natalium, which may be translated " grant of birth-right," a libertinus was put in all respects upon an equality with an ingenuus just as if he had in fact been born free. Since this had the effect of excluding the patron's right of succession it was rarely accorded and only with the patron's consent.[46] A licence to wear a gold ring (jus aureorum anulorum) put him in

---

[41] Girard, p. 135.
[42] This was part of the legislation on marriage of Augustus—lex Julia de maritandis ordinibus—de adulteriis—de fundo dotali—and the later lex Papia Poppaea (A.D. 9). Practically, these statutes constituted one marriage code and are so treated in the sources.
[43] Dig. 23. 2. 44 pr.
[44] Corbett, p. 39.
[45] Dig. 38. 1.
[46] Dig. 40. 11 ; Cod. 6. 4. 1.

the same position politically, leaving the patron's rights unaffected.[47] By Nov. 78. 1. (A.D. 539) Justinian bestowed upon all freedmen present and future both the above-mentioned rights, but without prejudice to the patron's rights unless expressly renounced, and, in any event, with reservation of the duty of obsequium and the liability to be reduced to slavery for ingratitude (§ 71).

80. THE HISTORY OF MANUMISSION.—From early times manumission afforded an escape from slavery. While slaves were few manumissions were correspondingly infrequent. In the last century of the Republic they became alarmingly numerous. Manumission by will was cheap and easy, and it might be some satisfaction to a dying man to think of a crowd of freedmen in new caps of liberty attending his bier.[48] Indiscriminate manumission had a bad effect upon the quality of the citizen body and Augustus sought to restrain it by the legislation to be presently mentioned, which remained in force until Justinian.

81. The civil law recognised only formal manumission by a master who combined Quiritary title with effective ownership. Bare title (nudum jus Quiritium) [49] gave no right to manumit.[50] If manumission was informal (§ 77), or the master "had the slave in his goods" merely (bonitary ownership, § 152) without civil law title, the man remained de jure a slave, though the praetor secured him in the de facto enjoyment of liberty. The lex Aelia Sentia of A.D. 4 added a further condition, viz., that, if the master was under twenty years of age, or the slave under thirty, manumission must be by vindicta after a just cause of manumission had been established to the satisfaction of a board (consilium) consisting at Rome of five senators and five knights (equites), and in the provinces of twenty Roman citizens chosen to be recuperatores.[51] In the first case, failure to satisfy this condition rendered the manumission void; in the second case the praetor gave the manumitted slave de facto protection. *(margin: G. 3. 56. / G. 1. 38. / G. 1. 18. / G. 1. 20.)*

82. LATIN STATUS—LEX JUNIA.—A new situation was created by the lex Junia, which, if correctly described by Justinian as the lex Junia Norbana, must be dated A.D. 19, but which perhaps

---

47 Dig. 40. 10. 5 and 6; 38. 2. 3, 1; vivit quasi ingenuus, moritur quasi libertus.
48 . . . at illum
    Hesterni capite induto subiere Quirites.
                                        (Persius, 3. 105).
49 See p. 112, n. 11.
50 Cod. 7. 10 5. Iteratio, a repeated (formal) manumission by an ex-Quiritary owner, is a curious anomaly, for which see Buckl. T. p. 94.
51 See p. 439, n. 41.

came before the lex Aelia Sentia. (Gaius describes it as lex Junia merely, which makes it possible to fix an earlier date).[52] From the early days of the Republic it had been the practice to establish " colonies " in Latium or other parts of Italy, whether as a military outpost or as a means of settling part of the urban population on the land. Later, the word " colony " described merely a particular form of civic government.[53] In a typical case the inhabitants of a colony, along with other privileges, enjoyed the right of trading with Roman citizens on equal terms and of employing Roman forms of contract and conveyance (jus commercii) as well as of making and taking under a Roman will (§§ 302, 307). The inhabitants of the oldest colonies, known as Latini prisci or veteres, enjoyed also the right of inter-marriage with Roman citizens (jus conubii). This was not accorded to any colony founded after 268 B.C. This condition, which reflected the relation in which Rome had formerly stood to her Latin neighbours, was known as Latinitas, and the inhabitants as Latini Coloniarii (Colonial Latins).[54] In Italy colonies of this class ceased to exist when, during the Social War (B.C. 91–88), Roman citizenship was extended to the whole of Italy south of the river Po. But new grants of Latinity were made to towns or larger areas outside Italy. Thus the region between the river Po and the Alps (Transpadane Gaul) received Latin status by a law promoted by the consul Gnaeus Pompeius Strabo in the year B.C. 89, and in a later age the Emperor Vespasian conferred Latin right on the whole of Spain. Latinity had long since lost any geographical association. It was an intermediate stage on the road to citizenship, which implied the jus commercii but not the jus conubii (the right of contracting a civil law marriage, § 91). The communities which enjoyed this privilege took with it the name of Colonial Latins.[55] The term " Latin " having received this wide extension, there was no difficulty in applying it to the manumitted slaves upon whom the lex Junia in combination with the lex Aelia Sentia (§ 84) conferred a statutory status. Such were slaves manu-

G. 1. 17. mitted informally, or by a bonitary owner (§ 152), or under the age of thirty, if the manumission did not satisfy the requirements

---

[52] G. 1. 22. Girard (p. 138) inclines to a date between B.C. 44 and B.C. 27.
[53] Moyle, p. 26.
[54] G. 3. 56. The term jus Latii is applied specifically to the right of access to Roman citizenship accorded either to decuriones (§ 105) and office holders (majus Latium) or to office holders only (minus Latium) G. 1. 96.
[55] Ulp. XIX, 4.

of the lex Aelia Sentia, not to speak of some other cases of less frequent occurrence. But though, in principle, the Junian Latins, as they were called, were assimilated to Colonial Latins, the statute denied them the right of making or taking under a Roman will or of being appointed tutors by will.[56] The reason why they could not make a will is plain enough. The statute wished to secure to the manumitter the same control over the manumitted slave's property as he would have had over the peculium of the imperfectly manumitted slave if the statute had not been passed; and so, as Justinian says, "though they lived free, they lost their liberty and their life together." Why the statute did not allow them to take under a will is not easy to see. Perhaps there is no answer, except that it was so interpreted. In any event it was evaded or restricted, for:— (a) though a Junian Latin might not take under a will directly, he might do so by testamentary trust (fideicommissum)[57] (§ 360); and (b) soldiers, amongst other special privileges, were permitted to leave legacies to peregrines and Latins by a military will and to institute them heirs.[58] A Latin might qualify himself for taking under a will by acquiring citizenship, in one of the various ways open to him, within one hundred days of the testator's death.[59]

G. 3. 56.

3. 7. 4.

83. Another statute—the lex Fufia Caninia (2 B.C.)—limited manumission by will to a varying proportion of the slaves owned and to one hundred at most.[60]   G. 1. 42.

84. LEX AELIA SENTIA.—The lex Aelia Sentia (A.D. 4), contained numerous provisions relating to manumission and in particular:—(a) prohibited manumission in fraud of creditors.[61] For particulars see the text. This clause, unlike the rest of the statute, applied to peregrini as well as to cives; (b) created a very inferior status for slaves who before manumission had been subjected to severe punishment. They were to be in the same position as surrendered enemies (peregrini dediticii). They might not make a will or take under a will. They might not reside within one hundred miles of Rome under penalty of being sold into slavery without hope of manumission and in case of a purported manumission becoming slaves of the Roman

G. 1. 47.
G. 1. 13.
G. 1. 25.

---

56 G. 1. 23. Colonial Latins usually had testamenti factio with Romans, Buckl. *T.* p. 289; de Zulueta, *Gaius*, II, 27. So had Junian Latins, but not the jus capiendi (§§ 309, 310).
57 G. 1. 24; 2. 275.
58 G. 2. 110.
59 G. 1. 28; Ulp. XVII, 1.
60 G. 1. 42; Inst. 1. 7.
61 G. 1. 36; Inst. 1. 6 pr.

People. They could not under any circumstances become citizens; (c) The provisions relating to the age of master and slave have been mentioned above (§ 81); (d) A slave manumitted under the age of thirty years without complying with the statute might become a citizen by marrying before seven witnesses a citizen or a Latin or a person of like status with himself, and, when he had a son one year old, proving these facts to the satisfaction of the praetor or provincial governor. This was called anniculi causae probatio (proof of a claim based on having a one-year-old child) or causae probatio ex lege Aelia Sentia. A senatusconsultum extended the privilege to all Junian Latins.

G. 1. 29.

G. 1. 31.

85. ALL FREEDMEN TO BE ROMAN CITIZENS.—The inferior types of free status were not affected by the constitution of Caracalla,[62] extending citizenship (with some uncertain limitations)[63] to the whole Roman world. But by the time of Justinian the status of dediticii, he tells us, had long since fallen into disuse, while the name of Latin had become infrequent. Accordingly by constitutions of 530 and 531 he put an end to both of them with the result, as he says, that " we have bestowed on all freedmen Roman citizenship with no discrimination as regards the age of the manumitted slave, the nature of the manumitter's ownership or the mode of manumission." This restored the law to its ancient simplicity by reducing all freedmen to a single type. It will be remarked that nothing is said as to the age of the master. In the Institutes Justinian allowed a master to manumit by will from the age of seventeen, which by Novel 119. 2. (A.D. 544) he reduced to fourteen for males, twelve for females, the age at which they were competent to dispose by will of their other property. After this nothing remained of the lex Aelia Sentia except the prohibition of manumission in fraud of creditors, and (it seems) the incapacity of masters under twenty to manumit inter vivos. The old consilium (§ 81) was plainly obsolete. We are not told what took its place.

1. 5. 3.

1. 6. 7.

---

[62] Dig. 1. 5. 17: In orbe Romano qui sunt ex constitutione imperatoris Antonini cives Romani effecti sunt. This is the only text except Nov. 78. 5, where the constitution is wrongly attributed to Antoninus Pius. (If anyone chooses to regard the fragmentary Giessen papyrus as a text he may add it to the list). The Emperor known to historians as Caracalla was known to lawyers as Antoninus. The constitution of 212 is often cited as the Constitutio Antoniana.

[63] Buckl. M. p. 59; Jolowicz, p. 357.

THE INSTITUTES

BOOK I (Tits. III–VII)

TITLE III

Of the law of persons

The principal division in the law of persons is that all men are §68. either free or slaves.

1. Freedom, from which we get the description of men as free, is a man's natural capacity of doing what he pleases unless he is prevented by force or law. 2. Slavery is an institution of the jus gentium by which one man is made the property of another contrary to nature. 3. Slaves (servi) are so-called because military commanders order their captives to be sold, and so are used to preserve them alive (servare) instead of killing them. They are also called mancipia because they are taken from the enemy by the strong hand (manu capiuntur). 4. Slaves are either born slaves or made slaves. §§69–71 They are born of our female slaves. They are made slaves either by the jus gentium, that is by being taken captive, or by civil law, as when a free man upwards of twenty years of age suffers himself to be sold in order to share the price. 5. There is no difference in the §75. condition of slaves. In the condition of free men there are many differences; for they are either born free (ingenui) or made free (libertini).

TITLE IV

Of persons born free

A free-born person (ingenuus) is one who is free from birth, §76 being the issue of parents both born free, or both made free, or one free-born, the other free-made. Even if the mother is free and the father a slave, the issue is free-born, just as is the case when a free woman bears a child and the father is unknown, because the child was conceived promiscuously. It is enough for the mother to have been free at the time of birth, though she may have been a slave at the time of conception. Conversely, if she was free at the time of conception, and became a slave before the child was born, it is settled that the child is born free, for an unborn child ought not to be prejudiced by the mother's misfortune. Suppose then that a slave-woman conceives, then is manumitted, then enslaved again, and bears a son. Is he slave or free? Marcellus [64] favours the view that he is free, on the ground that it is enough that the unborn child had a free mother in the interval between conception and birth, and this is good law. 1. If a person is free-born he is not prejudiced by being at some time in *de facto* slavery and afterwards manumitted. Imperial constitutions have very often declared that manumission does not prejudice a man's birth-right.

---

[64] Ulpius Marcellus was a jurist of the time of Marcus Aurelius, the author of a Digest, Responsa and other works.

TITLE V

Of freedmen

Freedmen are those who have been manumitted from legal slavery.[65] Manumission means a gift of freedom, for so long as a man is a slave he is under the hand and power of a master and by being manumitted, that is dismissed from hand, he is set free from power. This has its origin in the jus gentium. By natural law all men were born free, and manumission was unknown since slavery was equally unrecognised. Afterwards, the jus gentium introduced slavery and this was followed by the benefit of manumission; so whereas the word " men " is a common and natural appellation of all mankind, the jus gentium has made three classes of men, men who are free, men who are slaves, and thirdly, men who have ceased to be slaves, that is freedmen.   1. Manumission takes place in many ways, for it may be effected either in Holy Church, as the imperial laws provide, or by vindicta, or amongst friends, or by a letter, or by testament or other expression of a man's last will; and there are many other ways by which a slave may attain to freedom provided by the constitutions of earlier emperors and by our own. 2. Slaves may be manumitted by their masters upon any occasion, even in the street, as when the praetor or proconsul or governor is on his way to the bath or the theatre.   3. Formerly, there were three kinds of freedmen, for manumitted slaves either acquired complete freedom and became Roman citizens, or a lesser degree of freedom and became Latins by the lex Junia Norbana, or finally a yet lower degree of freedom and were reckoned as dediticii, as provided by the lex Aelia Sentia. But the degraded status of dediticii has long since passed out of use, while the name of Latin had become infrequent. Therefore, our benevolence, anxious always to enlarge and to improve, has in two constitutions amended the law and restored the original position; for from Rome's earliest infancy there was a uniform, single freedom, the same for the manumitted slave as for the manumitting master, except, of course, that the first was a freedman and the master was free-born. First, then, we have put an end to the status of dediticii. This is effected by a constitution[66] promulgated amongst our decisions,[67] by which at the suggestion of the eminent Tribonian we have settled the controversies of the old law. Next, by another constitution,[68] which is a conspicuous ornament of our legislation, we have abolished the status of Junian Latins and all the law relating to them, and, admitting no distinction as regards the age of the manumitted slave or the nature of the master's ownership or the mode of manumission, we have, as above observed, bestowed Roman citizenship on all freedmen, providing also many additional ways by which slaves may attain freedom and with it citizenship, the only kind of freedom now allowed.

§ 77.

§§ 80-4.

§ 85.

---

[65] Not from slavery *de facto*, as in the case of a free man wrongly supposed to be a slave (Tit. IV, 1, *supra*), or from slavery jure gentium.
[66] Cod. 5. 6.
[67] Quinquaginta Decisiones (*supra*, § 40).
[68] Cod. 5. 7.

Title VI

Who may not manumit, and why ?

Manumission is not permitted indiscriminately. Thus a manu-   § 84.
mission in fraud of creditors is without effect, for the lex Aelia
Sentia bars the way to freedom. 1. Nevertheless, an insolvent
master is permitted by his testament to institute a slave his heir
together with a gift of freedom, so that the slave becomes free and
sole and necessary heir, provided that there is no other heir under   § 335.
the will, either because no other person is instituted heir, or because
the heir instituted by the will for some cause or other does not take
the inheritance. This is provided by the same statute, and wisely;
for it was a thing very much to be kept in view, that men in dis-
tressed circumstances, who were not likely to get anyone to succeed
them, should have a slave as necessary heir who would satisfy the
claims of creditors, and that, if he failed to do so, the creditors
should sell the estate in the slave's name and save the reputation of
the deceased. 2. The law is the same if a slave is instituted heir   § 77.
without a gift of freedom. For our constitution [69] benevolently
provides, not merely in the case of an insolvent master, but as a
principle of general application, that an institution as heir imports
a gift of liberty; for it cannot be inferred from the fact that a
testator has omitted to add a gift of freedom that he intended that
the man whom he had chosen to be his heir should remain a slave,
and that he should have no heir at all. 3. Manumission is understood to be in fraud of creditors, if the manumitting master is
already insolvent, or will become insolvent in consequence of the
manumission. But the view has prevailed that a gift of liberty will
not fail to take effect, even though the property of the estate is
insufficient to meet the claims of creditors, unless the manumitter
intended to defraud them; for men often hope that their means are
more ample than they are in fact. So it is understood that manumission fails to take effect only when creditors are defrauded both
by the manumitter's intention and by the actual consequence of the
property being insufficient to satisfy their claims. 4. The same
statute forbids a master under twenty years of age to manumit otherwise than by vindicta, a just cause of manumission having been
established before the council. 5. There is a just cause of manumission, if, for example, a master manumits his natural father or
mother or son or daughter, or brother or sister, his pedagogue,[70] his
nurse, his governor,[71] his foster-brother, or foster-sister, or a slave
who is to manage the manumitter's affairs, or a female slave with a
view to marriage; provided, in this case, that marriage takes place
within six months, unless there is some good reason to the contrary.
A slave manumitted to manage a business must be not less than
seventeen years of age. 6. Once a cause has been approved, the
approval cannot be recalled, whether the cause be true or false.
7. Since, then, the lex Aelia Sentia prescribed a particular mode of   § 81.
manumission for masters under twenty years of age, it followed that,
though from the age of fourteen anyone might make a will and

[69] Cod. 6. 27. 5.
[70] A pedagogue was a slave who took little children to school.
[71] Or " tutor " in the English sense.

institute an heir and leave legacies, nevertheless, if he was still under the age of twenty, he could not in his will give freedom to a slave. But it was intolerable that a person who was competent to dispose of all his property by will was not allowed to manumit by this method a single slave. Accordingly, we allow this to be done, provided that the master has completed his seventeenth and entered on his eighteenth year. This was the age at which the old law allowed a man to plead another's cause, and why should not a person who has reached this age be credited with enough sense to be able to confer liberty on his slaves?

§ 85.

TITLE VII

Of the lex Fufia Caninia and its abolition

§ 83.

The lex Fufia Caninia set a certain limit to the number of slaves who might be manumitted by will. Since this was an obstacle to manumission and to some extent invidious we have thought proper to abrogate it, for it was scarcely reasonable that a man should be allowed in his lifetime to bestow freedom on all his slaves, unless there was some good reason to the contrary, but should not be allowed to do so by his dying disposition.[72]

II. THE SECOND DIVISION OF PERSONS

(Independent and dependent status)

1. 8 pr.

86. PATRIA POTESTAS.—All persons are either sui juris or alieni juris. Persons alieni juris are in the power of others, either of masters or of parents. The position of persons in the power of masters, i.e., slaves, has been considered above (§ 72). It remains to speak of children in the power of a father or remoter ascendant, in other words of the patria potestas. This was an institution which the Romans considered to be peculiar to themselves, but Gaius notes that something like it existed amongst the Galatians, and it is in fact an institution frequently found in a primitive state of society. We shall speak of the consequences of the patria potestas, first, as regards the persons, secondly, as regards the property, of descendants in power.

1. 9. 2.

G. 1. 55.

87. As regards the person of the son or other descendant, the power of the paterfamilias anciently included[73]:—1. the power of life and death (jus vitae necisque). The history of the Republic records instances of its exercise; 2. the power of sale either trans Tiberim into foreign slavery or within the city into the status of mancipium (§ 124); 3. the right to give the children in marriage and to divorce them at pleasure; 4. the

---

[72] Further particulars in Gaius 1, 42-6.
[73] Girard, p. 150.

right to give them in adoption and to emancipate them at pleasure.

88. With scarcely any exception these powers or rights disappeared before or during the Empire. 1. The jus vitae necisque, long obsolete in practice,[74] was formally abolished by Constantine,[75] who decreed that a parent who killed his child should incur the horrible penalty of parricide. Paulus in a text cited in the Digest from the *Sententiae*[76] treats the abandonment of children as homicide, but it is doubtful whether the practice was forbidden by law before 374.[77]

4. 18. 6.

2. Sale into actual slavery, not unknown in the third century,[78] survived in Constantine's legislation permitting the sale of new-born children. Justinian allowed it but only in case of extreme poverty[79] (§ 71). The noxal surrender of sons into mancipium was abolished only by Justinian.[80] 3. Marriage and divorce, from being a matter of arrangement between parents or an arbitrary exercise of paternal power, came to be regarded as questions which principally concerned the immediate parties.[81] Similarly, the consent of children came to be a necessary condition of adoption[82] or emancipation,[83] unless they were infants.[84]

89. As regards property, the son in power was originally in no better position than a slave. Whatever he acquired was acquired for the paterfamilias. Like a slave he might be allowed the *de facto* enjoyment of a peculium. But by degrees the principle came to be admitted that a filiusfamilias might have a peculium not merely on sufferance, but of right: — (a) From the time of Augustus soldiers were allowed to keep as their own what they acquired in military service (peculium

2. 9. 1.

---

[74] During the Catilinarian conspiracy (63–62 B.C.) Fulvius, the son of a senator had joined the conspirators. His father had him brought back and put to death (Sallust, *Catiline*, cap. 39. 5). Other fathers did the same. The jus vitae necisque is allowed by Papinian (*Coll.* 4. 8), Ulpian (Dig. 48. 8. 2), and Paul (Dig. 28. 2. 11, where " licebat " has been substituted for " licet ").
[75] Cod. 9. 17 1. But according to another view the jus vitae necisque was extinguished in 365 by a constitution of Valentinian I. Cod. 9. 15. 1.
[76] Dig. 25. 3. 4.
[77] Cod. 9. 16. 7 (8) ; Girard, p. 153.
[78] Cod. 4. 43. 1 ; 7. 16. 1.
[79] Cod. 4. 43. 2.
[80] Inst. 4. 8. 7.
[81] Bene concordans matrimonium separari a patre divus Pius prohibuit. Paul *Sent.* 5. 6. 15 ; Dig. 43. 30. 5. But Justinian retained in the Code a constitution of Diocletian (Cod. 5. 17. 5), which permitted a paterfamilias to dissolve his daughter's marriage—magna et justa causa interveniente.
[82] Dig. 1. 7. 5 ; Cod. 8. 47 (48) 10 pr. *in fine.*
[83] Paul *Sent.* 2. 25. 5.
[84] Cod. 8. 48. 5 *in fine*

castrense). This practically belonged to them for most purposes. They might dispose of it by will (§ 303), but **before** Hadrian only while still on service. If they failed to do so, it reverted to the father in its character of peculium. It was only Justinian who gave the children and brothers and sisters of a deceased *filius* a preferent right of intestate succession. (b) Constantine and later Emperors extended the principle to what the son earned in various civil employments or the service of the Church (*peculium quasi-castrense*), which, however, before Justinian the son might not (generally) dispose of by will. (c) It was Constantine also who reduced (in effect) to a usufruct the father's interest in property coming to the son by inheritance from his mother (*bona materna*) (§ 112). This was extended by later Emperors to all other acquisitions derived from the mother or from her relations (*bona materni generis*), and ultimately to all acquisitions from any source not otherwise classified. These are comprehended under the general term of *bona adventicia*. The son never acquired even under Justinian the right of disposing of them by will during the father's lifetime, though they became his absolute property when his father died. If he died first the property went to the father (subject to prior claims) [85] by right of succession, not by right of peculium. The expression *peculium adventicium*, therefore, should be avoided. In case of emancipation imperial constitutions allowed the father to retain one-third part of the *bona adventicia*, "as, so to say, the price of emancipation." Justinian substituted for this the usufruct of a half. (d) All this leaves unaffected the father's right to his own property confided to the son and to gains accruing from it. This was *peculium profectum a patre* or, as it is usually called on the analogy of *dos profecticia* (§ 222), *peculium profecticium*. To the same head may be referred gifts made to the son with the intention of conferring a benefit upon the father (*contemplatione patris*), and gifts made by the father to the son, which remained without effect during the father's lifetime.[86]

90. The patria potestas came into existence in a variety of ways, and in particular by: 1, civil law marriage; 2, legitimation; 3, adoption; 4, imperial rescript.

91. CIVIL LAW MARRIAGE (*justae nuptiae—justum matrimonium*).—Justinian summarises the conditions of marriage in the following sentence: "A civil law marriage is contracted

---

[85] Of descendants and of brothers and sisters; Cod. 6. 59. 11; 6. 51. 6.
[86] Girard, p. 155.

2. 12 pr.

2. 11. 6.

2. 9. 1.

by Roman citizens who are united according to law, males having reached years of puberty, females being of marriageable age, whether they be sui juris or in power, provided that children in power must have the consent of the paterfamilias." The requirements of a civil law marriage, therefore, were as follows: —

1. 10 pr.

- (a) the spouses must be qualified to contract a civil law marriage (§ 92);
- (b) they must be of marriageable age (§ 93);
- (c) there must be no rule of law forbidding them to marry or to intermarry (§ 94);
- (d) children in power must have the necessary consents (§ 95);
- (e) husband and wife must be consenting parties to the marriage (§ 96).

92 (a). JUS CONUBII.—The husband must have the right to contract a civil law marriage with the wife (conubium—jus conubii). In the earliest period of Roman history there was general conubium between Romans on the one hand, and the inhabitants of Latium and the oldest colonies (§ 82) on the other (prisci Latini). Children followed the status of the father, citizen if he was citizen, Latin if he was not. In either case there was a marriage recognised by the Roman courts. But to constitute a civil law marriage, both parties to the marriage must normally be citizens, for, in general, citizens alone had the power of contracting a civil law marriage. In the first two centuries of the Empire citizens individually, or as members of a community, were by special favour allowed to contract a civil law marriage with Latin or peregrine women.[87] Grants of the kind were frequently made to discharged soldiers.[88] After Caracalla's constitution the requirement of conubium lost most of its former importance. It continued to exclude marriage with Latini Juniani and peregrini dediticii, so long as either status existed.

93 (b). MARRIAGEABLE AGE.—The parties to the marriage must be of marriageable age. After controversy between the schools, this came to be fixed at fourteen for males, twelve for

---

[87] Ulp. V, 3 & 4. Conubium est uxoris jure ducendae facultas. Conubium habent cives Romani cum civibus Romanis; cum Latinis autem et peregrinis ita si concessum sit. Professor Last has kindly called my attention to the case of the municipality of Volubilis, which received from the Emperor Claudius a grant of citizenship and conubium with peregrine women. Cagnat & Merlin, Inscriptions latines d'Afrique (Paris, 1923), 634.
[88] G. 1. 56.

females.[89]　These ages passed into the Canon Law and through the Canon Law into most modern systems.　Now, however, the canonical age of marriage is sixteen for males and fourteen for females.[90]　England followed the old Canon Law until the age was raised to sixteen for both sexes by the Age of Marriage Act, 1929.

94 (c). LAWFUL MARRIAGE.—The parties must be united according to law, *i.e.*, they must be competent to marry and to intermarry.　The following could not marry at all: *viz.*, (i) persons already married.[91]　There is no record that the Romans ever admitted polygamy; (ii) castrati [92]; (iii) in the early Empire soldiers during the term of service [93]; (iv) (in the later law) persons who had taken vows of chastity or been admitted to priest's orders.[94]　Intermarriage was principally forbidden between persons too nearly related by birth, adoption or marriage.　For particulars reference may be made to the text. It is enough to say that marriage was forbidden between ascendants and descendants by blood or marriage, and between collaterals any one of whom was removed by one degree only from the common ancestor.　For some three centuries a paternal uncle was allowed to marry his niece.　This was because the law was changed to enable the Emperor Claudius to marry his brother's daughter Agrippina.[95]　The marriage was not a success.　Five years later she poisoned him with a dish of mushrooms.[96]　The old law was restored by Constantine in 339.[97]　In the later Empire it was forbidden to marry a deceased wife's sister or a deceased husband's brother.[98]　This was the starting point of the canonical doctrine that the prohibitions which apply to blood relationship (consanguinity) apply equally to relationship by marriage (affinity).[99]　Justinian

---

[89] G. 1. 196; Ulp. XI, 28; Inst. 1. 22 pr.
[90] *Cod. Jur. Can.* c. 1067.
[91] Inst. 1. 10. 6; Cod. 5. 5. 2.
[92] Dig. 23. 3. 39, 1.
[93] Corbett, p. 39.
[94] These are the impedimenta voti et ordinis of the Canon Law.
[95] G. 1. 62.
[96] Boletus domino, sed quales Claudius edit,
　　Ante illum uxoris, post quem non amplius edit.
　　　　　　(Juvenal, V. 147–8.)

" He feasts, secure, on mushrooms fine as those
　Which Claudius, for his special eating, chose,
　Till one more fine, provided by his wife,
　Finish'd at once his feasting, and his life."
　　　　　　(Gifford's translation.)
[97] Cod. Theod. 3. 12. 1.
[98] Cod. Theod. 3. 12. 2 (A.D. 355); Cod. 5. 5. 5 (A.D. 393).
[99] A. Esmein, *Le Mariage en Droit Canonique*, 2nd ed. (1929), t. I, p. 417.

must share with the Church the credit of having invented what
is called cognatio spiritualis (spiritual relationship) by prohibiting
the inter-marriage of god-parents and god-children.[1] More
reason may be found for prohibiting intermarriage between
guardians and their wards, or between provincial administrators
and the ladies of the provinces.[2]

95 (d). CONSENT OF PATERFAMILIAS.—If a party to a
marriage was in power the consent of the paterfamilias was a
necessary condition. A grandson in power with an unemancipated father still living required the consent of grandfather and
of father as well. This was in order that the father might not
have a suus heres imposed upon him without his consent. The
same consideration did not apply to a granddaughter. In her
case the grandfather's consent was necessary and sufficient.[3]
Difficulties arose in case the paterfamilias was insane or
unreasonably refused his consent. They were felt to be more
serious in the case of the son than of the daughter.[4] Justinian
decided that in either case the consent of an insane parent was
not required. The dos (§ 222) and donatio propter nuptias 1. 10 pr.
(§ 221) were to be settled by the appropriate authority. If
consent was unreasonably withheld the lex Julia allowed the
daughter, and, possibly, the son as well, to apply to a magistrate
for leave to marry.[5] At all events this was the law for
Justinian.

96 (e). CONSENT OF PARTIES.—The consent of the parties is
assumed to be necessary. It was so in Justinian's day as it had
been for centuries before his time.[6] It is likely enough that in
early times marriage was a matter of arrangement between the
parents on both sides in law as it always might be in fact (§ 88).

97. SPONSALIA.—Marriage, naturally, implies an antecedent
agreement to marry. Anciently, in Rome as in Latium
generally, this took the form of reciprocal stipulations
(§ 444) or sponsiones (whence the word sponsalia meaning
"betrothal").[7] The parties would normally be the intending
husband, or his paterfamilias, and the paterfamilias of the
intended bride. This practice was discontinued in Rome earlier
than in Latium, where it lasted until Roman citizenship and

---

[1] Cod. 5. 4.
[2] Corbett, pp. 42–4.
[3] Dig. 23. 2. 16, 1.
[4] Cod. 5. 4. 25.
[5] Dig. 23. 2. 19; Corbett, p. 66.
[6] Dig. 23. 2. 2 (Paulus).
[7] Dig. 23. 1. 2.

with it Roman Law were extended to Latium during the Social
War [8] (§ 82). In the classical period mutual promises to marry
created no legal obligation, so much so that to stipulate for a
penalty to be paid in the event of marriage not taking place
was held to be contra bonos mores.[9] In the later Empire a
practice of eastern origin came into use, namely, for the man or
woman or both to give something by way of earnest to
guarantee the engagement (arra sponsalicia).[10] Like arra in the
contract of sale (§ 464), with which it was closely allied, it
served to penalise the party who withdrew from the engagement
without just cause.

98. No Ceremony Required.—No ceremony, civil or
religious, was necessary. Marriage was concluded by consent.[11]
But something more precise was desirable to show that (and
when) marriage had taken place. This consisted in a traditio
of the wife to the husband, usually indicated by taking her to his
house (ductio in domum).[12] Consistently with this, it was held
that marriage might be concluded in the absence of the husband,
but not of the wife.[13] It was, of course, fundamental that the
parties had the intention to live together as husband and wife
(affectio maritalis). There was nothing but this to distinguish
marriage from concubinage (§ 104).

99. Wife's Status Unchanged.—Roman marriage, of the
type which became universal (or nearly so) in the classical age,
was a relation of remarkable freedom. Marriage per se did not
effect a transfer of the wife's property to the husband or give
him any right of administration. She retained her contractual
freedom, except that she could not make a gift to her husband,
any more than he could to her. This was one reason why it was
of importance to fix the moment at which marriage took place.[14]
As the wife controlled her own property, so in law (it is thought)
she was expected to provide for her own maintenance. It was
not her husband's business to provide for her needs.[15]

100. A marriage between peregrines, if valid by the laws
and customs of the community to which they belonged, was
matrimonium, but not justum matrimonium. The Roman

---

[8] By the leges Julia (B.C. 90) and Plautia Papiria (B.C. 89).
[9] Dig. 45. 1. 134 pr.   [10] Cod. 5. 1 ; Girard, p. 164, n. 2.
[11] Dig. 24. 1. 66.
[12] Buckl. T. p. 112 ; M. p. 67. This was not of the essence of
marriage. Dig. 23. 2. 5.
[13] Paul Sent. 2. 19. 8.
[14] Cod. 5. 3. 6.
[15] Hunter, p. 679. But the question is controversi juris. See Wind-
scheid-Kipp, III. § 491, n. 2.

courts recognised and gave effect to it. There was no patria
potestas, but the children were held to be legitimate and took G. 1. 55.
their father's status. By a senatusconsultum passed at the
instance of the Emperor Hadrian the same consequence followed
when a peregrine husband married a citizen wife. The son was
justus patris filius. Previously this would not have been the G. 1. 77.
case unless the peregrine by special favour had the jus conubii.
The senatusconsultum did not apply to the converse case of a
citizen husband marrying a peregrine wife. This was a relation
which the Roman Law did not encourage. Antony's marriage
with Cleopatra (B.C. 37) would not have been " marriage," even
if he had first divorced Octavia, which he did only five years
later.

101. DIVORCE.—There is a story that divorce was unknown
in Rome until about B.C. 227 (but different dates are given)
when one Spurius Carvilius Rufa put away his wife because
she was incapable of bearing children. Like Shakespeare's
Henry VIII he seems to have been troubled by conscience, for
the censors had required him to take an oath that he married
with a view to offspring.[16] The statement that divorce was
previously unknown cannot be accepted. Cicero connects
divorce with the Twelve Tables, Plutarch with Romulus. But
we may believe that in early times it was infrequent. In the
later Republic it became very common. As marriage came
into existence by agreement and marital affection, so it was
thought reasonable that it should cease to exist when these
conditions were no longer present. This meant that the
marriage bond might be severed by mutual consent (divortium
bona gratia) or at the will of either party (repudium). In the
latter event Augustus required, at least in some cases, a formal
repudiation before seven witnesses (lex Julia de adulteriis).
In the East it was the practice to send a bill of divorcement
(libellus repudii) and this was made obligatory by Theodosius II
and Valentinian III in A.D. 449.[17] This relates to the free
marriage, which was the only marriage then in existence. As to
the dissolution of manus marriages there is little information.
Marriages contracted by confarreatio were sometimes dissolved
by a contrary process called diffarreatio. The Christian
Emperors decreed penalties of fantastic severity for causeless
divorce, without, however, declaring it void until Justinian did
so, but, as it happened, in the case least open to objection,

---

[16] Aulus Gellius, IV. 3
[17] Cod. 5. 17. 8 pr.

namely, divorce by mutual consent. This was in the year 542.[18]
The law was repealed in the year following Justinian's death.[19]

102. There were cases in which marriage was terminated by
operation of law. If a father adopted his daughter's husband
or his son's wife, the marriage became incestuous and was *ipso*
jure dissolved (incestus superveniens). Loss of citizenship converted justum matrimonium into matrimonium non justum with
loss of potestas. Enslavement jure civili of either spouse
dissolved the marriage. There is some doubt as to the effect of
captivity. It is generally supposed that before Justinian the
marriage was dissolved and was not automatically re-established
by postliminium (§ 117).[20] Under Justinian captivity did not
per se dissolve the marriage, but if for five years the husband
had not been known to be alive the wife was free to remarry.[21]
Apart from this, absence, however prolonged, though without
news, left the marriage unaffected.[22]

103. THE STATUS OF CHILDREN.—Before leaving the subject
of marriage a few words may be said about the status of
children. Reference has been made above to the general principle that, where there is conubium between the parents, the
children follow the status of the father at the time of conception,
but where there is no conubium the status of the mother at the
time of birth (§ 69).[23] It would follow from this that the issue
of a peregrine father and a citizen mother would be citizen,
just as in the converse case the issue would be peregrine. But
this rule of the jus gentium was qualified by a lex Minicia which
laid down the rule that where one parent was peregrine, the
other citizen, the issue should always have the inferior status.
This statute, of uncertain date, but before the Social War,
included Latins under the head of peregrines. This meant the
inhabitants of Latin communities in Italy (§ 82). The statute
was not extended to Junian Latins. It followed that the issue of
a Junian Latin father and a citizen mother was citizen. There
had been some doubt with regard to marriages contracted under
the lex Aelia Sentia (§ 84). It was argued that in this case there
was a statutory conubium between the parties and "conubium
always has the effect that the issue follows the status of the
father." But a senatusconsultum promoted by the Emperor

Margin references:
1. 10. 2.
G. 1. 78.
G. 1. 79.
G. 1. 80.

---

[18] Nov. 117, c. 10.
[19] Nov. 140.
[20] Dig. 49. 15. 12, 4 ; 14, 1.
[21] Dig. 24. 2. 6 (interpolated?) ; Buckl. *M*. p. 40.
[22] Nov. 117, c. 11.
[23] Ulp. V, 8.

Hadrian provided that in any event the issue of a Latin father and a citizen mother should be citizen. If both parties were peregrine and lawfully married the child took the father's status (§ 100).

104. Concubinage was a tolerated condition which was only distinguished from marriage by the absence of affectio maritalis. Like marriage is was permanent—while it lasted—and monogamous. It was contrary to law for a man to have a wife and a concubine at the same time.[24] The issue was illegitimate (liberi naturales), but not promiscuous (spurii), and might be legitimated, as will presently appear (§ 105).

105. LEGITIMATION.—There were various ways in which natural children might be legitimated and brought under the power of their father. These were:—(a) by subsequent marriage (legitimatio per subsequens matrimonium). This was introduced by Constantine to encourage marriage with existing concubines. After much intermediate legislation Justinian established this method of legitimation subject to certain conditions:—(i) The parents must have been legally capable of intermarriage when the child was conceived or born [25]; (ii) a marriage contract must be drawn up in order that no doubt might exist as to the transition from concubinage to matrimony; and (iii) the child must acquiesce.[26] Previous Emperors had made it a condition that there should not be legitimate children by a previous marriage. Justinian dispensed with this requirement.[27] It will be remarked that this indulgence was given only in favour of the issue of concubinage. It did not apply to illegitimate children in general. The Christian Emperors had continued to tolerate an institution which they disapproved and discouraged. Justinian's legislation without a fundamental change of attitude in effect recognised it as what Hunter calls "a species of left-handed marriage." The Church made no distinction between the offspring of concubinage and of more promiscuous relations, but in any case admitted legitimation by subsequent marriage, excluding only the issue of an adulterous union, and with or without this limitation the institution has passed into modern systems of law. The desire of the clergy to make it part of the law of England was so successfully resisted by the barons, as recorded in the Statute of Merton, A.D. 1235-36, that very nearly

1. 10. 13.

---

[24] Paul *Sent*. 2. 20.
[25] Buckl. *T*. p. 129.
[26] Nov. 89. 11.
[27] Nov. 12. 4.

seven centuries elapsed before it found its way into the Statute-
book in the Legitimacy Act, 1926; (b) by making a son a
member (or marrying a daughter to a member) of the council
of a municipality (decurio). This was a function which entailed
heavy financial liabilities, and people were compelled or bribed
to undertake it. Legitimation in this case is said to take place
per oblationem curiae—" by offering to a municipal council ";
(c) by imperial rescript (per rescriptum principis). This method
of legitimation was admitted by Justinian when, the concubine
being already dead, marriage was out of the question,[28] and in
some other circumstances.

1. 10. 13.

106. ADOPTION.—This is another way in which patria
potestas was brought into existence. Adoption was of two
kinds, viz., (a) of a person sui juris, specifically called adrogatio,
and (b) of a person alieni juris, which had no specific name.[29]
We must inquire how each of these was effected and what were
its legal consequences.

G. 1. 99.

107. ADROGATION.—This was effected in the time of Gaius
by a legislative act of the comitia curiata or calata. Gaius says
that it was called adrogation because the adopting father was
asked (rogatur) whether he wished that the person he was going
to adopt should be his lawful son, the person to be adopted was
asked whether he suffered it to be so, and the People was asked
whether it was pleased so to enact. This last was what was
formally necessary. It is what Gaius means when he says that
adrogation was effected " by the authority of the People." But
this procedure was a formal survival from ancient times. The
essence of the matter was an inquiry by the pontiffs, who had to
be satisfied that the adrogation was desirable and that the
interests, religious and material, of the adrogatus and his gens
were duly protected. The adrogator had to be at least sixty
years of age and childless.[30] If the pontiffs gave their approval,
the question was submitted pro forma to the People, that is to
the thirty lictors who represented the thirty curiae. This method
of adrogation from its nature could only be resorted to in the
city of Rome.[31] In the provinces it was replaced by an
imperial rescript granted after inquiry by the local magistrate,
and this came to be used at Rome, first, as an alternative, and,
from the time of Diocletian, or later, to the exclusion of the

---

[28] Nov. 74.
[29] Aulus Gellius (V. 19) calls it adoptatio.
[30] Dig. 1. 7. 15, 2 ; 17, 3.
[31] G. 1. 100.

older procedure.   In the time of Justinian it was the only   1. 11. 1.
method in use. Adoption by will, common in the late Republic
and early Empire, has been supposed to be a kind of adrogation.[32] But perhaps it was merely an institution as heir with
a direction to take the testator's name.[33]

108. Women, according to the prevailing view, could not be
adrogated populi auctoritate, because they could not take part   G. 1. 101.
in the proceedings of the comitia.   There was not the same
difficulty in the case of adrogation by imperial rescript.[34]   But
essentially adrogation was intended to keep a Roman family
alive by providing for its continuance in the male line of
descent, so that the adrogation of females can only have been
admitted when the institution had already changed its character.

109. The adrogation of children under puberty, Gaius says,
was at one time prohibited, later permitted.[35]   The difficulty was
that the child could not consent unaided, and tutors were not
generally considered competent to give their authority in a
matter of such grave concern.[36]   The Emperor Antonius Pius
in a letter to the pontiffs allowed the adrogation of impuberes
subject to stringent conditions.   First, an inquiry must be held
(this indeed was common to all adrogations) ; secondly, the
child was not to be emancipated except for just cause after
inquiry ; thirdly, the adrogator must give security to restore the
child's property in the event of his death or emancipation while
still impubes ; fourthly, if the adrogator died first, the adrogatus
was to have his property returned to him and in addition, if
disinherited or emancipated without just cause, to receive one-   1. 11. 3.
fourth of the adrogator's estate.   This was known as the quarta
Antonia.   It was a special case of the provision for children
which came to be known as the legitima portio (§ 318).   It may
be that these or like conditions were usually required by the
pontiffs.   The imperial rescript dealt specifically with the adrogation of an impubes and termination of potestas while the child
was still impubes.[37]   It might be thought obvious that a female
could not adrogate, and indeed females could not adopt at all in
the proper sense of the word, but a quasi-adoption by women   1. 11. 10
even of a person sui juris was permitted by Diocletian whereby
the adopted person acquired the rights of a natural-born child.[38]

---

[32] Girard, p. 190.
[33] Buckl. *M.* p. 79.
[34] Dig. 1, 7. 21.
[35] G. 1. 102.
[36] Dig. 1. 7. 17, 1.
[37] Buckl. *M.* p. 76.
[38] Cod. 8. 47. 5.

1. 11. 11.   110. CONSEQUENCES OF ADROGATION.—The legal consequences of adrogation were as follows:—(i) The adrogatus and
children in his power, if any, passed into the power of the
adrogator; (ii) the property of the adrogatus of whatever kind,
and debts due to him, passed to the adrogator by a kind of
G. 3. 83.   universal succession (§ 402) [39]; (iii) debts due by the adrogatus
3. 10. 1.   and (before Justinian) the personal servitudes of ususfructus and
usus (§ 252) were extinguished as a consequence of the extinction
of his old persona resulting from the adrogation. Inherited
G. 3. 84.   debts were not thus affected. The reason was that an inheritance was treated as a single res (§ 149). The adrogator could
not take its benefit, if any, without taking the attendant burden.
He was regarded as heir of the deceased, as he would have been
ab initio if the adrogatus had been a natural-born son and had
accepted the inheritance by his father's order. Obligations
ex delicto also survived the adrogation. They became noxal
liabilities (§ 638) of the adrogator, but continued to be personal
liabilities of the adrogatus, enforceable against him directly, if
he again became sui juris.

111. Such was the situation at civil law. But to save
creditors from seeing their just claims defeated by an operation
over which they had no control the praetor gave them a utilis
actio (§ 701) against the adrogatus, based upon the fiction that
there had been no change of status (§ 777), and, if the adrogator
failed to defend the action in his name, allowed the property
which had come to him from the adrogatus to be taken in
execution to satisfy the plaintiff's claim.[40] Justinian says that
in such circumstances the adrogator is not liable in law, but may
be sued in the name of the son with the consequences above
3. 10. 3.   described. If he defends the action he does so at his own risk.

112. Gaius and Justinian agree in describing adrogatio as
a mode of universal acquisition. But Justinian goes on to say
that he had reduced it to a usufruct as in the case of natural
parents.[41] Since everything which the adrogatus took with him
into his new family (not being peculium castrense or peculium
quasi-castrense) necessarily came under the description of bona
adventicia,[42] in which the paterfamilias merely had a usufruct,
it is evident that acquisition by adrogation was in fact a thing
of the past. Justinian might very well have treated it as
obsolete. His change in the law was formal, not substantial.

[39] But see below, § 112.
[40] G. 3. 84; 4. 38. Though there was no express provision in the
Edict, the praetor gave a similar remedy in case of loss of liberty or
citizenship in eos ad quos bona pervenerunteorum. Dig. 4. 5. 2 pr.
[41] G. 2. 97, 98; 3. 83; Inst. 2. 9. 6; 3. 10. 2.
[42] Buckl. *T.* p. 398, n. 9

By the legislation of Constantine and his successors the pater remained technically dominus of the bona adventicia,[43] though without power of alienation, in effect a usufructuary. Constantine calls him dominus possessionis.[44] In Justinian's system he was usufructuary in law as he had previously been in fact. If the adrogatus died in potestate the property went to the father, subject to the prior claims of the issue of the adrogatus and of brothers and sisters.[45]

113. ADOPTION OF PERSONS ALIENI JURIS.—Adoption in the narrower sense was effected in the old law by a series of sales and manumissions terminating in a decree of the magistrate declaring the child to be the child of the adopting father.[46] This was a fictitious application of the rule of the Twelve Tables: "If a father sells his son three times, the son shall be free from his father's power." [47] Gaius describes the procedure as follows:—

> "The father mancipates his son to someone (§ 158): he G. 4. 67. manumits vindicta (§ 77) [48]; the son immediately reverts to the father's power. The father again mancipates to the same person or to another (usually to the same); he manumits; the son again reverts to his father's power; then the father mancipates for the third time to the same person or to another (usually to the same)."

This breaks the patria potestas. The son is now in the mancipium of the person to whom he has been mancipated (§ 124) who will usually be the adopter (infra). But he does not wish to retain him in mancipio but to have him for a son. To complete the process the son must be re-mancipated to the natural father, and claimed from him as son in a fictitious action brought by the adopter (in jure cessio).[49] If the last mancipation was made to a third person, re-mancipation to the father was unnecessary. But it was more convenient to make the mancipations to the adopter, for it reduced the *dramatis personae* from three to two. For the adoption of a daughter or grandchild one mancipation was held to be sufficient. For this elaborate fiction Justinian substituted a declaration before the magistrate followed by a magisterial order and registration 1. 12. 8. in court, all the parties concerned, the person to be adopted included, consenting. Both Gaius and Justinian say that the

[43] Buckl. T. p. 280, n. 16.
[44] Cod. 6. 60. 1.
[45] Buckl. T p. 281.
[46] G. 1. 99, 134
[47] G. 1. 132: Ulp. X. 1.
[48] G. 1. 138.
[49] G. 1. 134.

adoption of a person alieni juris is effected " by order of the magistrate " (imperio magistratus). But what for Gaius is the concluding step, for Justinian is substantially the whole process of adoption.

114. The effect of adoption before Justinian was, as in the case of adrogation, to pass the adoptatus into the power of the adopter. Justinian made a fundamental change by limiting this to the case of adoption by a natural ascendant, such as a maternal grandfather; or a paternal grandfather, if an emancipated son gave his son in adoption to his own father. The commentators call this adoptio plena (complete adoption) because it produced all the old effect of adoption. In other cases there was no change of patria potestas, but the adoptatus acquired a right of intestate succession to the adopting father. Apart from this, there was merely a *de facto* change of family with some legal consequences such as reciprocal duty of support. This is called adoptio minus plena (incomplete adoption). There is said to be another case of adoptio plena, *viz.*, when the person given in adoption is not a presumptive suus heres of the person giving him in adoption; *e.g.*, a grandfather gives his grandson in adoption, retaining his son in power. But it seems that in this case the potestas did not pass, or, if it did, it reverted if the death of the father before the grandfather made the grandson a presumptive suus heres of the grandfather (§ 336).[50]

I. 11. 2.

115. Imperial rescript was another way of creating patria potestas, *e.g.*, if a Latin or peregrine obtained by this method a grant of citizenship, children already born might at the same time be declared to be in his power. Without such a declaration they continued to be sui juris.[51]

116. There were other ways in which potestas might come into existence to which it will be enough to make a passing reference, such as anniculi causae probatio ex 'ege Aelia Sentia (§ 84), and numerous cases in which a person who had married in ignorance of his or his wife's real status was allowed to get the matter put right (erroris causae probatio). One instance may suffice: —

G. 1. 67.

"A Roman citizen marries a Latin or peregrine woman in ignorance as to her real status believing her to be a citizen and she has borne him a son, the son will not be in the father's power because he will not even be a Roman citizen but a Latin or a peregrine (there being no conubium between the parents he

---

[50] Buckl. *T.* p. 123; *M.* p. 78.
[51] G. 1. 93, 94.

follows the status of the mother); but by a senatusconsultum he
is permitted to prove the cause of error, and so his wife and his
son are admitted to Roman citizenship and thenceforward the
son begins to be in the power of his father."

With the extension of citizenship to the whole Empire this
method of acquiring potestas passed out of use.

117. POSTLIMINIUM.—During captivity the patria potestas
was in abeyance. If the paterfamilias returned from foreign
slavery he resumed his power over his children. Similarly, if a
child returned he reverted to his father's power. This was called
postliminium, because the person concerned re-crossed the   1. 12. 5.
threshold (limen) of the Roman State.

118. HOW PATRIA POTESTAS ENDED.—We have spoken of the
ways in which patria potestas came into existence. It remains
to speak of the ways in which it ceased to exist. These were:—
1. Death of the paterfamilias, but on the death of a grandfather
unemancipated grandchildren did not become sui juris, for they   1. 12 pr.
fell under the power of their father, if he too was unemancipated; 2. Any change of status in father or son involving loss
of freedom or citizenship or family; and, in particular, the
emancipation of the son or his being given in adoption, any
adoption before Justinian, but in consequence of his legislation,
adoptio plena only. Emancipation was effected in the time of
Gaius by a fictitious process similar to that used in the case of
adoption (§ 113),[52] the only difference being that in the final
stage the person concerned was claimed as free (vindicatio in
libertatem), not as a son. The Emperor Anastasius, A.D. 502,
where the absence of the son made this process impossible,
allowed the same effect to be produced by imperial rescript
followed by registration in court.[53] Justinian abolished the old
fictions [54] and made even the rescript unnecessary, believing that
the matter could safely be left to the persons concerned. He
required merely a declaration before the magistrate, the son   1. 12. 6.
consenting or at least acquiescing and registration in court, as in
the case of adoption; 3. In general, no public office or dignity
affected the relations of father and son. But Justinian enacted
that the eminent dignity of the patriciate should release the   1. 12. 4.
person thus honoured from patria potestas. By Novel 81 he
attached the same consequence to the consulship and other
dignities.

---

[52] G. 1. 132.
[53] Cod. 8. 49. 5.
[54] Cod. 8. 49. 6.

119. The emancipation of a natural-born son, we are told, terminated the rights of agnation, not of cognation. Thus the praetor allowed the emancipated son to succeed to his father ab intestato in the class unde liberi (§ 388). But the emancipation of an adopted son terminated all relations with the family of adoption. In his family of origin he counted as an emancipated son. Justinian says that there is scarcely any way in which natural or adoptive children can compel their parents to emancipate them. The impubes adrogatus could do so on reaching puberty, if he could show good cause.[55] A father instituted heir on condition of emancipating his children was bound to do so.[56] Trajan, we are told, compelled emancipation by a father who was ill-treating his son.[57]

120. CAPITIS DEMINUTIO.—The origin of this institution is obscure and has been the subject of much speculation. The following remarks are confined to the developed doctrine which is the same for Gaius in the second century as for Justinian in the sixth. Capitis deminutio means a change of status, which takes place: —(i) when a man loses freedom and citizenship by being reduced to slavery. This is called capitis deminutio maxima ; (ii) when a man loses citizenship, but retains his freedom. This happened in the old law when a man was interdicted from fire and water,[58] which meant, in effect, compelled to go into exile, as happened to Cicero in B.C. 58. Under the Empire a sentence of deportation (but not of relegation) to an island had the same effect. This is called capitis deminutio minor or media ; (iii) when citizenship and freedom are retained but a man's family is changed whether (according to our way of thinking) for the worse or for the better. This is capitis deminutio minima. It takes place when a person who is sui juris becomes alieni juris, or conversely. Thus, not only does a paterfamilias undergo capitis deminutio by being adrogated, but a filiusfamilias undergoes capitis deminutio by being emancipated. In the old process of emancipation every mancipation and every manumission was a capitis deminutio.[59] It is plain from all this that capitis deminutio in general cannot be described as a descent in the ladder of status. If a man having a son in power was adrogated, not only he but his son too underwent capitis deminutio. In each case there was a change of family.[60]

Marginal references: 1. 12. 10. / 1. 16. / 1. 16. 2. / 1. 16. 3.

---

[55] Dig. 1. 7. 32 pr.　　　　[56] Paul *Sent.* 4. 13. 1.
[57] Dig. 37. 12. 5.　　　　　[58] G. 1. 161.
[59] G. 1. 162.　　　　　　　[60] Dig. 4. 5. 3.

121. MANUS AND MANCIPIUM.—In Justinian's law potestas, in its two forms of dominica potestas and patria potestas, stands alone as a source of dependent status. But for Gaius there were two other institutions which subjected one person to the authority of another, namely manus and mancipium. They are not mentioned by Justinian because manus was obsolete (§ 122) and mancipium was abolished by his own legislation. But, since some knowledge of these institutions is necessary for the understanding of the course of historical development, they cannot be disregarded.

4. 8. 7.

122. MANUS.—There was an ancient custom by which a wife on or after marriage passed into the hand of her husband (in manum viri) with the consequence that she was like a daughter to her husband (filiae loco), and, if he was in power, like a granddaughter (neptis loco) to his father. If the husband died sui juris and intestate she shared the inheritance equally with her children. This system is commonly described as manus marriage, the other being called free marriage. Manus marriage was obsolescent in the time of Gaius. It may have lingered on for about a century longer. Anciently manus was brought into existence in one of three ways:—(a) by confarreatio. This was a religious ceremony, peculiar to patricians, which took place with a solemn form of words in the presence of ten witnesses. It took its name from the cape of spelt (far) which was offered to Jupiter Farreus (the Jupiter of the spelt cake) [61]; (b) by coemptio, an imaginary sale of the woman by the paterfamilias (or by herself if sui juris?) into the hand of the man she was to marry; (c) by use (usu). If a woman " remained married " for a whole year she passed into the hand of her husband, who acquired a proprietary right over her just as he might over any other movable property, by a year's unbroken possession (§ 174). The Twelve Tables allowed her to interrupt the usucapion by staying away for three nights in each successive year (trinoctium–trinoctio abesse). This may have been the starting point of the free marriage, but Gaius in the passage just cited implies, if he is not writing carelessly, that she was married already and not in course of becoming married during the currency of the usus period. This manner of acquiring manus, Gaius says, " had partly been abolished by statute and partly fallen into disuse." But he treats the other two methods as still in force, and says, in particular, that the

---

[61] Spelt was a kind of grain, the food of the primitive Romans.

greater flamines, that is priests of Jupiter, Mars and Quirinus, and the reges sacrorum had to be the issue of marriage by confarreatio, and themselves thus married.[62] Papinian and Paul speak of conventio in manum as an existing institution,[63] and in the *Liber regularum* attributed to Ulpian, but thought to date from the early part of the fourth century, it is said to be effected farreo.[64] It is improbable that it survived the third century except in the narrow circle of the priesthood.

123. Manus was not inseparable from marriage. It might also exist without marriage. Gaius tells us that coemption might be made either for the purpose of marriage or by way of trust [65] (fiduciae causa). This last was a contrivance which enabled a woman to change her tutor. She made a coemption to a male person, not her husband, for that would have placed her in the position of daughter. This person, termed the co-emptionator, into whose manus she had passed, mancipated her to another person of her choice, and he in turn manumitted her vindicta, thereby becoming her fiduciary tutor (§ 129), and if she wished to make a will (which may have been the object in view) she could do so by his authority (§ 306). It seems that the same trick was sometimes employed for evading the burden of family sacred rites.[66] Normally, a woman was released from manus by the process of emancipation in use in the case of a daughter, namely by a single mancipation followed by re-mancipation and manumission, but with the difference, as Gaius points out, that, whereas a daughter could not in any way compel her father to emancipate her, a married woman could escape from manus by sending a letter of divorce.[67] This is evidently a late development, which can only have been admitted when manus was already a decaying institution.

124. MANCIPIUM (CIVIL BONDAGE).—This was the status resulting from the mancipation of a free person.[68] It occurred when a father made a noxal surrender of his son (§ 638), or in the process of adoption or emancipation, or in the case of a woman in the circumstances above described.[69] In the first

---

[62] G. 1. 111–3. In A.D. 23 the Emperor Tiberius promoted a law providing that the wife of the priest of Jupiter (flamen Dialis) should pass in manum for religious purposes only (Tacitus, *Annals*, 4. 16). There had been earlier legislation. G. 1. 136 ; Buckl. *T.* p. 119 ; *M.* p. 72.
[63] *Coll.* 4. 2. 3 ; 4. 7. 1.
[64] Ulp. Tit. IX.
[65] G. 1. 114.
[66] de Zulueta, *Gaius*, II, p. 36.
[67] G. 1. 137
[68] G. 1. 117, 118.
[69] G. 1. 118 (a).

case, practically limited to male children, it created a relation
between the person mancipated and the person to whom the
mancipation was made which continued, at all events in
historical times, only until the delinquent had by his labour
made good the damage.[70] In the other cases the status was
usually momentary.[71] A person in mancipio remained a free
man and was not to be treated with contumely. If he was, he
had an actio injuriarum (§ 615). But he was in a quasi-servile
position. Like a slave he could not be instituted heir by his
master, unless at the same time given his liberty.[72] Like a
slave he acquired for his master.[73] Like a slave he was set
free by manumission ; which might be censu, vindicta or testamento.[74] By manumission he became sui juris and did not
revert into his father's power, the mancipation (it was disputed
whether it must be thrice repeated or one was enough (§ 639))
having extinguished the potestas (§ 113).[75] The noxal
surrender of free persons was abolished by Justinian.

THE INSTITUTES

BOOK I (Tits. VIII–XII, XVI)

TITLE VIII

Of persons sui juris and persons alieni juris

There follows another division of the law of persons. For some §86.
persons are sui juris, others are alieni juris: and of these last some
are in the power of parents, others in the power of masters. Let us
consider then the persons who are alieni juris, for when we know
who these are, we shall understand at the same time who are sui
juris; and first let us see who are in the power of masters.

1. In the power of masters, then, are slaves. This power is §72.
created by the jus gentium, for amongst all peoples it may be seen
that masters have over their slaves the power of life and death, and
whatever is acquired through a slave is acquired for the master.
2. But today no men subject to our rule are allowed to do violence
to their slaves without lawful cause or beyond measure. For a constitution of the Emperor Antonius Pius directs that anyone who
without cause kills his own slave is to be punished just as much as if
he had killed some other person's slave. More than this, a constitution of the same Emperor restrains excessive harshness of masters.
For, being consulted by certain provincial governors about slaves

[70] Coll. 2. 3.
[71] G. 1. 141.
[72] G. 1. 123.
[73] G. 2. 86.
[74] G. 1. 138.
[75] G. 1. 132

who fly for refuge to temples or to the statues of the Emperor, he directed that, if the masters appeared to have used intolerable severity, they should be compelled to sell their slaves on fair conditions, receiving the purchase price; and rightly so, for it is in the public interest that a man should not misuse his property. These are the words of the Emperor's rescript to Aelius Marcianus: "The power of masters over their slaves should not be restricted, and no one should have his right taken from him. But it is in the interest of masters that relief against cruelty or starvation, or intolerable wrong, should not be denied to slaves who justly invoke it. Do you, therefore, inquire into the grievances of those of the establishment of Julius Sabinus who have fled to our statue, and if you find that they have been treated with undue severity, or shamefully ill-used, order them to be sold on the terms that they are not to revert to their master's power. And let Sabinus take notice, that if he attempts to evade my decree, I will visit his offence with severe punishment."

Title IX

Of patria potestas

§ 86.

Children begotten in lawful wedlock are in the power of parents. 1. Wedlock or marriage is a union of male and female involving an undivided habit of life. 2. The legal power which we have over our children is peculiar to Roman citizens; for no other men have the power over their children that we have. 3. The child born to you and to your wife is in your power, also the child born to your son and his wife, that is your grandson and granddaughter, and your great-grandchild and so forth. But a child born to your daughter is not in your power, but in the power of the child's father.

Title X

Of marriage

§ 91.

A civil law marriage is contracted by Roman citizens who are united according to law, males having reached years of puberty and females being of a marriageable age, whether they be sui juris or in power, provided that children in power must have the consent of the paterfamilias. Civil law and natural reason agree in requiring this consent, and that the parent's authority should be given before marriage. Hence the question arises whether the daughter of a

§ 95.

madman can marry or the son of a madman take to himself a wife. As regards the son opinions differed, but our constitution [76] allows a son, as a daughter already might, to enter upon marriage without parental consent when the father is insane, in accordance with the procedure therein prescribed.

§ 94.

1. Marriage is forbidden within certain degrees of relationship. First, ascendants and descendants may not intermarry, for example

---

[76] Cod. 5. 4. 25.

father and daughter, grandfather and granddaughter, mother and son, grandmother and grandson, and so on *ad infinitum*. Marriage between such persons is wicked and incestuous. This is so far the case that even when the relationship of parent and child is created by adoption, marriage between them is impossible, and this continues to be so even after the tie created by adoption has been dissolved. Consequently, you cannot marry a woman who has become your daughter or granddaughter by adoption, even though you have emancipated her.

2. There is a similar prohibition of marriage between collaterals, but not so stringent. Of course, marriage is prohibited between brothers and sisters, whether they have in common both parents or one parent only. But if a woman has become your sister by adoption, so long as the adoption continues you cannot marry her, but you may marry her when the adoption has been dissolved by her being emancipated, and, similarly, if you have been emancipated, there is nothing to prevent your marrying her. It is therefore settled that if a man wishes to adopt his son-in-law, he should first emancipate his daughter; and if he wishes to adopt his daughter-in-law, he should first emancipate his son. 3. A man may not marry his brother's or sister's daughter, or granddaughter, though the latter is related to him in the fourth degree; for whenever it is not lawful to marry a person's daughter neither is it lawful to marry that person's granddaughter. But there seems to be no objection to your marrying the daughter of a woman whom your father has adopted as his daughter, because there is no bond between you either by natural or by civil law. 4. The children of two brothers or of two sisters or of brother and sister may intermarry. 5. A man may not marry his father's sister, even a sister by adoption, nor his mother's sister, because they are reckoned amongst parents. On the same principle marriage with a great-aunt, paternal or maternal, is forbidden. 6. Out of respect for affinity some marriages must not be contracted. For example, a man may not marry his step-daughter or daughter-in-law, for each of them stands to him in the relation of daughter. This must be understood to mean a woman who was his daughter-in-law or step-daughter. For if she still is your daughter-in-law, that is, if she is still married to your son, there is another reason why you cannot marry her, namely, that you cannot be married to two women at once: for the same reason you cannot marry your step-daughter while you are still married to her mother. 7. A man may not marry his mother-in-law or his step-mother, because each of them is deemed to be a mother to him. This holds good when the relation no longer exists, for if a woman is still your step-mother, that is, is still married to your father, on general principles you cannot marry her: similarly you cannot marry her if she is still your mother-in-law, that is, if her daughter is still your wife. 8. But a husband's son by a former wife and a wife's daughter by a former husband, or conversely, may intermarry, notwithstanding they have a brother or sister born of the second marriage. 9. If your wife has been divorced from you, and has had a daughter by a second husband, she is not your step-daughter, but Julian says that we should refrain from such a marriage. For neither is the woman betrothed to your son your daughter-in-law, nor is the

woman betrothed to your father your mother-in-law, but it is more right and proper (he says) to refrain from such marriages.

§ 74.   10. There is no doubt that the relationships of slaves are an obstacle to marriage, if, for example, father and daughter, or brother and sister have been manumitted. 11. There are other persons who for different reasons may not intermarry. These cases will be found enumerated in the Digest.

12. If a union is contracted which does not comply with these conditions, there is no husband or wife, no wedlock or marriage, no dower. Accordingly the children born of such a union are not in the father's power, but are in the same position as children born of a promiscuous union, who are considered to have no father, the paternity being uncertain. It follows that on the dissolution of such a union, there can be no question of claiming the return of dower. Persons who contract unlawful unions incur the penalties set forth in the imperial constitutions.

§ 105.   13. It sometimes happens that children are not in the power of parents from the very moment of birth, but are brought into power afterwards. Such is the case of a natural-born child who afterwards comes under the father's power by being made a member of a municipal council; or when the issue of a free woman, whom the father might have married, but with whom he was merely cohabiting, is afterwards in terms of our constitution brought into the father's power by a formal marriage settlement; our constitution [77] assures the same status to children subsequently born of the marriage.

TITLE XI

Of adoptions

We have in our power not only natural-born children as above described, but also adopted children.

§ 106.   1. Adoption takes place in one of two ways, either by imperial rescript or by order of the magistrate. By the authority of the Emperor we adopt persons of either sex who are sui juris. This kind of adoption is called adrogation. By order of the magistrate we adopt persons of either sex who are in the power of parents, whether in the first degree of descent, as a son or a daughter, or in remoter degrees of descent, as a grandchild, or a great-grandchild. 2. But

§ 114.   today by our constitution,[78] when a child in power is given in adoption by a natural father to an extraneous person, the rights of the natural father remain unimpaired, and nothing passes to the adoptive father, nor is the adopted child in his power, the only effect of the adoption being that we allow the adopted child the right of succeeding *ab intestato* to the adoptive father. But if the natural father has given his son in adoption not to a stranger, but to the son's maternal grandfather, or, if the natural father has been emancipated, even to the son's paternal grandfather, or, similarly,

---

[77] Cod. 5. 27 10 and 11.
[78] Cod. 8. 47 (48). 10.

to a maternal or paternal great-grandfather:—in any such case, since the rights of natural kinship and of adoption meet in the same person, the ancient right of an adopting father remains unimpaired and the child passes into his family and power. 3. When a child below puberty is adrogated by imperial rescript, adrogation is only allowed after inquiry into the circumstances. The adrogation must be shown to be honourable and for the pupil's advantage and is subject to certain conditions; namely, the adrogator must give security to a public officer or notary, that if the child dies before reaching puberty, he will restore the property to the persons who would have succeeded if the adoption had not taken place. Further, the adrogator may not emancipate the child, unless after inquiry he is found to deserve to be emancipated, and then he is to restore to him his property. If the adopting father has disinherited the child, or in his lifetime emancipated him without just cause, he is ordered to leave to him one-fourth of his own estate, that is to say over and above what the adopted child brought to the adopting father on adoption or has subsequently acquired for him. 4. It is settled that a younger person cannot adopt a person older than himself; for adoption imitates nature, and it would be outrageous that a son should be older than his father. It is necessary therefore that a person who adrogates or adopts another should be his elder by the complete term of puberty, that is by eighteen years. 5. A man may adopt a child as a grandchild, great-grandchild or remoter descendant, although he has no son. 6. He may adopt another man's son to be his grandson or another man's grandson to be his son. 7. But, if a person adopts a child to be his grandson as if born of an adoptive or natural son, the son must consent, so that he may not acquire a suus heres against his will. If a grandfather gives in adoption his son's son, his son's consent is not required. 8. In very many respects a son adopted or adrogated is assimilated to a son born in lawful wedlock. Therefore, if a person has been adrogated by imperial decree or adopted by an ascendant before the praetor or the governor of a province, he may be given in adoption by the adoptive father. 9. It is common to both kinds of adoption that persons naturally impotent may adopt, but not persons who have been castrated. 10. Women cannot adopt, because even their natural children are not in their power; but by the imperial clemency they are allowed to adopt as a solace for the loss of natural children.

§ 109

11. A consequence peculiar to adoption by imperial rescript is that if the person adrogated has sons in his power not only does he pass into the power of the adrogator himself, but his children do so too as grandchildren of the adrogator. This was the reason why the Emperor Augustus did not adopt Tiberius until Tiberius had adopted Germanicus, so that immediately on the adoption of Tiberius Germanicus became the grandson of Augustus.

§ 110

12. The old writers record an opinion happily expressed by Cato in his writings that slaves who are adopted by their masters may in this way obtain their freedom. In accordance with this we have in our wisdom enacted that if a master has by deed before the magistrate declared a slave to be his son the slave is thereby set free, though this has not the effect of giving him the rights of a son.

TITLE XII

How patria potestas comes to an end

§ 118.

Let us now see in what ways persons are freed from another's power. How slaves are freed from power may be understood from what has been said above concerning the manumission of slaves. Persons in the power of a parent become sui juris on his death. But a distinction must be made. When a father dies, sons and daughters [who were in his power] always become sui juris. But when a grandfather dies, the grandchildren do not necessarily become sui juris, but only if they do not fall into the power of their father. Therefore, if when the grandfather dies the father is living and in his father's power, the children fall into their father's power; but if when the grandfather dies the father is already dead, or is no longer in his father's power, his children, since they cannot fall into his power, become sui juris.

1. Since a man who is deported to an island for some crime loses his citizenship, it follows that when, in this way, he is removed from the number of citizens, his children cease to be in his power just as if he were dead. Similarly, if a filiusfamilias is deported to an island, he ceases to be in the power of his parent. If they are re-established by imperial clemency, they recover in all respects their former status. 2. But a father who is relegated to an island retains his children in his power, and conversely a child who is relegated remains in the power of his parent.[79] 3. If a man becomes a slave of punishment he ceases to have his sons in his power. Slaves of punishment are those who are condemned to labour in the mines or given over to wild beasts. 4. If a filiusfamilias is a soldier, or becomes a senator, or a consul, he remains in power; for military service or the consular dignity does not free a son from the power of his father. But our constitution[80] provides that the pre-eminent rank of patrician releases a son from paternal power from the very moment of the granting of the imperial patent. For how can it be tolerated that a father should be able to release a son from the bonds of power by way of emancipation, but that the imperial majesty should not be able to take out of the power of another the man whom the Emperor has chosen to be a father of the State? 5. If a father is taken captive, though he becomes the slave of his captors, none the less his power over his children continues to exist owing to the right of postliminium; because persons taken captive by the enemy, if they return from captivity, recover all their former rights. Accordingly, if he comes back he will have his children in his power, because the effect of postliminium is that the person who was taken captive is feigned never to have left the State; but if he dies in captivity the son is deemed to have been sui juris from the time when his father was taken captive. Similarly, if it is a son or a grandson who is taken captive we speak of the paternal power as in suspense. The word postliminium is derived from "post" and "limen," and a person who is taken captive and comes back within the limits of the

§ 117.

---

[79] Relegation was a less serious punishment than deportation. There is the well-known case of the poet Ovid, relegated to Tomi in Scythia.
[80] Cod. 12. 3. 5.

Empire is correctly described as returning by postliminium. By
" limen " (threshold) we mean the frontier of a house, and the old
lawyers applied the word to the frontier of the Roman State; so that
the word postliminium conveys the idea of recrossing the frontier.
If a prisoner is recovered from a beaten foe he is deemed to have
come back by postliminium.   6. Again, children are released from   § 118.
paternal power by emancipation.   Formerly, this was effected either
by an ancient ceremonial of pretended sales with manumissions
interposed or by imperial rescript.   But we have put an end to the
old fictions and provided that parents should go directly to the
competent judges or magistrates and in their presence release from
their power their child or grandchild.[81]   After this, as provided
by the praetor's edict, the emancipating parent has the same rights
in respect of the property of the emancipated child or grandchild as
a patron has in respect of the property of a freedman; and further,
if the emancipated child is below puberty, the emancipating parent
becomes his guardian.   7. It is to be noticed that an ascendant who
has a son in power and also a grandchild by that son, may emancipate the son, retaining the grandchild in power, or, conversely,
retain the son in power, emancipating the grandchildren (or any
further descendants), or make all of them sui juris.

8. But if a father gives a son in adoption to the son's natural   § 114.
grandfather or great-grandfather in the way provided by our constitutions,[82] that is to say, declares his purpose by a formal instrument
before the competent judge, both the person who is being adopted
and the person who is adopting being present and offering no objection, then the power of the natural father is determined and goes
over to the adopting ascendant, and, as we have observed above, the
adoption retains all its old effect.   9. It must be noted that if your
daughter-in-law has conceived by your son, and afterwards you
emancipate your son or give him in adoption while your daughter-
in-law is pregnant, none the less the child is born in your power.
But if the child is conceived after the father has been emancipated
or given in adoption, it will be in the power (as the case may be) of
its own emancipated father or of the adoptive grandfather.   There
is scarcely any way in which natural or adoptive children can compel   § 119.
the parent to release them from his power.

TITLE XVI

Of capitis deminutio

Capitis deminutio is a change of status, and takes place in three   § 120.
ways, for it is either maxima or minor (or as some say media) or
minima.

1. Capitis deminutio maxima, that is the greatest capitis
deminutio, occurs when a person loses at once citizenship and freedom.   This happens when men by a terrible sentence are made
slaves of punishment, or when freedmen who have shown themselves   § 71.

---

[81] Cod. 8. 48. 6.
[82] Cod. 8. 47 (48). 11.

ungrateful to their patrons are reduced to slavery, or when men have suffered themselves to be sold as slaves in order to share the price.

2. Capitis deminutio minor vel media, that is the less or middle capitis deminutio, takes place when citizenship is lost, but freedom is retained. This happens when a man is interdicted from water and fire or deported to an island.

3. Capitis deminutio minima, that is the least capitis deminutio, takes place when citizenship and freedom are retained, but a man's status is changed. This happens when persons who were sui juris become alieni juris, or conversely.

4. There is no capitis deminutio when a slave is manumitted, for a slave has no caput to be lost or changed.

5. If a man suffers a change not of status but of social standing, he does not incur a capitis deminutio, for example by being removed from the Senate.

6. When it was said that rights of cognation continue even after capitis deminutio, this must be understood to refer to capitis deminutio minima. For, if the greatest capitis deminutio is incurred, this destroys the right of cognation as well, as for example if a cognate becomes a slave, and even if he is subsequently manumitted, the relationship is not re-established. The same consequence follows if a person is deported to an island. 7. When tutelage devolves upon agnates it does not go to all of them simultaneously, but to those who are nearest in degree, and within that degree to all.[83]

III. The Third Division of Persons

(Some independent persons have a tutor or curator, others not)

1. 13 pr.
125. We pass to the third and last division of persons, namely, of persons sui juris some have guardians, others not. The Roman Law knew two kinds of guardianship distinguished as tutela and curatio or cura. We shall consider these severally.

1. 13. 1.
126. Tutela.—Servius quoted by Justinian defines tutela as " a right and power exercised over a free person [that is, a person sui juris] who on account of tender years cannot take care of himself, given and allowed by civil law." The Servius mentioned was Servius Sulpicius, consul B.C. 51 and author of the first commentary on the Edict (§ 19). No doubt, what he wrote was " on account of tender years or sex," for in his day women who were sui juris were in perpetual tutelage (perpetua mulierum tutela). This institution in a very attenuated form still existed in the time of Gaius, but had gone out of use a

---

[83] If the nearest refused or were disqualified (contrary to what was the case in succession) the tutela went to the next in degree. Inst. 3. 2. 7.

century or more before Justinian.[84]   We return to the subject
later (§ 138).

Tutela came into existence in various ways and the resulting
kinds are distinguished as follows:—

127. (1) Testamentary (tutela testamentaria).   A pater- 1. 13. 3.
familias might by his will appoint a tutor to sons or other
descendants in power beneath the age of puberty, who would
become sui juris on his death (not to grandsons therefore unless
their father was dead or emancipated).

128. (2) Statutory (legitima). Failing a testamentary tutor G. 1. 155.
the tutelage by the Law of the Twelve Tables went to the 1. 15 pr.
nearest agnates; for the principle was that the persons who had
the benefit of succession ab intestato should also have the right
(or burden) of tutelage.   This was the statutory guardianship of
agnates (legitima agnatorum tutela).   For agnates by Nov. 118
Justinian substituted cognates.

There were two other cases of statutory tutelage, namely of 1. 17.
patrons (legitima patronorum tutela) and of parents (legitima 1. 18.
parentum tutela).   The first of these was exercised by patrons
and their children over persons of either sex manumitted from
slavery while still under age.   This was not expressly enacted
by the Law of the Twelve Tables, but was an inference drawn
from the fact that the law called patrons and their children to
the succession ab intestato.[85]   A parent, who emancipated his
child under age, stood to him in the position of patron,[86] because
in the last stage of the proceedings the child was in mancipio
to his father.

129. (3) Fiduciary (tutela fiduciaria).   So long as the old
ceremonial emancipation by sales and manumissions remained
in force it might happen that the child had not been re-
mancipated to the father, and was manumitted by the person
in whose mancipium he was after the third sale.[87]   By the
manumission he became quasi-patron of the manumitted child,
but this tutelage was fiduciary, not legitima, because it was
usual to bind the extraneus manumissor, as he was called, by a
fiducia to hold the right of succession in trust for the emanci- 3. 2. 8.
pating father.

This type of tutelage did not survive the ancient form of
emancipation, which Justinian abolished by a constitution of
531.[88]   But the term fiduciary tutelage had another meaning,

---

84 G. 1. 144 et seq.; 157; 168 et seq.; 190; Ulp. XI. 25; 27; Buckl.
T. pp. 165 et seq.; M. pp. 101 et seq.
85 G. 1. 165; Inst. 1. 17.
86 G. 1. 175; Inst. 1. 18.
87 G. 1. 166a.
88 Cod. 8. 48. 6.

which is noticed by Gaius,[89] and is the only meaning given to it by Justinian. If the emancipating parent died leaving the emancipated child still under age the guardianship passed to the nearest male relatives of the child agnatically related to the deceased; namely the child's father (if a grandfather had emancipated), unemancipated brothers, uncles. They were called fiduciary because they had to be called something, and, at least, under the old mode of emancipation the train of events which resulted in their becoming guardians began with a fiduciary mancipation. They were not statutory, for unlike the children of the patronus (§ 128)[90] they were not called to the succession by the Law of the Twelve Tables, and by inference to the guardianship.

[It is not at first sight obvious what motive a parent would have for emancipating a child of tender years. It may be supposed that he, or someone else, perhaps the mother, wished to anticipate his death by making a provision for the child which would not be absorbed in the parent's estate. If through failing health or for some other reason he did not care to undertake the burden of tutelage he would allow the fictitious purchaser to manumit after the third mancipation, and thus become the child's guardian. In other words, the emancipating parent procured by act *inter vivos* the situation which would have arisen if by his will he had instituted the child as heir and appointed the extraneous person testamentary guardian.]

130. (4) **Dative** (*tutela dativa*). In default of other tutors an appointment was made by the magistrate. The tutor so appointed was called tutor dativus (though for Gaius a tutor dativus was a tutor appointed by will),[91] and in the older law tutor Atilianus, because appointed at Rome under the provisions of a lex Atilia (before B.C. 186). A mother could not, properly speaking, appoint a tutor by will, because she had no potestas over her children, but she could leave property and appoint a tutor to manage it.[92] The same course was open to any person who left property by will to a child under the age of puberty. Such tutors, appointed rather to the property than to the person, required confirmation by the magistrate.[93] They are known in modern systems of law as " tutors nominate."

I. 20 pr.

131. DUTIES AND FUNCTIONS OF TUTORS.—A tutor's functions were mainly two:—1. to interpose his authority (auctoritatem interponere); 2. to administer the property (negotia gerere).[94] Under the first head the tutor supplemented his ward's want of

---

[89] G. 1. 175; Inst. 1. 19.
[90] G. 3. 58.
[91] G. 1. 154.
[92] Dig. 26. 2. 4.
[93] Dig. 26. 3. 5.
[94] Ulp. XI. 25.

capacity and enabled him to contract in his own name. It was
a principle of law that the ward could not incur liability without
his tutor's authority. Without it he might make his condition
better (as by stipulating (§ 444) or accepting a gift), but not 1. 21 pr.
make it worse. Therefore, unaided, he could not accept an
inheritance (which from its nature involved, or might involve,
burdens as well as benefits), nor alienate property, nor bind 2. 8. 2.
himself by a contract involving reciprocal rights and duties,
though the other party was bound to him. Of course he could
not demand performance by the other party unless he was
himself prepared to do his part (§ 548). The idea of authority
is that the tutor augments or completes the deficient capacity of
his ward. The authority must be given by the tutor in person at
the time of the act to be authorised. If given by letter or after
an interval it was ineffectual. It was something more than a 1. 21. 2.
mere consent. Under this head may be included his duty to
furnish funds adequate for the ward's education in the station
of life to which he belonged.[95]

132. The other principal function of the tutor was negotia
gerere, that is to administer the property as trustee for his ward.

133. Of the two functions assigned to tutors each had its
special inconvenience.[96] Auctoritatis interpositio was only
possible when the ward was old enough to know what he was
doing. He must have intellectus. The tutor could only supply
judicium. Further, it required the co-operation of guardian and
of ward. The disadvantage of negotiorum gestio was that whatever the tutor did was done in his own name. It bound and
entitled him and not the ward. Modern systems get over the
difficulty by making the guardian the representative of the ward
(§ 143 ix). Roman Law with its imperfect theory of agency
went only a little way in this direction. But it partly attained
the same result when under the Empire it gave equitable actions
(utiles actiones, § 701) after the determination of the guardianship to and against the late ward in respect of the late guardian's
administration. the late guardian having no further right or
liability in relation to third parties.[97]

---

[95] This, I take it, is what Paulus means (as appears from the context)
when he says (Dig. 26. 7. 19, 3) cum tutor non rebus dumtaxat sed etiam
moribus pupilli praeponatur. The mother usually had the custody and
control of education (Cod. 5. 49. 1 ; cf. Hor. Epp. 1. 1. 22, Pupillis, quos
dura premit custodia matrum), failing her, some rear relation. In case of
dispute the last word was with the court.
[96] Girard, p. 229.
[97] Dig. 26. 9 ; Cod. 5. 39.

134. In the early law a testamentary tutor might decline to act. But in the time of Justinian tutela was a public duty which might not be declined except by leave of the magistrate. Numerous grounds of excuse were admitted. A whole Title of the Institutes is devoted to the subject.

1. 25.

135. Under the Empire the powers of a tutor were much restricted. First, the Oratio Severi of A.D. 195 forbade the alienation of praedia rustica and suburbana—agricultural land and undeveloped building land—unless directed by will, without an order of court,[98] and Constantine extended this to praedia urbana—houses—and to valuable movables.[99] The result was that in the later law the tutor's power of alienation without leave of the court was very limited.

136. The law had many contrivances to protect wards against maladministration and misconduct of guardians. The fact that so many precautions were taken shows that they were needed. Thus:—1. It was open to any person other than the ward [1] to take proceedings for the removal of a tutor on the ground of misconduct, actual or anticipated (accusatio or crimen suspecti tutoris). This action had its origin in the Twelve Tables. 2. The (late) ward after the termination of the tutorship [2] (or his heirs) had the actio rationibus distrahendis (action for liquidation of accounts). It lay for double damages against a tutor who had been guilty of embezzlement.[3] This also dated from the Twelve Tables. 3. A more general remedy was the actio tutelae dating from the later Republic.[4] It lay like the actio negotiorum gestorum (§ 590) in respect of an administration which had actually taken place, and was therefore brought only after the guardianship was at an end. Later, it assumed a more general character and could be brought in respect of any dereliction of duty. The standard of diligence demanded of a tutor is variously stated in the Digest. For Justinian it seems to be the diligentia quam suis rebus (§ 417). Perhaps he made it so.[5] Condemnation in this action (actio tutelae directa) entailed infamia. The ex-guardian on his side had a contrary action (actio tutelae contraria) for expenses and indemnity. 4. Guardians were sometimes required to furnish security for their faithful administration (satisdatio rem pupilli salvam fore). This applied to all tutores legitimi and to tutors appointed by the magistrate without previous inquiry in the case of small estates. If the estate was large the matter came before a higher magistrate, who, before making an appointment, satisfied himself

1. 26.

4. 16. 2.

1. 24.

---

[98] Dig. 27. 9. 1.
[99] Cod. 5. 37 22.
[1] Dig. 26. 10 7 pr.
[2] Dig. 27. 3. 1, 24.
[3] Dig. 27. 3. 2.
[4] Q. Mucius Scaevola mentions the actio tutelae in an enumeration of the judicia bonae fidei. (§ 702.) Cic. de Offic. 3. 17. 70.
[5] Dig. 27. 3. 1 pr. (interpolated?).

as to the sufficiency of the proposed tutor. In this case no
security was required, nor was it demanded of testamentary
tutors, whom the testator himself had selected for the office.
If, in a case requiring security, the magistrate had failed to take
any, or sufficient, security, he exposed himself to a subsidiary
action for consequential damage. 5. Lastly, the tutor had to
make an inventory of the pupil's estate, and his own property
was subject to a general tacit hypothec to secure the pupil's
claims (§ 263). This was introduced by Constantine and
retained by Justinian.[6]

1. 24. 2.

§ 256.

137. The reader will not have failed to notice that in the
course of its history tutela has undergone a fundamental change.
It begins as a projection of the patria potestas into the future
with a view to the protection of the family property after the
testator's death. In the Twelve Tables it is a tutela rei. Protection of the person came later and did not amount to much
until the institution of the tutela dativa. Ultimately the tutor
had extensive powers, but they were in the nature of a trust,
and under the Empire were limited by legislation. In the
Servian definition tutela is still jus ac potestas in capite libero
but it exists ad tuendum eum qui propter aetatem se defendere
nequit.

1. 13 1

138. PERPETUA TUTELA MULIERUM.—Reference has been
made above to the perpetual tutelage of women. This was
an institution for which parallels are found in other systems
of law ancient and modern. The principal design was to keep
the property in the family. The reason commonly given that
women owing to the levity of their minds are easily imposed
upon seemed to Gaius more specious than real.[7] In his time
the institution was already in decay. The Law of the Twelve
Tables had exempted Vestal Virgins from its operation. The
leges Julia and Papia Poppaea of Augustus freed from tutelage
married women who had acquired the jus liberorum by having
three children if ingenuae, four if libertinae.[8] Claudius (A.D.
49?) abolished the agnatic tutelage of women.[9] Consequently
even young girls could not have agnatic tutors while young boys
could. This anomaly was removed by Constantine.[10] The
statutory tutelage of patrons and parents remained and was to
some extent a reality.

"No doubt the statutory guardianships of patrons and of
parents are understood to have some effect, because these

6 Cod. 1. 37. 20.
7 G. 1. 190.
8 G. 1. 145. 194.
9 G. 1. 157.
10 Cod. 5. 30. 3.

guardians are not compelled to authorise their female wards to make a testament or to alienate res mancipi or to contract an obligation, unless there is a very good reason for the alienation or the obligation. All this is established in the interest of the guardians in order that their right as intestate heirs may not be excluded by the woman's will, or the amount of the inheritance reduced by the alienation of valuable property or by a burden of debt." [11]

The statutory guardians of women were allowed to get rid of the burden of guardianship by making a cession in court (cessio in jure, § 165) to another person called the cessicius tutor.[12]

The other guardianships—testamentary, fiduciary, dative— were a mere formality.

"For women of full age manage their own affairs and in some cases the guardian interposes his authority as a matter of form, and often the praetor compels him to do so against his will." [13]

If a woman wished to change her tutor she could do so with the authority of her existing tutor by the process described above in speaking of manus (§ 121).

The jus liberorum was sometimes conferred by imperial favour on women who had not the necessary qualification. Augustus conferred it on his wife Livia. A final blow was perhaps dealt to the perpetual tutelage of women, if in fact it had existed so long, by a constitution of Honorius and Theodosius A.D. 410, which adopted the curious expedient of giving all women the jus liberorum.[14] Nemo post haec a nobis jus liberorum petat, quod simul hac lege omnibus concedimus— "Let no one hereafter ask us the right of children, for by this law we grant it to all women." [15] But there is some doubt as to the effect of the original enactment (the words quoted are from Justinian's Code). Perhaps it is safer to say that the institution became obsolete by disuse.

139. CURA—CURATIO (curatorship).—Obviously boys of fourteen and girls of twelve cannot be left to manage their own affairs. Accordingly, curatorship succeeds to tutelage. This institution (cura minorum) had its origin in a lex Plaetoria (or Laetoria) of about B.C. 200 which punished persons who over-reached anyone under twenty-five years of age (minores viginti

---

[11] G. 1. 192.
[12] G. 1. 168, 169.
[13] G. 1. 190.
[14] Cod. Theod. 8. 17. 3.
[15] Cod. 8. 58 (59).

quinque annis—adolescentes).[16] Apart from the penalty, the nature of which is unknown, the praetor allowed the minor to plead the lex by way of exception to an action brought upon the impeached transaction (§ 745). It became usual for a person who wished to do business with a minor to require the minor to apply, or himself to apply, to the magistrate to appoint a curator for the purpose of the transaction in question.[17] At a later date the Emperor Marcus Aurelius initiated the practice of allowing a minor to get a permanent curator appointed for the general management of his affairs. Curators differed from tutors mainly in the following particulars: 1, They were appointed to administer the property, not to control the person ; 2, no one was obliged to have a curator unless he was a party to litigation and in some other cases, for example, a retiring tutor might demand the appointment of a curator for the purpose of settling accounts ; 3, a curator could not, strictly speaking, be appointed by will, but, if so appointed, was generally confirmed by the magistrate.

1. 23. 2.
1. 23. 1.

140. Up to about the time of Diocletian a minor was free to contract, with the qualification that if the contract was calculated to prejudice him he might obtain restitutio in integrum (§ 777) from the praetor, and this was so whether he acted with or without the consent of a curator,[18] though in the first case relief, obviously, would less easily be accorded. In the later law minors who had permanent curators came to be assimilated more and more closely to pupils and had in general the same liabilities, rights and remedies.[19] In consequence, just as the pupil could not bind himself without the authority of his tutor, so the minor could not incur more than a natural obligation (§ 406) without the consent of his curator.[20] Consent was not the same as authority. It might be indicated in any way. The curator need not be present at the transaction. Ratification had the same effect as antecedent consent. If the minor had no curator—as we have seen he need not have one—the old law continued to apply. Consent was not the only function of the curator. He came to have, like the tutor, a general power of administration. In the case of a female between the ages of twelve and twenty-five, the tutor, if there was one, had no

16 Buckl. *M.* p. 104 ; Monier (5) I. p. 333.
17 Cod. 5. 31 1.
18 Dig. 45. 1. 101. (Modestinus).
19 Girard, p. 252 ; Buckl. *M.* p. 106.
20 Cod. 2. 21. 3 (Diocletian and Maximian, A.D. 293).

power to administer (§ 138),[21] so that, though she had a tutor, she would need a curator as well.[22] Under the Empire the normal term of full age (twenty-five years—perfecta aetas) was occasionally anticipated by imperial licence. This privilege was accorded to young men who had completed their twentieth, and to young women who had completed their eighteenth, year.[23] It carried all the usual rights of majority except that, like minors generally, they could not alienate or hypothecate immovable property without a decree of court.[24] It might be convenient that a young man who had not reached full age should take over the administration of his dead father's affairs. In the case of a woman it may be supposed that the object usually was to release her from curatorship on marriage. This institution, known as venia aetatis, has been adopted with variations by many modern systems of law.[25]

141. Another and much older case of curatorship was that exercised over insane persons and prodigals. By the Law of the Twelve Tables madmen (furiosi) and prodigals interdicted from the management of their goods were placed under the curatorship of their agnates. This provision was of limited scope. It did not apply to any case of mental disorder short of madness, nor to prodigal freedmen (who had no agnates) nor to prodigal ingenui unless they were dissipating property which came to them *ab intestato* from a father or grandfather.[26] All these *lacunae* the praetor supplied by appointing curators to meet the special emergency in question, and ultimately the curatorship of the agnates fell into disuse, the praetor assuming a general jurisdiction to deal with all cases of mental disease or prodigality.

1. 23. 3.

THE INSTITUTES

BOOK I (Tits. XIII–XV, XVII–XXVI)

TITLE XIII

Of tutelage

§ 125.

Let us pass now to another division. Of persons sui juris some have tutors or curators, others not. We will consider, then, who

---

[21] G. 1. 190 ; Ulp. XI. 25.   [22] *Vat.* 110 ; Dig. 26. 5. 13. 2.
[23] Cod. 2. 44. 2.
[24] Cod. 2. 44. 3.   It seems that the oratio Severi (*supra*, § 135) which related to the tutor's administration (negotiorum gestio) was understood to apply also to his authorisation of the pupil's acts, so that in this case too an order of court was required and in both cases curators were assimilated to tutors.   *Cf.* Dig. 44. 1, 3 ; 26. 9. 1, 2.
[25] *B. G. B.* art. 3 : Swiss *C. C.* art. 15 ; and in South Africa and Ceylon, Lee, p. 44.   [26] Ulp. XII, 3.

have tutors or curators, for in this way it will be evident who are
not subject to any such control; and let us begin with tutors.
1. Tutelage, as Servius defined it, is a right and power exercised
over an independent person, given and allowed by the civil law for   § 126.
the protection of one who on account of his tender age is not able
to be his own defender. 2. The persons who exercise this right and
power are called tutors (from *tueri*=to defend). 3. Parents are
allowed to give tutors by will to children in power who have not yet   § 127.
reached puberty; but to grandchildren only if on the grandparent's
death they will not come under the power of their own father.
Consequently, if at the time of your death your son is in your
power, his children cannot have a tutor under your will, although
they were in your power, because on your death they will fall into
the power of their father. 4. Since posthumous children are for
many purposes deemed to be already born, it is settled that tutors
may be given by will to posthumous children no less than to
children already born, provided that if they were born in the
testator's lifetime they would be in his power and prospective sui
heredes. 5. If a father appoints a tutor by will to an emancipated
son, the appointment requires confirmation by the governor [27] which
is given as of course without inquiry.

Title XIV

Who may be appointed tutors by will

Not only a paterfamilias, but also a filiusfamilias may be   § 127.
appointed tutor. 1. A testator may even appoint his slave, giving
him at the same time his freedom, or even without doing so, for
the appointment as tutor tacitly implies a direct gift of freedom.
Of course, it is another matter if a slave supposed to be free is
appointed by mistake. Another man's slave cannot be appointed
unconditionally, but an appointment expressed to take effect " when
he shall be free " is good. A man cannot appoint his own slave on
such terms. 2. If a madman or a person less than twenty-five
years of age is appointed, the appointment will take effect when he
recovers his sanity or reaches the age of five and twenty.

3. A tutor may unquestionably be appointed until a certain time,
or from a certain time, or before the institution of an heir.[28] 4. But   § 291.
a tutor cannot be appointed for a certain property or for a certain
purpose, for tutors are appointed to the person and not for a special
purpose or thing.

5. If a testator has appointed tutors to his " daughters " or
" sons," he is understood to appoint to a daughter or son born
posthumously. What is to be said of grandchildren? Are they to
be understood to be included under the description " sons "? The
answer is that if the testator said " children," they are included,
but not if he said " sons," for there is a distinction between the

---

[27] *i.e.*, in the provinces, at Rome by the appropriate magistrate (*infra*,
1. 20. 4.).
[28] G. 2. 231 ; Inst. 2. 20. 34

words "son" and "grandson." The expression "after-born children" clearly includes sons and other descendants.

TITLE XV

Of the statutory tutelage of agnates

§ 128.   If no tutor has been appointed by will, by the Law of the Twelve Tables the agnates are tutors. They are termed statutory tutors. 1. By a man's agnates are meant persons related to him through males, for example a brother born of the same father, such brother's son, a grandson by such son, a father's brother, a father's brother's son, a grandson by such son. But persons related through females are not agnates, but cognates, that is, connected by a natural tie of relationship. Therefore, your father's sister's son is not your agnate, but your cognate, and conversely you are his cognate, because children belong to the father's, not to the mother's family. 2. When the law calls the agnates to the succession in the event of intestacy this does not necessarily imply that the deceased made no will at all; it means if he died intestate so far as concerns the appointment of a tutor. This would be the case also if the tutor appointed in the testator's will had died in his lifetime. 3. Rights founded on agnation are almost always [29] destroyed by capitis deminutio; for agnation is an institution of the civil law. But rights of cognation are not always affected,[30] because civil law principles may destroy civil law rights but certainly not natural rights.

TITLE XVII

Of the statutory tutelage of patrons

§ 128.   By the same Law of the Twelve Tables the tutelage of freed persons of either sex belongs to their patrons and the patrons' children. This too is called statutory, not that the law has any express provision with regard to it, but this consequence has been drawn from the law by interpretation. For, from the fact that the law directed that the inheritances of freedmen and freedwomen who died intestate should go to the patrons and their children, the old lawyers concluded that the law intended that the tutelage also should belong to them, since it directed that the agnates whom it called to the succession should also be tutors, and because, in general, the benefit of succession and the burden of tutelage go together. We say "in general" because if a child is manumitted under the age of puberty by a woman, the woman is called to the succession, but some other person is tutor.

---

[29] There were exceptions in the later Empire, *e.g.*, Anastasius allowed emancipated brothers and sisters to succeed as if they had not been emancipated. *Infra*, 3. 5. 1.

[30] Inst. 1. 16. 6.

Title XVIII

Of the statutory tutelage of parents

On the analogy of the tutelage of patrons another tutelage is §128.
admitted which is also called statutory. For, if a parent has
emancipated a son or daughter, a grandson or granddaughter by a
son or further descendants, below the age of puberty, he will be their
statutory tutor.

Title XIX

Of fiduciary tutelage

There is another tutelage which is called fiduciary. For, if a §129.
parent has manumitted a son or a daughter, a grandson or a granddaughter or a further descendant under puberty, he becomes their
statutory tutor; but when he dies, if he has male children, they
become fiduciary tutors of their sons or brother or sister and so
forth. Yet if a patron tutor dies, his children succeed him as
statutory tutors, because a son of the deceased, if he had not been
emancipated in his father's lifetime, after his death would be sui juris
and would not fall into the power of his brothers or have them for
tutors; but a freedman, if he had remained a slave would, of course,
have been in the same position in relation to his master's children
after his master's death.[31] The persons above-mentioned are only
qualified to be fiduciary tutors if they are of full age; this rule has
by our constitution [32] been extended to all tutors and curators.

Title XX

Of the tutor Atilianus and the tutor appointed under the lex Julia et Titia

If a child has no other tutor of any kind a tutor used to be §130.
appointed in Rome under the provisions of the lex Atilia by the
urban praetor and the majority of the tribunes of the people, and in
the provinces as provided by the lex Julia et Titia [33] by the governor
of the province. 1. Further, if a tutor was appointed by testament
subject to a condition, or from a certain date, a substitute might be
appointed under the same statutes to act while the condition was
pending, or until the day arrived. Again, if the testamentary
appointment was unconditional, application might be made under
these laws for the appointment of a tutor to act pending the acceptance of the inheritance. A tutor so appointed ceased to be tutor
on the occurrence of the contemplated event. 2. If a tutor was
taken captive by the enemy a tutor substitute might be appointed
under these laws, who ceased to be tutor when the captive returned,
for on his return he was re-instated as tutor by the rule of postliminium. 3. However, appointments ceased to be made under these

---

[31] See remarks in Buckl. *T.* p. 147 ; *M.* p. 93.
[32] Cod. 5. 30. 5.
[33] 31 B.C., Schulz, p. 168.

statutes from the time when the consuls began to appoint tutors to
pupils of either sex after inquiry, and, later, imperial constitutions
empowered the praetors to appoint; for the above-mentioned statutes
made no provision for taking security from tutors, nor for compelling
tutors to undertake the duty of administration. 4. The practice now
is that at Rome appointments are made by the praefect of the city
or the praetor, each within the limits of his jurisdiction, and in the
provinces by the governors after inquiry, or by magistrates to whom
the matter is referred by the governors, if the pupil's estate is of no
great value. 5. Our constitution,[34] dispensing with the governor's
order, provides that if the estate of a pupil or a minor amounts to
five hundred aurei the Defenders of the Cities together with the
Bishop of the City or other officials, or the magistrates or the Justice
of the City of Alexandria shall appoint tutors or curators, a statutory
security to be given as provided by the same constitution and the
magistrates accepting it to be responsible for its adequacy. 6. The
institution of tutelage is in accordance with the law of nature, which
places children of tender years under the direction and guardianship
of others. 7. Since tutors manage the affairs of their pupils, when
§ 136.   they reach the age of puberty the tutors may be required to account
in an action of tutelage (actio tutelae).

Title XXI

Of the authority of tutors

§ 131.   In some cases pupils require the authority of tutors, in others
not. For example, if a pupil stipulates for something to be given
to him, the tutor's authority is not necessary, but it is, if a pupil
makes a promise to another person. For it is a settled principle
that a pupil may make his condition better even without the tutor's
authority, but cannot make it worse without such authority. Consequently in contracts which give rise to reciprocal obligations, such
as purchase and sale, hire, mandate, deposit, if the tutor does not
give his authority, the other party to the contract is bound, but the
pupil is not bound. 1. Further a pupil cannot accept an inheritance,
or petition for possession of goods, or take up a fideicommissary
inheritance except with the tutor's authority, even if the estate is
profitable and does not entail any loss. 2. The tutor must be present
to give his authority at the time of the actual transaction, if he thinks
it for the pupil's advantage that he should do so. Authority given
after the transaction or by letter is of no effect. 3. If an action is
pending between a tutor and a pupil, since the tutor cannot give
authority in a matter which affects his own interest, it is no longer
the practice, as it once was, to appoint a praetorius tutor,[35] but a
curator is appointed to take the place of the tutor. The action then
proceeds with the intervention of the curator, whose function ceases
when the action is concluded.

---

[34] Cod. 1. 4. 30.
[35] G. 1. 184.

TITLE XXII

How tutelage is determined

Pupils of either sex are freed from tutelage when they reach puberty. In the case of males the old lawyers used to ascertain puberty not merely with reference to the child's age but also from an examination of the body.[36] This was long ago repudiated as indecent in the case of females and we hold it to be equally open to objection in the case of males. Accordingly, we have promulgated a constitution [37] fixing the age of puberty in males at the completion of the fourteenth year. For females we retain the old rule according to which women are deemed to be of marriageable age when they have completed their twelfth year. 1. Again, tutelage is terminated, if the child before reaching puberty is given in adrogation or deported, or reduced to slavery by a patron on account of ingratitude, or taken captive by the enemy. 2. If a tutor is appointed by will until a certain condition is realised, he ceases to be tutor when the condition takes effect. 3. Tutelage is determined by the death of tutor or pupil. 4. Again tutelage comes to an end if the tutor suffers capitis deminutio with loss of freedom or citizenship. If the tutor incurs the least capitis deminutio, as by giving himself in adoption, the statutory tutelage alone is determined, the other kinds of tutelage remaining unaffected. But any capitis deminutio of the pupil, even the least, puts an end to the tutelage. 5. Again, if a tutor is appointed by will up to a certain time, he ceases to be tutor when the time arrives. 6. Tutelage is determined if a tutor is removed on a suspicion of misconduct, or is excused for just cause and relieved of the burden of administration, as will be explained below.

§ 71.

§ 120.

TITLE XXIII

Of curators

Males who have arrived at the age of puberty and females of marriageable age have curators until they have completed their twenty-fifth year, for they are not yet of an age to manage their own affairs. 1. Curators are appointed by the same magistrates as appoint tutors. A curator is not appointed by testament, but if so appointed is confirmed by an order of the praetor or governor. 2. Persons below the age of twenty-five years are not obliged to have curators except for the purpose of a law-suit [38]; for a curator may be appointed for a specific purpose. 3. By the Law of the Twelve Tables madmen and prodigals (though above the age of five and twenty years) [39] are in the curatorship of their agnates. But the modern practice is for curators to be appointed at Rome by the

§ 139.

§ 141.

---

[36] G. 1. 196; Ulp. XI. 28.
[37] Cod. 5. 60 3.
[38] Or when a debtor wished to pay a debt, or the tutor to settle his accounts.
[39] *i.e.*, without regard to age. The age in the case of the curatorship of minors resulted from the lex Plaetoria, which was more than two centuries later than the Twelve Tables.

praefect of the city or the praetor, and in the provinces by the governors after inquiry. 4. Curators should also be appointed to persons who are of feeble mind or deaf and dumb, or suffer from an incurable disease, because they are unable to attend to their affairs. 5. There are cases in which even pupils receive curators, for instance if a statutory tutor is unfit to act, for if a person has a tutor already he cannot have another given him. Again, if a tutor appointed by testament or by the praetor or governor is not competent to administer the estate, and yet is not guilty of misconduct, the practice is to appoint a curator to act with him; and the same course is followed to supply the place of tutors who are excused not altogether, but for a limited time.

6. If a tutor suffers from ill-health, or is prevented by any other cause from attending to his pupil's affairs, and the pupil is absent or an infant,[40] the prae or or governor of the province will appoint the tutor's nominee to act for him, the tutor remaining responsible.

TITLE XXIV

Of the security to be given by tutors and curators

§ 136.   To prevent the property of pupils and of persons who have curators being dissipated or diminished, the praetor requires tutors and curators to give security for their administration. However, this is not invariably the case; for testamentary tutors are not compelled to give security because the testator has satisfied himself as to their fidelity and capacity; and tutors and curators appointed after inquiry are not called upon to furnish security, because they are chosen for their fitness. 1. If two or more persons are appointed by testament or after inquiry, any one of them may offer to give security to indemnify the pupil or minor and so be preferred to his fellow tutor or curator and administer the estate alone, unless the co-tutor [or co-curator] is prepared to give security and to be the sole administrator. This means that a tutor or curator cannot directly compel his fellow tutor or curator to give security, but he must offer security himself, so as to give the co-tutor [or co-curator] the choice of accepting or of giving security. If no one offers to give security, the tutor chosen by the testator to do so must administer, and if the will contains no direction, the tutor selected by the majority must administer, as is laid down in the praetor's Edict. If the tutors cannot agree amongst themselves as to the choice of one or more administrators, the praetor must interpose. The same course is to be adopted when there are several tutors appointed after inquiry, namely, the majority may decide who is to administer. 2. It must be known that not only are tutors and curators liable to pupils, minors and others in respect of their administration, but, further, a subsidiary action is available as a last resort against the magis-
§ 136.   trates who accept the security. This may be brought against magistrates who have entirely neglected to see that tutors or curators gave security, or who have accepted an inadequate security. The responses of lawyers and imperial constitutions have extended the remedy, so as to make it available against their heirs as well. 3. The said constitutions further provide that if tutors and curators fail to give security they may be coerced by execution upon their property. 4. This action does not lie against the praefect of the city or against a praetor or governor of a province or any other person authorised to appoint tutors, but only against those magistrates whose duty it is to demand security.

---

[40] If the pupil was present and above the age of infancy he could himself appoint with the tutor's authority.

Title XXV

Of the excuses of tutors or curators

Tutors and curators are excused for various reasons, particularly on §134. account of children, whether in power or emancipated. If they have at Rome three children surviving, in Italy four, or in the provinces five, they may be excused from tutorship or curatorship as from other public duties, for tutorship and curatorship are regarded as public duties. Adopted children are not taken into account, but a natural father may take credit for children given in adoption. Grandchildren by a son are reckoned as representing their father, but not grandchildren by a daughter. Only surviving sons are reckoned. But the question has been raised as to sons lost in war, and it is settled that only those are reckoned who fall in battle, for these, having given their lives for the State, are deemed to go on living in the annals of fame. 1. A rescript in the *Semestria* of the Emperor Marcus Aurelius decreed that an administrator of the Fisc [41] may be excused so long as he continues to act. 2. Absence on State business is a ground of excuse. In the case of existing tutors and curators this is allowed so long as the absence lasts, a special curator being appointed to act for them. They resume their functions on their return, and cannot claim the year's delay which is allowed in the case of new appointments. So Papinian wrote in the fifth book of his *Responsa.*

3. Office-holders are excused, as the Emperor Marcus decreed; but acceptance of office is no excuse for abandoning a guardianship already undertaken. 4. Litigation between the guardian and the pupil or minor is no excuse unless it relates to the whole property or to an inheritance. 5. Three burdens of tutorship or curatorship which the guardian has not solicited afford relief so long as the administration lasts. A guardianship exercised over several wards, such as brothers, in respect of one estate counts as one guardianship. 6. Poverty is a ground of excuse, if a person can show that he is unable to undertake the burden imposed upon him. 7. Ill-health is an excuse, if it prevents a person managing his own affairs. 8. The Emperor Pius decided by rescript that illiteracy was an excuse, though, of course, illiterate persons may be able to do business.

9. If a testator has appointed a person testamentary tutor from ill will, this without more furnishes an excuse. A person cannot be excused, if he promised the child's father that he would act. 10. The mere fact that the person nominated as guardian was unknown to the child's father is not in itself an excuse. 11. Enmity of a serious character between a tutor or curator and the father of the ward is a ground of excuse if no reconciliation has ensued. 12. Similarly, if the father has challenged the guardian's status. 13. A person upwards of seventy years of age may claim to be excused. Formerly, it was the practice to excuse persons under twenty-five years of age, but by our constitution [42] they are disqualified from acting as tutors or curators, so that no excuse is needed. This enacts that neither a pupil nor a minor shall be called to a statutory tutelage; for it was inconsistent with principle that persons who require help in managing their affairs and are under guardianship themselves should be allowed to have the guardianship of others. 14. Soldiers may not be guardians, even if they are willing to act. 15. At Rome grammarians, rhetoricians and medical men are exempted from tutorship and curatorship. The same applies to those who practise these professions in their native cities and are within the permitted number.[43]

16. When a person wishes to be excused and alleges several grounds of excuse, if he fails to establish some of them, he is not forbidden to rely

[41] The Imperial Treasury.
[42] Cod. 5. 30. 5.
[43] Only a limited number was allowed in each city.

on others within the periods allowed. Those who wish to excuse themselves do not appeal, but, whatever the nature of their tutorship, make their excuses, if they are within one hundred miles from the place of their appointment, within fifty days from the time when they have knowledge of it ; if they are living more than one hundred miles away, the time allowed is one day for each twenty miles and thirty days more. But, as Scaevola used to say, this must be so calculated that the period is not in any case less than fifty days.

17. Every tutor is considered to be appointed to the ward's whole estate. 18. A person who has acted as tutor is not obliged to be curator for the same person. Even if a father who has appointed a person tutor by his will has added that he appoints the same person curator, such person must not be compelled to act in this capacity. This is laid down in a rescript of the Emperors Severus and Antoninus.

19. The same Emperors decided by rescript that a husband appointed curator to his wife may excuse himself, even though he is intermeddling in her affairs. 20. If a person has got himself exempted by alleging false grounds of excuse, this does not discharge him from the burden of guardianship.

TITLE XXVI

Of tutors and curators who have come under suspicion

§ 136.　　The crimen suspecti (that is, the charge brought against a suspected tutor) goes back to the Twelve Tables. 1. The right of removing suspected tutors is vested at Rome in the praetor and in the provinces in the governors and the proconsul's legate. 2. We have told who may take cognisance of a case of suspicion. Now let us see who may come under suspicion. All tutors may, whether testamentary or of any other kind, a statutory tutor included. What is to be said of a patron? He too may be removed, only we should remember that his reputation must be spared. 3. Next, we must inquire who may take proceedings against suspected tutors. It must be known that the action is reckoned to be a public action, that is anyone may bring it. Even women are allowed to do so by a rescript of the Emperors Severus and Antoninus, but only such as act from motives of affection, for example a mother; so too a nurse, a grandmother, or a sister. But if the praetor observes that any other woman moved by a sense of duty not inconsistent with the modesty proper to her sex cannot endure that a child should suffer harm he allows her to make the accusation. 4. Children below puberty cannot accuse their tutors ; minors above that age may accuse their curators, acting on the advice of near relations. This was enacted by a rescript of Severus and Antoninus.

5. A tutor falls under suspicion if he does not administer his tutorship faithfully, even though he is solvent. This was Julian's opinion. The same jurist says that a tutor may be removed on the ground of suspicion before he has begun to act, and there is a constitution to this effect. 6. A tutor who has been removed for active misconduct incurs infamia, but not if removed for negligence. 7. If proceedings are taken against a tutor on the ground of suspicion, he is suspended from the administration pending the inquiry ; so Papinian held. 8. Proceedings come to an end if the tutor or curator dies pending the inquiry. 9. If a tutor fails to present himself in order to get determined the allowance to be made for the pupil's maintenance, the Emperors Severus and Antoninus decreed by epistle [44] that the pupil is to be put into possession of the tutor's goods, and a curator is to be appointed to sell wasting property. Accordingly a

---

[44] Dig. 26. 10. 7, 2.

tutor may be removed as suspected if he fails to provide maintenance.
10. If a tutor puts in an appearance, and falsely alleges that the pupil's
estate is too small to admit of an order for maintenance being made, he
is to be remitted for punishment to the praefect of the city just as is the
case if a person has purchased a guardianship by bribery.

11. If a freedman is found to have been guilty of fraud in the administration of the tutelage of sons or grandsons of his patron, he is sent to the
praefect of the city for punishment.

12. Lastly, it must be observed that tutors and curators who are guilty
of fraud in their administration must be removed, even though they offer
security, because giving security does not change the guardian's dishonest
intentions, but merely affords an opportunity of continuing to rob the
estate.

13. For we consider a person to be suspected when his character lays
him open to suspicion. A tutor or curator who is a faithful and careful
administrator is not to be removed on the ground of suspicion simply
because he is poor.

IV. JURISTIC PERSONS

142. The subject of juristic persons—not touched upon in
the Institutes—is too complicated and controversial to admit
of more than a brief reference within the compass of an
elementary textbook. If some texts in the Digest could be
taken at their face value we might conclude that the general
notion of a corporation as a legal entity distinct from its
members was as familiar to the lawyers of the classical age as
it was to the age of Justinian. Si quid universitati debetur,
singulis non debetur: nec quod debet universitas singuli debent.
"What is owed to the corporation is not owed to the individual
members, and what the corporation owes, the individual members do not owe." The quotation is from Ulpian's tenth book
on the Edict.[45] But we cannot be sure that Ulpian meant the
word "universitas" to include more than the municipal cor-
porations, of which, as appears from the context, he was
speaking. The general application of the word to every kind of
corporate body may belong to a later age. In any case the
process was complete by the time of Justinian. That the idea
of corporate personality was only gradually established appears
from the difficulty which was long experienced in admitting that
a municipality or its members collectively could possess,[46]
accept a legacy [47] or be instituted heir (§ 307).[48]

Juristic personality is sometimes attributed to foundations for
pious causes. But the notion of the foundation in some
mysterious way owning itself—an idea as incomprehensible to
English lawyers as the trust conception is to many continental
lawyers—if entertained at all, was, even in the Byzantine
Empire, still in embryo. Usually the property devoted to
charitable purposes was conveyed to the Church or to the
bishop of the diocese, for the purpose of administration. When,

---

[45] Dig. 3. 4. 7, 1 (Monro's translation). Duff, *Personality in Roman Private Law*, pp. 47, 48.
[46] Dig. 41. 2. 1, 22.
[47] Ulp. XXIV, 28.
[48] Ulp. XXII, 5.

as sometimes happened, a trust (so to call it) was created with no indication of a trustee, the question in whom ownership vested remains an enigma.[49]

The view, once general, which attributes juristic personality to a vacant inheritance (hereditas jacens, § 337) no longer finds favour.[50] But the subject may conveniently be considered in this connection. The question of ownership pending acceptance was never entirely settled. In the early law the inheritance (later the items comprised in it) might be acquired by usucapion (so Gaius tells us) though the acquirer knew that he had no title to the property, until this dishonest institution was abolished by the Emperor Hadrian (§ 175). The fact that it was acquired by usucapion, not by occupation, implies that what was acquired was not a res nullius. Gaius speaks of it as a case of acquiring what one knows to belong to someone else (accidit ut qui sciat alienam rem se possidere usucapiat). Yet the same Gaius in the Digest says that things belonging to an inheritance before anyone becomes heir are no man's property (nullius in bonis),[51] and there are other texts to the same effect. For a long time the law oscillated between the view that the title of the eventual heir related back to the time when the inheritance became vacant,[52] and the contrary view that the inheritance represented the person of the deceased,[53] though, on either hypothesis, the things comprised in it were meanwhile without an owner. Then, the idea emerged that the inheritance was owner—hereditas dominae locum obtinet [54]—and this goes a long way towards recognising it as a juristic person. But it cannot be said that this conclusion was positively reached. "It seems that even the compilers did not really regard the hereditas jacens as a person." [55] If it was a person, it remained a person of limited capacity. Thus, though in general a slave belonging to an inheritance acquired for the inheritance as for any other master, the inheritance could acquire through him neither another inheritance to which he had been instituted (because until the heir entered there was no one to authorise acceptance), nor a usufruct (because there was no living person to whom the usufruct could attach).[56]

G. 2. 52.

APPENDIX

The Influence of the Roman Law of Persons upon Modern Systems

143. This ends what we have to say on the Roman Law of Persons. But before passing to the Law relating to Things it may be of interest to consider shortly the influence of the Roman Law of

---

[49] Buckl. *T*. p. 178 ; *M*. p. 36.
[50] Sohm, p. 513.
[51] Dig. 1. 8. 1 pr.
[52] Dig. 45. 3. 28, 4.
[53] Inst. 2. 14 2 ; Dig. 41. 1. 34
[54] Dig. 43. 24. 13, 5.
[55] Duff, p. 166.
[56] Dig. 41. 1. 61.

Persons on modern systems of law, so far as this has not been already noticed. Where Roman elements are present they are generally due rather to inheritance than to reception, for the Law of Persons does not readily lend itself to export and import. It is true that some institutions of Roman Law have been tardily imitated by common law systems, but in such cases (and indeed this applies generally) the use of Roman terms sometimes conceals a difference of substance. We shall speak only of some of the principal institutions described in the foregoing pages so far as they have their counterpart in the modern law.

(i) *Patria potestas.* The French Code retains the rubric *de la puissance paternelle*, but what is meant in fact is parental authority, which belongs to both parents, though "the father alone exercises this authority during the marriage." [57] The German Code speaks of *elterliche Gewalt.* Both systems give the parent the usufruct of a child's property (except his earnings) during minority (in French Law until the age of eighteen or emancipation), subject to the duty of education and maintenance.[58] It is obvious that the modern parental authority is a very pale reflex of the Roman patria potestas even in the latest stage of its development.

(ii) *Marriage.* The Canon Law accepted and transmitted to the modern world the Roman principle that marriage is concluded by consent. The Council of Trent (1563) added the requirement of the presence of the parish priest and two or three witnesses. England followed the old Canon Law until 1753 (Lord Hardwicke's Act), Scotland until 1940 (Marriage (Scotland) Act, 1939), and this is still law in many of the states of the American Union. It seems that English Law recognises as valid the so-called common law marriage (concluded by mere consent), if contracted in a part of the world where formalities are inexistent or unsuitable.[59]

(iii) *Marriage of minors.* Certain consents are commonly required, in the first instance of parents. In France a marriage contracted without the required consents may be avoided at the instance of the persons whose consent is required, or of the minor [60]; in South Africa at the instance of the parents alone.[61] In England, want of consent does not *per se* make a marriage void or voidable, though a minor (infant) who falsely declares that consent has been obtained incurs a penalty.[62]

(iv) *Status of married women.* By the English common law, "the very being and existence of the woman is suspended during the coverture or entirely merged or incorporated in that of her husband. And hence it follows that whatever personal property belonged to the wife before marriage is

---

[57] *C. C.* art. 373.
[58] *C. C.* arts. 384 *et seq.*; *B. G. B.* arts. 1649, 1651, 1686.
[59] Cheshire, *Private International Law* (4th ed.), 320–2.
[60] *C. C.* art. 182.
[61] Lee, pp. 58, 59.
[62] Jenks, art. 1819.

by marriage absolutely vested in the husband." [63]   Further,
she was in general incapable of concluding a contract.
Equity came to her relief with the doctrine of the separate
estate of the married woman. Today by statute she enjoys
all the freedom of a feme sole.[64]   In France there are many
" matrimonial systems " including one like the dotal system
of Roman Law, but not one of them goes so far as the
English Law in the direction of freedom.   In South Africa
this degree of freedom can be secured by antenuptial
contract.[65]

(v) *Divorce.* From the first, the Christian Church set its face
against divorce, but many centuries elapsed before the
principle was established that a consummated marriage is
dissolved by death alone. This is law today in countries in
which ecclesiastical influences are predominant.[66] It was
the law of England until the Matrimonial Causes Act, 1857,
with the consequence that marriage could be dissolved only
by Act of Parliament. In countries which do not follow
the Canon Law divorce is admitted on more or less easy
terms. For the existing English Law see Matrimonial
Causes Act, 1950. A freedom of divorce commensurate
with the Roman Law existed in Soviet Russia from 1918 to
1944.[67]

(vi) *Legitimation by subsequent marriage.* See above, § 105.

(vii) *Adoption.* Most modern systems permit the adoption of
minors with various consequences. For French Law see
C. C. arts. 343 *et seq.* and Planiol I. 550 *et seq.*; for German
Law, B. G. B. arts. 1741 *et seq.*; for South Africa, the
Children's Act, 1937. Adoption *de jure* was unknown to
English Law before the Adoption Act, 1926. The Adoption
Act, 1950, for most purposes places an adopted child in the
same position as a child born in lawful wedlock. This was
Roman Law until Justinian distinguished adoptio plena and
adoptio minus plena (*supra*, § 114).

(viii) *Emancipation.* Many systems of law admit the emancipation of minors, but only with the effect of freeing them from
some of the disabilities of minority.[68] This is not emancipation in the Roman sense. Other systems of law have
adopted in place of emancipation the useful Roman institution of venia aetatis (§ 140). English Law affords no such
ways of escape from the disabilities of infancy.

---

[63] Blackstone, *Commentaries,* II, 433.
[64] Law Reform (Married Women and Tortfeasors) Act, 1935, ss. 1–5.
The first important statutory advance was made by the Married Women's
Property Act, 1882.
[65] Lee, p. 79.
[66] As in Italy and Southern Ireland. *Cf. Cod. Jur. Can.* c. 1118.
Matrimonium validum ratum et consummatum nulla humana potestate,
nullaque causa praeterquam morte dissolvi potest.
[67] *Nachimson* v. *Nachimson* [1930] P. 127.
[68] *e.g., C. C.* arts. 476 *et seq.*

(ix) *Guardianship.* Modern systems of law with a Roman background, such as the French, reproduce with variations the principal features of the Roman tutela and cura. Thus is France the tutor is charged with the care of the person of the ward (this was not so in Roman Law), is his legal representative and as such within limits competent to bind him by contracts made in his name, and administers the property,[69] but does not, as in Roman Law and many other countries (Germany, Switzerland, South Africa), " authorise " the minor's contract.[70] The " family council " is an intrusive element in the system, of customary origin, quite unsuited to modern conditions. In English Law the modern guardian may be guardian of the person or guardian of the estate or both. In the second of these capacities he acts as trustee for the ward. He neither contracts in his name, nor authorises his contracts. Here again the English Law affords the minor no means of escape from his disabilities. It is equally a stranger to interdiction on the ground of prodigality; and the court has even gone so far as to refuse recognition to a foreign conseil judiciaire, who corresponds in French Law to the Roman curator prodigi.[71]

---

[69] *C. C.* art. 450 (same in German law).
[70] Josserand, *Cours de droit civil positif français,* I § 419.
[71] *Re Selot's Trust* [1902] 1 Ch. 488 ; Cheshire, *Private International Law* (4th ed.), 148.

BOOK II

THE LAW OF PROPERTY

I. PRELIMINARY

144. The second principal branch of the Roman Private Law is the Law relating to Things. This is treated by Gaius in Books II and III. In Justinian's Institutes it extends also to the first five Titles of Book IV. By " Thing " (res) the Romans understand any unit of economic value. " The true point of contact between the various res seems in reality to be the fact that whoever has a res is actually or prospectively so much the better off " (Moyle). " Res . . . means any economic interest guaranteed by law, any right or rights having a money value, any interest expressible in terms of money which the law will protect " (Buckland). The Law relating to Things, therefore, is the Law relating to Property, understood in a sense wide enough to include the Law of Obligations and the Law of Succession. In this Book the term " Law of Property " is used in a more limited sense, exclusive of Obligations and Succession.

145. CLASSIFICATION OF THINGS.—Things may be classified according to their physical nature, or according to the technical rules of the legal system in question. Thus, if we classify things as movable and immovable we have regard to their physical nature ; if we classify them as real and personal, as in English Law, or as mancipable and non-mancipable (res mancipi—res nec mancipi), as in Roman Law, we have regard to arbitrary distinctions created by law. But the first principle of classification is not so simple as it looks ; for it is often difficult to say whether for legal purposes a thing is to be regarded as movable or immovable, and a thing which is treated as movable for one purpose may for another be treated as immovable. So that, in the last resort, we are concerned not with the question, what things are in themselves, but with the question, what is the attitude of the law with regard to them. The classifications adopted by the Roman lawyers are, in the main, the result of historical development or practical convenience. They display little inclination towards scientific analysis.

146. Justinian begins his second Book by saying, " Things are either in our patrimony or outside our patrimony "; by 2. 1 pr. which he means that there are certain things which are not the subject of private ownership.[1] These are: —(a) Things common to all men (res communes)—the air, running water, the sea and the sea-shore ; (b) things public (res publicae)—rivers and harbours ; (c) things belonging to a corporate body, such as theatres, race-courses and the like in cities (res universitatis) ; (d) things belonging to no one (res nullius), comprising : — (i) sacred things (res sacrae), i.e., churches and other things dedicated to the service of God ; (ii) religious things (res religiosae), i.e., graveyards and graves ; (iii) sanctioned things (res sanctae), such as city walls and gates. They are said to be sanctioned, because any offence against them is punished capitally ; and penalties imposed by law are termed " sanctions." The first two of these are said to be matter of divine right (divini juris), and the term applies in a way to the third as well (quodammodo divini juris sunt).

147. All this is very confused. The distinction between things common and things public is ill-defined, and has no practical value. As to the sea-shore, there is no reason in the nature of things why it should not be owned by private persons, as it may be in English Law by grant from the Crown. Indeed, there are texts which say that one may become owner of a portion of the shore by building upon it, remaining owner, however, only so long as the building stands.[2] But, in general, the shore was not owned by individuals. One text suggests that it was the property of the Roman People.[3] More often it is regarded as owned by no one, the public having undefined rights of use and enjoyment. Rivers are said to be public. But a river was not public unless it flowed perennially, i.e., all the year round, though it did not lose its character if it happened to go dry in a single summer.[4] The public had rights of fishing and navigation and of incidental use of the banks. Whether the river-bed belonged to the Roman People, or to the riparian owners, or to no one was never clearly defined. There was, no doubt, a tendency, which became more pronounced as time went on, to regard all res publicae as the property of the Roman

---

[1] In nostro patrimonio—extra nostrum patrimonium. Res in commercio —extra commercium—things susceptible or not of private transactions— mean much the same.

[2] Dig. 1. 8. 6 pr. (Marcianus) ; 41. 1. 14. (Neratius).

[3] Dig. 43. 8. 3 pr. (Celsus)

[4] Dig. 43. 12. 1, 2.

People, or, as we should say, of the State,[5] and, similarly, res universitatis were regarded as the property of the universitas.

148. The phrase res nullius is used in various senses:—
  (a) to include all things which according to Roman ideas are not susceptible of private ownership;
  (b) specifically, as above, of things sacred, religious and sanctioned;
  (c) of things which, though susceptible of ownership, are not at the moment owned, e.g., wild animals uncaptured, or things which have been abandoned by their owner (res derelictae).

149. RES CORPORALES—INCORPORALES.—Things are distinguished as corporeal and incorporeal (res corporales—res incorporales). "Corporeal things are things which can be touched, as land, a slave, a garment, gold, silver and other things innumerable." "Incorporeal things are things which cannot be touched. Such are things which consist in a right, as an inheritance, usufruct, obligations in whatever way contracted." It is commonly objected that this classification is illogical, because it confounds physical things with rights. But from the Roman point of view there is no confusion. I can own " this thing " and I can own " this right "; each is an asset of value to me and therefore a res. No doubt, ownership of a corporeal thing is a right or a bundle of rights. But usage identifies ownership of a corporeal thing with the thing owned, so that ownership, alone of rights, is regarded as corporeal; or, rather, the thing is substituted for the right. All other rights remain incorporeal.

150. RES MANCIPI—NEC MANCIPI.—Through the whole course of Roman Law, until the distinction was formally abolished by Justinian,[6] things were distinguished as mancipable and non-mancipable (res mancipi—res nec mancipi). Mancipable things were things which were transferred by mancipation. All other things were non-mancipable. Particulars will be given when we come to speak of modes of acquisition.

151. THINGS MOVABLE AND IMMOVABLE.—The classification of things as movable and immovable was not of cardinal importance in Roman Law, because for most purposes the law did not distinguish between them. It is true that Italian soil, as will be

2. 2. 1.

2. 2. 2.

G. 2. 22.

---

[5] Any State-owned property was in a sense res publica, but not in the special sense in which the term is used in this context. It was said to be in patrimonio or in pecunia populi (Dig. 41. 1. 14 pr.; 18. 1. 6 pr.) or in patrimonio fisci (Dig. 43. 8. 2, 4.).
[6] Cod. 7. 31. 1, 5.

seen, being a res mancipi, required a special method of conveyance. But this was limited in area and came to be an unessential formality. In the classical era land no less than movables might, in effect, be conveyed by simple delivery. But there were some differences between movable and immovable property. The periods of usucapion were not the same (§ 174). Movables could be stolen, land not (§ 601). In relation to possession and the possessory interdicts the rules were different.[7] Some distinctions result from the nature of the things themselves. What are called real or praedial servitudes (rights of way, rights of support, etc.) are naturally inapplicable to movables. In the later Empire the distinction between movables and immovables became more prominent owing to the introduction of special modes of conveyance, applicable to land (§ 210). In the Middle Ages this became the principal basis of classification and it has persisted in modern systems of law. In English Law it has tended more and more to replace the old classification of things as real and personal.

152. DOMINIUM EX JURE QUIRITIUM.—Roman ownership, or, as it was called, ownership by quiritary title (dominium ex jure Quiritium), implies a Roman owner of a Roman thing acquired by Roman process. It was not available (privileged cases apart) to peregrines, because they were not citizens. It was inapplicable (privileged cases apart) to provincial land, because provincial land (technically) was not owned by individuals, but by the Roman People or the Emperor.[8] It was not a consequence of transfer by tradition of a res mancipi, because ownership of a res mancipi could not be transferred by tradition. **G. 2. 7.** But long before Justinian these distinctions had become unimportant. The constitutio Antoniniana of A.D. 212 had extended citizenship to the whole Roman world (§§ 85, 92); the difference between Italian and provincial soil was merely formal; a perfectly satisfactory (praetorian) title to res mancipi could be procured by tradition.[9]

While these distinctions lasted they gave rise in classical law to " inferior modes of holding which may be called Ownership."[10] These were:—1, Ownership by peregrines; 2, ownership of provincial land; 3, the so-called " bonitary ownership " of mancipable things conveyed by tradition. The first two did

[7] Inst. 4. 15. 4a.
[8] G. 2. 7, 21. See note on Inst. 2. 1. 40, *infra*.
[9] The praetor protected the acquirer by the actio Publiciana in rem. See below § 176.
[10] Buckl. *T.* p. 189; *M.* 113.

not come within the normal vision of a Roman lawyer. The third is more important. We shall meet with it again when we come to speak of the law of usucapion (§ 172). It is effective ownership separated from civil law title.[11]

153. The Roman classification of things as corporeal and incorporeal obscures the separate position in the legal system of the Law of Succession and the Law of Obligations. Justinian does not, in fact, in any part of the Institutes consider " things," in the wider sense which he gives to the word, as a single and separate topic. After the preliminary observations on the classification of things summarised above, he goes on to consider the ways in which things are acquired by particular title (not things in general, but corporeal things). It is only when he has described the modes of acquisition by natural law, devoting to this subject the remainder of the first Title of his Second Book, that in Title II he distinguishes things corporeal and things incorporeal. This is made the occasion for a description of praedial servitudes, rustic and urban, and of usufruct, use and habitation, commonly described, but not in the Institutes, as personal servitudes, together with the ways in which these rights are created and determined (Tits. III to V). Then, reverting to the acquisition of things, he describes the principal subsisting mode of acquisition by civil law, namely, usucapion, and its later development, long-time-prescription (Tit. VI). Title VII is devoted to donation, described as " another mode of acquisition." The subject of Title VIII is " persons who may, and who may not alienate," of Title IX " Persons through whom we acquire." The last section of this Title prepares the reader for a transition to modes of acquisition by universal title. The subject of inheritance, testamentary and intestate, together with its praetorian equivalent, possession of goods, occupies the remainder of Book II and the first nine Titles of Book III. Titles X–XII of Book III treat of acquisition by adrogation and some other modes of universal succession. Then in Title XIII we are introduced abruptly to the topic of obligations with the remark " Let us now pass to obligations."

---

[11] G. 2. 40, 41. Normally civil law title and effective ownership go together. When they are separated the first is called " bare Quiritary title " (nudum jus Quiritium), the second has come to be known as " bonitary ownership." The term is an invention of the commentators. Theophilus has the phrase " bonitary owner." The classical writers say that a man " has a thing in his goods," or that " it is in his goods " (in bonis habere—in bonis esse) There were other cases of bonitary ownership besides that mentioned above; in particular the praetorian ownership of the bonorum possessor (§ 387) and of the bonorum emptor (§ 755). G. 3. 80; Buckl. M. p. 114.

154. This arrangement of the subject-matter, however imperfect, brings into view *seriatim* most of the topics, which in a textbook on the private law of Rome we might expect to find occupying a central position between the Law of Persons on the one hand and the Law of Actions on the other. But for some other such topics we look in vain. There is no discussion of possession, or of real rights other than servitudes.[12] Whatever may have been the Roman point of view, it is here that a modern reader expects to find these subjects treated. We supply these gaps, therefore, in this commentary; and, departing from the comprehensive terminology of the Institutes, divide the Law of Things into three principal sections, dealing with:—I. The Law of Property (including Ownership, Real Rights less than Ownership, and Possession); II. The Law of Succession; III. The Law of Obligations. It would be more logical to reverse the order of these last two topics, but in conformity with the purpose of this book we adhere to the order of the Institutes.

THE INSTITUTES

BOOK II (Tits. I and II)

TITLE I

Of the classification of things

In the first Book we have explained the law of persons. We are now to speak of things; which are either in our patrimony, or outside our patrimony. Some things are by natural law common to all men, some are public, some belong to a corporate body, some belong to no one, most things belong to individuals, and are acquired by various methods, as will appear from what follows. 1. By natural law the air, flowing water, the sea, and therefore the shores of the sea are common to all. Consequently, no one is forbidden to approach the shore, provided that he does not interfere with dwelling-houses, monuments and buildings, for these are not subject to the jus gentium, as the sea is. 2. All rivers and harbours are public; consequently the right of fishing in a harbour and in rivers is common to everyone. 3. The sea-shore extends to the limit reached by the highest winter flood. 4. The use of river-banks is public and juris gentium, like the use of the river itself; and so every one is free to put in at the bank, to fasten ropes to trees growing on the bank, or to land a cargo, just as every one is free to navigate the stream. But the ownership of the banks and of

§ 146.

---

[12] The explanation of the omission is that the Roman tradition did not assign these topics to the Law of Things. Buckl. *Main Institutions,* pp. 108, 144.

trees growing on them is vested in the riparian proprietors. 5. The
use of sea-shores too is public and juris gentium, like the use of the
sea itself, and so any one may set up a hut to retire into, may dry
his nets, and draw them up from the sea. But the ownership of the
shores may be supposed to be vested in no one, and to be governed
by the same law as the sea and the sea-bottom.

6. Things belonging to a corporate body, not to individuals, are,
for example, things in cities, such as theatres, race-courses and the
like, and any other things which are the common property of cities.

7. Things belonging to no one are sacred things, religious things,
sanctioned things; for a thing which is subject to divine law is
owned by no one. 8. Those things are sacred which are duly
consecrated to God by the Bishops, such as sacred buildings, and
offerings dedicated to the service of God; which things, as our
constitution [13] enacts, may not be alienated or pledged except for
the redemption of captives. If any one by his own authority
purports to make a thing sacred, it is not sacred, but profane. A
site on which sacred buildings have been built remains sacred (as
Papinian wrote) even after the destruction of the building. 9. Any
one may make a place religious at his pleasure by burying a corpse
in his own ground. If ordinary ground is owned in common one
co-owner may not use it for burial without the consent of the rest,
but it is different in the case of a burial-place owned in common.
Similarly, if property is subject to a usufruct the owner may not
make it religious without the consent of the usufructuary. A person
may bury in another man's land with the consent of the owner.
Subsequent ratification is equivalent to consent.

§ 245.

10. Sanctioned things too, such as city walls and gates, are in
a way matter of divine law, and, therefore, no one's property. City
walls are said to be sanctioned because capital punishment is
ordained against those who violate them. The part of a statute
ordaining a penalty in the event of its infringement is called a
sanction.

[For sec. 11, see p. 127.]

Title II

Of incorporeal things

Some things are corporeal, some incorporeal.

1. Corporeal things are things which by their nature are tangible,
such as land, a slave, a garment, gold, silver and other things
innumerable. 2. Incorporeal things are intangible; such are things
consisting in a right, for example an inheritance, usufruct, use, obligations howsoever contracted. Nor does it make any difference that
an inheritance includes corporeal things; for the fruits too, which are
gathered from land are corporeal, and what is due to us under
any obligation is usually corporeal, for example land, a slave or
money. But the right of inheritance, the right of usufruct, the
right of obligation, are incorporeal. 3. We refer to the same head

---

[13] Cod. 1. 2. 21.

those rights appurtenant to houses and land which are called servitudes.

II. Modes of Acquisition

155. We pass to the subject of modes of acquisition, the processes by which a thing becomes mine. These are distinguished as original and derivative, the first when the thing of which I become owner had no previous owner, or at least when my ownership stands in no necessary relation to that of the person who owned before me; the second when I derive my title from some one who owned before me, and take subject to any real burdens which attach to the property. This distinction is made by medieval and modern writers. It is not found in the texts of the Roman Law.

156. Justinian says that we acquire things either by natural law, which he here identifies with the jus gentium, or by civil 2. I. 11. law. The first, he adds, is plainly the older, since it is as old as the human race. It is said, with justice, that, so far as the Roman Law is concerned, this inverts the historical sequence. This does not mean that the early Romans did not recognise occupation and tradition as modes of acquisition. On the contrary, as regards the first, Gaius says that " they considered nothing so entirely theirs as what they had taken from the enemy." But in any legal system what is technical and peculiar G. 4. 16. engages attention before what is simple and universal; and, besides, some of the juris gentium modes of acquisition have all the air of an afterthought. Reversing, therefore, the order of the Institutes and preferring that of Gaius, we shall speak—first, of the civil modes of acquisition; afterwards, of the natural modes of acquisition. So far as the legal consequence is concerned there is no difference between them. Both alike made the acquirer owner of the thing acquired.

III. Acquisition by Civil Law

157. The civil law modes of acquisition described in the texts are usucapion and donation, and another of minor importance which Justinian abolished. In the earlier law the 2. 7. 4. two principal modes of acquisition by civil law were mancipation and cession in court (cessio in jure). Justinian does not mention them. They had passed out of use before his time. But they are of historical importance and must be considered in some detail. We shall speak, therefore, of: —

1. Mancipatio ; 2. In jure cessio ; 3. Usucapio. Donation, which was not in fact usually a mode of acquisition, is reserved for separate treatment (p. 147).

G. 1. 119.   158. MANCIPATIO.—Gaius described this as follows:—

" Mancipation is a fictitious sale, a process peculiar to Roman citizens. It is effected thus:—

" There are brought together not less than five witnesses. Roman citizens above the age of puberty and another person similarly qualified, who is to hold a bronze balance, and is called the libripens.   Then the person who is acquiring by mancipation, taking hold of the thing [14] to be transferred uses the following form of words:—' This man [15] I declare to be mine by quiritary right, and be he bought to me with this bronze and bronze balance ': then he strikes the balance with a piece of bronze and gives it to the transferor by way of price."

The declaration made by the purchaser was termed the " nuncupation " from the verb nuncupare meaning to make a public declaration.[16]

Ulpian [17] supplies some further particulars:—

" Mancipation takes place between Roman citizens and Latin colonists and Junian Latins and peregrines to whom commercium has been conceded.   Commercium is the right of buying and selling.[18] Movable things cannot be mancipated unless they are present, and not more than can be grasped in the hand. But several immovables, even though situate in different places, can be mancipated simultaneously."

G. 4. 17.   It may be supposed that, in the case of immovables, as in the procedure by legis actio sacramenti, a sod of earth or something of the kind was taken to represent the property which was being sold. There is no apparent reason why the same symbolism should not have been available also in the case of movables.

159. Gaius speaks of mancipation as a " fictitious sale," because, though in form of a sale, in his time the process was a general mode of conveyance, limited indeed to certain kinds of property, but applicable to any kind of transaction, sale, gift, constitution of a dos (§ 222) and others. But originally, the transaction was in fact, what later it was feigned to be, a sale for ready money.   Before the introduction of coined money, not, as was once supposed, by the Decemvirs, but nearly two centuries later, the medium of exchange was uncoined bronze

---

[14] Rem teners, not aes tenens—holding a piece of bronze—which some editors substitute on poor authority.
[15] The sale of a slave is taken as a typical transaction.
[16] G. 2. 104.
[17] Liber singularis Regularum, XIX, 4, 5.
[18] Scilicet, by the formal processes of the civil law.

(aes rude), which had to be weighed to determine the amount. This was the function of the libripens. When coined money came into use, the weighing became a fiction, the bronze currency being represented by an ingot of bronze, known as raudusculum. The ceremony was now merely dramatic. The actual contract, sale or whatever it might be, took place, so to say, off stage.

160. No doubt the transition from the real to the fictitious sale was gradual. There must have been steps in the process which are unknown to us. The formula preserved by Gaius raises more than one question to which no answer has been found. Why this declaration of ownership, recalling the procedure in the legis actio sacramenti (§ 672) and in the process of in jure cessio, to be mentioned later (§ 165)? Why the five witnesses? Some have imagined a connection with the five classes of the Servian constitution (§ 4). The formula employed must have admitted of modifications to meet the circumstances of the case. The transferor may in some cases have made a contemporaneous declaration, but this is disputed. In any event it was not necessary that he should do so. It must be borne in mind that it was the ceremony that vested the property in the "purchaser." Actual delivery was not essential.

161. We must now ask what things could be conveyed by this process. The answer is res mancipi and (it seems) only res mancipi. The term includes:—(a) land and houses in Italy and in certain privileged districts outside Italy; (b) rustic servitudes over such land; (c) slaves and beasts of draft and burden.[19] Everything else, including public land (ager publicus), provincial lands, and urban servitudes (§ 237) were res nec mancipi.

162. Why were the above-mentioned things grouped together to form one class? Because they constituted the principal wealth of a primitive rural community. These were the things which were entered upon the census roll and determined the assessment of the individual citizen. There may have been an earlier period when alienable property in land was unknown and res mancipi meant, as the etymology seems to suggest, movable property, things which could be grasped by the hand.[20]

163. We have seen that the mancipatory sale implies the use of uncoined bronze as a medium of exchange. There was an

---

[19] G. 2. 14a; Ulp. XIX. 1.
[20] Unde etiam mancipatio dicitur quia manu res capitur.

earlier time when cattle were the standard value. This is indicated by the etymological connection between pecus=cattle and pecunia=money. But the two stages overlapped. It may safely be said that the mancipatory sale goes a long way back. Perhaps it was common to Rome and her Latin neighbours.[21]

164. Mancipation was a living institution in the time of Gaius and was still in use two centuries later.[22] But the ceremonial became unnecessary because a recital in a written instrument that the forms had been complied with was allowed to serve the same purpose.[23] This eliminated balance and balance-holder, ingot of bronze and nuncupatio. In this form —the shadow of a symbol—it lingered on in the notarial style of what had been the Western Empire even after Justinian had formally abolished the distinction between res mancipi and res nec mancipi (§ 150) and with it the continued existence of an institution which had long since been useless and seldom employed. It had been superseded by the simple method of transferring ownership by tradition. While it lasted it had, indeed, the one advantage that ownership could be transferred by this method without transfer of possession (therefore, not necessarily on the spot) and was available to an owner of immovable (possibly also of movable) property, who for whatever reason was not in actual possession at the time.[24] But in the later Empire a deed of transfer was equally available for this purpose (§ 210), so that it was matter of indifference whether land was conveyed in one way or in the other. It was merely a question of the form of words employed, that is of notarial style.

165. IN JURE CESSIO.—This is another civil law mode of acquisition, for a description of which we again turn to Gaius.

G. 2. 24.   " In jure cessio takes place as follows:—
" Before a magistrate of the Roman People, such as the urban praetor, the person to whom the cession is made, holding the thing in question says: 'This man I declare to be mine by quiritary right'; and when he has vindicated the praetor asks the person who cedes whether he makes a counter-vindication. If he says no or says nothing, the praetor awards the thing to the person who has vindicated it. This is called a legis actio
G. 2. 25.   (statute-process). It may also take place in the provinces before the governor. We usually or almost always employ mancipations. For when we can do a thing for ourselves in the presence of witnesses, why should we give ourselves the greater trouble of resorting to the praetor or provincial governor? "

---

[21] Girard, p. 308, n. 6.
[22] Girard, p. 314.
[23] Arangio-Ruiz, p. 185.
[24] Girard, p. 314.

Ulpian describes the process succinctly [25]: —

> "In jure cessio is a method of alienation common to res mancipi and to res nec mancipi. It requires three persons—the person who cedes—the person who vindicates—the person who awards. The owner cedes: the cessionary vindicates: the praetor awards."

In jure cessio, then, is a fictitious real action or vindication, resembling the common recovery of English Law, but arrested in its initial stage by the alienor, who plays the part of defendant, admitting the claim of the alienee, who is the fictitious plaintiff.[26]

166. This form of conveyance was used for the following purposes: —

    (a) to alienate corporeal property of every kind whether res mancipi or res nec mancipi;

    (b) to transfer incorporeal things other than obligations, such as inheritance [27];

    (c) to create and extinguish [28] praedial servitudes and usufruct.

For urban servitudes this was the only method available. Rustic servitudes could also be created by mancipation (§ 161). In the Law of Persons we have met with in jure cessio in connection with manumissio vindicta (§ 77), adoption (§ 113), and the tutela legitima of women (§ 138).

167. Being a civil mode of acquisition, in jure cessio was available only to Roman citizens and in respect of things susceptible of Roman ownership (dominium ex jure Quiritium). It passed out of use in the post-classical period, and, as a mode of acquisition, had disappeared before the time of Justinian.

168. USUCAPIO.—It may happen that a person is in possession of property as owner but without legal title. In such a case all mature legal systems recognise him as owner, or, at least, give him the substantial advantages of ownership, if he continues to possess for the period defined by law and satisfies other necessary conditions. This is called acquisitive prescription. The Roman Law gave effect to this mode of acquisition under the name of usucapio. Later, an analogous institution grew up in the provinces called long-time-prescription (longi temporis

---

25 XIX, 9, 10.
26 For another theory see Buckl. *M.* p. 124.
27 G. 2. 38, 34.
28 G. 2. 29, 30; Girard, p. 403.

praescriptio). But it will be convenient to treat the whole subject under the head of usucapion.

169. In order that property may be acquired by usucapion the following conditions must be satisfied. There must be a thing susceptible of ownership—title—good faith—possession— lapse of time. They are summed up in the line—

> Res habilis, titulusque, fides, possessio, tempus.

170. (i) The thing in question must be capable of being the subject of transactions between Roman citizens (res in commercio), and must not be declared incapable of alienation by any rule of law. This excludes all res extra commercium, *e.g.*, res sacrae, religiosae, sanctae (§ 146). It excludes a free man, who is not a res, and provincial land, which is technically incapable of private ownership (§ 152). Dotal immovables cannot be acquired by this method because they are inalienable, nor the immovable property of pupilli and minores XXV annis for the same reason.[29] Stolen property (res furtiva) could not be acquired even by a possessor in good faith. This was enacted by the Twelve Tables and a lex Atinia of unknown date. But the "vice" of theft was purged, if the thing returned to its owner, or at least "if the owner knew where the thing was and there was no obstacle to his vindication of it."[30] After this, it ceased to be a res furtiva. Later legislation (lex Julia et Plautia) extended the same prohibition to things movable or immovable possessed by violence (res vi possessa).

171. (ii) There must be a just cause (justa causa) or just title (justus titulus). The phrases are equivalent. "Just cause" or "just title" means an antecedent or contemporaneous event which, in normal circumstances, makes acquisition of possession take effect as acquisition of ownership. A mere handing over of a thing is colourless. It may be for momentary convenience, or by way of deposit or loan. Equally, it may be made with the intention of transferring ownership and with the normal consequence that ownership passes. Thus, a man may acquire by way of sale, gift, legacy and so forth. Justinian says that a mistaken belief that a cause exists, when it does not, excludes usucapion. In other words, a putative title is insufficient. There must be an actual sale, an actual gift, etc.[31] In the case of legacy the person claiming to usucape must be a

2. 6. 2.

2. 6. 8.

2. 6. 11.

---

29 Girard, p. 330.
30 Buckl. *T*. p. 248.
31 Dig. 41. 4. 2 pr. ; 41. 6. 1 pr.

THE LAW OF PROPERTY

legatee.[32] If the thing in question is supposed to be a res
derelicta there must have been an abandonment by a non-owner
and something equivalent to occupation.[33] But a tendency
developed, evidenced by texts in the Digest, to admit usucapion
when the error was excusable, at all events in case of sale.[34]

172. (iii) There must be good faith. If a person finds 2. 6 pr.
himself honestly in possession as owner without civil law ownership this is usually due to one or both of the following facts: —
(a) He has acquired from a person who had no title to convey
the ownership; (b) he has acquired by a process not apt to make
him civil law owner. This second situation arises, in particular,
if a res mancipi is conveyed by tradition, not by mancipation,
but it exists also in any other case of so-called bonitary ownership (bonorum possessio—bonorum emptio, etc.).[35] To
constitute good faith the acquirer must honestly believe that the
transaction has made him owner at least by praetorian title.
This generally implies a belief founded in an error of fact, not
of law, that the person from whom he thinks that he derives
his title was owner or competent to alienate. I can usucape
if I have bought from a pupillus, not authorised by his tutor,
believing him to be pubes, or from an insane person believing
him to be sane, but not if I did not know that a pupil was by
law incompetent to manage his affairs without his tutor's
authority.[36] It was enough that possession originated in good
faith. It was not necessary that good faith should continue
during the period of possession. There was an exception in the
case of donation until Justinian altered the law.[37] The Canon
Law required good faith throughout (mala fides superveniens
nocet) and this has influenced modern codes.

173. (iv) There must be possession, i.e., juristic possession,
not mere detention (§ 267). This implies corpus and animus—
physical control and the intention to possess as owner. These
need not necessarily co-exist in the same person. A person may
acquire and hold possession through a slave, a son in power, or
a free agent (§ 230). In general both agent and principal must
have the appropriate animus. The agent must intend to acquire
possession for his principal, not for himself. The principal

32 Dig. 41. 8. (pro legato). But it was not fatal to usucapion that a
legacy had been revoked by codicil unknown to the claimant. Dig.
41. 8. 4. This is a titulus putativus.
33 Dig. 41. 7. 6.
34 Dig. 41. 4. 11 ; 41. 10. 3 ; 5. 1 ; Buckl. T. 246 ; M. 129.
35 Buckl. M. p. 126.
36 Dig. 41. 4. 2, 15 & 16—juris error nulli prodest.
37 Cod. 7. 31. 1, 3 ; Buckl. T. 244 ; M. p. 127.

must intend to acquire possession through the agent. But, if a slave or filiusfamilias makes an acquisition for the peculium, possession vests forthwith in the master or paterfamilias and usucapion begins to run in his favour although he is ignorant of the fact of acquisition.[38] This is because there is an implied authority to acquire by means of the peculium. If a free agent has a general authority to acquire possession for his principal, single acquisitions are acquired for the principal though he has not knowledge of each of them as it occurs, but in this case usucapion does not begin to run until he has knowledge of the single acquisition in question.[39]

2. 6 pr.

174. (v) The possession must continue uninterrupted for the period defined by law. This was fixed by the Twelve Tables at two years for immovables, for other things one year. In the latest period, as we shall see, the periods were longer. Interruption of usucapion is termed usurpatio. Any actual interruption for however short a time arrested the course of usucapion, and wiped out the effect of previous possession. In Justinian's system commencement of proceedings for the recovery of possession by the owner had the same effect.[40] In calculating the time of possession the heir or bonorum possessor was allowed credit for the unbroken possession of his predecessor in title joined to his own. This applied even if he knew that the title was defective. It was enough that his predecessor had the necessary good faith. This is called succession to possession (successio in possessionem). It applies only to the universal successor. The particular successor (purchaser, donee, legatee, etc.) stood in a different position. A constitution of Severus and his son Antoninus, commonly called Caracalla, allowed a purchaser to add to his own time that of his vendor, but both must have had bona fides at the moment of acquisition. Justinian allowed the same advantage in all cases of singular succession.[41] This is called accession of possession (accessio possessionis).

2. 6. 12.

2. 6. 13.

175. It is likely enough that the theory of usucapion was gradually developed. Gaius mentions cases in which good faith was not required. The most remarkable of these was usucapion as heir (usucapio pro herede). This is what he says: —

> Lib. II. 52. " Sometimes it happens that one who knows that he possesses a thing which does not belong to him may usucape;

---

[38] Dig. 41. 2. 1, 5; 41. 3. 47.
[39] Cod. 7. 32. 1; Dig. 41. 2. 49, 2.
[40] Girard, p. 334.
[41] Dig. 41. 4. 2, 17; Cod. 7. 31. 1, 3.

for example, if a person possesses a thing forming part of an inheritance (res hereditaria), of which the heir has not yet obtained possession; for he is allowed to usucape, provided the thing admits of usucapion. This kind of possession and usucapion is called usucapio pro herede. 53. This usucapion goes so far that even immovables are usucaped in one year. 54. The reason why in this case the usucapion of immovables is complete in one year is because formerly it was held that by possessing things belonging to an inheritance the inheritances themselves were usucaped at the end of a year. For the Law of the Twelve Tables ordained that immovables should be usucaped in two years, other things in one year : so an inheritance was thought to come under the description of " other things " since it is not an immovable : and, although it was afterwards considered that the inheritance itself could not be usucaped, none the less the usucapion of one year continued to apply to all things forming part of an inheritance, even immovables. 55. The reason why this iniquitous institution was allowed is because the ancients wanted inheritances to be accepted as soon as possible that there might be persons to perform the sacrifices to which in those days great importance was attached, and that creditors might know who was to be looked to for payment of debts. 56. This kind of possession and usucapion is also called ' lucrative,' because a person acquires gratis a thing which he knows to belong to some one else.

57. " But today, it is no longer lucrative; for at the instance of the late Emperor Hadrian a senatusconsultum was passed rescinding such usucapions; and so an heir by bringing an action for the inheritance may obtain any item of the inheritance from the person who has usucaped it just as if it had not been usucaped. 58. If there is in existence a suus et necessarius heres the law excludes the possibility of usucapio pro herede." [42]   2. 19 2.

It may be that the cases which Gaius treats as exceptional were survivals from a time when they were not exceptions, and that the usucapion of the Twelve Tables required neither good faith nor just title as a condition of usucapion.[43]

176. Until the process of usucapio had run its course, if the possessor lost possession, he could not vindicate the property from a third person, because he could not truthfully assert that the thing belonged to him by quiritary title (§ 726). But the praetor came to his aid by means of the Actio Publiciana in rem, which allowed him to recover the property as if time had already run in his favour.

177. Justinian says (Inst. 4. 6. 4) that the Actio Publiciana was so-called because a praetor Publicius first propounded it in

---

[42] For other cases—usureceptio ex fiducia—ex praediatura—see G. 2. 59-61 ; Buckl. T. p. 245 ; M. p. 128 ; de Zulueta, Gaius II, pp. 71 et seq. ; infra, §§ 264, 523. For suus et necessarius heres vid. inf. § 336.
[43] Girard, p. 327.

his edict. The date of this praetor has not been ascertained. It seems that the action came into use in the last century of the Republic. It was called a fictitious action, because the judex was directed to decide the case as if time had already run its course. This involved an adaptation of the usual formula of the vindicatio rei (§ 726) by substituting for the words "if it appears that the thing in question belongs to plaintiff by quiritary title" the words "if it appears that supposing the plaintiff had possessed the thing in question (for one year or for two as the case might be) it should be his by quiritary title" (*infra*, § 734).

The action was available—(1) to a bonitary owner (in particular to a person to whom a res mancipi had been made over by tradition without mancipation or cessio in jure (§§ 152, 172)); (2) to a bona fide possessor, who had acquired a thing by purchase or other just cause from a non-owner (§§ 172, 697). In the first case the Actio Publiciana gave an effective remedy against any person into whose hands the thing might have come; if the quiritary owner sought to get the thing back, relying on his legal title, he might be met (*e.g.*) by the exceptio rei venditae et traditae (Dig. 21. 3. 3). In the second case lost possession could be recovered from any one except the true owner. It was to meet this case that the praetor allowed him to assert his right by means of the so-called exceptio justi dominii—si ea res possessoris non sit—Dig. 6. 2. 16 and 17 (*infra*, § 746).

It is uncertain whether the action was applied *ab initio* to case (1) and to case (2) or only to one or other of them. In the classical period it was available to both, and in other cases as well. See Girard, p. 375; Buckland, *T.* pp. 192, 193; *M.* p. 115; Jolowicz, pp. 277 *et seq.*

178. LONGI TEMPORIS PRAESCRIPTIO.—The institution of usucapio above described was available only to Roman citizens and only in respect of things susceptible of Roman ownership (dominium ex jure Quiritium). It did not apply to provincials (anywhere), or to provincial land. In the provinces an analogous institution existed called "long time prescription" or "long possession prescription" (longi temporis vel longae possessionis praescriptio). It has no connection with the praescriptio of the formulary procedure described by Gaius (§ 740). At first available as a defence, it became in course of time a mode of acquisition, always subject to the qualification that the holder of provincial land was not technically owner. The person who had held such land for ten years as against an owner domiciled in the same civitas (district, or, as Justinian defined it, province) [44] or for twenty years against an owner domiciled in a different district (province) [45] was allowed an action to recover

---

[44] Cod. 7. 33 12. 1.

[45] Cod. 7. 39. 8 pr. This meant, in effect, that during absence the prescriptive period was doubled. Nov. 119. 8.

possession of the land, if he had lost it, not only from third persons, but from the original owner as well. This institution was subject to the same condition of just title, good faith,[46] etc., as usucapion. A similar term of prescription may have been available to provincials in the case of movables.[47] A Roman citizen, anywhere, acquired movables by the normal process of usucapion after one year's possession.

179. LIMITATION OF ACTIONS.—From the acquisitive prescription above described must be distinguished the law as to limitation or prescription of actions. By an enactment of Theodosius II (A.D. 424) actions (where the law made no other provision) were barred by the lapse of thirty (sometimes forty) years.[48] A person who had let the statutory period go by without prosecuting his claim could not maintain an action. This is (very inexactly) described as extinctive prescription. No substantive right was extinguished. If property passed into a third hand, the original owner could re-claim it, the long-possessor could not.[49] That is, he could not recover it as his property. He might no doubt have possessory remedies.

180. Justinian made extensive changes in the law:—

(i) By an enactment of 528 he allowed a person whose possession had originated in good faith, though without just title, and who had held for the Theodosian period of thirty (or forty) years an action to vindicate the property from the original owner or from any third person, provided that the property (even though stolen from the owner) had not originally been acquired by violence.[50] This created a new case of acquisitive prescription which the commentators have labelled longissimi temporis praescriptio. The existing law as to limitation of actions remained unaffected. It was available notwithstanding that possession had been acquired in bad faith or by violence ;

(ii) Three years later Justinian swept away the ancient distinctions between civil and praetorian ownership and between res mancipi and res nec mancipi, and fused the institutions of usucapio and longi temporis

---

46 *Semble.*
47 Dig. 44. 3. 3, 9.
48 Cod. 7. 39 ; Buckl. *T.* p. 251.
49 Girard, p. 326.
50 Cod. 7. 39. 8.

2. 6 pr. praescriptio.[51] For the acquisition of movables he retained the old name of usucapion, extending the period from one year to three. The term longi temporis praescriptio was applied to the acquisition of immovables. Subject to what has been said as to longissimi temporis praescriptio the old conditions of justus titulus, bona fides, res nec furtiva nec vi possessa, continued to apply to movables and immovables alike.

181. OTHER MODES OF ACQUISITION BY CIVIL LAW.—Property might vest in a person by statutory title (lege), e.g., by the lex Papia Poppaea, which denied to unmarried and childless persons the right to take as heirs or legatees and vested the inheritance or legacy in others.[52] Ulpian refers to this head a legacy by vindication (§ 345), the statute in this case being the Twelve Tables. Another case of statutory title was created by a constitution of Valentinian, Theodosius and Arcadius (A.D. 389), by which a person asserting a claim to property (movable or immovable), who took possession of it by 4. 2. 1. violence, forfeited it, if he was owner, to the person whom he had dispossessed.

182. Adjudicatio was another civil law title. In certain actions known as judicia divisoria the judge was directed to award property in severalty among the interested parties. These actions were:—(a) actio communi dividundo—for division of property owned in common ; (b) actio familiae erciscundae—for 4. 6. 20. division of an estate vested in co-heirs ; (c) actio finium regundorum—for determining boundaries. The word adjudicatio is applied both to this mode of acquisition,[53] and to the clause in the formula, which contained the instruction to the judex (§ 722).

183. Yet another mode of acquisition by civil law was litis aestimatio (assessment of the matter in issue). Since the formulary system did not admit decrees of specific performance (§ 718), but only condemnation in money, a defendant in a vindication who was willing to pay instead of restoring (§ 727) kept the property as his own, as if by purchase.[54]

---

[51] Cod. 7. 25 ; 7. 31.
[52] Ulp. XIX. 17.
[53] Ulp. XIX. 16.
[54] Dig 6. 1. 46.

THE INSTITUTES

BOOK II (Tit. I, sec. 11, Tit. VI)

TITLE I, sec. 11

Things become the property of individuals in many ways; of some things we acquire the ownership by natural law, which, as we have said, is called the jus gentium; of some things by civil law. It is more convenient to begin with the older law. Plainly, the older law is the law of nature, which nature brought into existence along with mankind, whereas civil laws came into being when cities began to be founded, magistrates to be created and laws to be written. § 156.

TITLE VI

Of usucapion and long possession

The civil law enacted that, if a person had in good faith bought a thing from a non-owner, believing him to be owner, or acquired it by donation or for any other just cause, he should usucape it, if a movable in one year everywhere, if an immovable in two years but only in Italian soil. This was to prevent the ownership of things remaining uncertain. The law was enacted because our ancestors thought that these periods gave owners time enough to look after their property. But we have taken a better course, so that owners may not be expropriated unreasonably soon, nor the benefit of the law confined to a particular area. Accordingly, we have published a constitution [55] providing that movables may be usucaped in three years, and immovables by long time possession, that is by ten years inter praesentes and by twenty years inter absentes; and ownership, if a just cause of possession precedes, may be thus acquired, not in Italy alone, but in every part of our Empire. § 180.

1. Sometimes, although a person has possessed in perfect good faith, no length of time will give ownership by usucapion; for example if a person possesses a free man or a thing sacred or religious or a run-away slave.[56] 2. Stolen things also and things possessed by violence cannot be usucaped even by bona fide possession for the above-mentioned periods; for the usucapion of stolen things is forbidden by the Law of the Twelve Tables and the lex Atinia, of things possessed by violence by the lex Julia et Plautia.[57] § 170. 3. When it is said that the usucapion of things stolen and possessed by violence is forbidden by statute, this does not mean that the thief or the person who possesses by violence cannot usucape. In their case there is another reason why usucapion is not allowed, namely because they possess in bad faith. What is meant is that not even a person who acquires from them in good faith by purchase or for any other just cause has the right of usucapion. Consequently, it seldom happens that possessors in good faith become

---

[55] Cod. 7. 31.
[56] A servus fugitivus was a res furtive. He had stolen himself. Dig. 47. 2. 61 ; Cod. 6. 1. 1.
[57] Of unknown date.

owners of movables by usucapion. For a person who sells or transfers for any other cause a thing which he knows does not belong to him commits theft. 4. However, this is not always so. For if an heir, thinking that a thing belongs to the inheritance, when it was in fact lent or let on hire to the deceased, or deposited with him, sells it or parts with it by way of gift or of dos to a person who acquires in good faith, there is no doubt that the acquirer can usucape, the thing not being affected with the vice of theft, since the heir who has in good faith disposed of the thing, supposing it to be his own, is not guilty of theft. 5. Again, if a person who has the usufruct of a female slave, supposing that her child is his property has sold or given it away, he is not guilty of theft, for

§ 601.   theft is not committed without theftuous intent.[58]   6. There are other ways too in which it may happen that a person may transfer to another a thing which does not belong to him without affecting it with the vice of theft, and so put the possessor in a position to usucape.   7. Usucapion more easily takes place in the case of immovables, as, for instance, if a person without violence gets possession of a site which is left vacant owing to the absence or carelessness of the owner, or because he has died and left no one to succeed him. He is himself a mala fide possessor, because he knows that he has seized another man's land; none the less, if he has transferred it to a person who takes it in good faith, the transferree

§ 601.   may acquire by long possession, because he has taken something which was neither stolen nor possessed by violence; for the opinion of some of the old lawyers that even land or a site could be stolen is no longer entertained, and imperial constitutions have consulted the interest of possessors of immovable property by providing that they are not to be deprived of long undisputed possession.   8. Some-times, even a thing stolen or possessed by violence may be usucaped,

§ 170.   as, for instance, if it has come back into the owner's power; for then, the vice which attached to the thing being purged, usucapion again becomes possible.   9. A thing belonging to our fiscus [59] cannot be usucaped. But Papinian wrote that if bona vacantia have not yet been reported to the fiscus and any item in such goods has been delivered to a bona fide purchaser, he may usucape it. There are rescripts of the Emperor Pius and of the Emperors Severus and Antoninus to this effect. 10. Finally, it must be known that a thing must not be affected by any vice,[60] if it is to be usucaped by a bona fide purchaser or by a person who possesses by any other lawful cause.

11. A mistaken belief that a cause exists, when it does not, cannot be the foundation of usucapion; for example, if a person possesses thinking that he has bought when in fact he has not; or

§ 171.   possesses by way of gift what has not been given.

12. Long-continued possession which has begun to run in favour of a deceased person is continued in favour of an heir or bonorum

§ 174.   possessor, although he knows that he has no title to the property; but if the deceased person's possession was initially unlawful, his possession does not help the heir or bonorum possessor, though

---

[58] This is error juris. Inst. 2. 1. 37.
[59] The Imperial Treasury.
[60] *Supra*, §§ 2, 4, 6.

himself innocent. Our constitution ordains that the principle of continued possession is to apply also to usucapion [of movables].[61]

13. A rescript of the Emperors Severus and Antoninus provides that a purchaser may join to his possession the possession of his vendor.

14. An edict of the Emperor Marcus decrees that if a person has bought from the fiscus the property of some third person and five years [62] have elapsed after the sale, he may repel by exception the owner's claim. A constitution of the Emperor Zeno, of sacred memory, has made special provision for the case of persons who acquire from the fiscus by sale or gift or other title, so as to give them security and confidence of success whether they are defendants or plaintiffs. Any person who supposes that he has a right of action §261. as owner of, or as having a hypothec over, any property so alienated has four years to bring his action against the Treasury (aerarium).[63] Our recent constitution extends to acquirers from our household or the household of the Empress the rule laid down by Zeno in the case of alienations by the fiscus.

IV. ACQUISITION BY NATURAL LAW

184. We pass now to modes of acquisition by natural law, *viz.*, 1, occupation ; 2, accession ; 3, specification ; 4, perception and separation of fruits ; 5, tradition or delivery.

185. (1) OCCUPATIO.—This means taking possession of a res nullius with the intention of becoming owner. The following are the principal cases:—(a) wild beasts, birds and fishes ; (b) things taken from the enemy ; (c) precious stones, gems, etc., found on the sea-shore ; (d) unoccupied islands in the sea ; (e) things abandoned by a former owner (res derelictae).

186. (a) Wild beasts, birds and fishes. These become the property of the captor, whether taken on public or on private land, one's own or someone else's. If you go on someone else's land for the purpose of hunting or fowling, he may warn you off, if he sees you coming. If you persist in spite of the prohibition, your action assumes a contumelious character, and exposes you to an actio injuriarum,[64] but, none the less, you are owner of what you take.

---

[61] Cod. 7. 31. 3. It applied to usucapion before Justinian's reforms. What is meant is that it is to continue to apply to his new term of three years' usucapion of movables.

[62] *i.e.*, if the circumstances did not admit of the usual usucapion of one or two years.

[63] Cod. 7. 37. 2. This meant that the purchaser or other acquirer from the fiscus got a clean title though the title of the fiscus might be defective. In the late Empire the Treasury of the Roman People (aerarium) was not distinguishable from the fiscus.

[64] And to other proceedings according to the circumstances, *e.g.*, actio legis Aquiliae, if damage is done. Roby I, 416, note.

2. 1. 12. 187. Beasts and birds are distinguished as: —

  (i) naturally wild (ferae naturae), and
  (ii) naturally tame (mansuetae naturae).

This is a question of the species to which they belong. Thus there are wild geese and tame geese. Creatures wild by nature may in individual cases be more or less tamed or domesticated. Wild beasts and birds become yours when you take them, and remain yours so long as they are under your control. They are deemed to be under your control so long as they are in your sight, and pursuit is not difficult. The same applies to bees which have swarmed from your hive.

2. 1. 14. Tamed beasts and birds are those which, though naturally wild, have acquired a habit of going away and coming back. they remain yours so long as the habit continues.[65]

2. 1. 15. Tame animals are owned like anything else and remain yours, however far afield they may chance to wander and however long they may chance to stay away.

2. 1. 16. 188. (b) Things taken from the enemy. These are said to become ours jure gentium. But the statement requires qualifica-
2. 1. 17. tion. Enemy property is usually at the disposal of the conquering State, and is not acquired by individuals. This applies both to land and to booty. This last was sometimes distributed amongst the soldiers. If enemy property happens to be in my possession at the outbreak of war I may appropriate it to my own use.[66]

(c). (d). (e). For other cases of occupatio it is sufficient to refer to the text of the Institutes (secs. 18, 22, 47).

189. (2) ACCESSIO.—This is the process by which a principal thing attracts to itself an accessory, so that the owner of the first becomes the owner of the second. The principal thing may be an immovable or a movable. The accessory may have been previously owned or unowned (res nullius). The accession may be effected by natural processes or by human agency or by a combination of both. The older commentators distinguish these cases of accession as natural, industrial (or artificial), and mixed. Numerous illustrations are given in the Institutes which may be

---

[65] Virgil supplies a pretty illustration.
  Cervus erat forma praestanti et cornibus ingens.
. . . .
  Ille manum patiens, mensaeque assuetus herili,
  Errabat silvis, rursusque ad limina nota
  Ipse domum sera quamvis se nocte ferebat.
      (Aen. VII. 483 et seq.)
[66] Dig. 41. 1. 51.

arranged under the following heads:—(a) natural increment;
(b) alluvion; (c) islands in rivers—river-beds; (d) building;
(e) planting and sowing; (f) miscellaneous cases of artificial
accession; (g) mixing of solids and liquids.

190. In the case of accession of a movable to a movable the
question may be raised which is principal, which accessory.
Usually the answer is obvious enough. If a hand is added to a
mutilated statue, plainly the hand is accessory. But cases may
be imagined in which the solution is not so simple. The Roman
Law texts suggest various criteria. In one place it is said to be
a question of appearance and the use to which the thing is
reasonably put.[67] In other texts the mental picture which we
form of a thing is made the test. This view, which has a
distinguished pedigree, is adopted by Paulus in the following
passage.[68]

> " Proculus points out that we follow the rule which was
> approved by Servius and Labeo, *viz.* that if anything be added
> to substances in which a special characteristic is kept in view,[69]
> the addition is merged in the whole; as a foot or hand (joined
> on) to a statue, a base or handle to a cup, a leg to a couch,
> a plank to a ship, a stone to a building, for the whole belongs
> to him who was previously owner."

If the accessory could be, and was, detached, so that it recovered
its individual character, it reverted to its former owner, who in
the meantime had an actio ad exhibendum to require it to be
disannexed.[70] If this was impossible, he was reduced to claiming compensation by an actio in factum. Much of this, it must
be confessed, suggests rather class-room discussions than
questions likely to occur in practice.

191. (a) Natural increment. The owner of the female parent   2. 1. 19.
is owner of the offspring. Perhaps this is not so much a case of
accession, as a continuation of the property which I already have
in the parent animal. The same applies to the offspring of
female slaves.[71] We may refer to the same head the natural
produce of the vegetable kingdom.

---

[67] Dig. 34. 2. 29, 1.
[68] Dig. 41. 1. 26 pr. (Walker's translation).
[69] In quibus propria qualitas expectaretur—" things with which what
we look for is a thing answering some particular description " (Monro)—
" objects which have a proper quality " (de Zulueta). In Dig. 6. 1. 23, 5.
Paulus says that if you attach to my statue an arm taken from another
statue the arm cannot be said to be yours " as the whole statue corresponds
to one idea " (Monro)—quia tota statua uno spiritu continetur.
[70] Dig. 6. 1. 23, 5.
[71] Inst. 1. 3. 4.

2. 1. 20.

192. (b) Alluvio. This is defined as " latent increment."
It takes place when a river-bank or an island in a river receives
accessions of silt deposited by the water. The owner of the
land is owner of the accessions. Alluvio does not apply to lands
granted by the State and defined by an arbitrary boundary (ager
limitatus), though this may more or less coincide with the line
of the stream.

193. (c) Islands in rivers—river-beds. An island may come
into existence in three ways:—(1) by the river dividing its
channel and so enclosing a tract of land between its two arms ;
(2) if part of the river-bed is left dry, but so that the water
flows on either side of it ; (3) when an island forms on the
water's surface.[72] In the first case there is no change of ownership. In the two other cases (which are indistinguishable) it is
necessary to consider the position of the island in the stream and
whether the riparian owners have or have not the right of
alluvion.

2. 1. 22.

194. Justinian says that, if the island is in the middle of
the river, it belongs to the riparian owners on the two sides.
This implies (though the text does not make it plain) that a
line is first drawn midway between the two banks (per medium
filum aquae).[73] All of the island which falls on either side
of the line is assigned to the owner or owners of the corresponding bank of the river ; if more than one in proportion to
their riparian frontage. All this supposes that they have the
right of alluvion. If they have not, the island is res nullius and
becomes the property of the first occupant.[74]

2. 1. 23.

195. If a river leaves its bed and flows in a new channel,
the old bed accrues to the riparian owners in the same way as an
island formed in the stream ; the new channel becomes public
like the river itself. If the river again shifts back to its old bed,
the new bed in turn accedes to the proprietors on either bank.
From which it follows that, if the whole of a man's land is
absorbed in the new channel, he loses it altogether, because his
field has ceased to exist, having lost its proper form, and he
cannot claim any share in the bed, since he owns no property
adjoining. So says Gaius, but he adds, " But it can scarcely be
that this would be maintained." [75] The Institutes has nothing
to say on the matter.

---

[72] Dig. 41. 1. 30, 2.
[73] Dig. 41. 1. 56, 1, alveus medius dividi debet.
[74] Dig. 43. 12. 1, 6.
[75] Dig. 41. 1. 7, 5.

196. (d) Building (inaedificatio). Normally, if a man builds a house, he owns the land and owns, or has the disposal of, the material. But there are cases where this is not so. A may build on A's land with B's material; A may build on B's land with A's or C's material. In both cases the result is the same. The building goes with the land and is the property of the owner of the soil (superficies solo cedit), but there is no change in the ownership of the material.[76] While the building stands, however, the owner of the material may not require it to be dis-annexed. This was enacted by the Law of the Twelve Tables. If the building fell down the material might be reclaimed—a barren consolation. But the law allowed the owner an alternative, viz., to sue for the value of the material. If the material was stolen the Twelve Tables gave him another remedy, the actio 2. 1. 29. de tigno injuncto, a penal action for double damages, which seems to have been a variant of the actio furti.

197. If a man builds upon land which he knows does not belong to him, i.e., if he possesses in bad faith, the Institutes says that he loses the materials, because he is presumed to have 2. 1. 30. parted with them by his own volition. It seems, however, that in the law of Justinian, if not before, he might prove that he had no such intention and recover the materials in the event of demolition.[77] Further, in the later law, anyone who had built on another's land, even knowing that it did not belong to him, might remove the building if he could do so without injury to the property (jus tollendi).[78] The builder was not in any event entitled to claim compensation by action, but a bona fide possessor might raise a plea of fraud against an owner seeking to recover his property, if he refused to indemnify him for his outlay, at least to the extent of the enhanced value of the land.[79]

198. (e) Planting and sowing (plantatio—satio). See text, secs. 31, 32.

(f) Miscellaneous cases of artificial accession. See text, secs. 26, 33, 34.

(g) Mixing of solids—of liquids (commixtio—confusio). For convenience this is treated in connection with accessio,

---

[76] Dig. 41. 1. 7, 10: non tamen ideo is qui materiae dominus fuit desinit ejus dominus esse. But Cod. 3. 32. 2, 1 says: sed et id quod in solo tuo aedificatum est, quoad in eadem causa manet, jure ad te pertinet. Si vero fuerit dissolutum, materia ejus ad pristinum dominium redit.
[77] Cod. 3. 32. 2, 1.
[78] Cod. 3. 32. 5, 1.
[79] Girard, p. 356.

though the legal consequences vary with the circumstances. If solids are mixed together there is, apart from agreement, no change of ownership. Plainly, if my sheep are mixed with

2. 1. 28. yours they remain mine. In theory the case is the same if our grains of wheat are accidentally mixed. If you are in possession of the whole, my action will be a vindication to recover my property, not an action for division of property owned in common. Practically, however, what I shall get is either part of the mass of mixed grain or compensation for the value of

2. 1. 27. the portion which belonged to me. If liquids are inseparably mixed so that one is absorbed in the other, it is a case of accessio; e.g., wine fortified with an admixture of brandy; the wine remains, the brandy disappears. If a new thing results from the mixture, it is a case of specificatio (see below). If both the components retain their character, e.g., wine mixed with wine, the whole, in the absence of agreement to the contrary, is owned in common in proportion to the value of the component parts. What is said of liquids applies equally to liquefied metals,[80] if fused together and inseparable.[81]

2. 1. 25. 199. (3) SPECIFICATIO.—This is the name given to the process of bringing into existence a thing of a new kind (nova species) out of existing material, e.g., wine out of grapes, a ship out of timber, a goblet out of gold. If the creator of the " new species " was not the owner of the material, a question arose as to the ownership, upon which the Sabinians and the Proculians took different views. The Sabinians decided in favour of the owner of the material, because without the material the finished product could not have existed. The Proculians preferred the creator of the new species, a thing which previously had no existence and no owner.[82] Justinian gave authority to an intermediate opinion. If the product could be reduced to its original state, as e.g., a gold cup can be resolved into the original lump of metal, there was no change of ownership; in the contrary case the specificator became the owner. In this case, therefore, specification is a mode of acquisition. It comes near to, but is not quite the same as the occupatio of a res nullius. In fact there never is a res nullius, for from the very moment that the new thing exists it has an owner. Justinian's solution

---

[80] Ut puta meum et tuum argentum in massam reductum est: erit nobis commune. Dig. 6. 1. 3, 2; though here, too, Pomponius prescribes a vindicatio pro rata ponderis. But see Dig. 41. 1. 27, 1, where he says, quite truly: nihil hic suum vere dicere potest prior dominus.

[81] Bronze and silver were separable, so lead and silver; bronze and gold, not. Dig. 6. 1. 5, 1; 41. 1. 12, 1.

[82] Dig. 41. 1. 7, 7.

is no better than either of the others. They are all arbitrary and dogmatic. The French code (arts. 570, 571) more reasonably takes account of the relative value of the material and the work.

Modern authorities do not agree whether good faith on the part of the specificator was a necessary condition of acquisition by this method, *i.e.*, whether he must have believed that the material belonged to him.[83]

200. (4) PERCEPTION AND SEPARATION OF FRUITS.—The term " fruits " includes:—(a) the natural and periodic increment of the animal and vegetable kingdoms; (b) the produce of cultivated fields and gardens; (c) (by an extension) rents and similar profits derived from property.[84] These various kinds of " fruits " are distinguished by commentators as natural, industrial and civil. In the texts of the Roman Law attention is principally directed to the second of these, which was of most practical importance.

201. The rules relating to the ownership of fruits varied according to the nature of the right upon which the claim was based. The owner in possession of land was entitled to the fruits because he was entitled to the land. " Fruits on the tree are deemed to be part of the land," [85] and they continued to belong to the owner of the land after separation. This mode of acquisition, if it can be called so, has been mentioned above. But there were cases, now to be considered, in which the fruits vested in some one other than the owner of the land. The emphyteuta (§ 256) and the bona fide possessor of land became owners of the fruits as soon as they were separated from the parent tree (fructuum separatio), but the usufructuary not until he had gathered them (fructuum perceptio). A lessee of land 2. 1. 36. (conductor) is said to become owner of the fruits by the will of the lessor (locator), which is interpreted as meaning by a kind of delivery, taking effect when the lessee gathers them.[86] From this it follows that if the lessor forbids him to gather them they do not become his, though he may have an action on the contract of hire.[87]

Though a bona fide possessor acquired the fruits by separation, if his title was challenged by the real owner of the

[83] Girard, p. 343, thinks that good faith was necessary. *Contra* Buckl. *M.* p. 144.
[84] Dig. 22. 1. 36.
[85] Dig. 6. 1. 44.
[86] Dig. 47. 2. 62, 8.
[87] Dig. 39. 5. 6.

property, he was accountable for fruits of which he was actually in possession at the time (fructus exstantes—fructus non consumpti). This rule, though in the Digest interpolated into texts of the classical jurists and in the Code into a constitution of Diocletian (A.D. 294) was " of much later origin, perhaps not much before Justinian." [88]

The mala fide possessor was accountable for all fruits, gathered and consumed, gathered and unconsumed, and for fruits which should have been gathered but were not.[89]

2. 1. 40. 202. (5) TRADITIO (delivery).—This means transfer of possession with the consequence that the ownership of the thing transferred vests in the transferee. Since our concern is with Roman Law we may assume the parties to the transaction to be Roman citizens and the subject of the transaction to admit of Roman ownership. But it may be noted that, being a mode of acquisition juris gentium, it was in effect available to peregrines, though technically they could not become owner by quiritary title. It was also the normal method of giving a title to provincial land.

203. The essential conditions of this mode of acquisition are:—(a) The thing must admit of delivery, and of acquisition by delivery. This includes in general all corporeal things movable and immovable. It excludes incorporeal things, which do not admit of delivery [90] (but see below (§ 242) as to quasi-tradition of incorporeals) ; and it excluded, before Justinian, res mancipi, which could not be acquired by this method (§ 152) ; and, of course, things which could not be acquired by private individuals (res extra commercium, § 146), but that is common to all modes of acquisition.

204. (b) The transferor must be competent to give and the transferee to acquire ownership by this method. To say nothing of rules of capacity applicable to both parties, this means, normally, on the side of the transferor that he must be owner, or convey the property as agent for the owner, ratification being here as in other cases equivalent to antecedent authority. Sometimes a non-owner may convey, e.g., a tutor in due course of administration may alienate the property of his ward (in the later law within narrow limits, § 135). On the other hand, there were cases in which an owner was competent to convey, e.g., a husband, though technically owner, could not alienate

[88] Buckl. *M.* p. 149.
[89] Inst. 2. 1. 35 ; 4. 17. 2. Cod. 3. 32. 22.
[90] Dig. 41. 1. 43, 1.

dotal immovables. Gifts between husband and wife being 2. 8 pr. prohibited, delivery by way of gift by the one to the other was ineffectual to convey the property (§ 215).

205. According to the Institutes, the Twelve Tables provided that the property in things sold and delivered did not pass unless the purchaser had paid the price to the vendor, or satisfied him in some other way, as by finding an expromissor (a third person who promised to pay), or giving a pledge.[91] The text goes on to say that the law of nature has the same effect, and adds (beyond what is attributed to the Twelve Tables) that if the vendor relies on the credit of the purchaser, the thing immediately becomes the purchaser's property. This passage has given rise to much controversy. Buckland says " the reference to the Twelve Tables is probably a misunderstanding." [92] Evidently so, if, as has been maintained, the rule was introduced into the law by Justinian himself some thousand years later, but this again is questioned. Whatever the source of the rule, it passed into the current Roman Law, and makes law today for the Union of South Africa.[93]

206. (c) The transferor must intend to convey, the transferee must intend to acquire the ownership of the thing transferred. Such an intention exists when, and only when, tradition takes place for some just cause. The meaning of cause has been explained above in speaking of usucapion (§ 171).

> " Mere tradition never transfers ownership, but only if sale or some just cause precedes, which supplies the motive for the tradition." [94]

But the cause need not, as usually in the case of usucapion (§ 171), have an objective existence. It is enough that it exists in the minds of the parties.[95] They may suppose that there is an obligation to deliver the thing in question, when in fact there is not. Nevertheless the property passes. The transferor's remedy will not be vindication, but condictio indebiti, a personal action based upon the quasi-contractual duty to restore (§ 594), always supposing that the minds of the parties were directed to the same thing, and not to different things.

---

[91] Inst. 2. 1. 41. There is no reference to the Twelve Tables in Dig. 18. 1. 19; 53, where the law is stated in similar terms.

[92] *Manual*, p. 137.

[93] Lee, p. 292. German law retains the principle that the property in things sold passes only on delivery, but without this qualification.

[94] Dig. 41. 1. 31 pr.

[95] The essential thing was the intent—animus transferendi et adquirendi dominii. The causa was only important as evidence of the intent: Buckl. *T.* p. 228.

The parties may even differ as to the supposed cause. You think it is gift. I intend sale. The property passes. You hand over money as a gift. I accept it as a loan.[96] The property passes. It would be otherwise if you handed over as a gift a thing not consumed by use, e.g., a goblet; I accept it as a loan. The difference is that a loan of money makes me owner, the loan of a goblet does not. In the first case we both contemplate a transfer of ownership. In the second case we do not.

207. (d) The transferor cannot give what he has not got.

> "Delivery ought not to transfer, and cannot transfer, to him who receives more than belongs to him who delivers. If, therefore, any one had the ownership of a field, he transfers it by delivery, but if he had it not, he transfers nothing to him who receives.
> "Whenever ownership is transferred it passes to the transferee such as it was in the hands of the transferor: if the land was burdened, it passes subject to the servitudes: if free from burdens, it passes unburdened: and if servitudes were owed to the land which was transferred, it passes to the transferee together with the servitudes owed to it."[97]

208. (e) There must be a physical transfer of possession or something which in law is an equivalent. The old commentators distinguished tradition as real and fictitious. Real tradition means an actual handing over of the thing, so that possession and ownership are simultaneously transferred. The term "fictitious tradition" includes various cases which are a little out of the ordinary. There is in fact nothing fictitious about them. They are: —

    (i) traditio brevi manu;
    (ii) constitutum possessorium;
    (iii) traditio longa manu;
    (iv) so-called symbolical delivery.

209. (i) Traditio brevi manu. This takes place when a person, who is already in possession, but not as owner, is to retain possession as owner; e.g., I have lent you a thing for use, now I give it you. You retain it as owner ex causa donationis. I have deposited with you a sum of money, now I lend it to you. My intention coupled with yours converts deposit into mutuum and makes you owner.[98]

2. 1. 44.

(ii) Constitutum possessorium. This is the opposite process. I am in possession as owner. I wish to make you a present of

---

[96] Dig. 41. 1. 36 (Julian); Dig 12. 1. 18 pr. (Ulpian).
[97] Dig. 41. 1. 20.
[98] Dig. 12. 1. 9, 9.

the thing, but to continue to have the use of it, for which I am willing to pay. I may without physical transfer make it yours, remaining in possession as hirer, not as owner.[99]

(iii) Traditio longa manu takes place when I do not assume actual physical control, but in order to make a thing mine it is placed in my sight, or I am placed in sight of it so that I can take possession at pleasure.[1]

(iv) Symbolical tradition (so-called) takes place when, *e.g.*, the keys of a warehouse are handed over to me in the neighbourhood of the building (or not in the neighbourhood of the building?), by which act the building and its contents are deemed to pass into my possession. But there is nothing fictitious or symbolical about this process. Rather, the keys are handed over as the readiest means of placing the person to whom they are delivered in the exclusive control of the warehouse and its contents; for, as Savigny says, the handing over of keys (as the keys of city-gates) may be symbolic, but keys have another and more frequent use—to unlock doors.[2]

210. The above-mentioned cases of "fictitious tradition" were the germs of a development which culminated in the later Empire, when the delivery of a written deed of conveyance took the place of delivery of the land. This was the traditio per cartam, which persisted into and through the Middle Ages. Sometimes even this was dispensed with. A recital that delivery had taken place served the same purpose. Contemporaneously, the practice grew up of registering transfers of land in the appropriate office (insinuatio apud acta).[3]

211. THESAURUS (treasure).—Paulus describes this as "an ancient deposit of money, of which no memory exists, so that it has no present owner."[4]   2.1.39

This is not quite satisfactory. Treasure is not a res derelicta. There has been no abandonment of ownership. Nor is treasure confined to money.

There are three possible claimants:—1, the owner of the soil (or of the movable [5]?) in which the treasure is found; 2, the finder; 3, the fiscus (always ready to pick up anything that is going). The Institutes attributes to Hadrian the decision

---

[99] Dig. 6. 1. 77; 41. 2. 18 pr.
[1] Dig. 46. 3. 79; 41. 2. 1, 21; 18, 2.
[2] *Das Recht des Besitzes*, § 22.
[3] Arangio-Ruiz, p. 190.
[4] Dig. 41. 1. 31, 1.
[5] There is no authority. See Sir George Hill, *Treasure Trove in Law and Practice*, p. 8. For English law see *Att.-Gen.* v. *Trustees of the British Museum* [1903] 2 Ch. 598.

that if a man found treasure on his own land he might keep it; if he found it by accident, not by deliberate search, on some one else's land, it went half to the finder, half to the owner of the soil. This is repeated in a constitution of Leo and Zeno (A.D. 474) with the addition that the landowner is not to have the treasure if he employs magic arts in the search, and treasure is defined as "movables hidden long ago by unknown owners." [6] We are not informed what happened if the treasure was found by deliberate search, or by magic arts.

From the place which this topic occupies in the Institutes and the Digest it appears that the discovery of treasure is referred to the natural modes of acquisition, but it does not readily fit in with the theory either of occupatio or of accessio. The fact is that it is a statutory, and therefore a civil law, mode of acquisition.

THE INSTITUTES

BOOK II

TITLE I (continued)

§ 186.
12. Wild animals, birds and fishes, that is all living creatures, which are natives of earth, sea or air, so soon as any one takes them, by the jus gentium immediately become his property, for if a thing has no owner natural reason assigns it to the man who takes it. It makes no difference whether wild animals and birds are taken by a man on his own land or on some one else's. Of course, if some one comes upon another man's land for the purpose of hunting or fowling and the owner sees him in time, he may forbid him. Anything you take remains yours so long as you have an effective control over it. When it has escaped from your control and recovered its natural liberty, it ceases to be yours and may once again be acquired by the first occupant. An animal is understood to recover its natural liberty when you have lost sight of it or when, though within your sight, it is difficult to pursue. 13. The question has been raised whether, if a wild animal is so seriously wounded that you can take it, it is supposed to be yours forthwith. Some take this view and hold that it remains yours so long as you continue to pursue it; if you abandon the pursuit, then it ceases to be yours and may again be acquired by the first person who takes it. Others maintain that it is not yours until you have caught it. We confirm this view, because many things may occur to prevent your taking it. 14. Bees also are naturally wild. So, if bees settle on your tree, before you have hived them they are no more yours than birds that have made their nest there; accordingly, if any one else has hived them he becomes their owner and if there chance to be

§ 187.

---

[6] Cod. 10. 15.

honeycombs any one may take them. Of course, before anything has been done, if you have seen some one coming on your land, you have a right to forbid him. A swarm which leaves your hive is understood to remain yours so long as it is in your sight and not difficult to follow; otherwise it goes to the occupant.

15. Peafowl and pigeons are naturally wild. It is irrelevant that they are in the habit of flying away and flying back; for bees do the same, and they are unquestionably wild; and people have deer so tame that they will go to the woods and come back, and no one denies that deer are naturally wild. In the case, however, of animals which are in the habit of going away and coming back, the accepted principle is that they are understood to be yours so long as they have the intention of returning; if they have ceased to have this intention, they are no longer yours and go to the first occupant. They are held to have ceased to have the intention of returning when they have lost the habit of returning.

16. Domestic fowls and geese are not naturally wild; this appears from the fact that there are birds which we distinguish as " wild fowl " and " wild geese." Consequently, if anything has occurred to disturb your geese or fowls so that they have flown away, even if they are out of sight, nevertheless, wherever they may be, they remain your property, and any one who keeps them with a view to his own profit commits theft. § 187.

17. Things taken from the enemy are immediately ours by the jus gentium. Indeed, even free men on capture become our slaves; if they escape from our power and return to their own people they resume their former condition. § 188.

18. Precious stones, gems and so forth, found on the sea-shore belong by natural law to the finder.

19. The young of animals belonging to you become yours by the same law. § 191.

20. Further, what a river has added by alluvion to your land becomes yours by the jus gentium. Alluvion means a latent increment, because what is added by alluvion is added so slowly that you cannot tell how much is added at any moment of time. 21. On the other hand, if the violence of the stream has carried away a piece of your land and driven it against a neighbour's land, it is plain that it remains your property. Of course, if the detached fragment has over a considerable time adhered to the neighbour's land, and the trees which it brought with it have struck root in it, they are understood from that time onwards to belong to the neighbour's land. § 192.

22. If a new island appears in the sea (which is not a frequent event) it belongs to the occupant as being a res nullius. In the more frequent event of an island forming in a river, if it occupies the middle part of the stream, it belongs to the riparian owners on either bank of the river in proportion to their river frontage. If the island is nearer to one side, it belongs to the owners on that side. If a river divides and again unites in a lower part of its course, so as to make an island of somebody's land, there is no change of ownership. 23. If a river wholly abandons its natural channel and takes a different course, the old bed belongs to the riparian owners in proportion to their frontage on the river; the § 194.

§ 195.

new channel acquires the legal character of the river, that is to say, it becomes public. If after some time the river resumes its old course, the new channel (now again dry) belongs to the riparian owners. 24. The case is different if a man's whole land is flooded, for flooding does not change the character of the land, and, therefore, if the water retires, it is plain that the land belongs to the same person as before.

§ 199.

25. When a man makes a thing from another person's materials the question is asked which of them is by natural reason owner. Is it the man who made it or the owner of the material? For example, suppose a man has made wine or oil or grain out of another man's grapes or olives or ears of corn, or has made some kind of vessel out of another man's gold or silver or bronze, or made mead by mixing another man's wine and honey, or compounded a plaster or eye-salve out of another man's drugs, or made a garment out of another man's wool, or a ship or chest or chair out of another man's timber. After prolonged controversy between the Sabinians and the Proculians the law has been settled in accordance with the intermediate opinion, namely, that, if the finished product can be reduced to its original material, it belongs to the owner of the material; if not, then the maker is preferred. For example, a vessel can by melting be reduced to a shapeless mass of bronze, silver or gold; but wine, oil or grain cannot be reconverted into grapes, olives or ears of corn, nor mead resolved into its original components of wine and honey. If a person has made a new thing partly from his own material, partly from some other person's material, for example, mead from his own wine and somebody else's honey, or a plaster or eye-salve from drugs which partly belong to him and partly to some one else, or a garment from wool partly his own and partly another's, there can be no doubt that in this case the maker is owner, because he has not only put his own work into it, but supplied, as well, part of the material.[7] 26. If a man has woven into his own garment another man's purple yarn, although the purple is the more valuable, it accedes to the garment, and the original owner of the purple [if it was stolen] has an action of theft against the thief, and a personal action (condictio), whether the man who stole it was the man who made up the garment or some one else. For though a thing which has ceased to exist [as in this case the purple] cannot be vindicated, a condiction lies against thieves and some other possessors.[8] 27. If materials belonging to two

---

[7] This sentence seems to continue a discussion which has been replaced by Justinian's own solution. It is not meant to qualify it, nor, in fact, does it do so. If the thing is reducible, there is no change of ownership. If it is irreducible, the specificator is owner in any event.

[8] This is understood to mean *mala fide* possessors, who would usually, but not necessarily, be themselves thieves (contrectatio fraudulosa). Against b.f. possessors there would be a condictio sine causa, or an actio in factum (Dig. 6. 1. 23, 5). The substantial difference was the measure of damages. Fur semper in mora est. If the defendant was a *mala fide* possessor, even if not technically a fur, he was treated as such. This is, in effect, what Theophilus says in his Greek paraphrase of the Institutes, *ad hunc loc.* Another view is that the text means that a condictio furtiva lies against the thief and some other kind of condictio against " some other possessors." Many of the older commentators replaced quibusdam (some) by quibusque (any).

persons are mixed with the consent of the owners the resulting whole belongs to them in common [9]; for instance, if wines have been mixed or lumps of silver or gold melted together. If the materials are of different kinds, and therefore a new kind of thing results from the mixing, for example, mead from wine and honey or electrum from gold and silver, the rule is the same, for in this case too there is no doubt that the resulting thing is owned in common. If things are mixed by accident and not by consent the same consequence follows, whether the materials are different or of the same kind.[10] 28. But, if grain belonging to Titius is mixed with yours, then, if the mixture was made by consent, the whole is owned in common, because the single bodies or grains, which were the separate property of each, are now owned in common by mutual consent. But, if the mixture took place by accident, or was effected by Titius without your consent, the resulting whole is not owned in common, because the single grains retain their original character, and in such cases the grain in bulk is no more owned in common than a flock or herd would be, if beasts belonging to Titius were mixed with yours; but if one or other of you keeps all the grain, the other may bring a real action to recover his rateable share, and it lies in the discretion of the judge to estimate the quality of each parcel of grain.

§ 198.

29. When a man builds on his own soil with another man's material, he is understood to be owner of the building, because everything which is built upon the soil goes with it. However, the owner of the material continues to be owner, though meanwhile he can neither vindicate it nor bring an action to have it produced (actio ad exhibendum) on account of the Law of the Twelve Tables, which provides that no one may be compelled to detach another person's tignum which has been built into his house, but may be sued for the double value in an action called the actio de tigno juncto. The word tignum means any building material. The object of the provision is to avoid the necessity of buildings being pulled down. But, if from any cause the building has been demolished, the owner of the material, if he has not recovered the double damages, may vindicate it and bring an action for its production.[11] 30. Conversely, if a man has built a house with his own material on another man's land, the house belongs to the owner of the soil. But in this case the owner of the material loses his right of ownership, because he is taken to have parted with it voluntarily, provided that he knew that he was building on another's land; therefore, even if the house is demolished, he will not be able to vindicate the material. To be sure, if the builder is in possession, and the owner of the soil sues for the recovery of his house, and does not pay the price of the material and the wages of the workmen, he may be repelled by the exception of fraud (exceptio doli mali), provided that the builder possessed in good faith; if the builder knew that

§ 196.

---

[9] This section relates to liquids and things which are mixed by liquefaction. The following section relates to mixture of solids. These are commonly (not by the Romans) distinguished as confusio and commixtio.

[10] i.e., provided the things are inseparable. Dig. 6. 1. 5. 1.

[11] Seemingly, the actio de tigno (in)juncto did not lie unless the material had been stolen by someone (tignum furtivum, Dig. 47. 3. 1.), but could be brought against a builder who had used the material in good faith. If he paid the penalty (so the text says) he might keep the material.

the land belonged to some one else, he may be blamed for thought-lessly building on land which he knew did not belong to him. 31. If Titius has planted another man's shrub in his own soil, the shrub is his; conversely, if Titius has planted his own shrub in soil belonging to Maevius, the shrub will belong to Maevius, provided in each case that it has struck root; until it has done so, there is no change of ownership. The principle that when a shrub has struck root there is a change of ownership is carried so far that if soil from land belonging to Titius has pressed against a neighbour's tree so that it drives its roots into Titius' land,[12] the tree becomes the property of Titius; for reason does not suffer a tree to belong to any other person than the person in whose soil it is rooted. Consequently, if a tree is planted near a boundary and drives its roots into the neighbour's land as well, it belongs to both proprietors.[13] 32. The principle that shrubs rooted in a man's land go with the soil, applies also to the sowing of grain. But the exceptio doli, which, as explained above, may be pleaded by the builder, if the owner claims the building, is equally available to one who at his own charge has in good faith sown in another man's land. 33. Written characters again, though they be of gold, accede to the paper or parchment on which they are written, just as buildings and crops are an accessory of the soil. Accordingly, if Titius has written a poem or a history or an oration on your paper or parchment, you are considered to be the owner, Titius not. But if you claim the books or parchment as being your property, and are not prepared to pay the cost of the writing, Titius may plead the exception of fraud, provided that he got possession of the papers or parchments in good faith.

G. 2. 78.

34. If a man has painted a picture on another man's canvas, some think that the canvas is an accessory of the picture; others maintain that a picture, whatever its value, is an accessory of the canvas.[14] But we think it better that the canvas should be an accessory of the picture; for it is absurd that a picture by Apelles or Parrhasius [15] should accede to a canvas of little value. Accordingly, if the original owner of the canvas is in possession of the painting and the artist claims it, but does not pay for the canvas, he may be repelled by the plea of fraud. If the artist is in possession, it follows that the original owner of the canvas has a utilis actio,[16] and if he does not pay the cost of the picture, he may be met with the plea of fraud, provided that the painter possessed the canvas in good faith. It is evident that if the canvas was

---

[12] Perhaps in consequence of a landslide. But the Digest (41. 1. 7, 13) has si vicini arborem terra presserim—if I have heaped soil about my neighbour's tree. *Qu.* read " presserit " ?

[13] *Contra,* Dig. 47. 7. 6, 2.

[14] So Paulus, Dig. 6. 1. 23, 3.

[15] Celebrated Greek painters. Apelles was Court painter to Alexander the Great, who died B.C. 323. Parrhasius lived about a hundred years earlier.

[16] Utilis actio (§ 701): in which the judex was instructed to treat him as still owner of the canvas. If the painter was out of possession he could recover the picture or its value on the condition of paying for the canvas. If he was in possession he could retain possession on the same condition. The original owner would merely recover his interest, namely the value of the canvas.

stolen by the painter or by any one else, the owner of the canvas
has the action of theft.[17]

35. If any one has in good faith bought land from one who was   § 201.
not its owner, believing him to be owner, or equally in good faith
acquired it by way of gift or for any other just cause, it has been
decided, as natural reason requires, that the fruits which he has
gathered should be his to reward the trouble he has taken in
cultivating the land.[18] Accordingly, if the real owner of the land
afterwards appears and claims his property, he cannot recover the
value of fruits which the possessor has consumed. But the same
indulgence is not extended to one who knows that he is in possession
of another man's property. Accordingly he has to give up the land
and is accountable for fruits even though consumed.

36. A usufructuary of land does not become owner of the fruits   § 201.
until he has gathered them. If he dies when fruits are ripe for
gathering, but have not yet been gathered, they do not belong to his
heirs, but go to the owner of the soil. The case of a lessee of land
is similar.[19]

37. In the case of animals the term " fruits " includes their
young, milk, hair and wool; consequently lambs and kids and calves
and foals immediately on birth are by natural law the property of
the usufructuary. The offspring of a slave-woman is not included
under the term " fruits " and therefore belongs to the owner of the
woman, not to the usufructuary; for it was considered ridiculous
that a human being should be included amongst fruits, when nature
has provided all fruits for the use of man. 38. If any one has the
usufruct of a flock he must make good losses by death from additions
by birth—so Julian held—and must replace dead vines and trees.
For every one must show proper husbandry and use the property   § 247.
as befits a good father of a family.

39. If a man found treasure on his own land the Emperor Hadrian   § 211.
in accordance with natural equity allowed the finder to keep it, and
he gave the same decision, in case any one found treasure by chance
in a place sacred or religious. But if one found treasure on another
man's land not by looking for it, but fortuitously, he allowed half of
it to the owner of the soil. Consistently with this, he decided that
if treasure was found on land belonging to the Emperor,[20] half was
to go to the finder, half [21] to the Emperor; if found in a place
which is public or belongs to the fiscus, half goes to the finder, half
to the fiscus, or to the city.[22]

40. Tradition or Delivery is another way in which things are   § 202.
acquired by natural law; for nothing is more in accord with natural
equity than to give effect to an owner's intention, when he wishes to
make his property over to some one else. Therefore, every kind of

---

[17] All of this follows Gaius (2. 78), who is also cited to the same effect
in Dig. 41. 1. 9, 2.
[18] This must not be understood to mean that his right to fruits is
limited to those which are the result of his own efforts. Dig. 41. 1. 48 pr.
(Paulus).
[19] Neither of them is owner of hanging fruits.
[20] His private domain.
[21] In this context publicus locus seems to mean civitatis.
[22] Somewhat inconsistent legislation of the divi fratres (Marcus Aurelius
and Verus) is recorded in Dig. 49. 14. 3, 10. Buckl. M. p. 145.

corporeal thing may be transferred by its owner and so alienated. Stipendiary and tributary lands (that is lands situated in the provinces) are alienated by this method.[23] However, by our constitution [24] there is no difference between provincial and Italian lands. 41. If things are delivered by way of gift or dos or for any other cause, the property undoubtedly passes. But things sold and delivered do not vest in the purchaser unless he has paid the price or satisfied the vendor in some other way as by getting some one

§ 205.   else to promise payment [25] or by giving a real security. This is so provided by the Law of the Twelve Tables, but it is truly said that the jus gentium, in other words natural law, has the same effect; and if the vendor gives credit to the purchaser, it must be allowed that the property immediately passes to him. 42. It makes no difference whether the thing is delivered by the owner himself, or by someone else with his consent. 43. Consequently, if the owner entrusts someone with the general management of his affairs, and such person sells and delivers something in the course of business, the property vests in the transferee.

§ 209.   44. Sometimes, without delivery, the owner's mere intention is enough to pass the ownership; for example, if some one has placed a thing in your hands by way of loan, or hire, or deposit, and then sells it or gives it to you. For though there is no delivery consequent upon the sale or gift, yet from the mere fact that he allows you to keep it, it becomes yours just as if there had been an actual delivery on that account.

45. If a person sells merchandise lying in a warehouse, as soon as he hands over the keys of the warehouse to the purchaser, he makes him owner of the goods.

46. Further, it sometimes happens that an owner's intention to benefit an indeterminate person passes the property; for example, praetors or consuls who throw largesse to a crowd do not know what any individual is going to get, and yet, since they intend that each man should keep what he gets, they make him owner as soon as he gets it. 47. On this principle [26] the better view seems to be that if the owner of a thing has abandoned it, and some one else takes possession of it, it immediately becomes his. A thing is said to be

---

[23] Under the Principate provinces were distinguished as senatorial and imperial. The first—the older provinces—were administered by proconsuls appointed by the Senate. The second—the frontier provinces—were administered by legati Caesaris. The tax imposed upon the first was called stipendium, that paid by the second tributum. Hence the distinction in the text: Gaius notices, but evidently without entirely endorsing (" intelliguntur "—" creduntur ") a current view that the first were owned by the Roman People (Tacitus, *Ann.* 1. 2, uses the phrase "*imperium* of the Senate and the People "), the second by the Emperor; which comes to much the same as the doctrine of English law that " every acre of land is technically held of the Crown " (Cheshire, *The Modern Law of Real Property* (4), p. 72). See A. H. M. Jones in *The Journal of Roman Studies* (1941), vol. 31, p. 26).

[24] Cod. 7. 31. 1.

[25] Either as surety, or by novation, or in any other way. Expromittere means to undertake to pay an existing debt. Buckl. *Textb.* p. 570.

[26] But the principle is not the same, because Justinian rejects the Proculian view that ownership of a res derelicta was not lost until another person took possession. Dig. 41. 7. 2, 1. He seems to hint at another view, namely, that the possessor's title was not perfect until usucapion.

abandoned when an owner throws it away with the intention of being rid of it with the consequence that he immediately ceases to be owner.

48. The case is different when, during a storm at sea, things are thrown overboard to lighten the ship. Such things continue to belong to their owners, for it is obvious that they are thrown away not to be rid of them but in order that the owner and the ship may escape the peril of the sea. Accordingly, if any one with a view to his own profit appropriates such things when they are cast ashore by the waves or found floating in the sea, he commits theft. The case is much the same as that of things which fall from a carriage in motion unknown to the owner.

V. Donation or Gift

212. Donation or Gift is an act of liberality which enriches the donee at the expense of the donor. The word covers a number of different transactions, which, if made for value and not gratuitously, are recognised as having each its own special character. Thus, I may give by transferring the ownership in a thing, or by creating or extinguishing a servitude, or by incurring or discharging an obligation and in other ways.[27]

Justinian describes donation as a mode of acquisition, and there are " one or two cases under his legislation " to which this description is fairly applicable,[28] but, in general, a gift may more properly be described, not as a mode, but as a cause or title, of acquisition (§ 171).

Gifts are distinguished as 1, gifts inter vivos; 2, gifts mortis causa.

When a gift, which is the most frequent case, takes the form of a transfer of ownership, it is usually effected by tradition. In Justinian's system a promise to give was enforceable as a vested pact (§ 529), which placed upon the donor a duty to deliver. 2. 7. 2.

213. Donatio Inter Vivos.—Gifts were the subject of special rules relating to:—(a) the amount; (b) the persons to whom they might be made; (c) the circumstances in which they might be revoked.

214. (a) Amount. A lex Cincia, a plebiscite of B.C. 204, prohibited gifts in excess of a certain (unknown) amount except in favour of a wide circle of relatives and some other privileged persons.[29] This law was a lex imperfecta,[30] i.e., it did not

---

27 Girard, p. 992.   28 Buckl. M. p. 150.
29 Vat. 298.
30 Ulpian, Regulae—ad init.—as reconstructed.

render the prohibited gift invalid, or even penalise it. The praetor gave effect to it by allowing an exceptio legis Cinciae, which might be pleaded by the donor (not by his heirs) if the donee claimed the gift in court.[31]

The lex Cincia had fallen into disuse before the time of Justinian and was replaced by legislation requiring registration in court of gifts in excess of 200, or, as Justinian enacted, 500 solidi. An unregistered gift in excess of this amount was void to the extent of the excess.

2. 7. 2.

215. (b) Persons. The chief restriction under this head was the prohibition of gifts between husband and wife. Such gifts were in general void,[32] but by an oratio of Antoninus (Caracalla) of A.D. 206 became valid if the donee survived the donor (the marriage not dissolved by divorce) and the donor at the time of death wished the gift to take effect.[33]

216. (c) Revocation. In the classical period gifts made by patrons to freedmen were revocable at discretion.[34] Under Justinian all gifts might be revoked on the ground of serious acts of ingratitude on the part of the donee[35]; and gifts by patrons to freedmen also on the ground of birth of issue to the donor, he being childless at the time of the gift.[36]

If a gift was made with a limitation or charge annexed to it (donatio sub modo) to which the donee failed to give effect, the gift might be recalled.[37]

217. Another peculiarity of donations (though not of donations alone) was the so-called beneficium competentiae, which the donor might plead if sued upon his promise to give. The purpose was to prevent the donor being ruined by his own generosity and also to protect his creditors. The debtor was to be left enough to supply his necessary maintenance after deduction of his debts.[38] The donee could only enforce the gift subject to these prior claims.

218. DONATIO MORTIS CAUSA.—This was a gift made in contemplation of death either generally or in view of a

---

[31] Buckl. *T.* p. 255; *M.* p. 152; *e.g.*, by vindication from a donor who had resumed possession. There would, of course, be no action on the gift before Justinian, unless it took the form of a stipulation.
[32] With some exceptions, in particular gifts mortis causa. Ulp. VII. 1.
[33] Dig. 24. 1. 32. Caracalla was joint Emperor with his father Septimius Severus from 198 A.D.
[34] *Vat.* 272.
[35] Inst. 2. 7. 2; Cod. 8. 55 (56). 10.
[36] Cod. 8. 55 (56). 8.
[37] Cod. 4. 6. 3; 8. 54 (55).
[38] Dig. 42. 1. 19, 1.

particular illness or hazard. It failed to take effect if the donor survived the donee (if they died simultaneously the gift held good),[39] and was subject to an unrestricted power of revocation inter vivos or by last will, which, however, might be expressly renounced. The condition of the gift, *viz.*, predecease or simultaneous decease of the donor, might be expressed to operate either as a condition precedent (suspensive) or as a condition subsequent (resolutive). In the first case the property did not pass, unless and until the condition was realised. In the second case it passed immediately but might be reclaimed (or reverted) if the condition was not realised.

219. Justinian says that gifts mortis causa have in all respects 2. 7. 1. been assimilated to legacies. This requires some qualification. A legacy implies a will and acceptance of the inheritance by an instituted heir. Neither of these things is necessary to a gift mortis causa, and there were other differences. On the other hand, there were close resemblances. Both took effect in consequence of death. In general, persons who could not make or take a legacy could not make or take a gift mortis causa. Both were postponed to the claims of creditors. Both were revocable. The provision of the lex Falcidia (§ 357) permitting the heir to retain one-fourth against legatees was extended by Septimius Severus to donationes mortis causa.[40]

220. So far as concerns form, a gift mortis causa could be constituted by any method appropriate to a corresponding gift inter vivos. By a constitution of A.D. 530, Justinian enacted that if a donatio mortis causa was made, in writing or without writing, in the presence of five witnesses, the number required for a codicil, registration and the usual notarial formalities were unnecessary.[41] It would be a mistake to regard this as laying down a general requirement of form for all gifts mortis causa.

221. DONATIO PROPTER NUPTIAS.—A special case of gift inter vivos was the donatio ante or propter nuptias. This was a 2. 7. 3. provision made by the husband for the benefit of the wife to take effect in the event of her surviving him, or being divorced without fault of her own. The institution, which was of oriental origin, developed in the later Empire. Originally, the gift was made before marriage, but Justinian's predecessor Justin having permitted the gift to be increased after marriage, Justinian changed the name from donatio ante nuptias to donatio propter

---

[39] Dig. 39. 6. 26 ; quia neuter alteri supervixit.
[40] Cod. 8. 56. 2, 2.
[41] Cod. 8. 56 (57). 4.

nuptias, and allowed such gifts to be made before and after marriage indifferently. Most frequently no property was actually transferred by the husband to the wife. He merely bound himself by contract to make the gift, and this promise was enforceable against himself in case of divorce, and against his heirs in case of his predecease. In Justinian's system the donatio propter nuptias was closely assimilated to the dos, of which we are next to speak.

VI. Dos

222. Dos was a gift made to the husband on the part of the wife as her contribution towards the expenses of the joint establishment. It was made by the wife or by another person on her behalf, usually before marriage and conditionally on the marriage taking place; but it might also be made or increased after marriage. If the dos was furnished by the wife's father or paternal ancestor it was called dos profecticia; if by the wife or any one else, dos adventicia; if on the express condition that it was to revert on the dissolution of the marriage, dos recepticia.[42]

223. Ulpian says that a dos may be constituted in three ways: "A dos is either given, or declared or promised."[43] These methods are distinguished as dotis datio, dotis dictio, dotis promissio. Dotis datio includes any mode of conveyance which vested the property in the husband. Dotis dictio was a verbal contract distinct from the stipulation (§ 442) applicable only in special circumstances. Dotis promissio was a promise to constitute a dos, made exclusively by way of stipulation until a constitution of Theodosius II and Valentinian III of A.D. 428 gave the same effect to an informal agreement (pactum de constituenda dote, § 529).

The above enumeration is not exhaustive. Any act of donation might be made to serve the same purpose. The amount of the dos and other particulars were usually settled by a written instrument executed before or after[44] marriage (instrumentum dotale).

224. In the course of its long history the legal incidents of dos were profoundly changed. We may distinguish three periods —the pre-classical—the classical—and the epoch of Justinian.[45]

---

[42] Ulp. VI, 3 and 5.   [43] Ulp. VI, 1.
[44] Inst. 2. 7. 3 ad fin.
[45] Girard, pp. 1008 et seq.; Buckl. T. p. 107; M. p. 64.

225. (1) Pre-classical period. If the woman was sui juris and married in manum everything that belonged to her vested automatically in her husband and was absorbed in his estate. The constitution of a dos, to the extent of the property composed in it, procured the same result. It was a provision made in the case of a manus marriage of a daughter in power by her father; in the case of a free marriage, by her father, or by herself, according as she was of dependent or independent status. Once vested in the husband, the dos remained his for all purposes and for all time. He was not accountable for it. It never reverted (unless it was dos recepticia, in which case the terms of restitution were determined in advance).

226. (2) The classical period. Divorces, and therefore second marriages, became increasingly frequent in the later Republic (§ 101). Correspondingly, the idea gained ground that the woman ought to have her dos back when the marriage was dissolved by divorce [46] or by the husband's death. This result was secured by stipulation (cautio rei uxoriae), defining the terms of restitution, enforced by the appropriate action (actio ex stipulatu). In the absence of stipulation, the lady was given another action (actio rei uxoriae), which enabled her to reclaim not the whole dos, but an equitable portion of it (quod aequius melius est), and in this action the husband was not condemned beyond his ability to pay.[47] In the case of the wife's predecease the dos could not be reclaimed, the actio rei uxoriae not being transmissible to heirs. Contrary to the general rule that the wife got back her dos, the dos profecticia reverted to the father, if alive; otherwise remained with the husband.[48] In principle, the husband was always owner of the dos, but, in the cases specified, subject to a duty of restitution. This was further emphasised by a provision of the lex Julia de fundo dotali (part of the lex Julia de adulteriis) of B.C. 18, which prohibited the alienation of a dotal immovable in Italy without the consent of the wife, and (as interpreted) its hypothecation even with such consent. In the cases in which the law required the husband to restore the dos to the wife, he was entitled to retain part of it on various grounds—on account of children (propter liberos), on account of the wife's misconduct (propter mores), for necessary expenses (propter impensas).[49]

---

[46] Ulp. VI, 6.
[47] Inst. 4. 6. 37; Cod. 6. 13. 17. The so-called beneficium competentiae § 217 (donation), § 511 (societas), § 756 (cessio bonorum).
[48] Ulp. VI, 4.
[49] Ulp. VI, 9.

227. (3) Justinian's legislation. Justinian by a constitution of 531 further limited the husband's power of disposition by prohibiting the alienation or hypothecation of dotal immovables wherever situated even with the consent of the wife. By the same constitution he fused the actio rei uxoriae and the actio ex stipulatu, abolishing the name of the former, but retaining most of its advantages. The reformed action was known as an actio ex stipulatu; not very happily, because it was available where there was no stipulation in fact, and, contrary to the nature of the actio ex stipulatu, was a bonae fidei judicium like the old actio rei uxoriae, but unlike it was transmissible to the woman's heirs. It was also known as actio de dote. The wife was given a tacit hypothec (§ 263) over all her husband's property to secure the restoration of the dos, and the husband had a similar hypothec over the property of the wife or her relations to ensure the dos being assigned to him in terms of the marriage contract.[50] The husband was liable to make compensation, if dotal property had been alienated without his wife's consent, or damaged through his failure to take as good care of it as he would of his own. The retentions of the classical age were gone, but the dos was *ipso jure* reduced to the extent of necessary expenses, and useful expenses [50a] could usually be recovered in an actio mandati or negotiorum gestorum.[51]

If, as often happened, movables were made over to the husband at a valuation (dos aestimata), the husband was liable for the estimated value, and not for the specific objects. He was answerable, whatever happened to the property. The general result of Justinian's legislation was that the dos always reverted to the donor or to the wife or her heirs, except that if the wife had been divorced for a permitted cause or had divorced her husband not for a permitted cause she forfeited the dos for the benefit of the husband, or of the husband and the children.[52] Through all this long course of development the husband was at first substantially and always formally owner of the dos.

During the Empire there was occasional legislation requiring parents to provide a dos for their daughters, but failure to do so did not invalidate the marriage.[53]

Margin references: 2. 8 pr. / 4. 6. 29. / 4. 6. 37.

---

[50] Cod. 8. 17 (18). 12 ; Girard, p. 1023.
[50a] See p. 323, n. 47
[51] Girard, p. 1022, n. 2.
[52] Nov. 117. 8 and 9.
[53] Corbett, p. 153 ; Buckl. *T.* p. 107 ; *M.* p. 65.

THE INSTITUTES

BOOK II

TITLE VII

Of donations

There is another kind of acquisition, donation.   § 212.
There are two kinds of donation, mortis causa and inter vivos.
1. Donatio mortis causa is a gift made in anticipation of death,   § 218.
when a person gives on the terms that, in the event of his death, the
donee is to have what is given, but that the donor is to get it back
in the event of his survival, or if he repents of the gift, or if the
donee dies first. These gifts mortis causa have been assimilated in   § 219.
all respects to legacies. It was a matter of controversy amongst the
jurists whether they were to be regarded as gifts or as legacies, for
they have resemblances with both, some taking the one view, some
the other. By our constitution[54] they are to be reckoned as
legacies practically in all respects and are to conform to the directions therein laid down. In a word, a gift is said to be mortis
causa when the giver would rather keep it himself than have it go
to the donee, and wishes the donee to have it rather than his heir.
So in Homer Telemachus is described as giving to Peiraeus.

> "Peiraeus, we cannot yet see how things will go. If the
> suitors manage to kill me traitorously in the palace and split
> up my heritage, I would rather you held these gifts. But if I
> succeed in dooming them to death, then shall I be just as glad
> to get them as you to let them go."[55]

2. There are other gifts, which are made without any thought of
death, and which we call gifts inter vivos. These have no resemblance to legacies and once perfected cannot be lightly revoked.
They are perfected when the donor has manifested his intention with
or without writing; and our constitution[56] ordains that, as in the case
of sale, the promise implies a duty to deliver, so that even before
delivery, it is fully and perfectly binding, and places on the donor   § 212.
a duty of delivery. Former imperial enactments required that gifts
in excess of two hundred solidi should be lodged in an official
registry. By our constitution[57] the limit is raised to five hundred
solidi; gifts up to that amount are valid without registration, and
there are special cases in which gifts are perfectly valid (to any
amount) without registration. Other provisions designed to secure
to gifts their full effect will be found in our constitutions. It must
be observed, however, that, even when gifts are quite complete, our   § 216.
constitution[58] allows donors, if the donees prove ungrateful, to
revoke them for certain specified reasons, lest otherwise their
generosity should be an occasion of injury or loss. 3. There is
another kind of gift inter vivos, unknown to the older lawyers, but

---

[54] Cod. 8. 56. 4.
[55] Od. XVII, 78–83.
[56] Cod. 8. 53. 35, 5b.
[57] Cod. 8. 53. 36, 3.
[58] Cod. 8. 55. 10.

§ 221.   introduced by the Emperors in modern times. This is the type of
gift which used to be known as donatio ante nuptias, so called
because it was concluded before (never after) marriage and was
conditional on marriage taking place. Our father, the late Emperor
Justin, having regard to the fact that it was lawful to increase the
amount of the dos after marriage, allowed, in the event of this being
done, a corresponding increase to be made in the donatio ante
nuptias. The consequence was to render the name "gift before
marriage" inappropriate, now that the gift could be increased after
marriage. Accordingly, since it is our desire that laws should be
carried to their logical conclusion, and that names should correspond
with facts, we have changed the name from donatio ante nuptias to
donatio propter nuptias, and ordained that like the dos this gift
may be not only increased, but also constituted after marriage.

4. Formerly there was another mode of acquisition by civil law,
namely, by right of accrual (per jus adcrescendi). This took place
in the following circumstances. Suppose a man, who owned a slave
in common with Titius, acting alone gave him his freedom by
vindicta or by testament; the consequence was that his share in the
slave was gone and accrued to Titius, the other co-owner. This was
open to the gravest objection. The slave was cheated out of his
freedom and kind masters suffered a loss, while masters who were
not so kind reaped an advantage. Our constitution provides a
remedy which favours freedom, gives effect to the benevolent
intention of the manumitting master, and indemnifies the other.[59]

VII. Competence to Alienate

228. In Title VIII Justinian considers some exceptional cases
in which owners may not alienate their own property, or persons
who are not owners may alienate the property of some one else.

Under the first head fall the cases of: —

2. 8 pr.   (1) the husband, forbidden to alienate dotal immovables
                         (§ 226);
                    (2) the pupillus incapable of alienating any property
2. 8. 2.   whatever without the authority of his tutor (§ 131).

There were many other cases. In the older law, a woman
G. 2. 80   of any age could not alienate res mancipi without her tutor's
authority. In the later Empire minors who had a curator were
assimilated to pupils and could not alienate without the curator's
consent (§ 140). Insane persons and interdicted prodigals
laboured under a general incapacity to act for themselves.

229. As an instance of a non-owner competent to alienate,
the case of the mortgagee is mentioned, who was empowered to

---

[59] The slave was free. The manumitting master had to compensate the
other.

      155

sell the pledge in order to realise his security. This right was 2. 8. 1.
not limited, as the text seems to imply, to the case where a
right of sale was a term in the contract. As early as Ulpian it
might be exercised without any agreement in that behalf, in
the absence of express agreement to the contrary [60] (§ 260).

In addition to the above Justinian might have mentioned
the case of tutors and curators who (within limits) have power
to alienate the property under their control (§ 135).

THE INSTITUTES

BOOK II

TITLE VIII

Of persons who may, and who may not alienate

It sometimes happens that an owner cannot alienate, and conversely one who is not owner has the power of alienation. Thus the
lex Julia forbids a husband to alienate dotal immovables, if his wife
does not consent, though the property is his, having been given him
by way of dos. This law we have changed and amended. The lex §§ 226,
Julia has reference only to Italian immovables, and while it prohibits 227.
alienation without the wife's consent, prohibits hypothecation even
with her consent. In respect of both these matters we have contrived
a remedy. The prohibition of alienation and pledge is extended to
provincial soil,[61] and neither is allowed even with the woman's
consent, lest the frailty of the sex should be the occasion of a
woman's financial ruin. 1. On the other hand, a creditor may by § 260.
agreement alienate a pledge, though the thing does not belong to him.
But this may be thought to take place with the consent of the debtor
who agreed from the beginning that the creditor might sell the
pledge, if the debt was not paid. Our constitution [62] prescribes a
procedure for realising pledges, which fully safeguards the interests
of both parties.

2. It must be observed that no pupil of either sex can alienate
any property without the tutor's authority. Accordingly, if a pupil § 131.
lends money without the tutor's authority no obligation is contracted,
because he does not make it the property of the borrower; so the
coins, if to be found anywhere, can be vindicated; if they have been
spent in good faith by the borrower, the sum may be claimed in a
personal action; if in bad faith, an action lies for their production.
Conversely, anything may properly be given to a pupil of either sex
without the tutor's authority. Accordingly, if a debtor pays to a
pupil what he owes, the tutor's authority is needed; otherwise he

[60] Dig. 13. 7. 4.
[61] Cod. 5. 13.
[62] Cod. 8. 33 (34). 3

will not be discharged from liability.[63] This is clearly enacted in a constitution, which at the suggestion of the eminent Tribonian, quaestor of our sacred palace, we have published to the advocates of Caesarea, providing that the debtor of a pupil may make payment to his tutor or curator, having first obtained permission from the court without any expense to the applicant.[64] If the judge makes the order, and payment follows, the debtor is completely secure. If the debtor pays without obtaining permission from the court, then, if the pupil has the money intact or has been enriched by it, and none the less sues for the debt, he may be met with a plea for fraud; but, if he has wasted the money or it has been stolen from him, the debtor cannot set up a plea of fraud, but will be condemned to pay over again, because he made the first payment carelessly, without the tutor's authority and without complying with our constitution. On the other hand, pupils cannot make a payment without the tutor's authority, because what they pay does not become the property of the creditor, since they are not allowed to alienate anything without such authority.[63]

VIII. Acquisition through Agents

230. The Roman Law of agency, whether in the field of property or of contract, developed slowly. It began in the family circle, *i.e.*, in connection with relations defined by status. It was gradually extended to relations established by contract. Thus we find the classes of persons through whom we acquire to be four, their relations to us being in the first three cases matter of status, in the fourth matter of contract. They are: (1) children and slaves in power; (2) slaves of whom we have the usufruct; (3) free men and other persons' slaves possessed in good faith; (4) free agents. We will consider these classes in order.

2. 9 pr. & 5.

231. Children [65] and slaves in power (with whom Gaius includes persons in our manus or mancipium). Until the end of the Republic the position of children in power and of slaves as regards acquisition was indistinguishable, for " a person in our power can have nothing of his own," and, therefore, whatever any such person acquired by any of the legal modes of acquiring ownership vested automatically in his superior, even without the superior's knowledge and consent. This did not

G. 2. 86.

G. 2. 87.

---

[63] Gaius (§ 93) states the law more clearly—" Therefore if a debtor pay money to a pupil, he makes that money the pupil's, but he is not himself discharged; because a pupil cannot dissolve an obligation without his tutor's authority, since he is not allowed to alienate anything without his tutor's authority. But if he has been enriched by the money, and nevertheless sues for it, he may be repelled by a plea of fraud."

[64] Cod. 5. 37. 25.

[65] The term includes all free persons in power of any age or either sex.

apply, however, to an inheritance or legacy, for a son or slave could not enter on an inheritance or accept a legacy except by **2. 9. 3.** the orders of the pater or dominus. Like ownership, possession (unaccompanied by ownership) was acquired through persons in **G. 2. 89.** power, for, " when they have acquired possession of a thing, we **2. 9. 3.** are deemed to possess it," provided that the child or slave had authority to acquire, special or general. The latter was the case when acquisitions were made with the peculium, which the father or master allowed him to retain.[66] Under the Empire the principle that the son acquired for the father was progressively narrowed, until the old law remained in force only in the case **2. 9. 1.** of the peculium profecticium (§ 89).

232. Slaves held in usufruct. The rule was that what they acquired in the affairs of the usufructuary (ex re nostra), or by letting their services on hire to a third person (ex operis suis),[67] vested in the usufructuary; what they acquired from other sources went to their owners. Thus, they acquired an **2. 9. 4.** inheritance or legacy for the owner, not for the usufructuary. Possession might be acquired subject to the same distinction.

233. Free men and other persons' slaves possessed in good faith. The rule is the same as in the last case, so that anything acquired in either of the above-mentioned ways vested in the possessor, but acquisitions from any other source went to the putative slave, if he was in fact free ; to his owner, if he was in fact a slave. The same applied to possession.

234. Free agents. The old rule was that nothing could be acquired through an extraneous person (*i.e.*, a person not falling under any of the above-mentioned classes). Gaius, after stating the rule, continues, " The only question is with regard to possession whether we can acquire it through a procurator." [68] Paulus, about fifty years later, expresses a more decided opinion : " It has been established in the interest of general convenience that we can acquire possession through a procurator." [69] A procurator was a general manager, but at an early date, perhaps in the course of the second century, the same principle was applied to any free agent (as well as to tutors and curators). **2. 9. 5.** Justinian attributes this result to a constitution of Severus and Caracalla of A.D. 196, but, as appears from the constitution

---

[66] Dig. 41. 2. 1, 5.
[67] Buckl. *T.* p. 279 ; *M.* p. 169.
[68] G. 2. 95. The palimpsest is illegible. The gap is variously supplied.
[69] Paul. *Sent.* 5. 2. 2.

itself, the Emperors were stating what in their time was established law. It followed that in any case in which acquisition of possession carried with it acquisition of ownership, ownership also could be acquired through a free agent.[69a] This was limited to cases of acquisition by natural law. It was inapplicable to the older forms of civil law acquisition, manicipatio and in jure cessio; for by these methods no one could acquire ownership except the person who actually took part in the ceremony, so that agency of any kind was out of the question. But in such cases (as in any other case of acquisition of possession through an agent) the principal's acquired possession would, if the conditions of usucapion were present, very soon ripen into ownership by lapse of time (§ 168).

THE INSTITUTES

BOOK II

TITLE IX

Of persons through whom we acquire

§ 230.

We acquire not only by ourselves, but also through those whom we have in our power; also through slaves in whom we have a usufruct; also through free men and other persons' slaves whom we possess in good faith. Let us investigate these cases separately.

§ 231.

1. Formerly, whatever came to children in power of either sex (with the exception of castrense peculium) was, without distinction, acquired for their parents; so much so, that what was acquired through one child might be given to another, or to a stranger, or sold, or disposed of in any way the parents pleased. This seemed to us inhuman. Accordingly, we have enacted that whatever comes to children through their father's property (ex re patris) is to be acquired for the father in accordance with the old law. What hardship can there be in attributing to the father an acquisition for which he has supplied the means? But in the case of all other acquisitions [70] the father is to have a usufruct, the ownership remaining with the son.[71] 2. If a parent emancipated a child in power, earlier constitutions allowed the parent to retain one-third of the property which did not vest in him as owner [i.e., the property of the child of which the father had the usufruct] as the price, so to say, of the emancipation. But it was not fair that on emancipation a son should lose part of his property, and that the honour of emancipation should entail a substantial diminution of fortune. Accordingly, we

---

[69a] Dig. 41. 1. 20 in fine.

[70] Always excepting peculium castrense and peculium quasi-castrense.

[71] Earlier Emperors from Constantine onwards had enacted this with regard to property derived from the mother and other special cases of bona adventicia. Justinian made the principle general. Cod. 6. 61. 6.

have decreed that instead of ownership of a third the parent is to retain the usufruct of a half.[72] In this way the son's property remains unimpaired, and the father has the enjoyment of a larger portion of the estate. 3. Again, you acquire what your slaves get § 231. by tradition, whether in consequence of stipulation or any other cause of acquisition. This goes to you, though you be ignorant of the acquisition, or unwilling to acquire. For a slave, being in his master's power, can have nothing of his own. But, if he is instituted heir, he cannot enter on the inheritance except by your orders; and if he does so, the inheritance vests in you, just as if you had yourself been instituted heir, and a legacy is acquired in the same way. You acquire through those in your power not only ownership but also possession; for if they get the possession of anything, you are deemed to possess it; and accordingly through their possession usucapion or long time possession runs in your favour. 4. With regard to slaves in whom you have merely a usufruct the rule is that whatever they acquire in your affairs (ex re vestra) or by letting their services on hire (ex operibus suis)[73] accrues to you, but anything acquired § 232. otherwise goes to their owner. Accordingly, if such a slave is instituted heir, or receives a legacy or gift, the acquisition, in each case, goes not to the usufructuary but to the owner. The same rule § 233. applies to any one whom you possess in good faith (as a slave), whether he is really free or is some one else's slave; for the rule which applies to the usufructuary applies equally to the bona fide possessor. Accordingly, anything acquired outside the two cases mentioned goes to the man himself, if he is in fact free, or to his real owner, if he is in fact a slave. When a bona fide possessor has usucaped the slave, he becomes his legal owner and entitled to all acquisitions from whatever source. But a usufructuary cannot usucape, first because he does not possess, but has merely a right of use and enjoyment; secondly, because he knows that the slave belongs to someone else. You acquire through the above-mentioned persons [slaves held in usufruct or bona fide possessed—a free person whom you in good faith treat as your slave] not only ownership but also possession—within the limits in each case defined above, that is if possession is acquired ex re vestra or ex operibus suis.

5. From what has been said it is evident that through free men, who are not subject to your power or possessed in good faith, and through another person's slave of whom you have neither a usufruct nor bona fide possession you cannot in any circumstances acquire. This is the meaning of the maxim that nothing can be acquired § 234. through an extraneous person (per extraneam personam nihil adquiri posse), except that it is settled in accordance with a constitution of the Emperor Severus[74] that through a free person such as a general manager you acquire possession, not only if you know of the acquisition but even if you do not; and you become owner as an immediate consequence of the possession, if the person who delivered the thing was owner, and, if he was not, by usucapion or long time possession.

[For section 6, see p. 185.]

---

[72] Cod. 6. 61 6, 3.
[73] This is a variant of the more usual *ex operis suis*.
[74] Cod. 7. 32. 1.

IX. SERVITUDES

235. Under the description of servitudes the later Roman
Law included two classes of rights which seem to have little
resemblance to one another, *viz.*, praedial servitudes, comprising such rights as English lawyers include under easements
and profits, and personal servitudes, the principal one of which,
viz., usufruct, bears more resemblance to a life interest in
immovable or movable property.

236. Nevertheless all servitudes have certain points in
common [75] : —

(1) They are all real rights (jura in re aliena) protected by
a real action called the actio confessoria, while a corresponding
action—the actio negatoria—is available to the owner of
property who wishes to take active steps to challenge another
person's claim to servitude in regard to it (§ 694).

(2) They are incorporeal things and as such are the subject
of special rules as to creation, extinction, and in other respects.

(3) They exist over the property of another for the benefit
of a thing or of a person. Therefore:—(a) in the case of a
praedial servitude the burden imposed on one property
(praedium serviens) must always be related to a benefit attached
to another property (praedium dominans). The Roman Law
did not recognise as a praedial servitude what English lawyers
call a profit " in gross." " A servitude cannot be created to the
effect that a man shall be at liberty to pluck fruit or to walk
about or to picnic on another man's ground." [76] ; (b) personal
servitudes last only so long as the person lasts in whose favour
they are created. They are determined, therefore, by death or
capitis deminutio. Further, being strictly personal in character,
they cannot be transferred to a third person.

X. REAL OR PRAEDIAL SERVITUDES

237. Real servitudes are either rustic or urban, according as
they are appurtenant to land or to buildings. The principal
rustic servitudes are iter, the right to go over another man's
land on foot or on horseback [77] ; actus, the right of passage
for a vehicle, the right to drive draught animals and cattle [78] ;

---

[75] Girard, p. 383.
[76] Dig. 8. 1. 8 pr.
[77] pedes vel eques. Dig. 8. 3. 12.
[78] armenta. Dig. *ibid.*

via, which included the above and something more, in par- 2. 3 pr.
ticular, the right to have a metalled track, which by the Law
of the Twelve Tables was to be eight feet wide and sixteen
feet where the road turned[79]; aquaeductus, the right to lead
water over another's land.

238. To the same head may be referred the right of drawing
water, of watering cattle and rights which in English law are
called " profits," such as the right of pasture, of excavating and
burning lime, of digging sand, as well as the negative right that
you shall not sink wells on your land, so as to diminish the
supply of water to mine.[80]

239. The principal urban servitudes are my right to have 2. 3. 2
a drain through your land serving my house (servitus cloacae
immittendae)[81]; servitude of support for a building (jus 2. 3. 1.
oneris ferendi); right to drive a balk of timber into my neighbour's wall (jus tigni immittendi); right to discharge rain-
water by drop from the eaves or from a spout on to neighbouring land (jus stillicidii vel fluminis avertendi vel recipiendi,
i.e., my right to divert or (the same thing) your liability to
receive)[82]; rights of light and prospect, *viz.*, jus altius non
tollendi, *i.e.*, my right to require you not to build so as to
interfere with my access of light; jus ne luminibus officiatur,
i.e., my right to access of light unimpeded by buildings or
trees; jus ne prospectui officiatur, *i.e.*, my right to a pleasing
and unimpeded view.[83] This last is unknown to English law,
for as an old judge said: " For Prospect which is matter only
of Delight, and not of Necessity, no action lies for the Stopping
thereof, and yet it is a great Commendation of a House, if it
has a long and easy Prospect." [84]

240. Besides the above, mention is made of a right of
building higher (jus altius tollendi) and a right that rain-
water shall not be received or discharged (jus stillicidii vel
fluminis non recipiendi aut non avertendi).[85] These servitudes

---

[79] Dig. 8. 3. 8.
[80] Dig. 8. 1. 15 pr.
[81] This is not mentioned in the Institutes, though it was, perhaps, the
oldest of the urban servitudes. Girard, p. 385.
[82] Or is it different—your *right* to receive?
[83] Dig. 8. 2. 17 pr.; 8. 2. 15.
[84] *Aldred's Case* (1611) 9 Rep. 58 b.
[85] G. 2. 31: jus altius tollendi aedes aut non tollendi, ne luminibus
vicini officiatur; Dig. 8. 3. 2 pr.: Rusticorum [sic] praediorum sunt licere
altius tollere et officere praetorio vicini etc. (Neratius); Dig. 8. 2. 2.
(Gaius): (jus) altius tollendi et officiendi luminibus vicini, aut non
extollendi: item stillicidium avertendi in tectum vel aream vicini aut non
avertendi; Inst. 2. 3. 1: ut stillicidium vel flumen recipiat quis in aedes
suas vel in aream, vel non recipiat.

are a puzzle. They seem to be not servitudes at all, but natural incidents of ownership. Various explanations have been given. Perhaps the following is as plausible as any. Servitudes were lost by non-user for the usucapion period of two years (§ 243). But in the case of urban servitudes mere non-user was not enough. The owner of the servient land must build against the servitude and maintain the obstruction for the statutory period. This was called "usucapion of freedom."

> "The better view is that freedom from servitudes may be acquired by usucapion, for the lex Scribonia put an end to the creation of servitudes by usucapion; not to their release. Accordingly, if for instance I owe you a servitude of not building higher, and I have maintained a higher building for the statutory period, the servitude is at an end." [86]

The same consequence follows if I obstruct your servitude of discharging rain-water on to my land.

In such cases my re-acquired right of doing as I please on my own land may have been regarded as a counter-servitude. If this seems improbable, the suggestion may be modified by supposing not a complete, but a partial, obstruction. This will leave your servitude still in existence, and I may be said *pro tanto* to have acquired a servitude against it. Another theory is that these anomalous servitudes were rights acquired in derogation of a municipal law or custom, restricting the height of buildings or allowing me to divert rain-water on to neighbouring premises. [87]

241. So far, it has been assumed that the enumerated rustic servitudes are appurtenant to land (*i.e.*, that the dominant praedium is land), and that the enumerated urban servitudes are appurtenant to a house (*i.e.*, that the dominant praedium is a house). But how are we to place, *e.g.*, a right of way appurtenant to a house, or, *e.g.*, a right that a neighbour shall not build appurtenant to a garden? Is the first urban, the second rustic? or does the general description continue to apply so that the first is rustic, the second urban? And if the character of the dominant praedium in each case determines the quality of the servitude what are we to say (as Buckland asks) if I acquire a right of way to land [or, rather, *for* land] and then build a house? "Does the servitude cease to be rustic and become urban?" [88] The texts give no consistent answer to these questions. Thus aquaeductus is usually

---

[86] Dig. 41. 3. 4, 28; *cf.* Dig. 8. 2. 6.
[87] Buckl. *T.* p. 264; *M.* p. 158.   [88] *T.* p. 263.

described as rustic, but one text speaks of a servitude to lead water through my house (according to this the character of the *servient* property seems to be decisive) as urban.[89] In the Institutes Justinian deals with normal cases and does not indulge in such speculations. The matter is not unimportant, for the law distinguishes in various ways between rustic and urban servitudes.[90] Thus in addition to a different mode of creation and extinction (§§ 242, 243), the interdict de itinere actuque privato applied to the first, not to the second[91]; and the rustic servitudes of via iter actus and aquaeductus could be hypothecated to a neighbouring land-owner,[92] urban servitudes not.[93] Girard makes the decision rest in each case upon the character of the dominant praedium. Buckland says " this opinion seems to create more difficulties than it solves."[94] For him, a right of way is always rustic, a right of light is always urban.

HOW PRAEDIAL SERVITUDES WERE CREATED AND EXTINGUISHED

242. (1) In the time of Gaius rustic servitudes were created by mancipation or by in jure cessio, urban servitudes only by in jure cessio. These modes applied to Italian soil. In the provinces similar rights were created " by pacts and stipulations." In the later law this mode was of general application. The pact settled the terms of the servitude. The stipulation was the promise to give effect to it, often combined with a penalty for failure to do so.[95] It is now generally agreed, contrary to the earlier doctrine, that the effect was to give a real right over the servient land, and not merely a personal right to have the servitude constituted by quasi-tradition.[96]

(2) Reservation (deductio). An owner might alienate land by mancipatio or in jure cessio, and in the later law by traditio, on the condition that it was to be servient to land retained.[97]

(3) Testament. I might give a legacy of a servitude, thus charging the land in the hands of my heir, or give a legacy of the land with reservation of a servitude, thus entitling my

G. 2. 29.

2. 3. 4.

2. 3. 4.

[89] Dig. 6. 2. 11, 1.
[90] Girard, p. 387.
[91] Dig. 43. 19. 1, 1.
[92] Dig. 20. 1. 12 (Paulus citing Pomponius).
[93] Dig. 20. 1. 11, 3.
[94] *M.* p. 157.
[95] Girard, p. 399.
[96] Moyle, p. 218; Buckl. *T.* p. 266; *M.* p. 159.
[97] Dig. 8. 4. 3.

heir to its exercise; or, finally, leave the servitude to one person and the land, less the servitude, to another.

(4) Lapse of time. Servitudes could not, strictly speaking, be acquired by usucapion, because they did not admit of physical possession (§ 272), but it seems that in the early law the distinction between ownership and servitude was not sharply defined and that servitudes (some or all?) could be acquired by this method, just as rustic servitudes might be acquired by mancipation. Late in the Republic a lex Scribonia forbade the usucapion of servitudes,[98] whether of some or of all is uncertain. But, in any event, it was forgotten or circumvented. The enjoyment of aquaeductus for a period reaching back beyond the limits of legal memory was construed as a grant (vetustatem vice legis tenere).[99] In the provinces, lapse of time, which came to be fixed at ten years inter praesentes and twenty years inter absentes (§ 178), gave a title to a servitude, if the servitude had been continuously exercised nec clam, nec vi nec precario (openly, without challenge or objection and not on sufferance), but without (it seems) the usual requirements of good faith and just title. Ultimately this became the general rule.[1]

(5) Quasi-tradition. From an uncertain date, but certainly in the later Empire, if the owner of land acquiesced in the exercise of a servitude by a neighbour (this can only apply to a positive servitude), the neighbour acquired the servitude by a kind of tradition, or by "a substitute for tradition."[2] If, as might well be the case, a document recorded the transaction, the document would in itself be sufficient to convey the right, as it ultimately did in the case of ownership (§ 210); and this method of acquisition would hardly be distinguishable from the constitution of a servitude by pacts and stipulations, which also would normally be reduced to writing[3] (§ 448).

(6) Adjudicatio. It was competent to the judex in a judicium divisorium (§ 182) to declare a servitude in favour of any of the parties to the litigation.[4]

243. Praedial servitudes were extinguished by:—

(1) Surrender or renunciation. In the old law this was effected by in jure cessio, an actio negatoria denying the

G. 2. 30.

---

[98] Dig. 41. 3. 4. 28 (29).
[99] Dig. 39. 3. 26; 43. 20. 3, 4; 39. 3. 1, 23.
[1] Cod. 7. 33. 12, 4; 3. 34. 1.
[2] Dig. 8. 1. 20 (pro traditione); 8. 3. 1, 2: Traditio plane et patientia servitutium inducet officium praetoris.
[3] Arangio-Ruiz, pp. 223, 224.
[4] Dig. 10. 2. 22, 3; 10. 3. 7, 1.

THE LAW OF PROPERTY 165

existence of the servitude, not defended by the owner of the dominant land. A rustic servitude might also be extinguished by re-mancipation. In the later law a servitude could be extinguished by mere agreement.[5]

(2) Merger (confusio), *viz.*, when the ownership of both the properties vested in the same hands, for no one can have a servitude over his own land (nulli res sua servit, § 254).

(3) Non-user for the statutory period, the period being the same as that required for acquisition, *viz.*, in the classical law, two years; under Justinian ten or twenty years.[6] In the case of urban servitudes, as remarked above, mere non-user was not sufficient. There must be obstruction on the part of the owner of the servient land maintained for the required period of years (§ 240).[7]

(4) Term or condition. A servitude might come to an end by expiry of the time for which it was constituted or by the effect of a resolutive condition. This might happen:—(a) if the ownership of the servient tenement was thus limited, in which case the servitude would expire with the expiry of the interest of the owner of the servient land[8]; (b) if the grant of the servitude was itself thus limited. This is a departure from the general quality of perpetuity, which is in principle characteristic of praedial servitudes, distinguishing them from personal servitudes, which are determined (at latest) by the death of the person entitled.

THE INSTITUTES

BOOK II

TITLE III

Of servitudes

Servitudes of rustic immovables are the following:—iter, actus, via, aquaeductus. Iter is the right of going or passing for a man, not of driving a beast of draught or a vehicle: actus is the right of driving beasts of draught or vehicles. Accordingly, if a man has iter (merely) he has not actus. If he has actus he has also iter, and therefore may exercise his right of way without driving a beast. Via is the right of going, passing, and driving. It includes iter and § 237.

[5] Girard, p. 404.
[6] Paul *Sent.* 1. 17; Cod. 3. 34. 13.
[7] Destruction or substantial alteration of either land is commonly said to extinguish a servitude. But reversion to the old state of things may revive it. Buckl. *T.* p. 267; *M.* p. 160.
[8] Dig. 8. 6. 11, 1.

§ 239.

actus. Aquaeductus is the right of leading water through another
man's land. 1. Servitudes of urban immovables are attached to
buildings. They are called "urban" because houses are called urban
properties, even though situated in the country. The following are
urban servitudes—a neighbour's liability to support the weight of an
adjoining building; to allow the adjoining proprietor to drive a
beam into his wall; to receive (or not to receive) on to his house or
yard the drip from his neighbour's eaves or the flow of water from
his spout; not to raise the height of his building so as to obscure his
neighbour's lights. 2. Some writers think that amongst rustic
servitudes are properly included rights of drawing water, of driving
cattle to water, of pasturage, of burning lime, of digging sand.

3. The reason why these servitudes are termed servitudes of immovables is because they imply the existence of immovable property
(praedia). For no one can acquire a servitude, rustic or urban,
unless he owns land, nor be charged with such a servitude, unless he
owns land. 4. If any one wishes to create a servitude in favour of

§ 242.

his neighbour, he should effect it by pacts and stipulations. A man
may also by his will condemn his heir not to build higher so as to
obstruct a neighbour's lights; or to suffer him to drive a beam into
a wall, or to receive his eaves-drip; or to suffer him to go or to drive
over his land, or to lead water from it.

XI. Personal Servitudes

244. The personal servitudes are (1) ususfructus; (2) usus;
(3) habitatio; (4) operae servorum.

2. 4 pr.

245. Ususfructus (usufruct). Justinian repeats from the
Digest Paul's definition of usufruct as "the right to use and
take the fruits of another man's property, the substance
remaining unimpaired"; and adds from the same source the
explanation of Celsus "for it is a right over a corporeal thing;
if this disappears, the right necessarily disappears with it."[9]
The effect of running the two citations together is that the
words "the substance remaining unimpaired" must be understood to mean "as long as the property in question lasts."
But it is usual to quote Paul's words without the added
explanation and to understand them to mean that the usufructuary may use and enjoy the property, but may not diminish
its substance. This is perhaps what Paul himself meant to
convey by the words salva rerum substantia. They are used in
this sense in Ulpian's *Regulae*.[10]

246. Whatever may be the precise intention of the definition,
it is obvious that the existence of the servitude depends upon the

---

[9] Dig. 7. 1. 1 and 2.
[10] Ulp. XXIV, 26: Ususfructus legari potest jure civili earum rerum
quarum salva substantia utendi fruendi potest esse facultas.

existence of a thing over which it can be exercised. Hence,
there cannot be a usufruct in things which are consumed in   2. 4. 2.
using them, including money. But a senatusconsultum of the
early Empire allowed a quasi-usufruct in such things. The
beneficiary became owner, but was required to give security for
the restoration of the equivalent upon the determination of his
interest. This development was rendered necessary by a practice
which became common under the Empire for testators to
bequeath a usufruct in the whole or part of their estate, thus
constituting the legatee a tenant for life with remainder to the
heir.

247. During the continuance of the usufruct the owner was
free to exercise any rights not inconsistent with it ; thus, to
alienate or hypothecate [11] the property. The usufructuary, on
the other hand, had all the ordinary rights of use and enjoyment
and of taking fruits, but he must exercise these rights in a
proper manner.   Thus the usufructuary of agricultural land
" must cultivate in the right way and use the property like a   2. 1. 38.
good father of a family." He might not cut timber trees.[12]
He might open and work quarries and the like, if he could do so
without undue disturbance of the course of agriculture.[13]   He
was required by the praetor to give security by stipulation for
proper use of the property and for its restoration on the expiry
of the usufruct.[14]   A usufruct could not be alienated, that is to
say a usufructuary could not convey his right and liability to a
third party, but there was nothing to prevent his contracting with
another person to allow him to enjoy the benefit of the usufruct
while it lasted, whether by way of gift, or hire or sale.   5. 1.

248. Usus (use), was a right of less extent than usufruct
and of less frequent occurrence. The usuary could only use
the property to satisfy the personal wants of himself and his
family. The usuary of a house might occupy it with his wife,   2. 5. 2.
family and servants, and receive guests. If he resided in the
house himself he might (in Labeo's opinion) take in a lodger,
but not lease the house to another person.[15]

249. Habitatio. This was the right to use a house. It had
been doubted whether it was a distinct servitude, or indeed a
servitude at all. Justinian pronounced it to be distinct from

---

[11] Cod. 3. 33. 2.
[12] Dig. 7. 1. 11.
[13] Dig. 7. 9. 1 pr.
[14] Dig. 7. 1. 13, 5.
[15] Dig. 7. 8. 2.

usufruct and use, and adopted the opinion of Marcellus that the person entitled might not only occupy the house himself, but also let it to others.

2. 5. 5.

250. Operae servorum was a right to use the services of slaves scarcely distinguishable from usus.[16] Like habitatio (and unlike usufruct and use) it was not lost by non-user or capitis deminutio (§ 120).[17] This is said to be reminiscent of an earlier view that the right was merely contractual and governed by the rules of contract.[18]

2. 4. 1 ;
2. 5 pr.

251. Personal servitudes were created in the same way as praedial servitudes : viz. by (1) in jure cessio,[19] later by pacts and stipulations ; (2) reservation on a grant ; (3) testament ; (4) lapse of time ; (5) quasi-tradition ; (6) adjudication ; to which must be added (7) statute (lege), particularly the usufruct which in the later law the father enjoyed in the bona adventicia of his son, and the usufruct of one-half which he retained upon emancipation (§ 89).

2. 4. 3 ;
2. 5 pr.

252. Personal servitudes were extinguished in the same ways as praedial servitudes : viz. by (1) surrender or renunciation ; (2) merger (consolidatio) ; (3) destruction or substantial alteration of the subject-matter. If a house was burnt down the usufruct was gone alike of the house, the site and the material [20] ; (4) non-user (except as mentioned above) ; (5) term or condition ; and finally (6) death and (except as mentioned above) capitis deminutio, any capitis deminutio before Justinian,

3. 10. 1

capitis deminutio maxima and media in his system.[21] If the usufructuary was a corporate body, such as a municipality, the usufruct was taken to be constituted for one hundred years, which was considered to be the longest duration of human life.[22] Though, normally, usufruct was a life interest it might be constituted for a definite period, e.g., for ten years, but, in any event, death put an end to it. Destruction by capitis deminutio was avoided by providing for a series of annual or shorter usufructs (in singulos annos—menses—dies), or for a new usufruct to come into existence immediately on the destruction of the first (" quotiens capite minutus erit "—repetitus

---

[16] Dig. 7. 7. Operae animalium is referred to in a single text (Dig. 7. 9. 5, 3). For usus of slaves and animals see Inst. 2. 5. 3 and 4.
[17] Dig. 7. 8. 10 pr. ; 33 2. 2.
[18] Arangio-Ruiz, p. 222.
[19] G. 2, 30.
[20] Dig. 7. 4. 5, 2 ; 8. 2. 20, 2.
[21] G. 3. 83.
[22] Dig. 7. 1. 56.

ususfructus). A grant of a usufruct for " so long as he lives," or for a definite term, was held to import a tacit renewal in the event of premature determination.[23]

253. ABNORMAL SERVITUDES.—Rights in the nature of personal servitudes might be created for a limited purpose, e.g., a right of passage or of taking water. They seem to resemble real servitudes, but are distinguished from them because they exist for the benefit of a person and not of a dominant tenement. They last no longer than the person entitled. But they are not merely contractual. They burden the land. The commentators call them abnormal or irregular servitudes. An English lawyer would call them easements or profits in gross. For instance, there is the case, mentioned in the Digest, of a legacy of a house together with a right of transit through other houses comprised in the inheritance.[24] This is described as a usus transeundi personae datus and contrasted with a legacy of a [real] servitude. Other texts speak of a " use of water." [25] Such rights being personal did not pass to heirs.

XII. RULES RELATING TO SERVITUDES IN GENERAL

254. Before leaving the subject of servitudes it may be well to direct attention to certain rules of general application to all servitudes, or, at least, to all real servitudes. They are these : —

(i) No one can have a servitude over his own property— nulli res sua servit.[26] Thus if I have a right of way over your field and acquire it by purchase, the right of way is extinguished, and does not revive if the field is again sold.[27] If I own two houses adjoining one another I may find it convenient to carry water from house A through a gutter on house B. That is, I make house B (in fact) servient to house A. If I sell house B can I claim to exercise a servitude over it without express reservation? The question is as old as the glossators. French Law allows the servitude. It is called a servitude ex destinatione patrisfamilias—par la destination du père de famille (" Destination du père de famille vaut titre ").[28]

---

[23] *Vat.* 63, 64 ; Dig. 7. 4. 1 ; 7. 4. 3.
[24] Dig. 33 3. 6.
[25] Dig. 7. 8. 21 ; 8. 3. 37.
[26] Dig. 8. 2. 26.
[27] Dig. 8. 4. 10.
[28] *C. C.* art. 692. For South African Law, see Lee, p. 174.

(ii) A servitude cannot consist in doing—servitus in faciendo consistere nequit. Servitude is a right to require the owner of the servient land to submit to something being done, or to abstain from doing something, on his own land—ut aliquid patiatur aut non faciat [29]—e.g., to allow me to go over his land (positive servitude), or not to build (negative servitude). He could not be called upon to do something except in the single case of the jus oneris ferendi, which placed upon the owner of the wall the duty of keeping it in repair.[30]

(iii) There cannot be a servitude of a servitude—servitus servitutis esse non potest.[31] Thus if I have a jus actus or a usufruct over your land I cannot create in favour of another a jus itineris (§ 237). The explanation is simple. A servitude is a burden on land. It cannot be laid on the land by one who is not the owner, or practically such (infra).

(iv) A servitude must be exercised civiliter, that is, in the way least burdensome to the owner of the land.[32]

(v) A servitude must have a perpetual cause.[33] This means that the thing over which the right is exercised, as well as the exercise of the right, must be capable of perpetual duration. There cannot be a servitude to take water from a pool or cistern, or, conversely, to discharge on to your land the waste water from my bath. But this does not prevent a servitude being limited to certain times and seasons, e.g., exercisable at certain times of the day or on alternate days.[34] In another sense a servitude must admit of perpetual duration, viz., that it can be created only by a dominus, or at least an emphyteuticarius or a superficiarius (§§ 256, 257), not by a usufructuary or a lessee. Though in strict law a real servitude could not be constituted from a fixed date, or to a fixed date or subject to a condition (ex tempore, ad tempus, sub conditione), any such qualifications of the grant were upheld by the praetor's jurisdiction.[35] Personal servitudes were free from these restrictions.

(vi) Remedies. The law gave for the protection of servitudes remedies the same as or analogous to those given for the protection of ownership. The actio confessoria asserting a servitude (§ 694) was a kind of vindication. For the denial of a servitude there was a corresponding negative action (actio

[29] Dig. 8. 1. 15, 1.
[30] Dig. 8. 5. 6, 2.
[31] Dig. 33. 2. 1. Qu. a usufruct of a usufruct? Girard, p. 391, n. 2.
[32] Dig. 8. 1. 9; C. C. art. 683.
[33] Dig. 8. 2. 28.
[34] Dig. 8. 1. 5, 1.
[35] Dig. 8. 1. 4 pr.

negatoria). The usual possessory remedies or variants of them were also available.[36]

THE INSTITUTES

BOOK II (Tits. IV and V)

TITLE IV

Of usufruct

Usufruct is the right to use and take the fruits of another man's property, the substance remaining unimpaired. For it is a right over a corporeal thing; if the thing disappears, the right necessarily disappears with it. §245.

1. Usufruct is separated from ownership in many ways. For example, by leaving a legacy of a usufruct; in which case the heir has the bare ownership the legatee the usufruct; conversely, if a testator bequeaths land with a deduction of the usufruct, the legatee has the bare ownership, the heir the usufruct; again the usufruct may be left to one person, the land, less the usufruct, to another. If it is desired to constitute a usufruct *inter vivos*, it must be done by pacts and stipulations. But in order that ownership may not be rendered valueless by the usufruct being for ever detached from it, the law provides that in certain events the usufruct shall be extinguished and re-absorbed in the ownership. §251.

2. There may be a usufruct not only of land and houses, but also of slaves or beasts, or of anything else, except things which are consumed in the use, for natural reason as well as civil law declares them not to be susceptible of usufruct; such are wine, oil, wheat, clothes; to which may be added coined money, for this too in a way is consumed in the use by passing from hand to hand. But in view of practical convenience, the senate has ordained that a usufruct can be constituted over such things, on condition of security being given to the heir. Accordingly, if there is a legacy of a usufruct of money, the money is paid over to the legatee and becomes his property, and the legatee gives the heir security for the return of an equivalent sum in the event of his death or capitis deminutio. Other things are similarly delivered to the legatee and become his property, but their value is assessed and security given for the return of the assessed value in the same events. The result is that the senate did not indeed create a usufruct of such things, for that was impossible, but by requiring security has made them susceptible of a quasi-usufruct. §246.

3. Usufruct is determined by the death of the usufructuary and by capitis deminutio maxima and media, and by failing for the statutory term to take advantage of the usufruct as constituted. All this is contained in our constitution.[37] Again, usufruct is determined if it is ceded by the usufructuary to the owner of the property (cession to a stranger has no effect): or, conversely, if the usufructuary acquires the ownership (consolidatio). Further, it is settled §252.

[36] Buckl. *M.* pp. 161, 165.
[37] Cod. 3. 33. 16.

that a usufruct of a house is extinguished if the house is burnt down or destroyed by earthquake or falls into ruin; there does not remain a usufruct even of the site.

4. When a usufruct is determined, it reverts to the owner of the property, who has from that time on full rights of ownership.

TITLE V

Of use and habitation

Usus (the bare use of a thing) is constituted and extinguished in the same ways as usufruct.

1. Use is a right of less extent than usufruct.

§ 248.

If one has the bare use of land, this is understood not to go further than taking vegetables, fruit, flowers, hay, straw and fuel for daily use, and the usuary is only allowed to remain on the land, so long as this is not inconvenient to the owner and does not interfere with the work of agriculture; and he may not make over his right to

§ 247.

another by way of sale or hire or gift, whereas a usufructuary may do all these things.

2. Again, one who has the use of a house may occupy it himself, but may not transfer his right of occupation to any one else; and the law has only reluctantly admitted that he may receive a guest and live in the house with his wife and children and slaves and servants; if a woman has the use of a house, she may live in it with her husband.

3. If a person has the use of a slave, he may employ his services, but he may not transfer his right to another. The same applies to the use of beasts of burden.

4. If the use of cattle or of sheep is left by will, the legatee has no right to the milk, or the lambs or the wool, for all these things are fruits. He may, of course, use the cattle to dung his land.

§ 249.

5. If a right of habitation is left by legacy or created in any other way, it seems to be neither use nor usufruct, but a distinct right. In the interest of practical convenience we have decided in accordance with the opinion of Marcellus [38] that persons who have the right of habitation may not only live in the house themselves, but also let the right to others.[39]

6. So much, then, of servitudes, and usufruct, use and habitation. We shall speak of inheritance and obligations in their proper place. We have given a summary account of the modes of acquisition jure gentium, let us now see how things are acquired by statutory and civil law methods.[40]

XIII. OTHER JURA IN RE ALIENA

255. In the preceding sections and the relevant Titles of the Institutes attention has been directed to one jus in re

---

[38] *Vid. sup. ad* Inst. 1. 4 pr.
[39] Cod. 3. 33. 13, 1.
[40] These topics have been dealt with above.

aliena, namely Servitude.   Other institutions may properly be
included under the same description, *viz.*, Emphyteusis and
Superficies and the forms of real security described as pignus
and hypotheca.   These topics are not systematically treated
in the Institutes.   We shall give a short account of them and
take occasion to say something of the Roman theory of
possession.   The Roman real security, as will be seen, in the
older law was not actually a jus in re aliena, for it took the
form of a conveyance of ownership with a pact to reconvey
if the debt to be secured was duly satisfied.   The Roman Law
of mortgage, therefore, if the description may be allowed, will
be found to include the earlier institution of mancipatio or
in jure cessio cum fiducia as well as its later developments
pignus and hypotheca.

XIV. EMPHYTEUSIS—SUPERFICIES

256. Emphyteusis [41] had two lines of ancestry, one Roman,
one Greek.   Under the early Empire it was the practice of
municipal authorities in Italy and elsewhere (less often of the
State) to grant leases of agricultural land in perpetuity or for
a long term of years conditionally on the payment of an annual
rent.   The rent was termed vectigal and land so granted was
called ager vectigalis.   The grantee was not owner of the land,
but in course of time came to be treated very much as if he
were.   The law protected his interest by giving him an action
in the nature of a vindication (actio vectigalis) to get possession
of the property from the owner or from any third party, and,
in addition, the usual possessory interdicts.   Another source of
the institution is to be found in grants made in the Greek States
under the name of emphyteusis, a Greek word meaning
" grafting " or " planting."   In the later Empire the word was
applied, generally, to all leases in perpetuity or for a long term
of years, and the institution was greatly developed.   Grants of
this character were made not only by the Emperor and public
authorities (usually of barren lands to be brought into cultivation), but also by private persons, and in particular by great
landed proprietors, ecclesiastical and civil.   But the nature of
the interest of the grantee remained undefined.   It was a
question whether he was to be regarded as a lessee or a purchaser.   The doubt was resolved by the Emperor Zeno who
decided that emphyteusis was neither hire nor sale, but a

---

[41] Girard, pp. 411 *et seq.*; Buckl. *T.* p. 275; *M.* p. 166.

contract of a special character, governed by its own rules.[42]
By this time the older ager vectigalis had faded out of sight.
Justinian in the rubric of Digest vi. 3 identifies the earlier and
the later institution—si ager vectigalis id est emphyteuticarius
petatur. The juristic position of the later emphyteuta was
much the same as that of the holder of the ager vectigalis.
He was similarly aided by action and interdict. His interest
passed to his heirs and was alienable subject to the proprietor's
right of pre-emption, or, in the alternative, of claiming a fine
of 2 *per cent.* of the purchase price. He held conditionally
on the payment of an annual quitrent (canon) and the duty
of keeping the land in cultivation. If he failed in these
particulars he might be ejected; in case of non-payment of
rent, as Justinian enacted, if the rent was three years in
arrear.[43]

257. Contrary to English Law, which permits separate
ownership of horizontal strata (as in Lincoln's Inn, where a
set of chambers on the ground floor may be owned by one
tenant in fee while the floor above is owned by another tenant
in fee), the Roman Law admitted no departure from the
principle *cujus est solum ejus est usque ad sidera et ad inferos*
and the allied rule *superficies solo cedit.* Therefore, no one
could own the surface except as owning the land.

> "If in a conveyance of land the alienor purports to convey
> the soil apart from the surface, this does not prevent the surface
> passing with the soil, for by its nature it is one with it." [44]

But this did not exclude the possibility of a jus in re exercised
over the surface. From an early date such a right was
admitted under the name of superficies, the person entitled to
it being known as superficiarius.[45] This was a right to the
enjoyment of a house built upon another person's land, either
in perpetuity or for a long term of years. The institution
originated in the case of erections set up by, or by permission
of, the magistrates upon land belonging to the State.[46] It
was adopted by towns in the form of what today would be
called building leases, and finally by private citizens. The
tenant paid a ground-rent called solarium. He had the benefit
of an interdict called the interdictum de superficie modelled

---

[42] G. 3. 145; Inst. 3. 24. 3; Cod. 4. 66. 1.
[43] Cod. 4. 66. 2.
[44] Dig. 44. 7. 44, 1.
[45] Dig. 43. 18; Girard, p. 411; Buckl. *T.* p. 276.
[46] *e.g.,* bankers' booths. Dig. 18. 1. 32.

upon the interdict uti possidetis (§ 772), and other remedies, in particular a praetorian action in rem in the nature of a vindication.

XV. REAL SECURITIES [47]

(Fiducia—Pignus—Hypotheca)

258. By a real security is meant a real right created to secure the performance of an obligation. It corresponds in general with what in English Law is called a mortgage. In Roman Law it assumed one of three forms: 1, transfer of ownership with a condition of re-transfer if the obligation was discharged; 2, transfer of possession, but not of ownership; 3, charge on property without transfer of either. The corresponding institutions are mancipatio (or in jure cessio) cum fiducia, pignus and hypotheca.

259. Mancipatio (or in jure cessio) cum fiducia.[48] This was a formal conveyance of property accompanied by an agreement as to the terms on which it was to be held (fiducia, § 523). These would include an undertaking to reconvey, if the debt was discharged. Originally, no doubt, as in the common law mortgage, failure to discharge a debt on the agreed date confirmed ownership (which had already passed by the conveyance) permanently and irrevocably in the creditor, but in the classical period this consequence did not follow unless there was an agreement to that effect (lex commissoria). It was more usual to authorise the creditor to realise his security by selling the property. As owner, it was in any event competent to him to do so and the right of sale could not be wholly withheld from him,[49] but it might be regulated, and if he sold contrary to the terms of the agreement he exposed himself to the debtor's actio fiduciae, in which condemnation involved infamia. This institution was in existence in the classical period of Roman Law. With the discontinuance of the formal methods of conveyance it passed out of use and Justinian's commissioners expunged all reference to it from the classical texts cited in the Digest. A very small oversight betrayed their handiwork. In a passage which speaks (or is made to speak) of pignus the pronoun which refers to it is " eam " not " id," a sure indication that the neuter noun pignus has been substituted for the

G. 4. 182.

---

[47] Girard, p. 814; Buckl. *T.* p. 473; *M.* 353.
[48] Girard, pp. 552 *et seq.*, 814; Buckl. *T.* 431, 474; *M.* 260, 353.
[49] Paul. *Sent.* 2. 13. 5.

feminine noun fiducia (*supra*, § 45). This was the starting point of a scholarly reconstruction of the history of Roman mortgage.

260. Pignus (pledge or pawn). This means the handing over of movable or immovable property by way of security. In the Institutes it is described amongst the contracts *re* (§ 437). but its aspect as a real right only receives incidental notice. The explanation given is that the Romans did not regard it as such but this has not deterred the moderns from treating it (and rightly) as a jus in re aliena. The pledgee had juristic possession (§ 267), and the advantage of the usual interdicts for retaining and recovering possession (§ 765) as well as the special interdict and action mentioned in the next section. Ususcapion-possession (§ 267) remained with the pledgor.[50] Originally, the creditor, like the pledgee in English Law, had merely the right to retain the property until his claim was satisfied, but no right of sale apart from agreement.[51] Later, a right of sale was taken to be implied unless expressly excluded.[52] In Justinian's law the parties might make their own terms as to time and conditions of sale,[53] short of excluding it altogether, which was not allowed.[54] In the absence of agreement as to sale, the creditor might sell after three notices or judicial sentence and two years' delay. If he could not find a purchaser he might petition the Emperor for an order allowing him to possess the property as owner[55] (impetratio dominii), but even after the order had been made the debtor still had a further two years within which to redeem.[56] The right to foreclose could no longer be a term in the contract, the lex commissaria having been prohibited by Constantine.[57]

261. Hypotheca was a real security created by mere agreement without delivery. It seems to have come into use in connection with the hire of land. It was usual to agree that the instruments of husbandry and the cattle on the land should be security for the rent, and similarly the rent of house property was secured by a hypothec of the furniture (invecta et illata). In the first case the praetor gave the landlord an interdict (interdictum Salvianum) to get possession of the property in

---

[50] Dig. 41. 3. 16; 41. 2. 36.
[51] Dig. 47. 2. 74 (73) (Javolenus); G. 2. 64; Inst. 2. 8. 1.
[52] Dig. 13. 7. 4 (Ulpian).
[53] Cod. 8. 33 (34). 3, 1.
[54] Dig. *ibid. in fine* (interpolated); Paul. *Sent.* 2. 13. 5.
[55] Cod. 8. 33 (34). In English law this is termed " foreclosure."
[56] Dig. 41. 1. 63. 4; Cod. 8. 33 (34). 3, 3.
[57] Cod. 8. 34 (35). 3.

the hands of the tenant [58] and later an action (actio Serviana) 4. 6. 7. to follow the property and recover it from the debtor or any third person. The principle of pledge without possession once admitted, the action was extended to house-tenants and finally to every other case in which the property was charged as a security without or with delivery.[59] This went far to eliminate any difference between pignus and hypotheca. In fact Marcian says that there was no difference between them except the sound of the words.[60] However, Ulpian, and Justinian after him, say that, if the words are used exactly, pignus implies transfer of possession, hypotheca not.[61] It must not be inferred from the use of the word hypotheca that the Roman hypothec was of Greek origin. Pledge without possession was a natural outgrowth of the Roman pignus ; the use of the Greek word to describe it came later.

262. The same property might be pledged (in the wide sense of the word) to two or more persons successively and every one of them was entitled, if he could, to have the benefit of the security. Apart from numerous cases of statutory privilege, in particular the privilege of the fiscus, successive incumbrances ranked in order of priority. Qui prior est tempore, potior est jure.[62] The first mortgagee alone could sell. He held the proceeds, after satisfying his own claim, in trust for subsequent incumbrancers. A later mortgagee might buy out an earlier one and step into his shoes. This was called the jus offerendi or jus offerendae pecuniae.

263. Legal or tacit hypothecs. Besides the conventional hypothecs above described, there were a great number of legal or tacit hypothecs, that is hypothecs created by law, either general, affecting the debtor's property in general, or special, affecting some property in particular. An instance of a general hypothec is the charge which the law created in favour of a pupil or minor over the whole of the tutor's or curator's estate (§ 136), or in favour of a legatee over the whole of the testator's estate in the hands of the heir (§ 349). An instance of a special

---

[58] G. 4. 147 ; Inst. 4. 15. 3.

[59] Under the names of actio pigneraticia in rem, actio hypothecaria and actio quasi Serviana the actio Serviana enlarged its original boundaries. It is not known whether the interdictum Salvianum equally did so.

[60] Dig. 20. 1. 5, 1 ; Inter pignus et hypothecam tantum nominis sonus differt.

[61] Dig. 13 7. 9, 2 : Proprie pignus dicimus quod ad creditorem transit, hypothecam cum non transit nec possessio ad creditorem.

[62] Cod. 8. 17 (18). 2 : Nam cum de pignore utraque pars contendat, praevalet jure qui praevenit tempore.

hypothec is the tacit hypothec given to a person who had spent money in repairing another person's house or ship. The landlord's hypothec, referred to above, developed into a tacit hypothec over the fruits in the case of land, and over the invecta et illata in the case of a house. Anything beyond this had to be the subject of agreement.

264. A real security might be extinguished as a consequence of the extinction of the principal debt secured by it, or independently. Amongst the latter modes of extinction the most important was release, which might be express, for which a bare agreement was sufficient,[63] or tacit. This would be the usual consequence of restoring a pledge to the debtor.[64]

Prescription was another mode of extinction. In the old law if a thing mancipated cum fiducia reverted to the owner, not under a contract of hire, or on sufferance (precario), and remained in his possession for a year, he re-acquired it by usucapion (usureceptio). This was a case of usucapio lucrativa (§§ 175, 523). Acquisition of ownership by usucapio did not extinguish a hypothec any more than a servitude.[65] But under the Empire acquisition of ownership by longi temporis praescriptio and under Justinian by longissimi temporis praescriptio had this effect (§§ 178, 180). The debtor himself was safe from attack if he had remained in possession with the passive acquiescence of the creditor for forty years.[66]

265. Charges on land created by bare agreement without delivery of possession and the numerous tacit hypothecs imposed upon it in the later Empire were a grave embarrassment to purchasers as well as to subsequent mortgagees, and there was no adequate system of land registration which might have mitigated this inconvenience.[67] The Emperor Leo went some way towards removing it by giving a preference to hypothecs registered in court, or subscribed by three witnesses of good repute.[68] But in spite of this the later Roman Law of mortgage continued to be in the highest degree complicated and unsatisfactory.

XVI. Possession

266. It is evident that possession is not the same as ownership. You may own without possessing. You may possess

---

[63] Dig. 13. 7. 9, 3.
[65] Dig. 41. 3. 44, 5.
[66] Cod. 7. 39. 8 pr.; Cod. 7. 39. 7, 1.
[67] Arangio-Ruiz, p. 189.
[64] Cod. 8. 25 (26). 9, 1.
[68] Cod. 8. 17 (18). 11, 1.

without owning. Possession implies physical control and the exclusion of adverse possessors. This may exist in very various circumstances. The person to whom you have handed your watch to look at is in possession of it, so is the watch-maker with whom you have left it for repair, so is the pawnbroker with whom you have pledged it, so is the thief who has taken it from you. Possession, to begin with, is matter of fact, not of right, but it is a fact which the law protects, by giving a possessor, merely as such, a remedy against another who disturbs him in his possession, or deprives him of it. In the Roman Law this takes the form of what is called the interdict procedure.

267. But the law will scarcely extend its protection to the possession (as distinct from the person) of every casual possessor. A line must be drawn. English Law gives a possessory remedy to any possessor who is not merely a servant. The Roman Law stops short of this. It protects the possession of the owner, of the bona fide and mala fide possessor, but not of one who holds under a contract as depositary, borrower, mandatory, hirer and so forth. From this there results a distinction between a higher and a lower degree of possession. The latter we describe as natural possession or detention. The Romans called it in possessione esse—naturalis possessio. The former we call interdict possession or juristic possession. The texts call it possessio merely, sometimes (perhaps by interpolation) possessio civilis.

It follows from this that the two kinds of possession may co-exist. If I, the owner, lend you my horse, I retain the juristic possession, you acquire the natural possession. But if you appropriate the horse to your own use, you have ousted me from possession and made the juristic possession your own.[69] There is yet another degree of possession, namely the possession which by lapse of time ripens into ownership (sometimes described as possessio ad usucapionem, § 173). This seems to be what the writers of the classical age commonly mean when they speak of possessio civilis.[70]

268. What is the meaning of the distinction in Roman Law between the two degrees of possession? According to the doctrine associated with the name of Savigny it is a question of mental attitude. All possession has two elements, a physical and a mental, which the Romans distinguish as corpus and animus. The first is the physical relation of the possessor to

---

[69] Dig. 41. 2. 3, 18; 20
[70] Buckl. T. p. 197; M. p. 120.

the object. The second is his sense of that relation. If he
is minded to deal with the thing as his own (animus domini—
animus sibi habendi), no matter whether rightfully or wrongfully, he possesses in the fullest sense, and is entitled to the
interdicts ; when he is not so minded, he has detention merely
without the use of the interdicts.

269. But there are cases which do not accommodate themselves to this classification. The emphyteuta (§ 256), the
superficiarius (§ 257), the pledgee (§ 260), the precario tenens
(§ 525) and the sequester (§ 436) have interdict possession,
though they have not the animus sibi habendi. These are cases
in which a dominus has parted with possession, but not with
ownership. Savigny gives them the name of derivative possession (abgeleiteter Besitz). In all four cases the animus of the
possessor is directed not to the exercise of dominium but to the
assertion of a right to possess derived from a previous possessor.
They are exceptions from the general rule and require explanation. They are explained on historical grounds, or on grounds
of necessity or convenience.

270. So far we have assumed the correctness of Savigny's
description of the animus required to constitute possession
(stricto sensu) as being the animus sibi habendi—the will to hold
as owner. But Ihering opposes to this " subjective theory " of
possession his own " objective theory " of possession. According
to this, intention is irrelevant to the distinction between detention
and possession. Any person has, in principle, possession, i.e.,
interdict possession, who consciously holds a thing whether for
himself or for another. If in any case a person so holding is
not a " possessor," it must be either because the thing in question
cannot in law be " possessed "—e.g., a res extra commercium, or
because the law for some reason does not accord " possession."
Such was the case with the contract of loan, mandate and the
like, the result of a development from a nucleus in the Roman
family, whose subordinate members might detain, but could not
" possess." It will be remarked that either theory must take
account of exceptions. But what is normal for Savigny (the
denial of possession to the borrower, mandatory, etc.) is exceptional for Ihering, and what for Savigny is exceptional (the
" possession " of the emphyteuta, etc.) for Ihering is normal.

271. Savigny's theory rests principally upon texts of Paulus
cited in the Digest. Ihering maintains that this jurist's views
were peculiar to himself and erroneous, and, besides, have been

misinterpreted. Not to embark upon a discussion which lies outside the scope of this book, we may be content to say that the Romans undoubtedly made use of the interdict procedure long before they had any theory of possession. Convenience, not logical consistency, determined the limits of its application. The classical jurists themselves had no single theory of possession. The Digest reflects their differences of opinion, as well as later doctrinal developments interpolated in the text.

272. Incorporeal things could not be possessed, but a usufructuary had in fact control of the property comprised in the usufruct, and if the law did not attribute to him juristic possession,[71] it allowed him the use of the usual possessory interdicts. If he had not possession, he had quasi-possession (possessio juris)[72] and the same reasoning was applied to praedial servitudes, to inheritance, and to a constantly increasing number of rights.[73] In the later law the principle that incorporeal things could not be possessed was an abstract dogma without practical significance. The quasi-possessor enjoyed the use of the usual interdicts or of special interdicts adapted to the particular case.

XVII. Summary

273. The topics which for convenience of treatment we have included under the description of "The Law of Property," so far as they find a place in Justinian's Institutes, belong to the very much more comprehensive class the Jus quod ad res pertinet. They form the subject of Titles I to VIII of Book II, which deal with little else than Ownership and Servitudes. This meagre record we have enlarged by including other jura in re aliena as well as an account of dos and possession. Dos might seem to be more at home in the Law of Persons, but since the compilers of the Institutes have not seen fit to consider it as part of the Law of Marriage, there is some excuse for assigning it to a context in which they have something to say about it, though not very much.

For Gaius, writing in the second century A.D., ownership meant primarily Roman ownership of Roman property, secured by the civil law action called vindicatio rei, in which the plaintiff, claiming a thing as his by quiritary title, sought to recover it from any wrongful possessor. A provincial might

---

[71] Dig. 41. 1. 10, 5.
[72] G. 4. 139.
[73] Arangio-Ruiz, Istituzioni, pp. 279 et seq.

hold land and be secured in its possession by an analogous
action, but he could not claim Roman ownership ; first, because,
generally, he was not a Roman citizen, and, secondly, because
provincial lands could not be privately owned, being deemed to
belong to the Roman People or to the Emperor (*supra*, p. 111).
The first obstacle was removed when Caracalla extended
citizenship to the whole Empire, and the second might be
thought to have become meaningless when Diocletian included
Italy within the provincial system and imposed the land-tax upon
Italian soil.   However, tradition was too strong for logic, and
more than two and a half centuries elapsed before Justinian
declared that the old distinctions had ceased to have any
meaning.[74]

In the field of servitude the triumph of provincial practice
over Roman tradition was complete.   The oldest praedial servitudes were res mancipi and could be created by mancipation as
well as by cessio in jure.   All other servitudes, real and personal,
could be constituted by cessio in jure.   In the provinces
servitudes of whatever kind were constituted by pacts and
stipulations and long before Justinian this had been applied to
all servitudes without distinction.

There were many cases of vindication besides the vindicatio
rei, such as vindicatio servitutis, to which Justinian gave the
name of actio confessoria, vindicatio ususfructus, vindicatio in
servitutem, vindicatio in libertatem.   The actio negativa or
negatoria denying the existence of a servitude has given some
difficulty.   According to Buckland it is a vindication with a
denial of the servitude.[75]

APPENDIX

INFLUENCE OF THE ROMAN LAW OF PROPERTY ON MODERN SYSTEMS

274. This concludes what we have to say on the Roman Law of
Property.   We shall not invite the student to travel far in what may
seem to him the wilderness of comparative law.   But something may
fitly be said about the impact of this branch of Roman Law on
modern systems.

(i) *Ownership in general.*   Rome has transmitted her conception
of ownership to the modern world.   It is not surprising,
therefore, that countries with a Roman Law background have
made use of its rules in framing their codes.   The Law of
Nations has done the same, with the result that " those parts

[74] Cod. 7. 25. 1 ; Biondi, *Istituzioni* (2) p. 208.
[75] Buckl. *T.* p. 676 ; *M.* p. 161 ; 30 L.Q.R. 447.

of the international system which refer to dominion, its nature, its limitations, the modes of acquiring and securing it are pure Roman Property Law."[76]   English Law has taken its own course, its debt to Roman Law for the most part forgotten or unacknowledged.

(ii) *Conveyance of land.* We have seen that the classical Roman Law made little difference between transfer of land and transfer of movables by delivery (§ 151). The Institutes of Gaius and of Justinian indicate no distinction. It was only in the Byzantine period that it became usual to record transfers of land in a public register (§ 210). In the Middle Ages feudalism together with the customary laws of the German nations and the survival of the Roman traditio per cartam engendered a vast variety of usage which has been replaced by various systems of land registration. In Holland this was made general by a law of the Emperor Charles V in 1529, which is the historical parent of the South African Registry of Deeds.[77]   England lags behind, and has no general system of land registration in actual use.

(iii) *Long continued possession.* This is generally, if the necessary conditions are satisfied, a title to property, but not in England (except in the matter of servitudes). By English Law, in the case of land, twelve years' adverse possession extinguishes the right of the original owner but does not give a positive title to the possessor. Possession of movables, however long continued, never gives title. The right to sue for their recovery is statute-barred by a term of six years, but that is another matter.[78]

(iv) *Servitudes.* The Roman Law of servitudes has left its mark on the modern law. In all civil law systems usufruct is the normal method of creating a life interest, and the praedial servitudes have a Roman complexion. Servitude is not a term of art in English Law, though it occurs in the Reports. Partly through Bracton and partly through texts of the Digest cited by Gale in his classic work on *Easements*, the rules of the Roman Law have " helped materially " to the making of the modern law.[79]

(v) *Mortgage.* Until 1926 the English mortgage of land was in form not very different from the Roman mancipatio cum fiducia (§ 259), but had been wholly transformed, in effect, by the equity of redemption. The forms of legal mortgage of land are now statutory. A mortgage of movables is effected (a) by transferring the ownership, but not usually the possession, by way of security for the payment of money (bills of sale), or (b) by transferring the possession, but not the ownership (pawn or pledge). French Law arrives at similar results. It distinguishes hypothecation of immovables with registration and pledge (*gage*) of movables with delivery. In a limited

[76] Maine, *Ancient Law*, p. 104.
[77] Lee, p. 139.
[78] Nor is the law altered by the Limitation Act, 1939.
[79] Holdsworth, vii, 324.

number of cases movables can be pledged without delivery, but with conditions calculated to secure publicity.

(vi) *Possession.* The French Law is substantially Roman. The German and Swiss codes reject the Roman theory of possession and in this respect at least are nearer to English Law. In French Law *en fait de meubles la possession vaut titre* (in the matter of movables possession is equivalent to title). This recalls the old adage mobilia non habent sequelam—movables cannot be followed. By the French Civil Code: (a) if I have parted with the possession of a corporeal movable voluntarily, as to a borrower, I cannot recover it from a third party who possesses in good faith; (b) if I have lost it or if it has been stolen from me, I can recover it within three years, but not later.[80] The principle that movables cannot be followed is commonly said to be Germanic. In fact it existed in the laws of some but not all of the German nations. After the reception (§ 37) it was displaced by the Roman rule, ubi rem meam invenio ibi vindico (I vindicate my property where I find it). It was called back to life by the German Commercial Code of 1861 and adopted in the Civil Code of 1900.[81]

In English Law a bona fide possessor is (exceptions apart) exposed to an action of detinue or conversion until time has run in his favour.

---

[80] *C. C.* art. 2279.
[81] *B. G. B.* art. 932.

BOOK III

THE LAW OF SUCCESSION

I. SUCCESSION (IN GENERAL)

275. After treating of the modes of acquisition of single things Justinian goes on to speak of the modes of acquisition per universitatem, that is of the ways in which all the property 2. 9. 6. of one person passed to another including, or together with, all transmissible rights and duties. Far the most important of these was inheritance, which is defined by Julian " as succession to the whole right of a deceased person " [1]; a phrase which must be understood to include whole liability as well. This took place equally under a will and upon intestacy, and the results were substantially the same, whether the succession devolved by civil law, or, under the name of possession of goods (bonorum possessio), was conferred by the praetor. The great importance of succession in the early law was its connection with religion. G. 2. 55. It was necessary that some one should replace the deceased in performing the duties of the family worship. At a later date another point of view asserted itself, namely, that creditors should know who to look to for payment of debts.

276. There can be no doubt that in the earliest times testamentary succession as we understand it was unknown to the Romans (or to the stock from which they came) as it was unknown to the ancient Greeks and Germans. But we have no historical knowledge of such a state of things. The peculiarity of the Roman Law is that it developed the institution and regarded it as normal from an epoch which, in comparison with other systems of law, was relatively early. From the earliest times of which we have any record testamentary disposition in one form or another was permitted. The Law of the Twelve Tables recognised it as already in existence.[2]

Institutes, II. 9. 6.

This may serve for the present as regards the modes of acquisition of single things, for legacies and fideicommissa, by

---

[1] Dig. 50. 17. 62.
[2] Girard, p. 842.

§ 402.

which also single things are acquired, will be more conveniently
considered below. Let us now investigate the modes of universal
acquisition. If you are made any one's heir or claim possession
of a deceased person's goods, or adrogate anyone, or if a
deceased person's goods are assigned to you in order to preserve
the liberty of slaves, in all these cases such person's property
passes to you in its entirety. Let us first consider inheritances,
which may come to you either under a will, or upon an
intestacy. We will speak first of testamentary inheritance, and
begin by explaining how wills are made.

II. Testamentary Succession

277. To speak, first, of testamentary succession, there are
three principal requisites for the validity of a Roman will,
viz.: —

   I. There must be a will valid *ab initio*;
   II. It must remain valid until the heir enters upon the
       inheritance;
   III. The heir must duly enter.

I. Initial validity of the Roman will. To constitute a will
valid *ab initio*: A. The will must be made in proper form;
B. An heir or heirs must be duly instituted; C. Testator, heir
and witnesses must have testamentary competence; D. Certain
persons must be either instituted or disinherited.[3]

III. The Formal Requirements of the Roman Will

278. The following types of will were in use at different
periods of Roman Law: —

(1) Testament made before the comitia (testamentum
comitiis calatis). The comitia curiata met twice in the year for
the purpose of making wills, and when it did so was known
as comitia calata.[4] It seems probable that this type of will
was, like adrogatio, a legislative act of the Roman People.
There is in fact a close parallelism between the two institutions.
As adrogatio effected an adoption inter vivos, so this testament
effected an adoption mortis causa. Perhaps, originally, in the
second case, as in the first, the design was to provide for the
continuation of the family in the absence of male issue, and it
may also have served to prefer one son to others as family
successor.

---

[3] Hunter, p. 766.
[4] *i.e.*, called or summoned.

279. (2) Testament made before the army (testamentum in procinctu). The word procinctus, Gaius says,[5] means "the army ready for battle," and this will was made "when the men were arming for battle." It consisted, as we learn from other sources, in a declaration made before a few comrades in the interval between the first and second taking of the auspices.[6] It was more limited in its application than the later military will, for it was only made in the circumstances described. Both these types of will passed out of use before the end of the Republic.

280. (3) Testament by bronze and balance (testamentum per aes et libram). This was an adaptation to the purpose of will-making of the mancipatory sale (§ 158). This is what Gaius says about it:—

> "Then there came to be a third kind of testament which is
> effected by bronze and balance; for if a person had not made his
> will in the comitia calata or in procinctu and was overtaken by
> the sudden menace of death he would mancipate his familia,
> that is his patrimony, to a friend and give instructions as to what
> he wanted given to each person after his death. This is called
> the testament per aes et libram because it is effected by manci-
> pation. The first two kinds of will have passed out of use, but
> the third kind remains in force. However, it has quite changed
> its character. Formerly the familiae emptor, that is the person
> to whom the familia was mancipated, was in the position of heir,
> and that is why he received the testator's instructions as to what
> he wanted to go to each person after his death. But nowadays
> an heir is instituted by the will and charged with the payment of
> legacies, and another person comes in as familiae emptor to
> maintain the tradition of the old law, but merely as a matter of
> form."

G. 2. 103.

281. The mancipatory testament then consisted originally in the mancipation of a person's whole estate by act inter vivos to another person called the purchaser of the estate (familiae emptor). It was a public and irrevocable act of disposition by which the property vested immediately in the transferee subject to the duty, at first moral rather than legal, of disposing of it according to the testator's instructions and of discharging his debts. Later it changed its character. The familiae emptor became merely a figure-head, the real heir being named in a written instrument, which was not made public until after the testator's death.

In its developed form the process was as follows:—

G. 2. 104.

(a) The testator commits his will to writing on tablets of wax; (b) in the presence of five witnesses, Roman citizens

---

[5] G. 2. 101.   [6] Jolowicz, p. 126.

above the age of puberty, and a balance-holder (libripens) mancipates the inheritance to the familiae emptor, who, pronouncing a solemn formula, strikes the balance with a piece of bronze and hands it to the testator by way of price.

The formula was as follows: "Thy estate (familium pecuniamque) [I declare to be] at thy orders and in my keeping [7] and, that thou mayest lawfully make a testament according to the public statute, with this bronze (and as some add "with this bronze balance") be the same to me purchased." [8] The public statute is the Law of the Twelve Tables.

(c) The testator, holding the will in his hand, says: "As is written in these tablets of wax, so I give, so I bequeath, so I declare my will, and so do you, citizens, bear witness."

An alternative, but less frequent method, was for the testator to dispense with the tablets, and declare his will orally in the presence of the witnesses and the libripens. This implies some adaptation of the testator's declaration as given above. It was by a will of this kind that the dying Horace appointed Augustus his heir, "for he had not the strength to seal the tablets of the will." [9]

The mancipatory testament was not entirely superseded by the other forms to be presently mentioned. It continued to exist as a written instrument reciting the use of a ceremony, which in fact did not take place. [10]

282. The concise account which Gaius gives of the mancipatory will leaves much unexplained. It is clear that the other two forms of will were of limited use and that recourse was had to a device for which there are parallels in other times and other lands of making a disposition inter vivos take effect as a disposition mortis causa. Unlike the comitial will, the whole purpose of which was to institute an heir, the mancipatory will was at first a legacy will, that is, disposed of specific things comprised in the dead man's estate. It is at least possible that it had existed in practice before the Law of the Twelve Tables, and that the famous clause

G. 2. 224.   Uti legassit suae rei, ita jus esto

2. 22 pr.   "As a man has disposed of his property so be the law"

gave it formal recognition. Later—perhaps under the influence

---

[7] There is some uncertainty as to the precise words used at this point owing to imperfections in the Verona MS.
[8] G. 2. 104.   [9] Suetonius, *Vita Horatii*.   *Cf.* Dig. 28. 1. 21 pr.
[10] Buckl. *T.* p. 285.   The will of Antonius Silvanus, executed in Egypt in A.D. 142 (F.J.R.A. iii, No. 47) is a very perfect example of a mancipatory will.

of the priests, who would wish to focus the liability for the sacra—it became the means of disposing of the inheritance, and the familiae emptor became a useless formality.

283. All this is speculation. But so is everything which has been written on the subject of the early history of Roman wills. Contrary to the views expressed above it has been maintained on the one hand that the function of the People in the comitial will was not to authorise it, but to witness its execution, and on the other that like the early mancipatory will the comitial will was a legacy will, which did not appoint an heir, but merely charged legacies upon the heir *ab intestato*. If this is so, the testamentary institution of an heir was a development, which came into use only in the later phase of the mancipatory will.[11]

284. (4) The Praetorian Testament. Strictly speaking, this was not a testament, for " the praetor cannot make an heir," G. 3. 32. but he could give possession of the estate (bonorum possessio), which came to have substantially the same effect. The praetor disregarded the solemnities of mancipation and was satisfied with an instrument executed in the presence of seven witnesses, who 2. 10. 2. affixed their seals. The seven witnesses corresponded with the five witnesses of the mancipatory will together with the libripens and the familiae emptor, who having no longer an active part to play had sunk to the level of witnesses.[12] The sealing was not a praetorian innovation. Some unknown statute required it in the case of the mancipatory will, when committed to writing.[13] This was a necessary precaution in order to identify the instrument which the testator held in his hand at the moment of mancipation. The bonorum possessio granted by the praetor in these circumstances was at first provisional in character. It might be successfully challenged by the civil law heirs *ab intestato*. But a rescript of the Emperor Antonius Pius made it an effectual answer to their claims to the inheritance. In technical language it was at first sine re—without abiding effect. It became cum re—with abiding effect.[14]

285. (5) Testamentum Tripertitum. This was the will of the later Empire prescribed by the Emperors Theodosius II and Valentinian III in A.D. 439. It was called " tripartite " because it was derived from three sources:—(a) The whole will must be 2. 10. 3.

---

[11] Jolowicz discusses these questions pp. 125 *et seq.*
[12] Girard, p. 861, n. 2.
[13] Cicero (*in Verr.* 2. 1. 45) says that the Edict of his time required tabulas testamenti obsignatas non minus multis signis quam e lege oportet.
[14] G. 2. 119-20.

made at one and the same time (uno contextu) in the presence
of witnesses. This came from the civil law ; (b) the witnesses
must be seven in number and must seal the instrument. This
came from the praetor's Edict ; (c) the testator (or, if he is
illiterate, another for him) and the witnesses must subscribe the
will. This came from imperial constitutions. " Subscribing "
meant something more than signing. It was the practice for the
testator to make a formal acknowledgment of the will. The
word " subscripsi "—I " have subscribed "—was enough, though
other formulae might be employed. Similar declarations in
writing were made by the witnesses. The document was then
enclosed in a wrapper and sealed on the outside by the
witnesses, who set their names against their respective seals
(superscriptiones).[15]

2. 10. 14.   286. (6) Nuncupative will. This was a declaration in the
presence of seven witnesses replacing the oral mancipatory will
(§ 281). It may have been allowed jure praetorio before
Justinian gave it the effect of a civil law will.[16]

287. (7) Abnormal or irregular wills. There were, besides
the above, a number of types of will applicable only to special
classes of persons, or in special circumstances. In most of
these the usual formalities were relaxed or dispensed with, but
2. 11.   in some additional formalities were required. The most important of these was the military will, to be distinguished from
the old testamentum in procinctu. This, introduced by Julius
Caesar as a temporary concession,[17] became an established
institution in the early Empire. A soldier (but, as Justinian
2. 11 pr.   enacted, only when on active service) might make his will as
he pleased and as he could ; it might be in a written instrument ;
it might be by an oral declaration in the presence of two or
three comrades, it might be by tracing characters in his blood
on scabbard or shield, or with sword in the dust.[18] Such a
will, if the testator survived, remained valid for a year after
honourable discharge from service. There were other cases in
which the usual forms were dispensed with, viz., a will made in
time of pestilence (witnesses need not be together at the same
time) ; will made in the country (five witnesses sufficient) ; will
of a parent disposing of property amongst his children (if
holograph, i.e., written wholly in testator's hand, no witnesses

---

[15] Girard, p. 863 ; Buckl. T. p. 287, n. 1 ; and especially Roby I. 181.
[16] Cod. 6. 23. 26, In testamentis sine scriptis faciendis omnem
formalem observationem penitus amputamus. Earlier texts are interpolated.
Girard, p. 862, n. 4.
[17] Dig. 29. 1 pr.   [18] Cod. 6. 21. 15, 1.

required). On the other hand, the will of a blind man required an eighth witness, the town secretary (tabularius) if available.[19]

288. (8) Finally, the later Empire admitted two public declarations of a man's last will, viz., a testament executed before a magistrate and lodged in court, and a testament presented to the Emperor.

THE INSTITUTES

BOOK II (Tits. X and XI)

TITLE X

Of the execution of wills

A testament is so called because it is evidence of a man's state of mind (testatio mentis).[20]

1. Not to neglect altogether our earliest institutions, it must be known that anciently there were two kinds of testament, of which one, known as the testamentum calatis comitiis was used in time of peace, the other termed procinctum [21] when men were making ready for battle. Then a third kind of testament came into use, which was known as the testament by bronze and balance; so called because it was effected by means of a mancipation, that is an imaginary sale, in the presence of five witnesses and a balance-holder, Roman citizens above the age of puberty, and another person known as the familiae emptor. The first two of these methods passed out of use in very early times: the third has persisted longer, but this too is partly disused.[22]   § 278.   § 280.

2. The above-mentioned types of will were creations of the civil law. Later, the praetor's edict introduced another way of making wills, for the jus honorarium did not require any mancipation, but were satisfied with the seals of seven witnesses, which by the civil law were not necessary.[23]   § 284.

3. Gradually, however, partly by usage, partly by imperial constitutions, the civil law and the praetorian law were brought into harmony, and it was enacted that testaments should be made at one and the same time (which was required in a way by the civil law), with seven subscribing witnesses (an innovation of the imperial constitutions), and the seals of the witnesses (in accordance with the praetor's edict) so that the law on this subject seems to be derived from three sources. The witnesses and their being present all at   § 285.

---

[19] Inst. 2. 12. 4; Cod. 6. 22. 8.
[20] A singularly absurd etymology.
[21] More correctly " in procinctu " (supra, § 279).
[22] This seems an understatement. The ceremonial part had been long since abolished. It became a question of a few words in a written instrument (§ 281).
[23] But see above, § 284.

once come from the civil law, the subscriptions of testator [24] and witnesses from the sacred constitutions, the sealing and the number of the witnesses from the praetor's edict.

4. To all this, to make sure that the will is genuine and for the avoidance of fraud, we have added in our constitution [25] the provision that the name of the heir is to be written by the hand of the testator, or of the witnesses,[26] and that everything must be done according to the tenor of the constitution.

5. All the witnesses may use a single seal, as Pomponius advised (why not, if they may use seven seals identical in design?), and a witness may use another person's seal.

12. It is indifferent whether a will is written on tablets, paper, parchment or any other material.

13. A person may make his will in any number of originals, every one of which must be duly executed. This is sometimes necessary, if a testator is going on a sea-voyage and wishes to take one original with him and to leave another behind, and there are innumerable other circumstances of life which may render this course desirable.

§ 286.

14. So far we have spoken of wills committed to writing. But if any one wishes to make an oral will in accordance with the rules of the civil law, he may be assured that a declaration of his wishes made in the presence of seven witnesses is a perfectly good and unimpeachable testament.

Title XI

Of the military testament

Imperial constitutions have dispensed with the formalities described above in the wills of soldiers, who have no knowledge of legal technicalities. Accordingly soldiers can make a valid testament without the proper number of witnesses or the observance of any other solemnity, provided, that is (as our constitution [27] very properly prescribes) that they are on active service. So in whatever manner a soldier is found to have declared his last will, in writing or without writing, his testament holds good as an expression of his intentions. But when he is not on active service, or is in his own home, he cannot avail himself of this privilege. He may make a will, even if he is a son in power, but with the usual formalities required in the case of civilians. 1. The following rescript addressed by the Emperor Trajan to Statilius Severus is very much to the point:—

§ 287.

> "The privilege accorded to soldiers of making their wills in any way they please must be understood in the sense that it must, of course, be established that there is in fact a will (civilians also may make a will without writing). If, therefore,

---

[24] Nov. Theod. 16. 1. 2 ; Cod. 6. 23. 21. If the will was holograph and declared to be so in the body of the will, an amending constitution (Cod. 6. 23. 28, 6) dispensed the testator from a further subscriptio—sufficiat ei totius testamenti scriptura et non alia subscriptio requiratur.

[25] Cod. 6. 23. 29.

[26] This was abrogated by Nov. 119. 2.

[27] Cod. 6. 21. 17.

the soldier whose succession is in question, called together some comrades, with the intention of declaring his will, and then used words indicating that he wished such a person to be his heir, and such a slave to be free, it may be concluded that he made an oral will, and his intentions must take effect. But if, as may happen in the course of conversation, he said to someone 'I make you my heir' or 'I leave you everything' this must not be construed as a testament. It is in the interest of soldiers them-selves that nothing of the kind should be admitted. Otherwise it will be easy for people to come forward after a soldier's death and say that they heard him declare that he left his property to any person they choose to name, and so his real intentions would be frustrated."

2. (A soldier who is deaf or dumb can make a will.)

3. But the imperial constitutions allow soldiers this privilege only so long as they are serving, and in camp. If veterans make a will after their discharge from the army, or if soldiers in service make a will away from camp, they must observe the usual for-malities. If they make a soldier's will in camp it holds good only for one year after their discharge. Suppose, then, a soldier dies within the year, but a condition is attached to the institution of an heir, which takes effect only after the year, is this valid as a military testament? It is decided that it is valid. 4. If before he was a soldier a man has made a will without observing the proper forms, and then while a soldier and on active service has broken the seals, and has made some addition, or cancelled some disposition, or in any other way manifested his intention that the instrument should take effect as a soldier's will, it must be pronounced valid as being in effect a new will made by a soldier.

5. If a soldier who is sui juris allows himself to be adrogated, or a soldier who is filiusfamilias is emancipated, a testament previously made holds good as a fresh declaration of a soldier's intention and is not deemed to be invalidated by the change of status.

[For section 6 of this Title, see p. 206.]

IV. INSTITUTION OF HEIRS

289. An heir or heirs must be duly instituted. This was essential. The institution of an heir was the essence and foundation of the whole testament (caput et fundamentum totius testamenti). The following points, in particular, are to be noticed.   2. 20. 34.

290. (a) Form of institution. The solemn form was "Be Titius my heir" (Titius heres esto); and, says Gaius, the form "I direct Titius to be my heir" (Titium heredem esse jubeo) seems now to be approved, but not "I wish Titius to be my heir" (Titium heredem esse volo); and the forms "I institute Titius my heir" or "I make Titius my heir" (Titium **heredem**

ELEMENTS OF ROMAN LAW

instituo—facio) are generally disapproved.[28]   In the later law
this insistence on form disappeared.   Constantius and Constans
A.D. 339 enacted that any form of words would avail which
clearly expressed the testator's intention,[29] and Theodosius II
and Valentinian III A.D. 439 allowed wills to be made in
Greek.[30]

291. (b) Place of institution in the will.   The institution of
the heir had to come first, because everything else depended
upon it.   Consequently, a legacy or a gift of freedom which preceded the institution of the heir was of no effect.   This
requirement was rendered unnecessary by Justinian.[31]

292. (c) The institution must be to the whole inheritance,
for no one can die partly testate, partly intestate.[32]   An
exception was admitted in the case of the military will.   A
consequence of the rule was that if an heir was instituted to a
fraction of the estate, e.g., to one-half, and no disposition was
made of the other half, he took this half also and was regarded
as sole heir.   The same situation arose if for any reason a
co-heir failed to take.   The other or others took the lapsed
share by accrual (jure adcrescendi).   Nor was the result different
if a testator had named a person heir to some specific thing,
e.g., to his estate at Capua.   The limitation was taken pro non
scripto (detracta fundi mentione).[33]   Under Justinian, if one
person was instituted to a specific thing and another generally,
the first institution was treated as a legacy, and other ways had
been found of giving effect to a testator's intention.[34]

293. (d) An institution might be absolute or conditional,
i.e., it might be subject to a suspensive condition (e.g., Be Titius
my heir if he has married my daughter within a year of my
death),[35] but not to a resolutive condition (e.g., Be Titius my
heir: if he has not married my daughter within a year of
my death, be Sempronius my heir); nor to take effect from a
fixed date or to a fixed date (ex die—ad diem).   This would be
contrary to the rule " once an heir, always an heir " (semel

2. 14. 5.

2. 14. 9.

---

[28] G. 2. 117.
[29] Cod. 6. 23. 15.
[30] Cod. 6. 23. 21, 6.
[31] G. 2. 229, 230 ; Inst. 2. 20. 34.
[32] Dig. 30. 17. 7.   The origin of this rule is much discussed.   If it is
primitive (which some deny) it points to a time when what passed on death
was a thing from its nature indivisible, the headship of the family.   Maine,
Ancient Law, p. 203.
[33] Dig. 28. 5. 1, 4.
[34] Cod. 6. 24. 13.   Further particulars in Buckl. *T.* p. 296.
[35] As to the position pending the condition and the cautio muciana, see
Moyle *ad* Inst. 2. 14. 9.

heres, semper heres).[36] One consequence was that an inheritance could not be limited to shift over from one person to
another. But under the Empire this was surmounted by means
of fideicommissa (§ 360), and it did not apply to military wills.
If an institution was expressed to take effect from an event
which must occur, but at an uncertain date, *e.g.*, be Titius
my heir when Seius dies (dies certus an—incertus quando), it
was construed as a suspensive condition and free from objection.
Any prohibited condition or time limit attached to the institution was ignored. It was taken " pro non scripto."

294. (e) A testator might institute one heir or several heirs.
If several, they might be instituted to equal shares or to any
shares the testator pleased. According to the Roman method
of calculation the whole inheritance was a single unit represented in terms of the standard pound weight, the *as* or *libra*.
A sole heir was said to be heir to the whole pound—heres ex
asse. If the inheritance was distributed amongst co-heirs,
their shares were usually calculated in terms of ounces (unciae)
or twelfths. An heir who took one-twelfth was said to be heir
to one ounce (heres ex uncia) and so forth. But it was essential
that the whole estate should be distributed somehow, for as
explained above, no one could die partly testate, partly intestate.
If a testator said, " Be Titius and Sempronius my heirs. Be
Titius my heir to one-half," and forgot to say what share
Sempronius was to take, he took the other half. It is unnecessary to enter into the problems of calculation, considered in the
text. A testator was not obliged to distribute his estate in
twelfths. He might divide it into fifths or sevenths or fifteenths
or any other fractions he pleased. But the fraction was still
called an ounce. The ideal pound might consist of as many | 2. 14. 5.
ounces as the testator pleased.[37]

295. (f) A testator might institute a free man duly qualified
to be instituted (a condition which will be explained below,
§ 307)—or a slave, his own or some one else's. If his own, | 2. 14 pr.
the old law required together with the institution an express
gift of liberty, but Justinian gave authority to the more
indulgent view that the institution in itself imported a gift of
liberty. If another person's slave was instituted he acquired
the inheritance for his master by accepting at his order, pro- | 2. 14. 1.
vided that the master was qualified. It may be asked why the
testator should institute a slave instead of instituting the master

---

[36] Dig. 28. 5. 89.
[37] Instances in Hunter, pp. 762–3.

directly. The answer is that the institution of a slave had
certain practical advantages ; in particular the law forbade any
kind of traffic in the succession to a living person, but the
slave with the prospect of succeeding formed part of the estate
of his master, who could manumit, if he chose (in which case
the manumitted slave might accept the inheritance for his own
account), or dispose of him *inter vivos* or by will. The slave
became, so to say, a promissory note entitling the holder to
claim the inheritance upon the testator's death.

THE INSTITUTES

BOOK II

TITLE XIV

Of the institution of heirs

§ 295.   One may institute as heirs free men or slaves, one's own or some
one else's. Formerly, the prevailing opinion was that one could not
institute one's own slave without a gift of liberty. But now by our
constitution [38] this is no longer necessary. This is no innovation,
for it was only reasonable, and Paulus in his commentaries on
Masurius Sabinus and on Plautius says that Atilicinus [39] was of this
opinion. A man's own slave is understood to include a slave of
whom he has the bare ownership, while another person has the usufruct. There is one case in which an owner cannot institute a slave
heir even with a gift of liberty, as appears from a constitution of
the Emperors Severus and Antoninus to the following effect :—" If a
slave is charged with committing adultery with his mistress he cannot, pending sentence, be manumitted by the will of the woman who
is charged with complicity in the same crime; from which it follows
that his institution as heir is without effect." [40] The expression
" some one else's slave " is understood to include a slave in whom
the testator has a usufruct. 1. A slave instituted heir by his master,
becomes free and a necessary heir (§ 335) by force of the testament,
if his condition has remained unchanged. If he has been manumitted by the testator in his lifetime, he may accept or decline the
inheritance, as he pleases, for he is not regarded as a necessary heir,
since he is not freed as well as instituted by his master's will. But
if his master has alienated him, he must enter upon the inheritance
by the order of his new master, who consequently becomes heir.
The slave himself, having been alienated, cannot become free or heir
under his (late) master's will, although he may have been instituted
heir with an express gift of liberty; for when he alienated him his

---

[38] Cod. 6. 27. 5.
[39] All these jurists belong to the first century. Atilicinus was later
than Sabinus (after whom the Sabinian school was named, § 30). Plautius
was the latest of the three.
[40] Dig. 28. 5. 49 (48), 2.

master is deemed to have abandoned his purpose of setting him free. If another person's slave is instituted heir and his position has remained unchanged, he must accept the inheritance at the bidding of his master. If he has been alienated in the testator's lifetime or, after the testator's death before he has accepted the inheritance, he must accept at the bidding of his new master. If he has been manumitted in the testator's lifetime or after his death before acceptance he may accept or decline the inheritance as he pleases on his own account.

2. Another person's slave may be properly instituted heir after his master's death, because it is competent to institute a slave belonging to an inheritance; for a vacant inheritance represents the person not of the future heir, but of the deceased. The slave of an unborn child may also be instituted heir. **§ 142.**

3. If a slave belonging to several masters, with all of whom there is testamenti factio, is instituted heir by a stranger, he acquires for each of the masters at whose bidding he accepts in proportion to the **§ 307.** share in which they are severally owners.

4. A testator may institute a single heir or as many heirs as he pleases without limit. 5. The inheritance is commonly divided into twelve ounces, which together make up the *as* or pound. These fractions of the pound are distinguished by appropriate names from the single ounce up to the complete pound. Thus we employ the **§ 294.** terms uncia (one ounce), sextans (two ounces or one-sixth), quadrans (three ounces or a quarter), triens (four ounces or a third), quincunx (five ounces or five-twelfths), semis (six ounces or one-half), septunx (seven ounces or seven-twelfths), bes (eight ounces or two-thirds), dodrans (nine ounces or three-quarters), decunx (ten ounces or five-sixths), deunx (eleven ounces or eleven-twelfths), and *as*, which comprises the whole inheritance. It is not obligatory that the estate should contain twelve ounces. The number of ounces which go to the pound is just what the testator pleases. For example if a man institutes a sole heir to the half, the half is understood to comprise the whole, for no one can die partly testate and partly intestate, **§ 292.** unless he be a soldier, in whose case it is simply a question of what he intends. Conversely, a testator may divide the inheritance into any number of ounces more than twelve. 6. In case of plurality of institutes, there is no question of distribution of shares unless the testator does not wish them to take equal shares, for it is well established that if no shares are mentioned all the heirs take equally. It may happen that some of the heirs are instituted to specified shares, and that there is another heir to whom no share is assigned; then if the specified shares do not make up a whole *as* he takes what is wanting to make up the twelve ounces; if there are more than one heir with no assigned shares, they divide the residue between them. If the whole *as* has been distributed, the heirs with assigned shares take half the estate, the other half goes to the heir or heirs with unassigned share or shares. It makes no difference whether the heir without an assigned share comes first or middle or last amongst the instituted heirs. In any case he takes the vacant share.

7. Now let us see what happens if there is a vacant share, but every heir has had a share assigned to him; if, for example, three persons have been instituted each to a quarter. It is settled that the

vacant share accedes rateably to the instituted heirs and the result is the same as if they had each been instituted to one-third. Conversely, if more than twelve ounces have been distributed, each share is rateably reduced, for example, four heirs have been instituted to one-third each, the result is the same as if each had been instituted to one-quarter.

8. If more ounces than twelve have been distributed, the heir who has no share assigned him takes what is wanting to make up the second pound, and similarly if the second pound is exhausted. But all these shares are ultimately reduced to a single *as*, whatever may be the number of ounces [so that what each heir takes is always represented as a fraction of the *as*].

§ 293.

9. An heir may be instituted unconditionally or conditionally; not from a certain time or to a certain time, for instance, " be he heir from five years after my death," or " from or to the kalends of such a month." It is settled that such an added date is disregarded, and that the result is the same as if the heir had been instituted in absolute terms.

10. In institutions, legacies, fideicommissa and grants of liberty an impossible condition is taken pro non scripto.

11. When several conditions are attached to an institution conjunctively expressed, as " if this *and* that be done," both or all of them must be satisfied; but if they are separate conditions, as " if this *or* that be done," it is enough to satisfy any one of them.

12. A testator may institute as heirs persons whom he has never seen, for example a brother's sons born abroad, though he does not know them; for a testator's want of knowledge does not render the institution void.

V. Substitution of Heirs (vulgar—pupillary—exemplary)

296. If a person was instituted as sole heir and for any reason could not, or did not, accept the inheritance, the will failed and the property went to the heirs *ab intestato*. To avoid such a catastrophe, it was usual for testators after instituting an heir, to substitute another who was to take, if the first heir did not. This was known as ordinary or vulgar substitution (substitutio vulgaris). The form would be: " Be Titius my heir ; if Titius shall not be my heir, then be Maevius my heir." The same rules applied to substitutions as to institutions. Thus a testator might name one substitute or several substitutes, and he might name several substitutes to one institute (" Be Titius my heir: if Titius shall not be my heir, be Seius and Sempronius my heirs "), or one substitute to several institutes (" Be Titius and Seius my heirs ; if Titius and Seius shall not be my heirs, be Sempronius my heir ") ; or he might substitute the institutes reciprocally one to another

2. 15 pr.

("Be Titius my heir to half; be Seius my heir to half. If Titius shall not be my heir, be Seius my heir; if Seius shall not be my heir be Titius my heir"). It was usual to name several substitutes one after another and last of all a slave of the testator, who because he could not refuse the inheritance was known as necessary heir (heres necessarius, § 335).

297. In the old law it was the practice to fix a time limit, usually of one hundred days, within which the heir was to make a formal acceptance, with the addition that if he failed to do so, he was to be disinherited and a substitute was to take the inheritance in his place.[41] This formal acceptance was known as cretio from the Latin verb cernere=to decide. The practice had fallen into disuse before Justinian, who formally abolished it.[42] It may be assumed, though there is no text, that the substitutus might, if there was undue delay, require the institutus to ask for a spatium deliberandi (§ 337).

298. Besides the ordinary or vulgar substitution, there was another substitution known as pupillary substitution. This took place when a paterfamilias appointed a child in power his heir and provided a substitute not only for the event of such child not being his heir, but also for the event of his becoming heir and dying before puberty, i.e., before acquiring testamentary capacity on his own account. The formula was— "Be my son Titius my heir: if my son Titius shall not be my heir, or shall be my heir and die before he becomes his own guardian, then be Seius heir." In this case, as Gaius and Justinian observe, there are, in effect, two wills, or one will disposing of two inheritances, for the testator provides for succession not to his own estate alone, but to his son's as well. At first this form of substitution was employed only if the child was instituted, and related only to property derived from the testator, but later the principle was carried so far that a paterfamilias might disinherit his son and still provide for the devolution of the son's estate, for example, property left to him by his mother after testator's death, in the event of his dying under the age of puberty. But the father could not make a will for his child unless at the same time he made a will for himself, for the pupillary testament was regarded as part of and accessory to the will of the parent. In a famous case of the time of Sulla (causa Curiana)[43] the question was whether

2. 16 pr.

2. 16. 2.

2. 16. 4.

---

[41] G. 2. 165.
[42] By interpolation in a constitution of A.D. 407 (Cod. 6. 30. 17); Girard, p. 924, n. 6.   [43] Cic. de Orat. I. 180; II. 141.

a pupillary substitution implied also a direct substitution. Under. the Empire, it was held that it did so, and conversely, a direct substitution was understood to imply a pupillary substitution in the absence of the expression of a contrary intention.[44]

2. 16. 1.

299. Justinian extended the principle of pupillary substitution to descendants who were insane. This has been termed quasi-pupillary or exemplary (*i.e.*, analogous) substitution. It was more restricted in its application than pupillary substitution, because the testator could not substitute any one he pleased. He had to appoint certain persons, *viz.*, descendants and, failing such, brothers and sisters of the insane person. Only in default of these, the choice was unrestricted. On the other hand, the power of appointment might be exercised by any ascendant, *e.g.*, a mother, who instituted the insane person heir, and not by the paterfamilias alone.

THE INSTITUTES

BOOK II (Tits. XV and XVI)

TITLE XV

Of vulgar substitution

§ 296.

A testator may make several persons heirs in succession, for instance " if such a person shall not be heir, be such other person heir," and so on, as often as he pleases; last of all he may institute his slave as necessary heir. 1. Several persons may be substituted to one person, or one person to several persons; or each heir may have a separate substitute, or again heirs may be substituted reciprocally, one to another. 2. If heirs instituted in unequal shares are reciprocally substituted and nothing is said about shares in the substitution it is understood that the testator meant the substituted heir to take the same share as the heir in whose place he is substituted. This was decided by the Emperor Pius. 3. If one co-heir has a substitute and is himself substituted to the other co-heir [and both co-heirs fail to take] the substitute is understood to be entitled without distinction to both parts of the inheritance. So decided by the Emperors Severus and Antoninus.[45] 4. If a testator has instituted another man's slave, believing him to be sui juris, and has substituted Maevius in the event of the slave so instituted not being heir; then, if the slave enters on the inheritance at his master's bidding, Maevius is admitted to half. For the words " if he shall not be heir," in case the testator knows that the person concerned is alieni juris, mean " if he is neither heir himself nor the means of some

---

[44] Dig. 28 6. 4 pr.
[45] This decision gave occasion for the rule substitutus substituto est substitutus instituto.

other person becoming heir "; but, if the testator supposed the person
instituted to be an independent person, then the words mean " if he
shall not have acquired the inheritance for himself or for any other
person into whose power he may afterwards fall." This was decided
by the Emperor Tiberius in the case of his slave Parthenius.[46]

Title XVI

Of pupillary substitution

If a person has children in his power who are below the age of
puberty he may appoint a substitute not only for the event of their
not being heirs but also for the event of their being heirs and dying
under puberty. For example, " Be my son Titius my heir; if my
son shall not be my heir, or if he shall be my heir and shall die
before he becomes his own guardian (that is reaches puberty), then
be Seius heir." In this case if the son is not heir, then the substitute is heir to the father; but if the son is heir and dies before
puberty, then the substitute is heir to the son. This is an institution
which owes its origin to custom, namely that if children are too
young to make wills for themselves, their parents should make wills
for them.

§ 298.

G. 2. 179.

1. Moved by this consideration we have placed a constitution [47]
in our code providing that if a person has a son or other descendant
of either sex and of any degree of descent who is not sane, he may
substitute certain persons to him on the analogy of pupillary substitution; if he recovers his sanity, the substitution is cancelled just
as it is in the case of pupillary substitution when the child reaches
the age of puberty. 2. Accordingly, in pupillary substitution as
above described there are, in a way, two wills, the father's will and
the son's will, just as if the son had himself instituted an heir; or,
we may say, if we please, that there is one testament with two
aspects, that is, involving two inheritances.

§ 299.

3. If a person is afraid that after his death his minor son may be
imperilled from its being known who is to take the inheritance in
the event of his death, he should make the vulgar substitution
openly in the first part of his will, and the pupillary substitution
lower down in another part of the will, which is separately fastened
and sealed; and he should insert in the first part of the will a direction that the lower part is not to be opened while the child is alive
and under puberty. It is obvious that the pupillary substitution is
not invalid if it is written on the same tablets as those in which the
testator appoints his own heir, though this may be unsafe for the
child. 4. Parents may substitute to their children as above described
not only when the children are heirs to their parents, but even when
they are disinherited; in which case if anything comes to the child
by inheritance, legacy or gifts from relatives and friends, it all goes
to the substitute [if the child dies under puberty]. Whatever is

---

[46] The argument is not very logical. What is meant is that, since the
testator never contemplated the actual situation, there is a case for an
equitable adjustment of the claims of both parties concerned.

[47] Cod. 6. 26. 9.

said of children must be understood to include after-born children.
5. No one can make a testament for his children, unless he also
makes a testament for himself, for the child's testament is a part and
consequence of the father's testament; so that if the father's will is
invalid, the son's will is invalid too. 6. Substitution may be made
to each child severally, or to the child who is the last to die under
puberty. The first method is adopted if the testator does not wish
any one of the children to die intestate; the second, if he is content
that as between themselves the law of intestate succession should
prevail.

7. The substitute may be described by name or in general terms,
e.g., "whoever shall be my heir"; in which case if the child dies
under puberty, the substitutes in his estate are the persons who are
named heirs and in fact become heirs under the father's will and
each in proportion to the share in which he is instituted. 8. Substitution in the case of a male child may be made up to the age of
fourteen; in the case of a female child up to the age of twelve. If
this age is passed the substitution is cancelled.

§ 360.
9. This kind of substitution cannot be made to a stranger, or to
a child above the age of puberty who has been instituted heir. What
a testator can do is to bind his heir by fideicommissum to make over
the inheritance to another person in whole or in part. The nature
of fideicommissum will be explained in its proper place.

VI. PERSONAL QUALIFICATION OF TESTATOR, HEIR AND WITNESSES (TESTAMENTI FACTIO)

300. Testator, heir and witnesses must be competent. All
of them must have the personal quality which is a necessary
condition of the validity of the will. The testator must be
competent to make it. The heir must be competent to be
2. 19. 4.   instituted by it. The witnesses must be competent to witness
it. This competence is called testamenti factio (will-making).
On the part of the testator it means a general competence to
make wills and a special competence to institute the person
in question. On the part of the heir and witnesses it means
a general competence to assume their several parts and a
special competence to be instituted by or to witness the
will in question. It is required that "they should have (or
that there should be) will-making with the testator" (testamenti
factio cum testatore). Thus, to anticipate what will be more
fully explained below, a peregrinus (as a rule) can neither
make, take under, nor witness a will. The disqualification is
absolute. An instance of a relative disqualification is the rule
prohibiting persons connected by potestas with the testator
from acting as witnesses (§ 308). A Junian Latin, who cannot
make a will (§ 82), can be a witness to a will " because there is

testamenti factio with him." [48]   This simply means that he has a general competence to witness a Roman will.

301. WHO MAY MAKE A WILL.—Justinian has a Title on "Persons who may not make a will," leaving us to infer the normal positive requirements,[49] which may be stated as follows:—

302. (1) The testator must be a Roman citizen, or a colonial G. 1. 23.
Latin.[50]   Junian Latins were disabled by the statute, which created the status. Peregrines could not make a Roman will. Their testamentary capacity was determined by the law of the community to which they belonged. The class of peregrini dediticii created by the lex Aelia Sentia (§ 84) could not make G. 1. 25.
a will at all. They could not make a citizen will, because they were not citizens, nor a peregrine will, because they did not belong to any peregrine community.[51]   Slaves could not make a will, except, Ulpian tells us, public slaves of the Roman People, who could make a will of half their peculium,[52] and a kind master like the younger Pliny might in effect allow his slaves to dispose of their peculia by will amongst themselves.[53] A citizen taken captive by the enemy was in the same position as a slave. If, however, he had made a will before he was taken captive, it was held good by right of postliminium (§ 117) if he returned, and by the operation of a certain lex Cornelia if he died in captivity. This is variously described as the benefit 2. 12. 5.
of the lex Cornelia (beneficium legis Corneliae) and the fiction of the lex Cornelia (fictio legis Corneliae). What was the nature of the fiction is unknown. Buckland says, " Probably the lex did not declare the will good, but provided that his estate was to be dealt with as if he had never been captured, and on this the lawyers built the further rule that the case was to be handled as if he had died at capture." [54]

303. (2) The testator (generally) must be sui juris. Persons in patria potestate could not make a will, because they owned nothing and therefore could leave nothing; but male descen- 2. 12 pr.
dants in power were competent to dispose by will of their 2. 11. 6.
castrense and under Justinian also of their quasi-castrense

---

[48] Ulp. XX, 8.
[49] But the rubric of Dig. 28. 1 is: Qui testamenta facere possunt et quemadmodum testamenta fiant.
[50] *Supra*, p. 54.
[51] Ulp. XX, 16.
[52] *Ibid.*
[53] Pliny, *Epistles*, 8. 16.
[54] Buckl. *T.* p. 289; Dig. 41. 3. 44, 7 *in fine*.

peculium. The bona adventicia could not at any time be disposed of by will (§ 89).

304. (3) The testator must be above the age of puberty and generally competent to form and express a sound judgment.

2. 12. 1, & 2.

Insane persons (unless in lucid intervals) and interdicted prodigals could not make a will. Persons who were either deaf or dumb could not make a mancipatory will because they were unable to take part in the ceremony,[55] but when the written will came into use, in principle these disqualifications disappeared.

2. 12. 3.

Justinian made special rules referred to in the text.

305. (4) There were cases in which incapacity to make a will was a penalty imposed by legislation, e.g., in the older law upon the author of defamatory writings (carmen famosum)[56] and in the late Empire upon certain heretics and apostates.

306. (5) Women could not take part in the business of the comitia and therefore could not make a will comitiis calatis; the mancipatory will they could, provided that they were sui juris and had anything to dispose of. But in order to obtain testamentary capacity they had to break away from their agnatic family by means of the fictitious coemption described by Gaius (§ 123), the object of which was to give the woman a fiduciary tutor, by whose authority she could make a will. Why her original tutor, whose authority in any event was necessary to enable her to make the coemption, could not equally give validity to her will remains obscure.[57] This tiresome formality was rendered unnecessary by the Emperor Hadrian,[58] though only to be replaced by the requirement of the tutor's authority so long as the perpetual tutelage of women remained in force. This was a reality in the case of the legitima tutela of parents and patrons. In other cases it could be compelled (§ 138). None of these restrictions upon testamentary capacity applied to women with the jus liberorum (§ 138) or to the praetorian will.[59] The last vestiges of any testamentary disability of women had disappeared long before Justinian.

---

[55] Ulp. XX, 13.
[56] Ulpian attributes this to a senatusconsultum (Dig. 28. 1. 18, 1). The Twelve Tables punished (with scourging?) the author of a malum carmen—qui malum carmen incantassit. This may refer to some form of magical incantation. Girard, p. 428, n. 4. It was misunderstood, even in the Augustan age, as appears from Horace, Sat. 2. 1. 82; Epp. 2. 1. 152. Another view is that both malum carmen (incantation) and carmen famosum (libel or vituperation) were punished by the Twelve Tables. Perhaps the idea of cursing is present in both.
[57] For a probable explanation, see Buckl. T. p. 120, n. 1.
[58] G. 2. 112; Ulp. XX. 15.
[59] G. 2. 119, 120.

THE INSTITUTES

BOOK II (Tit. XII, Tit. XI, sec. 6)

Title XII

Who are not permitted to make a will

Not every one can make a will. In the first place, those who are under power have not this right, so much so that even if their parents give them leave, this does not any the more give them testamentary capacity, except always in the cases mentioned above, and particularly in the case of soldiers in the power of parents who by imperial constitutions are permitted to make wills of their castrense peculium. At first this privilege was allowed only to men on actual service by the Emperors Augustus, Nerva, and Trajan, but afterwards by a rescript of the Emperor Hadrian it was accorded also to men who had received their discharge. Accordingly, if they have made a will of their castrense peculium it goes to the heir instituted in the will, but if they die intestate without leaving children or brothers [or sisters] [60] to survive them, it belongs to the parents on general principles of law [as peculium].[61] From this it may be understood that what a soldier in power has acquired on service his father cannot take from him, nor can the father's creditors sell it or interfere with it in any way, and when the father dies he does not share it with his brothers; in fact what he acquires on service is his property, though at civil law the peculia of sons in power belong to their parents, just as the peculia of slaves belong to their masters, with the exception of things which by imperial constitutions and in particular by our legislation are for various reasons not acquired by the parent. With the exception, therefore, of those who have castrense peculium or quasi-castrense peculium, if any son in power makes a testament it is without effect, even though he may die sui juris. 1. Further, children below the age of puberty cannot make a will, because they have no judgment; nor madmen, because they are devoid of reason: and it makes no difference if the child afterwards reaches the age of puberty or the madman afterwards becomes sane. However, if a madman makes a will in a lucid interval, it is deemed to be valid, and certainly wills made before insanity supervened remain valid, for neither wills nor any other transactions duly completed are avoided by supervening insanity.

2. Again, a prodigal who has been interdicted from the management of his property cannot make a will, but a will made before the interdiction is upheld. 3. Again, a person who is deaf or dumb cannot always make a will. We refer, of course, to a person who is completely deaf, not to a person who is hard of hearing; just as by a dumb person we mean one who cannot speak at all, not one who is slow of speech. But it often happens that educated and learned men for one reason or another lose the use of hearing and speech. Accordingly, our constitution [62] has come to their aid, allowing

§ 303.

§ 304.

§ 304.

---

[60] *Arg.* Cod. 6. 61. 4.
[61] Dig 49. 17. 2. Or by inheritance? Buckl. *T.* p. 376.
[62] Cod. 6. 22. 10.

them to make wills and perform other permitted acts in the cases and in the ways therein set forth. If after making his will a person becomes dumb or deaf from ill health or any other cause, his will none the less remains valid.

§ 302. 4. A blind man cannot make a will except in the way prescribed by our father the Emperor Justin.[63] 5. If a man taken captive by the enemy makes a will while in captivity it is invalid, even though he comes back. But a will made before capture, if he comes back is valid jure postliminii; if he dies in captivity, by the lex Cornelia.

TITLE XI, sec. 6

§ 303. It must be observed that on the analogy of the peculium castrense statutes of early date and imperial constitutions have allowed certain persons to have what is called quasi-castrense peculium, and some of them have been permitted, notwithstanding that they are in power, to dispose of such peculium by will. Our constitution has given this a wider application, and allowed all such peculia to be disposed of by will, that is by a will executed with the usual formalities. It is open to any one to peruse our constitution [64] and so inform himself as to its provisions.

2. 19. 4. 307. WHO MAY BE INSTITUTED HEIR.—The capacity to be instituted, to which the commentators have given the name of testamenti factio passiva, is naturally wider than the capacity to make a will, since it includes sons in power and slaves, young children and insane persons, though in the last two cases the question of acceptance raised difficulties.[65] But the following were disqualified, viz.: —

1. Peregrini (with an exception in favour of the military will) and in the older law peregrini dediticii [66];

2. Incertae personae (unascertained persons).[67] An incerta persona is any one whose personality is not precisely determined in the mind of the testator, e.g., " whoever is the first to come to my funeral," or " whoever gives his daughter in marriage to my son." [68] But the disability was extended beyond such cases to include postumi, that is persons not born at the date of the will, and corporate bodies.[69] By degrees, however, the disqualification of postumi was removed and under Justinian all such persons might be instituted unless the posthumous child was the issue of the testator and of a woman

---

[63] Cod. 6. 22. 8.
[64] Cod. 6. 22. 11.
[65] Buckl. *T*. p. 312 ; *M*. p. 190.
[66] G. 1. 25 ; 2. 110.
[67] Ulp. XXII, 4.
[68] G. 2. 238 ; Inst. 2. 20. 25.
[69] Buckl. *T*. p. 291, n. 10.

whom he could not legally marry, for instance another man's wife.[70] A practical limit was set by the rule that the heir must be in existence when the inheritance fell vacant.[71] In the case of corporate bodies the difficulty was that there was no specific person to accept the inheritance, and the idea of juristic personality only slowly emerged (§ 142). Ulpian says, " A municipality cannot be instituted, nor can its members collectively, because it is a fluctuating body (quoniam incertum corpus est)." Exceptionally, senatusconsulta allowed municipalities to be instituted by their freedmen and to take generally by way of fideicommissum. Gods and goddesses (with some favoured exceptions) fell under the same prohibition.[72] The State was reluctant to concede corporate personality to combinations of individuals or to foundations. In the later Empire, and particularly by Justinian, the permitted scope of such institutions was very much enlarged. It was now possible to institute municipalities, the Church and every kind of religious or charitable foundation, but private associations only by special licence. By a constitution, the text of which is not preserved, but which has been partially reconstructed from the *Basilica* (§ 46), Justinian seems finally to have abrogated the general principle that an incerta persona could not be instituted. There is a reference to this constitution in the text.[73]

3. By the lex Voconia (B.C. 168) a woman could not be instituted heir by a testator whose census amounted to 100,000 *asses,* which placed him in the first class.[74] This prohibition fell into disuse together with the census in the early Empire.

308. WHO MAY WITNESS A WILL.—The disqualifications were in general the same as in the case of the testator, but some persisted in the case of witnesses after they had ceased to apply to testators. Thus women and deaf or dumb persons could not be witnesses. {2. 10. 6.}

Close family relationship with the principal parties to the will was another disqualification. This excluded persons united by potestas with the testator (in his power, in whose power he is, in the same power), or with the familiae emptor, and in the {2. 10. 9.} later law with the heir. But legatees were competent witnesses {2. 10. 10.} and, contrary to English law, might witness the will without {2. 10. 11.}

---

[70] Inst. 2. 20. 28 ; 3. 9 pr. ; Dig. 28. 2. 9, 1.
[71] Buckl. *M.* p. 188.
[72] Ulp. XXII, 5 and 6.
[73] Inst. 2. 20. 27 ; Girard, p. 872, n. 5.
[74] G. 2. 274.

forfeiting the legacy.   Junian Latins might witness a will, though they could not make one (§ 300).

THE INSTITUTES

BOOK II

TITLE X, secs. 6–11

Of the execution of wills

§ 308.

6. Any persons with whom the testator has testamenti factio may be witnesses to his will. But a woman, a child below the age of puberty, a slave, a person who is deaf or dumb, an insane person, an interdicted prodigal, and any one who is by law an incompetent witness may not be included in the number of witnesses.

7. When one of the witnesses at the time of the execution of the will was thought to be free, and was afterwards found to be a slave, the Emperor Hadrian in his rescript to Catonius Verus, and afterwards, the Emperors Severus and Antoninus by rescript declared that they would graciously come to the aid of the will, and that it should be deemed to be validly executed, since at the time of its execution the witness was generally supposed to be free and no one had challenged his status.

8. A father and a male descendant in his power, or two brothers in the same power, may join in witnessing a will, for there is no harm in several witnesses to a stranger's will being taken from the same family. 9. But a person in a testator's power may not be a witness, and if a soldier after taking his discharge makes a will of his castrense peculium, his father cannot be a witness, nor any one in his father's power, for members of the same family as the testator are not admissible witnesses. 10. Neither may the heir, nor a descendant in his power, nor the ascendant in whose power he is, nor brothers in the same power with himself, be witnesses, for today the whole business of will-making is deemed to be a proceeding between the heir and the testator. Formerly there was much con-

§ 280.

fusion in this branch of the law, and the old jurists, while they did not allow the familiae emptor and those related to him by power to be witnesses, raised no objection to the heir and those related to him by power being witnesses, though urging that the right should not be abused. We have given their recommendation the force of law and applied the same rule to the heir and his connections as was anciently applied in the case of the familiae emptor, to whose place the heir has succeeded. 11. Legatees and fideicommissaries, not being universal successors, and persons connected with them are not debarred from being witnesses. Indeed one of our constitutions [75] expressly allows them to be so.

309. A person might have testamenti factio in the sense that he could be instituted heir (so-called testamenti factio passiva)

---

[75] Not extant.

and a will instituting him would be a valid will, and yet might not be able to take under the will, or might be able to take, but not keep. These cases are the subject of the next three sections.

VII. Jus Capiendi—Caduca—Ereptoria

310. There were cases in which by statute law an institutus was denied the jus capiendi—the right of taking under a will. By the lex Junia a Junian Latin was under this disability unless he acquired Roman citizenship within one hundred days after the " delation " of the inheritance (§ 337).[76] By the marriage laws of Augustus—the lex Julia 18 B.C. and the lex Papia Poppaea A.D. 9—unmarried persons, males over twenty-five and under sixty, females over twenty and under fifty (caelibes) and childless married persons (orbi) were penalised unless they qualified by marriage (or by birth of issue?) within the same limit of time, the first by the loss of the whole, the second by the loss of half the inheritance. The inheritance, or half of it, as the case might be, fell vacant (caducum) and went to other persons benefited by the will as heirs or legatees who were married and had children, and failing such to the Treasury (aerarium, later fiscus).[77] But if the heir was within the sixth degree of relationship to the testator [78] these disabilities had no application, and there were other exemptions. We might well be amazed that a penal law so diluted in its effect should have been calculated to encourage marriage, were it not that the legacy hunter is a familiar figure in the pages of the Latin satirists. Though Horace invited the blessing of the goddess Lucina on the marriage law,[79] it may be questioned whether it was more successful than such attempts " to make men good by Act of Parliament " have proved in other ages and other lands. But these " leges caducariae " remained on the Statute-book until abrogated by Constantine in A.D. 320.[80]

311. Another case of incapacity to take under a will, which has been the occasion of many decisions in the South African courts, was created by the senatusconsultum Libonianum of A.D. 16 and an edict of the Emperor Claudius.[81] These enactments forbade any person to write a benefit for himself in another person's will even at the testator's dictation. Transgressors incurred the penalties of the lex Cornelia de falsis (Inst. 4. 18. 7) and the disposition was taken pro non scripto. It will be remembered that in English Law an attesting witness of a will or codicil (and his or her wife or husband) cannot take any beneficial interest in property thereunder.[82]

---

[76] G. 1. 23, 24; Ulp. XVII, 1.
[77] Ulp. XVI, 1. XVII, XVIII; Buckl. T. pp. 319, 320; infra. p. 224.
[78] Or the seventh in the case of the issue of second cousins Vat. 216.
[79] Carmen Seculare.
[80] Cod. 8. 57 (58). 1.
[81] Dig. 34 8 : 49. 10; Cod. 9. 23. 3.
[82] Wills Act, 1837, s 15.

312. There were cases in which a person might be instituted and might take, but could not keep. This happened when the heir was deemed " unworthy " of the intended benefit, which by consequence was " snatched from him " and as a rule escheated to the Treasury. There were many such cases. The most flagrant instance was when the heir had culpably caused testator's death ; and it may be observed that the same rule exists in English Law. The commentators have given to this kind of forfeiture the name of ereption on the ground of indignity.[83]

VIII. Who must be Instituted or Disinherited

313. Certain persons must be instituted or disinherited : —

(1) By civil law sons in power must be either instituted or disinherited in express terms (nominatim). The proper form of disherison was, " Be my son Titius disinherited " (Titius filius meus exheres esto), or simply, " Be my son disinherited " (Filius meus exheres esto) when there was only one. If the testator failed to institute or disinherit a son in power, the will was invalid. This was the case even though the son died subsequently to the will but before the testator. The law was settled in this sense in accordance with the Sabinian doctrine. The Proculians had maintained that the will was valid, on the ground that the omission of the son did not render the will void *ab initio*, but only in the event of the son's survival. Other descendants in power, who on the testator's death would be his sui heredes, must also be instituted or disinherited, but in their case a general clause of disherison—" Be all the rest disinherited " (ceteri omnes exheredes sunto)—was sufficient.

This applied to daughters and to the children of sons who owing to the death or emancipation [84] of their father were potential sui heredes of the testator. If they were passed over in silence the will was not void, but the person omitted was let in to share along with the instituted heirs, *i.e.*, took a rateable share in competition with sui heredes instituted by the will and half of the inheritance if the person instituted was a stranger to the family (extraneus), which would include an emancipated son. Grandsons in power would take a son's share between them as representing their deceased, or emancipated, father.

314. (2) The praetor extended the rule requiring institution or disherison to include all descendants whom he admitted to intestate succession in the class *unde liberi* (§ 388).

2. 13 pr.

2. 13. 1.

2. 13 pr.

2. 13 pr.

---

[83] Dig. 34. 9 ; Cod. 6. 35. The word *ereptorium* occurs only in Ulp. XIX, 17.
[84] Provided that they were born or conceived before the father's emancipation (§ 336).

This meant that he ignored emancipation and placed emancipated sons and their issue in the same position as sui heredes. He required all males (grandsons as well as sons) to be disinherited nominatim, females inter ceteros, failing which he gave them bonorum possessio contra tabulas (§ 387).   The effect was to upset the will, not technically, but practically (for most purposes),[85] and to admit to the succession not only the descendant who invoked the relief, but also all others entitled to succeed *ab intestato* who had not been duly disinherited (disherisons were not affected by the grant of bonorum possessio contra tabulas).   The praetor made no distinction between men and women, but the Emperor Antoninus Pius reverted to the rule of the civil law by providing that women were not to take more by bonorum possessio contra tabulas than they would have taken by right of accrual at civil law.[86] `2. 13. 3.`

315. (3) Justinian maintained the praetorian system, but with the more stringent requirement that every disherison must be made in express terms (nominatim).   Failing this, the sui heredes could impeach the will as wholly void, other liberi could upset it by obtaining bonorum possessio contra tabulas.   It is to be noticed that under Justinian adoptive children need not be taken into account (except in case of adoptio plena), because they did not any longer leave their family of origin (§ 114).[87] `2. 13. 5.`

THE INSTITUTES

BOOK II

TITLE XIII

Of the disherison of children

It is not enough for the complete validity of a will to observe the forms above described.   It is further necessary that a testator who `§ 313.` has a son in power should take steps to institute him heir or to disinherit him specially.   If he passes him over in silence the will is void, so much so that even if the son dies in his father's lifetime, no one can take as heir under the will, because the will was invalid from the beginning.   In ancient times this did not apply in the case of daughters and the issue of sons and other descendants through males.   If these were not instituted or disinherited, the will was not void, but they were allowed to take a certain portion of the inheritance.   Further, it was not required that such persons should be disinherited specially.   They might be excluded in general terms. 1. A special disherison is expressed in the formula, " Be my son Titius disinherited " or " Be my son disinherited " without naming

---

[85] Buckl. *M.* p. 198.
[86] G. 2. 126.
[87] Inst. 2. 13. 5. *in fine*.

him, that is, in case there is only one son. Posthumous children too should be either instituted or disinherited. With regard to them there is no difference between sons and other descendants of either sex. The will is valid *ab initio*. But as soon as a child of either sex is born into the family, the will is broken and wholly fails to take effect. (No such consequence follows if a woman suffers a miscarriage.) The practice used to be that females born after the will might be disinherited either specially, or by a general clause, provided in the latter case that they received some legacy to show that they had not been overlooked; but male descendants (sons and remoter descendants) had to be disinherited in express terms by the formula " If any son be hereafter born to me, be he disinherited." 2. Under the general description of " posthumous " are included descendants who take the place of a suus heres, and are, so to say, by an afterbirth [88] brought into the position of sui heredes. For instance, if a person has in his power a son and a grandson or grand-daughter by that son, as the son is in the first degree of descent, he alone has the position of suus heres, though the grandchildren are in the same power. But if the son dies or in any way goes out of his father's power in the father's lifetime, his children take his place and are in the position of sui heredes just as if they had been newly born into the family. Accordingly, just as it is necessary to institute or disinherit a son specially to prevent the will being void from the beginning, so it is necessary to institute or disinherit grandchildren by a son, lest if the son dies in the testator's lifetime they should take his place and break the will by being (so to say) born into the family. This is provided by the lex Junia Velleia, which also indicated a mode of disherison appropriate to such cases.[89]

§ 314.

3. By civil law emancipated children need not be instituted or disinherited, because they are not sui heredes. But the praetor requires all children of either sex who are not instituted to be disinherited, males specially, females specially or by a general clause. If they are neither instituted nor disinherited in the manner described, he promises them possession of goods against the will. 4. Adoptive children, so long as they are in the power of their adoptive father, are in the same position as children born in wedlock, and, therefore, must be instituted or disinherited, as described above. But if they are emancipated by their adoptive father they are not reckoned as children either at civil law or by the praetor's edict. Conversely, so long as they are in the adoptive family they are strangers to their natural parent, so that there is no need for him to institute or disinherit them. But when they have been emancipated by their

---

[88] " quasi adgnascendo." " by an event analogous to subsequent birth " (Moyle); " like the after-born " (Poste, Gaius, 2. 133).

[89] This is the situation dealt with in the second chapter of the lex Junia Velleia (A.D. 26?). The order of events is—birth of grandchild, will of grandfather, death of father, death of grandfather. A person thus promoted by succession to the rank of suus heres is termed by the commentators a quasi-postumus. The first chapter of the lex related to one case of postumi properly so-called (persons born after the date of the will). The statute enacted that the will was not to be broken in either case if the person concerned had been instituted or disinherited by anticipation. See Poste, Gaius, p. 196.

adoptive father, they are in the same relation to their natural father
as if he had emancipated them himself. 5. Such was the old law on
the subject. But we, bearing in mind that both sexes contribute to
the procreation of children and that neither the Law of the Twelve
Tables nor the praetor's edict makes any difference between them,   § 315.
have by our constitution [90] established one simple law applicable
alike to sons and daughters and all descendants through males,
unemancipated and emancipated, born or after-born, requiring them
all to be instituted or individually disinherited with the same
consequence of failure to do so in every one of these cases. With
regard to adoptive children we have introduced a distinction which
may be found in our constitution [91] on the subject of adoption.
6. But if a soldier on active service makes a will and has not individually disinherited his children born or after-born, but has passed
them by in silence well knowing that he has children, imperial constitutions provide that his silence is equivalent to an express
disherison.

7. Mothers and maternal grandparents have no need to institute
or disinherit their children, but may omit to mention them. For
the silence of a mother or maternal grandmother and other maternal
ascendants has the same effect as disherison by a father. Neither
the civil law nor the praetor's edict, which promises bonorum
possessio contra tabulas to children passed over in silence, requires
a mother, or maternal grandparent, to disinherit a son or daughter,
or a daughter's children of either sex if they are not instituted.
But in such cases there is another remedy which will be explained
below.

IX. The Plaint of the Unduteous Will

316. The rules considered in the last chapter secured that
parents should not pass over their children in silence and that
if they chose to disinherit them they should use the appropriate
form. Failing this, the children were said to be praeteriti
(passed over) and might avail themselves of the remedies above
described. These rules did not prevent a father from disinheriting his children. They merely said how he was to do
so. Further, the rule applied to the father's (or grandfather's)
will only—not to the mother's. But from the end of the   2. 13 pr.
Republic, or the beginning of the Empire, a new principle
asserted itself, namely that a testator was not free to dispose
of his property as he pleased, that certain near relations must
be provided for. If he failed in this duty the will might be
impeached and rescinded by a procedure known as the plaint
of the unduteous will—querela inofficiosi testamenti. This was
an action brought against an instituted heir who had entered on

[90] Cod. 6. 28. 4.
[91] Cod. 8. 47 (48). 10.

the inheritance. It originated in the court of the centumviri (§ 690), and took the form of a fictitious allegation that the testator was insane, and that the will was therefore invalid or must be set aside. Later, this fiction disappeared from view and the querela was considered to be based upon the unjust reflection cast upon the person passed over or insufficiently provided for.

2. 18 pr.

317. Who might bring the querela? Descendants, ascendants, brothers and sisters, but these last only if turpes personae had been preferred to them. The law seems to have been settled in this sense as early as Ulpian.[92] The term turpes personae (base persons) is not precisely defined. It includes persons technically infamous (infames) and persons of bad character or low social standing.[93] If there were no children, or none who impeached the will successfully, the querela was available to ascendants, and, in the same way, ultimately to brothers and sisters.[94]

2. 18. 1.

318. Under what circumstances might the querela be brought?

(a) The person bringing it must show that he had received less than a fair share of the testator's estate. He need not have been instituted heir, but he should have been provided for by institution or legacy or gift mortis causa. The amount to which he was entitled was originally left to the discretion of the court. Later, it came to be fixed by statute at one fourth part of what he would have taken upon intestacy. This was the proportion of the estate which by the lex Falcidia (§ 357) the heir was allowed to retain against legatees. In connection with the querela it was known as the portio legibus debita or the legitima portio (the statutory portion) and in modern usage is termed " the legitim."

2. 18. 6.

(b) He could not bring it, if he had been disinherited on just grounds.

(c) He must have no other means of attacking the will. The querela is described as " a last resort " (ultimum adjutorium). If the complainant could avail himself of any other remedy the querela was excluded. Thus a suus heres passed

2. 18. 2.

---

[92] Dig. 5. 2. 1.

[93] Cod. 3. 28. 27. The origin of infamia was the black mark attached to a person by the censor. Under the Empire the word covered certain disqualifications created by the praetor or by statute, which under Justinian were mainly procedural. The subject is too complicated to be summarised in a footnote. For fuller information, see Buckl. T. p. 91; M. p. 53; Sohm, p. 183; Moyle ad Inst. 4. 16. 2.

[94] Dig. 5. 2. 31 pr.

over could not bring it since he had his remedy by petitio
hereditatis at civil law (§ 694) and an emancipated son, who had
been passed over, could not bring it because he could get
bonorum possessio contra tabulas from the praetor (§ 314). But
either of them could bring it if he was disinherited without just   2. 13. 7.
cause, for in that case no other remedy was available. In a
woman's will passing-over (praeteritio) had the same effect as
disherison (exheredatio).

(d) The querela was barred by the lapse of five years from
the time when the heir entered on the inheritance, and there
were other circumstances in which it could not be brought,
e.g., if the person who might have brought it recognised the
validity of the will by accepting a benefit under it or compromised his claim.

319. What was the effect of the querela, if successful? It
upset the will and produced an intestacy.[95] If there were two
or more instituted heirs, to upset the will wholly it was necessary to challenge it as regards each or all of them. If the
complainant attacked one only or successfully attacked one only
the will was upset pro tanto. This produced the anomalous
result that the testator was taken to have died partly
testate and partly intestate, contrary to the general rule. The
same consequence followed if two persons were entitled pari
passu to attack the will (e.g., two sons both alleged to be
unjustly disinherited) and only one did so or did so successfully.

320. A testator might miscalculate the amount of his fortune
or might increase it after the date of the will. This made no
difference. If the person entitled did not receive his just proportion, the will could be successfully challenged. To avoid
this result, it was usual to insert a clause to the effect that if the
share was found to be too small it should be referred to a fair-
minded man to bring it up to the right amount (boni viri
arbitratu). This saved the will.

321. So far we have stated the law as it stood before
Justinian. He made many changes: —

(a) The querela was only to lie if the person entitled received
nothing at all. If something, however little, was left to him,
the will could no longer be impeached and upset, but an action
lay to have what was left made up to the statutory amount.
This meant, in effect, that the arbitration clause (as we should   2. 18. 3.
call it) was read into every will. The result of this action (actio

---

[95] Dig. 5. 2. 28 in fine.

ad supplendam legitimam) was to reduce the amount which went to the instituted heirs, the will otherwise remaining intact. It was a good defence to this action, as it was to the querela, that the complainant had been justly disinherited.

(b) After the date of the Institutes, Novel 18. 1 (A.D. 536) increased the amount of the legitim in the case of children. If there were not more than four, it was to be one-third of the intestate share, otherwise one-half. The share of ascendants and of brothers and sisters remained fixed at one-quarter.

(c) The just grounds of exheredation were defined by Novel 115 (A.D. 542)—fourteen in the case of children, eight in the case of parents, three in the case of brothers and sisters. The burden of justifying disherison lay upon the instituted heir.

(d) Lastly, by the same Novel, Justinian introduced an entirely new condition by requiring the persons entitled to the legitim, if descendants or ascendants, to be instituted heirs, but not necessarily to the amount of the legitim. If they were disinherited without just cause (though otherwise well provided for) the will might be upset by the querela, but only as concerns the institution of heirs. The other provisions of the will remained unaffected.[96] This enactment carries the law a stage further as regards recognition of the claims of next-of-kin. In the earliest stage descendants might be disinherited, but not passed over in silence. In the classical and post-classical periods, they might still be disinherited, but some provision must be made for them. In the latest stage descendants and ascendants must be both instituted heirs and provided for up to the statutory amount. If they were disinherited, however amply provided for, they could bring the querela. If they were instituted, but insufficiently provided for, they had the actio ad supplendam legitimam. If they were passed over in silence, they might have recourse to the civil law remedy of petitio hereditatis or the praetorian remedy of bonorum possessio contra tabulas. Such at least is a probable explanation of the situation. But the procedural consequences of Justinian's latest change in the law are as obscure as they are unimportant.

322. The expectations of descendants and others might be defeated by alienation *inter vivos* no less than by last will. To provide against this contingency an aggrieved person was allowed to bring querela inofficiosae donationis or inofficiosae dotis. "The effect was that both under wills and in intestacy

---

[96] Nov. 115, c. 4, 9; Girard, p. 920.

there was machinery similar to the *querela* [inofficiosi testamenti] by which immoderate *donationes* and *dotes* might be set aside." [97]

323. THE MODERN LAW OF LEGITIM.—The principle of the legitim is an integral part of those modern systems of law, which have a Roman ancestry more or less direct. German writers on Roman Law use the phrase " succession by necessity " (die Noterbfolge) to cover both the rules requiring certain persons to be instituted or disinherited and the rules requiring certain persons to be provided for. These are distinguished as formal succession by necessity (das formelle Noterbrecht), and material succession by necessity (das materielle Noterbrecht or Pflicht-teils-recht). The French writers speak of " succession against the will " (succession à l'encontre du testament). In French Law the part of the estate which a testator may dispose of is called la quotité disponible. This is the equivalent of a child's portion if there are three children or less, and in any event is not less than one-quarter of the estate. In German Law the testator may in any event freely dispose of one-half of his estate.

The English Law has tardily and to a very limited extent recognised the duty of a testator to provide for his family in the Inheritance (Family Provision) Act, 1938. In South Africa, where the legitim has been abolished by statute, the courts none the less regard the duty of educating and maintaining minor children as " a debt resting upon the estate." [98]

THE INSTITUTES

BOOK II

TITLE XVIII

Of the unduteous will

Since it often happened that parents unreasonably disinherited or passed over their children a rule was introduced allowing children who complain that they have been unjustly disinherited or unjustly passed over to bring the plaint of the unduteous will on the pretended ground that the parents were in a way insane when they made their will. It is not alleged that the testator was really insane (if he had been there would have been no will at all); the supposition is that testator has made his will validly, but not in accordance with the claims of natural affection. §316.

1. It is not merely children who may thus impeach the will of their parents, but parents similarly impeach the will of their §317.

---

[97] Buckl. *T.* 332.
[98] Lee, p. 41.

children. Brothers and sisters are by imperial constitutions preferred to base persons instituted heirs. Consequently they cannot take proceedings against any and every heir. Relatives more distantly related than brothers and sisters cannot take proceedings with any hope of success.

§ 114.

2. Natural children and adoptive children (with due observance of the distinction in our constitution) may bring the plaint of the unduteous will if they have no other means of coming at the deceased person's estate. For no one can bring the plaint who can claim the inheritance in whole or in part by any other form of proceeding. Posthumous children too, if they have no other remedy, may bring the querela.

§ 321.

3. All this must be understood to apply only if the testator has left them nothing at all by his will. This has been enacted by our constitution out of regard for the claims of nature. If they have been left any share of the inheritance great or small, or any thing whatever, the querela cannot be brought, but the aggrieved party may have what he takes under the will brought up to a fourth part of what he would take in the event of an intestacy, although there is no direction to this effect in the will. 4. If a tutor has accepted a legacy given by the will of his own father to a ward whose affairs he is administering, while the tutor himself received nothing under his father's will, this does not prevent him impeaching his father's will on his own account.

§ 318.

5. Conversely, if he has brought the querela in the name of a ward to whom nothing was left and has failed in the suit, he does not forfeit a legacy left to himself in the same will.[99] 6. Accordingly, in order to exclude the querela a person must have his quarter, either as heir, or by way of legacy or fideicommissum or gift mortis causa, or gift inter vivos but only in the cases mentioned in our constitution, or in the other ways specified in the constitutions.[1]

7. When we say " quarter " this must be understood in the sense that, whether there be one person, or more than one, entitled to impeach the will, there is one-quarter for them all, so that each person gets his rateable share of the quarter.

X. How Wills Fail to Take Effect

324. It is not enough that a will should be valid *ab initio*. It is further necessary that it remain valid until the heir enters upon the inheritance. A will valid *ab initio* (jure factum) may fail to take effect in any of the following ways:—

325. (1) By the subsequent introduction into the family of a new suus heres (§ 336), which takes place:—

---

[99] If a relative impeached the will unsuccessfully, anything given to him by the will was forfeited to the fiscus. Dig. 5. 2. 8, 14. It was a case of ereption for indignity (§ 312).

[1] *viz.*, if made propter nuptias or by way of dos and in some other exceptional cases (Moyle, *ad loc.*).

(a) by birth, *i.e.*, when after the date of the will a child is born to the testator who has not been instituted or duly disinherited [2];

(b) (in the older law) when a woman became a wife in manu of the testator and thereby acquired the status of daughter [3];

(c) when owing to the death or emancipation of a son during the testator's lifetime the son's children take his place as sui heredes (§ 336);   2. 13. 2.

(d) when the testator acquires a new suus heres by adoption.   2. 17. 1.

326. Anciently, any one of the above events was fatal to the will and there was no way of avoiding the consequence. But ultimately jurisprudence and legislation combined to make it possible to save the will by instituting or disinheriting in advance any one who in the course of nature might come to rank as suus heres of the testator. Failing this precaution the will was destitute of effect. Adoption, however, which was not an accident of nature, continued to avoid the will, just as marriage (usually) does in English law, except, perhaps, when the adopted son had been previously instituted.[4] There could, of course, be no question of previous disherison, since he was not a suus heres at the date of the will.[5]

327. (2) By making a subsequent will, even though in the event no one accepted the inheritance. If the second will was 2. 17. 2. a praetorian will the first will was not technically revoked, but the praetor gave bonorum possessio according to the second will, not according to the first.

328. In the above two cases the will was said to be " broken " (ruptum).

329. (3) If the testator underwent change of status (capitis deminutio) subsequently to the will. In this case the will was 2. 17. 4. said to become inoperative (irritum). But the praetor came to the aid of the instituted heir, if the will satisfied the praetorian requirements and the deceased was a Roman citizen and sui juris at the time of his death, by giving him bonorum

---

[2] Ulp. XXIII, 3.

[3] Since coemptio, which produced manus (§ 121) might be used for other purposes than matrimony (coemptio fiduciae causa), a woman might be in a man's manus without being his wife and having the status of daughter. In that case she would acquire the status of daughter only if she afterwards married him—si quae in manu fuit nubat. G. 2. 139.

[4] Dig. 28. 2. 23, 1 ; 28. 3. 18.

[5] G. 2. 140.

possessio secundum tabulas.[6] At first the grant was provisional
merely—sine re—and was unavailing against civil law heirs *ab
intestato*.[7] Later, it was cum re, *i.e.*, an effective answer to
their claim.[8]

330. (4) By civil law the only way to revoke a will was to
make a new one. But the praetor gave an exceptio doli if a
testator had burnt, torn or defaced his will or erased the
institution of the heir animo revocandi.[9] The effect was that
he died intestate or revived an earlier will, if it appeared that
such was his intention. In the later law destruction animo
revocandi annulled the will *ipso jure*.[10]

331. (5) The later imperial law (Theodosius and Honorius
A.D. 418) made a will void after a lapse of ten years from its
execution. Justinian qualified this by allowing a will after
such lapse of time to be revoked by a declaration made before
three witnesses or lodged in the archives.[11]

332. A will might fail: (6) through being set aside as
inofficious, in which case it was said to be rescinded (rescis-
sum)[12]; or, (7) if no heir accepted the inheritance, in which
case the will was said to be abandoned (destitutum). This might
happen because the heir or heirs died before the testator, or,
surviving him, died before acceptance or repudiated the
inheritance.

333. Just as a former will could not in general be formally
revoked except by a later one, so a later one always revoked
the old one. Two valid testaments could not co-exist. However, under the Empire this was modified. If in the second will
the heir was instituted to some specific properties merely, and
the testator expressed the wish that the first will should remain
in force, though the second will revoked the first, the heir was
affected with a fideicommissum (§ 360) in favour of the heir
instituted in the first will, retaining only the property expressly
given him in the second will, or so much as together with this
was required to bring his share up to the statutory fourth which

---

[6] Moyle *ad* Inst. 2. 17. 6. says: " The only kind of capitis deminutio
whose effect, in making the will irritum, could be overridden in this manner
by bonorum possessio secundum tabulas was capitis deminutio minima."
So Poste *ad* G. 2. 147. But this is questionable. Windscheid, III, § 563,
n. 7. The language of the text " si modo defunctus et civis Romanus et
suae potestatis mortis tempore fuerit " suggests the opposite.
[7] G. 2. 148 ; Ulp. XXIII, 6.
[8] Girard, p. 891.
[9] G. 2. 151.
[10] Dig. 28. 4. 1 ; Girard, pp. 889, 890.
[11] Cod. 6. 23. 27, 2.
[12] Dig. 5. 2. 8, 16.

by the senatusconsultum Pegasianum a fiduciary heir was
entitled to retain against fideicommissaries (§ 366). This was so
provided by a rescript of the Emperors Severus and his son
Antoninus (or Caracalla).

THE INSTITUTES

BOOK II

TITLE XVII

In what ways wills fail to take effect

A will duly executed remains valid until it is broken or becomes
inoperative. 1. A will is broken when, though the testator's status
remains unchanged, the legal effect of the will is impaired. For if § 325.
after making his will the testator adrogates a person sui juris by
imperial decree, or adopts a person alieni juris before the praetor
as provided by our constitution, his will is broken, just as if he had
acquired a new suus heres by birth. 2. Again, a later will, validly § 327.
executed, breaks an earlier will. And it makes no difference whether
an heir accepts the inheritance under the later will, or does not
accept; for the only question asked is whether there could be an heir
under the later will. Accordingly, if the instituted heir renounces
the inheritance, or dies either in the lifetime of the testator or after § 332.
his death before entering upon the inheritance, or if he is instituted
conditionally and the condition fails, in all these cases the testator
dies intestate; for the earlier will is invalid, being broken by the
later will, and the later will is equally without effect, since no one
takes up the inheritance. 3. If a testator makes a valid will and
afterwards a second will also valid, although in the second will he
institutes an heir to certain specified properties only, the first will is
destroyed, as was decided by a rescript of the Emperors Severus and
Antoninus. The words of this constitution we have directed to be
inserted here, since there is another matter to which the constitution
gives expression. It runs as follows:—" The Emperors Severus and
Antoninus to Cocceius Campanus. There should be no doubt that
the second testament, although the heir is instituted merely to certain
specific properties, is just as valid as if no such things had been
mentioned, but the instituted heir is bound to be content with the
properties given to him, made up if necessary to the amount of the
Falcidian quarter,[13] and to restore the inheritance to the heirs § 333.
instituted in the earlier will. This results from the clause in the
second will expressing the intention that the first will should take
effect." This, then, is the way in which a will is broken. 4. There
is another way in which wills validly executed are rendered invalid, § 329.

---

[13] More precisely Pegasian, but the quarta Pegasiana is frequently
called quarta Falcidia, the s.c. being in effect read as one enactment with
the lex. The words of the constitution are quoted also in Dig.
36. 1. 30 (29).

namely when the testator is capite deminutus. How this happens
has been explained in Book I.

5. In this case wills are said to become inoperative. No doubt
wills which are broken become inoperative and wills which are *ab
initio* invalid are inoperative, and valid wills which are rendered
inoperative by capitis deminutio may also be said to be broken. But
since it is more convenient to distinguish different events by appropriate names we say that some wills are invalid, and that some valid
wills are broken or become inoperative. 6. (5) However, wills *ab
initio* valid which are rendered inoperative by capitis deminutio are
not wholly destitute of effect. For, if they are sealed with the seals
of seven witnesses the instituted heir may claim bonorum possessio
secundum tabulas, if at the moment of death the testator was a
Roman citizen of independent status. But if the will was rendered
inoperative by the testator's loss of citizenship or of liberty, or by his
giving himself in adoption and at the time of his death he was in the
power of his adoptive father, the instituted heir cannot ask for
possession of goods in terms of the will. 7. (6) A will cannot be
invalidated merely because the testator did not want it to remain in
force and still less if after making one will he has begun to make
another, and either because he was prevented by death or because he
changed his mind has not carried it through to completion. This is
laid down in an Oration of the Emperor Pertinax,[14] providing that
valid wills are not to be deprived of effect except by a subsequent
will duly executed and completed. If a will is incomplete it is, of
course, no will at all.

8. (7) In the same Oration the Emperor declared that he would
not accept an inheritance to which the Emperor was instituted
merely in order to involve some one in litigation, nor would he
approve a will irregularly executed in which he was instituted heir
from the same motive, nor would he accept the title of heir on the
strength of spoken words, nor take anything by virtue of any writing
not authorised by law. The Emperors Severus and Antoninus have
issued many rescripts to the same effect, " For though, " say they,
" we are above the law, yet we live obedient to the law."

XI. Different Kinds of Testamentary Heir—
Acceptance of the Inheritance

334. The third and last condition of the effective validity
of the Roman will was that an heir or heirs should duly enter
upon the inheritance (§ 277). Failing this, the will was destitutum (§ 332) and there was an intestacy. There were three
classes of testamentary heirs, *viz.*, (1) necessary (necessarii);
(2) family and necessary or family (sui et necessarii or sui);
(3) extraneous (extranei).

2. 19. 1.   335. Necessarii Heredes.—These were slaves instituted heirs
with a gift of liberty. In the later law the gift of liberty was

---

[14] A.D. 193.

implied from the institution. The slave was called "necessary heir" because he could not refuse the inheritance, but as a set-off the praetor gave him the right of separation (beneficium separationis, so called), *i.e.*, allowed him to apply for "separation of goods," with the consequence that he kept intact anything that he acquired as his own property after the death of the testator and creditors had to be content with the assets of the estate. The object of instituting a slave in the last resort was to relieve the memory of the deceased from the ignominy of *post mortem* bankruptcy. It may be remarked in passing that the phrase "separation of goods" had another application, *viz.*, when creditors of the estate claimed separation as against creditors of the heir,[15] a very necessary precaution if the heir was heavily indebted, for the normal consequence of succession was to absorb the patrimony of the deceased in the patrimony of the heir.

336. SUI ET NECESSARII—SUI HEREDES.—These were descendants in the power of the testator who became sui juris upon 2. 19. 2. his death, and children or further descendants born after his death (posthumous, therefore, in the modern sense of the word), who would have been in this position, if born during his lifetime. A grandchild satisfied these conditions if conceived during testator's lifetime and if his father had ceased to be in power (by death or otherwise) before the testator's death. Gaius and Justinian say that sui heredes are so called because they are "family heirs" (domestici heredes) and even during testator's lifetime have, in a way, a vested interest in the family estate: "Even in the lifetime of their parent they are deemed to be in a certain sense owners." By the civil law they could not decline the inheritance, but the praetor gave them the privilege of abstaining (the so-called beneficium abstinendi); which, however, they lost, if they intermeddled with the estate. But minors and soldiers who had done so might petition for relief by restitutio in integrum (§ 777).

337. EXTRANEI HEREDES, *i.e.*, persons not subject to testator's power. These might accept or not as they pleased and by civil 2. 19. 3. law might take their own time to do so. It was usual, however, for the testator to prescribe a limit of time (normally, one hundred days) within which the heir must make a formal acceptance, if he meant to accept at all. This institution was known as cretio (§ 297). Apart from this, any indication of 2. 19. 7.

---

[15] Dig. 46. 2. 1. 1.

intention to accept the inheritance (adire hereditatem), and in particular, acting as heir (pro herede gerere) was sufficient. An acceptance or refusal, once made, could not be retracted, except by minors and soldiers. The practice of directing the heir to make cretio had fallen into disuse before Justinian. Instead of this it was usual for the heir, under pressure from the creditors or at his own instance,[16] to apply to the praetor to fix a period for him to deliberate (spatium deliberandi), within which he must accept (if he meant to),[17] or (as Justinian enacted) [18] disclaim, if he meant to, the inheritance, *i.e.*, failure to disclaim was construed as acceptance. The time allowed was not less than one hundred days and usually not more than nine months. Meanwhile, the inheritance was vacant (hereditas jacens, § 142) and with reference to the heir was said to be delated (delata), *i.e.*, offered, or open for his acceptance: " A delated inheritance means one which one can acquire by entering upon it." [19]

338. Lapsed Portions—Caduca.—If a single heir for any cause did not in due course take the inheritance there was an intestacy. If one of several co-heirs was dead or disqualified when the will was executed his institution was wiped out. It was taken pro non scripto. If the institution, though initially valid, subsequently failed from whatever cause (death, disqualification, repudiation, etc.) there was a lapse and the lapsed portion went to the other heirs by right of accrual (jure adcrescendi). The marriage laws of Augustus made fundamental changes. First, they created a new statutory class of lapses by withholding from caelibes and orbi the jus capiendi (§ 310). Secondly, they decreed that all lapses (caduca), statutory or other, should escheat to the aerarium (later replaced by the fiscus),[20] unless there was a co-heir or legatee blessed with issue to arrest the caducum on its way to the public chest,[21] (caducorum vindicatio). Thirdly, the same laws, or later senatusconsulta, postponed acceptance of the inheritance and, by consequence, the vesting of legacies to the opening of the will and thus prolonged the possibility of lapse.[22] The effect was to exclude the jus adcrescendi except in the case of descendants and ascendants of the testator to the third degree, who enjoyed the jus antiquum (§ 310). Constantine relieved caelibes and orbi of their disabilities, but the law of lapses remained otherwise unchanged until Justinian abolished it by his constitution *de caducis tollendis* (A.D. 534) [23] and re-established the jus adcrescendi with the difference that the accrued portion was to carry with it any attached burdens of legacy, etc., which had not been the case in the old law. He also reverted to the old rule that an heir

(margin left) 2. 19. 5.

(margin left) 3. 1 pr.

---

[16] Girard, p. 932.
[18] Cod. 6. 30. 22. 14a.
[20] Ulp. XVII, 2.
[22] Ulp. XVII, 1 ; XXIV, 31.

[17] G. 2. 167.
[19] Dig. 50. 16. 151.
[21] G. 2. 207.
[23] Cod. 6. 51.

who knew that he was instituted might enter upon the inheritance immediately upon the death of the testator without waiting for the opening of the will.

339. TRANSMISSION OF THE INHERITANCE.—But acceptance might for various reasons be delayed. If the heir survived the testator but died before entry he did not transmit the inheritance to his heirs, because it was not yet his to transmit. Such was the principle, but it was modified by legislation. Theodosius II made it inapplicable to descendants of the testator who died before the opening of the will (transmissio Theodosiana).[24] Thus, a grandson took the place of his deceased father instituted by the grandfather's will. Justinian made the right of accepting the inheritance transmissible from and to any heirs, but only within a year of its becoming available (transmissio Justinianea) [25] and the heirs of the heir must accept, if at all, within the remainder of the year.

340. BENEFICIUM INVENTARII.—A constitution of A.D. 531 made a revolution in this branch of the law by providing that any heir (testamentary or *ab intestato*) who had doubts about accepting or refusing might accept with benefit of inventory (beneficium inventarii). If he did so, he had to begin an inventory of the assets within thirty days of becoming aware of his right to claim the inheritance and complete it within another sixty days. By satisfying this requirement he escaped liability for the debts of the deceased beyond the extent of the assets. In effect he was converted from a universal successor into an executor and residuary legatee. Reluctantly, " that we may not be thought to have a complete disregard of antiquity," Justinian retained the alternative of applying for the spatium deliberandi. An heir who accepted after deliberation incurred all the old liabilities of the universal successor. But he was not relieved from the duty of making an inventory. If he failed to do so, he was denied the benefit of the lex Falcidia (§ 357).[26]

THE INSTITUTES

BOOK II

TITLE XIX

Of the different kinds of heir

Heirs are either necessarii or sui et necessarii or extranei. 1. A heres necessarius is a slave of the testator, whom he institutes heir, and is so called because, whether he wishes it or not, he becomes free

---

[24] Cod. 6. 52. (A.D. 450). Compare Wills Act, 1837, s. 33.
[25] Cod. 6. 30. 19 (A.D. 529).
[26] Inst. 2. 19. 6; Cod. 6. 30. 22, 14c.

§ 335.   and necessary heir immediately on the death of the testator. Hence it comes that testators who have doubts about their solvency are in the habit of instituting a slave, or substituting a slave in the second or any remoter place, so that if creditors are not satisfied, it may be the estate of the heir rather than that of the testator which is possessed by the creditors, or sold or divided between them. In compensation for this disadvantage the necessary heir has the advantage that he keeps for himself everything that he acquires after the death of his patron, and, if the estate proves insufficient to satisfy the creditors, his own property cannot afterwards be sold to make good the deficiency.

§ 336.   2. Sui et necessarii heredes, are, for instance, a son, a daughter, a grandson, or granddaughter by a son, and other descendants [through males], provided they were in the power of the deceased. But it is not enough that a grandchild should have been in the grandfather's power at the time of death; it is further necessary that his father should have ceased to be suus heres to *his* father, either carried off by death or in some way released from power; for then the grandchild takes the place of his father as suus heres of the grandfather. Sui heredes are so called because they are family heirs and are in a way deemed to be owners even in the lifetime of their father. This again is the reason why if a man dies intestate the succession goes in the first instance to the children. They are called "necessary" because in every event, whether they wish it or not, they are heirs *ab intestato* or testamentary. But the praetor allows them, if they wish it, to abstain from the inheritance so that it is the parent's estate and not their own of which the creditors take possession.

§ 337.   3. Others who are not subject to the testator's power are called extranei heredes, and so even our children, if they are not in our power, when we institute them as heirs, are considered to be extraneous heirs. If children are instituted heirs by their mother they are in the same position, because women do not have children in their power. Also a slave who is instituted heir by his master and manumitted after the execution of the will is in the same position.

    4. With extraneous heirs there must be a testamenti factio whether they are instituted themselves, or those in their power are instituted. In regard to this two moments of time are taken into account, the time when the will is made, and the time when the testator dies, the first to give validity to the institution, the second to give it effect.

§ 307.   Further, there should also be testamenti factio with the heir when he enters on the inheritance, whether the institution is absolute or conditional. But change in the status of the heir in the interval between the execution of the will and the death of the testator or the realisation of the condition does not hurt the heir, because, as we have said, three times must be taken into account. The term testamenti factio is applied not only to a testator who is competent to make a will, but also a person who is competent to take for himself or to acquire for another under a will, though he may not be competent to make a will himself. Therefore, persons who are insane or dumb, posthumous children, infants, sons in power and another person's slaves are said to have testamenti factio; for although they cannot make a will themselves, they can take under a will either for themselves or for some one else. 5. Extraneous heirs are allowed to deliberate whether they will accept or renounce the inheritance. But if a family heir who has the privilege of abstaining § 337. has intermeddled with the property, or if an extraneous heir, who may deliberate, has entered on the inheritance, he may not afterwards abandon it, unless he is under twenty-five years of age; for if persons within this limit of age have taken up a ruinous inheritance, the praetor comes to their aid, just as he does in any other matter in which they have been misled. 6. It must be observed, however, that the Emperor Hadrian once extended indulgence even to a person above twenty-five years of age in a case in which a heavy liability unknown when the heir entered on the inheritance afterwards came to light. This was a special favour granted to an individual. At a later date the Emperor Gordian [27] extended the privilege to soldiers in general. But our constitution has put this benefit within the reach of all the subjects of our Empire. By § 340. complying with its provisions any one may enter upon an inheritance and be liable only to the extent of the value of the estate, so that there is no longer any need to have recourse to deliberation, unless an heir thinks best, instead of acting in terms of our constitution, to take time to deliberate and to incur the old liability consequent upon the acceptance of an inheritance.

7. An extraneous heir, whether instituted in a will, or called to the succession *ab intestato*, becomes heir either by acting as heir or even by a mere expression of intention to take up the inheritance. A § 337. person is deemed to act as heir, if in the character of heir he deals with things belonging to the estate, as by selling them, by cultivating or giving a lease of landed property, or indeed by declaring in any way whatever by word or deed his purpose of entering on the inheritance, provided that he knows that the owner of the property has died testate or intestate and knows that he himself is his heir. To act as heir is equivalent to acting as owner, for in the old language the word heres was often used in the sense of dominus. Just as an extraneous heir becomes heir by a mere declaration of intention, so a contrary decision effects an immediate repudiation. There is nothing to prevent a person who is born deaf or dumb or becomes so afterwards from acting as heir and acquiring the inheritance for himself, provided that he understands what he is doing.

XII. LEGACIES

341. The topic of legacy is intimately connected with testamentary succession, for though there may be a will without a legacy, there cannot be a legacy without a will. Legacy is 2. 20. 1. vaguely described in the Institutes as " a gift left by a deceased person," and more precisely in the Digest as " a diminution of the inheritance whereby the testator directs that something which would otherwise form part of the whole estate going to the heir

---

[27] A.D. 238.

is to go to some other person." [28] Thus, while inheritance was
a form of universal succession, legacy was a form of particular
succession ; and while the heir was liable for the debts of the
deceased, the legatee was not liable for debts, but could not
take, or having taken keep, his legacy until the debts were
satisfied.

342. A legacy commonly consisted in a gift of a corporeal
thing or things, determined specifically or generally—" my black
horse," " five hundred aurei," etc., but it might assume a great
variety of forms. Thus a usufruct or a praedial servitude might
be created by way of legacy ; the testator might discharge his
debtor by leaving him a legacy of the debt (legatum libera-
tionis) ; or bequeath the debt to a third person (legatum
nominis) ; or charge his heir with some duty of action or
abstention, for example, to build a bath or theatre for a municipality.[29] A legacy might take the form of a gift of an *aliquot*
part of the inheritance [30] (" Be Sempronius my heir. Let my
heir divide my inheritance with Titius "). This was called a
" partition," and the legatee was termed a " partiary legatee."
In the instance given he takes one-half. Any other proportion
might be arranged. But in all such cases the legatee took by
particular not by universal title. He was not liable for the
debts.

343. The distinguishing marks of a legacy in contrast with
a fideicommissum of a single thing was that a legacy was left
by imperative words and was legally binding upon the heir,
while a fideicommissum was created by words of request [31] and
imposed at first a merely moral obligation. A legacy might be
left by a will and from the beginning of the Empire by a codicil
confirmed by will either by anticipation or subsequently.[32] A
fideicommissum could be left by an unconfirmed codicil. There
were other differences which will be noticed below (§ 371).
Most of the differences between legacies and fideicommissa had
already ceased to exist before Justinian fused the two institutions
as described in the text.

344. Until Justinian's legislation (§ 349) legacies were (in
point of form) of four kinds :—*viz.*, (1) per vindicationem (by
vindication) ; (2) by damnationem (by condemnation) ; (3)

Marginal references:
2. 20. 13.
2. 20. 21.

2. 23. 5.

2. 23. 1.

2. 20. 2.

2. 20. 2.

---

[28] Dig. 30. 116 pr. (Florentinus).
[29] Dig. 35. 2. 80, 1.
[30] Ulp. XXIV, 25.
[31] Ulp. XXIV, 1.
[32] G. 2. 270a ; Girard, p. 968.

sinendi modo (by way of sufferance) ; (4) per praeceptionem (by taking in advance). Each of these was created by an appropriate form of words and had its own special consequences.

345. LEGATUM PER VINDICATIONEM.[33]—This entitled the legatee to vindicate the subject of the legacy, that is to claim it from the heir or any one else in a real action. A testator could leave by this method only a thing which belonged to him by quiritary title, both at the date of the will and at the time of death, unless the legacy consisted in " things which are weighed, counted, or measured " (fungible things, § 420), in which case it was sufficient that they belonged to the testator at the time of death.[34] The effect of the legacy was that the thing bequeathed became the property of the legatee by quiritary title from the moment of the acceptance of the inheritance. The only doubt was if this was so, whether he knew of it or not. The Sabinian view was that it vested forthwith subject to repudiation. The Proculians held that the legacy did not vest until the legatee knew of it and wished it to belong to him. The Sabinian (not, as Gaius says, the Proculian) view prevailed.[35] The correct formula was: " I give and bequeath the slave Stichus." But either " give " or " bequeath " was enough, and there were other alternatives. This type of legacy was also available to constitute a usufruct or praedial servitude over property which belonged to the testator by quiritary title, for in this case also the right vested directly in the legatee and he could enforce it by the appropriate real action (actio confessoria).[36]

346. LEGATUM PER DAMNATIONEM.[37]—The testator might give by this method anything whatever, whether it belonged to himself, to his heir, or to a third person. If it belonged to a third person the heir must acquire it, if he could ; otherwise, pay its value. A thing not yet in existence might be bequeathed by this method, as an unborn slave or next year's harvest. The legatee's remedy was a personal action against the heir. The formula was: " Be my heir condemned to give (dare damnas esto)," or, simply, " my heir must give (dato) the slave Stichus." If the subject of the legacy was a thing precisely ascertained, the double value was recoverable in case of denial of liability. This G. 4. 9. was a survival from the legis actio procedure and was one of several cases in which denial had this consequence (§ 593).

---

[33] G. 2. 193.
[34] G. 2. 196.
[35] G. 2. 195 ; Dig. 8. 6. 19, 1 ; Girard, p. 981, n. 1.
[36] Paul. *Sent*. 3. 6. 17 ; Girard, p. 969.
[37] G. 2. 201.

347. LEGATUM SINENDI MODO.[38]—The formula was: " Be my heir condemned to allow Lucius Titius to take and have for himself the slave Stichus." On the face of it, the duty imposed upon the heir is negative, a duty of sufferance. But the view prevailed that the heir was required to transfer the thing to the legatee by any appropriate method. In the result, therefore, there was little to distinguish this form of legacy from the last, except, principally, that by this the testator could only dispose of what belonged to himself or to his heir at the time of death and not of what belonged to a third person. Since the property did not vest immediately in the legatee, the appropriate remedy was a personal action against the heir.

348. LEGATUM PER PRAECEPTIONEM.[39]—This was a direction that the legatee might take something out of the estate before it was distributed amongst the heirs. The formula was: " Let Lucius take the slave Stichus in advance." Since an heir could not be charged with a legacy to himself,[40] this meant that if, for example, Sempronius and Titius were instituted heirs each to one-half, and Sempronius was given a legacy per praeceptionem of the slave Stichus, he took one half share in the slave in his quality of heir, and the other half share in the slave by virtue of a legacy charged upon the share of his co-heir Titius, but the inheritance to be divided between Sempronius and Titius was the inheritance *minus* the slave Stichus, which Sempronius had " taken in advance." The question was debated between the schools whether a legacy could be left in these terms to a person who was not a co-heir.[41] The Sabinian view was that it could not. It followed that the only action appropriate to such a legacy was the action given to co-heirs for a division of the inheritance, in which it would be the duty of the judge to see that the subject of the legacy was adjudicated (§ 722) to the person entitled. The Proculians, on the contrary, held that a legacy expressed in these terms could be left to a stranger, the direction that the legatee should " take in advance " being construed simply as a direction that " he should take." In Latin this meant that the first syllable of the word was to be ignored and the word praecipito read as if it were capito. Gaius adds that this opinion " is said to have been confirmed by a constitution of the late Emperor Hadrian."[42] This is one of the passages which lend colour to the view that Gaius was a provincial and that the latest sources of information were not accessible to him. According to this view the legatee's remedy would vary with the circumstances. If the slave was the quiritary property of the testator the legatee could vindicate it, whether he was a co-heir or a stranger (the formula " heres meus capito " was a permitted variant in the legacy per vindicationem)[43]; if the slave was in bonis (merely) of the testator, a

[38] G. 2. 209.
[39] G. 2. 216.
[40] Ulp. XXIV, 22.
[41] G. 2. 217, 218.
[42] G. 2. 221.
[43] G. 2. 193.

co-heir could take advantage of the action for the division of the inheritance.

349. SENATUSCONSULTUM NERONIANUM.—Such was the old law as stated by Gaius. But these distinctions had already been rendered less important by a senatusconsultum of the Emperor Nero, which enacted that if a legacy was expressed in inappropriate terms (for example, if a testator gave a thing which did not belong to him by quiritary title by a form of words appropriate to a legacy by vindication) it should take effect in the way most favourable to the legacy, that is, by condemnation.[44] If, however, a legacy was expressed in appropriate terms it retained its former effect.[45] This enactment was in turn superseded by a law of A.D. 339 providing that in legacies or fideicommissa no form of words need be observed,[46] so that it was indifferent how a testator expressed his intention. Finally, Justinian by constitutions of 529 and 531 enacted that legacies and fideicommissa indifferently should give rise, according to circumstances, to a real, personal or hypothecary action.[47] This last was a consequence of the tacit or legal hypothec which Justinian gave the legatee or fideicommissary over all the items of the estate in security of his claim (§ 263). Words of command and words of request were to have the same effect. There was to be no difference between legacies and fideicommissa. All the advantages of each were to attach to the other. In case of conflict the humaner character of fideicommissum was to prevail.

350. In general the same testamenti factio was required in a legatee as in an heir. But there were differences. The lex Voconia (§ 307), which incapacitated women from being instituted by testators who were in the first class of the census did not apply to legacies.[48] Conversely, before Justinian, a postumus alienus could not take a legacy (§ 371), though if instituted heir he could get bonorum possessio from the praetor.[49]

351. Justinian devotes a short title to ademption and transference of legacies. Ademption (taking away) is the

2. 20. 24.

---

[44] G. 2. 197; Ulp. XXIV, 11a.
[45] Buckl. *M.* p. 207.
[46] Cod. 6. 37. 21. Buckland says this " seems to mean that where ambiguous forms were used, the court would have to determine which form was meant. But it may signify that in practice the distinctions of form were beginning to be disregarded."
[47] Inst. 2. 20. 2; Cod. 6. 43. 1 & 2.
[48] Buckl. *T.* p. 341; *M.* p. 207.
[49] G. 2. 241; Inst. 2. 20. 26; 3. 9 pr. A postumus alienus was a person born after the execution of the will who was not in testator's power.

technical term for revocation. This might be effected by any apt words in the will itself or in a subsequent codicil, or by erasure of the legacy animo recovandi. Transference of the legacy from one person to another necessarily revoked the original disposition. In general, if the will failed, the legacy failed with it, in the absence of a codicillary clause (§ 377). But if the instituted heir was also entitled to succeed *ab intestato* he was not allowed to get rid of the burden of the legacy by repudiating the testamentary succession.[50]

352. VESTING OF LEGACIES.—A few words must be said about the vesting of the legacy, *i.e.*, the legatee's right to claim it. Two stages were distinguished, one of expectancy, the other of realisation. On the death of the testator or the opening of the will (§ 338) the legatee acquired an expectancy transmissible to heirs, but if the legacy was conditional not unless and until the condition was satisfied.[51] When the inheritance vested in the heir, *ipso jure* in the case of the suus heres, by acceptance in the case of the extraneus heres (§ 337), the legatee's right was complete, except that, if the legacy was expressed to take effect from a fixed future date (ex die), he must wait till the date arrived. It will be noticed that, if the legacy was unconditional and not postponed and the heir was suus, there was no interval of expectancy. The legacy might be claimed immediately. The Roman lawyers employed technical terms to describe the two events. In the first case—the expectancy—they said *dies cedit*—" the date is on its way " ; in the second case—the realisation—they said *dies venit*—" the date has arrived." [52]

353. The subject of gifts mortis causa, which in many respects resembled legacies, has been treated above (§ 218).

THE INSTITUTES

BOOK II (Tits. XX, XXI)

TITLE XX

Of legacies

§ 341.

We pass to the subject of legacies. This topic may seem foreign to the matter which now occupies us, namely, universal acquisition.

---

[50] Dig. 29. 4. 1 pr., 13.
[51] Ulp. XXIV, 31.
[52] Buckl. *T.* p. 343 ; *M.* p. 211. The exercise by a suus heres of his *jus abstinendi* was not fatal to legacies if the estate was solvent. Buckl. *T.* p. 305.

But since we have been discussing the whole subject of wills and
testamentary heirs, we may properly go on to speak of legacies.

1. A legacy is a gift left by a deceased person.

2. Formerly there were four kinds of legacy, per vindicationem,
per damnationem, sinendi modo, per praeceptionem, and certain
forms of words were appropriate to each kind of legacy. But this
verbal technicality has been entirely abolished by imperial legislation; and now our constitution [53] ordains that there is to be but
one kind of legacy, and that legatees may enforce their claim whatever be the words of the will not only by personal, but also by real
and hypothecary actions.

§ 344.
§ 349.

3. Not only so, but, observing that in old times legacies were
strictly construed, while fideicommissa, which were in a greater
degree the expression of a deceased person's intention, received a
more indulgent interpretation, we have thought fit to assimilate the
two institutions, so that there shall be no difference between them,
but that each shall supply whatever may be wanting in the other.[54]
But lest we should put some difficulty in the way of the young
student by treating the two in combination, we have judged it best
to consider them separately; first, legacies, and afterwards fideicommissa. If the nature of each is understood, the trained lawyer
will easily appreciate the combined result.

4. A testator may bequeath not only what belongs to himself or
his heir, but also what belongs to a third party. In the last case the
heir must acquire the thing and give effect to the legacy, or, if he
cannot acquire it, pay its value. But if the subject of the legacy is a
res extra commercium, for example, the Campus Martius, or a law-
court or consecrated buildings or things dedicated to public use, the
legacy is without effect. When we said that another person's property may be the subject of a legacy, we must be understood to mean
if the testator knew that the thing belonged to some one else, not if
he was ignorant of the fact; for, if he had known, perhaps he would
not have given the legacy. There is a rescript of the Emperor Pius
to this effect. The better view is that the plaintiff, that is the
legatee, must prove the knowledge of the testator, not that the heir
must prove his ignorance, for the burden of proof always lies on the
plaintiff.

5. If a testator bequeaths a thing which is pledged to his creditor,
the heir must redeem it. The rule just mentioned applies in this
case also, namely that the heir must redeem it only if the deceased
knew that it was pledged. This was so decided by a rescript of
Severus and Antoninus. But if the testator intended the legatee to
redeem it, and said so, then the heir need not redeem it. 6. If a
testator bequeaths a thing which does not belong to him, and the
legatee acquires it in the testator's lifetime, then, if he bought it,
he can recover its value from the heir in a testamentary action; but
if he acquired it from some lucrative cause, such as donation, he
cannot do so. For it is a long-established rule that two lucrative
causes cannot concur in the same person in relation to the same
thing. On this principle, if one and the same thing is due under two

[53] Cod. 6. 43. 1.
[54] Cod. 6. 43. 2.

separate wills, it is material whether the legatee has in the first instance acquired the thing or its value; if the thing, he cannot make any further claim, because he has got it by a lucrative title; if the value, he can.

7. A thing which is not in existence may be the subject of a legacy, if some day it will exist, for example the future fruits of land, or the unborn child of a female slave.

8. If the same thing is left to two persons, whether conjunctively or disjunctively and both accept the legacy, it is divided between them; if one legatee falls out, because he renounces the legacy, or has died in the lifetime of the testator, or in any other way failed to take, the whole goes to the other legatee. A legacy is conjunctive, if for example, a testator says, " I give and bequeath the slave Stichus to Titius and Seius "; disjunctive if he says, " I give and bequeath the slave Stichus to Titius "—" I give and bequeath the slave Stichus to Seius." If he says " the same slave Stichus " the legacy is equally disjunctive.

9. If a legacy is given of land which is not the property of the testator, and the legatee has bought the property less the usufruct, and afterwards the usufruct comes to him [by lucrative title] and he brings an action on the testament, Julian says that his claim to the land is well-founded, because the existence of the usufruct, which is regarded as a servitude, is no obstacle to plaintiff's claim, but it is incumbent on the judge to order the heir to pay the value of the land, less the value of the usufruct.

10. If the subject of a legacy is a thing which belongs to the legatee, the legacy fails to take effect, because a man cannot be made owner of a thing which is his already; and even if he has parted with it, he cannot claim either the thing or its value. 11. If a person has left a legacy of a thing belonging to him believing it to belong to someone else the legacy is good, because the actual fact carries more weight than the mistaken belief. Even if he thought that the thing belonged to the legatee, the legacy holds good because effect can be given to the testator's intention. 12. If a testator has bequeathed a thing which belonged to him and has afterwards alienated it, Celsus holds that if he sold it with no intention of revoking the legacy, the thing is still due. Severus and Antoninus gave a rescript to this effect. They also decreed that if a man after making his will has pledged land which he had given as a legacy, he is not to be taken to have revoked the legacy, and therefore the legatee can sue the heir to have the property redeemed. If the testator has alienated part of the thing bequeathed, the part which has not been alienated is of course owing, the other party only if it was alienated with no intention of revoking the legacy. 13. If a person has bequeathed to his debtor release from the debt the legacy is valid; and the heir of the deceased cannot claim payment from the debtor or from his heir, or from anyone who is in the position of heir to him. Nay more, the debtor can sue the heir to be discharged from the debt. The testator may also direct the heir not to call in the debt for a certain time.

14. On the other hand, if a debtor has left to his creditor a legacy of what he owes to him, the legacy is void, if there is nothing more in the legacy than there is in the debt, because he gets no advantage

from the legacy. But if the debt is subject to a term or a condition and the legacy is not so limited, the legacy is valid, because the legatee gets his money sooner. Papinian held that if the time limit expires or the condition is satisfied during the testator's lifetime the legacy none the less holds good, because it was valid at first, and this is correct, for we cannot accept the view that a legacy is extinguished because circumstances have arisen which if they had existed at the date of the will would have made it invalid. 15. If a husband gives his wife a legacy of her dos the legacy is valid, because there is more in a legacy than is to be got by suing for the dos.[55] If he bequeaths a dos which in fact he has never received the Emperors Severus and Antoninus pronounced the legacy void, that is, when the legacy is simply a legacy of the dos; but if the testator has given by way of pre-legacy a certain sum of money, or a certain thing or a sum or thing mentioned in a dotal instrument, the legacy holds good.[56] 16. If the subject of the legacy has perished without any responsibility of the heir, the legatee loses it. If the testator has bequeathed a slave belonging to someone else and the slave has been manumitted without the heir having done anything to bring the manumission about, he is not liable to the legatee. But if the heir's own slave was the subject of the legacy and he manumits him, he is liable, Julian says, and it makes no difference whether he knew or did not know that the slave had been left away from him. It is the same if he has given the slave to someone, and the donee has manumitted him. 17. If slave-women have been left together with their children, although the women have died, the children are attributed to the legacy. Similarly, if there is a legacy of skilled slaves together with their assistants, if the skilled slaves are dead, the assistants none the less pass to the legatee. But if a slave is bequeathed together with his peculium, in the event of the slave dying or being manumitted or alienated the legacy of the peculium is also lost. The same is the case if there is a legacy of land " fully furnished " (fundus instructus) [57] or " with the instruments of husbandry " (cum instrumento); if the land is alienated the legacy is extinguished.

18. If there is a legacy of a flock, and the flock is reduced to a single sheep, this single sheep can be claimed in a real action. Julian says that any additions which accrue to the flock after the making of the will go to the legatee; for a flock is a single entity made up of distinct individuals, just as a building is a single thing made up of stones in combination. 19. It follows that a legacy of a house includes pillars of marbles added to the house after the date of the will. 20. If there is a legacy of a peculium anything added to or taken from it in the lifetime of the testator is the legatee's gain or loss. But, if the slave has acquired anything after the death of the

---

[55] The action on the legacy had certain advantages over the action on the dos, principally that plaintiff got his money, or whatever it might be, sooner.

[56] If a sum of money or a thing was specified, the rule falsa demonstratio non nocet (sec. 30, infra) applied even though nothing had in fact been received (Cod. 6. 44. 3). The legacy is called a " pre-legacy " because it anticipated the payment of the dos in the ordinary course.

[57] This is the more comprehensive term. It includes furniture (in the ordinary sense) and other useful accessories.

testator before the heir has entered, Julian says that if the peculium
was left to the manumitted slave himself, everything acquired by the
slave before the heir enters goes to the legatee, because the legacy
takes effect and is calculated from the entry of the heir; but, if the
peculium was left to a stranger, acquisitions are not included in the
legacy unless the peculium was augmented from its own resources.
The manumitted slave has no claim to the peculium unless it was
left to him, though if an owner manumitted a slave in his lifetime
it is enough if the peculium is not expressly withheld. This was so
decided by a rescript of Severus and Antoninus. The same Emperors
by another rescript pronounced that if a peculium is left by legacy,
it does not carry the consequence that the manumitted slave can
claim a refund of money expended for his master's account. Again,
they decided that if the direction is that a slave is to be free when
he has rendered his accounts, and that he is to make up an adverse
balance, this implies a legacy of the peculium. 21. Things incorporeal no less than things corporeal may be the subject of a legacy.
Therefore, a man may leave by will a debt due to him with the
result that the heir must place his right of action at the disposal
of the legatee, unless the testator has recovered the debt in his
lifetime, for in that case the legacy is extinguished. Again, a legacy

§ 342.

of this kind is valid: " Be my heir condemned to repair such a
man's house " or, " to discharge such a man's debt."

22. If a slave or anything else is left in general terms, the
legatee has the choice, unless the testator has expressed a different
intention. 23. The legacy of an option, that is when the testator
has said that a legatee may choose from his slaves or other property
which or what he pleases, used to imply a condition, and so, unless
the legatee had exercised the option in his lifetime, he did not transmit
any right to his heir. But our constitution [58] has improved upon
this and allowed the legatee's heir to exercise the option although
the legatee has not done so in his lifetime. If there are several
legatees to whom the option is left, or several heirs of one legatee,
and they cannot agree in their choice, to prevent the failure of the
legacy (the unkind conclusion generally drawn by the jurists) we
have decreed that fortune is to be the arbiter, and that the matter
is to be decided by lot.[59]

24. Legacies can be left only to persons with whom there is
testamenti factio. 25. Formerly, legacies and fideicommissa might
not be left to uncertain persons, even by a soldier, as the Emperor

§ 307.

Hadrian decided by rescript. By " an uncertain person " was meant
a person of whom a testator had no clear mental picture, for
example, " Whoever shall give his daughter in marriage to my son,"
or " the first persons to be appointed consuls after the date of my
will." It was held too that freedom could not be given to an
uncertain person, because it was considered that slaves should be set
free by name. Similarly, a guardian appointed by will had to be
precisely indicated. But a legacy with a certain demonstration, that
is to an unascertained member of an ascertained class, was good; for
example, " let my heir give such a thing to any one of my relations

---

[58] Cod. 6. 43. 3.
[59] Simonds J. in *Re Knapton* [1941] 2 All E.R. 573, citing this text,
allowed the same expedient.

now in being who takes my daughter in marriage." But imperial
constitutions directed that, if legacies or fideicommissa had been left
to uncertain persons and paid in error, they could not be recovered.
26. A legacy to a person not in existence at the date of the will,
who if he had been then living would not have been a suus heres of
the testator (postumus alienus) was formerly invalid, from which it
followed that a grandfather could not leave a legacy to the unborn
child of an emancipated son. 27. But the law relating to these
matters has been amended by our constitution as regards not only
institutions of heirs but also legacies and fideicommissa.[60] However,
it is still the law that an uncertain person cannot be appointed tutor,
because a testator must have a clear idea of the person he appoints
to be tutor to his children.

28. Indeed, a person born posthumously not in testator's power   § 307.
might be instituted heir even before our constitution, as he still
may be, unless he be a child conceived of a woman who cannot
be testator's wife. 29. A legacy is good, though the testator may
have made a mistake as to the legatee's name. The same applies
in the case of heirs; and rightly, for names were invented in order
to identify individuals, and it is just the same if this can be done
in any other way. 30. Closely akin to this is the rule, " A false
demonstration does not avoid a legacy," for example, " I give as
a legacy my slave Stichus born on the estate "; the legacy is good,
though Stichus was not born on the estate, but bought, provided
that his identity is ascertained. Similarly, if a testator writes, " the
slave Stichus, whom I bought from Seius," the legacy is good, though
the slave was bought from some one else, always provided that there
is no doubt which slave is meant. 31. Much less is a legacy prejudiced by a false cause; for example, " I bequeath my slave Stichus
to Titius, because he managed my affairs when I was away," or to
Titius, " because I was acquitted on a capital charge through his
undertaking my defence," for though Titius did not in fact do either
of these things the legacy none the less holds good. But if the cause
is expressed in the form of a condition, it is otherwise; for example,
" I give such an estate to Titius, if he managed my affairs." 32. Is a
legacy to the slave of the heir instituted by the will valid? It is
settled that such a legacy if unconditional is ineffectual, and it is not
helped by the fact that the slave has ceased to be in the power of
the heir in the testator's lifetime, for a legacy which would be invalid
if the testator had died immediately after making his will ought not
to be valid merely because he has lived longer.[61] But such a legacy
may be left conditionally, so that we have to ask whether when the
right to the legacy vests (dies cedit) the slave has ceased to be in   § 352.
the power of the heir.[62] 33. On the other hand, if a slave is
instituted heir, there is no doubt that a legacy may be properly given

---

[60] This constitution is not included in our text of the Code. Its effect
is given in Krueger's edition of the Code (Cod. 48. 6) from an abstract in
the *Basilica*.

[61] This is the regula Catoniana (Dig. 34. 7. 1; Buckl. *M.* p. 207)
domiciled and expanded in English law in the form *quod ab initio non
valet in tractu temporis non convalescit*. Broom's *Legal Maxims* (9),
p. 123.

[62] The question has been much discussed: G. 2. 244; Buckl. *T.* p. 341.

to the slave's master, even unconditionally. For even if the testator has died immediately after making his will, still the right to the legacy is not understood to vest in the heir, for the inheritance has been separated from the legacy, and another person may become heir through the slave, if, before entering on the inheritance by his master's order, he has passed into another person's power, or by being manumitted has become heir himself, in which cases the legacy is good; but if there has been no change in his condition and he enters upon the inheritance by order of his master [who thus becomes heir] the legacy is extinguished.

34. Formerly, a legacy which preceded the institution of the heir was bad, because wills derive their force and effect from the institution of an heir, which is therefore considered to be the starting-point and foundation of the whole will. For the same reason a gift of freedom before the institution of the heir was invalid. But since it seemed unreasonable to pay attention to the order of the words—a thing which the ancient lawyers themselves condemned—and to disregard the testator's intention, we have amended the law in this regard, so that now a legacy (and much more a gift of liberty, which is always favoured) may be placed before the institution of an heir, or between the institutions of different heirs.[63]

§ 291.

35. A legacy expressed to take effect after the death of the heir or of the legatee himself was formerly invalid; for instance, " I give such a legacy when my heir shall be dead," or " on the day before the death of the heir or legatee." But this too we have corrected, putting legacies on the same footing as fideicommissa,[64] in order that the former may not be at any disadvantage in comparison with the latter.

36. Formerly, a testator could not give, revoke or transfer a legacy by way of penalty. A disposition is said to be by way of penalty when it is designed to bring pressure to bear upon a person as an inducement to act or forbear; for example, " Let my heir, if he gives his daughter " (or, as the case may be, " does not give his daughter ") " in marriage to Titius, pay Seius ten aurei "; or, " If my heir alienates (or ' does not alienate ') his slave Stichus, let him give Titius ten aurei "; and the rule was so strictly observed that very many imperial constitutions indicated that even the Emperor would not accept any such legacy; nor were such legacies valid in soldiers' wills, though generally any expression of a soldier's will was effectual. Even a gift of liberty thus made was void. Further, Sabinus held that an additional institution could not be made by way of penalty; as if a testator said, " Be Titius my heir: if Titius gives his daughter in marriage to Seius, be Seius also my heir "; for it made no difference how pressure is exercised on the heir, whether by imposing a legacy or by adding a co-heir. But these refinements we have not approved, and we have enacted in general terms that legacies left or revoked or transferred by way of penalty are not to differ in any way from other legacies, with the exception of such as

---

[63] Cod. 6. 23. 24.
[64] Cod. 4. 11.

are impossible or prohibited by law or immoral [65]; for the principles of our age do not tolerate any such testamentary dispositions.

TITLE XXI

Of the ademption and transference of legacies

The ademption of legacies is effective, whether it is made in the same will as that in which the legacy was given or by codicil, and whether by contrary words, as, when the testator has said, " I give and bequeath," he revokes the legacy by saying, " I do not give and bequeath," or by words which are not contrary, in short by any words whatever. §351.

1. A legacy may be transferred from one person to another, as for example if a person says, " The slave Stichus, whom I bequeathed to Titius, I give and bequeath to Seius," whether he says this in the same will or in a codicil. By this form of words he both takes the legacy from Titius and gives it to Seius.

XIII. THE LEX FALCIDIA

354. By the Law of the Twelve Tables a testator might leave legacies to any amount. This was deduced from the words of the statute: Uti legassit suae rei ita jus esto—" As a man has disposed of his property, so let the law be." The consequence was that there were many intestacies, because heirs did not think it worth while to accept an inheritance, which might prove of little or no value. Three laws were passed to remedy this state of things. The first two failed. The third 2. 22 pr. succeeded.

355. Lex Furia testamentaria.[66] This statute, passed at some date between B.C. 204 and 169, provided that no one, who was not related to the testator within the limit which the praetor later set for the intestate succession of cognates (viz., the sixth degree and the seventh in the case of the issue of second cousins),[67] might take by way of legacy or gift mortis causa more than a thousand asses under a penalty of four times the excess, recoverable by manus injectio (§ 686). This failed because a testator might distribute the whole of his estate in legacies within the permitted limit.

356. Lex Voconia,[68] B.C. 168. This applied only to the wills of persons who were in the first class of the census. It enacted that no one might take under any such person's will more than

---

[65] Cod. 6. 41.
[66] G. 2. 225 ; 4. 23 ; Ulp. I, 2.
[67] Vat. 301.
[68] G. 2. 226.

the heir, or heirs collectively. Under this statute the heir must have something, but it might be very little, because the testator might leave numerous legacies of small amount.[69]

357. LEX FALCIDIA, B.C. 40. This was more successful. It provided that a testator might not dispose of more than three-quarters of his estate in legacies. This secured to the heir at least one-fourth.

2. 22 pr.

358. The statute was interpreted as follows:—

(a) If there were two or more heirs, each must have a clear fourth part of the share of the estate to which he was instituted (quarta Falcidia). It was not enough that the heirs collectively took one-fourth of the estate between them.

2. 22. 1.

(b) The value of the estate was computed as it was at the time of death. Subsequent increase or decrease did not affect the valuation. But, since an extraneous heir need not accept the inheritance unless he chose, he could always come to terms with the legatees and so guard against the risk of the estate depreciating in value.

2. 22. 2.

(c) In arriving at the valuation, deduction was first made of debts, funeral expenses, and the value of slaves manumitted by the will. The residue was distributed so as to secure at least one-fourth of the inheritance to a single heir, or one-fourth of each heir's share of the inheritance when there were several heirs, the residue going to the legatees in proportion to the amount of their respective legacies.

2. 22. 3.

(d) If the subject of the legacy was indivisible, e.g., a right of way, it vested in the legatee, but if he took steps to assert his right against the heir, and failed to make compensation to the extent of the heir's statutory claim, he could be met by a plea of fraud (exceptio doli, § 742).[70]

359. The lex Falcidia did not apply to military wills.[71] Before Justinian it applied to other wills without exception. But Justinian withheld its benefit from heirs who claimed a spatium deliberandi and did not make an inventory, and in every case allowed a testator to exclude it by express provision in his will.[72] If an heir took advantage of it, when it was open to him to do so, he was required to make his inventory with special formalities.[73]

§ 340.

---

[69] For another provision of the lex Voconia vide supra, § 307.
[70] Dig. 35. 2. 80, 1.
[71] Dig. 29. 1. 17, 4.
[72] Cod. 6. 30. 14c.
[73] Nov. 1. 2. 2.

THE INSTITUTES

BOOK II

Title XXII

Of the lex Falcidia

It remains to examine the lex Falcidia, which is the latest statute limiting the amount of legacies. Anciently the law of the Twelve Tables, providing that " As a man has disposed of his property so let the law be," allowed complete freedom of testamentary disposition, so that a man could, if he pleased, distribute his whole estate in legacies. But it was found desirable to restrict this power of giving legacies; indeed testators themselves had an interest in the matter, for intestacies were very frequent, owing to the refusal of instituted heirs to accept an inheritance which promised them little or no advantage. The matter was dealt with by the lex Furia and the lex Voconia, but neither of them procured the desired result. Accordingly, last of all the lex Falcidia was enacted, which provided that a testator might not dispose in legacies of more than three-quarters of his estate, that is to say that a fourth part of the estate was to remain with the instituted heir or heirs. 1. Thereupon the following question arose. If two heirs are instituted, say Titius and Seius, and the share of Titius is wholly exhausted by legacies expressly charged upon him, or burdened beyond the permitted proportion, while the share of Seius is not burdened at all, or burdened, let us say, only to the extent of one-half, is it to be said, because Seius gets one fourth part, or more, of the whole inheritance, that Titius is not allowed to retain anything against the legacies charged upon him? The answer is that he may keep intact a fourth part of his own share in the inheritance, for the principle of the lex Falcidia must be applied to each heir separately. 2. The value of the estate for the purpose of the statute is the value which it has at the time of the testator's death. So, for example, if a person whose estate is worth one hundred aurei, has left legacies to that amount, the legatees will not be any better off, if, before the heir enters on the inheritance, the estate has received accessions through slaves belonging to the estate or from birth of issue to female slaves or from natural increase to flocks and herds sufficient to leave one-fourth of the inheritance with the heir after the legacies have been paid, but, none the less, the legacies must be reduced by one-fourth. Conversely, if the testator has left legacies amounting to seventy-five aurei, and before the heir has entered, the property has been so much reduced by fire or shipwreck or death of slaves that it amounts to no more than seventy-five aurei, or even less, the legacies must be paid in full. But this does not really hurt the heir, who need not accept the inheritance unless he pleases. Consequently, the legatees must come to terms with him, so as not to lose their legacies through the inheritance being abandoned. 3. In calculating the Falcidian share deduction is first made of debts, funeral expenses, and the value of slaves manumitted by the will; then one-fourth of the residue stays with the heirs and three-fourths are distributed amongst the legatees in proportion to their several legacies. For example, if

§ 282.

§ 357.

§ 358.

we suppose that four hundred aurei have been left in legacies, and
the estate amounts to four hundred aurei, each legatee loses a fourth
part of his legacy. If three hundred and fifty have been given in
legacies, a sum equal to an eighth part of the whole estate, *viz.*, fifty,
must be deducted. If five hundred have been left, we deduct first
one-fifth [of the whole], then one-fourth. For we must deduct first
the amount by which the legacies exceed the value of the estate and
then the fourth part which is to stay with the heirs.

XIV. FIDEICOMMISSA

360. The fideicommissum was a contrivance to surmount
some of the technicalities of the Roman will. It was a request
to the heir to make over the property or part of it to some
other person not qualified to take as heir or legatee at civil
law. Thus a peregrinus (who might actually be the child of
the testator, if he had married a peregrina) could not be heir
or legatee, but for a considerable period of time he was allowed
to take by way of fideicommissum ; and this, according to
Gaius, was the principal reason for the introduction of fideicommissa.[74] In course of time fideicommissum came to serve
many other ends, for example, to give freedom to slaves (§ 77),
and on the other hand was deprived of many of its initial
advantages. In essence it was a trust or confidence reposed
upon a person's good faith. The person to whom the property
was given in the first instance was termed the fiduciarius, the
person to whom it was to be handed over was termed the
fideicommissarius.

2. 23. 1.   361. Originally the fideicommissum created merely a moral
obligation. Augustus made it enforceable by legal process.
This he did by ordering the consuls to interpose their authority,
and this developed into a regular jurisdiction, which was shared
by the consuls with a praetor specially appointed for the purpose
known as praetor fideicommissarius. But this did not affect the
position of the heir as universal successor. " Once an heir
always an heir." It was he and he alone who could sue and be
sued in the name of the estate.

362. The heir might be requested to hand over the whole
(or part) of the inheritance, or some specific thing. Thus the
fideicommissum was employed as a substitute either for the
civil law inheritance or for the civil law legacy. Justinian
treats of these topics in separate Titles, and it will be convenient
to follow this arrangement, though so far as the fideicommissum

---

[74] G. 2. 285.

itself is concerned the same principles apply to one as to the other. But a direction to hand over the inheritance or part of it raised a problem as to the relation of the fideicommissarius to creditors of the estate, which did not normally arise when his position was analogous to that of legatee. It will be necessary to consider this question in some detail.

363. FIDEICOMMISSARY INHERITANCE.—The form of words employed might be the following:—" Be Lucius Titius my heir. I request you, Lucius Titius, as soon as you can enter upon my inheritance to make it over to Gaius Seius." But any other words which conveyed the testator's meaning would do as well. If the heir accepted the inheritance, he had to give effect to the trust imposed upon him, by conveying the items of the estate to Gaius Seius by appropriate methods. But he remained liable to creditors of the estate, just as debtors of the estate remained liable to him alone, though he had to hand over whatever he recovered from them. This was a situation which few heirs would be willing to accept. Some method must be found to ensure that the person who took the benefit of the estate should also sustain its burdens. The steps taken to secure this result are an interesting and complicated chapter in legal history.

2. 23. 2.

364. An heir might be desired to hand over the whole inheritance or part of it. If the whole, it was the practice for the heir to sell the inheritance for a nominal price to the fideicommissarius; and the parties entered into the stipulations (§ 444) which were usual when an inheritance was sold, the heir stipulating for an indemnity against claims, and promising on his part to make over to the fideicommissarius any property which might come to him as heir and to make cession to him of rights of action.[75] These stipulations were called stipulationes emptae et venditae hereditatis (stipulations on the sale of an inheritance). If part of the inheritance was to be made over, there was no pretence of a sale, but stipulations directed to the same ends were entered into to secure a proportionate division of benefit and burdens. They were modelled upon the stipulations in use when an heir was directed to hand over a portion of the estate by way of legacy to the " partiary legatee " (§ 342). They were known as stipulationes partis et pro parte (of a part and in proportion to a part). It will be seen, therefore, that Gaius is right when he says that formerly, *i.e.*, before the legislation to be presently mentioned, the fideicommissarius to whom

---

[75] G. 2. 252.

the whole inheritance was made over was in the position neither of heir nor of legatee, but of purchaser. If he took a portion of the estate he was in the position of a partiary legatee. This system had many inconveniences. In particular it exposed each party to the risk of the other's insolvency; if the heir became insolvent the fideicommissarius got nothing; if the fidei-commissarius became insolvent the heir lost the benefit of his indemnity.

2. 23. 4.   365. A reform was effected by the senatusconsultum Trebellianum of A.D. 56. This rendered the stipulations unnecessary and placed the fideicommissary in a position analogous to that of an heir, as soon as the inheritance or part of it was restored to him; and " restoration " simply meant consent on the part of the heir to give effect to the fidei-commissum.[76] The result was to give the fideicommissary an interest to which the praetor (not specifically the praetor fidei-commissarius) would give effect in relation to third parties. From this time actions lay for and against the heir and the fideicommissarius in proportion to their interest in the inheritance; for and against the heir at civil law; for and against the fideicommissarius by praetorian law. If the heir sued or was sued after handing over the inheritance, " the plea that the inheritance had been restored " (exceptio restitutae hereditatis) was available as a defence.[77]

2. 23. 5.   366. Fideicommissa were still liable to fail by refusal of the heir to enter upon the inheritance. This inconvenience was removed by the senatusconsultum Pegasianum, passed in the reign of Vespasian (A.D. 69–79), which offered the heir an induce-ment to enter in imitation of the fourth share which the lex Falcidia allowed him to retain against legatees (§ 357). But the analogy was unfortunate, for it was considered that just as the heir was solely liable, whatever the amount of the legacies, so, in a case to which the senatusconsultum Pegasianum applied, he was solely liable, whatever the amount of the fideicommissum. The result was that when the heir was not required to hand over more than three-quarters of the inheritance, he enjoyed the benefit of the senatusconsultum Trebellianum and was liable
2. 23. 6.   only to the extent of the one-fourth or larger fraction which he

---

[76] Dig. 36. 1. 30 pr.

[77] " In civil law he remained capable of suing and liable to suit for the whole, but the praetor controlled and protected him, so that in fact he sued and was sued only so far as he retained any share of the estate, while the heir in trust sued and was sued by analogous actions for what he received." I Roby, p. 372.

retained. But, if he was required to hand over more than three-quarters, the senatusconsultum Pegasianum applied, and he was solely liable, as he was under the lex Falcidia ; and this result followed (says Gaius, but on this point Paulus differs from him), whether he chose to retain his Pegasian fourth, or did not.[78] The consequence was that in such cases it became necessary to have recourse once more to the old stipulations. By another clause of the senatusconsultum Pegasianum, an heir who declined to enter might be compelled to do so *pro forma*, and to make over the inheritance. But in this case he was merely a conduit-pipe to transmit the inheritance with all its incidents to the fideicommissary, just as if the case had fallen within the scope of the senatusconsultum Trebellianum.

367. Justinian combined the two senatusconsulta in one enactment, which continued to bear the name of senatus-consultum Trebellianum. Henceforward :—(1) whether the 2. 23. 7. heir was required to hand over much or little, the benefit and burden were in every case to be rateably divided between the heir and fideicommissary ; (2) the heir was in every case entitled t⌐ retain a clear quarter against fideicommissaries ; (3) he could be compelled to make formal entry. These two last provisions were retained from the senatusconsultum Pegasianum.

The commentators speak of the quarter which the heir was allowed to retain against fideicommissaries as the quarta Trebelliana, but in the texts of the Roman Law it is called the quarta Falcidia. There was in fact no difference between them. We have mentioned above that Justinian enacted that an heir who did not avail himself of the benefit of inventory was not allowed to retain the fourth, and that a testator might in express terms deprive his heir of the right to do so (§ 359).

368. FORMAL REQUIREMENTS OF FIDEICOMMISSUM.—For long there were not any. Ulpian says, " It is established that a fideicommissum can be given by a nod of the head." [79] But in practice fideicommissa were usually contained in a will or codicil, which in Justinian's system required the presence of seven and five witnesses respectively (§ 374). If the writing was insufficiently witnessed or if there was no writing at all Justinian enacted that a person who alleged a fideicommissum might put the alleged fiduciary to the oath in the manner described in the text of the Institutes. Apart from this and 2. 23. 12.

---

[78] G. 2. 257 ; Paul. *Sent.* 4. 3. 2.
[79] Ulp. XXV, 3.

from an oral will or codicil duly witnessed oral evidence of a fideicommissum was now inadmissible.

369. Any person could leave a fideicommissum who could make a will.[80] Originally many persons could take a fideicommissum who could not be instituted heirs or take a legacy or who though they had testamenti factio passiva had not the jus capiendi (§ 310). Thus peregrini could take, and caelibes and orbi. But most of these loopholes were closed by legislation.

370. FAMILY SETTLEMENTS.—An important use of the fideicommissum to which the Institutes afford no clue was to enable testators to tie up their property through successive generations. Thus a testator might leave his property to A whom he appointed his heir, and charge him to make it over on his death to B, and B might be similarly charged in favour of C; or there might be a general direction that the property was not to be alienated out of the family (fideicommissum familiae).[81] The will of a certain Dasumius, assigned to the year A.D. 108, which has been reconstructed from fragments of an inscription on marble, contains a gift of land to freedmen, with a direction that it is to remain with their descendants in perpetuity.[82] But not long afterwards Hadrian prohibited fideicommissa in favour of incertae personae (§ 371). It is not clear how far this was intended to restrict, and in fact restricted, family settlements. There is some indication that in the third century they were not allowed to extend beyond persons in being and the next (unborn) generation.[83] Justinian removed previously existing restrictions on gifts to incertae personae, thus opening the door to perpetual fideicommissa. By Novel 159, dealing with a particular will, he decreed that in that and all future cases the property might not be tied up beyond the fourth generation. This may be described as the Roman Law against perpetuities. It passed into the modern systems derived from Roman Law, and though most of them have confined a testator's power of tying up property within more reasonable limits, it still exists in the law of Malta [84] and South Africa.[85] Justinian's rule was bad enough. The post-glossators made it worse by allowing a testator by sufficiently definite words to exclude its operation and to tie up the property in perpetuity. There was difference

80 Ulp. XXV, 4.
81 Dig. 31. 32. 6.
82 Girard, *Textes*, p. 801.
83 Buckl. *T.* p. 363 ; *M.* p. 225.
84 *Strickland* v. *Strickland* [1908] A.C. 551.
85 Lee, p. 384.

of opinion and of practice as to the meaning of the fourth generation. In South Africa it is understood to mean four generations after the first, *i.e.*, four generations of fideicommissarii, the first fiduciarius not being taken into account. The property is free at last in the hands of the fifth fideicommissarius.

371. FIDEICOMMISSA OF SINGLE THINGS.—As we have seen above, a fideicommissum might serve as a substitute for the civil law legacy, and as a means of escape from the restrictions which attached to it. There were many differences between them, of which some persisted until and even after Justinian; others had disappeared before his time. The following enumeration is principally taken from Gaius.

1. A legacy was a charge imposed upon a testamentary heir. A fideicommissum might be charged upon an heir *ab intestato*,[86] or a legatee,[87] or a fideicommissary.[88]

2. A legacy could only be left by will, or by a codicil confirmed by will. A fideicommissum could be left by an unconfirmed codicil.[89]

3. Legacies were expressed in imperative terms and called for the use of the form appropriate to the particular kind of legacy intended. Fideicommissa were expressed in the language of request, and no form of words was required.[90]

4. Legacies (originally) must be in Latin. Fideicommissa might be in Greek or any other language.[91]

5. A legacy could not benefit a person who had not testamenti factio passiva, or who had not the jus capiendi. Originally fideicommissa were free from these restrictions. But in course of time this advantage was taken from them. Thus peregrini were forbidden to take by fideicommissum and by a senatus-consultum made on the proposition of the Emperor Hadrian, any such gifts were forfeited to the fiscus.[92] The disabilities of caelibes and orbi were extended to fideicommissa by the senatusconsultum Pegasianum.[93] But Junian Latins, so long as the class existed, remained capable of taking by fideicommissum, though they could not take directly as heirs or legatees (§ 82).[94]

6. Incertae personae and postumi alieni could not take by legacy. They could take by fideicommissum, until a senatus-consultum passed at the instance of the Emperor Hadrian applied the same rule to fideicommissa as to institutions and legacies.[95]

---

86 G. 2. 270; Inst. 2. 23. 10.　　　87 G. 2. 271; Inst. 2. 24 pr.
88 Inst. 2. 23. 11.
89 G. 2. 270a.
90 Ulp. XXIV, 1; G. 2. 249.
91 G. 2. 281.
92 G. 2. 285.
93 G. 2. 286.
94 G. 1. 24; 2. 275.　　　95 G. 2. 287.

7. A gift of liberty could not be made directly to another man's slave; it could be made by fideicommissum.[96] This was done by directing a beneficiary to buy the slave and free him, or by leaving something to his owner with a direction to free him.[97] This usually, but not necessarily, produced the desired result.

8. While the formulary system lasted, legacies were sued for by formula, fideicommissa by "extraordinary" procedure before the consul or the praetor fideicommissarius and in the provinces before the praeses (§ 758).[98]

9. Legacies did not carry interest, if payment was unduly delayed; fideicommissa did.[99]

372. There had been a progressive assimilation of legacies and fideicommissa in the classical and post-classical periods, though the statement attributed to Ulpian in the Digest that "legacies have in all respects been made equal to fidei-commissa"[1] has plainly been doctored. Justinian, as we have seen, completed the fusion of the two institutions, so that—to give one example—ownership now vested directly under a fidei-commissum in any case in which it would have vested under a legacy. But a gift of liberty to another man's slave was necessarily made by way of fideicommissum, and a direction to the heir to manumit continued to be construed as fidei-commissary, which gave the manumitting heir the rights of patronage, though it might have been construed as direct.

2. 20. 3. (margin)

THE INSTITUTES

BOOK II (Tits. XXIII, XXIV)

TITLE XXIII

Of fideicommissary inheritances

§ 363. (margin)

We now pass to fideicommissa, and let us first consider fidei-commissary inheritances.

§ 361. (margin)

1. It must be observed that in early times fideicommissa were not legally binding, for no one was compelled to give effect to a request unless he chose to do so. In those days if testators wished to leave an inheritance or a legacy to a person who was not legally competent to take under the will they committed it to the good faith of those who were. Such dispositions were called fidei-commissa, because they created no legal obligation, but reposed merely on the conscience of those to whom the request was

---

[96] G. 2. 272.
[97] Buckl. *M.* p. 221.
[98] G. 2. 278.
[99] G. 2. 280.
[1] Dig. 30. 1.

addressed. It was the Emperor Augustus who first ordered the consuls to interpose their authority so as to give them legal effect. It may be that on one or two occasions he wished to show favour to particular persons, or that a request had been made in the name of the Emperor's safety, or that there had been some signal instances of bad faith. This procedure seemed equitable and commended itself to the people, and so it developed into a regular jurisdiction. It was so much favoured that after a time a special praetor was appointed to exercise jurisdiction in the matter of fideicommissa, who was known as the praetor fideicommissarius.

2. The first condition of a fideicommissary inheritance is that some one should be directly instituted heir in the will, and that he should be charged with a trust to make over the inheritance to some one else. Without such an institution the will would be void. So when a testator has written, " Be Lucius Titius my heir " he may go on to say, " I request you, Lucius Titius, the moment you are able to enter on the inheritance, to render and restore it to Caius Seius." A testator may also request his heir to restore part of the estate. He may leave a fideicommissum absolutely or subject to a condition or to take effect from a stated future date. § 363.

3. When the inheritance has been restored the person who restores it none the less remains heir; the person to whom the inheritance is made over was sometimes regarded as heir, sometimes as legatee.[2] 4. In the days of Nero, when Trebellius Maximus and Annaeus Seneca were consuls, a senatusconsultum was passed, providing that if an inheritance was restored in pursuance of a fideicommissum, all actions which at civil law could be brought by the heir or against the heir should be available to and against the person to whom the inheritance was restored. After this enactment the praetor began to give equitable actions to and against the person who took the inheritance, just as actions at law are brought by and against the heir. 5. But since the heirs who were usually requested to restore either the whole or nearly the whole of the inheritance often refused to accept an inheritance which offered no prospect or little prospect of gain, with the consequence that the fideicommissa failed to take effect, afterwards in the time of the Emperor Vespasian in the consulship of Pegasus and Pusio the Senate resolved that an heir who was requested to restore the inheritance might retain a quarter of it, just as the lex Falcidia allows him to retain a quarter against legacies. The same retention is allowed in the case of single things left by fideicommissum. After this senatus-consultum the heirs used to bear all the burdens of the inheritance, and a person who took part of the inheritance by fideicommissum was in the position of a partiary legatee, that is, of a legatee to whom part of the inheritance went by way of legacy. This kind of legacy was called " a partition " (partitio), because the legatee divided the inheritance with the heir. Accordingly the stipulations which were made by the heir and the partiary legatee began to be employed between the heir and the person to whom the inheritance was restored, the object being to secure that the benefit and burden of the inheritance should be rateably apportioned between them. § 364.
§ 365.
§ 366.

---

[2] i.e., after the enactment described in s. 4.

6. It followed that if the instituted heir was requested to restore not more than three-quarters of the inheritance, then, restoration was made as provided by the senatusconsultum Trebellianum and actions relating to the inheritance were given against each of the parties concerned in proportion to their shares, against the heir by civil law, against the person to whom the inheritance was made over by the senatusconsultum Trebellianum as if he were heir. But if the heir was desired to restore more than three-quarters or even the whole inheritance, the senatusconsultum Pegasianum applied, and the heir, once he had entered on the inheritance, if he entered voluntarily, whether he retained the quarter or not, bore the whole burden of the inheritance. If the fourth was retained, the parties entered into the stipulations partis et pro parte which were usual between the partiary legatee and the heir; if the whole inheritance was made over, the stipulations usual in the case of the sale of an inheritance were employed. But if the instituted heir refuses to enter upon the inheritance on the ground that he has doubts as to its solvency, the senatusconsultum Pegasianum provides that, on the demand of the person to whom he is requested to restore, the praetor shall order him to enter and to restore the inheritance, and actions are to be given to and against the person who takes the inheritance just as in cases coming under the senatusconsultum Trebellianum. In this case no stipulations are needed, because the heir is secured against loss, and actions arising out of the inheritance are transmitted to and against the person to whom the inheritance is made over, for in such an event the two senatusconsulta have the same effect.

G. 2. 257.

§ 367.

7. Even the old lawyers were dissatisfied with these stipulations and the eminent Papinian describes them in some cases as legal quibbles. We have decided therefore, aiming, as always, at simplicity in our legislation, to abrogate the senatusconsultum Pegasianum and to lend full authority to the senatusconsultum Trebellianum, so that fideicommissary inheritances will in future be restored under this enactment, whether the testator has allowed the heir to retain one-fourth or less or more or nothing at all. But if by the terms of the will the heir is to keep nothing or less than one-fourth, he is to be allowed to retain a fourth or so much as is needed to make up a fourth, or to recover it, if already paid; and in any case actions are to lie rateably against the heir and the fideicommissary as under the senatusconsultum Trebellianum. If the heir has voluntarily restored the inheritance, all actions connected with the inheritance are to be available for and against the fideicommissary exclusively. Lastly, we have transferred to the senatusconsultum Trebellianum the special provision of the senatusconsultum Pegasianum that when the instituted heir refused to enter, he might be compelled, if the fideicommissary desired it, to make over to him the whole inheritance, and then all actions were to be given to and against the fideicommissary, neither profit nor loss from the inheritance remaining with the heir. 8. It makes no difference whether it is a sole heir who is requested to restore the whole or part of the inheritance, or an heir instituted to a share of the inheritance who is asked to restore the whole or part of his share. The rules are the same in both cases.

9. If an heir is desired, after deducting or first taking some specific thing equivalent to one-fourth of the estate, for instance, a piece of land or any other thing, to restore the inheritance, restitution must be made as described above under the senatusconsultum Trebellianum, just as if the heir had been desired to retain the fourth part of the estate and make over the remainder. But there is this difference. In the first case all actions are transferred *in solidum*, and the heir retains the thing given to him free of any burden, just as if he were a legatee. In the second case the actions are divided in the proportion of one-fourth and three-fourths for and against the heir and fideicommissary respectively. Even though the thing which the heir is allowed to retain, or first take, may constitute the greatest part of the estate, none the less actions are transferred *in solidum* against the fideicommissary, and he must consider whether it is in his interest to have the inheritance transferred. The same principle applies if two or more things are to be deducted or taken first. It is the same if a sum of money amounting to a fourth or even to the greatest part of the estate is to be deducted or taken. All of this applies equally to an heir instituted to a share of the inheritance.

10. Moreover, a man who is going to die intestate may desire his civil law or praetorian successor to restore his whole inheritance or part of it or a specific thing, such as land, a slave, or money, to a named person. But there can be no legacy where there is no will.

11. A fideicommissary may in turn be requested to make over what he has received in whole or in part, or some other thing, to another person. 12. Fideicommissa then, as we have seen, depended at the beginning on the good faith of the heirs and this was what gave them their name and essential character. It was Augustus who made them legally binding, and now we, in our anxiety to surpass that Emperor, have made a constitution, suggested by a case brought to our notice by the most eminent Tribonian, quaestor of our sacred palace, which provides that if a testator has trusted his heir to restore his inheritance or a special fideicommissum, and the matter cannot be proved by a written instrument or by five witnesses (the statutory number in the case of fideicommissa) because there are less than five witnesses, or no witnesses at all, then if the heir perfidiously denies the existence of any fideicommissum, the fideicommissarius, § 368. having first sworn to his own good faith, may put the heir under the necessity of either taking an oath that he never heard the testator say anything of the kind, or, if he declines to do so, of giving effect to the fideicommissum. The same procedure may be followed when the person charged to restore is a legatee, or himself a fideicommissary. If the person charged admits that something was left away from him, but seeks to take advantage of legal technicalities, he will unquestionably be compelled to give effect to the trust.

TITLE XXIV

Of single things left by fideicommissum

A man may leave single things by fideicommissum, for example, § 371. land, a slave, a garment, plate, or money, and desire the heir to restore it to some one, or similarly a legatee, though a legatee cannot be charged with a legacy. 1. A testator may leave by way of fideicommissum a thing which belongs to himself, or to his heir, or to a legatee or fideicommissarius or to anyone else. Consequently, a legatee or fideicommissarius may be requested to restore not only the thing left to him, but any other thing, whether his own or some one else's. The only thing to be observed is that a man must not be asked to give up more than he takes under the will. Any direction in excess of this is without effect. When some one else's property is left by fideicommissum, the person charged must buy it

§ 372.

and make it over or pay its value. 2. Freedom may be given to a slave by fideicommissum, when an heir, or a legatee or fidei-commissarius is desired to manumit him. It makes no difference whether the slave belongs to the testator, or to his heir, or to a legatee or even to a stranger. If the slave belongs to some one else, he must be purchased and manumitted. If the owner refuses to sell, as he may, provided he has taken nothing under the testator's will, the gift of freedom does not immediately fail, but is postponed, because, as time proceeds, an opportunity may occur of buying the slave and making him free. If manumission takes place by way of fideicommissum the manumitted slave is not the freedman of the testator, although he owned him, but of the person who manumits.

§ 77.

If, on the other hand, a slave is set free directly by a man's will, he is the testator's freedman (libertus orcinus); and no slave can get his freedom under a will directly, unless he belonged to the testator both when the will was made and at the time of death. A gift of freedom is understood to be direct, when a testator does not desire some one to manumit the slave, but desires that he should derive his freedom, so to say, from the will. 3. Fideicommissa are usually constituted by such words as " I ask," " request," " desire," " authorise," " entrust." Any one of them has as much effect as all of them in combination.

XV. CODICILS

373. Codicils and fideicommissa were closely connected in their origin and their subsequent history. Introduced, we are told, by Lucius Lentulus, who is credited with being the first to employ fideicommissa, they were approved by Trebatius, and when Labeo had made codicils their validity was no longer open to question.[3]

374. Codicils, in the Roman meaning of the word, were informal written directions to an heir, often conveyed in a

[3] Inst. 2. 25 pr. Nothing is known of Lucius Lentulus. Cicero mentions cases of fideicommissa (Roby I, 356). Perhaps Lentulus gave his name to a " leading case." Trebatius was a teacher of Labeo ; Pomponius says that he wrote several books, which were not much in use in his time. Dig. 1. 2. 2, 45, 47. Horace introduces him in *Sat.* II. 1.

letter. For the first three centuries of the Empire no solemnity **2. 25. 3.**
of form was required. Justinian, following earlier legislation,
required seven witnesses for a will, five for a codicil (§ 368).
A codicil might be written or unwritten.[4] This gave a new
meaning to the word codicil by converting it into a slightly less
formal type of will, which like the more formal will might be
either written or nuncupative.

375. It was not a necessary condition of the validity of a
codicil that the deceased should have made a will. It might
take effect as a direction to the heir *ab intestato*. If, however, **2. 25. 1.**
there was a will, the codicil stood or fell with it, and avoidance
of the will avoided the codicil also.[5] Codicils might precede
or follow a will. In the former case they had *ab initio* the
character of instructions to the heir *ab intestato*, and it might
be supposed that they would be superseded by a subsequent
will. Papinian required express confirmation if they were to
retain their effect. The Emperors Severus and Antoninus
allowed dispositions contained in them to take effect as fideicommissa, if the will did not indicate a contrary intention.
Codicils more often followed the will. It was usual to confirm
them by anticipation by a special clause in the will. The will of
Dasumius (*supra*, § 370), contains a clause which, as recon- **3. 2. 6.**
structed, runs as follows: " If I shall have left anything written
and sealed in codicils or by any other kind of disposition I
desire it to be as valid as if it were written and sealed in my
will." In another and later will executed in Egypt by a soldier,
Caius Longinus Castor, in the year A.D. 189, which has been
preserved almost intact, the formula runs [6] :—" If I have left
anything hereafter written in my own hand, I wish it to be valid
in any way soever." This gave effect to any subsequent codicil,
provided that it was holograph, *i.e.*, written wholly in testator's
own hand. It may be that this continued to be admitted in the
later Empire as an exception from the general requirements
of form. It is interesting to note that an almost identical
clause, known as the reservatory clause, was until lately in use
in South Africa.[7]

---

[4] Cod. 6. 36. 8, 3. In omne autem ultima voluntate excepto testamento
quinque testes . . . debent adhiberi, sive in scriptis sive sine scriptis
voluntas conficiatur. This is interpolated at the end of a constitution of
Theodosius II. Buckl. *T.* p. 360. Inst. 2. 25. 3 is not up to date.

[5] Dig. 29. 7. 3, 2.

[6] Girard, *Textes,* p. 808.

[7] Lee, p. 361.

376. An unconfirmed codicil, if valid *qua* codicil, was adequate to create a fideicommissum,[8] but not, in the time of Gaius, to confer a legacy or to appoint a testamentary tutor.[9] After Justinian's legislation assimilating fideicommissa and legacies it made little difference whether a codicil was confirmed or unconfirmed. There remained one important difference between codicils and wills. A codicil could not regulate the devolution of the civil law inheritance. Therefore, it could neither appoint an heir, nor disinherit, nor attach a condition to an instituted heir, nor make a direct substitution. If a person purported to dispose of an inheritance by a document valid as a codicil, invalid as a will, it was a question of construction whether he meant to affect his heir *ab intestato* with a fideicommissum, or to institute a testamentary heir. In the first case the disposition held good, in the second, not.[10] But even as early as Papinian it was admitted that a codicil might at least *ascertain* the heir. The case is put of a testator who leaves some part of the inheritance undisposed of by his will, and adds: " Be the person heir whom I make heir by codicil." Afterwards he instituted Titius by codicil. Papinian held that this was a good institution to the undisposed fraction of the estate, for the institution was deemed to be made under the will.[11]

2. 25. 2.

377. To prevent a will miscarrying through some defect of form, it was usual to insert a clause desiring that the writing should also have the effect of a codicil.[12] This is known as the codicillary clause (clausula codicillaris). It imposed upon the *ab intestato* heir the duty of giving effect to the directions contained in the invalid will. Sometimes the codicillary clause was implied, *i.e.*, the *ab intestato* heir was held bound even in the absence of such a clause to give effect to the deceased's wishes.[13] Generally, a person claiming the estate or any part of it had to elect whether to claim under the will or under the codicillary clause as upon an intestacy. Having chosen the one alternative, he could not fall back upon the other. But in the case of near relatives this rule was not applied. " For it is not the same thing to lose what is your due and to miss a gift of fortune." [14]

---

[8] Dig. 29. 7. 3, 2.
[9] G. 2. 270a ; G. 2. 289. *Secus*, if confirmed, Dig. 26. 2. 3.
[10] Dig. 29. 7. 13, 1.
[11] Dig. 28. 5. (78) 77.
[12] Dig. 29. 7. 1 ; Cod. 6. 36. 8, 1a.
[13] For instances, see Hunter, p. 829.
[14] Cod. 6. 36. 8, 2.

THE INSTITUTES

BOOK II

Title XXV

Of codicils

Before the time of Augustus there was no law of codicils. They § 373.
were introduced by Lucius Lentulus, with whom fideicommissa also
had their origin. For when he was dying in Africa he wrote
codicils, confirmed in advance by his will, in which he desired
Augustus by way of fideicommissum to do something. The Emperor
carried out his wishes, and others following his example discharged
fideicommissa, and, in particular, the daughter of Lentulus paid
legacies which were not enforceable at law. Thereupon, Augustus is
said to have called together the lawyers and amongst them Trebatius,
whose authority was very great at the time, and to have asked them
whether this could be admitted and whether there was anything in
the use of codicils which was contrary to legal principle; and
Trebatius is said to have recommended Augustus to allow them,
because (as he said) the practice was very useful and necessary for
Roman citizens, on account of the long residence of men of those
days away from home and often in distant countries, where, if a man
could not make a will, he might at least make a codicil. After this
when Labeo too had made codicils their perfect admissibility was no
longer questioned.

1. A man may not only make codicils when he has made a will § 375.
but if he is dying without a will he may leave fideicommissa by
codicil. When codicils had been made before the will Papinian held
that they were without effect unless subsequently confirmed by a
special declaration. But the Emperors Severus and Antoninus
decided by rescript that fideicommissa could be claimed under
codicils preceding the will if it appeared that the person who had
subsequently made a will had not changed the intention which he
had expressed in the codicils.

2. By codicils an inheritance can neither be given nor taken § 376.
away—were it otherwise there would be confusion between the law
of wills and the law of codicils—and consequently no one can be
disinherited by codicil. What is meant is that an inheritance cannot be given or taken away directly. There is nothing to prevent
an inheritance being left in a codicil by way of fideicommissum.
Codicils cannot impose a condition on the instituted heir nor effect
a direct substitution.

3. A man may make as many codicils as he pleases and they may § 374.
be executed without any solemnity.

APPENDIX

The Modern Law of Testamentary Succession

378. This concludes what we have to say about the Roman Law
of testamentary succession. It has profoundly affected modern

systems of law. We may distinguish three causes which have contributed to this result. The first was the influence of the Church, steadily exercised against intestacy. To die without having made a pious disposition of a considerable part of his estate was not good for a man's soul—or for the Church. The second was the survival, or reception, of Roman Law, which had the effect of driving competing principles out of the field or into the holes and corners of local custom. The third has been the absorption of much of the accumulated material in modern codes. In England there was no general reception, but much Roman Law found its way into the practice of the ecclesiastical courts and the Court of Chancery, particularly in the matter of legacies. A fundamental difference between continental (and other civil law) systems on the one hand and English Law (and other common law systems) on the other is that the former retain the Roman Law heir, the successor *in universum jus quod defunctus habuit*, liable—saving the benefit of inventory—for the deceased person's debts even beyond the extent of the assets. This applies equally to testamentary and to intestate successors. In English Law the place of the heir is taken by the testamentary executor and in case of intestacy by an administrator appointed by the court. If the deceased has made a will, but forgotten to appoint an executor, an administrator is appointed *cum testamento annexo*. The executor is not unknown to foreign systems, but his functions are limited. It rests with a testator to appoint an executor or not, as he pleases, and the court does not supply the want, if no appointment is made. In South Africa, in spite of the civil law background, the English system of administration has been adopted. Heirs are commonly named in a will, but they are in fact merely residuary legatees.[15]

On the continent various types of will are in use, including *inter alia* the notarial will and the holograph will, that is a will written wholly in the handwriting of the testator, and signed by him, but not necessarily witnessed. This type of will is permitted also by the law of Scotland. In England, apart from the privileged will of soldiers and mariners [16] there has, since the Wills Act, 1837, been one will only, namely the will executed, as required by the statute, in the presence of two or more attesting and subscribing witnesses. This type of will has been introduced into South Africa and apart from the soldiers' will is now the only permitted form of testamentary disposition.[17] A peculiarity of South African Law is that it is perhaps the only existing system of law which allows a testator to tie up his property for ever by a perpetual series of fideicommissa.[18]

XVI. INTESTATE SUCCESSION

379. The Roman law of intestate succession was derived in order of historical sequence from four sources, namely:—

---

[15] Lee, p. 353.
[16] Wills Act, 1837, s. 1; Wills (Soldiers and Sailors) Act, 1918, s. 1.
[17] So provided by the Wills Act, 1953, which took effect from January 1, 1954.
[18] Lee, p. 385.

I. The Twelve Tables; II. The Praetor's Edict; III. Imperial Legislation before Justinian's Novel 118; IV. Justinian's Novels.

380. I. THE LAW OF THE TWELVE TABLES.—By the Law of the Twelve Tables the succession went to (A) sui heredes; (B) the nearest agnate (proximus agnatus); (C) the members of the gens (gentiles).

381. SUI HEREDES.—To be precise these were not successors to the deceased.[19] They had a vested interest during his lifetime.[20] This class consists of free persons in the power of the intestate who become sui juris on his death. It includes sons and grandsons, natural and adoptive, but grandsons only if their father has predeceased them or passed out of power by being given in adoption or emancipated while they continued in the power of their grandfather. In the old law a wife married to the deceased in manu counted as a daughter; his son's wife, similarly married, counted as a granddaughter, but was not a sua heres unless her husband has ceased to be in power before his father's death. Posthumous children were sui heredes if they would have been so if born during the ancestor's lifetime. G. 3. 3.

382. Sui heredes became such even though they might be ignorant of the death of their ancestor, or insane. No authority of tutor, or consent of curator, was needed if they were under age. The family ownership was, as it were, continued in the descendants immediately upon the death of the paterfamilias— statim morte parentis quasi continuatur dominium. Exceptionally, a person not in power on death might qualify as suus heres, e.g., by returning from slavery and recovering his status jure postliminii (§ 117). Conversely, it might happen that a person in power at death did not qualify as suus heres, as when the ancestor was posthumously pronounced guilty of treason and his estate was forfeited to the fiscus, though as Justinian suggests it might be more correct to say that he became suus heres, but ceased to be so when the condemnation was pronounced. The condemnation, however, had retrospective effect. 3. 1. 3. / 3. 1. 4. / 3. 1. 5.

383. If all the sui were in the first degree of descent they took share and share alike with no preference of males over females. Children in the second or remoter degree took per

---

[19] Dig. 28. 2. 11: post mortem patris non hereditatem percipere videntur, sed magis liberam bonorum administrationem consequuntur.
[20] G. 2. 157: Inst. 2. 19. 2: sed sui quidem heredes ideo appellantur quia domestici heredes sunt, et vivo quoque parente quodammodo domini existimantur.

258 ELEMENTS OF ROMAN LAW

3. 1. 6.
3. 1. 7.

3. 1. 8.

stirpes, as representing their deceased parent. In determining who was suus heres regard was had not to the time of death, but to the time when it was ascertained that deceased died intestate. Therefore, if an extraneus who had been instituted heir ultimately refused the inheritance, and deceased left a son, who died after his father, but before the refusal of the inheritance, the son's son, if he had one, was suus heres to the deceased grandfather. It was not necessary that he should have been born, but he must have been conceived, in his grandfather's lifetime.

384. PROXIMUS AGNATUS.—Failing sui heredes the succession by the Law of the Twelve Tables went to the nearest agnate of the deceased. Si intestato moritur cui suus heres nec escit adgnatus proximus familiam habeto. "If a man who has no suus heres dies intestate, the nearest agnate shall have the estate." [21] By "nearest" is meant the nearest when the fact of

3. 2. 6.
3. 2. 4.

intestacy is ascertained. Succession in this class was per capita, not per stirpes, all agnates of equal degree taking equally and without representation. If the nearest agnate declined to enter or died before entry, the inheritance did not pass to a remoter

3. 2. 7.

agnate, nor to the next class, the gentiles.[22] By the civil law it was vacant, and any person might assume its rights and responsibilities. By doing so he became owner of the things comprised in the inheritance at the end of a year (usucapio pro herede, § 175).[23] Subsequently to the Twelve Tables a rule came into existence unfavourable to female agnates. Beyond the second degree, i.e., unless they were sisters of the deceased,

3. 2. 3.

they were excluded from the succession. Justinian attributes this to what he calls the media jurisprudentia, i.e., juristic interpretation, subsequent to the Twelve Tables, but antecedent to imperial legislation. Paul says that this seems to have come about from applying the principle of the lex Voconia (Voconiana ratione).[24] This law, as has been seen, was unfavourable to women in the matter of testamentary succession (§ 307).

385. GENTILES.—Failing agnates the succession went to the members of the gens, which probably means to the gens as a unit. Si agnatus nec escit, gentiles familiam habento. "If there is no agnate the members of the gens shall have the estate." This was not strictly speaking succession, but a reversion to the

---

[21] G. 3. 9 ; Inst. 3. 2 pr. ; Ulp. XXVI, 1.
[22] Buckl. M. 228.
[23] G. 2. 52, 53.
[24] Paul. Sent. 4. 8. 20.

gentile community from which the individual paterfamilias derived his right. This order of succession (so to call it) still existed in the time of Cicero, and even in the beginning of the first century A.D.[25] But the whole law of the gens was obsolete by the time of Gaius.   G. 3. 17.

386. The civil law canons of succession as time went on were felt to be open to serious objection. Thus:—

(a) relations through females were wholly excluded ;   G. 3. 24.
(b) there was no succession between mother and child except in case of marriage in manu ;
(c) nor of emancipated children or children given in adoption ;   G. 3. 19.
(d) nor of collaterals, when the agnatic bond had been broken by capitis deminutio ;   G. 3. 21.
(e) nor of remoter agnates, when the nearest agnate refused ; G. 3. 22.
(f) nor of female agnates beyond the degree of sisters ;   G. 3. 23.
(g) nor, generally, of cognates who were not at the same time agnates.   G. 3. 24.

These disadvantages were removed by the praetor. This brings us to the second period in the history of intestate succession.

387. II. SUCCESSION UNDER THE PRAETOR'S EDICT.—The praetor could not " make an heir," [26] but he could give bonorum possessio and enforce it by the interdictum quorum bonorum, the hereditatis petitio possessoria, and other remedies.[27] Bonorum possessio was the praetorian counterpart of the civil law succession. It was granted by the praetor, later by any magistrate, to persons who claimed to be entitled.[28] In general this was matter of course, like, in our system, a grant of probate. Serious question as to the right of the applicant would only arise when he sought to take advantage of the interdict procedure. Bonorum possessio under the Edict was given in the event of a deceased person dying either testate or intestate, and in the first event either in conflict with the will or in accordance with it (b. p. contra tabulas—b. p. secundum tabulas). Failing a will, various classes of persons were entitled to claim as praetorian successors *ab intestato*. In the case of a free-born intestate four such classes were recognised and the corresponding   3. 9. 3.

---

[25] Girard, p. 897, n. 1.
[26] G. 3. 32 ; Inst. 3. 9. 2.
[27] Buckl. *M.* p. 238. This would make the bonorum possessor praetorian (bonitary) owner of the items of the estate with the right to become civil law owner by usucapion.
[28] Buckl. *T.* p. 387 ; *M.* p. 236.

bonorum possessiones were known as b. p. unde liberi (children), unde legitimi (statutory heirs or agnates), unde cognati (cognates), unde vir et uxor (husband and wife). The part of the Edict which determined the order in which the various persons or classes might advance their claims was known as the edictum possessorium, and they were entitled to claim in the order just stated. The word unde—" whence " or " by which "—has reference to the relevant section of the Edict—that part of the Edict " by which " children, etc., are called to the succession. The order of intestate succession was the result of a process of historical development. The four classes did not obtain recognition at the same time, and in the first case (unde liberi) it is probable that the praetor gave bonorum possessio sine re (without conclusive effect) before he gave it cum re (with conclusive effect), i.e., to begin with, it was provisional merely, and could not be maintained against a petitio hereditatis of the civil law heir. It seems that bonorum possessio unde legitimi was known to Cicero, and the list of bonorum possessiones was probably complete by the time of Labeo.[29] We proceed to consider them in order.

G. 3. 35.

388. (1) Bonorum possessio unde liberi. Under this head the praetor called to the succession together with the sui heredes emancipated sons and daughters (including sons and daughters given in adoption and subsequently emancipated by the adoptive parent) and the issue of emancipated sons, but not children adopted by the deceased and subsequently emancipated nor children given in adoption and not subsequently emancipated. It must be remarked that this order of succession only exists in relation to a male ascendant, for it is a praetorian enlargement of the civil law class of sui heredes.

3. 1. 10.

3. 1. 11.

389. (2) Bonorum possessio unde legitimi. This corresponds with the civil law succession of the proximus agnatus. The praetor made no addition, unless, as some thought, he admitted remoter agnates in this order.

3. 9. 3.

G. 3. 28.

390. (3) Bonorum possessio unde cognati. This class comprises all blood relations through males or females as far as the sixth degree and the seventh in the case of the issue of second cousins; it includes children in an adoptive family, female agnates remoter than sisters, agnates who had undergone capitis deminutio, remoter agnates (unless admitted in the class above),

3. 9. 3.

3. 5. 5 ;

3. 5. 3.

G. 2. 29.

G. 2. 27.

---

[29] Girard, p. 899.

mothers (unless, in the older law, married in manu) in succession
to children and vice versa.[30]

G. 2. 28.

3. 9. 3.

391. (4) Bonorum possessio unde vir et uxor. Failing cognates within the above-mentioned degrees the husband was
admitted to the succession of the wife, and the wife to the
succession of the husband.

392. Since the praetor called these four classes to the
succession one after the other it was necessary to fix a limit
of time within which persons entitled in each class must make
their claim. This was (normally) one year for children or
parents, one hundred days for all other persons.[31] However,
if the members of one class failed to claim within the time
allowed, they had the opportunity of coming in in a later class.
Thus liberi might claim in the unde legitimi class, or, if they
failed to do so, in the unde cognati class. Similarly legitimi
had another chance of claiming unde cognati.[32] But persons
who had failed to claim in their proper class might find themselves bound to share with others to whom they would otherwise
have been preferred.

393. When the praetor let in emancipated children along
with children in power,[33] he did so only upon condition that
they brought into account all property which had accrued to
them since emancipation ; for, if they had not been emancipated,
all their gains would have increased the fund available for
distribution. This contribution was called collatio bonorum.[34]
A difficulty arose when a grandfather had emancipated a son,
retaining the son's children in power. Clearly, it would be
unfair to the other children of the deceased to allow the emancipated son and his children to take together a double share in the
succession. Julian provided for this case by introducing into
the Edict a new clause, providing that in such case the father
and his children should take one share between them (nova
clausula de conjungendis cum emancipato liberis ejus).[35] The

---

[30] G. 2. 24 ; Inst. 3. 3 pr.
[31] Inst. 3. 9. 9. *in fine* ; Dig. 38. 15. 4, 1. By " days " understand *dies
utiles, i.e.,* " days on which it was both lawful and *de facto* possible for the
claim to be made." Buckl. *M.* p. 236.
[32] Dig. 38. 9. 1, 11.
[33] By giving the emancipated child bonorum possessio ab intestato, as
here, or contra tabulas, when he had been passed over in his father's will
(*supra*, § 314).
[34] Buckl. *T.* p. 325 ; *M.* p. 198.
[35] Dig. 37. 8. 3.

father made collatio bonorum, but only for the benefit of the children, since his coming in left the other sui no worse off than they were before.[36]

394. It will have been noticed that the praetor did not in every case depart from the civil law canons of succession. Sometimes he confirmed the civil law, *e.g.*, by giving bonorum possessio to sui or to the nearest agnate; sometimes he supplemented the civil law, *e.g.*, by admitting emancipati along with sui, or by allowing husband or wife to succeed in the last resort; sometimes he corrected the çivil law, *e.g.*, by giving bonorum possessio to heirs instituted in a will which satisfied his requirements, but was not valid by civil law, or by substituting the class of cognati for the gentiles. His intervention therefore assumed three forms, to confirm, to supplement, to correct, adjuvandi vel supplendi vel corrigendi juris civilis gratia.[37] This, perhaps, represents the historical order of development. The praetor first confirmed, later supplemented, finally corrected.[38]

395. III. IMPERIAL LEGISLATION BEFORE NOVEL 118.—Many changes were made, which principally had the effect of promoting certain relatives whom the praetor admitted only as cognates to the more privileged position of sui or legitimi. The result was a complicated system which, including changes made by Justinian's own constitutions, unfortunately, is perpetuated in the Institutes. The only part of it to which we need direct attention is that which relates to the succession of mothers to children, and of children to mothers.

396. SUCCESSION OF MOTHERS TO CHILDREN.—Justinian tells us that in a special case the Emperor Claudius gave a mother the succession to her children. A general rule was laid down by the senatusconsultum Tertullianum, which gave mothers who had the jus liberorum (§ 138) a statutory title to succeed to their children. Contrary to what might be inferred from the language of the Institutes, this enactment was not so much a recognition of a mother's claim to an early place in the scheme of succession as one more device to encourage the procreation of children. It is a belated application by the Emperor Hadrian of the policy of the leges Julia and Papia Poppaea.[39] This explains why the succession of mothers to children was taken in

3.

---

[36] Dig. 37. 8. 1, 13.
[37] Dig. 1. 1. 7, 1.
[38] This is Girard's view (p. 845), but other views are held.
[39] Buckl. *T.* p. 374.

hand before the much more frequent case of the succession of children to mothers.

397. SUCCESSION OF CHILDREN TO MOTHERS.—This was given by the senatusconsultum Orfitianum of A.D. 178, but limited 3. 4. to the first degree of descent. Later legislation extended it to grandchildren. It was not affected by capitis deminutio minima. Like the senatusconsultum Tertullianum it applied to illegitimate not less than to legitimate issue.[39a]

398. IV. JUSTINIAN'S NOVELS.—In Novels 118 and 127 (A.D. 543, 548), Justinian superseded the old agnatic scheme of succession in favour of the claims of natural relationship. Under this system the succession went to the following classes : —

1. Descendants, the nearer excluding the more remote, with representation per stirpes in infinitum ;

2. Ascendants, the nearer excluding the more remote, and brothers and sisters of the whole blood, the children, but not the grandchildren, of a deceased brother or sister representing the deceased (but only if a brother or sister remained alive). All of these (subject to representation) took equally. If there were ascendants only, equally near, the estate was divided, first by lines (paternal and maternal), and within each line by heads (thus a surviving paternal grandfather took half, surviving maternal grandparents divided the other half between them). Nephews and nieces, if no brother or sister were living, were not admitted in this class, but came in later in class 4 (or in class 3 if a half-brother or -sister survived) ;

3. Half-brothers and -sisters and the issue of deceased half-brothers and -sisters in the first degree of descent with the same qualification ;

4. Other collaterals without representation and with no limit of remoteness ;

5. Husband and wife. This last order of succession is included on the authority of the *Basilica*. It is not mentioned in Novels 118 and 127.

[39a] The praetor had admitted to bonorum possessio unde cognati a mother's illegitimate children and the mother in succession to them, Dig. 38. 8. 2. Modern systems have derived from Roman Law the rule that a mother makes no bastard. For the law of South Africa, see Lee, p. 31. In England s. 9 of the Legitimacy Act, 1926, admits reciprocal succession of a mother and her illegitimate children, provided she leaves no legitimate issue.

399. Such in its latest phase was the Roman Law of intestate succession, which has profoundly affected the legal systems of Europe and through Europe of the remotest regions of the world. In France the districts of the written law adopted it from an early date. The " reception " made it part of the common law of Germany. In other countries, often under the patronage of the Church—ecclesia vivit lege Romana—it came into competition with rules of customary and feudal law. All three elements are present in the English Statutes of Distribution (1670, 1685), which were adopted in some other parts of the English-speaking world, and remained in force in this country until replaced by the provisions of the Administration of Estates Act, 1925.

400. Apart from matters of detail, two matters of general application mark the triumph of Roman principles in the modern law. The first is the admission of the principle of representation unknown to the customary law, first in the descending line, later in collateral lines. The second is the universal adoption of the Roman conception of relationship as a tree with its branches. The Germans from of old pictured it in the shape of the human body. The common ancestors made the head. Their children were in the neck, grandchildren in the shoulders, and so on through elbow and wrist to the three joints of the finger. This was the scheme of the *Sachsenspiegel,* a compilation dating from between 1220 and 1235. The *Schwabenspiegel* (1274–5) placed the children in the shoulder not in the neck, but included the nail. Both systems agreed, therefore, in carrying relationship to the fourteenth Roman degree. Before the fourth Lateran Council (A.D. 1215) this marked the limit of the prohibited degrees for marriage (*viz.,* sixth cousins). The Lateran Council cut this down to the fourth canonical degree (third cousins), and the codex juris canonici limits the prohibition to the third canonical degree (second cousins).[40]

---

[40] c. 1076, § 2. In linea collaterali [matrimonium] irritum est usque ad tertium gradum inclusive. In calculating collateral relationship the Canon Law reckons degrees down from the common ancestor, and, if the persons whose relationship is in question are not equally remote from the common ancestor, the longer line marks the degree of relationship. Thus a grandson is in the second degree of relationship to his grandfather, but also to his uncle and to his first cousin, and in the third degree to his first cousin's children. The Roman Law traces the degrees up and then down. A grandson stands in the second degree to his grandfather, the third to his uncle, the fourth to his first cousin. Blackst. *Commentaries,* II, p. 206.

THE INSTITUTES

BOOK III (Tits. I–VI, IX)

TITLE I

Of intestate succession

A man dies intestate if he has made no will, or if he has made an invalid will, or if his will has been broken or rendered inoperative, or if no heir has accepted the inheritance.   § 328.

1. By the Law of the Twelve Tables the inheritances of intestates belong in the first instance to the sui heredes. 2. Those persons are said to be sui heredes who were in power of the deceased at the time of his death, as son and daughter, grandson and granddaughter by a son, great-grandson and great-granddaughter by a grandson born of a son. It makes no difference whether children are natural or adoptive; and we must include also children legitimated by oblatio curiae or per subsequens matrimonium. This takes place in terms of our constitutions when a man has been living with a woman not as his wife, but whom he could have married, and has had children by her; if afterwards, wishing to make her his wife, he has executed a marriage contract, and had children by her, then not only the children born after the constitution of the dos, but those born before, who have been the occasion of the legitimacy of those born afterwards, are to be legitimate and in the power of the parent. This is to apply even if no children have been born after the execution of the dotal instrument, or if they have been born, and subsequently died.[41] Grandchildren and great-grandchildren are not reckoned among sui heredes, unless the person in the preceding degree has ceased to be in power in consequence of death or for any other reason such as emancipation; for if at the time of death a son was in power, a grandson by that son cannot be suus heres. The same applies to remoter descendants. Posthumous children too who would have been in power, if born in the parent's lifetime, are sui heredes. 3. Descendants become sui heredes even though they are ignorant of their right, or chance to be insane; for in any case in which an inheritance is acquired in spite of ignorance, it is equally acquired in spite of insanity. From the moment of the parent's death the ownership is, so to say, continued in the successor. No authority of tutor is required in the case of pupilli, nor consent of curator, when the heir is insane. The inheritance vests by mere force of law.   § 381.   § 105.

4. It may happen that though a person was not in power at the time of death, he nevertheless is suus heres to his parent, as when a person returns from foreign slavery after his father's death. This is the effect of postliminium.   § 117.

5. Conversely, although a person is a member of the family at the time of death, he may, nevertheless, not be a suus heres. This happens if a father has been adjudged guilty of treason after his death, so that a stigma of infamy is attached to his memory. He   § 382.

---

[41] Cod. 5. 27. 10 & 11.

cannot have a suus heres, since the estate escheats to the fiscus. Perhaps, it would be more correct to say that the successor becomes suus heres, but ceases to be so.

§ 383.

6. When there are children and grandchildren by another child they are called together to the succession, and the nearer in degree do not exclude the more remote; for it seems fair that a son's children should take their father's place. Similarly, grandchildren and great-grandchildren are called together; and since it is settled that grandchildren and great-grandchildren succeed to their parents' place, it is consistent with this that the inheritance should be distributed not in capita, but in stirpes, so that, for example, a son takes half the inheritance, and two or more grandchildren by another son take the other half between them. Again, if there are grandchildren by two sons, say, one or two by one son, three or four by another, then half the inheritance goes to the one or two, the other half to the three or four. 7. When the question arises whether a person can be a suus heres, we must look to the time at which it is certain that a man has died intestate, which may occur because no one accepts the inheritance. Therefore, if a son has been disinherited, and a stranger instituted in his place, and then the son dies, and afterwards it is ascertained that the instituted heir does not become heir under the will because he will not or cannot be heir, then, the grandson will be suus heres, because at the time when it was ascertained that the paterfamilias died intestate, the grandson was the only survivor. This is settled law.

8. Even if he was born after his grandfather's death, still if he was conceived in his grandfather's lifetime, and his father dies and no one is heir under the will, he becomes suus heres to his grandfather. Of course, if he is both conceived and born after his grandfather's death, he will not in these circumstances be suus heres to his grandfather, because there was no bond of relationship between him and his father's father. Again, the adopted son of an emancipated son is not reckoned amongst the grandfather's children. Such persons not being entitled to succeed in the quality of children are just as little entitled to claim possession of goods in the character of nearest cognates.

§ 388.

9. Emancipated children have no right to the inheritance by civil law, for they are not sui heredes, having ceased to be in the power of their parent, and the Law of the Twelve Tables does not admit them by any other title. But the praetor, moved by considerations of natural equity, gives them possession of goods in the unde liberi class, just as if they had been in power at the time of the parent's death, whether they are the only children or whether they concur with children who remained in power. Therefore, if there are two children, one emancipated and one who was in power at the time of death, the latter is the sole heir at civil law, but since the emancipated child is by the praetor's indulgence admitted to a share in the inheritance, the suus heres will in effect be heir only to one half. 10. Emancipated children who have given themselves in adoption are not admitted to the succession of their natural father in the class of children, that is, if when he dies they are in the adoptive family; for if in his lifetime they have been emancipated by the adoptive father they are admitted to the succession of their natural father,

just as if he had himself emancipated them and they had never
been in the adoptive family. Consistently with this, they become
strangers to the adopting father. But if they are emancipated by
the adoptive father after the death of their natural father, they are,
as before, strangers to the adopting father, and are not, any the more
for that, entitled to rank as children in succession to their natural
father. The law has been settled in this sense, because it would be
unfair that the adoptive father should be able to determine whether
the natural father's estate should go to his children or to his
agnates.

11. Adoptive children, therefore, are in a worse position than
natural children. The latter after emancipation by the indulgence
of the praetor retain the rank of children, though they lose it by
civil law. But adoptive children after emancipation lose the position
of children by civil law, and are not aided by the praetor. This is
as it should be; for the theory of the civil law cannot destroy the
claims of nature, and if they cease to be sui heredes, they do not
therefore cease to be children or grandchildren. But adoptive
children on emancipation become strangers to the adoptive parent,
for the right and name of son or daughter which they acquired
by adoption they lose by another process of civil law, namely
emancipation.

12. The same applies in the case of the possession of goods which § 314.
the praetor gives in opposition to the will to children who have been
passed over, that is, neither instituted nor duly disinherited. For
the praetor admits to this possession children in power at the time
of death, and emancipated children, but not children who are in an
adoptive family when the natural parent dies. But adoptive children
who have been emancipated by the adoptive parent have no claim to
succeed upon his intestacy, and still less are entitled to contra-
tabular possession, for they have ceased to be reckoned as children.
13. It must be remarked, however, that children who are in an
adoptive family, or who have been emancipated by their adoptive
parent after the death of their natural parent, though not admitted
to the succession of their natural parent in the class of " children,"
nevertheless come in under another part of the edict, which calls
cognates to the succession, provided always that they are not
excluded by " children " (sui heredes or emancipated) nor by any
agnatic relation; for the praetor calls to the succession first " children," then the statutory heirs, then the nearest cognates. 14. All this
was the old law. But our constitution [42] has amended the law with
regard to children given in adoption by their natural fathers.
Cases occurred in which sons by being given in adoption lost the
right of succeeding to their natural parents, and then, the adoption
being easily dissolved by emancipation, were not called to the
succession of either parent. This our constitution corrects by providing that when a natural parent gives his son in adoption to
another, the son is to retain all his rights, just as if he had remained
in his natural father's power and no adoption had taken place, the
only change being that he acquires the right of intestate succession to
his adoptive father. But if the adoptive father has made a will the

---

[42] Cod. 8. 47 (48). 10.

adoptive son is to have no claim to the estate either by civil law or by praetorian law, neither by applying for possession of goods against the will, nor by bringing the querela inofficiosi testamenti; for the adoptive father is not under any obligation either to institute him heir or to disinherit him, since there is no natural relationship between them, not even in the case of the adoption of one of three male children under the senatusconsultum Afinianum.[43] There is one exception, namely, when the adopting father is a natural ascendant, for since the rights of civil law and of nature meet in his person we have left the old law to take its course, just as when a paterfamilias gives himself in adrogation; all of which may be gathered from the above-mentioned constitution.

§ 114.

15. Further, the old law, giving a preference to the issue of males, called to the succession as sui heredes only grandchildren by sons; grandchildren by daughters, on the other hand, and great-grandchildren by granddaughters ranked merely as cognates, and were postponed to the agnates, in succession to a maternal grandfather or great-grandfather or to a grandmother or great-grandmother, paternal or maternal. But the Emperors have not left this outrage on nature without amendment, and since the words grandson and great-grandson apply indifferently to descendants through males and through females, they have given them the same degree and order of succession. But, in order to give some advantage to those whose claim is based not only on natural relationship but also supported by the rules of the old law, they decided that the share of grandsons or granddaughters or remoter descendants through females should be somewhat reduced, so that they should take one-third less than their mother or grandmother would have taken, or their father or grandfather, paternal or maternal, when succession to a female was in question. When any of the above-mentioned persons, even if they were the only descendants, took up the succession, the agnates were excluded; and just as the Law of the Twelve Tables when a son is dead, calls to the succession grandsons or granddaughters, great-grandsons or great-granddaughters to take the place of their father in succession to their grandfather, so imperial legislation calls them, subject to the deduction above mentioned, to the succession in place of their mother or grandmother. 16. But since a question still remained between the agnates and descendants through females, the agnates claiming a quarter of the estate by virtue of a certain constitution, we have not admitted this constitution into our code, or allowed it to be reproduced from the Code of Theodosius.[44] The constitution which we have promulgated has deprived it of all authority, and we have enacted [45] that if any such grandchildren by a daughter, or great-grandchildren by a granddaughter, and so on, are in existence, the agnates are to have no share in the succession, so that collateral relations may not be preferred to the direct line of descent. Division of the inheritance is to be made as under the old law in stirpes, so that, for example, if in one line there are one or two children, in another three or four, one half of the inheritance goes to the one or two, the other half to the three or four.

---

[43] Cod. 8. 47 (48). 10, 3. The date and the motive of this S.C. are unknown. Girard, p. 195, n. 4.
[44] Cod. Theod. 5. 1. 4.
[45] Cod. 6. 55. 12.

TITLE II

Of the statutory succession of agnates

If there is no suus heres, nor any of those whom the praetor or the imperial constitutions call to the succession along with the sui heredes to take the succession in any way, the inheritance by the Law of the Twelve Tables belongs to the nearest agnate. 1. Agnates, as we have explained in the first book, are relations through males. Thus brothers born of the same father are agnates to one another and are termed consanguinei, and it is not necessary to inquire whether they have the same mother. Similarly, a father's brother is an agnate to his brother's son, and conversely. To the same class belong brother's sons (patrueles—consobrini) and the same principle applies to remoter degrees of relationship. Children born after their father's death are similarly related. The law does not give the inheritance to all agnates simultaneously, but only to those who are in the nearest degree when it is ascertained that the deceased died intestate.

2. Agnatic relationship is also created by adoption, as between natural sons and sons whom the father has adopted. These too are called consanguinei in relation to one another. Similarly, if another of your agnatic relations, a brother, a father's brother or one further remote has adopted a son, you are agnates to one another. 3. Male relatives (through males) are admitted to the inheritance by title of agnation in any degree, however remote. But in the case of females the rule was that sisters might succeed, but no remoter female agnate; while in succession to them any male agnate was entitled, however remote. Consequently, you succeeded to the daughter of your own brother or of your father's brother, or to your father's sister, but they did not succeed to you. This was so ordained, because it was thought better that inheritances should, as a rule, go to males rather than to females. But, since it was unfair that they should be entirely excluded as if they were strangers to the family, the praetor admitted them in the unde cognati group, but postponed them to agnates and to nearer cognates. 3a. This rule is not to be found in the Law of the Twelve Tables, which did not distinguish between male and female agnates, whatever the degree of relationship. It was the invention of an intermediate jurisprudence, subsequent to the Twelve Tables, but anterior to the imperial constitutions. The praetor's edict went some way towards correcting this anomaly, but not far enough. 3b. Our constitution, therefore, reverts to the rule of the Twelve Tables, and admits all female agnates to the succession equally with male agnates of the same degree. 4. And it [46] makes one further change, by transferring one degree only of cognatic relationship to the agnatic group, with the result that in succession to an uncle are called not only his brother's children but also the children (not remoter descendants) of his sister, whether of the whole or of the half blood on either side, just as if they were agnatically related to the deceased. This must be understood to be the case only if there are no brothers or sisters in existence, who accept the inheritance. For they being nearer in degree exclude the more remote, since in this class the inheritance is divided

§ 384.

1. 15. 1.

---

[46] Cod. 6. 58. 14.

not ad stirpes but in capita, *i.e.*, equally amongst relatives nearest in degree. 5. If there are agnatic relatives of different degrees of remoteness, the Law of the Twelve Tables expressly calls to the succession the nearest. Therefore, if the deceased is survived by a brother and another brother's son, or by a father's brother, the brother is preferred. Although the Law speaks of "the nearest agnate" (in the singular number), there is no doubt that if there are several agnates of the same degree they are all admitted. Similarly, though "nearest" properly implies nearest of several, there is no doubt that though agnates are found in one degree of remoteness only, the inheritance belongs to them. 6. To ascertain who is nearest, if the deceased died without having made a will, we ask who was nearest at the time of death; but if the deceased made a will we ask who was nearest when it was ascertained that there was not going to be any testamentary heir, for it is not till then that a person can properly be said to have died intestate. Sometimes this takes place only after a considerable interval of time, and it often happens that owing to the nearest having died the person who eventually is nearest was not the nearest at the time of death.

7. At first no succession of members of this class was admitted, that is to say, if the person entitled as nearest refused the inheritance or died before accepting it, this did not any the more entitle remoter agnates to succeed. Here again the praetors found a partial remedy, admitting them as cognates. But we, desiring to bring the law to the highest possible state of perfection, have decreed in our constitution [47] relating to the rights of patrons that succession shall not be refused to remoter agnates; for it was really absurd to withhold from agnates a right which the praetor made available to cognates, particularly in view of the fact that the burden of tutelage passed to remoter agnates failing the nearest degree, and that the existing law withheld an advantage where it imposed a burden.

§ 129.
8. Another case of statutory succession is that of the parent who has emancipated a son or daughter or other descendant with a trust agreement. Under the old law an express agreement was necessary, but by our constitution [48] it is implied in all emancipations of children.

TITLE III

Of the senatusconsultum Tertullianum

§ 386.
The Law of the Twelve Tables applied so strictly the principle of preferring issue through males and excluding issue through females that it did not admit a reciprocal right of succession between a mother and her children. The praetors, however, allowed them to succeed to one another in the class unde cognati. 1. But this narrow-

§ 396.
ness of the law was afterwards amended. It was the Emperor Claudius who first allowed a mother a statutory succession to her children as a consolation for their loss. 2. Afterwards the senatus-consultum Tertullianum, enacted in the time of the Emperor Hadrian, made full provision for the melancholy succession of a mother (not

§ 138.
of a grandmother) by providing that a mother who had the jus

---

[47] Cod. 6. 4. 4, 20.   [48] Cod. 8. 48 (49). 6.

liberorum, that is, who had three children, if she was free-born, or
four, if she was a freed-woman, might succeed *ab intestato* to her
sons or daughters, even though she was in the power of an ascendant,
in which case she would require his order to accept the inheritance.
3. The mother is postponed to children of a deceased son, whether
sui or ranked as such, whether of the first or a further degree of
descent; and by imperial constitutions the son and daughter of a
deceased daughter are preferred to the daughter's mother, that is to
their own grandmother. The father in each case is preferred to the
mother, but not a grandfather or great-grandfather, that is to say
when it is a question simply between them and the mother.[49]
Further, a brother born of the same father excluded the mother in
succession to a son or daughter, but a sister born of the same father
was admitted together with the mother. If there were brother and
sister, they took in equal shares excluding the mother. 4. But by a
constitution which we have placed in our code we have thought
proper to come to the aid of the mother, having regard to the claims
of nature and the perils of child-birth. For why should a woman be
punished for not having the required number of children? We have
therefore given mothers, whether free-born or freed, a full right of
succession in the statutory class even though they may not have had
any child except the one whose succession is in question.[50]

5. The earlier constitutions partly aided the mother, and partly
put her at a disadvantage by reducing her share by one-third in
favour of certain agnatic relations. But we have decided to take the
straight simple course of preferring the mother to all statutory
claimants in succession to her children without any deduction; except
that brothers and sisters, whether related by agnation or by cognation
to the deceased (who by our legislation are placed first in the order
of statutory succession) are called to the succession along with the
mother; if there are sisters only the mother takes one half, the sisters
divide the other half amongst them; if the deceased is survived by a
brother or brothers with or without sisters, the inheritance is distributed in capita between him or them and the mother.[51] 6. But as
we have provided for mothers, so they ought to consult the interest
of their children; and mothers must know that if they have failed to
apply within a year for guardians to be appointed to their children
or to take the place of a guardian who has been removed or excused,
they will deservedly be excluded from the succession to their children
who die under the age of puberty.[52] 7. By the senatusconsultum
mothers succeed even to their illegitimate children.

TITLE IV

Of the senatusconsultum Orfitianum

Conversely, children are admitted to the succession of mothers § 397.
who die intestate by the senatusconsultum Orfitianum, which was

---

[49] If a grandfather had emancipated a grandson, retaining the father
in power, the father excluded the mother, and by so doing was the occasion
of the grandfather succeeding as parens manumissor. If the father was
dead, the mother was preferred to the grandfather, excluding the father.
[50] Cod. 8. 58. 2.
[51] Cod. 6. 56. 7.   [52] Cod. 6. 58. 10.

passed in the consulship of Orfitus and Rufus in the time of the
Emperor Marcus. This gave a statutory succession to sons and
daughters, even though in power, in preference to brothers and
sisters and remoter agnates of a deceased mother. 1. The senatusconsultum did not call grandchildren to the succession of a grandmother, but this was afterwards amended by imperial constitutions.
2. It must be remarked that rights of succession under the Tertullian
and the Orfitian senatusconsulta are not lost by capitis deminutio.
This is in accordance with the rule that new statutory inheritances
are not destroyed in this way, but only those which are given by
the Law of the Twelve Tables. 3. Even illegitimate children succeed
to their mother under this senatusconsultum.

§ 338.

4. If of several statutory heirs, some have renounced the
inheritance or failed to accept it, either because they have died before
acceptance, or have been prevented from accepting by some other
cause, their share accrues to the rest who accept, or to their heirs
if they die before the accrual of the lapsed portion.

Title V

Of the succession of cognates

§ 390.

After sui heredes, and those whom the praetor and the constitutions call to the succession together with them and after statutory
successors (that is agnates and those whom the above-mentioned
senatusconsulta and our constitution advance to the rank of agnates)
the praetor calls the nearest cognates. 1. In this class of successors
regard is had to natural relationship. Agnates who have undergone capitis deminutio and their issue do not rank as statutory
heirs by the Law of the Twelve Tables, but are called by the praetor
in the class of cognates, except that the law of the Emperor
Anastasius calls to the succession of a deceased brother or sister
emancipated brothers and sisters (not their children) together with
those whose right of succession remains unimpaired, not indeed on
equal terms, but with a certain deduction, as appears from the
language of the constitution [53]; they are preferred, however, to
remoter agnates, even those that have not suffered capitis deminutio
and, undoubtedly, to cognates. 2(1). Relatives through females
in a collateral line are called by the praetor in the third order of
succession unde cognati.

3(2). Children who are in an adoptive family are in the same
order of succession to their natural parents.

4(3). That illegitimate children have no agnatic relations is
evident, for agnation means relationship on the father's side (while
cognation means relationship through the mother as well) and illegitimate children are supposed to have no father. On the same principle
they cannot be held to be related to one another as consanguinei
(i.e., as having a common father), because consanguinity is a species
of agnation. They are therefore merely cognates to one another, as
they are too to their mother's cognates. So all such persons may
take advantage of the bonorum possessio unde cognati.

[53] Cod. 5. 30. 4.

THE LAW OF SUCCESSION

5(4). It must be added that a person may be admitted to the inheritance by title of agnation, though he is in the tenth [or any remoter] degree,[54] whether under the Twelve Tables or in the class to which the praetor offers bonorum possessio unde legitimi. But the praetor does not promise succession in the class of cognates beyond the sixth degree and the seventh in the case of the children of second cousins.

Title VI

Of the degrees of relationship

Some explanation of the degrees of cognatic relationship may be useful. This is calculated either in the ascending line, or in the descending line, or in the side line (or, as we say, collaterally). 1. Relations in the first degree are father and mother in the ascending line, son and daughter in the descending line. 2. In the second degree, grandfather and grandmother ascending, grandson and granddaughter descending, and in the collateral line brother and sister.

3. In the third degree, ascending great-grandfather and great-grandmother, descending great-grandson and great-granddaughter, in the collateral line a brother or sister's son and daughter, a father's or mother's brother or sister.

4. In the fourth degree, ascending great-great-grandfather and great-great-grandmother, descending great-great-grandson and great-great-granddaughter, in the collateral line great-uncles and great-aunts, that is a grand-parent's brothers and sisters, and first cousins, that is, the sons and daughters of one brother or sister in relation to the sons and daughters of another brother or sister.

[Sections 5 and 6 illustrating the fifth and sixth degrees are omitted.]

7. This may suffice to explain the method of calculation. Remoter relationships are reckoned on the same principle, each birth making one more degree. 8. Agnatic degrees of relationship are similarly calculated. 9. For all of this consult the Table of Degrees annexed hereto.

10. The praetorian law of succession has no application to slaves. But by our constitution [55] in case of manumission children succeed to either parent and reciprocally between themselves [details obscure and of no importance], the right of patronage being so far in abeyance.

11. From what has been said it is apparent that persons in the same degree of cognatic relationship are not always called simultaneously to the succession, and that a nearer cognate is not always preferred to a remoter cognate. For since the first class consists of sui heredes and those who are admitted together with them, it is evident that a great-grandson, or a great-great-grandson (who are in the third and fourth degree respectively) are preferred to a father or mother (who are in the first) and to a brother (who is in the second). It makes no difference in this class whether the person claiming the succession was in power at the time of death or not in power, having been emancipated or being the child of an

---

[54] The tenth degree is mentioned merely by way of illustration.
[55] Cod. 6. 44.

emancipated child or of a child of the female sex.   12. Similarly
an agnate, who retains his right of agnation unimpaired, however
remote in degree, is usually preferred to a nearer cognate; for
example the grandson or great-grandson [born of a grandson] of a
father's brother comes before a mother's brother or sister.   So whenever we say that a nearer cognate is preferred, or that cognates are
called together to the succession, this must be understood to be so
only if there are no sui heredes (or others reckoned with them) or
any agnate with prior claims, except that in this last order of
succession brothers and sisters who have been emancipated, in spite

3. 5. 1. of the capitis deminutio are preferred to remoter agnates in the
succession to a deceased brother or sister.

<h3 style="text-align:center">TITLE IX</h3>

Of possession of goods

§ 387. The law of possession of goods was introduced by the praetor to
amend the old law; not only in the case of intestate successions, as
above explained, but also when the deceased had made a testament.
For if a testator had instituted a stranger to the family not born
at the date of the will (alienus postumus), though he could not
succeed at civil law, since the institution was invalid, yet the
praetor afforded a remedy by giving him possession of goods.   However, today our constitution [56] allows him to be instituted directly,
as no longer unrecognised by the civil law.   1. But sometimes the
praetor gives bonorum possessio not to amend or impugn the civil

§ 394. law, but rather to confirm it.   For example, he gives possession of
goods in accordance with the will (bonorum possessio secundum
tabulas) to heirs instituted by a valid will, and to sui heredes and
agnates, though quite apart from bonorum possessio these are
entitled to succeed by civil law.   2. When the praetor calls to the
succession persons who have no civil law title they do not become
heirs *ipso jure* (the praetor cannot make an heir; it is only by a
statute or an enactment which has the force of a statute such as a
senatusconsultum or an imperial constitution that men become heirs);
but since the praetor gives them bonorum possessio they are placed
in the position of heirs and are called " possessors of goods."   The
praetor has created many other degrees of succession in giving possession of goods, his object being that no one should die without a
successor.   Thus he has on equitable principles (ex bono et aequo)
extended the right to succeed to an inheritance beyond the very
narrow limits of the Law of the Twelve Tables.

§ 314. 3. There are two kinds of bonorum possessio when the deceased
has left a testament.   The first which is given to children who have
been passed over unnoticed [that is, neither instituted nor expressly
disinherited] is called possession of goods against the will (b. p.
contra tabulas).   The second is given to all duly instituted heirs
and is called possession of goods in terms of the will (b. p. secundum
tabulas).   From testamentary succession he goes on to speak of
succession *ab intestato*.

---

[56] See note to Inst. 2. 20. 27.

In the first place he gives possession of goods to sui heredes, and those whom the edict admits in this class. This is called bonorum possessio unde liberi. Next come the statutory heirs who are admitted in the order unde legitimi. [The third order of bonorum possessio relates to the succession to an emancipated son.] [57] In the fourth place come the nearest cognates (b. p. unde cognati). Then (after two classes of succession to freedmen [57]) in the seventh place comes the reciprocal succession of husband and wife (b. p. unde vir et uxor). Lastly, in the eighth place, [another class of successors to freedmen].

4–7 (abbreviated). Of the above-mentioned possessions of goods six only are retained in our system, viz., contra tabulas—secundum tabulas—unde liberi—unde legitimi—unde cognati—unde vir et uxor.

8(7). There is a seventh which the praetors very reasonably introduced. For last of all the edict promises possession of goods to any persons to whom any statute or senatusconsultum or imperial constitution says that it shall be given, and whom the praetor has not definitely included in any of the above-mentioned classes of testamentary or intestate successors, but to whom he afforded this ultimate and extraordinary remedy, adapted to the special circumstances created by legislative enactment. 9(8). Thus the praetor introduced several kinds of succession and arranged them in order, but within each class it often happened that there were several persons in different degrees of relationship to the deceased. So in order that creditors should not suffer delay in bringing their actions, but might have some persons against whom they might proceed, and on the other hand might not too readily be allowed to consult their own interest by being let into possession of the goods of the deceased, the praetor defined certain periods for claiming possession of goods.

(9). These were in the case of children and parents natural and adoptive one year, in all other cases one hundred days. 10. If any § 392. one fails to claim within the time allowed, his right accrues to other persons of the same degree; and if no one claims, the praetor offers possession of goods to persons subsequently entitled, as laid down in the part of the edict dealing with succession, just as if there had not been any one in the preceding class. If any one has renounced the bonorum possessio offered to him, it is not necessary to wait until the time limited for his acceptance has expired, but the edict immediately admits the persons next entitled.

11. In calculating the periods dies utiles only are taken into account. 12(10). Earlier Emperors have very wisely provided that a claimant need not trouble to apply for possession of goods, but may take full advantage of its benefit, in whatsoever way he may have manifested (of course within the time prescribed) his intention of asserting his claim.

XVII. SUCCESSION TO FREEDMEN

401. This is a subject which most manuals of Roman Law dismiss with little, if any notice, and we shall be content to

[57] The parts of the text omitted here will be found below, p. 278.

do the same, merely referring the reader, if he wishes to pursue the subject, to the text and to Buckland's *Textbook* and *Manual*, where the subject is treated in some detail. As appears from the Institutes, the law passed through several stages and in all of them the patron (or his family) was in certain circumstances entitled to claim the whole or part of a deceased freedman's estate. Though by Novel 78 Justinian for most purposes abolished the distinctions which had previously existed between ingenui and libertini, this did not affect the law of succession unless expressly renounced by the manumitter (§ 79).

THE INSTITUTES

BOOK III (Tits. VII–IX)

TITLE VII

Of the succession to freedmen

Let us now consider the succession to freedmen. In ancient times a freedman was allowed to pass over his patron in his will with impunity; for the Law of the Twelve Tables called a patron to the succession of his freedman only if the freedman died intestate without leaving a suus heres. So if he died intestate and left a suus heres, the patron had no right of succession. If the suus heres was a natural-born child there was no ground of complaint; but if he was an adopted son, it was clearly unfair that the patron should be entirely excluded. 1. Accordingly the praetor's edict introduced an amendment. If the freedman made a will he was required to leave his patron half of his estate. If he left him nothing at all, or less than half, the patron was given bonorum possessio for one half against the tablets of the will. If he died intestate leaving as his suus heres an adopted son, equally the patron was given bonorum possessio of the half against this son. The patron was excluded by natural children, not only such as were in power at the time of death, but also those that had been emancipated or given in adoption, provided that they had been instituted to some share in the inheritance, or, being passed over, had obtained contra-tabular bonorum possessio. Disinherited children did not in any way exclude the patron. Subsequently the lex Papia enlarged the rights of patrons who had wealthy freedmen. It provided that if a freedman left a fortune of one hundred thousand sesterces and less than three children, whether he died testate or intestate, a child's portion should go to the patron. Accordingly, if the freedman left one son or daughter, the patron took half the estate just as if he had died childless; if he left two children the patron took one-third; if three children, nothing. 3. The whole matter is now regulated by a constitution which we have issued in the Greek language.[58] If a freedman or a freedwoman leaves an estate of less than one hundred aurei (we take this to be the equivalent of the one hundred thousand sesterces of the lex Papia, counting each thousand sesterces as one aureus) and has made a will, the patron is excluded. If he or she dies intestate without children

---

[58] Cod. 6. 4. 4. The original text does not exist. Its substance is repeated in the *Basilica*.

the patron succeeds as under the Law of the Twelve Tables. If the estate amounts to [one hundred aurei or] more than one hundred aurei and there are children of either sex or of any degree entitled to succeed as heirs or to have possession of the goods, they take to the exclusion of patrons and their issue. If the freedman or freedwoman dies intestate and without children the whole estate goes to the patron or patroness. If they have made a will and passed over the patron or patroness, having no children or having disinherited the children (or in the case of a mother or maternal grandmother having passed them over in silence in circumstances excluding the querela inofficiosi testamenti), then by our constitution the patron or patroness is to have, not as before one-half, but a clear third of the estate unburdened by legacies or fideicommissa (these to be charged on coheirs). If they have been given less than a third the deficiency is to be made good to them. When patrons are called to the succession this must be understood to include patrons of either sex, their children and collateral relatives to the fifth degree. If, however, there are several descendants of a patron or patroness, or of two or more such, the nearest in degree is to take the succession of the freedman or freedwoman, which is to be divided not among the stocks (*per stirpes*), but by counting the heads of those nearest in degree (*per capita*). And the same rule is to be observed with collaterals; for we have made the law of succession to freedmen almost identical with that relating to freeborn persons.[59]

4. All this applies to freedmen who are Roman citizens, for today there are no others, the status of dediticii and of Junian Latins having been abolished; and in fact there could not be any question of succession to Junian Latins, because, though they lived free, they lost their freedom with their last breath, and the manumitting masters retained their goods under the lex Junia in a way by right of peculium as if they were slaves. But afterwards the senatusconsultum Largianum [60] provided that children of the manumitter, not expressly disinherited, should be entitled to the goods of a Latin in preference to the manumitter's extraneous heirs. This was followed by an edict of the Emperor Trajan, which directed that if a Latin obtained a grant of citizenship by imperial favour without or without the knowledge of his patron, he should live a citizen, but die a Latin. But all these enactments are repealed by our constitution,[61] and the roads which formerly led to the Latin status together with some others are now the means of access to Roman citizenship.

§ 82.

TITLE VIII

Of the assignment of freedmen

Before leaving the subject of succession to freedmen we may observe that the senate resolved that a patron might assign a freedman to one of his children, so as to entitle him to succeed as patron after his father's death, to the exclusion of the other children. But if the child to whom the freedman is assigned dies childless their right revives.

1. Assignment may be made not only of a freedman, but also of a freedwoman, and not only to a son or grandson, but also to a daughter or granddaughter. 2. This right of assignment is given to a father who has two or more children in power. What then if he has made an assignment to one of them whom he afterwards emancipates? Does this destroy the assignment? It is settled that it does, as held by Julian and most other jurists.

---

[59] Moyle's translation has proved helpful in this passage.
[60] A.D. 42.
[61] Cod. 7. 6. 1.

3. The assignment may be made by testament or without testament, and in any terms whatever as allowed by a senatusconsultum made in the time of the Emperor Claudius in the consulship of Suillus Rufus and Ostorius Scapula.

Title IX

Of possession of goods

§ 129.

3. In the third place the praetor gives the possession to the ten persons whom he preferred to the extraneous manumissor (b. p. unde decem personae). These are father, mother, grandfather and grandmother (paternal and maternal), son and daughter, grandson and granddaughter (by a son or by a daughter), brother and sister (issue of the father or of the mother). . . . Fifthly, to the nearest member of the family of the patron (b. p. tum quem ex familia); sixthly to the patron or patroness, their children and parents (b. p. unde patronus, patrona, liberi et parentes eorum) . . . eighthly, to the cognates of the manumissor.

5. The succession unde decem personae we have shown to be superfluous, for our constitution,[62] which we have made about the emancipation of children, directs that manumitting parents shall have the privilege of succession formerly secured to them by a fiduciary contract, so that this bonorum possessio is no longer required. 6(5). As to the b. p. tum quem ex familia and the b. p. unde patronus et patrona, etc., these have been entirely removed by our constitution relating to the right of patronage, for we have put the succession to freedmen on the same footing as the succession to ingenui, with this difference only that the succession of freedmen does not go beyond the fifth degree.[63] Consequently the usual bonorum possessiones meet all their needs. 7(6). The eighth bonorum possessio, viz., unde cognati manumissoris has also been abolished for the reasons above stated.

XVIII. Other Cases of Universal Succession

402. Inheritance and bonorum possessio are not the only modes of universal succession. Gaius mentions, besides, emptio bonorum, adrogation and conventio in manum.[64] Of these Justinian describes adrogation alone, but he adds another case, namely when a deceased person's estate is assigned to a person who is not an heir for the purpose of securing the liberty of slaves manumitted by will or codicil, and mentions as obsolete emptio bonorum and succession under the senatusconsultum Claudianum.[65] Emptio bonorum was a method of execution on property or a procedure in insolvency to be described when we come to speak of the Law of Actions (§ 755). Adrogation and the consequences of marriage in manum have received attention under the head of the Law of Persons. The other topics are explained in the text. We need not therefore give further

---

[62] Cod. 8. 48 (49). 6.
[63] Cod. 6. 4. 4.
[64] G. 2. 98.
[65] Inst. 2. 9. 6; 3. 11; 3. 12.

attention to any of these modes of universal succession and may proceed at once to the subject of Obligations.

THE INSTITUTES

BOOK III (Tits. X–XII)

TITLE X

Of acquisition by adrogation

There is another kind of universal succession created not by the Law of the Twelve Tables or by the praetor's edict but by the law which rests upon consent.

1. This takes place when a paterfamilias gives himself in adoption. Formerly all his property corporeal and incorporeal and debts due to him vested in the adrogator by full legal title except such things as are destroyed by capitis deminutio such as are the obligation of freedmen to render services [66] and rights derived from agnation. The same formerly applied to use and usufruct, but our constitution [67] provides that they are not to be destroyed by the lowest degree of capitis deminutio (c. d. minima). G. 3. 83.

2. But by our law the adrogator is placed in the same position as the natural parent; for today the father, whether natural or adoptive, acquires through his sons merely the usufruct of what comes to them from outside, the sons themselves retaining the ownership.[68] But if the adrogated son dies in the adoptive family, the ownership too passes to the adrogator, unless there are other persons who by our constitution are preferred to the father in respect of such acquisitions of the son as do not vest immediately in the father.[69]

3. Debts owed by the adrogatus do not in strict law bind the adrogator, but the adrogator may be sued in the name of the son, and if he is unwilling to undertake his defence creditors may go to the competent magistrate and get an order allowing them to take possession and dispose in the manner prescribed by law of the property which together with the usufruct in it would have belonged to the son if he had not given himself in adoption.

TITLE XI

Of persons to whom an estate is assigned to preserve gifts of freedom

Another case of succession was created by a constitution of the Emperor Marcus, which allows slaves, who have been manumitted by testament, if no one accepts the inheritance, to ask for the property of

---

[66] By jurata promissio operarum (§ 443) or stipulation. Buckl. *T.* p. 458.
[67] Cod. 3. 33. 16.
[68] Cod. 6. 61. 6.
[69] Cod. 6. 59. 11, *i.e.*, not falling under the description of peculium profecticium. The father was postponed to children and brothers and sisters of the deceased filius. Moyle, *ad* Inst. 3. 1. 15.

the deceased to be assigned to them in order that gifts of freedom may take effect. This is contained in a rescript of the Emperor addressed to Popilius Rufus, which runs as follows:—

1. "If the estate of Virginius Valens, who has made certain gifts of freedom in his will, is in the way of being sold as insolvent, there being no successor *ab intestato*, the magistrate who has cognizance of the matter, will on application give effect to your desire to have the estate assigned to you for the preservation of the gifts of freedom whether direct or fidei-commissary, if you give the creditors adequate security for the discharge of their claims in full. The slaves to whom a direct gift of freedom is made will be free in the same way as if the inheritance had been taken up, and those whom the heir was requested to manumit will receive their freedom from you, unless you are unwilling to have the estate assigned to you except on the terms that the slaves also directly manumitted shall be your freedmen. We approve this too if the individuals concerned consent. This our rescript is not to be rendered inoperative by any claims of the fiscus, for the cause of freedom is to be preferred to any considerations of pecuniary advantage; and if the estate is sequestrated, it must be done without prejudice to gifts of liberty which would have taken effect if the testamentary heir had accepted the inheritance." 2. This rescript comes to the aid both of manumitted slaves and of deceased persons to prevent their goods being possessed and sold by their creditors. Certainly, if goods are assigned for this cause, there will not be any sale in solvency; for the deceased has some one to take up his cause, and well qualified too, for he gives the creditors security to answer their claims in full. 3. Primarily this rescript applies when freedom is given by testament. What is to be said if a person dying intestate has given freedom to slaves by codicil, and no one takes up the succession *ab intestato*? The boon of the constitution should be extended to this case. Undoubtedly it applies when a testator has given freedom by codicil. 4. The constitution, as its words import, applies only when there is no successor *ab intestato*. Accordingly, so long as it is uncertain whether there is any such heir, the constitution remains in suspense. So soon as it is certain that no one is going to take up the inheritance, the constitution applies. 5. Suppose a person has abstained from the inheritance, but in circumstances which entitle him to claim *restitutio in integrum*. Does the constitution take effect? Yes, the estate must be assigned. What then if the heir subsequently gets restitution? Of course freedom once bestowed cannot be recalled. 6. This constitution was introduced to preserve bequests of freedom; if then there are none such, it does not apply. What then if the deceased made gifts of freedom in his lifetime or mortis causa and the slaves so manumitted wish to have the estate assigned to them to prevent any question being raised of manu-mission in fraud of creditors? Can this be allowed? The better view is that it can, though the constitution does not say so. 7. The constitution of the Emperor Marcus is in many respects incomplete. Accordingly we have dealt with the whole matter in the fullest detail in our own constitution [70] to which reference may be made.

TITLE XII

Of successions now obsolete, namely, by Sale of Goods and under the senatusconsultum Claudianum

There were formerly other forms of universal succession, which existed before the succession last described. Such was the purchase of goods, a complicated process of selling a debtor's estate, which

---

[70] Cod. 7. 2. 15.

was in use in the days of the ordinary procedure. But when the extraordinary procedure became general, the system of bonorum venditio passed out of use along with the ordinary procedure; and now creditors are allowed by order of the magistrate to possess the insolvent debtor's goods and dispose of them as they consider to be for their advantage, as will appear more fully from the treatment of the subject in the Digest. 2. There used also to be a deplorable case of universal acquisition under the senatusconsultum Claudianum when a free-woman by cohabiting with a slave lost her freedom and with it her substance. We have thought this unworthy of our age § 71. and have not allowed it to be inserted in our Digest.

BOOK IV

THE LAW OF OBLIGATIONS

I. Obligations in General

3. 13 pr.

403. Obligation is defined in the Institutes as juris vinculum quo necessitate adstringimur alicujus solvendae rei secundum nostrae civitatis jura—" a legal bond whereby we are constrained by a necessity of performing something according to the laws of our country."   The word vinculum like the word obligatio suggests a physical constraint.   Vinculum means a fetter, obligatio means a tying or binding.   It is surmised that in the most primitive phase of Roman Law the fetter and the binding had a sinister reality.   A person was said to be bound, who had pledged his body by the solemn process of nexum (§ 522) as security for the payment of a debt, just as a thing was said to be bound when it was given in pledge for the same purpose.[1] But by the classical period of Roman Law, still more in the age of Justinian, all this had faded into a remote background.   It cannot be supposed that it was present to the mind of the author (whoever he was) from whom Justinian borrowed his definition. For him the words vinculum and obligatio were metaphors, just as we use the language of metaphor when we speak of " bonds of affection," or say that a man is " bound " to act or to forbear. Obligation had come to mean, as in the above definition, a duty of performance or abstention imposed by law.   Sometimes it meant the corresponding right of the person entitled, as in the phrase " to acquire an obligation."   Lastly, by a slight extension, rather implied than expressed in the texts of the Roman Law, obligation is the relation which exists between two persons, one of whom is bound to act or to forbear for the benefit of the other, a relation of creditor and debtor.[2]   The first is the person who has the right, the second is the person who owes the corresponding duty.   This is the sense in which the word obligation, when used precisely, is understood at the present day.

1. 2. 2.

404. Obligation is a res incorporalis and as such belongs to the jus rerum or Law of Things.   But it creates a jus in personam, i.e., a right available against a specific person, not a

---

[1] Buckl. *T.* p. 407.
[2] Moyle, p. 476.

jus in rem, *i.e.*, a right available against persons generally, or, as it is sometimes expressed, against the whole world. This distinction is emphasised by Paulus in a well-known passage. Obligationum substantia non in eo consistit ut aliquod corpus nostrum vel servitutem nostram faciat, sed ut alium nobis obstringat ad dandum aliquid vel faciendum vel praestandum.[3] "The essence of obligation does not consist in making us owner of a thing or entitling us to a servitude, but in binding a person to us to give something, or to do, or to make good." This essential difference is somewhat obscured by the Roman inclusion of obligation under the general head of the Law relating to Things. It is true that an obligation commonly has some value for the person entitled and, so far, forms part of his estate. But there is a very substantial difference between having five pounds in your own pocket, and having a claim to get five pounds out of someone else's pocket. The French Code, strangely, includes the whole topic of Obligations in Book III, which treats of "The different ways in which property is acquired." But more recent codes assign to the subject a place commensurate with its importance in the modern law, and make it, along with the Law of Property, of Family Relations and of Succession, one of the principal divisions of the Private Law.

405. Justinian's definition of obligation is in terms very wide. It seems to embrace all rights in personam. But by Roman usage it included only rights in personam capable of estimation in money or (in other words) "pertaining to the sphere of proprietary rights."[4] It did not include rights arising out of family relations, or rights created by public law.[5] In Gaius the term is limited to rights and duties recognised by the jus civile. In Justinian it includes some, but not all, praetorian rights and duties.[6] Whether a right is or is not regarded as a source of obligation seems to be a question of usage rather than of definition. Thus the obligationes quasi ex maleficio (§§ 406, 634) are all praetorian, but the praetorian liability of the master or father in the actiones adjecticiae qualitatis (§ 563) is not represented as an obligation. It is reserved in the Institutes for Book IV, which treats of the Law of Actions.

406. CLASSIFICATION OF OBLIGATIONS.—Obligations are 3. 13. 1. variously classified:—(a) Civil and praetorian or honorary.

3 Dig. 44. 7. 3 pr.
4 Salmond, *Jurisprudence*, p. 630.
5 Sohm, translated by Ledlie, p. 358.
6 Buckl. *M.* p. 248.

This classification is peculiar to Roman Law. It distinguishes obligations according as they derive their authority from the civil law or from the praetor's Edict. Though Justinian describes this as "the principal devision of obligations," he makes no further use of it.

3. 13. 2.

(b) Ex contractu, quasi ex contractu, ex delicto (or maleficio) quasi ex delicto (or maleficio)—arising from agreement, based upon the analogy of agreement, arising from delict, based upon the analogy of delict. This four-fold classification is adopted in the Institutes and was anticipated by Gaius (if he was the author) [7] in the third book of the *Aurea*, as appears from a passage cited in the Digest.[8] In his Institutes he speaks of obligations as having two sources only, *viz.*, contract and delict,[9] while in the second book of the *Aurea* he makes a three-fold division, "Obligations arise from contract or from delict or by special rules of law from various types of cause." [10] Justinian's classification is open to objection, first because the group of obligations described as arising quasi ex contractu seems to resemble obligations arising from contract merely in having the

3. 27 pr.

negative character of not arising from delict ; secondly, because the distinction between obligationes ex maleficio and obligationes quasi ex maleficio has no logical foundation. On the other hand, the two-fold division leaves many obligations unaccounted for. The three-fold classification has practical utility, if no scientific value. Obligations arise from agreement, or from wrongdoing, or from various other causes, which cannot conveniently be brought under any more precise description.

(c) Civil—natural. A civil obligation is one which is fully protected by law and enforceable by action. A natural obligation is one which is only imperfectly protected by law. It is not enforceable by action, but has legal consequences, which vary with the circumstances.[11] Thus, a natural obligation may support a contract of suretyship (§ 573) or be converted into a civil obligation by novation (§ 660), at least in certain cases. It seems that the only consequence which is common to all cases of natural obligation is the exclusion of the condictio indebiti, for, where there is a natural obligation to pay, a payment which discharges it cannot be described as undue.[12]

---

[7] *Supra*, § 45.
[8] Dig. 44. 7. 5.
[9] G. 3. 88.
[10] Dig. 44. 7. 1 pr.
[11] Moyle, p. 480.
[12] Dig. 44. 7. 10 ; 46. 1. 16, 4 ; Buckl. *T.* p. 552.

Natural obligations resulted from the contracts of slaves and from contracts between a paterfamilias and a filiusfamilias, or between persons subject to the same potestas. These cases are peculiar to Roman Law. Other cases of natural obligation have their counterpart in modern systems. Such is the case of the contract of an impubes made without his tutor's authority, and, in the later law, of a minor made without the consent of his curator (§ 140). It was formerly thought that a nude pact, *i.e.*, an agreement which did not fall within the scope of any recognised class of contract or actionable pact (§ 526) produced a natural obligation. But the better opinion is that this was not so, except in the case of an agreement to pay interest on a money loan (§ 421).[13]

II. Obligations Arising from Contract

407. The texts of the Roman Law do not supply a definition of contract. The words contractus—contrahere—like " contract " in English, are used in various senses, sometimes wider, sometimes narrower. Labeo gives contractus the meaning of a reciprocal obligation, such as purchase and sale, hire, partnership.[14] But when the Romans speak of obligations arising from contract, they mean obligations arising from convention or agreement. In Roman Law it was far from being the case that all agreements which might be expected to produce a legal obligation did so. Agreements were not (subject to later developments) actionable unless they could be referred to one or other of four categories, and it was only then that they were said to give rise to obligations from contract. Corresponding with these four categories, obligations arising from contract are subdivided into four classes which are distinguished as obligations:—(a) re—*i.e.*, by the handing over of a thing (res); (b) verbis, *i.e.*, by a form of words; (c) litteris, *i.e.*, by a special kind of writing; (d) consensu, *i.e.*, by agreement without anything further. The last class was limited to four specific cases. This classification, it will be observed, is a classification not of contracts, but of obligations. But it is commonly applied to the agreements from which the obligations arise. We distinguish, therefore, the contracts known to Roman Law as Real, Verbal, Litteral and Consensual. These several classes of contract will be considered in this order. But, first, mention must be made

3. 13. 2.

---

[13] Girard (8), p. 682; Moyle, p. 479; Buckl. *T.* p. 553; *M.* p. 336.
[14] Dig. 50. 16. 19.

of some other principles of classification and of general standards of liability.

408. Contracts are unilateral or bilateral. A unilateral contract is one in which the duty of performance is all on one side; thus in a loan of money the borrower alone is bound. In bilateral contracts there are reciprocal obligations. These again are subdivided. In some a duty exists on both sides from the moment of the conclusion of the contract; thus in sale the seller is bound to deliver, the buyer is bound to pay. They are said to be perfectly bilateral. In others there is an immediate duty on one side only, but on the other a contingent duty; thus, in deposit, the depositary is bound to restore the thing deposited, the depositor is bound, but only if circumstances call for it, to compensate the depositary for expenses. Such contracts are said to be imperfectly bilateral. Sometimes instead of "bilateral" we say "synallagmatic," a word derived from the Greek word for reciprocal contracts.

409. Contracts are stricti juris or bonae fidei. This classification properly applies to actions (stricti juris judicia—bonae fidei judicia (§ 702)), but usage permits its extension to the corresponding contracts.[15] All unilateral contracts are stricti juris. They bind the promisor to the very thing he has promised, neither more nor less. If action is brought upon them, equitable defences must be raised by way of plea (exceptio, § 741). All bilateral contracts are bonae fidei. Under the formulary procedure it was an instruction to the judex to decide according to good faith (§ 733); this empowered him to take into consideration equitable defences though not raised on the pleadings, and allowed him a greater latitude of interpretation and of decision, so as to do substantial justice between the parties. This distinction survived the formulary procedure and persisted in the later law.

410. Contracts are formal or informal. A contract is formal when the form makes the contract. An informal contract depends upon the intention of the parties. This distinction is not made by the Roman lawyers but is implicit in any legal system. Thus in Roman Law stipulatio (§ 444) and expensilatio (§ 455) are formal; the contract of sale is informal.

411. Formal contracts are sometimes called abstract, because they are dissociated from events outside themselves. They are

---

[15] The phrase bonae fidei contractus occurs. Dig. 22. 1. 32, 2.

self-contained. The stipulation, as will be seen, consists in
question and answer: " Do you promise to give? " " I
promise." Why? The inquiry is irrelevant. I am bound
because I have promised. In informal contracts the why is
relevant. For this reason they are also called " causal "
contracts.

412. In course of time abstract contracts tend to become
causal. An important movement in this direction took place
when Aquilius Gallus, Cicero's colleague in the praetorship
(B.C. 66) introduced into his Edict the exceptio doli [16] (§ 742).
After this it was possible, as it had not been before, to go
outside a formal contract and to inquire into the circumstances
in which it was made. Thus, if a defendant alleged that he had
been induced by plaintiff's fraud to bind himself by a formal
contract, he could raise this issue by pleading the exceptio doli.
In English Law the contract under seal has undergone the same
development. " It is only in modern times that special defences,
on the ground of fraud and the like, have been allowed to avail
a man against his own deed." [17]

413. It must be remarked that a contract is not necessarily
formal in the sense of the above description because the law
prescribes a particular form. Thus Justinian under penalty of
nullity required certain formalities for contracts which the
parties had agreed to reduce to writing,[18] and by English law,
equally under penalty of nullity, contracts of marine insurance
must be executed in the form of a policy.[19] But in neither
case is the contract a formal contract in the technical sense;
still less if the writing is not of the essence of the contract, but
only needed for proof of its existence and terms.[20]

414. DOLUS—CULPA.—Every party to a contract, whatever
the nature of his undertaking, is required to come up to a
certain standard of conduct, which varies with the circumstances,
and determines the general measure of his responsibility. Everyone is answerable for intentionally wrongful acts, that is to say
for dolus. An agreement not to be answerable for dolus is
without effect.[21]

---

[16] Hunter, p. 595. But see p. 438, n. 58.
[17] Pollock, *Principles of Contract* (10), p. 7.
[18] Non aliter vires habere sancimus. Cod. 4. 21. 17. The rule was
general, not limited to contracts of sale, in connection with which it is
mentioned in the Institutes (*infra*, § 463).
[19] Stamp Act, 1891, s. 93.
[20] *e.g.,* Sale of Goods Act, 1893, s. 4; Law of Property Act, 1925,
s. 40.
[21] Dig. 2. 14. 27, 3; 50. 17. 23.

415. But, generally, something more is required, *viz.*, a certain measure of diligence. In principle the party who benefits by the contract incurs the higher liability. Thus less is required of the lender than of the borrower, less of the depositary than of the depositor. When the contract is for the benefit of both parties, each is required to exhibit the same degree of diligence.[22]

416. Diligence is the duty seen from the positive side. If a person fails to exhibit in his conduct the required measure of diligence, he is guilty of negligentia or culpa. To say that a person is liable for culpa is another way of saying that he must exhibit diligence.

417. The texts distinguish two standards of diligence, a higher and a lower. The higher is the diligence which the good father of a family habitually exhibits in his own affairs (diligentia exacta or exactissima—diligentia boni patrisfamilias).[23] The lower is the diligence which the person in question exhibits in his own affairs (diligentia quam suis rebus).[24] This may, in fact, reach a high degree of diligence or it may not. But, at least, where this standard is applied nothing extraordinary is expected. It is a concrete standard. It is enough that the person in question pursues his normal course. He need not concern himself with ideals. According to a traditional terminology, where the first standard is applied, there is said to be liability for culpa levis in abstracto—slight negligence in the abstract; in the second case there is liability for culpa levis in concreto—slight negligence in the concrete. The only reason for introducing the word levis into the description is to indicate that the liability goes beyond liability for gross negligence (culpa lata) which, we are told, is scarcely, if at all, distinguishable from wrongful purpose. " Lata culpa is extreme negligence, that is not understanding what everybody understands." [25] It is a degree of negligence which indicates a complete obtuseness of mind and conduct; " for, if a man does not come up to the standard of diligence which human nature demands of him he is not free from guilt," says Celsus; with the qualification (evidently an intrusive gloss), " unless (in the case of deposit) he comes up to his own standard," [26] a qualification scarcely admissible if culpa lata is equivalent to dolus.

---

22 Dig. 13. 6. 5, 2 *in fine*.   23 Dig. 13. 6. 18 pr.; 13. 7. 14.
24 Dig. 10. 2. 25, 16. This is the common abbreviation of diligentia quam suis rebus adhibere solet—the diligence which he is in the habit of applying to his own affairs, Inst. 3. 14. 2.
25 Dig. 50. 16. 213, 2.
26 Dig. 16. 3. 32.

418. It has been said that the two degrees of culpa are of post-classical origin. Modestinus in an extract cited in the *Collatio* (§ 47) is unaware of them.[27] On the other hand, the classical law had a standard of liability which has almost disappeared from the later law. In some cases there was an absolute liability for all loss not attributable to vis major. The party to the contract had to keep the thing safe. He was said to be liable for custodia. Here, there was no question of negligence, except so far as it might negative the defence of vis major, and no degree of diligence saved the party from liability. In Justinian's system the duty of custodia was usually reduced to the duty of exact diligence. It remained in the liability of innkeepers, shippers and stable-keepers under the praetorian Edict (§ 528). The difference between custodia and exacta diligentia is seen particularly in the case of theft. In the first case the liability to make good the loss is absolute apart from vis major (§ 502),[28] which includes violence offered by pirates and robbers, but not ordinary theft ; in the second case there is no absolute liability, but " an obligation to show the care of a bonus paterfamilias in guarding against theft," the burden of proving diligence being as usual upon the person responsible.[29]

THE INSTITUTES

BOOK III

TITLE XIII

Of obligations

Let us now pass to obligations. Obligation is a legal bond whereby we are constrained by a necessity of performing something according to the laws of our country. 1. The principal division of obligations is into civil and praetorian. Civil obligations are created by statutes or, at least, approved by the civil law. Praetorian obligations are those which the praetor has created in the exercise of his jurisdiction. They are also called honorary. 2. The next division of obligations is into four species. For they arise either from contract, or on the analogy of contract, or from delict or on the analogy of delict. We shall first examine those which arise from contract, which, again, are of four kinds. For they are contracted re or verbis or litteris or consensu; all of which we proceed to examine in order.

§ 403.

§ 406.

§ 407.

---

[27] *Coll.* 10. 2. 1.
[28] quia custodia adversus vim parum proficit, Dig. 19. 1. 31 pr.
[29] Buckl. *T*. 560 ; *M*. 340. The whole question of custodia is obscure. Very different views are held.

III. REAL CONTRACTS

419. This group includes four particular contracts, *viz.*, 1, mutuum—loan for consumption; 2, commodatum—loan for use; 3, depositum—deposit; 4, pignus—pledge or pawn.

The common elements are:—(a) agreement, (b) the handing over by one person to another of a res. In the first case the ownership of the thing transferred passes to the transferee, in the other cases it does not.[30]

420. MUTUUM.—This is a loan for consumption of money or of other things which are weighed, numbered or measured (res fungibiles).[31] The effect of the contract is to vest the ownership of the thing transferred in the transferee, and, normally, the lender must be owner of the thing lent, and competent to alienate. But commercial dealings do not always conform to this requirement. If A owes me money, and I direct him to make payment for my account to B, who is to have the money on loan, I am lender, but I have never been owner of the coins lent. The contract of mutuum is unilateral, *i.e.*, it gives rise to a duty on one side only, *viz.*, the duty of the transferee (borrower) to make over to the transferor (lender) at the time expressly or impliedly agreed, or at a reasonable time after demand, other money or goods equal in quantity and quality. He cannot escape doing so on the ground that the subject of the loan has perished by accident, as by fire or shipwreck. The duty of the borrower was enforced by an action called condictio, which in the case of a money-loan was known as actio certae pecuniae creditae or condictio certae pecuniae (§ 730), and in the case of any other fungible thing as condictio triticaria (§ 731), from triticum = grain, a loan of corn being taken as typical of all loans other than a loan of money. The procedure in the case of money-loan was marked by the peculiarity that the plaintiff might challenge the defendant to a wager of one-third of the amount in suit, with the result that if judgment went against him the defendant had to pay the amount of the loan and one-third more. Conversely, if the plaintiff failed in his action he had to pay one-third to the defendant. This was effected by reciprocal stipulations known as sponsio et restipulatio tertiae partis.[32]

3. 14 pr.

3. 14. 2.

---

[30] For the historical origin of these contracts, see Buckl. *T.* pp. 462 *et seq.*; *M.* p. 272.
[31] Things within a class are said to be fungibiles, when they are equivalent (in genere suo functionem recipiunt. Dig. 12. 1. 2, 1) or interchangeable (mutua vice funguntur). The word fungibilis was invented by the German humanist Zasius in the sixteenth century.　　[32] G. 4. 13; 171.

421. Interest on money lent. The parties might agree that
the loan was to bear interest (faenus—usurae), but this was not
binding as a contract (with some exceptions) unless expressed
in the form of a stipulation (stipulatio usurarum), and consequently it was usual to reduce any loan at interest to the form
of a verbal contract by which the borrower bound himself to
repay the capital and to pay the agreed rate of interest (stipulatio sortis et usurarum). In general, a bare agreement for
interest was not actionable, but created a natural obligation,
which excluded the condictio indebiti (§ 406). The principal
exception was the case of money lent to be carried over sea, or
to be converted into goods to be carried over sea, at the risk of
the lender (pecunia trajecticia). This was known as nauticum
faenus. There were some other exceptions, viz., loans by cities
(in the classical law), loans of grain (Alexander Severus), loans
by bankers (Justinian).[33]

422. Rate of interest. The permitted rate of interest was
variously defined at different periods. The Twelve Tables are
thought to have fixed it at one-twelfth of the capital per month
(unciarium faenus), which means that the debt had doubled
itself at the end of the year. A lex Genucia of B.C. 342 is said
to have prohibited interest altogether, but had no lasting effect.
In the time of Cicero the highest permitted rate was 1 p.c. per
month or 12 p.c. per annum (usurae centesimae seu calendariae
—so-called because the interest fell due on the first day of the
month—kalendae). This remained substantially unchanged
until Justinian made the rate vary with the circumstances, the
standard rate being 6 p.c. In the contract of nauticum faenus,
in which the lender lost his money if the ship did not reach its
destination, the parties had been free to fix their own rate of
interest[34]; Justinian limited it to 12 p.c. per annum.

423. Accumulation of interest. In the classical period
arrears of interest might not be recovered in any one action in
excess of the capital. Justinian enacted that the capital might
not in any circumstances yield in interest a sum greater than
itself. This meant that when the capital had doubled it ceased
to bear interest.[35]

424. Compound interest (anatocismus). Before Justinian
the law forbade the parties to agree in advance that the loan
should bear compound interest.[36] Justinian (very absurdly)
forbade it as regards accrued interest as well; that is to say,
the parties were not allowed to convert accrued interest into an
interest-bearing loan by a new agreement.[37]

---

[33] Dig. 22. 1. 30 ; Cod. 4. 32. 11 (12) ; Nov. 136, c. 4.
[34] Paul. Sent. 2. 14. 3.
[35] Girard, p. 549.
[36] This, perhaps, may be inferred from Cod. 4. 32. 28 pr. There is
much uncertainty as to the classical law. Cicero, when governor of Cilicia
(B.C. 50), allowed compound interest calculated on annual (not monthly)
accruals. Apparently, it had been forbidden by a recent senatusconsultum.
Cic. Epp. ad Attic. 5. 21, 11 and 13.
[37] Girard, p. 550.

425. SENATUSCONSULTUM MACEDONIANUM.—This measure enacted in the reign of Vespasian (A.D. 69–79), forbade loans of money to sons in power,[38] so that a lender could not recover the loan even after the father's death. But senatusconsulta still took effect as instructions to the magistrates, and not precisely as legislation (§ 9). Consequently the transaction remained technically valid. If a son borrowed money he was still liable jure civili and the father was liable jure praetorio to the extent of the son's peculium in the actio de peculio (§ 565). But the praetor gave effect to the senatusconsultum by allowing either son or father a plea known as the exceptio senatusconsulti Macedoniani (§ 745).

426. However, there were cases in which the exception was not available: viz., 1. if the son was generally supposed to be sui juris, or had given himself out as such; 2. if the father had consented to the loan or subsequently ratified it, or been enriched by it; 3. if the son had a peculium of his own (castrense or quasi-castrense), and the loan was covered by it; 4. if the son had renounced the benefit of the exception after becoming sui juris; 5. if, being away from home for the prosecution of his studies, he had borrowed a moderate sum, not in excess of his usual allowance. Even apart from these exceptions the loan produced a natural obligation (§ 406), which excluded the condictio indebiti and might be made a civil obligation by novation (§ 660), when the son was sui juris.[39]

427. OTHER CONTRACTS RE.—Commodatum—depositum—pignus. These have certain common characteristics:—

1. They are all real contracts created by the transfer of a res, and consequent displacement, not as in mutuum of ownership, but of detention (commodatum—depositum) or of possession (pignus) (§§ 267, 269).

2. They are all bonae fidei contracts, imperfectly bilateral, giving rise to a direct action on the one side, to a contrary action on the other.

428. COMMODATUM.—This was a gratuitous loan for use of movables, or, more rarely, of immovables. It might even relate to fungible things if they were to be returned in specie, as when I lend you goods to dress your shop window.[40] The lender is termed the commodans—commodator; the borrower is termed the commodatarius.

---

[38] Dig. 14. 6. 1 pr. Son was taken to include grandson. Dig. 14. 6. 14 and (later) female descendants in power were brought within the scope of the S.C., Inst. 4. 7. 7.

[39] Dig. 12. 6. 40 pr.; 14. 6. 10; Buckl. T. p. 553.

[40] Dig. 13. 6. 3. 6.

429. The duties of the borrower were:—

1. to return the thing lent at the time or in the event agreed or implied in the contract ;

2. to return it as good as he received it, reasonable wear and tear excepted ;

3. to exercise the highest degree of diligence (exacta diligentia). He was liable, therefore, for dolus and for culpa levis in abstracto (§ 417). He was not liable (subject to 4) if the thing perished from a cause entirely outside his control (casus). He was answerable for theft unless he could show that he was free from fault [41] ;

4. not to use the thing except in terms of the contract. If 4. 1. 6. he used the thing in an unauthorised way he was liable also for casus ; and, if he did so in bad faith, for theft.

430. The duties of the lender were:—

1. to allow the borrower to use the thing for the time agreed or reasonable in the circumstances [42] ;

2. to indemnify him for extraordinary expenses. Thus heavy expense incurred in medical treatment of a sick slave, or in pursuing and bringing back a runaway was charged to the lender ; but the ordinary costs of food and medicine fell on the borrower [43] ;

3. to indemnify him for damage caused by the thing lent owing to some defect or mischievous quality of which the lender was aware, e.g., if vessels were lent to hold wine or oil, which the lender knew to be leaky or otherwise defective.[44]

Since the contract is (normally) for the advantage of the borrower alone the lender's liability is less extensive.

431. Actions. The lender had the actio commodati directa to enforce the duties of the borrower ; the borrower had the actio commodati contraria to enforce the duties of the lender. We learn from Gaius that there were alternative formulae in this action—in factum concepta and in jus concepta (§§ 697, G. 4. 47. 735, 736). The formula in factum was the earlier.[45]

432. DEPOSITUM.—This is a contract whereby one person 3. 14. 3. (depositor) gives to another (depositarius) a thing to be kept for him gratuitously and returned on demand.

---

[41] Dig. 13. 6. 21 ; 18. 1. 35, 4.
[42] Dig. 13. 6. 17, 3.
[43] Dig. 13. 6. 18, 2.
[44] Dig. 13. 6. 18, 3.
[45] Buckl. M. pp. 274, 276

433. The duties of the depositarius were: —

4. 1. 6.
1. to keep the thing—not to use it. If he used it in bad faith he was guilty of theft;

2. to restore it on demand as good as he received it with any produce or accessories.[46] According to the Institutes and texts in the Digest [47] the depositarius was liable for dolus, not for culpa. He was also liable for culpa lata (scarcely to be distinguished from dolus). One interpolated text in the Digest seems to make him liable for so-called culpa levis in concreto (§ 417).[48]

434. The duties of the depositor were: —

1. to compensate the depositary for all expenses;

2. to indemnify him for all damage attributable to the dolus or any culpa of the depositor; e.g., if he deposited a slave whom he knew or should have known to be given to stealing.[49]

435. Actions. The depositor had the actio depositi directa, the depositary the actio depositi contraria. As in the case of
G. 4. 47.
commodatum there were alternative formulae. The direct action has certain peculiarities: —

4. 16. 2.
1. Condemnation involved infamia;

2. No set-off, deduction, exceptio doli or right of retention was permitted as an excuse for not restoring the property on demand.[50]

436. Special cases of depositum.

(a) Depositum necessarium or miserabile. This was a deposit made upon occasion of civil disturbance, fire, earthquake
4. 6. 17.
4. 6. 26.
or shipwreck. It gave rise to a claim for double damages, if the property was not returned on demand.

(b) Depositum sequestre, giving rise to a special action called actio depositi sequestraria. This was a deposit made by two or more persons of a movable or immovable thing, particularly of a thing in litigation (res litigiosa) with a third party called a sequester, on the terms that it was to be delivered to one or other of them in a certain event, particularly in the event of the decision of the litigation. Unlike an ordinary deposit this type of deposit conferred juristic possession, not detention merely, upon the depositary. The object of this was to prevent usucapion running in favour of one of the parties pending the decision of the event.[51]

---

[46] Dig. 16. 3. 1, 16 and 24.
[47] Dig. 13. 6. 5, 2; 16. 3. 1, 47. Cf. G. 3. 207.
[48] Dig. 16. 3. 32.
[49] Dig. 47. 2. 62 (61), 5 in fine.
[50] Inst. 4. 6. 30; Cod. 4. 34. 11 pr.
[51] Dig. 16. 3. 17, 1; 41. 2. 36; 39.

(c) Depositum irregulare. This was a deposit subject to a condition of restitution in genere and not in specie.[52] It took place when money was placed in the hands of a banker or other person, on the understanding that the amount, not the actual coins, should be returned on demand. This contract resembled mutuum, but its economic purpose was different, because it was a deposit made with a capitalist, not a loan made by a capitalist,[53] and its legal effect was different. It was bonae fidei, not stricti juris. It might give rise to infamia. The senatusconsultum Macedonianum did not apply. Interest might be claimed under a simple pact, or in case of mora.[54] It may be remarked that in English and South African Law a deposit with a banker is regarded as a loan.

437. PIGNUS (Pawn or Pledge).—This may be defined as a contract whereby a corporeal thing is handed over by one person to another as security for a debt. It was one of the modes of creating a real security, differing from mancipatio cum fiducia because it did not involve transfer of ownership, and from hypotheca because it did involve transfer of possession. But this is a topic belonging to the Law of Property (§ 258). Here we are concerned with pignus as a contract. 3. 14. 4.

438. The duties of the pledgee (creditor) were:—

1. to restore the thing when the debt was extinguished;

2. if the property was sold, to restore the surplus, if any, after satisfying the debt;

3. to exercise exacta diligentia. Thus, he must realise the fruits of the property (if any) and set them off, first, against interest; then, against capital, unless it was agreed that he was to keep the fruits in lieu of interest (antichresis—pactum antichreseos);

4. in the case of an ordinary pledge of a movable not to use the thing unless expressly authorised by the contract. If he did so in bad faith, he was guilty of theft.

439. The duties of the pledgor (αebtor) were:— 4. 1. 6.

1. to pay necessary and (within reasonable limits) useful expenses (§ 498), incurred by the creditor about the thing pledged, e.g., repairing a house or medical attendance on a slave [55];

2. to indemnify the creditor for damage or mischief caused by the thing pledged, if he knew or ought to have known of its

---

[52] Dig. 19. 2. 31.   [53] Girard, p. 565.
[54] Dig. 16. 3. 25, 1. In bonae fidei contractibus ex mora usurae debentur, Dig. 22. 1. 32, 2. Mora means wilful delay in discharging an obligation.
[55] Dig. 13. 7. 8 pr. and 25.

3. 14. 4.

harmful or mischievous quality. The standard of diligence—the contract being for the benefit of both parties—is the same as that required of the creditor, *viz.*, exacta diligentia. Thus, the pledgor was answerable, if he knowingly or carelessly pledged a slave who was given to stealing. If he was without fault in the matter, he had the alternative of noxal surrender [56] (§ 638);

3. to pay damages, if he had pledged a thing which did not belong to him and the creditor had in consequence lost the benefit of his security.[57]

440. Actions. The pledgor had the actio pigneraticia directa to enforce the duties of the pledgee, particularly the duty of restoring the property, when the debt was extinguished. The pledgee had the actio pigneraticia contraria. The real actions and interdicts arising out of pignus have been described above (§ 261).

THE INSTITUTES

BOOK III

TITLE XIV

How an obligation is contracted re

§ 420.

An example of an obligation contracted re is the giving of a mutuum. The obligation of mutuum consists in things which are weighed, counted or measured, such as wine, oil, grain, coined money, bronze, silver, gold, things which by counting, weighing or numbering we give to a person with the intention of making them his, and on the understanding that not the same things, but others of like kind and quality shall some time be given back. The transaction is called mutuum, because from being mine the thing becomes yours (ex meo tuum fit). It gives rise to an action called a condictio. 1. If a person has received what was not due from another who pays him in error, he is bound re, and the other may bring a condiction to recover what he has paid, for he can make use of the formula, " if it appears that he ought to give," just as if he were suing on a loan. From this it follows that a pupil, to whom a payment has been made in error without the authority of his tutor, is no more liable in an action for the recovery of an undue payment than he would be in an action on a loan. But it may be said that this kind of obligation does not rest on contract because a person who gives something in payment intends rather to discharge an existing contract than to conclude a new one.

§ 428.

2. Again a person who receives a thing that he may make use of it, that is on loan (commodatum), is bound re and may be sued

---

[56] Dig. 13. 7. 31 ; 47. 2. 62, 1.
[57] Dig. 13. 7. 9 pr.

in an action on the loan. But this kind of loan is very different
from mutuum, for the thing is not given to him with the intention
of making it his property and therefore he is bound to give it
back. If a thing received as a mutuum has been lost by some accident, as by fire, earthquake, shipwreck, or the onset of robbers or
foes, the borrower remains bound just the same. But if a person has
received something as a loan for use, no doubt he must exercise the
highest diligence in keeping the thing, and it is not enough for him
to have shown the degree of diligence which he usually applies to his
own affairs, if a more diligent person might have kept the thing
safe. But he is not answerable for vis major or inevitable accident,
provided that it is not due to his own fault; for if I have lent you
something, and you choose to take it abroad with you, and you lose
it in consequence of an attack of enemies or pirates or from shipwreck, you are undoubtedly liable for its restoration. A thing is
said to be lent, if you receive a thing for use without making or
agreeing to make any payment. If payment is part of the transaction it is a contract of hire, for commodatum must be gratuitous.
3. If a person receives a thing as a deposit, he is bound re, and can   § 432.
be sued for its return in the actio depositi. But he is liable only
for dolus, not for culpa, that is carelessness and neglect; and so a
person is not liable, if through his failing to keep it carefully, it
has been stolen; for if a person has given a thing for safe-keeping
to a careless friend, he must thank his own want of caution, if it is
stolen. 4. A creditor who receives a thing as a pledge is bound re   § 437.
and can be sued for its restoration in the actio pigneraticia. But
since a pledge is given for the advantage of both parties, of the
debtor in order that he may get credit, and of the creditor in
security of the debt, it is settled that it is enough for [58] the creditor
to exhibit exact diligence in the keeping of the thing: if he does so,
and the thing is lost by some chance occurrence, he is secure from
attack, and is not prevented from suing for the debt.

IV. VERBAL CONTRACTS

441. There were three verbal contracts: —

    1. dotis dictio ;

    2. jusjurandum liberti or jurata promissio operarum ;

    3. stipulatio.

The first two were of comparatively small importance.
They are mentioned by Gaius.[59] The text of the Verona
palimpsest, which at this point is defective, is supplied by the
epitome included in the Lex Romana Visigothorum (§ 33).

442. DOTIS DICTIO.—A formal constitution of a dos made
by the woman herself, an agnatic male descendant, or her debtor

---

    [58] The text seems intended to exclude the higher liability for custodia
(§ 404) suggested by some apparently classical texts (Dig. 13. 7. 13, 1 ;
Cod. 8. 13. 19).
    [59] G. 3. 95a.

(§ 223).[60]   It was superseded by an enactment of Theodosius II of A.D. 428, which permitted the constitution of a dos by an informal agreement (§ 529).

443. JUSJURANDUM LIBERTI.—When a master manumitted a slave it was usual to require him to undertake an engagement (frequently onerous) to render services after manumission (§ 79).   Since a slave could not bind himself by a civil law contract, his undertaking was secured by an oath, which, repeated after manumission, created a civil liability.   This persisted under Justinian.

444. STIPULATIO.—This was immeasurably more important. It consisted essentially in a formal question and answer.   One party (stipulator or reus stipulandi) said to another (reus promittendi), e.g., " Do you promise to give me one thousand sesterces? "   The other said, " I promise."   This concluded the contract and gave rise to a legal obligation on the part of the promissor to do what he had promised.   It was essential that there should be precise correspondence between question and answer.   The contract was unilateral and stricti juris The meaning of the word is unexplained.   Justinian, following Paulus, derives it from a word stipulus (otherwise unknown), said to mean " firm," and some other doubtful etymologies have been suggested.

445. ORIGIN AND HISTORY OF THE STIPULATION.—The remote origin of the stipulation is obscure.   At one time the idea was entertained that it was derived from the nexum, itself a specialised form of the mancipation.   Thus Maine says, " The question and answer of the stipulation were unquestionably the nexum in a simplified shape." [61]   But this theory is rejected on many grounds.   It is enough to mention one, namely (to quote Girard) that " a dialogue cannot be a simplification of a monologue." [62]   Girard's own view was that the origin of the stipulation was to be looked for in the oath.   Some support for this view is found in the earliest recorded form of the verbal contract consisting in the solemn formula—spondesne?— spondeo—" Do you pledge your word? "—" I pledge my word," which there is reason to believe originally implied an oath.   It is significant, too, that Gaius tells us that, though in civil transactions this form of words was confined to citizens, it was also employed when negotiating peace with a foreign prince in the

G. 3. 96.

3. 15 pr.

---

[60] Ulp. VI, 2.
[61] *Ancient Law,* p. 339.   As to nexum, see Buckl. *T.* p. 429 ; *M.* p. 259 ; Jolowicz, p. 166 ; and below, § 522.   [62] Girard, p. 516.

words, " pacem futuram spondes? "—" Do you pledge your G. 3. 94.
word that peace shall be? " But such negotiations were
commonly accompanied by some religious ceremonial. It is
not too adventurous, therefore, to conclude that the stipulation
in its early form of sponsio had its origin in religion and
possibly in an oath. Later, the religious element was dropped
and a civil contract came into existence sanctioned by civil
remedies. As to the starting point of this " secularisation,"
various views are held. The civil contract may have begun as a
guarantee in connection with legal process. It is pointed out
that frequently the formula is not, " Do you promise to give? "
(active voice), but, " Do you promise giving? " (passive voice), a
phrase more applicable to performance by a third person than
by the promisor.

446. As we have seen, the civil contract at first required
the use of the words spondesne? spondeo, which were available
only to Roman citizens. The next stage of development consisted in admitting other and less formal words such as [63]
promittis? promitto—fidepromittis? fidepromitto—fidejubes?
fidejubeo—dabis? dabo—and in making these forms available
also to foreigners. This made them part of the jus gentium, 3. 15. 1.
viz., the law which the Romans applied to aliens and to citizens
alike (§ 58).

The Greek equivalent of the above words was also admitted ;
or the question might be in Greek, the answer in Latin (or
vice versa) ; and, ultimately, any language might be employed,
provided that question and answer corresponded. Even the
requirement of precise correspondence was relaxed. If Titius
says, " Do you promise ten? " and Gaius replies, " I promise
five," or if Titius says, " Do you promise five? " and Gaius
replies, " I promise ten," there was in either case a good
stipulation for the lesser sum. At least this was the later law,
though in the Digest it appears under the name of Ulpian.[64]
If one person says, dabis?—" Will you give? " and the other
replies, quidni—" Why not? " (or " of course "), Ulpian says
(or by interpolation is made to say) that there is a binding
promise.[65]

447. Another development was to reduce the stipulation
to writing. This practice goes back at least to the time of

---

[63] Or " namely." Veluti has either meaning, Barry Nicholas in 69
L.Q.R., p. 65.
[64] Dig. 45. 1. 1, 4: Ulpian (perhaps interpolated) ; secus G. 3. 102, and
Inst. 3. 19. 5 reverting per incuriam to the older law. Girard, p. 519, n. 7.
[65] Dig. 45. 1. 1, 2.

Cicero, and became very common under the Empire.[66] It was usual to conclude the written record with the words, " Rogavit Titius—spopondit Maevius " (Titius questioned—Maevius promised), or a similar turn of phrase.[67] What if the writing recorded the promise, but not the preceding interrogation? Even this was enough, at least in the later law. We read in the Institutes (the passage repeats Paulus, who states the effect of a rescript of Severus and Caracalla of A.D. 200), " If a written instrument records that a person has promised the effect is the same as if he had replied to a preceding question." [68]

448. The oral stipulation continued to exist, consisting, as it did from the beginning, in question and answer. Even this requirement may have been rendered unnecessary by the Emperor Leo, who, by a constitution of A.D. 472, enacted that

3. 15. 1.

any expression of intention should be sufficient to create a valid stipulation.[69] If this is to be understood to refer to oral contracts, we get a liberty of contracting by mere word of mouth admitted in few modern systems of law. But it is at least possible that Leo's enactment refers to stipulations reduced to writing. This would be in accordance with the predilection of the Eastern Empire for the use of written instruments. There are those who hold that, notwithstanding the manipulation of Justinian's commissioners, the Digest remained in many respects an ancient monument, and, in particular, the oral stipulation may have been for practical purposes replaced by the written cautio.

449. All these developments left unaffected the cardinal principle that the parties must come together for the conclusion of the contract, a feature which throughout its history distinguishes the stipulation from the consensual contracts of modern law. This requirement is affirmed in the Institutes when it is said that no verbal contract can be validly concluded without the presence of the parties (item verborum obligatio inter absentes concepta inutilis est). But this, too, was reduced to a

3. 19. 12.

shadow by Justinian's rescript to the advocates of Caesarea mentioned in the text.

450. The result, then, of a long process of development is that a contract effected by a solemn form of spoken words, and,

---

[66] Girard, p. 520, n. 1 ; Roby II. 11.   [67] Dig. 2. 14. 7, 12.
[68] Inst. 3. 19. 7 ; Paul *Sent.* 5. 7. 2 ; Cod. 8. 37. 1. Of course, Paul of the *Sentences* is not always the genuine Paulus and it has even been maintained that the rescript betrays the hand of Justinian's editors.
[69] Cod. 8. 37 (38). 10. Omnes stipulationes, etiamsi non sollemnibus vel directis, sed quibuscumque verbis pro consensu contrahentium compositae sint, legibus cognitae suam habeant firmitatem.

possibly, secured by the sanction of religion, has ended in a formless written contract. It is almost, but not quite, true to say that in the latest Roman Law any written agreement was enforced as a stipulation, for it remained necessary that the instrument should be intended to take effect as a stipulation and not as a mere pact,[70] or a mere acknowledgment of a debt.

451. SCOPE OF THE STIPULATION.—Unlike the rest of the Roman contracts, which had a limited field of operation, the stipulation was applicable to any kind of agreement. Thus a man might stipulate for:—(a) a specific sum of money; (b) some other specific thing; (c) any act or abstention, even of an uncertain or indefinite character. These three types of obligation were the occasion of corresponding actions, *viz.*—for (a) and (b) the condictions (certae pecuniae—triticaria—§ 420), and 3. 15 pr. for (c) actio ex stipulatu—" an action on the stipulation." This seems to cover all three, but in practice was limited to cases to which the condictions were inapplicable (§§ 730–2).

452. A particular use of the stipulation was to novate 3. 29. 2. (§ 660) an existing debt. This had the advantage of facilitating proof and of permitting the creditor to sue by condictio. The jurist Aquilius devised a form of stipulation known as the stipulatio Aquiliana, by which all outstanding claims which one person might have against another were novated and then (if this was desired) discharged by acceptilatio (§ 655).

453. PROCEDURAL STIPULATIONS.—Besides their common use as a form of contract between parties, stipulations were also employed as an incident of judicial procedure corresponding to what we call a recognisance. Such stipulations might be required (a) by the judex; (b) by the praetor (or aedile); (c) by either judex or praetor (aedile). This is the basis of Justinian's 3. 18 pr. classification of stipulations as judicial praetorian, conventional, and common. For instances see the text.

THE INSTITUTES

BOOK III (Tits. XV, XVIII, XIX, Secs. 12, 17)

TITLE XV

Of the verbal obligation

A verbal obligation is contracted by question and answer, when § 444. we stipulate for something to be given to us or done for us. It gives

---

[70] Dig. 2. 14. 7, 12.

§ 451.   rise to two actions, a condictio, if the stipulation relates to something certain, an actio ex stipulatu, if it relates to something uncertain. The word stipulation is derived from an old word stipulus meaning firm, which perhaps itself comes from stipes—the trunk of a tree.

§ 446.   1. Formerly certain traditional words were employed. Spondes? Spondeo. Promittis? Promitto. Fidepromittis? Fidepromitto. Fidejubes? Fidejubeo. Dabis? Dabo. Facies? Faciam.[71] It makes no difference whether the stipulation is made in Latin or Greek or any other language, provided that both parties understand the language used. Nor need they use the same language. All that is required is that the answer should correspond with the question. Two Greeks may contract in Latin. Such were the verbal solemnities formerly in use. But afterwards the Emperor Leo made a constitution, which put an end to verbal solemnities and required merely that the

§ 448.   parties should agree and understand one another's meaning, expressing their intention in any words they please.

2. Stipulations are either absolute, or with an indication of time, or conditional. Absolute, as when one says, " Do you promise to give five aurei? " in which case demand can be made at once. With an indication of time, as when a date of payment is added; for instance, " Do you promise to give ten aurei on the next first of March? " If a time is specified in the stipulation, a debt is contracted immediately, but demand cannot be made before the day arrives, nor indeed on the actual day, for the debtor has the whole of that day in which to make payment, since it is not certain that he has not paid on the promised day until the day is over.

3. If you stipulate, " Do you promise to give ten aurei each year I live? " the obligation is understood to be absolute and without limit of time, for a debt cannot be contracted so as to last only up to a certain time.[72] But if your heir sues he may be met with a plea founded upon the terms of the agreement (exceptio pacti).
4. A stipulation is conditional when the obligation is to take effect subject to some event, so that the stipulation comes into operation, if something is done, or if something is not done; for example : " If Titius is made consul do you promise to give five aurei? " If a person stipulates, " If I have not gone up to the Capitol, do you promise to give? "; this is equivalent to a stipulation for something to be given when he dies. A conditional stipulation merely gives rise to a hope that the thing will fall due, and we transmit this hope to heirs if we die before the condition is realised.

5. A place of performance may be introduced into the stipulation, for example, " Do you promise to give at Carthage? " This stipulation seems to be in terms absolute, but actually it involves a delay sufficient to give the promisor time to make payment at Carthage. Consequently, if any one at Rome stipulates, " Do you promise to give at Carthage today?" the stipulation is ineffectual, because it is impossible to contract on such terms. 6. Conditions

---

[71] Do you engage yourself? I do engage myself—Do you promise? I do promise—Do you pledge your credit? I do pledge my credit—Do you guarantee? I do guarantee—Will you give? I will give—Will you do? I will do.
[72] Dig. 44. 7. 44, 1. But see Buckl. *M.* p. 266.

which are expressed with reference to an event which is past or present either render the obligation void from the beginning or do not postpone its operation; for instance, " If Titius was consul, or if Maevius is alive, do you promise to give? " If the facts are not so, the stipulation is invalid; if they are so, the stipulation takes effect immediately. For, if things are certain in themselves, they do not delay the obligation, though they may be uncertain in our own mind.

7. Not only things but also acts may be the subject of a stipulation, as when we stipulate for something to be done, or not to be done. In stipulations of this kind it is best to add a penalty, lest the amount at issue should remain uncertain and the plaintiff be compelled to prove the amount of his interest. So if a person stipulates for something to be done, he should add a penal clause—" If this is not done, do you promise to pay ten aurei by way of penalty? " But if the stipulation comprises in one and the same contract both things to be done and also things not to be done the penal clause will run— " If anything is done contrary to what is stipulated or if anything is not done as stipulated, then by way of penalty do you promise to pay ten aurei? "

Title XVIII

Of the different kinds of stipulation

Stipulations are classified as judicial, praetorian, conventional and common, that is both praetorian and judicial. 1. Judicial stipulations are incidental to the functions of the judge alone, such as security against fraud, or for pursuit of a runaway slave or payment of his value.[73] 2. Praetorian stipulations are incidental to the functions of the praetor alone, such as security against apprehended damage or for payment of legacies. The term praetorian must be understood to include stipulations required by the aediles, for these too depend upon the jurisdiction of a magistrate. 3. Conventional stipulations are not contracted by the order of a judge or praetor, but express the agreement of the parties. One may say that of such stipulations there are as many kinds as there are things about which men may conclude agreements. 4. Common stipulations are, for example, a stipulation for the security of a pupil's estate; for the praetor directs the guardian to give such security, and sometimes the judge does the same, if the circumstances call for it. Another example is when a procurator is required to give security that his principal will ratify his acts.

§ 453.

Title XIX, Secs. 12, 17

12. There can be no verbal obligation unless the parties come together. This requirement, however, often led to litigation, when, sometimes after a considerable lapse of time, persons disposed to take captious objections alleged that they or the other parties were not present when the contract was concluded. Accordingly, in order to

§ 449.

[73] Dig. 4. 2. 14, 11 ; 6. 1. 21.

bring such disputes to a speedy conclusion, we have promulgated a constitution addressed to the advocates of Caesarea, which provides that complete credit is to be given to writings which declare the parties to be present, unless the party who makes such unworthy allegations produces the most convincing proof either by writing or by the word of competent witnesses that he or the other party were in some other place during the whole of the day on which the

§ 447.

instrument was executed.[74] 17. If a written instrument states that a person has promised, the promise is deemed to have been given in answer to a preceding question.

V. The Contract Litteris

454. The written contract or contract litteris finds a place in the classification of contracts both in Gaius and in Justinian, but the literal contract of Gaius is not the literal contract of Justinian. Long before Justinian the old literal contract was a thing of the past. Justinian substitutes for it a written instrument, which was produced in proof of a loan and was governed by special rules of evidence.

455. In the old law the contract litteris consisted in an entry in a creditor's ledger (codex accepti et expensi) of a payment, either actually made, or supposed to be made, to a debtor.[75] "Supposed to be made," for this contract was usually employed to novate a pre-existing debt, e.g., for goods sold and delivered. The effect was to replace a bonae fidei contract by a stricti juris contract (§ 409) and to give a creditor the severer remedy of the condictio (§ 420), besides which he was relieved from the necessity of proving the items of the account. In order to effect the novation without disturbing the account between the parties it was necessary to feign that the old debt had been discharged and a new debt contracted in its place. This involved cross entries (nomina transcripticia). In the case put above the debt was said to be transferred from the thing to the person (a re in personam); but sometimes the purpose was to substitute one debtor for another, and then the debt was said to be transferred from person to person (a persona in personam).[76] It must be observed that it was the writing which made the obligation, not the fact (if it was the fact) that money had changed hands. The contract was formal (§ 410). Gaius distinguishes these nomina

---

[74] Cod. 8. 37 (38). 14, 2.
[75] This is the commonly accepted view, but little is known. The term *expensilatio*, usually applied to this contract, is not found in the texts.
[76] G. 3. 128-30.

transcripticia from nomina arcaria or cash entries (arca=cash-box), which were evidence of a mutuum, but did not in themselves constitute a contract.[77]

456. The literal contract was in most respects inferior to the stipulation. It was only available for a money-debt. Only citizens could be creditors, and it was questioned whether peregrines could be debtors.[78] But it had one advantage, *viz.*, that it could be contracted *inter absentes*.[79] It implied a special system of book-keeping, and when this fell into disuse, the literal contract became obsolete. It was the only written contract known to the Roman Law. But in the Greek parts of the Empire other written contracts were in use known as syngraphae and chirographa.[80] It seems that in these cases by Greek Law the writing produced an obligation in itself and was not merely evidence of an independent contract.

457. Justinian devotes a Title to "Obligation by writing." He is not referring to the old ledger contract, which, as the text says, was no longer in use, but to the practice of giving an acknowledgment of a debt in a written instrument. In principle this was evidence of a mutuum, unless the instrument could be construed as a promise to repay a loan, in which case it was evidence of a stipulation. It might happen that no money had in fact changed hands. If sued on the contract, the alleged debtor could plead the exceptio doli or the exceptio non numeratae pecuniae [81]; in the alternative he could bring an action to be released from his engagement and to have the instrument returned to him (condictio sine causa, § 595). In either event the burden of proof lay on him to show that the money had not been paid. But from about the end of the second century A.D. the burden of proof changed, and the rule was established that if the alleged debtor denied his liability, he could cast upon the other party the burden of proving pay-ment.[82] As before, he could raise the issue by way of exception or by bringing an action.[83] The proceeding was known by the general name of querela non numeratae pecuniae—the complaint that money had not been paid. To prevent abuse of this defence Justinian enacted that a defendant who denied the writing, or admitted the writing but said that he had not received the

3. 21.

---

[77] G. 3. 131.
[78] G. 3. 133.
[79] G. 3. 138.
[80] G. 3. 134.
[81] G. 4. 116; Inst. 4. 13. 2.
[82] Cod. 4. 30. 3. (Caracalla A.D. 215).
[83] Cod. 4. 30. 7.

money, if the case went against him, was to be liable for double the amount claimed as in the actio legis Aquiliae (§ 632).[84]

458. This procedure was very beneficial to the alleged debtor, but it would have been unreasonable to allow him to raise the issue without limit of time. Accordingly a limit was fixed, first of one year, later of five, and by Justinian of two years, after which the querela was no longer available to the alleged debtor (unless, as Justinian enacted, he made his exception perpetual by formal notice to the creditor, or in certain circumstances, by lodging a protest with the court).[85] He was, in fact, as the Institutes say, bound by the writing and liable to the condictio. The text adds the qualifying words, " in the absence, that is, of a verbal obligation." This means that if the instrument could be construed as a stipulation, he would be liable on the verbal contract, which it was no longer open to him to impugn. If it could not be so construed, he was liable on a mutuum, which it was no longer open to him to deny. This is the truth of the matter. But Justinian hesitates to say that he is bound by a mutuum, for there may not in fact have been any mutuum at all. So he says that he is bound by the writing.

459. It is generally supposed that in Justinian's day there was no genuine written contract, and that in the Institutes a written contract is invented so as to conform to the four classes of contract to be found in Gaius. Thus Moyle says, " Justinian's attempt to pass off the instrument as a literal contract, which is due merely to the habit of reproducing, if possible, the arrangement and terminology of Gaius, is forced and unhappy." [86] But it must be remembered that a written contract persisted in the Greek provinces of the Empire notwithstanding its inconsistency with Roman Law, and the late Professor Collinet contended that Justinian deliberately incorporated the Greek usage in his own system, but only to the very limited extent indicated in the text. It seems more probable that the whole question is one of evidence. After the lapse of the two years the alleged debtor is, as an English lawyer would say, estopped from saying that he is not liable. There does not seem to be anything particularly " forced, or unhappy " in saying that he is bound by the writing. But this is not the same thing as to say that he is bound by a written contract.[87]

---

[84] Nov. 18. 8.   [85] Cod. 4. 30. 14, 4.
[86] Moyle, p. 498.
[87] Buckland (*T.* p. 461) seems to come to much the same conclusion.

THE INSTITUTES

BOOK III

TITLE XXI

Of the obligation litteris

Formerly an obligation used to be contracted by writing, namely § 455. by ledger entries, but these are no longer in use. Of course, if a person has stated in writing that he is indebted for a sum of money, which in fact has not been paid to him, he cannot after a considerable lapse of time raise the plea that the money was not paid. This has often been laid down in imperial constitutions. Thus it happens § 458. that even today he is bound by a writing when the querela is no longer available and a condictio may be brought upon the writing, always supposing that there is no verbal contract. The lapse of time which excluded the querela was formerly defined by imperial constitutions as a period of five years; but to prevent the possibility of creditors being for a long time defrauded of their money, our constitution has cut it down to a period of two years, after which this defence is no longer available.

VI. THE CONSENSUAL CONTRACTS

460. In four cases consent alone makes a contract. These are:—1. sale (emptio venditio); 2. hire (locatio conductio); 3. partnership (societas); 4. mandate (mandatum). The presence of the parties is not required, as it is in stipulation, consequently, the contract can be concluded by letter or by messenger. All these contracts are bonae fidel and bilateral, giving rise to reciprocal actions. In the first three, which are " perfectly bilateral " (§ 408) the duty of performance is reciprocal. A plaintiff will not succeed in his action unless he can show that he has performed or is ready and willing to perform his corresponding part of the contract.[88]

THE INSTITUTES

BOOK III

TITLE XXII

Of obligation by consent

Obligations are contracted by consent in the contracts of sale, hire, partnership and mandate. 1. The reason why in these cases obligation is said to be contracted by consent is because writing is

---

[88] Girard, p. 567; Sohm (Ledlie's translation), p. 397; infra, p. 316.

not required, or the presence of the parties, nor need anything be transferred to give substance to the obligation. All that is required is that the parties should agree. 2. Consequently contracts of this kind may be concluded though the parties do not come together, as by letter or by messenger. 3. Again, in these contracts each party is bound to the other to do what good faith requires, whereas in the stipulation one party is the stipulator (or promisee), the other party is the promisor.

VII. Sale

461. Sale may be defined as a contract whereby one person promises to transfer to another a thing and to procure to him the undisturbed and permanent possession of it, and the other on his part promises to pay a price.

The essential elements in the contract are: Consent—Thing —Price.

462. Consent.—When is the contract of sale complete?

The answer differs according as the parties intend to conclude it by spoken or by written words.

3. 23 pr.　　463. A. If the parties do not intend to reduce their contract to writing, it is complete as soon as the thing and the price are ascertained.

B. If the parties do intend to reduce their contract to writing, i.e., do not intend to be bound until they have done so, it is not complete until it has been reduced to writing accordingly, viz., the instruments must be written in the hand of the contracting parties, or, if written by a third person, must be subscribed by the contracting party, and, if they are notarial, must be formally completed and released to the parties.[89] This is the effect of Justinian's enactment (Cod. 4. 21. 17) summarised in the Institutes, by which contracts which the parties have agreed to put into writing (quos in scriptis fieri placuit) are to be invalid (non aliter vires habere sancimus) unless the required formalities are observed.

464. Arra.—Sometimes a special element was introduced into the contract in the form of arra or earnest. The word has two different applications.

(1) Originally it meant a coin, or other thing, handed over by one party to the other, usually by the buyer to the seller, as we say, "to bind the bargain," i.e., to indicate that the bargaining of the parties had ended in a firm agreement. It

---

[89] I am indebted to Professor de Zulueta (*The Roman Law of Sale*) for this translation of "partibus absoluta."

was proof of the conclusion of the contract—argumentum emptionis et venditionis contractae. The wide diffusion of this practice (not limited to the contract of sale) appears from the etymology of the word, which came to the Romans from the Phaenicians through the Greeks and in turn was transmitted through the French to the English in the word "earnest." But it must not be inferred from this that the institution was a foreign importation into Europe. In English and the allied languages it was popularly known as God's penny, because, if not consumed in drink, it was given to the poor; unless we accept from Grotius the cynical suggestion that it was so called " since it generally does not much exceed the amount which it is usual to give to the poor in God's name." [90] The commentators call this primitive type of arra " arra confirmatoria." It was in use for simple transactions among simple people.

(2) By an extension the word came to include a deposit on sale, *i.e.*, an instalment of the purchase price. If the purchaser failed to pay the balance at the time or times agreed the seller might treat the sale as cancelled and keep the deposit. This was the consequence of a special clause in the contract providing that in such event the property should be unsold (ut fundus inemptus sit).[91] It took effect as a resolutive condition and was termed a lex commissoria (condition of forfeiture).[92] This penalised the defaulting purchaser. In the later Empire the penalty worked both ways. If the party who gave the earnest withdrew without just cause the other party kept it. If the party who received the earnest withdrew he had to return it and as much again. From Egyptian documents it appears that the deposit might actually amount to more than half the purchase price.[93] This rendered repudiation of the contemplated sale extremely unlikely. On the other hand, either party was free to withdraw if he was willing to incur the forfeit. The commentators call this type of arra " arra poenitentialis." In these cases there was as yet no contract between the parties. This awaited a written instrument to be executed later. Meanwhile, the conditions of the arra were determined by a preliminary agreement verbal or in writing (pactum arrale). All this reflects the Greek contractual system, which did not recognise an executory contract of sale. Arra served to supply the *lacuna*. But it is plain

---

[90] *Introduction to Dutch Jurisprudence*, 3. 14. 27.
[91] Dig. 18. 1. 6, 1. It rested with the seller to treat the contract as cancelled or sue for breach. Dig. 18. 3. 3 and 4 pr.
[92] Dig. 18. 3. 1. For this and other special terms in contracts of sale see de Zulueta, p. 55.
[93] Girard, p. 577, n. 5.

from Justinian's constitution, to be mentioned presently, that the Greek and the Roman theories of sale were in unreconciled conflict.

3. 23 pr.

465. Justinian does not treat the subject of arra as a whole, but refers to it in a constitution included in the Code, and again in the Institutes, in connection with his legislation on the subject of written contracts. There was to be no binding contract until the instrument was executed with the statutory formalities. Until this was done, but not afterwards, either party might withdraw, subject to the usual penalty. This was to be so even though the parties had not made it an express term in the contract. In the case of contracts without writing Justinian made no change. The arra was probative, and at the same time penal, if the parties meant to make it so. Whether the contract was written or unwritten, the party who withdrew after completion incurred the usual consequences of breach of contract.

466. SUBJECT MATTER.—The next essential element in the contract of sale is the thing or res. This must be:—(a) in existence or capable of existing. You cannot sell a dead slave or a live unicorn; (b) in commercio, i.e., capable of being owned. You cannot sell a free man, or a res sacra, religiosa or sancta; (c) something in which the buyer acquires an interest under the contract. You cannot buy a thing which is yours already. If these conditions are satisfied, the most various things may be the subject of the contract; a thing corporeal or a thing incorporeal (as a servitude, a debt, an inheritance), a thing now in existence, or a thing which will or may come into existence hereafter—venditio rei speratae, e.g., next year's crop —venditio spei, e.g., what I catch in my net [94] (in the first case the sale goes off if there is no crop, in the second case you take your chance); a thing which belongs to the seller (res sua), a thing which belongs to someone else (res aliena).[95]

But contrary to our modern notions, a thing generally described (genus) cannot be the subject of a contract of sale. Thus, I cannot contract to buy or sell "a thousand bushels of wheat." It seems that bargains of this sort were effected by stipulation. But I may contract to buy "a thousand bushels of

---

[94] Dig. 18. 1. 8.
[95] Dig. 18. 1. 28. But if a vendor knew that the thing did not belong to him and the purchaser did not, he was liable ex empto even before eviction. Dig. 19. 1. 30, 1.

the grain in your barn." This was considered to be sufficiently specific.[96]

467. PRICE.—The third element is price. This must:—(a) consist in money; (b) be certain (certum); (c) genuine (verum); and (d) in certain cases, reasonable (justum), as defined by law.

468. (a) The price must consist in money. On this point the Sabinians and Proculians held divergent views. The Proculian view prevailed. 3. 23. 2.

469. (b) The price must be certain or ascertainable (certum). 3. 23. 1. This it was held to be if it was to be fixed by a third person, but not if it was left to the discretion of one of the parties to the contract. If the third person did not fix the price the contract failed. In English Law, where the price is not determined the buyer must pay a reasonable price.[97] This means that there is a contract to sell at a reasonable price. In Roman Law this would not be a contract of sale. If the goods were delivered, there would be an innominate contract, giving rise to an actio praescriptis verbis (§ 524).

470. (c) The price must be genuine (verum). It must not be merely pretended, as when a price is named *pro forma,* but there is no intention that it should be demanded or paid; or merely derisory, as when a valuable property is expressed to be sold for a single sesterce. In both these cases the transaction (if anything) is not sale, but gift.

471. (d) The price (in certain cases) must be reasonable (justum). This element in the contract finds expression in the principle of relief on the ground of so-called laesio enormis, *i.e.,* more than ordinary prejudice. It is thought to have been introduced into the law by Justinian, though in the Code it is attributed by interpolation to Diocletian.[98] A vendor who had received less than half the fair price, as it was at the time of the sale, might recover what he had sold, returning the money paid for it, subject, however, to the alternative that the purchaser might supplement what he had paid, so as to make up a fair price. Two questions (in particular) have been raised with regard to this rule:—1. whether it applied to movables as well as to land; 2. whether the purchaser had a corresponding right, if he had paid more than twice the fair price. So far as Roman

---

[96] Buckl. *T.* p. 484 ; de Zulueta, p. 14.
[97] *S. G. A.,* s. 8 (2).
[98] Cod. 4. 44. 2 and 8.

Law is concerned, a negative answer must be given to both questions. But the medieval lawyers extended the rule in both directions and applied it by analogy to other bonae fidei contracts such as hire and partnership. It has passed into some modern systems derived from the Roman Law. By the French Code, art. 1674, " if the vendor has suffered prejudice to the extent of more than seven twelfths in the price of an immovable he has the right to demand the rescission of the sale." Relief on the ground of laesio enormis is admitted in Ceylon, but no longer in South Africa.[99]

472. We proceed to consider the effect of the contract of sale as regards the duties of the parties.

473. DUTIES OF THE SELLER.—The seller was bound:—
1. to deliver the thing and to give vacant possession ;
2. to take care of it until delivery ;
3. to guarantee against eviction ;
4. to guarantee against undisclosed defects.

474. (1) Duty to deliver and to give vacant possession. The seller was bound to take all necessary steps to transfer to the buyer whatever right he had in the thing sold together with accessories, and in particular to convey it by mancipation, if a res mancipi, or by tradition, if it was not.[1] The object of the contract of sale being to make the buyer owner, an agreement that the ownership should not pass was inconsistent with the nature of the contract.[2] But the seller was not bound to make the buyer owner immediately and directly (rem dare).[3] He satisfied his duty to deliver, in the absence of expression to the contrary, by giving vacant possession (rem praestare—vacuam possessionem tradere—rem habere licere). This proposition may be split into two. First, he must put the buyer in physical possession, which he cannot do, for example, if some other person is in possession by the authority of the praetor, such as legatees or fideicommissaries who have been let into possession in security of their claim, or creditors placed in possession of the estate (§ 754),[4] or if there is an outstanding usufruct. Secondly, the seller must give vacant possession, that is to say " exclusive possession, not defeasible by interdict, and

---

[99] Abrogated by Union Act, No. 32 of 1952 ; Lee, p. 231.
[1] Paul. *Sent.* 1. 13a. 4.
[2] Dig. 18. 1. 80, 3.
[3] Dig. 18. 1. 25, 1: qui vendidit necesse non habet fundum emptoris facere, ut cogitur qui fundum stipulanti spopondit.
[4] Dig. 19. 1. 2. 1.

free from burdens interfering with it except such as had been agreed upon." [5] Thus a civil law heir does not give vacua possessio if a praetorian successor can displace the purchaser by the interdict quorum bonorum (§§ 387, 765), and if land is burdened with a hypothec, a purchaser may require its liberation.[6] But a praedial servitude was not considered to interfere with possession. Consequently a vendor was not bound to deliver land free of such servitude unless he had expressly sold it as free (uti optimus maximusque).[7] But if he knew that the land was burdened, it was his duty to say so.[8] A lease was no burden on the land, because it gave no real right (§ 494).

475. (2) **Duty to take care of the thing until delivery.** It may be that in the classical period the vendor was liable for custodia, had to keep the thing safe.[9] But in Justinian's system no more was required of him than that he should exercise exacta diligentia (diligentia in custodiendo).[10] He was liable for dolus and for so-called culpa levis in abstracto (§ 417), but not if the thing perished by accident or was lost by theft or suffered deterioration, unless he had undertaken to be so, or was in default in making delivery or otherwise to blame. This meant that, in general, the thing was at the risk of the purchaser. We return to this subject later. If the thing was stolen, destroyed or damaged by a third person, the purchaser was entitled to call upon the vendor for cession of actions (§ 649), e.g., vindicatio, actio furti, actio legis Aquiliae.

3. 23. 3

476. (3) **Duty to guarantee against eviction.** The law on this matter went through successive phases.[11] In the earliest period a purchaser by mancipation whose title was not defended or not effectually defended by his vendor, so that he suffered eviction, had an action for double the price, the (so-called) actio auctoritatis.[12] This was of limited application and in cases to which it was inapplicable, or as a substitute for it, the practice grew up of entering into stipulations in certain cases for double the price to be paid in the event of eviction (stipulatio duplae); in other cases, where the property was less valuable, for a simple guarantee against eviction (stipulatio habere licere), which gave

---

[5] Buckl. *T.* p. 488; Dig. 19. 1. 11, 13.
[6] Dig. 19. 1. 52. 1.
[7] Dig. 18. 1. 59.
[8] Dig. 19. 1. 1, 1.
[9] Jörs-Kunkel, p. 228.
[10] Dig. 18. 1. 35, 4; 18. 6. 2, 1 & 3; 19. 1. 31; Buckl. *T.* p. 560; de Zulueta, p. 33
[11] Girard, p. 588.
[12] Paul. *Sent.* 2. 17. 3.

rise to a claim for an indemnity, if the title proved defective. At a later date these stipulations could be compelled or were implied in the sale, and, ultimately, a purchaser whose right to possess was called in question could in any event sue for an indemnity in an action on the contract.[13] This replaced the stipulatio habere licere express or implied. But if the property sold was of considerable value it continued to be usual to make an express stipulation for double the price or for less or more as might be agreed,[14] though even where this had not been done, an action might be brought for a multiple of the price, when this was in accordance with local usage.[15]

The action on the stipulation, express or implied, differed from the action for an indemnity in the conditions of its exercise and in the nature of the remedy.[16] The first lay when an action had been brought against or by the purchaser terminating in an adverse decision on his right to possess.[17] In the second, it was enough that his right to possess as purchaser was seriously menaced. In the first the measure of damages was the price or a multiple of the price. In the second the purchaser claimed general damages, and, in particular, the market value of the property at the time of eviction. In the first he must have suffered actual eviction or escaped it by paying the amount of the condemnation (litis aestimatio, § 183). In the second he might be still in possession, though by a title not derived from the vendor, e.g., if the thing was given to him by the real owner.[18]

477. (4) Duty to guarantee against undisclosed defects. Here too the law went through a long process of development.

(a) In the most ancient period, if land was sold by mancipation and the vendor had misrepresented its extent, the purchaser had the so-called actio de modo agri for double the difference in value—in duplo ejus quod mentitus est [19]; and he could also sue upon special terms attached to the mancipation (leges mancipii).

478. (b) Later, the vendor was bound by informal representations and guarantees (dicta et promissa) made at the time of sale, and was liable for undisclosed defects of which he was aware.[20] But the law did not cast upon him any general duty of warranting the absence of latent defects.

---

13 Girard, pp. 595-6 ; Buckl. *T.* p. 489.
14 Dig. 21. 2. 56.
15 Dig. 21. 1. 31, 20 ; 21. 2. 6
16 Girard, p. 594 ; Buckl. *T.* p. 490 ; *M.* p. 284.
17 Dig. 21. 2. 16, 1 ; 24.
18 Paul. *Sent.* 2. 17. 8.
19 Paul. *Sent.* 2. 17. 4.
20 Moyle, *Contract of Sale in the Civil Law,* p. 189.

479. (c) Therefore, if a purchaser wished to protect himself, he had to do so by stipulation, and this came to be the usual course. It might be supposed that this guarantee, like the guarantee against eviction (with which it was frequently combined in a single stipulation) would have come to be implied in every contract of sale, but the law took a different line of development.[21]

480. (d) The curule aediles (§ 18), acting under their powers of police, drew up rules requiring sellers of slaves and cattle to make a public declaration of certain specified defects, moral (in the case of slaves) and physical, and gave actions against them when defects became apparent, whether the sellers knew of them or not.[22] These were the actio redhibitoria, and the actio aestimatoria or quanti minoris. The first lay within six months to have the sale rescinded against restoration of the price, if the thing had defects (so-called redhibitory defects) which destroyed or impaired its usefulness to the purchaser. In the second action, which in similar circumstances could be brought within the year, the purchaser affirmed the sale and claimed a reduction in the price.

481. (e) The edict of the aediles protected purchasers of slaves and live stock (at first in the market, later anywhere). The civil law gave a remedy only in the circumstances above described (§ 478). But ultimately the aedilician remedies came to be extended to every kind of sale. If the texts could be taken at their face value, this development would seem to have taken place as early as Ulpian or even Labeo.[23] But it is generally agreed that they are interpolated. The development was complete in Justinian's system, if not before.

482. The general result was that if a vendor had guaranteed the existence of certain qualities, or the absence of defects, or if he had failed to declare defects of which he was aware, he was liable for general damages in an actio empti. In other cases he was limited to the remedies given by the actio redhibitoria and the actio quanti minoris. The defect complained of must have existed at the time of the sale,[24] and the purchaser must keep his eyes open—Ignorantia emptoris prodest, quae non in

[21] Girard, p. 598. " The variety of the cases prevented universal forms from becoming established," de Zulueta, p. 47.
[22] Dig. 21. 1. 1, 2: dummodo sciamus venditorem etiamsi ignoraverit ea quae aediles praestari jubent, tamen teneri debere.
[23] Dig 21. 1. 1 ; 63.
[24] Cod. 4. 58. 3.

supinum hominem cadit—" It is only such ignorance as does not argue carelessness that will avail the purchaser." [24a]

483. DUTIES OF THE BUYER.—The buyer was bound:—

1. to pay the price, with interest if payment was overdue,[25] but not unless the seller was ready and willing to do his part. Therefore, he might refuse to pay, if the seller failed to deliver, or had sold in bad faith a thing which did not belong to him, or did not give vacua possessio, or if proceedings had been instituted contesting the buyer's title.[26] In all these cases, if sued upon the contract, he could plead the defence traditionally known as the exceptio non adimpleti contractus—a plea that plaintiff had not carried out his part of the contract. It was not really an exceptio (§ 741), but an unqualified denial of plaintiff's claim, and " the plaintiff must prove his performance, while in a true exception the burden of proof was normally on the defendant " [26a];

2. to take delivery as soon as the seller tendered it, or at the time agreed. Any costs properly incurred by the seller between the date of the contract and delivery were charged to the buyer.[27]

484. THE THEORY OF RISK.—It has been said above that as soon as the contract was concluded the risk passed to the purchaser. This will require some qualification, but for the present may be accepted as the general rule. It followed that if the thing perished, or was stolen, or suffered deterioration, while in the hands of the seller without fault on his part, the buyer had to pay the price just the same. This is inconsistent with the general principle that delivery and payment are concurrent conditions, each dependent on the other—no delivery, no payment—no payment, no delivery—as well as with the natural expectation that risk and ownership should go together.[28] It may be conceded that the rule is anomalous, but it does not follow that it is unreasonable or unfair. The same consequences follow in modern systems (as the English and the French), which make ownership pass as soon as the contract is concluded.

[24a] Dig. 18. 1. 15, 1 (Mackintosh's translation).

[25] Dig. 22. 1. 32, 2; Paul. *Sent.* 2. 17. 9; Cod. 4. 32. 2; 4. 49. 13; Buckl. *T.* p. 493, n. 8; de Zulueta, p. 51.

[26] Girard, p. 603.

[26a] Buckl *T.* p. 493. This applies equally to the seller and to the other perfectly bilateral contracts, hire and partnership (*supra*, § 460).

[27] Dig. 19. 1. 13, 20.

[28] The maxim res perit dimino is not Roman. For its use in English Law see *Bayne* v. *Walker* (1815) 3 Dow. 233.

Various attempts have been made to account for the Roman rule. It has been supposed to be a survival from an earlier time when the consensual contract of sale was unknown or in its infancy; thus, it is suggested that there was a time when the bargain was concluded by reciprocal stipulations, each creating an absolute duty of performance—on the one side a duty to deliver, on the other side a duty to pay; or, again, it is said that the rule is reminiscent of the mancipatory sale, which passed the property forthwith without delivery. All this is speculation. In sharp contrast with such theories is the view that the rule is post-classical and that in the classical period of Roman Law the risk did not pass to the purchaser until delivery, i.e., risk and ownership went together.[29] The question must be regarded as still open.

485. The rule that the risk passed when the contract was complete did not always mean that it passed as soon as there was a contract binding the parties. The emptio must be perfecta. This implies that the subject-matter and the price are exactly ascertained and the sale is unconditional.[30] Failing any of these conditions, the risk does not pass. Thus it does not pass:—(1) if the sale is subject to a suspensive condition, which has not yet been satisfied; (2) if the subject-matter of the sale or the amount of the purchase money has not been precisely determined, e.g., if you buy one hundred sacks of wheat from the stock in my granary, and specific sacks have not yet been appropriated to the contract, or if specific goods are sold at so much the pound and have not yet been weighed. The case would be different if the whole lot were sold for a lump sum (per aversionem—in aversione).[31]

486. If things are sold in the alternative, e.g., if the vendor is to deliver either the slave Stichus or the slave Eros as he pleases, the risk of the first is with the vendor, i.e., if one has perished, he must deliver the other. The risk of the second is with the purchaser, i.e., if both slaves have perished without fault of the vendor the purchaser will nevertheless have to pay the agreed price. The result is the same if the selection is left to the purchaser.[32] The risk of destruction or total loss

[29] Buckl. T. pp. 486–7; M. p. 282.
[30] Dig. 18. 6. 8 pr.: si id quod venierit appareat, quid, quale, quantum sit, sit et pretium, et pure venit, perfecta est emptio—" Sale is perfect, if the identity, quality and quantity of the thing are ascertained, and the price determined and the sale is unconditional."
[31] Dig. 18. 1. 35, 5; 62, 2.
[32] Provided that this is all that is left to his choice and not whether he would buy or not, Dig. 18. 1. 34, 6.

(periculum interitus rei) and the risk of depreciation (periculum deteriorationis) usually go together, but where there is a choice of alternatives this is not so. If a vendor has to deliver Stichus or Eros as he pleases, and Stichus goes blind, he may deliver Stichus. The risk of depreciation is with the purchaser, not with the vendor.

487. Actions. The vendor had the actio venditi, the purchaser the actio empti and the aedilician actions (§ 480) which were ultimately absorbed in the actio empti.[33]

488. When did the property in the thing sold pass to the purchaser? Not until delivery, nor even then unless the price was paid or credit given (§ 205).

THE INSTITUTES

BOOK III

TITLE XXIII

Of purchase and sale

§ 463.

The contract of purchase and sale is concluded as soon as the parties are agreed on the price, although the price has not been paid, and even earnest has not been given. For earnest is merely proof that the contract has been concluded. This must be understood of contracts of purchase and sale which are not reduced to writing. For with regard to this kind of sale we have made no change. But when the contract is put into writing our constitution provides that there shall be no concluded contract, unless the instruments of sale have been written out in the hand of the contracting parties or if written by some one else have been subscribed by the party to the contract, and if the documents are drawn up by a notary unless they have been formally completed and released to the parties. So long as any of these requirements is wanting, there is a locus poenitentiae and either party may withdraw from the contract without incurring a penalty. But this is only so, if nothing has been given by way of earnest; for if earnest has been given (whether the

§ 465.

agreement for earnest[34] was written or verbal), and either party refuses to complete the contract, then, if it is the purchaser he forfeits what he has given; if it is the vendor he has to return what he has received and as much again. This applies when the parties have not come to any understanding about the earnest.

1. There must be a price. Without a price there can be no sale.

§ 469.

Further, the price must be certain. It was much discussed amongst

---

[33] Buckl. *M*. p. 285.

[34] The language of the Institutes, sive in scriptis sive sine scriptis venditio celebrata est, is confused and clumsy, but means the same as Cod. 4. 21. 17, 2, from which it is evidently taken, and refers not to the principal contract of sale, but to the collateral agreement for arra (pactum arrale).

the ancients whether there was a sale if it was agreed that a thing should be sold at a price to be fixed by Titius. We have decided that in all such cases there is a sale conditionally on the price being fixed by the person named. But if he will not or cannot fix the price, there is no sale since there is no agreed price. The same principle may reasonably be extended to the contract of hire.[35]

§ 468.

2. The price must consist in money. It was formerly a great question whether it could consist in some other thing, as a slave, a piece of land, or a toga. Sabinus and Cassius think it may; and in accordance with this view it was commonly said that the contract of purchase and sale is effected by an exchange; and barter (it was said) was the most ancient kind of sale. An argument for this was found in the poet Homer, who in a certain passage describes the army of the Achaeans as getting wine by giving other things in exchange. The passage runs as follows: " So the long-haired Achaeans bought them wine, some for bronze and some for gleaming iron and some with hides and some with whole kine and some with captives " (Iliad VII, 472–5). The other school took the opposite view, and maintained that exchange was one thing, sale another. Otherwise it would be impossible to distinguish the thing sold from the price given for it, for reason does not allow us to say that each thing is at once the object of the sale and the price. So the opinion of Proculus, who said that exchange is a special contract distinct from sale, has very properly prevailed, since this was supported by another passage in Homer and by more weighty reasons besides. This was admitted by earlier Emperors and will be found treated at large in our Digest. 3. So soon as the contract of sale is concluded (which, as we have said, when there is no writing takes place as soon as the parties are agreed on the price) the risk of the thing sold immediately

§ 475.

attaches to the purchaser, although the thing has not yet been delivered to him. Accordingly, if a slave has died, or has suffered some bodily injury, or if a house has been totally or partially con-

§ 484.

sumed by fire, or land has been wholly or partially swept away by the violence of a stream, or has been seriously diminished in area or value from flood or from trees being blown down by a high wind, the loss falls on the purchaser, who has to pay the price, though he does not get the thing. For the vendor incurs no responsibility for accidents which happen without wrongful intention or negligence on his part. Conversely, if, after the sale, land gains any accession by alluvion, the purchaser profits by it; for the person who incurs the risk should also take the profit. If a slave, who has been sold, has run away or has been stolen without wrongful intention or negligence on the part of the vendor, we have to ask whether the vendor undertook to keep him safe until he delivered him to the purchaser. If he did, the risk is his. If he did not, he is not responsible. The same applies to animals and anything else. But the seller must put at the disposal of the buyer the right to vindicate the thing and to bring a personal action, for these remain with the seller by virtue of his ownership until the thing is handed over. The same may be said of the actio furti and the actio damni injuriae [under the lex Aquilia].

---

[35] Cod. 4. 38. 15.

4. A sale may be conditional as well as absolute; for example, " If you approve the slave Stichus within such a time, you will be the purchaser for so many aurei."

5. If a person buys a sacred or religious place, or a public place such as a forum or a basilica knowing it to be such, there is no sale; but, if deceived by the vendor he has bought it as private or profane, because he cannot have what he meant to buy he will have an action on the contract to recover as damages what it was worth to him not to be deceived. It is the same if he has bought a free man, believing him to be a slave.

VIII. Hire

489. The second consensual contract is letting and hiring (locatio conductio), which may be defined as a contract, whereby one person agrees to give to another the use or the use and enjoyment of a thing or his services or his labour in return for remuneration, usually in money. This contract closely resembles sale. Like sale, it may be analysed into three elements: consent, subject-matter, remuneration.

490. Consent.—No form is needed. The contract being consensual does not depend for its validity upon the presence of the parties. It may be concluded by letter or by messenger. It is complete so soon as the parties are agreed upon its essential terms.

491. Subject-Matter. — The commentators distinguish (though the distinction is not sharply drawn in the texts of the Roman Law) three types of this contract: —

(a) the hire of a thing (locatio conductio rei);

(b) the hire of services (locatio conductio operarum);

(c) the hire of a piece of work (locatio conductio operis).

In the first two cases the person who supplies the thing or the services is termed the locator, the person who pays is the conductor. In the third case the person who gives the order for the work, and pays for it, is the locator (he " places " the order), the person who executes the work, or gets it executed, is the conductor. This perplexed terminology is due to the different meanings attached to the word locare and its derivatives, and suggests that the contract of hire had outgrown its original limitations. It may be that in the earliest forms assumed by the contract there was always something " placed." In (a) I place a thing at your disposal; in (b) I place myself or my slave or son at your disposal; in (c) I place in your hands something on which you are to expend your labour, e.g., goods to be carried, clothes to be washed or mended, material to construct a house, a slave or son to be taught a trade. In these cases the employer " places " not the work merely, but the material for doing the work. If the other party is to furnish the material, the contract is, usually not hire, but sale (§ 497).

492. What from one point of view is placing of an order, from another point of view is the rendering of a service, and it may be thought that locatio operis and locatio operarum are different ways of looking at the same thing. Thus if a contractor is to build for me a block of flats and supply all the materials at his own expense, I am said to place the order (insulam aedificandum loco) and the contractor is said to place his services (locat operam). This, says Paulus, makes the contract a contract of hire,[36] notwithstanding the fact that I become owner of the materials, which, as remarked above, would usually bring it under the head of sale. But it must not be concluded from this that a locatio operis is always a conductio operarum, for there is a substantial difference between serving for a wage and undertaking to do a piece of work as an independent contractor.[37]

493. Not all services could be the subject of a contract of hire. It was generally limited to services which were commonly rendered by slaves. Members of what are called the liberal professions were supposed to do their work for nothing. But they could recover an honorarium for their services by means of the extraordinaria cognitio of the magistrates (§ 758).

494. As regards the hiring of a thing, in principle there was no difference between a movable and an immovable. A lease of land did not create a real right. It was merely contractual. This was once so in English Law, but for many centuries a lease has been reckoned as an estate in the land. On the Continent, the idea that a lease does not create a right in rem has persisted longer, and it seems that in French Law a leasehold interest is still regarded as a personal, not a real right,[38] though this does not carry the consequence, as in Roman Law, that the lessee can be ejected by a purchaser of the land.[39] In modern systems

---

[36] Dig. 19. 2. 22, 2. Sabinus (Dig. 18. 1. 20) gives a better reason, viz., the principal thing comes from me (quoniam a me substantia proficiscitur), i.e., the building accedes to the soil.
[37] Dig. 50. 16. 5, 1.   [38] Amos & Walton, p. 104.
[39] Cod. 4. 65. 9; C. C. 1743. From the middle ages onwards it was matter of controversy whether " sale breaks hire " or " hire goes before sale." The question was variously decided. To say that " hire goes before sale " does not necessarily mean that the lessee has a real right. It may give him security only against the lessor and persons claiming under him, not against third parties.

of law lessees can usually protect themselves against disturbance by taking steps to have their lease registered against the lessor's title. In South Africa leases in longum tempus, *i.e.*, for ten years and upwards, require registration if they are to affect purchasers without notice.[40]

495. What has been said relates to ordinary leases of land, which were usually of short duration, and in the case of agricultural tenancies did not exceed five years. But in ager vectigalis, and later under the name of emphyteusis, the Roman Law recognised a lease for a long term of years or in perpetuity. This has been described above (§ 256).

496. REMUNERATION.—The third term in the contract of hire is the remuneration or rent (merces). This must consist in money, though it appears that this was at one time a disputed question as in the case of price in the contract of sale. It must be certain or ascertainable. It must be genuine.[41] It need not be fair (in the technical sense), *i.e.*, the rule of laesio enormis does not apply. Suppose the remuneration is to be fixed by a third person, is there a contract of hire? Yes, if he actually fixes the amount; no, if he does not. Suppose the amount is left to the discretion of one of the parties. Clearly there is no contract of hire, but there would be a right to compensation for services rendered which could be enforced by the actio praescriptis verbis (§ 524). The rule that the remuneration must consist in money admitted of one exception. In the case of agricultural tenancies it might consist in a portion of the fruits, whether determined absolutely, *e.g.*, so much oil from an olive garden (pars quanta), or in a fixed proportion of the yearly yield (pars quota). A hiring of this kind was known as colonia partiaria.[42]

497. In certain cases the dividing line between hire and other contracts was not easy to draw. Such were:—(a) emphyteusis, which resembled both hire and sale, and was finally decided to be neither, but a special contract governed by rules of its own (§ 256)[43]; (b) the case of the gladiators. I supply you with gladiators on the terms that you are to pay me twenty denarii for each man who survives unharmed, and a thousand denarii for each man who is killed or maimed. The prevailing opinion, says Gaius, is that it is hire of those that come out unharmed,

3. 24. 2.
3. 24. 1.

---

40 Lee, p. 153.
41 Dig. 41. 2. 10, 2: quia conductio nulla est quae est in uno nummo.
42 Dig. 19. 2. 25, 6; Cod. 4. 65. 21; Girard, p. 605.
43 G. 3. 145; Inst. 3. 24. 3.

but sale of those who are killed or disabled: which it is the event declares, there being understood to be a conditional sale or hire of each gladiator [44] ; (c) the case of the goldsmith. He is to make rings, supplying the material. It was ultimately decided that this was sale, not hire, nor, as Cassius held, sale of the materials and hire of the goldsmith's labour [45] ; (d) the case of the fuller or tailor. Clothes are to be cleaned or mended. If the charge is fixed, the contract is hire. If the man is to be paid for his services, but the amount is to be determined later by agreement, there is no contract of hire, but if the service has been rendered, he can recover the value of his services in the actio praescriptis verbis (§ 524). If he is to do the work for nothing (quod raro accidit) it is mandate.[46]

498. The duties of the letter of a thing (locator rei) were: — 1. to procure to the hirer its use and enjoyment for the purpose contemplated by the contract; 2. to keep it in repair (except that the hirer was responsible for trifling repairs): 3. to compensate him for necessary and useful expenses.[47]

To the first head may be referred the letter's liability to deliver the thing free from defects. The extent of this liability varied with the circumstances. If I hire from you wine-vats, it is obvious that you must supply vats which do not leak. If you fail to do so, you have not supplied what I was entitled to get. Your ignorance of the defect is irrelevant. But if I take a lease from you of pasture lands, which produce poisonous herbs, you will be liable in damages if this was known (or should have been known) to you; otherwise I can only claim a remission of the rent.[48] The aedilician edict did not apply to the contract of hire,[49] but the letter's duty to supply a thing fit for its purpose had substantially the same effect.

The letter was not responsible for disturbance or eviction due to a cause which came into existence after the conclusion of the contract unless it was attributable to his own act. Thus he was not liable if land which he had given on lease was

---

[44] G. 3. 146. The explanation is designed to get over the difficulty that I cannot sell a dead slave (§ 466). It is not entirely satisfactory.

[45] G. 3. 147; Inst. 3. 24. 4. Compare for English law, *Lee* v. *Griffin* (1861) 1 B. & S. 272; *Robinson* v. *Graves* [1935] 1 K.B. 579.

[46] G. 3. 143; Inst. 3. 24. 1; 3. 26. 13; Dig. 19. 5. 22.

[47] Dig. 19. 2. 55, 1. Necessary expenses are such as are required to preserve the property from destruction or depreciation. Useful expenses increase the value of the property, though their omission would not render it less valuable.

[48] Dig. 19. 2. 19, 1.

[49] Dig. 21. 1. 63.

expropriated by public authority. But he must forgo his claim to rent.[50]

499. The duties of the hirer of a thing (conductor rei) were mainly:—1. to retain possession of the thing for the time agreed [51] ; 2. to take proper care of it—thus, to keep agricultural land in proper cultivation,[52] not to overload a hired beast of burden [53] ; 3. to pay the agreed merces, subject to just ground of excuse.

500. Both parties were required to exercise exacta diligentia, in other words were answerable for dolus and culpa levis in abstracto (§ 417).[54]

501. In the case of hire of services the parties were bound, on the one hand to render, on the other hand to accept, the agreed services. Wages fell due de die in diem. Consequently an employee could claim no wages for time in which he was absent from illness. But it was otherwise if work was suspended by an entirely impersonal cause such as the flooding of a mine,[55] though in this case employers sometimes excluded their liability for wages by a special term in the contract.[56]

502. Just as the hirer of services need not pay for services not rendered, so the hirer of land need not pay for land the use of which had not been enjoyed. Consequently, he was entitled to a remission of rent, if there was failure of crops due to storms of extraordinary violence, earthquake, flood, hostile incursion, or other causes falling under the general description of vis major.[57] But good years must be set off against bad, and if the landlord had remitted the rent and subsequent years were unusually productive, he might claim to be reimbursed.[58]

---

[50] Dig. 19. 2. 33.
[51] Dig. 19. 2. 55, 2. Was the hirer bound to accept delivery and enter into possession, as stated by Girard (p. 608) and Buckland (T. p. 500)? No text says that he was. I learn on good authority that no such duty exists in French or in German Law. If, as has been thought, the contract was real before it was consensual, it may well have been the same in Roman Law.
[52] Dig. 19. 2. 25, 3 ; 30, 2. He was liable for diligentia in custodiendo (§§ 418, 475), sometimes for custodia. G. 3. 205 ; Cod. 4. 65. 28.
[53] Dig. 19. 2. 25, 3 ; 30, 2.
[54] Inst. 3. 24. 5 (conductor rei) ; Dig. 19. 2. 24, 7 (conductor operis).
[55] Dig. 19. 2. 38, qui operas suas locavit totius temporis mercedem accipere debet, si per eum non stetit quo minus operas praestet.
[56] Girard, p. 608, n. 3.
[57] Dig. 19. 2. 25, 6. Vis major (or major casus) means inevitable accident, cui humana infirmitas resistere non potest, Dig. 44. 7. 1, 4. Casus fortuitus and damnum fatale mean much the same.
[58] Dig. 19. 2. 15, 4 ; Cod. 4. 65. 8.

503. The contract of hire was determined:—1. by expiration
of the agreed term, if any; otherwise at the will of either party.
In the case of agricultural tenancies, if the tenant remained
in possession after expiry of the term with consent, but without
special agreement, there was an implied renewal (tacita relocatio)
for one year.   In other cases it seems that the hirer remaining
in possession was required to pay merely for the actual period
of use or enjoyment (prout quisque habitaverit) [59]; 2. by mutual
consent; 3. by either party for just cause; thus *by the lessee*:—
if the premises were not kept in adequate repair, or if he was
otherwise prevented by the lessor or even by a third party from
using the property as agreed (*e.g.*, Titius lets a house to Gaius.
An adjoining proprietor builds so as to obscure his lights.   Gaius
may repudiate the contract) [60]; *by the lessor*:—if the lessee was
wasting the property; or failed to pay the rent for two years;
or if the lessor had urgent need of the property for his own use,
or required possession in order to effect repairs; 4. by merger
of the titles of both parties in the same person; 5. by destruction
of the subject-matter of the contract; 6. by death of a locator
operarum.

504. A special case of locatio conductio was carriage by sea,
regulated by the so-called lex Rhodia, which is the source of the
mercantile law of average.[61]

505. Actions.   The locator had the actio locati, the conductor the actio conducti.   The interdictum Salvianum and the
actio Serviana were available to a landlord to secure his rent
(§ 261).

THE INSTITUTES

BOOK III

TITLE XXIV

Of letting and hiring

The contract of letting and hiring comes very near to purchase   § 489.
and sale and is governed by the same rules.   For just as sale is
concluded by an agreement as to the price, so hire implies an agreement as to the rent or remuneration.   The letter has an action on the
letting (actio locati); the hirer has an action on the hiring (actio
conducti).

---

[59] Dig. 19. 2. 13, 11.
[60] Dig. 19. 2. 25, 2.
[61] Dig. 14. 2; Paul, 2. 7; Girard, p. 610; Buckl. *T*. p. 506.

§ 524.

§ 496.

1. What was said above as to the ascertainment of the price in the contract of sale being left to a third party applies equally to the ascertainment of the remuneration in the contract of hire. Accordingly, if any one gives clothes to a fuller to be cleaned or attended to, or to a tailor for mending, and there is no agreement at the moment as to what is to be paid, but the sum is afterwards to be fixed by agreement, properly speaking there is no contract of hire, but the fuller or tailor will have the actio praescriptis verbis.

2. Again, just as the question was commonly raised whether there was a contract of sale, when things were to be given in exchange for things and not for money, so it was questioned whether there was a contract of hire, if, for example, someone gave you a thing for use or enjoyment and received from you some other thing for use or enjoyment. It is settled that this is not hire, but a contract of a special kind. For example, there are two neighbours. Each owns an ox. They agree each to lend his ox to the other for ten days for a certain work, and then one of the oxen dies while working for the man to whom it does not belong. An action does not lie on a contract of hire, nor on a contract of loan, for there was no gratuitous loan, but an action must be brought on the special circumstances of the case (actio praescriptis verbis).

§ 497.

3. Sale and hire are so closely allied that sometimes it is a question whether a contract is one or the other. For example, when land is given to be enjoyed in perpetuity, that is to say on the terms that so long as the rent is paid to the owner of the soil, he may not reclaim the land from the lessee or his heir, or from any one to whom the lessee or his heir may have transferred the land by way of sale, gift, constitution of a dos, or by any other title. The old lawyers doubted whether a contract of this nature was hire or sale, some taking one view, some the other. Consequently, Zeno's

§ 256.

constitution was enacted, which decided that the contract of emphyteusis was a thing apart, not to be referred either to hire or to sale, but resting upon its own special terms. If the parties came to any special arrangement this was to be regarded as an essential part of the contract. If there was no express agreement as to risk, then the risk of total destruction was to be with the owner of the soil, the risk of partial destruction with the emphyteutic tenant. This is still law.

§ 497.

4. Again, the question was raised—if Titius agrees with a goldsmith that he is to make rings of a certain weight and a certain pattern out of his own gold and is to receive, say ten aurei, is this sale or hire? Cassius said that it was sale of the material, and hire of the goldsmith's labour. But it is decided that it is sale and sale only. If Titius furnishes the gold, and the goldsmith is to do the work for an agreed reward, the contract is undoubtedly hire.

§ 417.

5. The hirer must observe in all respects the terms of the hiring and, if anything is not provided for, he must do what is right and fair in the circumstances. If a person has paid or promised to pay a sum for the use of clothes, or plate, or a beast of burden, he is required to take the same care of it as a very careful father of a family applies to his own affairs. If he does this and has lost the thing by accident, he will not be liable for failing to restore it.

6. If the hirer dies while the period of the hire is still running his heir succeeds to the contract on the same terms.

IX. Partnership (Societas)

506. Partnership is " a contract for reciprocal performances directed to a common purpose " (Sohm)—" It was essentially the union of funds, skill or labour, or a combination of them, for a common purpose, which often had, but need not have, profit for its aim " (Buckland).

507. The following kinds of partnership are distinguished: — [62]

1. universal partnership (societas universorum bonorum). This, no doubt, grew out of the ancient institution of consortium, which was the name given to the relation between sui heredes holding together after the death of the paterfamilias (§ 513). But in later times universal partnership existed only by agreement. Perhaps Ulpian had this type of partnership in view when he said that partnership is a relation of brotherhood [63] ;

2. partnership in all business transactions (societas universorum quae ex quaestu veniunt) ;

3. partnership in a particular business (societas alicujus negotiationis) ;

4. partnership in farming the revenues (societas vectigalis or vectigalium). The Roman way of collecting taxes, particularly the land-tax (vegtigal), was to sell to a company of speculators for an agreed price the right to collect and retain the tax paid by individuals. Such partnerships belong to the sphere of public law and have little in common with the " private partnerships " above described. In particular, partnerships of this kind were not determined by death, as were the ordinary partnerships.[64] These speculators were known as publicani, for which the English equivalent is " tax-farmers " or " farmers of the revenue." [65]

5. partnership in a thing or a particular transaction (societas unius rei). Partnership in a thing is not easily distinguished from co-ownership. It was a question of intention. If the parties intended to create the partnership relation, there was partnership, otherwise not. A case is put in the Digest of a joint purchase by neighbours of a site adjoining their houses to prevent interference with the access of light.[66] This constituted

---

[62] Dig. 17. 2. 5 pr.; 7; Inst. 3. 25 pr.
[63] Dig. 17. 2. 63 pr.: cum societas jus quodammodo fraternitatis in se habeat.
[64] *Infra*, § 510.
[65] To farm the taxes means to sell or buy the right to collect them. For particulars, see Jolowicz, pp. 36, 37, and, more fully, Greenidge, p. 230.
[66] Dig. 17. 2. 52, 13.

a partnership relation. In another case there was a partnership, but it was doubtful whether it was in a thing or in a transaction. You have three horses and I one, and we enter into a partnership on the terms that you shall take my horse, sell the whole team of four and give me a quarter of the price received. According to Celsus it is a question of construction whether there is a partnership in the horses before sale or only in the selling of them (as he held to be the case). On the second hypothesis, my horse having died before sale, the partnership fails to take effect and I have no claim to any share in the price realised by the sale of your horses. On the other hypothesis the death of my horse is a partnership loss and the three remaining horses are sold for partnership account.[67]

508. ESSENTIAL ELEMENTS IN THE CONTRACT.

1. A contribution by each of the partners. The contribution need not be equal or similar. One partner may contribute his capital, another his industry, for one man's services may be worth as much as another man's money. But each must contribute something.

2. A common interest. Each partner must be entitled to some (not necessarily an equal) advantage. The shares in profit and loss may be fixed by agreement; failing which, they are deemed to be equal. If the share in profits is fixed, but not in losses, or conversely, the share in the one is taken to be the same as in the other. An agreement that a partner should have a larger share in profits than in losses was good, and it might even be agreed that a partner should share in profits and not in losses. But a contract that one should share in losses but not in profits was a lion and jackal arrangement, which was not permitted (leonina societas).[68]

3. The intention to form a partnership (affectio societatis). This was sometimes the only thing to distinguish partnership from joint ownership.[69]

4. A lawful object.[70]

509. DUTIES OF THE PARTNERS INTER SE.—Partners are bound reciprocally:—

1. each to contribute his share as agreed;
2. to share profits and losses as agreed;

Margin notes: 3. 25. 2. / 3. 25. 1. / 3. 25. 3 / 3. 25. 2.

---

[67] Dig. 17. 2. 58 pr.
[68] Dig. 17. 2. 29, 2.
[69] Dig. 17. 2. 31.
[70] Dig. 17. 2. 57.

3. each to indemnify the other *pro rata* against all expenses and liabilities properly incurred on behalf of the partnership;

4. in all partnership business to exhibit the diligentia quam suis rebus. So the law was settled, perhaps by Justinian, though the words of the Institutes repeat a passage in the Digest attributed to Gaius.[71] The actual functions of each partner in the business were in each case matter of arrangement.

3. 25. 9.

510. HOW PARTNERSHIP IS DETERMINED.—Ulpian says that partnership is dissolved [72]:—1. by events connected with the person (ex personis); 2. by events connected with the subject-matter (ex rebus); 3. by an act of the will (ex voluntate); 4. by a juridical act (ex actione). Expanding this summary we may say that a partnership is determined:—

(a) by any change in the persons composing the group, particularly by the death of one of the partners; or if one of the partners incurred a forfeiture of the whole of his estate (publicatio), or becoming insolvent, made a cession of his goods to his creditors (cessio bonorum).

3. 25. 5.

Gaius notes that, " partnership is said to be dissolved by capitis deminutio," [73] which suggests a doubt. In Justinian's law capitis deminutio had no effect except in the case of c. d. maxima, which involved forfeiture of goods. It is not mentioned in the Institutes amongst the causes of dissolution.

When it is said that death dissolves the partnership, what is meant is that it does not continue between the surviving partners nor between them and the heir of a deceased partner. An exception was admitted in the case of a societas vectigalium.[74] But the death of a partner did not put an end to the partnership until the other partners had knowledge of it,[75] and until an unfinished business was brought to completion the heir of a deceased partner was expected to exhibit the same diligence as a socius, and succeeded to the rights and duties of the deceased, so that he might be a party as plaintiff or defendant in an actio pro socio (§ 511). Partners might agree *ab initio* that if one died the survivors should remain in partnership,[76] but this was a new partnership, not a subsistence of the old one [77];

3. 25. 5.

---

[71] Dig. 17. 2. 72.
[72] Dig. 17. 2. 63, 10.
[73] G. 3. 153.
[74] 17. 2. 52 ; 59 pr. ; 65. 9.
[75] Dig. 17. 2. 65, 10.
[76] Inst. 3. 25. 5 ; Dig. 17. 2. 65, 9.
[77] Buckl. *T.* p. 519.

3. 25. 6.
(b) when the object of the partnership has been accomplished or becomes impossible of realisation, or when the partnership capital is exhausted ;

3. 25. 4.
(c) by the will of the partners or any one of them (renuntiatio), or by the arrival of the date, or the happening of the event, fixed in advance for the determination of the partnership. A partner might at any time renounce the partnership ; either expressly, or tacitly as by selling his share in the partnership property. But, if he renounced unreasonably in breach of an agreement that the partnership was to continue for a certain time, he exposed himself to an actio pro socio. If he renounced with the fraudulent design of getting a benefit for himself, *e.g.*, if one of the partners in a universal partnership renounced in anticipation of an inheritance coming to him with the design of keeping it to himself, he was obliged to share it, if profitable, with the other partners. If it proved a source of loss, he had to bear the loss himself. As Cassius puts it, he freed his partners from himself, but not himself from his partners [78] ;

(d) by bringing an action for the liquidation of the partnership. This was equivalent to renunciation. Paulus using the word actio " in its widest sense to denote any juristic act " refers to the same head a stipulation [79] changing the character of the partnership (changing the terms or the parties). This would effect a novation (§ 660), and might have been referred to the head of renunciation.

4. 16. 2.
511. The actio pro socio lay to enforce the duties of the partners *inter se*, and, in particular, for an account. Condemnation involved infamia (§ 317). On the other hand, a defendant might plead the beneficium competentiae (§ 217).[80] Since
4. 6. 38.
partners were usually joint owners, they had also the actio communi dividundo for division of the common property and adjudication (§ 722).

512. THE GENERAL ASPECTS OF PARTNERSHIP IN ROMAN LAW.

1. A societas was not generally a juristic person, but it is questioned whether the great partnerships formed to undertake public works or to farm the revenues (societates publicanorum) were or might be so.[81]

2. By English Law (Partnership Act, 1890, s. 5) " Every partner is an agent of the firm and his other partners for the

---

[78] Dig. 17. 2. 65, 3.
[79] Dig. 17. 2. 65 pr. ; Buckl. *T.* p. 512.
[80] Dig. 17. 2. 63 pr.
[81] Buckl. *T.* p. 513 ; *M.* p. 298.

purpose of the business of the partnership." In Roman Law this was not so. One partner had no implied authority to bind the others even in matters strictly within the business of the partnership. But the other partners might be liable:—(a) if they had made the partner their agent or ratified his action; (b) if he contracted in the name of the partnership and they had been benefited. If he contracted in his own name and on his own account they would not in any case be liable to third parties.[82]

3. In English Law partnership is defined (P. A., s. 1 (1)) as, "the relation which subsists between persons carrying on a business in common with a view of profit." A view of profit is not essential to the Roman conception of partnership.

4. In English Law, subject to any agreement between the parties, every partnership is dissolved as between all the parties by the death of any partner (P. A., s. 33 (1)). In Roman Law no such agreement was permitted in ordinary partnerships.

513. APPENDIX.—Fresh and unsuspected light has been thrown upon the ancient institution of consortium by the fragments of Gaius discovered in Egypt and published in 1933.[83] The opening words of the fragment relating to societas coincide with the concluding words of Gaius III, 154 in the Verona palimpsest. What follows (154a; 154b) is new matter not found in the Verona text. The passage runs as follows:—

154. The partnership of which we are speaking, namely, that which is contracted by mere consent, is juris gentium, and so it exists amongst all men by natural reason.

154a. But there is another kind of partnership peculiar to Roman citizens. For, anciently, on the death of the paterfamilias, there was a partnership between sui heredes which was statutory and at the same time natural (legitima simul et naturalis), which was called ercto non cito, that is, partnership with undivided dominium. The word erctum means dominium, from which we get erus meaning dominus. The word ciere means to divide, whence we say cedere [? caedere] and secare.

154b. Others too who wanted to have this partnership could accomplish their object before the praetor by a certain legis actio. In this partnership of brothers and of others who contracted a partnership after the model of brother co-heirs, there was this peculiarity that any one of the partners by manumitting a slave owned in common, made him free and acquired a freedman (i.e., rights of patronage) for all the co-owners; and, similarly, by mancipating . . .

---

[82] Moyle, p. 448.

[83] The text with translation and notes by Prof. de Zulueta under the title *Supplements to the Institutes of Gaius* was published by the Clarendon Press in 1935.

Here the fragment ends. It confirms the view that the earliest form of partnership arose by operation of law, when sui heredes held together in a joint family without dividing the estate. A voluntary association of the same kind might be brought into existence by means of a legis actio, possibly a fictitious allegation of co-heirship.

G. 2. 219.
[It has been maintained that the explanation given in the text of the ancient phrase ercto non cito is wrong, since (it is said) the idea of division is contained in the word ercto, as appears from the judicium familiae erciscundae—the action for division of the estate. On this hypothesis the phrase means, " division not being put in motion," or, " promoted " (cito from ciere = to put in motion). But it is more likely that Gaius is right. Erctum means property. The judicium familiae erciscundae is the action for appropriation of shares in the estate.

The word " cito " in the combination " ercto non cito " is not the past participle of the classical verb ciere, for it is cīto, not cito (Servius ad Aen. VIII. 642; Bruns. ii. 79). It may well belong to a forgotten verb meaning " cut " or " divide." Perhaps the judicium familiae erciscundae got its name from ercti ciendi, which, being read as one word, suggested a fictitious verb ercisci, unknown except in this connection.] [84]

THE INSTITUTES

BOOK III

TITLE XXV

Of partnership

§ 507.
A partnership may relate either to all the goods of the partners or to a particular business, for example the purchase and sale of slaves, or of oil, wine or grain. 1. If there is no express agreement
§ 508.
as to the proportion in which the partners are to share in profit and loss, the shares in each are understood to be equal. Any express agreement must be respected; for there has never been any doubt as to the validity of an agreement that one partner should share in profit and loss to the extent of two-thirds, the other to the extent of one-third.

2. But the question was raised whether an agreement could be upheld by which, for example, Titius is to have two-thirds of the profit and bear one-third of the loss, while Seius is to bear two-thirds of the loss and take one-third of the profit. Quintus Mucius thought that such an agreement was contrary to the nature of partnership and therefore could not be approved. Servius Sulpicius took the opposite view, and this has prevailed, for it often happens

---

[84] I have borrowed this suggestion from the Notae Varieorum to Aulus Gellius (1. 10. q. in vol. III of the Delphine edition of 1824 (p. 1074)).

that a man's services are so valuable to the partnership that it is fair that he should be accepted as a partner on more advantageous terms. Indeed, there is no doubt that a partnership may be concluded on the terms that one partner is to make a contribution in money and the other is not to do so, and yet profits are to be shared equally, for a man's services are often equivalent to money, Accordingly, against the opinion of Quintus Mucius and in accordance with the view entertained by Servius consistently with his principle, it is established that a partnership may be constituted on the terms that one of the partners shall share in profit but not be liable for loss. This must be understood in the sense that if one transaction proves profitable, another the reverse, a balance is to be struck, and the net gain (if any) is to be regarded as profit. 3. It is clear that if the shares are expressed in respect of profit only or of loss only, nothing being provided for the opposite event, the shares will be the same in the one case as in the other. 4. Partnership continues so long as the § 510. partners remain of the same mind, but as soon as any one partner renounces the partnership it is dissolved. Of course, if any one renounces the partnership with the cunning design of keeping to himself some anticipated gain, for example, if there is a universal partnership, and one of the partners, being instituted heir, renounces with the purpose of enjoying the inheritance alone, he is obliged to share the gain with the others. But if he acquires any other gain without such fraudulent design, it goes to him alone and, similarly, the partner to whom the renunciation is made keeps for himself anything acquired after the renunciation.

5. Again, the death of any partner dissolves the partnership [and his heir does not take his place], for when a man enters into a partnership, he selects a particular person to be his partner. If several persons have agreed to form a partnership, the death of any one of them dissolves it, though there may be several survivors, unless there was an agreement to the contrary when the partnership was formed. 6. If a partnership is formed for a specific purpose it comes to an end when the business is accomplished.

7. It is evident that forfeiture of goods puts an end to a partnership, that is to say, if the whole estate of one of the partners is forfeited, for, since the fiscus takes his place, he is considered to be civilly dead.

8. If one of the partners finding his circumstances embarrassed has made cession of his goods and his estate is sold to satisfy his public or private debts the partnership is dissolved. But, in this case, if all agree to remain in partnership, a new partnership is deemed to be formed.

9. It was formerly a question whether in the actio pro socio a § 509. partner was answerable for dolus merely, like the depositary, or also for culpa, that is for slackness and negligence, and this second view has prevailed. But negligence is not to be measured by the standard of most exact diligence. It is enough for a partner to apply to partnership business as much care as he exhibits in his own concerns. If a man takes to himself a careless partner, he must blame himself and no one else.

X. Mandate (Mandatum)

514. Mandate is a contract whereby one person (mandator) gives another (mandatarius) a commission to do something for him without reward, and the other accepts the commission. It is imperfectly bilateral (§ 408), because, though it may give rise to reciprocal rights and duties, the duty of the mandatarius arises immediately upon the acceptance of the commission, while the duty of the mandator, *viz.*, to indemnify the mandatarius against loss and liability, is merely contingent.

3. 26. 7.

515. Essential Elements.—1. The object of the contract must be lawful. It may consist either in general management (procuratio omnium bonorum) or in the doing of a specific act (procuratio unius rei). It may, but does not necessarily, imply entering into legal relations with a third party.

3. 26 pr.

2. The mandator (it is said) must have an interest in the thing to be done by the mandatarius.[85] I may give a mandate in the interest of (a) myself alone (mea gratia); (b) myself and you (mea et tua gratia); (c) myself and a third party (mea et aliena gratia); (d) a third party alone (aliena gratia[86]); (e) you and a third party (tua et aliena gratia); (f) you alone (tua gratia). If the requirement of interest is strictly construed the first three constitute a mandate properly so called, the last three not. But some mandates which were not directly in the interest of the mandator came to be upheld as a valid contract because by giving a mandate aliena gratia or tua et aliena gratia I placed myself as regards the third party in the position of a negotiorum gestor (§ 585), and as such acquired a personal liability and consequent interest in the execution of the mandate; and, further, if you do an act at my instance and suffer loss in consequence you are held to be entitled to an indemnity because, if left to yourself, you might not have acted as you did. Such was the opinion of Sabinus in the case of my having given

3. 26. 6.

you a mandate to lend money at interest to Titius, " because but for the mandate you would not have given him credit." This introduces into the law a new principle. The binding character of the mandate is no longer based upon interest which the mandator has in its execution, but upon the detriment to the mandatarius in changing his position at the mandator's instance. In fact, so far was a mandate of this character from being invalid that under the name of mandatum credendae pecuniae or, as the commentators call it, mandatum qualificatum (§ 574),

[85] Dig. 17. 1. 8, 6.
[86] Dig. 17 1. 2.

it became a common method of creating the relation of principal and surety. There is a passage in the Digest in which Ulpian is made to apply the same reasoning to any mandatum tua gratia, but it is clearly interpolated.[87] It marks, however, in the law of Justinian a complete abandonment of the rule that a mandator must have an interest in the subject of the mandate; though, even so, it remained important to distinguish mandate from mere advice, which, however unfortunate for the person who acted upon it, did not entitle him to claim an indemnity from the person who gave it.

3. The mandate must be gratuitous. This rule, like the last, did not persist in practice, or was matter of form rather than of substance. If a reward was agreed upon, and the affair was capable of falling under the contract of hire (§ 493), the contract would be locatio conductio. In other cases an agreed remuneration (honorarium—salarium) could be recovered by means of the extra-ordinary jurisdiction of the magistrate (§ 758). 3. 26. 13.

516. DUTIES OF THE PARTIES.—The mandatarius was bound:—1. to execute the mandate, subject to the right of renouncing it re adhuc integra, i.e., while he can do so without prejudice to the mandator and subject to just excuse for failure to renounce at all, or in good time; 2. not to exceed the mandate; 3. to exercise exacta diligentia.[88] In the classical law he was liable only for dolus[89]; 4. to render accounts; 5. to make over to the mandator all benefits accruing from the mandate including rights of action against third parties. 3. 26. 11.

3. 26. 8.

517. The duties of the mandator were principally:—1. to indemnify the mandatarius against expense, loss and liability incurred in the execution of the mandate[90]; 2. not to revoke the mandate to his prejudice.

518. Mandate may be determined:—

(a) by mutual consent, viz., either by arranging in advance for the termination of the mandate after a certain time or in a certain event; or by subsequent agreement;

(b) by unilateral revocation or renunciation, but not without liability unless made re integra, viz., by the mandator before the mandatarius has done anything in execution of his commission; by the mandatarius, so that by renouncing he does not put the

---

[87] Dig. 17. 1. 6, 5; Girard, p. 620, n. 5; Buckl. *T.* p. 515; *M.* p. 300.
[88] Cod. 4. 35. 13.
[89] Modestinus in *Coll.* 10. 2. 3.　　　　[90] Dig. 47. 2. 62 (61), 5.

mandator in a position in which he cannot conveniently do the thing himself or get some one else to do it for him;

(c) by the death of either party. But if the mandatarius has proceeded to act, or continued to act, in ignorance of the mandator's death he is entitled to be indemnified by the heirs; conversely, the heirs of the mandatarius are bound to take necessary steps to wind up the business in hand.[91]

The texts of the Digest leave some uncertainty as to the effect of a mandate to do something after the death of the mandator (mandatum post mortem), *e.g.*, a mandate to my debtor to pay such person after my death, a mandate to see to my funeral or to raise a monument to my memory. Such a mandate was exposed to two objections, first, that a mandate is determined by death; secondly, that an obligation could not begin in the person of the heir. But in some cases such mandates are stated to be valid, and in Justinian's system they were free from objection, the second of the above rules having been formally abolished.[92]

The death of the mandatarius always determined the mandate except to the limited extent above mentioned.

519. Actions. The mandator had the actio mandati directa, the mandatarius the actio mandati contraria. Condemnation in the direct action involved infamia. There was besides the extraordinaria cognitio for remuneration.

520. MANDATE AND AGENCY.—We are apt to think of mandatum in terms of agency, and the word agency is sometimes employed to translate the word mandatum. But this is incorrect. In the law of contract agency implies a contractual relation established between one person termed the principal and a third party by another person termed the agent, who acts as intermediary. In English Law, at least, the topic " Principal and Agent " is mainly concerned with this relation, though also with the relation of Principal and Agent *inter se*. But mandate is essentially a contract of employment and its rules are concerned only with the reciprocal rights and duties of the mandator on the one hand and the mandatarius on the other. It is true that the contract of mandate played a part in other branches of the law, and contributed in an important degree to their development. These are:—

(a) Agency (as above defined) (§ 571);

---

[91] There is no text, but no doubt it was so as in partnership. Dig. 17. 2. 40.
[92] Buckl. *T.* p. 517; *M.* p. 301.

(b) Suretyship (§ 574) ;

(c) Assignment of Obligations (§ 649).

But the employment of the contract of mandate in these several spheres is best reserved for future consideration as occasion arises.

THE INSTITUTES

BOOK III

TITLE XXVI

Of mandate

There are five modes of mandate. A man may give you a mandate for his own benefit alone, for his and yours, for a third party's alone, for his and a third party's, for yours and a third party's. If you are given a mandate in your own interest alone, it is an empty mandate, and gives rise to no obligation or action of mandate between you two. 1. A mandate is solely in the interest of the mandator when, for example, a man gives you a mandate to look after his affairs, to buy a property for him, or to be his surety. 2. A mandate is in the interest of yourself and of the mandator, when, for example, a man gives you a mandate to lend money at interest to some one who is borrowing the money in connection with the mandator's business; or if when you are about to proceed against him in a matter in which he has gone surety, he gives you a mandate to proceed instead against the principal debtor at his risk, or, at his risk to stipulate from a person whom he delegates to you for payment of what was due to you from himself. 3. There is a mandate in the interest of a third person alone if, for example, you are given a mandate to manage the affairs of Titius, or to buy a property for Titius, or to go surety for Titius. 4. A mandate is in the interest of the mandator and a third person if, for example, some one gives you a mandate to manage affairs in which he and Titius are jointly interested, or to buy property for himself and Titius, or to go surety for himself and Titius. § 515.

5. A mandate is in the interest of yourself and a third person, if you are given a mandate to lend money at interest to Titius. But a mandate to lend free of interest is a mandate in the interest of a third person alone. 6. A mandate is given in your interest alone if for example some one gives you a mandate to invest your money in the purchase of land rather than to lend it at interest, or conversely. But a mandate of this kind is rather advice than mandate, and, therefore, creates no obligation, for no one is liable to an action on mandate for giving mere advice, even though the advice does not turn out well for the person to whom it is given, for any one may form his own opinion as to the value of the advice given. Accordingly, if you have money lying idle and some one advises you to buy something with it, or to lend it, he is not liable to you on a mandate, even though the affair has not been to your advantage. This is so far the case, that it was a question whether a person was

liable on a mandate, if he gave you a mandate to lend money at interest to Titius. Sabinus held that such a mandate was binding, because but for the mandate you would not have let Titius have the money and this view has prevailed. 7. A mandate creates no obligation if it is contrary to good morals, for example, if Titius gives you a mandate to commit a delict, for, even though you incur a penalty in consequence, you have no action against Titius.

§ 516.   8. A mandatary must not go beyond the terms of his mandate. For example, if you have a mandate to buy or to go surety up to one hundred aurei, you must not buy for more, or go surety to a greater amount. Otherwise you have no action of mandate. Sabinus and Cassius went so far as to say that you cannot maintain an action even to the extent of the hundred. The other school took the opposite view and this is certainly the kinder solution. If you buy for less you will, of course, have your action, for a mandate to buy for a hundred implies a mandate to buy for less, if possible.

§ 518.   9. A valid mandate ceases to exist if it is revoked before the mandatary has acted upon it.

10. Again, the death of either party in similar circumstances [93] puts an end to the mandate. But from motives of convenience it is settled that if, in ignorance of the mandator's death, you have carried out the mandate, you have your action on the contract; otherwise you would be prejudiced by an excusable ignorance. Similarly, if persons who owe money to Titius pay his steward not knowing that he has been manumitted, they are discharged from the debt, though in strict law they could not be discharged, since they have paid some one to whom payment should not have been made.

11. No one is obliged to accept a mandate; but if a mandate is accepted it must be executed or renounced at the earliest possible moment, so as to give the mandator the opportunity of doing the thing himself, or getting some one else to do it for him. If this opportunity is not afforded him while things remain as they were, he will have his action on the mandate, unless the mandatary had good reason for not renouncing, or for not renouncing in time.

12. A mandate may be expressed to take effect from a future date or subject to a condition.

§ 515.   13. Finally, it must be remarked that if a mandate is not gratuitous it must be referred to some other type of contract. Thus, if the service is to be remunerated, it is a contract of hire; and it may be stated as a general principle that where in the absence of remuneration there is a contract of mandate or deposit, if there is agreement for remuneration there is a contract of hire. Therefore, if you give clothes to a fuller to be cleaned or attended to or to a tailor for mending, and there is no present agreement for remuneration or promise to fix it at a future date, an action of mandate is available.

---

[93] *integro mandato.* This means the same as dum integra res sit (sec. 9). Death dissolves the mandate in any event—mandatum solvitur morte, Dig. 17. 1. 26 pr.; but (and this is why the qualifying words are introduced) without prejudice to outstanding obligations. Julianus quoque scripsit mandatoris morte solvi mandatum, sed obligationem aliquando durare. *Ibid.*

XI. Nexum—Fiducia

521. We have now passed in review the "named contracts," real, verbal, literal and consensual. Before going on to consider some other types of actionable agreement a few words may be devoted to two institutions which find no place in Justinian's scheme—nexum and fiducia.

522. Nexum.—This goes back to a remote antiquity. In the early days of the Republic debtors used to bind themselves by a process per aes et libram resembling mancipation, which reduced them either (as some think) immediately (self-mancipation) or (as some think) on failure to repay (contract) to a position little better than slavery.[94] This state of things was ended by a lex Poetelia of B.C. 326 or some years later, which is described by Livy as follows: —

> "The consuls were ordered to bring before the people a measure providing that no one save one who had incurred a noxa (committed a guilty act)[95] should be kept fettered or bound until he discharged the penalty; that the debtor's property, not his person, should be liable for a money loan. So the bondsmen were set free and it was enacted that in future none should be bound."[96]

The subsequent history of this obscure institution is unknown. The contrary process of formal discharge per aes et libram is described by Gaius as existing (§ 656), but it must not be inferred from this that nexum was not already obsolete.

523. Fiducia (Trust).—We have met with this above in various connections (§§ 123, 129, 259). Here it will be useful to recall the passage in which Gaius mentions it in speaking of usucapion. This is what he says: —

> Lib. II, 59. There are other cases besides in which a man usucapes a thing which he knows does not belong to him. If a person has given a thing in trust (fiduciae causa) by mancipation or in jure cessio, and has come into possession of it, he can usucape it in one year, even though it be an immovable. This kind of usucapion is called usureception, because we recover by usucapion what once was ours. 60. But since a trust is contracted either with a creditor by right of pledge, or with a friend that our things may be safer in his keeping, if it is contracted with a friend usureception takes place in any event; if with a creditor always if the money is paid, but before payment only if the debtor has not hired the thing from the creditor or asked to have it on sufferance. If he has obtained possession in any other way lucrative usucapion is allowed (§ 175).

---

94 Buckl. *M*. p. 259.   95 Nisi qui noxam meruisset.
96 Livy, VIII, 28.

This passage gives the clue to the nature of fiducia. At a time when the distinction between possession and ownership was not yet sharply drawn transactions which later assumed the character of the real contracts pignus and depositum (and by inference commodatum as well) were effected by a transfer of ownership by one or other of the old civil law methods of mancipatio or in jure cessio ; the acquirer on his part giving an undertaking (pactum conventum) to re-transfer the ownership on payment or (as the case might be) on demand. Meanwhile the original owner easily recovered ownership by usucapion. The duty to re-convey was made good by the actio fiduciae, which was a bonae fidei judicium and relatively late.[97] The other party had a contraria actio for any claim for expenses, etc., which he might have against the original owner.[98]

Fiducia does not occur except as an incident of the conveyance of a person or a thing. It is a parasitic institution and was not looked upon as a contract. In the classical age it was still in common use to constitute a pledge.

XII. Innominate Contracts

524. There were cases in which there seemed to be undoubtedly a contract, but it was difficult to determine the precise juristic nature of the transaction in question. It might, for example, be on the border-line between sale and hire, or within the limits of the contract of hire it might be doubtful whether it was conductio rei or locatio operis (§ 491). In a case of this kind Labeo held that an action at civil law should be given upon the facts (civilem actionem in factum esse dandam Labeo scribit),[99] and the principle was applied in other similarly ambiguous cases. Ultimately, the action was extended beyond its original scope to include cases which clearly did not conform to any existing type of contract.[1] It was the practice to insert at the beginning of the formula a statement of fact (praescripta verba).[2] The plaintiff was said praescriptis verbis agere. This action, variously described as actio civilis incerti, actio civilis in factum and (ultimately) actio praescriptis verbis, came to be

---

[97] G. 4. 62. But it is at least as old as Q. Mucius Scaevola (fl. 100 B.C. § 11), who includes fiducia in his list of bonae fidei judicia. Cic. de Off. 3. 17. 70.

[98] Buckl. M. pp. 260, 261.

[99] Dig. 19. 5. 1, 1.

[1] Girard, p. 625.

[2] Cod. 2. 4. 6, 1: utilis actio quae praescriptis verbis rem gestam demonstrat.

available wherever there was an agreement for reciprocal performances, not referable to one of the recognised types of
consensual contract, and one party had done his part, while
the other had not. It was an action brought, as an English
lawyer would say, upon an executed consideration. Transactions of this kind are commonly described as innominate
real contracts. They are innominate, because they do not fall
within the definition of any of the recognised and named
contracts,[3] though in fact, as will be seen, they are sometimes
distinguished by appropriate names. They are real, because, as
in the case of the real contracts, it is the fact that something
has been done on one side that gives rise to the liability on the
other. But, whereas in the case of the real contracts proper,
this doing consists in the handing over of a res, to be returned
in kind or in specie, in the case of the innominate contracts one
party has done what he had undertaken to do in terms of an
antecedent agreement. It is said that there is no true analogy
between the two cases, and it is, perhaps, preferable to omit
the word " real " from the description, and to speak merely of
" innominate contracts." [4]

525. There were many transactions of this kind, some so
frequent as to be distinguished by particular names (though
not, therefore, technically " named " contracts). Thus—to
mention first the case of exchange (permutatio)—if I agree
to give you my ox in exchange for your horse, there is no
obligation, because exchange is not a consensual contract, but,
if in execution of the agreement I have given you my ox, I
shall have an action against you if you fail to give me your
horse. In the alternative I can reclaim my ox by a condictio.
To ground my action on the contract, it is necessary that I
should have made you owner of the ox, for it is not sufficient,
as in sale, merely to give quiet possession.[5] Another frequent
case was the bargain known as aestimatum, which gave rise to
an action known specifically as the actio de aestimato, and was
of sufficient importance to be the subject of a special chapter in
the Edict. This is a bargain, admitting of variations, by which
I deliver goods to you on the terms that you are to sell them for
what they will fetch, and pay me an agreed price. If you do
not sell them I am to have them back. If you sell them, as you
expect to do, for more than the agreed price you keep the

---

[3] Dig. 2. 14. 7 ; 19. 5. 1 pr.
[4] Buckl. *T.* p. 521 ; *M.* p. 303.
[5] Dig. 19. 4. 1, 3.

difference. This case falls under the head of the earlier type
of ambiguous transactions. Ulpian says that it was a great
question whether it was sale, or locatio operis, or conductio
operarum, or mandate, and consequently it seemed best (to the
praetor) to make it the subject of a special action.[6] Another
case was precarium, which was " a gratuitous grant of enjoyment
of land or goods, revocable at will." [7] This gave rise not only
to the interdict de precario for the recovery of the property from
the grantee (precario accipiens) but also (under Justinian) to the
actio praescriptis verbis. Yet another case was transactio or
compromise, in which the performance which grounds the action
was the renunciation of a contested claim. Many other cases
may be supposed in which something has been given or done on
one side on the terms that something is to be given or done (or
not done) on the other. A formula attributed to Paulus covers
most, but not all, of these cases. Aut enim do tibi ut des, aut
do ut facias, aut facio ut des, aut facio ut facias [8]—" Either I
give you that you may give, or I give that you may do, or I do
that you may give, or I do that you may do." As it happens,
aestimatum, perhaps the first agreement of the kind to receive
legal recognition, does not exactly conform to any one of these
four types.[9] It exhibits, however, the feature which is common
to all these cases, something done or given on one side giving
rise to a duty on the other.

XIII. Pacts

526. An agreement which did not conform to any type of
contract, nominate or innominate, was termed a " pact " or a
" bare pact." It did not ground an action, but might be
pleaded as a defence. Nuda pactio actionem non parit, sed
parit exceptionem.[10] Progressively, however, certain pacts were
made actionable, and so became contracts (or terms in a contract) in effect though not in name. Pacts raised to this higher
value are called by the commentators pacta vestita, i.e., pacts
which are not bare, and are, therefore, clothed. They fall into
three classes : —

(a) pacta adjecta ;

<hr>

[6] Dig. 19. 3. 1. In another text Ulpian says that it might be partnership. Dig. 17. 2. 44.
[7] Buckl. T. p. 524 ; M. p. 305. But like what we call a long loan it
might be practically as good as ownership.
[8] Dig. 19. 5 5 pr.
[9] Girard, p. 627.
[10] Dig. 2. 14. 7, 4.

(b) pacta praetoria ;

(c) pacta legitima.

527. Pacta Adjecta.—These are pacts annexed to some principal contract, intended to form part of it and to modify it ; for example, an agreement annexed to a contract of sale that the vendor shall not be liable in the event of eviction, or, conversely, that he shall add to his implied liability a personal security against eviction. In the law of Justinian, as a rule, pacts entered into contemporaneously with the principal contract (pacta in continenti adjecta) were taken to be part of it, whether the effect was to increase or to diminish the principal obligation, and whether this was a bonae fidei or a stricti juris contract.[11] The only exception was that interest could not be claimed upon a money loan, unless there was a stipulation to that effect (supra, § 421). But pacts made subsequently to the principal contract (pacta ex intervallo adjecta) were ineffectual to increase it, so as to enlarge a party's right of action, though they might be pleaded by way of defence (exceptio pacti).[12] In the case of the consensual contracts it was always open to the parties, omnibus integris manentibus, i.e., if nothing had been done on either side, to discharge the contract by mutual agreement and to make a new contract in its place.

528. Pacta Praetoria.—These were agreements which were recognised as binding by the praetor. The principal case was constitutum debiti, an informal agreement, to pay, usually on a named date, a sum of money (or to give some other fungible thing) due to the promisee from the promisor or a third person. In the first case it resembled what we call an account stated ; in the second case it was one of the ways of creating a suretyship (§ 575). It gave rise to an action called the actio de pecunia constituta.[13] 3. 29. 4. 4. 6. 8.

Other praetorian pacts of less importance were the voluntary oath (so-called jusjurandum voluntarium),[14] and various transactions of disparate nature known by the name of receptum. The receptum argentarii was an undertaking by a banker to honour his client's draft in favour of a third party. It resembled constitutum, with the difference that in this case there was no antecedent liability. Justinian put an end to it as a separate 4. 6. 11.

---

[11] Dig. 2. 14. 7, 5 ; 12. 1. 40.
[12] Dig. 18. 1. 72.
[13] Buckl. T. p. 529 ; M. p. 306 ; Schulz, pp. 560 et seq.
[14] To be distinguished from the jusjurandum necessarium, which was an incident of judicial procedure. See Inst. 4. 6. 11 and Moyle, ad loc. : Buckl. T. pp. 529, 633 ; M. pp. 308, 383.

institution. The receptum nautarum cauponum stabulariorum was the express (or implied?) undertaking of carriers by water, innkeepers or stable-keepers to be answerable (vis major excepted) for the safety of goods committed to their charge.[15] This must be distinguished from the liability quasi ex delicto to be mentioned below (§ 637). The receptum arbitri—an agreement to act as arbitrator—was binding in the sense that the person who had taken upon himself this function was (by administrative methods) compelled to act, but the parties to the submission had no action against him if he failed to do so.[16]

Hypotheca cannot be regarded as a praetorian pact, for the praetorian action to which it gave rise was an actio in rem, not an actio in personam. The topic belongs to the Law of Property (§ 261).

529. PACTA LEGITIMA.—Three pacts were made actionable by imperial legislation. These were:—

(a) an agreement to constitute a dos (pactum de constituenda dote), made actionable by Theodosius II in A.D. 428,[17] superseding the formal dotis dictio (§§ 223, 442);

(b) a promise to give (pactum donationis), made actionable by Justinian (§ 212);

(c) an agreement to refer a matter to arbitration (compromissum). This too was made binding by Justinian, but only to a limited extent, viz., if after the sentence of the arbitrator had been pronounced, the parties accepted it in writing or did not impugn it within ten days.[18] Until one or other of these conditions was satisfied the authority of the arbitrator to act was merely a mandate, revocable at will by either party. It may be remarked that compromissum is not equivalent to the English word compromise, which corresponds with the Latin transactio. It is the French compromis. In the literature of international law it is in common use, meaning the terms of a submission to arbitration.

XIV. UNILATERAL DECLARATIONS OF INTENTION

530. The contracts and pacts of which we have spoken have the common quality of being agreements—duorum pluriumve in idem placitum consensus[19]—duorum consensus

---

[15] Dig. 4. 9. 1.
[16] Buckl. T. p. 531; M. p. 309.
[17] Cod. 5. 11. 6.
[18] Cod. 2. 55 (56). 5.
[19] Dig. 2. 14. 1, 2.

atque conventio.[20]   There were two institutions, each of limited application, which were unilateral expressions of intention and sources of obligation—votum and pollicitatio.

531. VOTUM.—This was a vow made to a god. Ulpian in the Digest says: " If a person has vowed a thing, he is bound by his vow." Patresfamilias, that is persons sui juris of the male sex, could so bind themselves and so could sons and slaves in power by the authority of father or master. The obligation was transmitted to heirs.[21]   Nothing further is known. The institution seems to belong to the jus sacrum.

532. POLLICITATIO.—An   offer   or   unilateral   promise— offerentis solius promissum [22]—which in certain circumstances could not be withdrawn. It seems to be confined to the field of municipal or public law. If a person promised to finance or execute a work of public utility [23] in consideration of a magistracy or priesthood conferred or to be conferred upon him or for any other lawful cause, or if there was no such evident motive and the work had been begun by himself or by the town authority or either party had done something to give effect to it or he had transferred property to the town, the philanthropist was bound by his promise or could not reclaim the property, " for it is very right that benefits bestowed on cities should not be revoked because the donor changes his mind." [24] We are not told how the obligation was enforced.

Girard [25] mentions the case of offers of reward, e.g., for the pursuit and capture of a fugitive slave, and concludes that they did not create a legal obligation as they do in some modern systems of law.[26]

XV. Of Contract in General

533. There was a Roman law of contracts, but scarcely a law of contract, i.e., there was no theory of contract in general apart from the special classes of contract of which the law took account. However, the stipulatio occupies a position by itself, inasmuch as any promise to which the law would give effect could assume this form, and in connection with the stipulation, principles are stated which to a great extent are applicable to contracts in general. Most of these are to be found in Institutes

---

[20] Dig. 50. 12. 3 pr.   [21] Dig. 50. 12. 2.
[22] Dig. 50. 12. 3 pr.
[23] Dig. 50. 12. 13, 1.
[24] Dig. 50. 12. 1 & 3.
[25] p. 488.
                                                          [26] e.g., B. G. B., art. 657.

III, 19. With some re-arrangement they may be made to supply
a general theory of contract. We shall consider first, the formation of contract, *i.e.*, what is necessary to its initial validity;
secondly, the operation of contract, or the persons affected by it.

534. FORMATION OF CONTRACT.—In order that a valid contract may exist there must be:—(1) an agreement; (2) intended
to create, and (3) apt to create a legal obligation between the
parties; (4) relating to an object (act or forbearance), which is
possible, and lawful; (5) made between competent persons;
(6) not voidable on the ground of fraud or fear.

535. (1) The parties must be agreed, *i.e.*, there must be
consensus ad idem. This is absent if the expressed intention of
one party does not coincide with the expressed intention of the
other, *e.g.*, " Do you promise to give ten? " " I promise to give
five," or conversely. This is the illustration given in the
Institutes,[27] but in the Digest [28] Ulpian says, or is made to say,
that the stipulation was in either event good for the lesser
amount (§ 446).

536. There may be an apparent agreement where there is
no real agreement. This will be the case when a person thinks
that he is contracting with a certain person, when in fact he is
not, or when he thinks that the contract has a certain content
when in fact it has not. In such circumstances the apparent
contract is usually void, *i.e.*, no contract at all, because the
essential conditions of every contract, *viz.*, persons who agree
and something agreed upon are wanting. This brings us to the
topic of error or mistake.

537. The commentators distinguish different kinds of error
as (a) in persona, (b) in negotio, (c) in corpore, (d) in substantia.

538. (a) Error in persona. This occurs if I am mistaken as
to the identity of the person with whom I am contracting, *e.g.*, I
borrow money from A thinking that he is B. There is no contract of mutuum. But since it clearly would be unfair that I
should keep the money, Celsus advised that an action could be
brought for its recovery.[29] In modern systems mistake as to

---

27 Inst. 3. 19. 5.
28 Dig. 45. 1. 1, 4.
29 Dig. 12. 1. 32. This has been called the condictio Juventiana after
its author P. Juventius Celsus. Another case of error in persona is when
a person falsely represents himself as agent for another, with whom I
mistakenly su⌐ ɔse that I have contracted, as in a South African case, in
which an imposter, fraudulently representing himself as having authority
by buy horses for Government, sold them to a bona fide purchaser:
Beyers v. *McKenzie* (1880) Foord 125.

the person does not affect the contract unless there is some good reason why it should, as, for example, where there is a question of personal confidence or aptitude. The French civil code says, "mistake as to the person with whom one intends to contract does not cause the contract to be void unless the consideration of this person was the principal cause of the agreement." [30]

539. (b) Error in negotio. I hand over to you a thing by way of deposit. You accept it as a loan. No contract.[31] Intending partners are not agreed as to the terms of the partnership. No contract.[32]

540. (c) Error in corpore. I stipulate for the slave Stichus, you assent, but think I mean the slave Pamphilus, whom you suppose to be Stichus. No contract. I think I am buying the Cornelian estate. You think you are selling the Sempronian 3. 19. 23. estate. No contract.[33]

541. (d) Error in substantia. It may be that the parties are agreed as to the thing which is the object of their contract, but that they both are, or one of them is, mistaken as to an essential quality. The texts of the Corpus Juris consider this question principally in connection with the contract of sale.[34] The conclusion to be drawn from them is that if the difference between the thing as it is and as it is supposed to be makes it in effect a different thing, the sale is void.

> "You have unwittingly sold me a table overlaid with silver for one of solid silver without my knowing it to be so, the sale is void and a condictio will lie to recover the money paid for it." [35]

The case is the same if a thing is sold as gold, both parties believing it to be such, when in fact it is bronze.[36] These are cases of error common to both parties. But the same consequence follows if the error is on one side alone, provided that it is reasonable in the circumstances. You sell this thing knowing it to be bronze (but without saying that it is bronze, or is not bronze). I buy it supposing that it is being sold as gold. I am not bound by the contract. For, "in the civil law the sale was always avoided by the buyer's essential error, no matter

---

[30] C. C. 1110.
[31] Dig. 12. 1. 18, 1.
[32] Dig. 44. 7. 57.
[33] Dig. 18. 1. 9 pr.
[34] In the case of stipulation if the parties were agreed as to the corpus mistake as to the quality was irrelevant. Dig. 45. 1. 22.
[35] Dig. 18. 1. 41, 1.
[36] Dig. 18. 1. 14 in fine.

whether the seller shared in it or not." [37]   But in English Law
a mistake as to quality "will not affect assent, unless it is a
mistake of both parties and is as to the existence of some
quality which makes the thing without the quality essentially
different from the thing as it was believed to be." [38]

542. It seems that the Roman Law limited the application of
error in substantia (the phrase is not found in the sources) to
two cases, viz., when the thing is not of the material supposed,
as in the cases mentioned above, and mistake as to the sex of a
slave.[39]   In the course of the centuries it has been extended to
include any case of mistake as to a quality judged to be essential,
as, for example, when a picture supposed to be the original work
of a famous master is found to be a copy. This tradition has
passed into modern systems which have a Roman Law
foundation.[40]

543. It is said that where there is error of the kind considered
in the Roman texts there is no contract—nulla est emptio [41]—
but it would be more correct to say that there is a contract, but
one which may be avoided by the party who is the victim of the
mistake. If I have got bronze when I thought I was getting
gold, presumably I may keep the bronze if I choose to do so,
unless you sold it equally in error, and have a good reason for
wanting to have it back. The texts of the Roman Law look
at the question from the buyer's point of view. I, the buyer,
have got bronze instead of gold. But what if you, the seller,
have given gold instead of bronze? In principle you should
be entitled to the same relief. But in both cases the error
must be reasonable, what the commentators call justa et
probabilis error,[42] and it is more likely to be so on the part
of the buyer than on the part of the seller. A seller should as a
rule know what he is selling.

544. Whether the mistake is sufficiently serious to entitle
the mistaken party to relief depends upon the circumstances of
the case. If the thing is represented as having qualities which
in fact it has not, the disappointed purchaser will in any event,
if there is a contract, have his action on the contract. But this
is not the point now in question. What we are asking is not
whether a contract has been broken, but whether any binding

---

[37] Mackintosh, *Roman Law of Sale*, p. 34.
[38] Lord Atkin in *Bell* v. *Lever Bros.* [1932] A.C. at p. 218.
[39] Dig. 18. 1. 11, 1.
[40] de Zulueta, pp. 26, 27.
[41] Dig. 18. 1. 41, 1.
[42] Dig. 41. 10. 5.   *Cf.* 18. 1. 15, 1.

contract exists. The purchaser's mistake may have been induced by misrepresentation, but it is not necessary that it should have been so. It is important to remember that mistake will not have any defect at all, unless, so to say, it impinges upon the orbit of the agreement. Mistake external to the contract leaves it intact. For instance, I buy a picture supposing it to be the work of Apelles. This is why I buy it. In fact it is not the work of Apelles. I have no remedy, unless:—(a) the picture was sold as a work of Apelles; or (b) the seller fraudulently led me to think it was such or acquiesced in my self-deception. This is sometimes called error in causa. It is a question of motive; and motive, generally, is irrelevant except as an indication of intention.

545. (2) The agreement must be intended to create a legal obligation between the parties. If the parties do not intend to be bound, the law will not bind them.[43] This rules out merely social engagements.

546. (3) The agreement must be apt to produce the intended result. It must conform to one or other of certain types; that is it must be concluded re, verbis, litteris or (in specific cases) consensu, or be an innominate contract or actionable pact. The type is called by the commentators the causa or the causa civilis of the contract. It is " the mark, whatever that may be in the particular case, which distinguishes any particular class of agreements from the common herd of pacta and makes them actionable." [44]

547. (4) The agreement must relate to an object which is possible and lawful. Every agreement must be an agreement about something. The something is the content or object of the agreement. It may consist in giving, doing or forbearing. In general, the parties fix their own terms, but when the contract is silent the law supplies matters of detail, e.g., as to time and place of performance. In principle, if performance is *ab initio* 3. 19. 1. physically or legally impossible the contract is void. But in the contract of sale the rule was modified so as to give a bona fide purchaser of a free man supposed to be a slave, or of a res sacra or religiosa supposed to be in commercio, an action on the contract [45] to recover his so-called negative interest, *i.e.*, compensation for the loss he had sustained in consequence of his reliance upon the validity of the contract (*e.g.*, out-of-pocket

[43] Dig. 2. 14. 7, 12.
[44] Pollock, *Principles of Contract* (11), p. 562.
[45] Dig. 18. 1. 4; 62. 1.

expenses, loss of another contract), if the seller was in good faith, and general damages for breach of contract (so-called positive interest) if he was not.[46] Impossibility merely relative to the promisor did not relieve him from liability. " If I stipulate from a person who cannot carry out the contract, though another person might, Sabinus writes that there is a valid obligation." [47]

If the object of a contract is unlawful it is deemed to be impossible.[48]

548. (5) The parties must be competent to contract.

The following were entirely or partly incompetent, *viz.*: —

(a) Persons of unsound mind, except during lucid intervals.[49]

3. 19. 8.   Furiosus nullum negotium gerere potest. Whether the other party knew of the disability or not was irrelevant.

(b) Infantes. Anciently this meant children who could not

3. 19. 10.   talk. In Justinian's law it meant children under seven years of age. In English law all persons of either sex below the age of twenty-one are " infants."

(c) Pupilli, *i.e.*, children under fourteen (males) or twelve (females), who are not in the power of an ascendant. If below seven years of age they came within the last class. If between seven and fourteen (or twelve) they could contract exclusively for their advantage, as by stipulation or by accepting a donation, but could not bind themselves by a contract which involved liability alone or reciprocal rights and duties without the auctoritas of their tutors. In other words, they could bind others

3. 19. 9.   to themselves, but could not bind themselves to others.[50] But in bilateral contracts a pupil could not require the other party to perform unless prepared to carry out his own part of the contract.[51]

(d) Slaves could not contract at all, being destitute of civil

3. 19. 6.   capacity, but could incur a natural obligation (§ 406).

(e) Sons and other male descendants in power could not contract by civil law with their paterfamilias (by natural law they could), but might do so with any one else, provided they

---

[46] Mackintosh, *The Roman Law of Sale*, p. 111. But see Girard, p. 474, n. 5.
[47] Dig. 45. 1. 137, 5.
[48] Dig. 28. 7. 15.
[49] Cod. 5. 70. 6.
[50] Dig. 19. 1. 13, 29: Si quis a pupillo sine tutoris auctoritate emerit, ex uno latere constat contractus; nam qui emit obligatus est pupillo, pupillum sibi non obligat. This is called negotium claudicans, " a limping transaction."
[51] Dig. 18. 5. 7, 1 ; Buckl. *T.* p. 159 ; *M.* p. 98.

were above the age of puberty. If below that age, but no longer infantes, they could acquire for their paterfamilias but could not bind themselves by contract even with his authority.[52] 3. 19. 9.

(f) Interdicted prodigals could not bind themselves by contract, but like pupils might stipulate for an advantage.[53]

(g) Independent persons under the age of twenty-five but above the age of puberty were originally capable of binding themselves without limit, but the praetor gave restitutio in integrum in case of prejudice (§ 777). Under the later Empire minors who had permanent curators were assimilated to pupilli with the result that they could not bind themselves by contract without the consent of their curators (§ 140). If a minor had no curator (for he was not bound to have one) the old law continued to apply.

(h) Women. In the old law women in potestate and in manu could not bind themselves by contract.[54] Other women were in perpetual tutelage and counted as pupillae. With the disuse of manus marriage and the perpetual tutelage of women these disabilities disappeared, and women as such were no longer subject to any incapacity, except that by the S.C. Velleianum they could not bind themselves as sureties or by any other kind of intercessio (§ 583). There was also the prohibition of gifts between husband and wife (§ 215).

(i) In contracts which required a spoken form of words deafness and dumbness were disqualifications. This applied 3. 19. 7. particularly to the stipulation.

549. (6) The contract must not be voidable on the ground of fraud or fear.

(a) Fraud (dolus). This might be raised as a defence to any action. In stricti juris actions it had to be pleaded (exceptio doli). In bonae fidei actions the judge took account of equitable defences without their being specially pleaded. There was also an actio doli or de dolo which was available as a last resort in the absence of any other remedy. A contract procured by fraud might be set aside by restitutio in integrum, and in bonae fidei contracts any fraudulent dealing gave rise to an action on the contract, e.g., the actio empti or venditi in case of sale.

---

[52] A tutor could " authorise " the pupil's act. A father could not " authorise " his child's acts. Since the pupil could acquire for himself it was convenient that he should be able to bind himself *tutore auctore*. This did not apply to the child in power.
[53] Dig. 45. 1. 6.
[54] G. 3. 104.

550. (b) Fear (metus) had the same effect as fraud as regards the avoidance of the contract. It might be set up by way of defence (exceptio metus) or be the ground of restitutio in integrum, or give rise to an action (actio metus).[55] The action had some peculiar features. It was an actio in personam available during one year against any person into whose hands property had come, which the plaintiff had parted with under the influence of fear. It was not an actio in rem, i.e., to assert title; for the plaintiff had parted with the property voluntarily, though under the influence of fear—coactus volui—being compelled I had the will to do it[56]; but since the intentio of the formula did not indicate any specific person as defendant it so far resembled a real action. It belonged to a class of actions which are described as actiones in personam in rem scriptae[57]— personal actions with a declaration in rem (§ 695). The action lay for four-fold damages if the property was not restored. By making restoration the defendant escaped liability. It was not any kind of fear which grounded this action. The evil threatened must be of a serious character, though metus seems to have been more comprehensive than duress in English Law.

4. 6. 25.
4. 6. 27.

> "The praetor says: Where an act is done through fear I will not uphold it.
>
> "Fear, according to Labeo, must be understood to mean not simply any apprehension whatever, but fear of some evil of exceptional severity."
>
> "The fear which we must hold to be referred to in this Edict is not the fear felt by a weak-minded man, but such as might reasonably occur even in the case of a man of thorough firmness of character."[58]

551. Force (vis) is the counterpart of fear. Ulpian says that formerly the Edict contained the words "force or fear," but that the reference to force was omitted as unnecessary.[59] However, moral compulsion is one thing, physical constraint another. A man's reaction to external control is no act of his. The old commentators distinguish vis compulsiva, which renders an act voidable, and vis absoluta, which makes it void. Cases of the latter may perhaps be imagined without resorting with the editors of Sohm to the hypothesis of hypnotic suggestion.[60]

---

[55] Commonly, but incorrectly, called the actio quod metus causa.
[56] Dig. 4. 2. 21, 5.
[57] Dig. 4. 2. 9, 8.
[58] Dig. 4. 2. 1 ; 4. 2. 5 & 6 (Monro's translation).
[59] Dig. 4. 2. 1.
[60] Sohm-Mitteis-Wenger (1933) § 51.

552. OPERATION OF CONTRACT—PERSONS AFFECTED BY IT.—
The principal rule is that a contract affects the parties to it and
no one else; from which two conclusions are drawn:—

    1. No one can stipulate for another;
    2. No one can promise for another.

553. No one can stipulate for another. This means,
primarily, that I cannot enforce a contract in the performance
of which I am not personally interested. It means, further, that
a third party cannot call for performance of a contract to which
he is a stranger. Therefore if A says to B, " Do you promise
to give ten aurei to C? " and B answers, " I promise," the
stipulation is invalid. A acquires no right, because he has no
interest. C acquires no right, because he is not a party. The
severity of this rule was mitigated to a considerable extent in
favour of A and to a less degree in favour of C.   3. 19. 4.

554. (a) If A has in fact an interest, the stipulation is valid. 3. 19. 20.
Thus, if A, on retiring from the administration of his ward's
affairs, stipulates from a co-tutor for the safe administration of
the estate (rem pupilli salvam fore), the stipulator has a direct
interest, because, if the ward's affairs are mismanaged, he will
himself be answerable in the actio tutelae; so, again, if a debtor
stipulates for payment to his creditor, in order to escape a
penalty which he will incur in the event of payment being
overdue.

(b) A may artificially create an interest by stipulating for a
penalty in the event of B failing to perform in favour of C. 3. 19. 19.
Then, if B fails to perform he incurs the penalty and A can sue
him for it.

555. C does not fall within the scope of the above exceptions, that is to say, he has not in either case a right to call
for performance from B. But exceptions existed in his favour
also, some of them more apparent than real.

(i) If A was in C's power, whether as slave or as filius
familias, the benefit of A's contract vested in the dominus or
paterfamilias, who could sue upon it in his own name. The
same result followed if the dominus or paterfamilias stipulated
in favour of a slave or son in power. But this is no real
exception, for as Justinian says, " Your voice is the voice of
your son, just as his voice is yours." There are, in fact, in the 3. 19. 4.
eye of the law two parties only involved in this transaction. It
is a question of agency or representation.

3. 19. 13.   (ii) A stipulation for something to be given to me after my death, or after yours, was held to be invalid; and the result was the same if something was to be given to my heir, or by your heir; for as Gaius says, "It was thought contrary to principle that an obligation should begin in the person of the heir." But Justinian remedied this by legislation.[61]

556. (iii) The stipulation, "Do you promise to give to me *or* to Titius," was free from objection. Titius was considered to be named, not in order to confer upon him the benefit of the contract but merely as a person to whom payment might be made on my account (solutionis gratia adjectus). It is like authorising your debtor to place the money to your credit with 3. 19. 4. your banker. A stipulation, "Do you promise to give to me *and* to Titius" (a stranger to the family) gave no right to Titius, but was valid as concerns myself. It was a moot question between the schools whether I was entitled to claim the whole (Sabinian view) or only the half (Proculian view). Justinian decided in favour of the latter alternative.[62]

557. (iv) Real exceptions existed in the later law. The principal case was donatio sub modo, *i.e.*, when a person accepted a gift subject to a charge, the third party in whose favour the charge was imposed had an action against a donee who failed to implement it.[63] A similar situation arose if a thing was lent or deposited with a direction that it was to be restored to a third party, and there were other cases.[64]

558. No one can promise for another. Therefore, if A says to B, "Do you promise that C will pay ten aurei?" and B 3. 19. 3. answers "I promise," the stipulation is invalid. B incurs no liability, because he undertakes nothing on his own account; nor does C, because he is not a party to the contract.

559. However, this rule, like the last, came to be modified or even abrogated in practice so far as concerns the liability of B. For:—(i) As in the case of stipulatio alteri B may be made 3. 19. 21. personally liable by an added stipulation for a penalty to be incurred in the event of C not doing what B promised he should 3. 19. 3. do; (ii) B would in any event be bound if he promised to procure C's performance, and a promise that C would perform was easily construed as having this effect.

---

[61] G. 3. 100; Cod. 4. 11. 1; 8. 37 (38). 11.
[62] G. 3. 103; Inst. 3. 19. 4.
[63] Cod. 8. 54 (55). 3 (Diocletian).
[64] Girard, p. 480; Buckl. *T.* p. 427.

But C could not incur a liability under a contract to which he was not a party except so far as the law might hold him liable on the ground of representation. This brings us to the subject of Principal and Agent which we shall consider presently.

560. The principle that a contract affects the parties and no one else, though illustrated by the verbal contract, is of general application to every kind of contract.[65] It is, in fact, a fundamental and a necessary consequence of the conception of a contract as a juristic act directed to establishing a relation *inter partes*. It is also plain that A and B cannot in general by their contract impose a duty of performance upon C. But it is not equally necessary that a contract between A and B should not confer a right upon C. The French Code, while asserting in terms (subject to qualifications) the rule that one cannot in general bind oneself or stipulate in one's own name except for oneself, has in practice given effect to stipulations for a third person even outside the cases contemplated by art. 1121.[66] English Law has stoutly refused to recognise a jus quaesitum tertio, but equity has undermined the juristic fortress, and legislation will (or may) complete the work of destruction.[67]

THE INSTITUTES

BOOK III

TITLE XIX

Of invalid stipulations

Anything which admits of private ownership may be the subject of a stipulation, whether it be movable or immovable. 1. But a stipulation is invalid if it relates to a thing, which either has not, or cannot have, any natural existence; for example if one stipulates for the slave Stichus, believing him to be alive, when he is in fact dead; or for the mythical hippocentaur, which cannot exist.

2. It is the same if one stipulates for a sacred or religious thing, believing it to be a matter of human right,[68] or for a thing which is public because it has been permanently dedicated to the use of the

---

[65] Neque stipulari neque emere vendere contrahere ut alter suo nomine recte agat possumus (Paulus). Dig. 44. 7. 11.
[66] C. C. arts. 1119–21.
[67] *Law Revision Committee, Sixth Interim Report* (1937) Cmd. 5449.
[68] But if a man purports to sell as profane land which is in fact religious the purchaser may be entitled to an indemnity. Dig. 11. 7. 8, 1 : si locus religiosus pro puro venisse dicetur, praetor in factum actionem in eum dat ei ad quem res pertinet.

people, such as a forum or a theatre, or for a free man, believed to be a slave, or for a thing which is not in the stipulator's commercium,[69] or for a thing which is already his own. Nor will the stipulation be in suspense because a public thing may become private, or a free man become a slave, or the stipulator afterwards acquire commercium of the thing in question, or the thing cease to be his; but the stipulation is invalid from the beginning. Conversely, if a thing can initially be the subject of a stipulation, and afterwards, without the stipulator having brought it about, comes under any of the above-mentioned descriptions, the stipulation is extinguished. Further, if I stipulate, "Do you promise to give Lucius Titius, when he shall be a slave," or anything of the kind, the stipulation is bad from the beginning, because things which from their nature we cannot own, cannot in any way whatever be made the subject of an obligation. 3. A promise that another person will give or do, for example that Titius will give five aurei, is not binding, but one

§ 553.

may be bound by a promise to see that he gives. 4. A stipulation for a person, other than one in whose power one is, is without effect. Of

§ 556.

course, one may stipulate for payment to be made to a stranger—for instance—"Do you promise to give to me or to Seius?" In this case the stipulator acquires the right, but payment may be made to Seius, even against the stipulator's will, so that the promisor gets his discharge, but the stipulator has his action of mandate against Seius. If one stipulates for ten aurei to be given to himself and to another in whose power he is not, the stipulation is valid, but it was a moot question, whether the whole sum could be claimed, or only a half. It has been settled that the stipulator does not acquire more than the half. If you stipulate for one who is in your power you acquire for yourself, for your voice is the voice of your son, just as your son's voice is taken to be yours in respect of things which you

§ 554.

can acquire through him (Inst. 2. 9. 1.). 5. Further, a stipulation

§ 535.

is invalid if the answer does not conform to the question; for instance, I stipulate for ten, you promise five, or conversely; or if one stipulates unconditionally, you promise conditionally, or conversely; that is, provided that you express this in your answer; for example, if a person introduces a condition, or a term into his stipulation, and you answer, "I promise for today." For if you simply say, "I promise," you are understood by this expression of assent to have promised subject to the term or condition of the stipulation, for it is not necessary to repeat the exact words used by the stipulator.

6. Again, you cannot validly stipulate from one who is subject to your power, nor can he stipulate from you. A slave cannot be civilly bound either to his master or to any one else, but sons may

§ 548.

be bound to any one other than their paterfamilias. 7. It is evident that a person who is dumb can neither stipulate nor promise. The same applies to a person who is deaf, because each party must hear who the other party says. By "deaf" must be understood, a person who has no power of hearing, not a person who hears with difficulty.

---

[69] "For instance, if in the days of Gaius a peregrinus had stipulated for a fundus Italicus, or if, in the times of the Lower Empire, a heathen had stipulated for a Christian slave" (Sandars).

8. A madman cannot contract at all, because he does not understand what he is doing.

9. A pupil is competent to conclude any contract, provided that the tutor must be present whenever his authority is necessary, for instance if the pupil binds himself, for he can bind another to himself even without his tutor's authority.

10. What we have said about pupils must be taken to apply to those who are old enough to have some understanding; for an infant and a child who is not far removed from infancy is not very different from a person of unsound mind, for pupils of this age have no understanding. But in the case of pupils not far removed from infancy the law has in their own interest received an indulgent interpretation, so that they have the same rights as children approaching puberty. But a child below the age of puberty cannot bind himself even with his father's authority.

11. A stipulation is void if an impossible condition is attached to it. A condition is impossible if its happening is contrary to the natural order of things, for example, " Do you promise to give if I touch the sky with my finger? " But if the stipulation is, " Do you promise to give if I do not touch the sky with my finger? " the obligation is understood to be unconditional, and performance can be demanded immediately.

12. [*Supra*, p. 303.]

13. Formerly no one could stipulate for something to be given to him after his death, or after the death of the person from whom he stipulated; nor could a son or slave in power stipulate for performance after the death of his master or paterfamilias, for slaves and sons speak with the master's or father's voice. Similarly a stipulation for performance on " the day before I die " or " on the day before you die " was invalid. But since, as has been already said, all stipulations derive their effect from the consent of the parties, we have thought fit to amend the law in this matter and pronounce all such stipulations valid. § 555.

14. Again, a stipulation expressed in such terms as these was invalid :—" If the ship shall have come from Asia, do you promise to give today? " because it contemplates performance of a conditional promise before the condition takes effect. But the Emperor Leo permitted such so-called preposterous stipulations in matters of dower and we have decided to give them general validity.

15. A stipulation conceived in the terms, " Do you promise to give when I die," or, " when you die? " was allowed to be good even by the old lawyers and is good today.

16. We can properly stipulate for performance after the death of a third person.

17. [*Supra*, p. 304.]

18. When several things are included in a single stipulation, if the promisor answers simply, " I promise to give," he is answerable for all of them. But if he promises one or more of them he is bound only to the extent of his promise. It is as if there were several distinct stipulations and only one or more of them had taken effect; for each particular thing must be included both in the question and in the answer.

19. As has been said above, no one can stipulate for another, for obligations of this character were designed to enable every one to get the thing in which he was personally interested. A stipulator is not interested in a thing being given to some one else. Of course if this is what he wants done it will be well for him to stipulate for a penalty which he will be entitled to claim if the thing is not done, although he is not personally interested. For when a person stipulates for a penalty the question is, not what is his interest but what is the amount of the penalty. Therefore, a stipulation for something to be given to Titius is without effect, but if a penalty is added, for example, " If you shall not have given, do you promise to give so many aurei? " there is a binding stipulation.

20. However, if a person stipulates for another, when he has an interest in the thing being done, it is settled that the stipulation is valid. For example, if a person who has been acting as tutor retires from the administration in favour of a co-tutor and stipulates for the security of his pupil's estate, the stipulation is binding, for he has an interest in its performance, since he will be personally liable if the estate is not properly administered. Again, one may validly stipulate for payment to one's manager; or to one's creditor, to the extent of one's interest, for example to avoid a penalty being incurred, or mortgaged land sold, in the event of failure to discharge the debt. 21. Conversely, if one has promised that some one else will do something, the position seems to be that the promisor is not bound unless he has promised a penalty on his own account. 22. If a thing is to become mine in a certain event a stipulation that it shall be made mine in that event is without effect.[70]

23. If the stipulator is thinking of one thing, the promisor of another, there is no obligation, any more than there would be if the answer did not correspond with the question; for instance, if some one stipulates with you for the slave Stichus, and you have in mind Pamphilus, whom you mistake for Stichus.

24. A promise which has an immoral cause is not binding, for example if the man promises to commit homicide or sacrilege.

25. If a person stipulates subject to a condition and dies before the condition takes effect, and it takes effect later, his heir may sue upon the stipulation, and similarly the promisor's heir may be sued. 26. If one stipulates for something to be given this year or this month, he cannot maintain an action until the whole year or month has expired. 27. If you stipulate for an estate or a slave, you cannot take proceedings immediately, but must give the promisor time to make delivery.

XVI. PRINCIPAL AND AGENT

561. The rules considered above, which render void stipulations in favour of a third person and promises directed to making a third person liable, if strictly applied, are fatal to the admission of agency in contract, and this was their effect in

§ 553.
§ 554.

§ 558.

§ 540.

---

[70] Thus, if a legacy and a stipulation are subject to the same condition and the legacy takes effect, the stipulation fails (Theophilus).

early Roman Law. However, a relation of Principal and Agent was gradually evolved, though it never reached the point of development which it has attained in modern systems.[71]

562. To illustrate the situation, let us suppose that A has given B a mandate to buy a horse for him from C. What are the resulting legal relations—first, as regards the liability of A to C, *i.e.*, the rights of C against A; secondly, as regards the liability of C to A, *i.e.*, the rights of A against C? Or, to state the problem in more general terms—In what circumstances and to what extent can a person be made liable, or become entitled, under, or by virtue of, a contract entered into by his agent with a third party?

563. As regards A's liability to C, C's recourse in the first instance is against the party who contracted with him, namely B, the agent; but in certain cases he can look beyond the agent B to the principal A. The law in this matter passed through three stages of historical development: —

(1) In the earliest period A incurred no liability whatever. He was not a party to the contract.

(2) In the classical period the praetor admitted along with the primary liability of B, the agent, a secondary liability of A, the principal, but only in a limited number of cases; and in these cases gave actions against A as well as against B. They have been named actiones adjecticiae qualitatis, because they were actions of an additional or supplementary character.[72] There were five such actions, *viz.*: —

(a) actio quod jussu; (b) actio de peculio et in rem verso; (c) actio tributoria; (d) actio institoria; (e) actio exercitoria.

564. (a) The actio quod jussu lay against a dominus or 4. 7. 1. paterfamilias when he had authorised or ratified a contract entered into by his slave or son in power.[73] The jussus was directed to the third party, not to the slave or son.[74]

565. (b) The actio de peculio et in rem verso lay, indepen- 4. 7. 4. dently of authorisation or ratification, when a slave or son who had a peculium had bound himself by contract. It was directed against the master or father, who was liable to the extent of the peculium (de peculio) or to the extent to which he had

---

[71] Girard, pp. 705–20.
[72] The phrase, which, of course, is not Roman, is also applied to other, *e.g.*, noxal, actions. Buckl. *T.* p. 692; *M.* p. 371.
[73] Dig. 15. 4. 1.
[74] Windscheid, II, § 482; Girard, p. 709, n. 33, Buckl. *Slavery*, p. 166.

derived a profit from the transaction (de in rem verso), whichever was the greater.

In calculating the amount of the peculium the defendant was allowed to deduct what was owed by the slave or son to himself or (with one exception) to any person in his power.

4. 7. 3.

566. (c) The actio tributoria was of more limited application. It was available when a slave or son had been trading with his peculium with the knowledge of his master or father. The superior was required to distribute the assets *pro rata* amongst the creditors, amongst whom he ranked without preference. The fund available for this purpose included the capital invested in the business and profits derived from it (merx peculiaris). If a creditor considered that he had been unfairly treated he might have recourse to this action to have his dividend brought up to the proper amount.[75] It offered the advantage that the defendant could not first deduct what was due to himself. On the other hand, the total peculium might largely exceed the portion invested in trade. Obviously, a creditor would not bring this action if he could get better satisfaction in the actio de peculio et in rem verso.

4. 7. 2.

567. (d) The actio institoria lay when a dominus or paterfamilias allowed his slave or son or an independent free person to carry on a business as his manager (institor). The superior was liable for the trade debts.

568. (e) The actio exercitoria was a similar action which lay when the owner of a ship (exercitor) had appointed his son or slave or an independent free person master of the ship (magister). He was liable for the debts incurred by the master in the exercise of his functions.

569. The common element, so far, in all these actions is that they arose out of transactions entered into by subordinate members of the family. Agency, therefore, had its origin within the circle of the Roman family. But in the last two of the above-mentioned actions the same consequences followed when a person unconnected with the family of the principal was appointed to manage a business or to be master of a ship. This marked a step in advance, but it was limited to these two cases.

570. (3) The last stage in the process of development was reached when the principle of these actions was extended to

---

[75] Dig. 14. 4. 7. 2.

other cases of agency of independent persons. This was the work not of the praetor, but of the jurists. Papinian advised that when a principal had given his procurator authority to raise loans the lender might maintain a utilis actio based upon the analogy of the institoria [76]; similarly if the procurator had a mandate to sell.[77] Practice may even have gone the length of including cases of mandate to do a particular act. If so, the ultimate result was that a principal might in every case be rendered liable to a third party in respect of a contract entered into by an agent in the principal's name and within the scope of the agent's authority. But the agent also was liable.[78]

THE INSTITUTES

BOOK IV

TITLE VII

Of contracts made with persons in power

Since mention has been made above of the action which is taken against the peculium of sons in power and of slaves, it is necessary to discuss in some detail this action, as well as the other actions which arising out of the contracts of sons and slaves are given against their parents and masters. Since very much the same rules apply to both, it will shorten the discussion if we confine our remarks to slaves and masters. If there is anything peculiar to the case of sons and parents it will be mentioned as occasion arises.

1. If then any one has contracted with a slave by his master's authority (jussu domini) the praetor allows him an action to the full extent of the contract against the master, because the other party to the contract is deemed to look to the master's credit. 2. On the same principle the praetor gives two other actions in solidum, the actio exercitoria and the actio institoria. The actio exercitoria lies, when a master has appointed his slave master of a ship, and a contract has been made with him in relation to the business in hand. The action is so called because a person who takes the ordinary profits of a ship is termed an exercitor. The actio institoria lies when a master has put a slave in charge of a shop or some other business and a contract has been made with him in the course of the business in question. The action is known by this name because a person put in charge of a business is called an institor. The praetor allows these two actions also if the person put in charge of a ship or a shop or other business is a free man or another person's slave, for the same principle of equity applies in this case as well. § 564. § 568. § 567.

---

[76] Dig. 14. 3. 19 pr.: utilis ad exemplum institoriae dabitur actio.
[77] Dig. 19. 1. 13, 25.
[78] Dig. 14. 1. 1, 17; est autem nobis electio utrum exercitorem an magistrum convenire velimus.

§ 566.

3. The praetor has introduced yet another action which is known as the actio tributoria, which is of the following nature. If a slave with the knowledge of his master trades with his peculium, and a contract is made with him incidental to the trade in question, the praetor requires the capital invested in the business and the proceeds to be distributed rateably between the master, if anything is owing to him, and the other creditors; and since he leaves to the master the duty of making the distribution, if any one of the creditors complains that the share assigned to him is less than it should be, he gives him the actio tributoria.

§ 565.

4. There is another action known as the action de peculio et in rem verso. The effect of this is that, although a slave has contracted without his master's approval, the master is liable to the full extent of what has been applied to his use, and, where this is not the case, then to the extent of the peculium. There is understood to be an application to the master's use when a slave has made any necessary expenditure on his account, for example, if he has borrowed money and with it paid his creditors or repaired buildings which were falling into ruin, or bought wheat for the use of the household, or acquired land or any other thing that was needed. Therefore, if for example, your slave has borrowed ten aurei from Titius and has paid five of the ten to your creditor, and has spent the remaining five in any general way, you must be condemned in solidum in respect of the first five, but, as regards the second five, only to the extent of the peculium. It is evident that, if the whole ten have been applied to your use, Titius can recover the whole. For, although there is but one action de peculio et in rem verso, nevertheless, it has two condemnations. So the judge must first inquire whether there has been an application to your use, and it is only when he finds that the amount claimed has not been so applied, or only partly so, that he goes on to estimate the amount of the peculium. In making this calculation, deduction is first made of what the slave owes to his master, or to a person in his power, and it is only what remains that counts as peculium. It may happen, however, that what the slave owes to another person in the master's power is not deducted from his peculium, as when the creditor is a slave who is part of the peculium. This means that what he owes to a vicarius is not deducted.

5. No doubt, a person who has contracted by the master's authority or who is in a position to bring the actio institoria or the actio exercitoria may also bring the actio de peculio et in rem verso. But it would be very foolish if, failing to take advantage of an action which would give him the full amount of his claim under the contract, he should put himself to the difficulty of proving that there had been an application to the defendant's use, or that the slave had a peculium, and one sufficient to meet his claim in full. Similarly, a person who can bring an actio tributoria, can also bring the actio de peculio et in rem verso; but, in this case, it is sometimes expedient to bring the one action, sometimes the other. The advantage in bringing the actio tributoria is that in this the master's position is not privileged, that is to say, there is no deduction of what is owed to the master and he has just the same right as the other creditors; but in the actio de peculio deduction is

THE LAW OF OBLIGATIONS

first made of what is owed to the master, and he is condemned to
the extent of what remains. On the other hand, the actio de peculio
has the advantage that in it account is taken of the whole peculium,
but in the actio tributoria only of so much of the peculium as is
embarked in trade, which may be a third or a fourth or a very small
part of the whole, while the greater part of the peculium is invested
in land, or slaves, or put out at interest. So everyone must choose
the action appropriate to the circumstances. Certainly if it can be
proved that there has been an application to the defendant's use the
actio de in rem verso is to be preferred.

6. What we have said about slave and master must be understood
to apply equally to a son and daughter, grandson and granddaughter
on the one hand, and to the father or grandfather in whose power
they are on the other.

7. There is, however, a rule which is peculiar to children in
power, namely, that the senatusconsultum Macedonianum forbids   § 425.
loans of money to be made to them; and the lenders are denied an
action either against son or daughter, grandson or granddaughter,
whether still in power or released from power by death of the paterfamilias or by emancipation, or against father or grandfather,
whether the child is still in power or has been emancipated. This
the Senate provided because it often happened that persons who were
heavily in debt from having borrowed money, which was wasted in
riotous living, entertained designs against their parents' lives.

8. Finally, it must be remarked that if a son or slave has
contracted by the authority of parent or master, or if the subject
of the contract has been applied to his use, a condictio may be
brought against the parent or master directly, just as if he had been
the original party to the transaction. Similarly, where the actio
exercitoria or institoria can be brought, the condictio is also
available, for in this case too the contract is taken to have been
made by the authority of the principal.[79]

XVII. Principal and Agent

(continued)

571. Next, as to the rights of the principal against the party
who has concluded a contract with his agent. Here, again,
agency begins in the family. A master or parent acquires the
benefit of contracts entered into by slaves or sons in power,
whether they contract in their own name, or in his, or in the
name of another person in the same power ; and within defined
limits contractual rights accrue to a master or putative master
through a slave in whom he has the usufruct or through a free
man, or another person's slave, bona fide possessed. But no   3. 28.
rights could be acquired through a free man, known to be free,

---

[79] Plainly what is stated in this section was a later development.

and a stranger to the family.[80] It followed that (to revert to our illustration), if A gives B a mandate to buy a horse from C, though in the latest stage of Roman Law A is liable to C, it is not the case that C is liable to A. Apart from novation, which means a new contract substituting A as C's creditor in place of B (§ 660), the only way in which A can sue C is by making use of B's action upon the contract. This is effected by means of a mandate to sue given by the agent B to his principal A, which the agent might be compelled to give in an actio mandati.[81] Further than this the Roman Law did not, in principle, go; that is to say, A could not sue except as the assignee of the right of action of his own agent B; and B, notwithstanding the assignment of his right of action to A, continued to be liable to C. This falls very far short of true agency. It is true that there is a text in the Digest in which Ulpian, after speaking of the adapted action on the analogy of the institoria (utilis actio ad exemplum institoriae, *supra*, § 570) is made to say " and so, conversely, it must be said that an adapted action on the sale is available to the principal " (ergo et per contrarium dicendum est utilem ex empto (better ex vendito) actionem domino competere),[82] *i.e.*, that the principal has a corresponding action against the third party; but this is clearly interpolated. Buckland says, " This is Justinian and probably does not really represent the law even for his time." [83] Exceptionally, to encourage the import of grain the Praefect of the Market allowed owners of vessels engaged in the trade to sue the debtors of their captains.[84] There were some other cases in which the principal might by special favour be allowed to bring the mandatory's action as an actio utilis,[85] as, for instance, if the agent was insolvent,[86] or would suffer no prejudice by the principal bringing the action, *e.g.*, when the contract was unilateral, and the agent therefore incurred no liability, or when the principal had satisfied the third party's claim under the contract.[87] But these are all cases of a special character, and go little way to invade the principle that A could not, at any period of Roman Law, acquire a contractual right against C through an intermediary B.

---

[80] Dig. 14. 3. 1; 45. 1. 126, 2.
[81] Dig. 41. 2. 49, 2.
[82] Dig. 19. 1. 13, 25.
[83] Buckl. *T*. p. 519.
[84] Dig. 14. 1. 1, 18.
[85] Dig. 14. 3. 1 & 2.
[86] Dig. 46. 5. 5.
[87] Girard, p. 719; Buckl. *T*. p. 519; *M*. p. 302.

THE INSTITUTES

BOOK III (Tits. XVII, XXVIII)

TITLE XVII

Of the stipulations of slaves

A slave has a power of stipulating derived from his master, and since an inheritance in many respects represents the person of the deceased, if a slave who belongs to an inheritance stipulates for anything before the heir has entered, he acquires for the inheritance and by consequence for the person who afterwards becomes heir.

1. A slave acquires for his master whether he stipulates for his § 571. master or for himself or for a fellow slave or without mentioning any one in particular. The same principle applies to children in power so far as the acquisition of a child can benefit a parent.   2. 9. 1.

2. When the subject of the stipulation is something to be done by the stipulator, this is always understood to mean the stipulator in person, for example, if a slave stipulates for a licence to go or to drive. This implies a duty not to interfere with the exercise of the licence by the slave himself. It does not extend to the master.

3. If a slave who is owned in common by more than one master stipulates, he acquires for each of them in proportion to his ownership, unless he stipulates by the authority of, or expressly for, one or other of them. In that case he acquires for him alone. If what he stipulates for cannot be acquired by one of his masters it goes wholly to the other, for example, if it belongs to one of them already.

TITLE XXVIII

Of the persons through whom obligations are acquired

Now that we have explained the kinds of obligation which arise ex contractu or quasi ex contractu, it must be remarked that you may acquire not only in your own person, but also through persons in your power, as slaves or sons, but with a distinction. What you acquire through your slaves is entirely yours, but as regards what you acquire from obligations through children in your power the distinction made by our constitution between ownership and usufruct takes effect, with the result that the father enjoys the usufruct in any profit accruing from an action, while the ownership is reserved to the son [88]; it being understood that the father brings the action in conformity with the rules laid down in our recent constitution.

1. Further, you acquire through free persons and another person's § 233. slave whom you possess in good faith, but only in two events, namely, if they acquire by their own exertions or in connection with your affairs.

2. The same applies to a slave in whom you have the usufruct § 232. or use.   3. It is a settled rule that a slave owned in common acquires

---

[88] Cod. 6. 61. 6; *supra*, p. 158, n. 71.

for each of his masters in proportion to their interest, except that,
if he stipulates or takes delivery expressly for one of them. he
acquires for that one alone; for example, if he stipulates, " Do you
promise to give to my master Titius? "; and the result is the same,
as observed above, if the slave stipulates by the authority of one
master alone. This was formerly matter of doubt, but has been
settled in this sense by our constitution.[89]

3. 17. 3.

XVIII. PRINCIPAL AND SURETY

572. A contract of suretyship is a contract whereby one
person binds himself to be answerable for the debt of another.
The person primarily liable is called the principal debtor or
principal; the person secondarily liable is called the surety or
guarantor. The relation of principal and surety was constituted
in Roman Law in various ways, and the merely secondary
nature of the surety's liability, as will be seen, was only gradually
established. The methods of creating suretyship were three,
viz., the verbal contract, mandate and constitutum debiti.

573. (1) The verbal contract. In the classical period there
were three types of suretyship by stipulation, which were distinguished by the form of words used by the stipulator (creditor)
in addressing the intended surety. After first stipulating from
the person who was to be the principal debtor he turned to the
person who was to be surety and said, " Do you promise the
same? " The words of the question might be Idem dari spondes
or Idem fideprommittis or Idem (or Id) fide tua esse jubes? [90]
The three resulting contracts were distinguished as sponsio, fidepromissio, and fidejussio, and the surety was known as sponsor,
fideprommissor and fidejussor, the term adpromissor being
applied indifferently to all three. Of these sponsio was available
to Roman citizens alone; sponsio and fidepromissio could only
be incidental to a principal liability created by stipulation, as
in the illustration given above.[91] By the time of Justinian the
only type of verbal suretyship remaining in use was fidejussio,
which might be created by any appropriate form of words
spoken or written; and might be incidental to any kind of
liability, contractual, quasi-contractual or delictual,[92] and in the
first case to any kind of contract, re, verbis, litteris or consensu.
Unlike the earlier forms, it bound the surety's heirs.[93]   The

3. 20 pr.

3. 20. 1.

---

[89] G. 3. 167a ; Cod. 4. 27. 2.
[90] G. 3. 116 ; Dig. 45. 1. 75, 6.
[91] G. 3. 119.
[92] Dig. 46. 1. 8, 5 & 6 ; 56, 3 ; 70, 5.
[93] G. 3. 120 ; Inst. 3. 20. 2.

surety might undertake an obligation equal to or less, but not greater, than that of the principal debtor. Thus the principal might be bound absolutely, the surety conditionally, but not conversely. The principal obligation might be civil or natural. 3. 20. 5.
3. 20. 1

574. (2) **Mandatum.** The relation of principal and surety might also be created by mandate. Thus, if I am willing to be surety for a loan to be made by you to Titius, I give you a mandate to lend to Titius, with the result that if you fail to recover the money from Titius you can proceed against me by the actio mandati contraria.[94] A mandate of this kind was known as mandatum credendae pecuniae. Tradition has attached to it the name of mandatum qualificatum (§ 515).[95]

575. (3) **Constitutum debiti.** This was an informal promise by a third party to discharge a debt due to you from Titius, made actionable by the praetor (§ 528). But Titius was not released. He remained liable as principal debtor.

576. **Nature of surety's liability.** On the face of it fidejussio creates not a secondary, but a primary, liability. B does not say, " I promise to pay if A does not." He says, " I pledge my credit for the same " (or " for it ") or " I pledge my credit for what Titius owes." The result is that, if he chooses to do so, the creditor can proceed against B before proceeding against, or even demanding performance from, A.[96] Indeed, he will have good reason for wishing to do so, even at the risk of exposing himself to an actio injuriarum (§ 615) by a principal debtor, who might choose to resent the reflection on his solvency [97] ; for if he took proceedings against the principal debtor, the obligation of the fidejussor (this does not apply to the mandator,[98] or to the constituens) was before Justinian extinguished by operation of law in consequence of the litis contestatio (§ 714), and the creditor would lose the benefit of his security. The surety, therefore, was in a very unpleasant position. He might be called upon to pay, even though the principal debtor was completely solvent. He could be sued for the whole debt, though there were other sureties. If he paid, he usually had recourse against the principal debtor in an actio mandati or negotiorum gestorum, but he was not, in principle, entitled to claim contribution from co-sureties.[99]

---

[94] G. 3. 156 ; Inst. 3. 26. 6.
[95] *i.e.*, a mandate of a special character.
[96] Cod. 8. 40 (41). 19.
[97] Dig. 47. 10. 19.
[98] Paul. *Sent.* 2. 17. 16 ; Dig. 13. 5. 18, 3.
[99] Cod. 8. 40 (41). 11.

577. In process of time these consequences of suretyship were avoided or overcome in practice or by legislation. A creditor might be willing to accept as a substitute for the usual absolute guarantee an undertaking by the surety to be answerable for what the creditor failed to recover from the principal debtor (fidejussio indemnitatis).[1] This meant that he had to go against the principal debtor before suing the surety. Or a creditor, who was pressing a surety for payment, might be induced to accept the surety's mandate to sue the principal debtor, thus retaining his recourse against the surety in the actio mandati. But these contrivances did not go far to improve the surety's position. Better relief was afforded by the three "benefits," of cession of actions, of division and of order.

578. Benefit of cession of actions (beneficium cedendarum actionum). From the early days of the Empire, if not earlier, it became the practice for a surety to demand cession of actions (§§ 649, 650) as a condition of satisfying the creditor's claim.[2] A creditor who unreasonably refused it could be met by a plea of fraud, but perhaps it was not until Justinian that a surety could demand it as of right. Cession of actions gave the surety both a recourse against the principal debtor and a means of obtaining contribution from co-sureties. It was open to the serious objection that satisfaction of the creditor's claim extinguished his right of action, so that nothing remained to cede. This was evaded by the fiction that the payment made by the surety was not a satisfaction of the claim, but a purchase of the right of action.[3] It was distinctly advantageous to the surety to get cession of actions against the principal debtor; for it might happen that the creditor had a privilege, giving him preference over other creditors, or was secured by a hypothec. A surety suing the principal debtor on a mandate (§ 576) had not these advantages.[4]

579. Benefit of division. Cession of actions, desirable in the last-mentioned case, was essential in relation to co-sureties, for without it (apart from the improbable event of one co-surety having received a mandate from another) there was no right to claim contribution. In the early law there had been some legislation on the subject, to which reference will be made below. But in the classical and post-classical periods a surety's right to

contribution was secured by an enactment of the Emperor
Hadrian which allowed a surety to require the creditor to divide
his claim *pro rata* between those sureties who were solvent at
the time of action brought. This was known as the beneficium
divisionis. A surety who failed to take advantage of it had
(except as above-mentioned) no right to contribution, and, as
Justinian says, he had only himself to thank for this, since he
might have availed himself of the Emperor's rescript. This
benefit was available from the beginning when the suretyship
was created by fidejussio or mandatum. It was only Justinian
who made it available to the constituens.[5]

3. 20. 4.

580. Benefit of order or excussion (beneficium ordinis seu
excussionis). During the whole of the Imperial period, as we
have seen (§ 560), the creditor had the strongest possible motive
for proceeding against the fidejussor before suing the principal
debtor. When Justinian in 531 abolished the consumptive effect
of litis contestatio (§ 661), this ceased to be so, and he completed
his reform by requiring the creditor to proceed in the first
instance against the principal debtor, if within the jurisdiction.
If he was not, the judge was to give the surety time to produce
him, and it was only if the time elapsed without his having done
so that he was himself exposed to the creditor's action.[6]

581. The above-mentioned benefits have been transmitted to
many modern systems of law, such as the French, but they are
of doubtful value. Cession of actions is unnecessary where the
law provides, as is usually the case, that the surety who has paid
is subrogated into the rights of the creditor. Where the other
benefits are admitted by law, it is usual to exclude them by
contract.

582. Gaius mentions a number of early statutes, which were
no longer in use in the later law. A lex Publilia gave a sponsor
who had discharged the debt and was not reimbursed within six
months an action known as actio depensi, giving rise to manus
injectio pro judicato, and later to two-fold damages in case of
denial.[7] A lex Apuleia introduced a kind of partnership
between sureties. As between themselves each surety was liable
only *pro rata* and could recover what he had paid in excess of
his share from the others, but each surety continued to be liable
to the creditor in solidum.[8] By a lex Furia a surety's liability
only endured for two years and where there were co-sureties the
creditor was required to divide his claim between such of them

[5] Cod. 4. 18. 3.
[6] Nov. 4. 1 (A.D. 535).
[7] G. 3. 127; 4. 22 & 25.
[8] G. 3. 122.

as were in existence at the time when the debt fell due.[9] This meant that the risk of insolvency of any one of them fell on the creditor and not, as under the Epistola Hadriani, upon the others. These two statutes applied only to sponsors and fidepromissors, and the second of them only to suretyship in Italy. All three are of very early date, not later than B.C. 200. A lex Cicereia required a creditor who accepted sponsors or fidepromissors as sureties to make a public declaration of the nature of the liability and of the number of sureties he intended to take. Any one of them might demand a praejudicium (§ 724) within thirty days to inquire whether the required declaration had been made. If it was found that it had not been made, their liability was discharged.[10]

Lastly, a lex Cornelia forbade any surety to bind himself for the same debtor to the same creditor in one year for more than 20,000 sesterces, and limited liability to that amount.[11] Of all these statutes this one alone applied to fidejussors as well as to sponsors and fidepromissors. But like the others it passed out of use in the later law.

583. By edicts of Augustus and Claudius women were forbidden to " intercede " for their husbands.[12] Intercession meant undertaking liability for another's debt whether instead of him (privative intercession) or together with him, e.g., as surety (cumulative intercession). The senatusconsultum Velleianum (A.D. 46) extended the prohibition to all cases of intercession by women.[13] Effect was given to the S.C. by the exceptio senatusconsulti Velleiani (§ 745). Justinian in a Novel dealing with a variety of matters declared invalid any instrument by which a wife bound herself for her husband, unless it was clear that it related to moneys applied to her own use.[14] This law from the summary of it made by the glossators is usually cited as the authentica siqua mulier (§ 43). The two enactments passed into the medieval and modern law and were the subject of extensive comment. Many exceptions were admitted, and it was generally allowed that a woman might renounce the benefit of both laws provided that she did so with full understanding of what she was doing. All this load of tradition is retained today in the law of South Africa,[15] but it is widely held that these privileges (or disabilities) of women are not required in an age (relatively) of feminine emancipation. In France they were abolished by Henry IV in 1604.

---

[9] G. 3. 121.
[10] G. 3. 123.
[11] G. 3. 124.
[12] Dig. 16. 1. 2 pr.
[13] Dig. 16. 1. 2, 1.
[14] Nov. 134. 8.
[15] Lee, p. 313.

THE INSTITUTES

BOOK III (Tit. XX)

Of fidejussors

It often happens that when a man makes a promise, other persons, known as fidejussors or sureties, bind themselves for him, as is the usual practice when creditors wish to have a better security. 1. Fidejussors may be accepted in respect of any obligation, whether arising re, verbis, litteris or consensu. It makes no difference whether the principal obligation is civil or natural, so much so that a man may bind himself for a slave, whether the slave's creditor is a stranger, or the slave's own master, in respect of the slave's natural obligation. 2. The obligation undertaken by a fidejussor is transmitted to his heirs. 3. The fidejussor's obligation may precede or follow the principal obligation. 4. If there are several fidejussors, however many they may be, each is liable for the whole debt, so that the creditor has the option to claim the whole from any one he pleases. But the Epistle of the Emperor Hadrian compels him to divide his claim amongst such of the sureties as are solvent at the time of the litis contestatio. Consequently, if at such time one of the sureties is insolvent, a heavier burden is laid on the others. If the creditor obtains payment of the whole amount from one of the sureties, the whole loss falls upon him alone if the principal debtor is insolvent, and he has only himself to blame, for he might have been aided by the Emperor's rescript and have required that he should be sued merely for his rateable share.[16] 5. Fidejussors cannot undertake a greater liability than the principal debtor, for their liability is merely accessory to his, and there cannot be more in an accessory than there is in the thing to which it accedes. But a fidejussor may be bound for less than the principal debtor. Thus, if the principal promises ten aurei, the fidejussor may be bound for five, but not conversely. Similarly, the principal debtor may promise unconditionally, the fidejussor conditionally, but not conversely. For " more " and " less " are not merely a question of quantity, but also of time. There is more in giving immediately than in giving after an interval of time. 6. If a fidejussor has discharged the debt he has an actio mandati to recover an indemnity from the principal debtor. A fidejussor may bind himself by using appropriate words in the Greek language. 8. With regard to the stipulations of fidejussors it may be accepted as a general principle that if anything is stated in writing to have been done it is deemed to have been done, and therefore if a person declares in writing that he has bound himself as fidejussor, it is presumed that all necessary forms have been observed.

§ 579.

3. 27 pr.

XIX. Quasi-contract

584. The expression " quasi-contract " is, as has been seen (§ 406), open to objection. The essence of contract is agreement. But in the relations of which we are now to speak there

---

[16] Or obtained cession of actions against the other sureties (§ 578).

is no agreement. Justinian, however, says that the resulting obligations arise as it were from contract (quasi ex contractu), though they resemble obligations arising from contract, positively only in being obligations and negatively in not arising from delict. Some of them, however, seem to have an analogy to particular contracts. Thus negotiorum gestio has an affinity with mandate, indebiti solutio with mutuum, co-ownership with societas. But these analogies cannot in principle justify the extension of the term quasi-contractual to other cases to which it is wholly inapplicable. We must be content, therefore, to say that the description is consecrated by usage and includes certain specific obligations, which we proceed to consider.

3. 27. 1.   585. NEGOTIORUM GESTIO.—The essence of this transaction consists in the fact that one person, termed the negotiorum gestor, has rendered a service to another, termed the dominus negotiorum or dominus rei gestae, without mandate or other legal obligation. It emerged into the field of law when the praetor gave an action for an indemnity to a person who in the absence of another had undertaken his defence in judicial proceedings. Later, under the influence of the jurists, it was extended to include services of every kind whether they took the form of general administration or of single acts. There was now a civil law action with reciprocal obligations. It was essential that the gestor should have acted in the interest of another person, not in his own interest. For this reason the action was not available to a bona fide possessor who had spent money on property, supposing it to be his own.[17] It was also required (in principle) that the gestor should have acted with the intention of binding the other party, *i.e.,* in the expectation that he would have a legal claim to an indemnity. This condition was absent if he intended to render a gratuitous service.[18] Lastly, he could have no claim in respect of an act which the dominus had forbidden him to do,[19] except that he might be able to recover his expenses so far as the dominus had been enriched by it.[20]

586. There is no impropriety in translating dominus and gestor by principal and agent, though these words usually imply an authority which in the case of negotiorum gestio is absent. This prefaced, we proceed to speak of the duties of the parties.

---

[17] Dig. 10. 3. 14, 1.
[18] Dig. 3. 5. 4.
[19] Dig. 3. 5. 7 (8), 3 ; 17. 1. 40.
[20] Dig. 3. 5. 5, 5, in id quod ego locupletior factus sum, habet contra me actionem.

587. The agent was bound (a) to render account of his 3. 27. 1.
proceedings; (b) to exercise exacta diligentia [21]; but if he acted
in an emergency he was liable only for dolus.[22]

588. The principal was bound to indemnify the agent in
respect of expenses and liabilities usefully incurred (si utiliter
gessit).[23] This means that the gestor was not entitled to an
indemnity unless what he did was in the circumstances a right
thing to do in the interest of the dominus. Good intentions
were not enough. An element in the case might be what was in
the mind of the principal. If I repair a house, " which the
owner had abandoned because he could not afford the expense
of it or one which he did not think that he required," I cannot
claim compensation; for " to have an action on negotia gesta
a man must have managed the affair beneficially, but he does not
manage it beneficially where he undertakes something which is
not wanted or which would lay a burden on the householder." [24]
It is the state of things at the moment which is taken into
account, not the actual event. I spend money for the treatment
of a sick slave. I can claim reimbursement, though the slave
happens to die.[25]

589. A negotiorum gestor is in a worse position than a
mandatory, who, provided he exhibits the proper degree of
diligence, can claim to be indemnified for all expenses incurred
in the execution of his mandate. By ratifying the gestor's act,
the dominus puts himself in relation to the gestor in the same
position as if he had given an antecedent mandate, so as to give
the gestor the actio mandati contraria, but this does not ex post
facto convert the negotiorum gestio for all purposes into a
contract of mandatum, so as to give the principal the actio
mandati directa, for condemnation in this action involved
infamia, and the dominus could not by his unilateral act put this
heavier burden on the other party to the transaction.[26]

590. ACTIONS.—The actio negotiorum gestorum directa lay
against the gestor, the actio contraria against the dominus.

591. INDEBITI SOLUTIO.—When a person has paid in error 3. 27. 6.
what he was not bound to pay the law lays upon the person
who has received payment a duty of restitution.

[21] Dig. 3. 5. 5, 14.
[22] Dig. 3. 5. 3, 9.
[23] Dig. 3. 5. 2. For the meaning of " useful expenses," see p. 323,
supra.
[24] Dig. 3. 5. 9 (10). (Monro's translation).
[25] Dig. 3. 5. 9, 1.
[26] Girard, p. 665.

592. Has paid. Payment (solutio) includes any performance whereby one person has been enriched at the expense of another. Usually it will be the handing over of money or of some other thing, but it may also consist in undertaking a new liability or in discharging an existing liability.

in error, *i.e.*, believing the payment to be due. The mistake must be reasonable in the circumstances, and except in the case of privileged persons, particularly women and minors, must be a mistake of fact and not of law. Regula est juris quidem ignorantiam cuique nocere, facti vero ignorantiam non nocere— the rule is that ignorance of law affects a man's rights, not ignorance of fact.[27] If one pays in doubt, does one pay in error? " In classical law the dominant view was that the doubt did not suffice, but Justinian put it on the same level as error." [28]

not bound to pay. The payment must have been undue (indebitum), *i.e.*, not due either by civil law, or by natural law, for even a natural obligation excludes the condictio indebiti (§ 406). A payment is said to be undue if (1) the supposed debt does not exist, whether it cannot exist, or has ceased to exist, or has not come into existence (except that a debtor does not pay unduly, if he pays in anticipation of the due date or of a condition which is certain to occur) [19]; (2) it has been made to a person who was not the creditor or entitled to receive payment on his behalf; (3) by a person who was not the debtor unless in the name of the debtor and with the intention of discharging the debt.[30]

593. There were cases in which the condictio indebiti was excluded, even when the above conditions were present, namely, those in which denial of liability involved the payment of double damages, if the claim was established to the satisfaction of the court. These were, principally, action on a judgment (actio judicati), action under the lex Aquilia and actions on certain legacies (§ 632). The reason for this exceptional treatment is obscure. Perhaps payment, in these cases, was regarded as " a sort of compromise by which the risk involved in defending the action was avoided." [31]

594. ACTIONS.—The case was treated as analogous to mutuum. The appropriate action was the condictio indebiti, which might be according to circumstances condictio certae pecuniae or condictio triticaria (§ 420), or (which was not the

3. 27. 7.

4. 6. 19.

---

[27] Dig. 22. 6. 9 pr.   [28] Buckland, *Main Institutions*, p. 293.
[29] Dig. 22. 6. 10 ; 18.
[30] Dig. 12. 6. 65 ; 9.   [31] Buckland, *ubi supra.*

case with mutuum) a condictio incerti, *e.g.*, to obtain release
from an obligation (§§ 420, 702, 732). Gaius, after describing
mutuum, goes on to say: " Another case in which a person is
bound *re* is when one has received what was not due to him
from another who paid in error; for a condictio lies against G. 3. 91.
him with the formula ' If it appears that he ought to give,'
just as if he had received a loan." Justinian retains the passage,
though he was to speak of indebiti solutio later on under the
rubric of obligationes quasi ex contractu.

595. The other cases of quasi-contractual obligation mentioned in the Institutes are those which exist between tutor and
pupil, co-owners, co-heirs, heir and legatee. But the phrase
admits also of a wide extension to include many cases of
unjustified enrichment, of which indebiti solutio is merely one
example. These cases are distinguished by particular names,
condictio ob causam datorum, or condictio causa data causa non
secuta (*e.g.*, I make a payment by way of dos, but the marriage
does not take place); condictio ob turpem vel injustam causam
(the payment was illegal or immoral—if I am innocent I can
recover); condictio sine causa (a comprehensive phrase applied
to cases other than the above, *e.g.*, when the parties are not
agreed as to the causa—I intend to lend, you think I intend to
give). To these the commentators have added condictio ob
causam finitam (there was a causa, which has ceased to exist [32]
—I have gone on paying an annuity not knowing that the
annuitant was dead); and a condictio ex lege was available
when a statute created an obligation without prescribing a
particular remedy.[33] Finally, there was the condictio furtiva
(§ 610), distinguished from the rest by the fact that the plaintiff
had parted with the property involuntarily. It was an abnormal
remedy allowed odio furum (§ 610).[34]

THE INSTITUTES

BOOK III

TITLE XXVII

Of quasi-contractual obligations

Having enumerated the different kinds of contract, let us now
consider obligations which cannot properly be understood to arise
from contract, but since they are not substantially delictual may be

---

[32] Dig. 19. 1. 11, 6.   [33] Dig. 13, 3.
[34] G. 4. 4; Inst. 4. 6. 14.

said to be analogous to contract. 1. For example, if in a man's absence another person has managed his affairs for him, there are reciprocal actions known as actions on the management of affairs (actiones negotiorum gestorum), the person whose affairs have been managed having the direct action, the manager of affairs (negotiorum gestor) having the contrary action. It is evident that in such cases

§ 585. there is no contractual obligation properly so-called, for these actions are available when a person without mandate has undertaken another man's affairs, and the man whose affairs are undertaken incurs a liability even though he does not know what is being done. This principle was received into the law from motives of convenience, lest persons who were obliged to go abroad on business at short notice without making arrangements for the conduct of their business at home might find that their affairs had been completely neglected, because no one was likely to attend to them unless he had a legal right to recover what he had spent. But just as one who has advantageously managed another person's business may hold him bound, so he, in turn, is bound to give an account of his administration. He is accountable up to the standard of most exact diligence. It is not enough to use the degree of diligence which he usually exercises in his own affairs if a more diligent person would be likely

§ 587. to manage the business to better advantage.

2. Again, tutors who may be sued in connection with their guardianship cannot be said to be bound by contract, because there is not any contract between guardian and ward, but since they are not liable ex maleficio, they seem to be liable quasi ex contractu. In this case too there are reciprocal actions; for not only has the ward the actio tutelae directa, but the guardian has the actio tutelae contraria, if he has incurred expense for his ward's account, or accepted a liability for him, or pledged his own property with a creditor of the ward. 3. Again, if there is community of property without partnership, for example in case of a joint legacy or gift, and one of the parties is liable to the other in an actio communi dividundo, because he has taken all the fruits of the property, or because the other has incurred necessary expenses upon it, the obligation is quasi-contractual.

4. The law is the same when in similar circumstances an action for division of the estate (judicium familiae erciscundae) is available between co-heirs.

5. Again, an heir is not understood to be bound by contract to a legatee, for a legatee cannot be said to have contracted either with the deceased or with the heir; so the relation is taken to be quasi-contractual.

§ 591. 6. A person who has received a payment made in error of what was not owed, may be said to be liable quasi ex contractu. Indeed, so far is he from being bound by contract, that, as observed in an

3. 14. 1. earlier Title, properly considered, he may be said to be bound not by the making of a contract, but by the (purported) unmaking of a contract; for a person who gives money with the design of payment, intends to discharge a contract, not to create one. None the less the person to whom money is paid in error is bound just as if he had received a loan and may be sued by condiction.

7. There are cases in which an undue payment made in error §593.
cannot be recovered. The old lawyers laid down the rule that whenever denial of liability has the effect of increasing [*i.e.*, doubling]
the amount for which judgment may be given, an undue payment
cannot be recovered, as in the case of the lex Aquilia and of legacy
(§ 632). The ancients restricted this to the case of legacies of a
specific sum left per damnationem, but since our constitution has
placed all legacies and fideicommissa on an equality, we have made
this increase correspondingly general, but we do not allow it to all
legatees. It is only legacies and fideicommissa left to churches and 2. 20. 2.
other sacred places which, if unduly paid, cannot be recovered.

XX. Obligations from Delict

596. Delicts are of two kinds, public and private. The first
are crimes, the second torts. They are not mutually exclusive,
for the same wrongful act may give rise both to criminal and to
civil process. But we are now concerned with delict only as
giving rise to a civil action. The Institutes is a treatise on
private law. It is only in the last Title of Book IV that something is said about public prosecutions and only in a cursory
manner.

597. The Roman law of delict had its roots in a distant past
and even in Justinian's system retained many archaic features.
In modern systems criminal process is usually directed to
punishment, civil process to compensation. It is a peculiarity
of the Roman Law that the civil law of delict is largely penal
in character. The sum in which a wrong-doer was condemned
might exceed and often greatly exceeded an estimate of the
damage sustained. It was a fine imposed as a punishment for
the wrong, which went, however, not to the State, as in criminal
process, but to the injured person.

598. The nucleus of the Law of Delict consists in three
wrongs which from the earliest times had given rise to criminal
or civil process. These were furtum, injuria, and damnum
injuria datum—theft, injury (in a special and technical sense)
and wrongful damage to property. Having their origin in the
civil law they were greatly modified and expanded by jurists
and the praetor. There were many other delicts, civil,
praetorian and statutory, but these three, together with rapina,
a variety of furtum, are the only delicts particularly described
in the Institutes. We shall pass them in review and then refer
briefly to some other delicts which escaped Justinian's attention.

599. Every delict gives rise to its appropriate action. But these are features which, in principle, are common to all actions ex delicto, *viz.*: —

1. Being penal they are not passively transmissible (§ 704);
2. A noxal action lies if the delinquent is in power (§ 638);
3. Co-delinquents are liable each severally for the whole penalty (§ 646).

In brief, they are penal, noxal and cumulative.

The first rule applies without restriction to all delicts, the second and third to civil law delicts, not so completely to others (§§ 642, 646). All of this will be illustrated in the following pages.

XXI. FURTUM—RAPINA

600. Paulus, as cited in the Digest, defines furtum in the following terms. Furtum est contrectatio rei fraudulosa lucri faciendi gratia vel ipsius rei vel etiam usus ejus possessionisve: quod lege naturali prohibitum est admittere.[35]

" Theft is a dishonest handling of a thing with a view to gain either of the thing itself or of the use or possession of it,[36] an action prohibited by the precept of natural law."

4. 1. 1. This is repeated in the Institutes with the omission of the words lucri faciendi gratia—" with a view to gain." We will consider the elements in this definition.

4. 1. 7. 601. Dishonest. There must be a theftuous intent. Furtum sine affectu furandi non committitur. Such an intention cannot be imputed to insane persons and very young children.[37]

4. 1. 6. handling. There need not be a carrying away or " asportation," as in common law larceny. Each person who successively handles a thing with guilty purpose commits a fresh act of theft. If a person who has received a thing on deposit denies the fact, this does not in itself make him a thief; but he is guilty of theft if he conceals the thing with the design of appropriating it.[38]

2. 6. 7. of a thing—a movable thing. Some of the old lawyers (Sabinus amongst them) thought that land might be stolen, but this view did not prevail. Things growing on the land, as

---

[35] Dig. 47. 2. 1, 3.
[36] An alternative translation is " in order to make gain either out of the thing itself or else out of the use or possession thereof " (Jolowicz, *Digest*, XLVII, 2 *de furtis*, Cambridge Univ. Press, 1940, *ad loc.*). The definition in the Institutes, of course, does not admit of this interpretation.
[37] Dig. 9. 2. 5, 2; Inst. 4. 1. 18.
[38] Dig. 47. 2. 1, 2.

trees or fruit, or forming part of it, as sand or chalk or minerals,
might be stolen.[39]

or of the use or possession. The use of a thing may be
stolen, as when a depositary uses, or a borrower misuses, a   4. 1. 6.
thing deposited or lent. The possession of a thing may be
stolen, as when an owner fraudulently resumes possession of a
thing which he has given in pledge or takes possession of a
thing which is possessed in good faith by a non-owner.

with a view to gain. This seems to be a necessary part of
the definition. If intending to cause you loss and with no
eye to gain I throw your silver cup into the sea it is not theft.[40]
But the requirement of gain is easily satisfied. If I lend to a
third person a thing which has been lent to me I commit
theft: —

> " for there is a kind of gain in making a present of what
> does not belong to me and so putting the person who
> receives it under an obligation to do something in return." [41]

prohibited by the precepts of natural law. Theft is
unreasonable in itself and universally condemned, for, as Cicero
says, " Nature does not suffer us to increase our capacities,
resources or wealth by despoiling others." [42]

602. There is no theft if the person interested consents to
what is done. This is normally the owner, so we are told that
theft takes place against the will of the owner (invito domino),[43]
though, as we have seen, there are cases in which the owner is
himself the thief, to which may be added the case of the owner
who " handles " a thing of which another person has the usufruct.[44] There was a difference of opinion on the question
whether there was theft when a person with guilty intent appropriated a thing which the owner was willing that he should have.
Pomponius thought that it was theft, and, indeed, it does not
follow that because you wish me to have you are content that I
should take. But Ulpian does not accept this view.[45] Suppose
I attempt to induce your slave to steal something from you ; he
informs you, and you let him take the thing to me wishing to
catch me in the act ; some of the older lawyers took the view
approved by Gaius that you cannot sue me for corrupting a

---

[39] Dig. 47. 2. 25, 2 ; 52, 8 ; 58 (57).
[40] Dig. 19. 5. 14, 2.
[41] Dig. 47. 2. 55 (54), 1.
[42] Cic. de Off. c. 3.
[43] Inst. 4. 1. 7 ; Dig. 47. 2. 46, 7.
[44] Dig. 47. 2. 20, 1.
[45] Dig. 48. 2. 46, 8.

slave, who has not been corrupted, nor for stealing a thing which has not been stolen. Justinian illogically allowed both actions.[46]

603. **Kinds of theft.** According to Labeo, whose view prevailed, there were two kinds of theft, furtum manifestum, and furtum nec manifestum. Sulpicius and Sabinus had included in the list furtum conceptum and furtum oblatum (§ 609), making four in all. But, as Gaius remarks, these two last are names of actions, not distinct kinds of theft.[47]

604. There was much controversy as to the extension to be given to the term furtum manifestum. Gaius continues:—

G. 3. 184.
" Some have said that theft is manifest when the thief is taken in the act; others go further and include the case of his being taken in the place where the theft is committed, for example in the olive garden where he has been stealing olives, or in the vineyard, where he has been stealing grapes, or so long as the thief is in the house, where the theft has been committed; others go further still and include the case of the thief being taken before he has carried the thing away to the place to which he meant to take it; lastly, there are those who say that theft is manifest whenever the thief is seen with the thing in his hands. This view has not been accepted; and the opinion that theft is manifest so long as the thief has not reached his destination cannot be approved because of the great uncertainty whether this is to be taken to be limited to a single day or extended over several days. The point is that thieves often intend to remove the stolen property to another city or to another province. Accordingly, one of the two first-mentioned opinions is preferred, and of them the second is most in favour."

4. 1. 3.
Justinian admits the first three cases and rejects the last, which, nevertheless, recalls the " hand-having thief " of English Law,[48] and may be the starting-point of the whole story, as it is of Ulpian's text in the Digest.[49]

605. Any one who helps another to commit a theft is a
4. 1. 11.
thief, but his intervention must amount to something more than mere advice.

---

[46] G. 3. 198 ; Inst. 4. 1. 8.

[47] G. 3. 183 ; Inst. 4. 1. 3. The word furtum like " theft " in English (see *Oxford-English Dictionary*) means both the act of stealing and the thing stolen. Furtum conceptum = receiving a theft—furtum oblatum = passing on a theft—furtum prohibitum (§ 607) = withholding a theft—furtum manifestum = theft carried in the hand. Mommsen (*Strafrecht* 750, n. 5) says that it is *durchsichtig* that -festus is connected with fendere as in offendere. I respectfully suggest that it is *durchsichtig* that it is the missing past participle of fero.

[48] P. & M. ii, 160, 495 ; Holdsworth, iii, 319.

[49] Dig. 47. 2. 3 pr. Fur est manifestus . . . qui deprehenditur cum furto. The qualifications which follow reflect later speculation.

606. Penalties for theft—Actions. By the Twelve Tables the punishment of manifest theft was "capital," that is to say a free man was beaten and assigned to the person from whom he had stolen. Whether the effect was to reduce him to slavery or to place him in a position of an adjudicatus (§ 681) was an open question with the early lawyers. Slaves were beaten and put to death. Afterwards this punishment was disapproved as too severe, and an action for a four-fold penalty was created by the praetor's Edict applicable to slaves and to free men alike. For non-manifest theft the Twelve Tables imposed a penalty of double damages, and this the praetor retained.[50]

The above account is taken from Gaius. The actions were the same in the time of Justinian.   4. 1. 5.

607. There had been other actions or proceedings in the earlier law. Particular interest attaches to the ancient ritual of search, for which parallels have been found in Greek law and other systems. Gaius again is our principal authority:—

Lib. III. 188. "There is also an actio prohibiti furti which lies against one who prevents search being made [on the premises] for stolen property."

192. "The actio prohibiti for fourfold value was introduced by the edict. The Twelve Tables had not provided any punishment for this offence; all they required was that he who proposed to search another's premises for stolen property should do so naked, wearing nothing but a linteum and carrying a platter; and, if he found anything, then according to the Twelve Tables, the case was to be dealt with as one of manifest theft. 193. What this linteum was has been doubted; but it seems to have been some sort of cloth or towel worn round the loins for decency's sake. But the whole thing is ridiculous; for he who would prevent a man wearing his ordinary dress from making a search, would equally prevent him when naked, especially as the discovery of a thing when sought for would subject the prohibiter to a heavier penalty. And as regards the platter, whether it be said that its use was enjoined in order that, the hands of the holder being occupied in carrying it, he could not surreptitiously take anything into the premises, or in order that he might place upon it anything found by him, neither reason could be satisfactory when the article sought for was of such a size or nature that it could neither be smuggled into the premises nor put upon the platter. There is no doubt that the law was complied with if a platter was there, no matter of what material it might be." [51]

---

[50] G. 3. 190.

[51] Muirhead's translation. For *linteum*, the reading of the Verona palimpsest, most editors substitute *licium*, following Festus and Aulus Gellius, who speak of search *lance et licio*.

608. It is plain that this ancient ritual was as much a mystery to Gaius as it is to ourselves. From Aulus Gellius it appears that it did not survive the lex Aebutia,[52] which was some three centuries before Gaius, and the Twelve Tables were another three centuries further back. Gaius wrote a commentary on the Twelve Tables, but like other commentators he may have made mistakes. In particular, it is suggested that a householder who resisted search was treated as a fur manifestus; hence the fourfold penalty in the later actio furti prohibiti.[53] It may be so, but we must concede to Gaius that he knew more about the Twelve Tables than we do. For the rest, speculation has been busy in exploring the origins of the quaestio cum lance et licio. Whether the lanx was really a magic mirror and the linteum or licium was really a halter to lead away the discovered beast are problems raised by persons of fertile imagination which we are not competent to decide.[54]

609. The other actions mentioned by Gaius are the actio furti concepti and the actio furti oblati. The first lay against a person on whose premises stolen property was found after search in the presence of witnesses though he were not the thief.[55] The second was available to one on whose premises stolen property was found against another who had given him the thing with the design that it should be found on the plaintiff's premises rather than on his own.[56] These actions, in each case for treble damages, were given by the Twelve Tables and retained by the praetor. Finally, there was the actio furti non exhibiti given by the praetor against a defendant who failed to produce a thing sought for and found upon his premises. This action—damages not stated—is recorded by Justinian, not by Gaius. All these actions had passed out of use before Justinian.

4. 1. 4.

610. The actio furti in all its forms was a penal action. In addition, the victim of a theft was entitled to recover his property, if he could, from the thief or any third person. For this purpose he had the actio ad exhibendum, a personal action for its production; the rei vindicatio, a real action available against any person in possession, or who had ceased to possess

[52] *Noctes Atticae*, 16. 10.
[53] Girard, p. 435.
[54] Jörs-Kunkel, p. 254, n. 10.
[55] G. 3. 186, 187. The relation of this action to the formal process of search described above is an unsolved problem. Buckl. *T.* p. 583; *M.* p. 322; Jolowicz, *Digest XLVII.* 2, p. lxxv.
[56] G. 3. 191.

in bad faith ; and the anomalous condictio furtiva,[57] a personal
action available against thieves and their heirs ; for unlike the
actio furti this action was passively transmissible (§ 704). The 　4. 1. 19.
Roman Law did not admit even the limited security which the
English Law gives to an innocent purchaser in market overt,[58]
still less the principle that possession is equivalent to title (§ 274).
Consequently an innocent purchaser from a thief could offer no
defence to the claim of the true owner. Ubi meam rem invenio
ibi vindico—" Where I find my property I vindicate it "—is the
traditional expression of this principle.

611. Who may bring the actio furti? Any person whose
interest it was that the thing should not be stolen. This was 　4. 1. 13.
usually the owner, but not always. A bona fide possessor
might bring the action. A usufructuary might bring it, but not
to the exclusion of the owner. Each sued to the extent of his
interest.[59] The owner might have placed the thing in the hands
of another person under contract. Which of them was entitled
to sue depended upon the nature of the transaction and the
interest, or relative want of interest, of the parties. In the cases
in which the other person was answerable to the owner in case
of theft, it was his interest that the thing should not be stolen
(the commentators call this the negative interest) [60] ; the owner
on the other hand was considered to be sufficiently protected by
his action on the contract, unless the bailee [61] was insolvent, in
which case the owner had an interest in suing the thief. In case
of pledge, the pledgee as well as the pledgor has a right of
action,[62] because it is more expedient for him to rely upon the
pledge than to sue the pledgor on the contract. If things are 　4. 1. 14.
placed in the hands of a fuller or tailor under a contract of hire,
it is he who has the actio furti, provided he is solvent, otherwise it is the owner who sues, " for in this case he is himself
interested in the thing being safe." Before Justinian, the same 　4. 1. 15.
principle applied in the case of loan,[63] but Justinian gave the
lender the option of proceeding against the borrower or the thief

---

[57] G. 4. 4 ; Inst. 4. 6. 14.
[58] S. G. A., ss. 22, 24.
[59] Dig. 47. 2. 46, 1.
[60] Jolowicz, p. xxix.
[61] The term " bailment," borrowed from English Law, conveniently
includes all cases, in which goods have been delivered upon condition that
they shall be restored in a contemplated event. The parties are termed
" bailor " and " bailee."
[62] Ideo autem datur utrique quia utriusque interest. Dig. 47. 2. 12, 2.
But the calculation of damages in each case was difficult. Jolowicz,
op. cit., p. XL.
[63] G. 3. 206.

as he thought best; and having adopted one alternative he was not allowed to change his mind and fall back on the other, except in the case of his having taken proceedings against the borrower without knowledge of the theft. If the borrower was sued upon the contract and satisfied the lender's claim, he was allowed the actio furti against the thief. A depositary was not considered to have an interest in the thing not being stolen, because in the absence of guilty intention on his part, he incurred no liability through his failure to restore, and if he was guilty of dolus no doubt the risk was his, but he was not allowed to acquire a right of action by his own wrong.[64] The owner, therefore, alone was competent to bring the action.

4. 1. 16.

4. 1. 17.

612. Wide as is the definition of furtum given in the text, it is not wide enough to include all the cases which in the Digest are brought under the head of furtum, *e.g.*, maliciously summoning a muleteer to court with the consequence that his mules, left unattended, are lost.[65] The definition speaks of the dishonest handling of a thing. This of course includes a slave as being an object of ownership, but free persons too could be stolen, a child in the law of Justinian, in the older law also a wife in manu.[66]

613. It must be observed that there could not (in general) be an action of theft within the family circle. A son could not bring an actio furti against his father (unless it were in respect of something included in his castrense peculium), nor a father against his son; nor a husband against his wife (or vice versa),[67] but, if either spouse had taken the other's property in contemplation of a divorce which actually followed, redress might be claimed in an action which bore the " polite name " of actio rerum amotarum—the action for taking things away.[68]

4. 1. 12.

614. For the praetorian delict rapina see the Text (Tit. II). It is commonly said that the peregrine praetor Lucullus distinguished this delict from furtum when he created the actio vi bonorum raptorum by his Edict in B.C. 76. But " the history of this action is curious and in some respects obscure." [69] The specific delict rapina developed gradually.[70]

---

64 Dig. 47. 2. 14, 3.
65 Dig. 47. 2. 67, 2.
66 G. 3. 199; Inst. 4. 1. 9.
67 Dig. 47. 2. 52, 6; 47. 2. 16; 36, 1.
68 Jolowicz, p. lxxxvii.
69 Jolowicz, p. 291.
70 Moyle, p. 523; Buckl. *T.* p. 584; *M.* p. 323; Girard, p. 444, n. 4.

THE INSTITUTES

BOOK IV (Tits. I, II)

TITLE I

Of obligations which arise from delict

In the last Book we explained the obligations which arise ex contractu and quasi ex contractu. We now turn to obligations from wrongdoing. Of obligations from contract there are, as we have seen, four kinds. But of obligations from wrongdoing there is only one kind, for they all arise re, that is from the wrongful act, such as theft, robbery, damage or injuria.

1. Theft is the dishonest handling of a thing, either of the thing itself or of the use or possession of it, such action being prohibited by the precepts of natural law. § 600.

2. The word furtum is derived from furvus, a word which means black, because theft is committed secretly and stealthily and usually by night; or from fraus; or from ferre in the sense of auferre—to carry away, or from the Greek word for thief, which likewise is derived from the verb meaning to carry away.[71] 3. There are two § 603. kinds of theft, manifest and non-manifest. The terms furtum conceptum and furtum oblatum are rather the names of actions connected with theft as distinct kinds of theft, as will be seen below. A manifest thief is not only one who is taken in the act, but also one who is taken on the spot; for example, if a man has stolen in a house and is caught before he has passed out through the door, or if he has been caught in a plantation or a vineyard where he has been stealing olives or grapes. Indeed, the term must be extended to include the thief who is seen or caught with the stolen property in his hands in a public or private place by the owner or by any one else before he has reached the place where he meant to take and leave it. But if he has taken it to its destination, though he is afterwards caught with the thing in his possession, he is not a manifest thief. What non-manifest theft is may be understood from what we have said already, for any theft which is not manifest is non-manifest.

4. We speak of furtum conceptum when in the presence of witnesses stolen property is looked for and found in a person's possession. A special action lies against him, even though he may not be the thief, called the actio furti concepti.

Oblatum furtum occurs when a person passes on to you stolen property and it is found as just described, that is if he passed it on with the design that it should be found with you and not with him; you have a special action against him, although he may not be the thief, called the actio furti oblati. Then there is the actio prohibiti furti against the man who has obstructed another who was set on making search in the presence of witnesses. Further, the

---

[71] This is taken from Paulus (Dig. 47. 2. 1 pr.) who attributes the first etymology to Labeo, the second to Sabinus. Furtum looks very much like a past participle of an earlier form of furari. So tono and sono in early Latin had third conjugation forms.

praetor's edict penalises the man who has not produced the thing which has been sought for and found in his possession. This is the actio furti non exhibiti—for not producing the stolen property. All these actions are disused as a consequence of the discontinuance of the ancient ceremonial requisition of stolen property, and it is very evident that any one who with guilty knowledge receives and conceals stolen property is guilty of non-manifest theft.

5. The penalty for manifest theft is fourfold, whether the thief be slave or free; for non-manifest theft twofold.

§ 601.

6. Theft is committed not only when a person removes a thing which belongs to some one else with the purpose of appropriating it, but in general when a person handles a thing which does not belong to him contrary to the will of the owner. Accordingly, theft is committed if a person to whom a thing is given in pledge or by way of deposit uses it, or if a person to whom a thing is lent for use misapplies it to some other use than that for which it was given. For instance, if a person has borrowed plate on the pretext that he was going to ask friends to dinner, and has taken it abroad with him, or if a man has borrowed a horse for riding and has taken it on a distant journey—taken it into battle, to cite the instance given by the ancients. 7. But it is settled that borrowers who apply the things for a purpose other than that for which they were lent, are not guilty of theft unless they knew that they were acting against the will of the owner and that, if he had known, he would not have allowed them to do it. If they thought that he would allow it, they are guiltless. This is a very proper distinction, for there is no theft where there is no theftuous intent.

8. Further, if a person thinks that he is using a thing lent to him contrary to the will of the owner, but in fact the owner is willing that he should so use it, it is said that there is no theft. This suggests the following question. Titius tried to suborn the slave of Maevius to steal some things from his master and bring them to Titius. The slave told his master, who, wishing to catch Titius in the act, allowed the slave to take some things to him. Is Titius liable for theft, or for corrupting a slave, or for neither ? The old lawyers entertained very different views on this matter, some admitting neither action, others the action for theft alone. But when the question was submitted to us we decided that both actions can be brought [72]; for though the conditions of the actio servi corrupti are not present, still he tried to corrupt the slave, and it is proper that he should be punished as if he had done so. For, if he escapes, others may attempt the corruption of a more corruptible slave.

9. Sometimes even free persons are stolen, as when a child in power is kidnapped.

10. It may happen that a man steals his own property, as when a debtor dishonestly resumes possession of a thing given in pledge.

§ 605.

11. Sometimes a man is liable for theft, who has not committed theft himself, as when a theft has been committed with his aid and at his instigation. For instance, some one knocks coins out of your hand in order that another may get away with them, or stands in

---

[72] Cod. 6. 2. 20.

your way in order that another may steal from you, or drives your
sheep or oxen in order that another may intercept them, as in the
case put by the ancients of a herd put to flight by waving a red
cloth. If anything of the sort is done mischievously and not with
the design that a theft may be committed the action should be on
the case (in factum). If Maevius helps Titius to commit theft,
both are liable for theft. Again, it is a case of aiding and abetting
if a man puts a ladder to a window, or breaks a window or door, in
order that another may commit theft, or lends tools for house-
breaking, or a ladder to be put against a window, knowing the
purpose for which they were borrowed. A person who does not help
another to commit a theft, but stops short at advice and encourage-
ment, is not guilty of theft.

12. If children or slaves in power steal from the paterfamilias § 613.
or dominus they commit theft, and the thing taken is a res furtiva,
and cannot be usucaped until it returns to the owner's power; but
there is no actio furti, as, indeed, there cannot be any other action
between the persons concerned; but if a third person has aided and
abetted the act, he is liable for theft, for the property has in fact
been stolen at his instigation.

13. The actio furti may be brought by the person whose interest § 611.
it is that the thing should be safe, even though he is not the owner;
and the owner cannot bring it unless he has that interest. 14. It
follows that if a thing given in pledge is stolen the creditor (pledgee)
may bring the action, even though the debtor (pledgor) is solvent,
because it is more to his advantage to rely upon the pledge than to
sue the pledgor upon the contract; this is so far the case that if the
pledgor himself steals the thing the pledgee may bring the actio furti
against him. 15. If a fuller or tailor has received clothes to be
attended to in the way of his trade for an agreed reward, and they
are stolen, it is he, not the owner, who has the action, for the owner
has no interest in the clothes not being stolen, since he can get
compensation for their loss in an action on the contract. So, again,
a bona fide purchaser may maintain the action just as the pledgee
may, though he is not the actual owner. The fuller or tailor cannot
bring the action of theft unless he is solvent, that is to say, able to
pay the value of the clothes to the owner; if he is not, so that the
owner cannot get his indemnity from him, it is the owner who brings
the action, because in this case he has an interest in the thing not
being lost. The same applies if the fuller or tailor is only partly
able to pay.

16. The ancients thought that the same principle should be
applied when property is lent, for the borrower too is answerable
for keeping the thing safe (necesse habet custodiam praestare). But
by one of our Decisions (§ 41) the law has been altered so that the
owner has the option of suing the borrower, or of proceeding against
the thief, and if he chooses the one alternative, he cannot fall back
upon the other. If he chooses to sue the thief, the borrower is
discharged. If he sues the borrower, he cannot go against the thief,
but the borrower may. This is on the assumption that the owner
knew that the thing had been stolen when he sued the borrower.
But if he did not know that the thing was not in the possession of
the borrower, or had his doubts about it when he sued the borrower,

and afterwards, when he comes to know about it, wishes to drop the action against the borrower and to go against the thief, he is free to do so (unless, of course, the borrower has made good his loss, in which case the owner has no longer any right of action against the thief, the borrower taking his place). If in these circumstances he decides to proceed against the thief, the borrower is discharged from liability, whatever may be the result of the action against the thief, and similarly [if he decides with knowledge of the theft to prosecute his claim against the borrower, he loses his recourse against the thief] whether the borrower is able to pay in whole or only in part.[73]

17. A person with whom a thing is deposited is not liable for safe keeping, but only for dolus. Consequently, since he is not liable to make good the loss if the thing is stolen, and, therefore, has no interest in the thing being safe, he cannot bring the actio furti. It is the owner who is competent to bring it. 18. The question has been asked whether a child beneath the age of puberty can commit a theft. It has been decided, since theft implies a theftuous intent, that a child is not liable for theft, unless he is very near to puberty and therefore understands that he is doing wrong. 19. The actio furti, whether brought for double or for fourfold damages, is concerned merely with the penalty. Apart from this, the owner is entitled to recover the thing or its value. For this purpose a vindication may be brought against the person in possession of the stolen property, whether the thief or any one else; and a condiction is available against the thief, or his heir, though not in possession.

§ 610.

TITLE II

Of robbery

A man who takes by force what belongs to another is liable for theft—for who is more completely a thief than the man who robs?—and so robbers are very properly said to be " impudent thieves." None the less, the praetor has made this delict the subject of a special action called the actio vi bonorum raptorum, which may be brought within the year for fourfold damages, after the year for single damages. This action is available even if a single thing is taken, and that of the smallest value. The fourfold damages are not wholly penalty with a further claim for the value of the thing, as in the case of manifest theft, but the fourfold assessment includes the value of the thing, so that it is penal to the extent of three-quarters, and the threefold penalty applies whether the robber is caught in the act or not. It would be ridiculous if a robber got off more lightly than an ordinary thief.[74]

1. This action lies only if a person has laid hands on a thing in bad faith. Consequently, if a person erroneously supposing that

---

[73] Cod. 6. 2. 22 (*verbatim*). I have supplied the words in brackets to make the meaning clearer.

[74] This reads like an extract from an earlier author retained *per incuriam* supporting the view that the damages were wholly penal. *Cf.* G. 4. 8. Papinian says (Dig. 47. 2. 81, 3.), raptor . . . manifestus fur existimandus est.

a thing is his and thinking that the law allows an owner forcibly to resume possession of his property has seized it with that design, he ought to be absolved in this action, and equally so if charged with theft. But to prevent robbers giving free rein to their avarice, imperial constitutions have introduced a better principle, namely, that no one may take forcible possession of movables or live-stock, even though he thinks that the thing belongs to him. Any one who offends against the law, if he is owner, forfeits his ownership, if he is not owner, must give the thing back and pay its value in addition. These enactments have applied the same rule to forcible entries on land, in order to prevent any kind of violence perpetrated under pretext of ownership.[75]

2. In this action the question is not whether the thing is the property of the plaintiff or not. It is enough that it forms part of his belongings. Accordingly if Titius has a thing on loan, or on hire, or as a pledge, or on deposit, so that he has an interest in its not being taken (this is so in the last case if he has undertaken to be liable for culpa), or if he is a bona fide possessor, or a usufructuary, or has any other right, so that he has an interest in its not being seized, this action may be said to be available, to recover not the ownership, but the loss which his estate has sustained in consequence of the robbery. And, generally, it may be said that whenever an action of theft is competent if a thing has been taken stealthily, this action is competent if it has been taken violently.

XXII. Injuria

615. The history of this delict begins with the Twelve Tables, where it comes into view as an aggression, more or less serious, upon a man's person. The penalty for a maimed limb was retaliation, unless the parties came to a composition—si membrum rupit, ni cum eo pacit, talio esto (§ 659)—for a broken bone three hundred asses if the injured person was a free person, one hundred and fifty if he was a slave (in the later law this was a case rather of damage to property). For every other injury there was a uniform penalty of twenty-five asses.[76] There is no record, even legendary, of retaliation having been applied. The pecuniary penalties were arbitrary and became inadequate. The system of fixed penalties gave way to an action in which the praetor fixed the sum up to which the judex might condemn (actio injuriarum aestimatoria) in view of the circumstances of the case. In particular, higher damages were given if the injury was of an atrocious character. Contemporaneously with, or in consequence of, this development, the meaning of injuria was

---

[75] The latest of these enactments was a constitution of Valentinian, Theodosius and Arcadius of A.D. 389, Cod. 8. 4. 7.

[76] G. 3. 223 ; Inst. 4. 4. 7.

greatly enlarged. No longer limited to physical violence, it came to embrace every kind of wanton aggression upon a man's person or personality.[77]   Essentially, it is an affront, a contumely, which easily passes into the associated wrong of defamation.[78]   But they are different. It is one thing to injure my reputation, another to injure my feelings. Wherever the Roman tradition exists, as on the continent and in Scotland and South Africa, both are actionable wrongs. But it is not so in English Law. " Our law [said Lord President Inglis in a Scottish case] says that a man may have damages for injury done to his feelings. The law of England repudiates that doctrine." [79]

616. For a general description of this delict it is sufficient to refer to the text. One or two particulars may be mentioned. Since the gist of injuria is injury to my feelings, if my feelings are not injured there is no injuria. If I do not show resentment it is supposed that I do not feel it. This is what is meant when it is said that the action is destroyed by dissimulation (haec actio dissimulatione aboletur), *i.e.*, if the victim of the affront conceals his feelings. For the same reason the action is barred after an unusually short time, *viz.*, one year.[80]   Contrary to the usual rule in penal actions this action is not actively transmissible (no penal actions are passively transmissible (§ 704)). This is because an action for injured feelings must be brought by the person whose feelings are injured, not by his heir.

4. 4. 12.

4. 12. 1.

617. Just as without theftuous intention there is no theft, so in principle there is no injuria without injurious intention—animus injuriae faciendae—animus injuriandi.[81]   But a man's intentions must usually be inferred, and sometimes conclusively inferred, from what he says and does. This applies particularly when injuria takes the form of defamation.

618. It will be noted that a man may suffer injuria not only in his own person but in the person of another. An injuria offered to a slave, if of an atrocious character or otherwise insulting to the master, gave the master a right of action. A father and a husband might maintain an action in respect of an injury offered to a child in power or to a wife ; a father-in-law in respect of an injury offered to his daughter-in-law, wife of a son in power.

4. 4. 2.

---

[77] Omnemque injuriam aut in corpus inferri aut ad dignitatem aut ad infamiam pertinere (Labeo ait). Dig. 47. 10. 1, 2.
[78] Dig. 47. 10. 15, 27
[79] *Mackay* v. *M'Cankie* (1883) 10 R. 537.
[80] Cod. 9. 35. 5.
[81] Dig. 47. 10. 26.

619. Condemnation in the actio injuriarum involved   4. 16. 2.
infamia, and compromise of the action had the same effect.[82]
But there was always the danger that the action might recoil
upon the plaintiff. A wise man would not bring it without
good cause. If he did so, he ran the risk of a contrary action
by the defendant.[83] Besides the civil action given by the
Edict, one of Sulla's laws, the lex Cornelia de injuriis, provided
a criminal process, in which the penalty went to the prosecutor
if the injuria took the form of personal violence or the invasion
of a man's house.[84] From the time of Caracalla, if not before,
the injured person had the alternative of bringing a civil action
based upon the same facts.[85] In the later Empire injuries were
punished criminally by extraordinary process and this procedure
tended to take the place of the civil action.[86]

THE INSTITUTES

BOOK IV

TITLE IV

Of injuries

In its most general sense injuria means anything done contrary   § 615.
to law; in a special sense it means sometimes contumely or insult,
sometimes fault (or a faulty act), as the lex Aquilia speaks of
damnum injuria datum, that is loss caused by fault, sometimes it
means iniquity or injustice. Thus, if the praetor or judge decides
contrary to law we say that the person against whom the decision
is given has suffered an injury or injustice.

1. An injury [in the special sense of contumely or insult which
is the subject of this Title] is committed not only when a man
is struck with the fist, or struck or beaten with a club, but also when
an outcry is raised against him, or when one has caused possession
to be taken of another person's goods on the false pretext of his
being his debtor, or has written or composed or published anything
in prose or verse to bring any person into disrepute, or has with
guilty purpose procured any such thing to be done, or has pursued a
married woman or a young boy or girl, or attempted anyone's
chastity; and, in short, it is plain that an injury may be committed
in a great variety of ways.

2. A man may suffer an injury not only in his own person, but   § 618.
also in the person of children in his power, or (according to the

---

[82] Dig. 3. 2. 4, 5 ; 6 ; Cod. 2. 11 (12). 18.
[83] G. 4. 177.
[84] Dig. 47. 10. 5 pr.
[85] Dig. 47. 10. 7, 6: Posse hodie de omni injuria, sed et de atroci
civiliter agi imperator noster rescripsit (Ulpian).
[86] Dig. 47. 10. 45 (Hermogenianus) ; Inst. 4. 4. 10.

better and accepted view) of his wife. So, if you commit an injury against a man's daughter, married to Titius, you may be sued not only in the name of the daughter, but of her father and her husband as well. But, conversely, if injury is done to a husband, the wife has no right of action, for it is the business of husbands to defend their wives, not of wives to defend their husbands. A father-in-law may maintain an action for injuries in the name of a daughter-in-law, whose husband is in his power. 3. An injury cannot be committed against a slave. But an injury may be done to a master through his slave, not indeed in the same way as through children and wives, but only if the injury is of an atrocious character and clearly intended as an insult to the master. For example, an action lies if some one beats another person's slave. But if a man abuses a slave or strikes him with his fist, the owner has no action against him.

4. If injury is done to a slave owned in common, it is reasonable that damages should be assessed not proportionately to each owner's share in the slave, but having regard to the personal status of the several owners, for it is their person which is affected by the injury.

5. If Titius has the usufruct of a slave, and Maevius the bare ownership, an injury done to the slave is understood to be directed against Maevius rather than against Titius.

6. If an injury is done to a free man, who is bona fide serving you as a slave, you will have no action, but he can sue in his own name; unless he was assaulted with the design of insult to yourself, for in that case you too can bring the action for injuries. The same applies if another man's slave is serving you in good faith, that is to say, you can bring the action whenever injury was done to him as an insult to yourself.

7. The Law of the Twelve Tables said that injuries were to be punished as follows:—for a maimed limb retaliation; for a broken bone there were pecuniary penalties of small amount in keeping with the prevailing poverty of the time. Afterwards, the praetor permitted any one who had suffered an injury to put a value upon it, so that the judge could condemn a defendant to pay the amount of the assessment or a less amount as he might see fit. The penalties fixed by the Twelve Tables have passed out of use. But the praetorian or honorary penalty (as it is also called) is in use in the courts. The assessment of the injury rises or falls according to the rank and reputation of the plaintiff; and the same principle is quite properly observed when the immediate victim is a slave, so that the assessment is highest when the slave is a steward, less when he is of middle rank, and least of all when he is a slave of no account or one condemned to wear fetters.

8. There is a lex Cornelia too which relates to injuries and gives an actio injuriarum. This lies when there is a complaint that a man has been struck or beaten or that forcible entry has been made upon his house. The word house is understood to apply to the house in which a man is living, whether it belongs to him or he has hired it or is occupying it gratis or as a guest.

9. An injury is accounted atrocious either on account of the nature of the act, as if a man is wounded or beaten with clubs; or on account of the place where the injury is committed, for example

in the theatre or the forum or in the presence of the praetor; or on account of the person injured, for example, a magistrate, or if a senator is injured by a person of low condition, or a parent or patron by a child or freedman; for the assessment is not the same when a senator or parent or patron suffers injury and when the victim is a stranger to the aggressor or a person of low condition. Sometimes the part of the body affected makes the injury atrocious, as when a man is struck in the eye. In such a case it makes little difference whether the injury is done to the father of a family or to a son in power. In either case the injury will be atrocious.

10. Finally, it is to be remarked that in every case of injury the person who has suffered it may proceed either criminally or civilly. It he takes civil proceedings an assessment is made as described above 'and a penalty decreed accordingly. If he proceeds criminally the judge determines the penalty in the exercise of his extraordinary jurisdiction. A constitution of Zeno enacted that viri illustres and persons of yet higher rank may bring and defend criminal proceedings for injury through procurators in the manner therein provided. § 619.

11. It is not alone the person who has actually done the injury or struck the blow who is liable, but also any one who with evil intent has effected or procured that some one should strike another in the face with his fist.

12. The right of action is lost if a man conceals his feelings. Therefore if a man " abandons his injury," that is, does not immediately resent it, he may not afterwards change his mind and revive an injury which he has once condoned. § 616.

XXIII. Damnum Injuria Datum

620. Unlike the delicts above described this is statutory. It has its foundation in the lex Aquilia, a plebiscite attributed without much reason to the year B.C. 287. The Twelve Tables and subsequent laws had dealt with specific cases of damage to property, but this legislation was abrogated or superseded by the statute, which contained provisions of a more general character.[87] The subject is contained in the first and third chapters of the lex, which so far as the text can be inferred from the Digest and the Institutes were substantially as follows: —

621. Chapter I. Si quis servum servamve alienum alienamve quadrupedemve pecudem injuria occiderit, quanti ea res in eo anno plurimi fuerit, tantum aes ero dare damnas esto.[88] 4. 3 pr.

" If any one shall have wrongfully killed another person's male or female slave or four-footed beast, be he condemned to pay to the owner the highest value in that year."

Chapter III. Ceterarum rerum praeter hominem et pecudem occisos si quis alteri damnum faxit, quod usserit, fregerit, 4. 3. 13.

---

[87] Dig. 9. 2. 1 pr.
[88] Dig. 9. 2. 2 pr.; Grueber, *The Lex Aquilia*, p. 199.

ruperit injuria, quanti ea res fuerit in diebus triginta proximis tantum aes ero dare damnas esto.[89]

"In respect of other things apart from the killing of slave or cattle if any one shall have caused damage to another by wrongful burning, breaking, or spoiling, be he condemned to pay to the owner the value which the thing has had in the last thirty days."

We will speak first of the general principles of liability under the statute and then consider the language of each chapter so far as it calls for comment.

622. To constitute liability under the statute there must be (a) an act, (b) which is wrongful, and (c) causes damage.

623. (a) An act. Mere omission does not render a person liable, but one who assumes to do a thing must, as a rule, carry it through to its proper completion. A surgeon will be liable if after operating he fails to give his patient proper attention.

4. 3. 6.

4. 3. 3
& 14.

624. (b) which is wrongful. The act must be wrongful, that is to say intended or negligent and without lawful justification or excuse. Any intended or negligent act which causes damage is prima facie wrongful. There are many grounds of justification and excuse—self-defence, accident, an authority conferred by law, and others. No liability attaches to a madman or a very young child as being incapable either of dolus or of culpa.[90]

4. 3. 2.

625. (c) and causes damage. This means a pecuniary detriment consequent upon the act. This may be positive or negative —positive, if my property has ceased to exist, or has been rendered less valuable; negative, if I have lost a reasonable prospect of profit. These kinds of damage are distinguished by the commentators as damnum emergens and lucrum cessans, which may be rendered " positive damage " and " loss of profit." The first may be immediate (e.g., my slave is killed or has lost an eye), or consequential (I have lost his services—I have incurred medical expenses—he was one of a troupe of singers and the whole troupe is less valuable in consequence of his death or injury). Where there is no pecuniary loss there is no action. An action does not lie under the statute for striking a slave if his value to me has not been depreciated by the blow nor for trespass to land unattended by damage.

4. 3. 10.

---

[89] Dig. 9. 2. 27, 5; Grueber, p. 199. There has been much speculation as to the original character of the statute. The language of the above extracts has plainly been modernised.

[90] Dig. 9. 2. 5, 2.

626. With regard to the construction of the statute the following points may be noticed. In chapter I : —

killed. This implies an act of direct violence, but the praetor extended it to include any way of causing death.[91]

another person's. Generally the owner is the person who suffers loss, and this is the only case contemplated by the statute, but there were cases in which an owner might himself be liable to an action on the analogy of the statute. These are noticed below.

four-footed beast—see the text.   4. 3. 1.

the highest value in that year. The year was reckoned back, according to the prevailing view, from the date of the fatal injury, not (if later) from the date of death.[92]

627. In chapter III : —

apart from the killing of slave or cattle. This is, perhaps, a gloss upon the words " in respect of other things " and not part of the original text of the statute, or it may be that all that precedes " if any one " is a later addition.

burning, breaking or spoiling. The word spoiling (ruperit) was widely construed so as to include any damage, however, caused.   4. 3. 13.

the value. This was construed to mean " highest value," as in chapter I. What was the measure of damages under   4. 3. 15. chapter III of the Lex Aquilia is a difficult question. The text seems to imply that a wound inflicted on a slave entailed a penalty equivalent to the [highest] value of the slave within the last thirty days. Wholly unreasonable as this seems, there are writers who accept it as illustrating the highly penal character of an early statute. Many ignore the difficulty. But Buckland (M. p. 324) says, " not necessarily the whole value, but the difference between this highest value and the value after the damage," and Roby (Vol. 2, p. 191), " Under the third clause the measure was the depreciation caused in what was the value to the plaintiff within the last thirty days." There is little, if any, textual authority for this view, but there are, none the less, good reasons for accepting it. If we turn to Gaius we find that in speaking of the damages recoverable under chapter I he remarks that these may exceed the value of the slave at the time of the killing if he had become lame or lost an eye within the year (G. III 214). Surely, if the law had awarded the full value

---

[91] Inst. 4. 3. 16; Dig. 9. 2. 7, 1; 7, 6; 51 pr.
[92] Dig. 9. 2. 21, 1.

of the slave in the case of a broken arm, Gaius would have commented upon such an extraordinary consequence. But he does not say a word about it. Nor is there any hint of anything of the kind in the title of the Digest (IX 2) *Ad Legem Aquiliam*. The inference is that no such idea occurred to the classical lawyers. Further, the phrase quanti ea res est (erit) is commonly used to mean "the appropriate damages" (see the formulae given on pp. 443, 445), and, in fact, is so used in the second chapter of the Lex recorded by Gaius III 215. Capite secundo adversus stipulatorem qui pecuniam in fraudem stipulatoris acceptam fecerit quanti ea res est tanti actio constituitur. "By the second chapter an adstipulator who defrauds a principal stipulator by releasing the promisor can be sued for the amount of the loss occasioned" (Poste). We are justified, therefore, in coming to a conclusion which is consonant with common sense. It corresponds with the solution suggested by C. H. Monro in his edition of the Lex Aquilia (Cambridge, 1898), pp. 35 *et seq.*, of a question which he begins by saying "presents to me insuperable difficulty."

628. The scope of the statute, as has already appeared, was greatly enlarged by the jurists and by the praetor. The particular contribution of the jurists (apart from the verbal interpretation of the statute) was to extend it, so as to include consequential damages. The result is sometimes surprising. It is plain that "foresee-ability" was not an element in the case. If I kill your slave, who has been instituted heir, and thus make it impossible for him to accept the inheritance by your order, I am liable to you for the value of the lost inheritance. The Digest puts the case of a master, whose slave has been guilty of serious falsification of his accounts. The master intended to examine him under torture with a view to extracting from him the names of his accomplices. I have killed him. Labeo says (and according to Ulpian, "very rightly") that the damages will include the interest the master had in the discovery of the frauds.[93] It is difficult to see how the damage could be assessed, particularly in view of another passage where Labeo and Proculus are quoted as holding that if you have fouled my nets by careless navigation I can get compensation for the value of the nets, but not for the lost catch of fish, for I might not have caught any.[94] Sentimental damages cannot be recovered in this action. "If you kill my slave (says Paulus) I am of opinion

4. 3. 10.

---

[93] Dig. 9. 2. 23, 4.
[94] Dig. 9. 2. 29, 3.

that my sentiments are not to be taken into account (as, for example, if one kills your natural son for whom you would willingly pay a high price), but only the market value." [95] Originally, the third chapter applied only to movables, but it was early extended to land.[96]

629. The praetor went much further in extending the usefulness of the action. First, he made it available to others than the owner, to the usufructuary, the bona fide possessor, the pledgee,[97] but not usually to one who had merely a right ex contractu, as a borrower, or a purchaser before delivery. The only exception was the lessee of land, who was given an action in respect of damage to his crop, but conditionally upon giving security to the defendant against further proceedings by the owner.[98] Secondly, the action, which under the statute lay only in case of direct violence by the body to the body (corpore corpori), was extended to cases of death or injury caused corpori but not corpore, and ultimately to cases where the defendant's act caused loss, but inflicted no injury (nec corpore nec corpori). Illustrations will be found in the text.

Lastly, by a still bolder departure from the original purpose of the action the praetor made it available in case of personal injury either to the plaintiff himself, or to children in his power.[99] This must be carefully distinguished from the actio injuriarum, for (a) the actio injuriarum implies wanton aggression, the actio legis Aquiliae lies also where dolus is absent if the defendant has been guilty of culpa ; (b) the actio injuriarum is brought for " sentimental " damages, the action on the statute only for " patrimonial " damages, that is for actual pecuniary loss.

630. In all the above cases the praetor is said to allow an actio utilis (quasi ex lege Aquilia) [1] or an actio in factum (ad exemplum legis Aquiliae).[2] The phrases seem to be used indifferently. It is only in the Institutes that a distinction is made between (a) the actio directa, when the damage is corpore corpori ; (b) the actio utilis (corpori non corpore) ; (c) the actio in factum (nec corpore nec corpori). The distinction has no 4. 3. 16. practical interest.

---

95 Dig. 9. 2. 33.
96 Dig. 9. 2. 27, 7-9 ; Buckl. *T.* p. 588 ; *M.* p. 325.
97 Dig. 19. 2. 11, 10 ; 11, 8 ; 30, 1.
98 Dig. 9. 2. 27, 14.
99 Dig. 9. 2. 13 pr. ; 5, 3.
1 Dig. 47. 2. 51.
2 Dig. 9. 2. 53.

4. 12. 1.
631. The actio legis Aquiliae was transmissible actively; not passively (§ 704), unless the action had reached the stage of litis contestatio before the death of the defendant (§§ 580, 714). But the author of a wrong was not allowed to make it a source of profit to himself. He was liable, therefore, to make compensation to the extent of his enrichment. This was not an action on the statute, but a condictio ob injustam causam (§ 595), which was passively transmissible.[3]

4. 6. 19.
632. The actio legis Aquiliae was one of the group of actions in which if liability was denied the damages were doubled— adversus infitiantem lis crescit (§ 593). This taken together with the use of the words damnas esto in the text of the law suggests that the original remedy may have been by way of manus injectio.[4]

4. 9 pr.
633. We have now passed in review the four delicts which Gaius and Justinian enumerate as giving rise to obligationes ex delicto. There were many others. Some of these were survivals from the Law of the Twelve Tables, like the action for cutting trees (actio de arboribus succisis (§ 689),[5] for arson (actio de aedibus incensis),[6] for damage done by pasturing cattle (actio de pastu),[7] all of which found a serious competitor in the actio legis Aquiliae. The actio de pauperie, which is referred to the same source, afforded a more general remedy for damage done by animals. Justinian devotes a Title to this subject in the Fourth Book (infra, p. 407). Other delicts were of praetorian origin, such as dolus and metus, giving rise to the actio doli and the actio metus (§§ 549, 550), and fraud on creditors (fraus creditorum), giving rise amongst other remedies to the action, commonly known as the actio Pauliana, to rescind dispositions made with fraudulent intention. To these may be added various statutory wrongs such as taking forcible possession of movables or forcible entry on land, which has been

4. 6. 6.
4. 2. 1.
mentioned in the text of the Institutes in connection with rapina. Many obligations originally regarded as delictual came to be regarded as contractual, though retaining sometimes traces of their origin. A conspicuous example is the action for double

4. 6. 17.
damages given in the case of so-called depositum miserabile (§ 436). Finally, there are the four cases which Justinian brings together under the description of obligationes quasi ex delicto. Some account of these will be given below.

---

3 Dig. 9. 2. 23, 8; 50. 17. 38.   4 Girard, p. 441.
5 G. 4. 11; Dig. 12. 2. 28, 6.
6 Dig. 47. 9. 9.   7 Dig. 19. 5. 14, 3.

THE INSTITUTES

BOOK IV

TITLE III

Of the lex Aquilia

The action for damnum injuria is given by the lex Aquilia. **§ 621**
The first chapter provides that if anyone shall have wrongfully
killed another person's slave or beast that pastures he is to be condemned to pay to the owner the highest value in that year.

1. Inasmuch as the law does not speak in absolute terms of a
beast, but only of beasts that pasture, we are to understand that it
does not relate to wild animals or to dogs, but only to beasts which
can properly be said to pasture such as horses, mules, asses, oxen,
sheep and goats. The same may be said of swine, for they also may
be termed beasts that pasture, for they feed in herds. Aelius
Marcianus quotes from the Odyssey:—

"Thou shalt find him sitting by the swine: they pasture by   **Od.**
the rock of Corax hard by Arethusa's fount."   **XIII,**
                                                                 407–8.

2. A man is said to kill wrongfully, if he kills without right.
Accordingly, one who kills a robber is not liable, provided that this **§ 624**
was the only way of escape. .

3. Nor is a man liable, if he kills by accident, if he is found
not to have been negligent; for one is liable under the statute for
negligence no less than for wrongful intention.

4. Therefore, if a person is hurling a javelin in sport or in
practice and has hit your slave who was passing by, we must
distinguish. If the event took place when a soldier was exercising
in the Campus or in any other place where such exercises are usual,
he is free from blame; but if any one else has done such a thing, he
is guilty. The same may be said of a soldier if he was throwing the
javelin in a place not reserved for the purpose. 5. Again, if a man
who was lopping a tree has let fall a branch and killed your slave
who was passing by, if this took place near a public road or a local
road, and he did not shout out, so that any one might keep out of
the way of the accident, he is in fault; if he shouted out, and the
other man did not look out for himself, he is free from blame; and
so he is, if he was cutting the tree away from the road or in the
middle of a field, though he did not shout out, for a stranger had no
right to be in such a place.

6. If a surgeon who has operated on your slave neglects the after **§ 623**
treatment and the slave dies in consequence, he is guilty of
negligence.

7. Want of skill is reckoned as a fault; for example, if a medical
man has killed your slave by operating unskilfully or giving him a
wrong medicine.

8. If your slave has been run over by a team of mules which the
muleteer had not the skill to hold back, the man is to blame; and
so he is too if he was not strong enough to check them when a
stronger man might have done so. The same applies to a horseman,
who was unable to hold in his horse either from want of strength
or from want of skill.

9. The effect of the words, "the highest value in that year," is as follows:—If some one has killed a slave of yours who today is lame, or has lost an eye, or is otherwise maimed, but who within the year was sound, or of great value, he is liable not for the present value of the slave, but for the highest value in the year. This is why an action under the statute is understood to be penal in character, because a man is liable not merely for the damage he has caused, but sometimes for much more, and so it is settled that the action does not pass against the heir of the wrongdoer, as it would have passed if the amount at issue never exceeded the damage actually sustained.[8]

10. It is settled not from the words of the statute, but from the interpretation which has been placed upon it, that regard must be had not merely to the value, calculated as above, of the slave or beast that has perished, but also to all the further loss which you have sustained in consequence; for example, if your slave has been instituted heir by some one, and he has been killed before he could enter upon the inheritance by your order, account must also be taken of the value of the lost inheritance. Or suppose one of a pair of mules, or one of a team of chariot horses has been killed, or a slave who was one of a troupe of comedians; account is taken not merely of the animal or slave killed, but also of the depreciated value of the rest.

11. A man whose slave has been killed may besides bringing the civil action also prefer a capital charge against the wrong-doer.

12. The second chapter of the lex Aquilia is no longer in use.[9]

13. The third chapter relates to all other damage. So, if a person wounds a slave or beast that pastures or wounds or kills a quadruped which is not a beast that pastures, as a dog or a wild animal, an action lies under this chapter, and equally so in the case of any other living creature, or inanimate property. The action is given, "if anything is burnt, broken or fractured," though the word "broken" is wide enough to cover all these kinds of damage, for it is construed as meaning spoilt in any kind of way. So the word includes not only burning and fracturing but also tearing, bruising, pouring away, in short any sort of destruction or deterioration; indeed, it has been advised, that if a person has mixed something with another's wine or oil, so as to impair its natural quality, he is liable under this part of the statute.

§ 624.

14. It is evident that under this chapter, as under the first, liability is incurred by dolus or culpa. But the liability relates to the value not in that year, but in the last thirty days. 15. In this chapter there is no mention of "highest value." But Sabinus held, and rightly, that the assessment should be the same as if the word "highest" had been inserted in the text of the statute. The plebeians, he said, who passed this law on the proposition of the

---

[8] This is incorrect. An action might be penal and therefore not transmissible against the heir, even though it entitled the plaintiff to compensation and no more (§ 704).

[9] As we learn from G. 3. 215 it gave an action for damages against an adstipulator who released the debtor by acceptilatio in fraud of the stipulator See above, p. 396 and below, p. 408, n. 36.

tribune Aquilius were content with having used the word in the first part of the Act.

16. It is settled that an action lies on the statute only if a person § 629. has caused damage with his body.   Accordingly, if damage is caused in any other way, it is usual to give a utilis actio; for instance, if some one shuts up and starves to death another man's slave or beasts; or drives an animal so furiously that it founders; or frightens an animal over a precipice; or persuades another man's slave to climb a tree or go down a well, and the man has been killed or injured. If a person has thrown another man's slave from a bridge or river-bank, and the man has been drowned in the stream, it may be readily admitted that the loss was caused by the wrongdoer's body, and so there is a direct liability under the statute. But if the injury is not caused by the body, nor to the body, but damage is caused in some other way, since it is not a case either for a direct action or for an action on the analogy of the statute, it has been decided that the wrongdoer may be sued by an actio in factum; for example, if a man from motives of compassion frees a slave from his fetters, thus enabling him to escape.

XXIV. Quasi-Delict

634. Justinian enumerates four cases of obligations said to arise quasi ex delicto. The implication seems to be that in all of them the law creates a liability though the defendant may not in fact be to blame. The cases are the following: —

(1) The judge who "makes the case his own" (si judex 4. 5 pr. litem suam fecerit) incurs a penalty fixed by the magistrate at discretion. "To make the case your own" is to behave as if you were a party, not a judge ; but the phrase came to apply to any irregularity even of the most innocent description. Grave dereliction of duty was punished criminally.   At the dawn of Roman Law the Twelve Tables enacted the death penalty against a judex or arbiter convicted of taking a bribe.[10]   From Augustus onwards judges who accepted bribes incurred severe penalties under the lex Julia repetundarum.[11]

635. (2) If anything was thrown, or poured, from an upper room, causing bodily injury to a free person passing or standing 4. 5. 1. below, the occupier was liable for double the damage calculated on general principles (damnum emergens—lucrum cessan, § 625), to the exclusion of damage to the man's property, e.g., to his clothes, for the Edict said " if he is living and it is averred that *he* is injured." [12]   If a free man was killed there was a

---

[10] Aul. Gell. 20. 1. 7.
[11] Inst. 4. 18. 11 and Moyle *ad loc.*
[12] Dig. 9. 3. 1, 6.

fixed penalty of fifty aurei ; anyone might sue for it, *i.e.,* the actio was popularis (§ 708), but preference was given to a person interested or to near relatives.[13]   There could be no question of damages in this case, for the human body does not admit of estimation.[14]

636. (3) If a thing was kept placed or suspended over a way used by the public, which might cause injury if it fell, there was a penalty of ten aurei, which might be recovered from the occupier in an actio popularis.[15]   If it actually fell, it was taken to have been thrown down and so came under the case last mentioned [16] ; or an action might be brought against the person who put it in the place from which it fell.[17]

637. (4) Ship-owners, innkeepers and stable-keepers were liable for damage or theft committed by slaves or free persons in their employ in the ship, inn or stable.   Innkeepers were also liable for the like acts of residents.[18]   The action lay for double damages, was penal and not passively transmissible (§ 704).   It must be distinguished from the contractual liability mentioned above (§ 528).   The advantage was mainly with the latter, in which it was not necessary to show that the damage or loss was caused by a person in the employ of the defendant and in the inn, ship or stable.   On the other hand, in the action ex contractu receptum must be proved or inferred.   This lay for single damages and not being penal was passively transmissible.

4 5. 3.

THE INSTITUTES

BOOK IV

TITLE V

Of quasi-delictual obligations

§ 634.

If a judge has made the cause his own, he does not seem to be properly speaking bound ex maleficio.   But since he is not bound by contract either and yet seems in a way to have done wrong, though it were by inadvertence, he is deemed to be liable quasi ex maleficio and will incur a penalty, which it lies in the discretion of the magistrate to determine.

---

[13] Dig. 9. 3. 5, 5.
[14] Dig. 9. 3. 1, 5.
[15] Dig. 9. 3. 5, 13.
[16] Dig. 9. 3. 1, 3.
[17] Dig. 9. 3. 5, 12.
[19] Dig. 44. 7. 5, 6 ; 47. 5. 1, 6.

1. If anything is thrown down or poured out from an upper storey so as to cause damage to any one, the occupier is liable quasi ex maleficio, whether the room was his own, or hired, or occupied gratuitously. He cannot be said to be bound properly speaking ex maleficio, because, generally, it is some one else, a slave or a free man, who is actually in fault. The case is similar when a person has something placed or suspended over a way frequented by the public, which might cause damage if it fell. There is a penalty of ten aurei. In the case of throwing down and pouring an action lies for double the damage. If a free man is killed, there is a fixed penalty of fifty aurei; if a free man is injured, the judge assesses the damages at his discretion. He must take into account the fee paid to doctors and other expenses of treatment, as well as loss of employment, actual or prospective. 2. If a filiusfamilias is living away from his father, and something is thrown down or poured from his apartment, or if he has something placed or suspended which is dangerous, Julian held that no action lies against the father, but that proceedings should be taken against the son. The same should be applied in the case of a filiusfamilias who is a judge and makes the case his own. § 635.

3. The owner of a ship, or inn, or stable, is liable quasi ex maleficio for wrongdoing or theft committed in the ship, inn or stable, provided that it is not committed by himself, but by some one employed about the ship, inn or stable. This action is not based upon contract, and since he is in a way to blame for employing bad men, he seems to be bound quasi ex maleficio. In these cases there is an action in factum, available to the heir but not against the heir. § 637

XXV. Noxal Actions

638. If a slave, or, before Justinian, a son in power, committed a delict, for which he would have been liable if sui juris, the appropriate action (furti, legis Aquiliae, injuriarum, etc.) lay against the dominus or paterfamilias for damages or the surrender of the culprit. So the law is stated by Gaius and Justinian.[19] But the primary duty was to surrender. If the slave or son had died (without fault on the part of the defendant) before litis contestatio he was not liable at all.[20] There was no substituted liability to make compensation.

639. The word noxa, which gives the name to this class of actions, means " mischief " done by a slave or son. It means also the person who does the mischief. Noxal surrender means " handing over the mischief " to the aggrieved person.[21] The 4. 8. 1.

---

[19] G. 4. 75; Inst. 4. 8. pr.
[20] Dig. 9. 4. 39, 4.
[21] The Latin is noxam dedere—noxae deditio. We find also noxam merere—" to commit a mischief "—noxam sarcire—" to repair a mischief." The phrase noxae dedere (for noxam dedere) is a solecism, suggested by noxae deditio. Such reflected action of a substantive is not surprising, and in any case it is a question of usage, not of grammatical analysis.

proper way of doing this was by mancipation, but tradition followed by usucapion would have the same effect. The slave became the property of the transferee; the son went into his mancipium (§ 124). In the case of the son it was a question between the schools whether three mancipations were necessary or one sufficient. Sabinus and Cassius took the latter view, holding that the three mancipations required by the Twelve Tables meant only voluntary mancipations. From the classical period (perhaps it had always been so) a son remained in mancipio only until he had by his labour made compensation for the mischief.[22] At the end of this time he was entitled to be manumitted, thereby becoming sui juris (§ 124). Justinian allowed the slave in the same case to demand manumission. This had the singular consequence that a slave who had committed a delict had a chance in this indirect way of obtaining his freedom.

640. Noxal liability is inseparable from the person of the offender (noxa caput sequitur). If a slave or son who had committed a delict was (in the one case) sold or (in the other case) given in adoption, the noxal action lay against the new dominus or pater. If the slave had been manumitted or the son emancipated the action was no longer noxal, but direct, i.e., lay against the wrongdoer personally. Conversely, if the wrong was committed by a person sui juris who afterwards became a slave or (by adrogation) a filiusfamilias, the direct action became noxal. In the case of a slave de facto control was sufficient to constitute noxal liability. The action might be brought against a bona fide or mala fide possessor.[23] This was the general rule. But for some reason (perhaps the words of the statute) it did not apply to proceedings under the lex Aquilia. In this case the dominus alone could be sued.[24] If the dominus had instigated the delict, or failed to prevent it when he could have done so, he was directly liable on his own account.

641. With litis contestatio the defendant's liability underwent a change. From a duty (merely) to surrender, it became a duty to compensate if the defendant did not surrender. If the slave died the liability to compensate remained. Such at least was the law in the time of Justinian. But it seems that in the time of Gaius a defendant condemned in a noxal action might satisfy the judgment by surrender of a dead slave (if he was not

---

[22] *Coll.* 2. 3. 1 (Papinian).
[23] Dig. 9. 4. 13.
[24] Dig. 9. 2. 27, 3.

responsible for the death). The text of the palimpsest is at this point for the most part illegible. The fragmentary Autun Gaius continues:—" And not only if he gives the whole body is he set free, but, also, if he gives any part of the body ; and the question is raised whether hair and nails are part of the body . . . a dead animal cannot be noxally surrendered " [25]—still less " a hair from the dog that bit you."

642. Noxal liability was attached to furtum by the Twelve Tables to damnum injuria datum by the Lex Aquilia ; to rapina, injuria and many other wrongs by the Edict.[26] It was in principle inapplicable to actions on contract, but in the later law a master sued on his slave's contract was sometimes allowed to make noxal surrender, when the same state of facts also gave an action ex delicto.[27] The Digest puts the case of a slave who is acting as exercitor of a ship (§ 568) without the will of the master. Goods placed on board are lost. There are alternative liabilities ex contractu from the receptum nautarum (§ 528) and quasi ex delicto (§ 637). If a plaintiff brings an actio de peculio on the contract he must see that the formula is so framed as to give the master the alternative of noxal surrender.[28]

THE INSTITUTES

BOOK IV

TITLE VIII

Of noxal actions

For delicts committed by our slaves, such as theft, robbery, damnum or injuria, noxal actions are given, with the consequence that if the master is condemned he may either pay the estimated damage or deliver the guilty slave. § 638.

1. The word noxa means the offending body, that is the slave. § 639.
Noxia means the wrongful act, theft, robbery, damnum, injuria.
2. It is very reasonable that masters should be allowed to settle any claim by surrendering the delinquent. It would not be fair that they should incur any loss beyond the body of the wrong-doer. 3. If a master is sued in a noxal action on account of his slave, he frees himself by surrendering the slave to the plaintiff. The effect is to

---

[25] Girard, *Textes*, p. 366.
[26] Buckl. *M.* p. 333.
[27] Buckl. *M.* p. 333.
[28] Dig. 47. 2. 42 and Jolowicz *ad loc*. The action is de peculio because the slave is conducting the business sine voluntate domini. If he had been acting voluntate domini the master would have been liable in solidum in the actio exercitoria. Dig. 14. 1. 1, 20.

divest him permanently of the ownership. But if the slave gets enough money to compensate his new master for the damage he has suffered the praetor will order his manumission without asking for the master's consent. 4. Noxal actions are established by statute or by the praetor's edict;—by statute as in the case of theft by the Twelve Tables, or in the case of damnum injuria by the lex Aquilia; by the praetor's edict as for example for injuria and robbery.

§ 640.

5. Every noxal action follows the person of the delinquent. Thus, if your slave has committed a delict, so long as he is in your power the action lies against you. If he has come into some other person's power the action is against that person; if he has been manumitted, the action lies against him directly and there is no further question of noxal surrender. Conversely, a direct action may become noxal; for if a free man has committed a delict and afterwards becomes your slave (how this can happen has been explained in the First Book) the action which began by being direct is now a noxal action against you. 6. If a slave commits a noxal act against his master there is no action, for no obligation can exist between a master and a person in his power; consequently, if the slave comes into another person's power or is manumitted no action lies against the new master or the manumitted slave. It follows that if another person's slave commits a delict against you and afterwards comes into your power the right of action disappears because a situation has arisen in which it cannot exist; and if he afterwards quits your power you cannot bring an action. It is just like the case of a master having done some wrong to his slave; even if the slave is manumitted or alienated, he cannot have any action against him. 7. The old lawyers admitted the principle of noxal surrender in the case of children in power of either sex. But modern sentiment has rightly rejected this cruel practice and it has passed entirely out of use. For who would endure to hand over to another a child, particularly a daughter, and to suffer, perhaps, in the person of his son more than the son himself?—and in the case of daughters considerations of decency condemn the practice. Accordingly, it has been decided that noxal actions are to be given against slaves alone, for we find it many times said by the old commentators that sons in power may be sued directly for their delicts.

XXVI. Damage by Animals

4. 9 pr.

643. The Twelve Tables gave a general action for damage by quadrupeds, known as the actio de pauperie. Pauperies, we are told, means damage done without legal wrong on the part of the doer, and, of course, an animal cannot be said to have done any legal wrong as it is devoid of reason. The action was noxal, and subject to the usual conditions of noxal actions. If the animal died before litis contestatio the action failed [29]; if after, the defendant in case of condemnation had

---

[29] Dig. 9. 1. 1, 13.

to satisfy the plaintiff's claim, the alternative of surrender being gone.[30] The action was given in the case of all four-footed animals and extended as a utilis actio to other animals.[31] But the jurists limit it to domestic animals, with a curious disposition to moralise the situation and to treat them (notwithstanding the account just given of pauperies) as responsible beings. Domestic animals were expected to behave decently. If they acted contrary to the nature of their kind they were answerable. It was an excuse that the animal was irritated by some external cause, e.g., a horse stung by a wasp, or provoked by the person attacked, or if it was a question of a fight between animals and the other animal was the aggressor. The same liability did not attach to animals ferae naturae. Good behaviour was not to be expected of them. Besides, if they had escaped from captivity—and this would be the usual case—they had no owner and no one was responsible for them. If a wild animal, retained in captivity, caused an injury, some one would usually be at fault; if the victim, he would not be entitled to redress; if the owner of the animal, he could be sued under the lex Aquilia. However, the aedilician edict gave an action for damages against any person who kept savage animals near a public road, and Justinian says that the actio de pauperie was also available. Another action, also given by the Twelve Tables and noxal, was for damage caused by cattle, whose owner had let them pasture on another man's land (actio de pastu pecoris).[32]

4. 9. 1.

THE INSTITUTES

BOOK IV

TITLE IX

Of damage by quadrupeds

Animals are devoid of reason, but if they have caused damage through wantonness, rage or savagery, the Law of the Twelve Tables gives a noxal action, the effect of which is (for so the law provides) that if they are surrendered the defendant is free from liability. Suppose, for example, some one has been kicked by a horse given to kicking or attacked by a savage bull. This action applies to animals which are moved to do something contrary to their nature. It has no application to animals naturally savage. Consequently, if a bear has escaped from its owner and done mischief, the former

§ 643.

---

30 Dig. 9. 1. 1, 14: noxae autem dedere est animal tradere vivum
31 Dig. 9. 1. 1, 2; 4.
32 Dig. 19. 5. 14, 3.

owner cannot be sued, for he ceased to be the owner when the animal escaped. The word pauperies means mischief caused without legal wrong, for an animal wanting in reason cannot be said to have done wrong. Thus far as concerns the noxal action.

1. It must be further remembered that the aedilician edict forbids us to keep a dog, a boar, a bear, or a lion, near a public road; if this prohibition is disobeyed and a free man is injured, the owner is liable to pay such amends as to the judge may seem equitable, and for any other harm double damages. In addition to these aedilician actions an action de pauperie is also available. For when more than one action can be brought on the same state of facts, bringing one does not exclude recourse to another, particularly if the actions are penal.

XXVII. Plurality of Creditors and Debtors

644. Two or more persons may be associated as creditors or debtors in respect of the same transaction. In contract each one of them is, in general, entitled or bound rateably. Thus, if A and B agree with C to sell to him, or to buy from him a house for 1,000 aurei, each is entitled to receive or bound to pay 500, and neither is entitled to receive or bound to pay 1,000.[33] (The same consequence follows if a man dies leaving two or more co-heirs.) However, this may be varied by agreement, so as to make each of them entitled to receive or bound to pay the whole. In the verbal contract, whether reduced to writing or not, the precise form of words used determines the character of the obligation. Thus, if A says to M, " Do you promise to give me five aurei? " and before he has answered B says to M, " Do you promise to give me the same five aurei? " and M answers " I promise to give to each of you," there are two creditors, either of them, but not both, entitled to receive five aurei from M. If M says to A, " Do you promise to give me five aurei? " and before he has answered M says to B, " Do you promise to give me the same five aurei? " and A and B both say, " I promise " or " We promise," [34] there are two debtors, either of them, but not both, bound to pay five aurei to M. The creditors are described as rei stipulandi. The debtors are described as rei promittendi or debendi. Such a relation may arise not only from stipulation, but from any other contract,[35] by testament,[36] and in various other ways. Each creditor or

3. 16 pr.

---

[33] Dig. 45. 2. 11, 1 & 2.
[34] Dig. 45. 2. 4. The question may also be put in the plural " spondetis "? *Ibid.* [35] Dig. 45. 2. 9 pr. (Papinian).
[36] Ut puta, si pluribus heredibus institutis testator dixit: Titius et [read " aut "] Maevius Sempronio decem dato (*ibid.*); Dig. 30. 8. 1, Lucius Titius heres meus aut Maevius heres meus decem Seio dato.
This case must be distinguished from adstipulatio. If two persons by arrangement stipulate independently for the same thing, the second is termed adstipulator. Possumus ad id quod stipulamur alium adhibere qui idem stipuletur, quem vulgo adstipulatorem vocamus. G. 3. 210. The adstipulator was a mandatary, though so far resembling a true correal creditor (§ 648) that he could discharge the debtor by acceptilatio (§ 645); *supra ad* Inst. 4. 3. 12 ; p. 400.

debtor is said to be entitled or liable in solidum, *i.e.*, to the whole. From this the moderns have coined the word "solidarity," which is distinguished as active solidarity in the case of creditors, passive solidarity in the case of debtors.

645. The essence of solidarity is that notwithstanding plurality of creditors or of debtors there is only one matter involved (una res vertitur). Consequently, any juristic act which extinguished the rights of a single creditor, or the liability of a single debtor, extinguished the rights of all creditors and the liability of all debtors. Solutio (§ 653), acceptilatio (§ 655) and novatio (§ 660) had this effect. So too had litis contestatio (§ 661), for it substituted for the original liability the duty to abide the result of the trial (§715). But a pact not to sue (pactum de non petendo), since it did not extinguish the obligation *ipso jure* but might be pleaded by way of exception, was, as a rule, limited in its effect to the creditor who gave it and the debtor who received it.

3. 16. 1.

G. 3. 180.
D. 45. 2.
2.
D. 46. 3.
34, 11.

646. The case of co-delinquents requires separate treatment. As a rule every one of them was as fully liable as if he were the only delinquent, for the law regarded actions for delict as cumulative. Satisfaction by one delinquent did not release the others. This applied to the ancient civil law delicts—furtum—injuria—damnum injuria datum.[37] But in the case of the praetorian delicts, and quasi-delicts a tendency manifested itself to regard the action as compensatory rather than penal, with the result that satisfaction by one delinquent discharged the rest. But litis contestatio never had this effect. This was the law before Justinian and he left it as he found it.

647. But as regards obligations ex contractu Justinian made sweeping changes. First, generalising a practice which had already been established by law in some cases and which it was matter of daily usage to make a term in contracts, he abolished the consumptive effect of litis contestatio (§ 661), thus putting obligations ex contractu on the same footing as praetorian obligations ex delicto.[38] Secondly, by Nov. 99 he allowed co-debtors, like sureties, the benefit of division, the effect of which was to compel the creditor to divide his claim between co-debtors who were solvent at the time of action and within the jurisdiction. This reduced very much the practical value of solidary obligation.

648. From what has been said, it will be seen that there was a class of cases in which any event which extinguished the obligation as regards one creditor or one debtor extinguished it as regards all creditors or all debtors, and that there was another class of cases in which nothing but payment or its equivalent had this effect. The current terminology distinguishes them by different names. The first is described as " correality " (from

---

37 Dig. 9. 2. 11, 2 : nam ex lege Aquilia quod alius praestitit alium non relevat, cum sit poena ; Dig. 47. 2. 21, 9 (furtum).

38 Cod. 8. 40. 28, 2 & 3.

correus=co-debtor. Dig. 34. 3. 3, 3), the second as " solidarity "
(in a special and limited sense), or simple solidarity.[39]

THE INSTITUTES

BOOK III

TITLE XVI

Of stipulations which have two creditors or two debtors

§ 644.
Two or more persons may be parties to a stipulation as creditors
or debtors. They are joint creditors if after they have all put
a question to him the person addressed answers " I promise." For
example, if two persons stipulate separately and the promisor
answers, " I promise to give to each one of you." For, if he
promises first to Titius, and then to another person putting the
question separately, there will be two separate obligations and no
plurality of creditors. There is plurality of debtors if, for example,
Titius says, " Maevius, do you promise to give five aurei? " and then
[before he has answered] says, " Seius, do you promise to give the
same five aurei? " and then each of them separately answers, " I
promise."

§ 645.
1. In obligations of this kind each stipulator is entitled to
demand, and each promisor is bound to give or do, the whole thing
stipulated for. But in each of the obligations there is only one thing
involved and either creditor by accepting, or either debtor by making,
payment destroys the obligation of all of them, and releases all the
parties.

2. Of two promisors one may be bound absolutely, another up to
a certain time or subject to a condition; and the time limit or
condition which attaches in the one case will not prevent performance being demanded from the one who is bound absolutely.

XXVIII. ASSIGNMENT OF OBLIGATIONS (CESSION OF ACTIONS)

649. The law relating to the assignment of the benefit of
obligations took in the main the same course as the Law of
Agency. Three stages may be distinguished.

1. In the earliest period the assignment of a right was
effected by novation. If A wished to transfer to B his claim
against C an agreement was come to between all three parties
by which C's liability to A was discharged and replaced by
G. 2. 38.
C's liability to B. If as might be the case, the object was
to discharge A's liability to B this was also extinguished by
the novation,[40] known in this case as delegation (the creditor-
debtor delegates his debtor to his creditor), which had the same

---

[39] Buckl. *M.* p. 349.   [40] Dig. 21. 2. 68, 1.

effect as payment.[41] This process was open to two objections: —
(a) it required the consent of the debtor, (b) it extinguished any
real or personal securities which might have been given for the
primary debt.

2. The next stage was to employ the machinery of mandate,
A gave B a mandate in his own interest (mandatum in rem
suam) to sue for and recover in A's name and as A's agent
what was due from C. In the period of the formula the intentio
was expressed in the name of A, the condemnatio in the name
of B., *e.g.*, " If it appears that C ought to give ten aurei to A,
judge, condemn C to give ten aurei to B." This is a praetorian
adaptation of a civil law action (§ 700). But the right which
B asserted was still the right of A, and until B made the right
his own by litis contestatio it was always liable to be destroyed
by a settlement between A and C; and, further, since B's
right to sue C depended upon mandate, if the mandate was
determined by revocation or by the death of either party, the
assignment lost its effect.

G. 2. 39.
G. 4. 86.

3. Finally, B was allowed to maintain an actio utilis (§ 701)
in his own name when the mandate had been determined by
death or revocation. But the risk remained that the assignor
might demand and obtain payment from the debtor before B
had made good his claim. This was overcome by allowing
B to secure his position by formal notice of the assignment
(litis denuntiatio) or by accepting part payment.[42] If after
this the debtor chose to settle with the assignor he did so
at his peril. As time went on there was an ever increasing
number of cases in which the assignee was allowed to sue in
his own name without mandate, particularly where there was
a legal duty to give the mandate, but these cases, though
numerous, remained exceptional.[43]

650. What English lawyers call assignment, in the Roman
Law and the systems derived from it is termed cession of
action or cession of the right of action. The assignor is the
cedent; the assignee is the cessionary. In the modern law,
mandate being unnecessary, cession is effected by agreement,
with or without the handing over of relevant documents of
title. But the cessionary's position is not secure unless the
debtor has notice, or, at least, knowledge of the cession before
he has satisfied the cedent.[44]

---

[41] Dig. 16. 1. 8, 3.
[42] Cod. 8. 41 (42). 3.
[43] Buckl. *M.* p. 342.
[44] *C. C.* 1689, 1690; *B. G. B.* 398, 407.

651. Cession of actions was open to abuse. Justinian forbade the cession of res litigosae [45]—things in litigation—a term which included rights of action. To prevent speculation in doubtful claims the Emperor Anastasius by a constitution commonly known as the lex Anastasiana (A.D. 506) enacted that the purchaser of a right of action might not recover from the debtor more than he gave for it with interest.[46] This ghost of the Roman Law, as a Dutch writer calls it, retained in the Roman-Dutch Law, has been pronounced obsolete in South Africa and Ceylon.[47]

652. In principle a debtor could not transfer his liability except by novation. The apparent exceptions belong to the Law of Actions (representation in litigation).[48]

XXIX. How Obligations are Determined

The principal modes of determination are performance, release and substituted agreement.

3. 29 pr.

653. (1) Performance (solutio). In the classical period any material satisfaction of the creditor's claim discharged the obligation. But there was probably an earlier stage in which an obligation voluntarily assumed could only be discharged by a reversal of the process by which it was created. Thus obligations contracted per aes et libram or litteris or verbis were discharged respectively per aes et libram or litteris or verbis. As actual payment or performance was not in itself sufficient to effect a discharge, so the fact that payment or performance was not made did not prevent the formal discharge from taking effect. When at a later stage performance was regarded as sufficient to extinguish an obligation, the formal processes retained an independent validity as a means of effecting a release, when a creditor was content to forgo his claim to performance. We return to this subject below.

654. The words solvere—solutio—are applied to any performance of a contractual [49] or other obligation. Performance may consist in doing the very thing which the creditor was entitled to demand from the debtor and the debtor was bound

---

[45] Cod. 8. 36 (37). 5.
[46] Cod. 4. 35 22.
[47] Lee, p. 246, n. 1.
[48] Inst. 4. 11.
[49] Dig. 50. 16. 176: solvere dicimus eum qui fecit quod facere promisit.

to render to the creditor or in doing something which the creditor was willing to accept in its place (datio in solutum—substituted performance). In the time of Gaius it was a moot question whether (as the Sabinians held) this discharged the obligation *ipso jure*, or (as the Proculians held), merely entitled the debtor to plead the exceptio doli, if sued upon the contract. The Sabinian view prevailed. Contrary to the English Law, performance might be made not only by the debtor but by a third party on his behalf, even without his knowledge or consent. Performance by a principal debtor discharged sureties, and performance by a surety discharged a principal debtor (subject, however, to the contrivance mentioned above (§ 578) by which payment by a surety was regarded as a purchase of the creditor's right of action and not as a satisfaction of the debt). *G. 3. 168.*

655. (2) Release (acceptilatio). Gaius and Justinian describe this as a fictitious payment. If you have promised Titius by stipulation to pay him 500 aurei, and he is willing to release you, you may be set free by a contrary stipulation in which you say to Titius, " Have you received the 500 aurei which I promised you? " and Titius replies " I have received," or " I have received them." This method of discharge applies only to verbal obligations and illustrates the effect of the contrarius actus (§ 653). But it might be made available to discharge any other kind of obligation, if the obligation to be discharged was first converted into a verbal contract by novation (§ 660). Gallus Aquilius invented a form of stipulation called after him the stipulatio Aquiliana by which all present and future liabilities of B to A might be reduced to a stipulation and then discharged by acceptilatio. It seems reasonable to suppose that as long as the contract litteris remained in use, it might be similarly discharged by a contrary entry in the creditor's ledger. *3. 29. 1.*

656. Gaius mentioned another kind of " imaginary payment " obsolete before the time of Justinian. This is what he says:—

> Lib. III. 173. "There is another kind of imaginary payment, namely, by bronze and balance. This is employed in certain cases, for example, if a debt has been contracted by bronze and balance, or if something is owing on a judgment. 174. The process is as follows. There are brought together not less than five witnesses and a balance-holder; then the party who is being discharged should speak as follows. ' Inasmuch as I have been condemned to you (condemnatus) in so many thousand sesterces, I loose and free myself from you in respect thereof with this bronze and bronze scale: I weigh out to you this the first and last pound in accordance with the public

statute.' Then he strikes the balance with an *as* and gives it to the person by [or from] whom he is being freed, as if in payment.

"175. Similarly a legatee by the same process releases an heir from a legacy left per damnationem (§ 346) except that instead of using the word condemnatus, which is the word pronounced by the judgment-debtor, the heir declares himself to have been damnatus by the will. An heir can only be released in this way from what can be weighed or counted, and only if it is of ascertained amount; some think that the same applies to what can be measured."

657. In the above passage we see the process of discharge per aes et libram converted from an actual to a fictitious payment. The law passed through three stages. In the first stage the ceremonial and material discharge of the debt coincide. A certain number of pounds of uncoined copper are weighed and given to the creditor in payment. In the second stage a payment in coined money discharges the debt, but a symbolic weighing of the first and last pound is still necessary to discharge the debtor. Finally, if actual payment is made, nothing more is needed to free the debtor from his obligation, but the ceremony remains available as a formal method of release.

658. Gaius says that this method of release was available in certain cases; he mentions three, viz., when the debt was contracted by bronze and balance, when it was due on a judgment, when it arose out of a legacy per damnationem (§ 346). The principle of contrarius actus applies in the first case, but not in the others, and it is not immediately obvious why they are treated in the same way. The explanation seems to be that in all three cases the person of the debtor was pledged to the creditor to secure the debt. A process of release precisely appropriated in the case of the nexus was easily extended to the closely related cases of the judicatus and the testamento damnatus.

659. Another way of release was by informal agreement. From the earliest times this was available to extinguish civil law liability ex delicto. Thus the Law of the Twelve Tables said: si membrum rupit, ni cum eo pacit, talio esto—" if he has broken a limb, unless he comes to terms with him, let there be retaliation " (§ 615), and this method of release was available, generally, in cases of injuria and theft.[50] But an obligation ex contractu could not be discharged in this way, until Justinian, applying the principle of contrarius actus,

---

[50] Dig. 2. 14. 17, 1.

allowed contracts concluded by consent, that is the consensual
contracts, to be discharged in the same way, provided that the
contract was still outstanding on both sides (re nondum secuta). 3. 29. 4.
If a consensual contract had been executed on one side, or if an
obligation had been contracted re, the debtor's liability might
be novated by stipulation (§ 660) and then discharged by
acceptilatio. A mere agreement to release the debtor did not
extinguish the obligation, but would be construed as a pactum
de non petendo, and might be pleaded by way of defence ; or,
as the phrase is, would take effect not by mere force of law but
by aid of an exception—non ipso jure, sed ope exceptionis
(§ 749).

660. (3) Novation, as the word implies, was the substitution
of a new obligation for an old one. It was effected by stipulation and in the older law also by literal contract (§ 455). It 3. 29. 3.
was necessary to its validity that there should be an existing
liability civil or natural, arising from any source, and that the
substituted liability should be different, but not too different,
from the old one. There was no novation if a stipulation
merely reiterated a previous stipulation or promised a part of a
whole already promised by stipulation. There was no novation
if the content of the new obligation was substantially different
from the content of the old, though the new obligation might in
a fit case be pleaded as a pactum de non petendo (§ 749).
Finally, as Justinian enacted, there was no novation without an 3. 29. 3a.
intention to novate (animus novandi). Within these limits
novation might assume several forms. It might consist merely
in the substitution of the formal stipulation for another kind of
obligation, as, for example, for a liability arising from a contract of sale. It might vary the substance of an existing
obligation, as by adding or taking away a condition or a time
limit or a surety. Lastly, it might take the form of substituting
a new creditor or a new debtor—" Do you promise to pay me
what you owe to Titius? "—Do you promise to pay me
what Titius owes me? " The substitution of a creditor could
not take place without the consent of all three parties ; but a
new debtor might be substituted without the consent of the old
one. For, just as I can discharge your debt by payment without
your knowledge or consent, so I can discharge it by substituted
agreement without your knowledge or consent. It was not
necessary that the novating stipulation should be legally enforceable. It was enough that it created a natural obligation, as in
the case of a pupillus promising without the auctoritas of his

tutor. Indeed, the older view was that if the novating stipulation was formally correct it acted automatically to extinguish the
old obligation, as in the case mentioned by Gaius of a stipulation for performance after the death of the promisor.[51] On the
other hand, a stipulation made with a slave, according to the
view which prevailed, had no novating effect. The original
obligation remaining intact. If the novation took the form of
adding a condition, the novation was only operative if the
condition took effect. Servius Sulpicius held that it extinguished
the old obligation in any event, and he took the same view with
regard to the stipulation of a slave, but Gaius, who records this
opinion, adds, " but in both cases the law is settled in the
opposite sense." [52]

661. Besides the novation above described, which the
commentators distinguish as novatio voluntaria, there was
another kind of novation, which took effect by operation of
law and has been termed novatio necessaria. This was a
consequence of litis contestatio, which novated and thereby
extinguished and consumed the pre-existing obligation, creating
in its place a new obligation to accept the result of the sentence,
which in turn was novated by judgment. But the two types of
novation differed in their effect. While voluntary novation discharged all collateral securities given in respect of the original
obligation, this consequence did not follow from litis contestatio
or judgment. Justinian extinguished novatio necessaria by
enacting that where there was plurality of debtors litis contestatio against one should not discharge the other or others.
This is what is meant when it is said that he put an end " to the
consumptive effect of litis contestatio." [53]

662. An obligation might be extinguished in other ways
which Justinian does not mention in this context. Such were
(a) impossibility of performance, e.g., when the subject-matter
perished ; but the debtor was liable in damages if he had caused
the impossibility or was in mora [54] ; (b) death of either party, if
his obligation was merely personal (not transmitted to heirs), as
in societas (§ 510) and mandatum (§ 518) ; (c) lapse of time,
when this extinguished the right (extinctive prescription, properly
so-called) and did not merely bar the remedy (limitation of
actions). Which was the effect of the Theodosian long-term

---

[51] G. 3. 176.
[52] G. 3. 179.
[53] Cod. 8. 40. 28, 2 ; Buckl. T. p. 454.
[54] Dig. 46. 3. 107 ; 45. 1. 82, 1. For mora, see p. 295, n. 54.

prescription (§ 705) is questioned [55] ; (d) confusio, *i.e.*, when the character of creditor and debtor met in the same person.

663. Capitis deminutio extinguished obligations ex contractu at civil law, but this was amended by the praetor (§ 111). In Justinian's law it had no such consequence. The effect of compensatio or set-off belongs to the subject of civil procedure.[56]

THE INSTITUTES

BOOK III

TITLE XXIX

Of the modes in which obligations are determined

Every obligation is determined by the performance of what is owed, or if some one with the consent of the creditor performs something else in its place. It makes no difference who performs, whether the debtor himself, or another person on his behalf; for the debtor is released from his obligation if another person performs, whether the debtor knows of it or not, and even against his will. If a principal debtor performs, this releases sureties; and, conversely, performance by a surety releases not only the surety, but the principal debtor as well. 1. Another method of discharge is by acceptilatio, or fictitious performance. This takes place as follows: — If something is due to Titius under a stipulation, and Titius is willing to release the debt, he must allow the debtor to use these words: — " What I have promised you have you received?" Titius answers, " I have received it." This method of discharge applies only to obligations contracted verbis, not to any other; for it has been considered in harmony with principle, that an obligation formed by words should be extinguished by words. But what is due from any other cause may be converted into a stipulation, and discharged by acceptilatio. Just as a debt may be satisfied in part, so it may be released in part by acceptilatio.

2. There is a particular kind of stipulation, commonly called the Aquilian stipulation, by which all the debtor's obligations are converted into a stipulation and then discharged by acceptilatio. This stipulation, which novates all pre-existing obligations, was contrived by Gallus Aquilius, and is in the following form: —

" Whatsoever from whatsoever cause you are, shall, or may be, bound to me to give or to do, presently or in time to come; whatever I am, or shall be, entitled to claim from you by personal or real action, or by extraordinary process; whatever of mine you have, hold, or possess, or might possess, or have fraudulently brought it about that you do not possess; how much so-ever is the value of each of these claims, so much money Aulus Agerius stipulated should be paid to him, and Numerius Negidius promised to pay." Then,

§ 653.

§ 655.

---

[55] Girard, p. 775.
[56] See Inst. 4. 6. 39, and comment.

in his turn, Numerius Negidius puts this question to Aulus Agerius. "Whatsoever this day I have promised to you by the Aquilian stipulation, all that have you received?"; to which Aulus Agerius replies, "I have received it," or "I have credited it as received."

§ 660. 3. Obligations are also discharged by novation. This takes place, for example, if Seius stipulates from Titius for what you owe to Seius. For the introduction of a new person gives rise to a new obligation, and the original obligation is extinguished by being converted into the later obligation. This is so far the case that, sometimes, the first obligation is extinguished even by a later stipulation which is itself ineffectual. For instance, if Titius stipulates from a pupil acting without his tutor's authority for what was due from you to Titius; in which case Titius loses his claim altogether, for you, the original debtor, are released, though the second obligation is not legally binding. But the law is different if a stipulation is made with a slave, for, in that case, the original debtor remains bound just as if no subsequent stipulation had been made. If the second stipulation is made with the same person (no change of parties taking place), there is no novation, unless the second stipulation introduces some new term into the obligation, for example by adding or taking away a condition, a time limit, or a surety. When we say that the addition of a condition effects a novation, this must be understood to mean, if the condition in fact is realised; if the condition fails to take effect, the original obligation still continues. The old lawyers were agreed that novation only took place when the second obligation was concluded with that design. But there were doubts as to when this purpose was to be inferred, and various presumptions were admitted in various cases. Accordingly, we have made a constitution [57] which states in the clearest terms that novation is only to take place when the parties have expressly stated that they have made the new agreement with the intention of novating the first. Otherwise, the old obligation remains in force and the second accedes to it, so that the promisor is bound by both obligations, as prescribed by our constitution.

§ 659. 4. Lastly, obligations contracted by consent alone are discharged by a contrary agreement. Thus, if Titius and Seius have agreed that Seius is to buy property at Tusculum for one hundred aurei, and then, before anything has been done on either side, that is before the price has been paid or the property delivered, the parties agree to abandon the sale, they are mutually released. The same applies to the contract of hire and to all the consensual contracts.

APPENDIX

ROMAN LAW AND THE MODERN LAW OF OBLIGATIONS

664. We have come to the end of the Roman Law of Obligations and conclude this Book like the ones which have gone before with some reference to the modern law. It must be brief, for it is plainly out of the question to go into matters of detail. To a large extent

[57] Cod. 8. 41 (42). 8.

the Roman Law *is* the modern law. If anyone doubts this, a glance at the French Civil Code should carry conviction. For the greater part of the last century this served as a model for codifiers the world over and if later codes have departed from it, it has at least been the point of departure.

Doubtless, in the field of contract there is one great difference between the Roman Law and modern systems. The Roman Law had no law of contract, only a law of contracts (§ 533). In the modern law—with reservations in regard to personal capacity, legality of object and so forth—every agreement intended to create a legal obligation does so. The later Roman Law was moving towards this conclusion and according to Prof. Riccobono had reached it. But the revival of the Roman Law in the eleventh and twelfth centuries meant a throw-back to the earlier law of the Digest. The glossators were preoccupied with the intricate learning of "vestments," *i.e.*, the question what converts a pact into a contract. Oceans of ink had to be spilt before the "doctors" reached the simple result that ex nudo pacto nascitur actio, or in the language of the Scottish adage, "Every paction begets an action." The practice of the courts had long anticipated this conclusion. In English Law the doctrine of consideration survived the assault of Lord Mansfield—a Scotsman and therefore a civilian—in *Pillans* v. *van Mierop*.[58] But today it has few friends and lies under sentence if not of death, at least of amputation.[59]

Civil law systems reproduce the Roman rubric of quasi-contract. This has scarcely been known to English Law except in the pages of authors who endeavour to introduce order into the system,[60] and the English law of quasi-contract, so far as there is one, differs from the Roman Law.

The Roman Law of Delict had a simple beginning in a small number of narrowly defined wrongs. In the course of the ages these have expanded into a compendious theory which meets the demands of modern societies. In South Africa it has been said, "With us all wrongs are either damna injuria data or injuriae proper."[61] If the learned author had written "almost all" the statement would have been correct.

The French Law has given a strange turn to the term *quasi-délit* by making it mean "an unlawful act which causes damage to another without the intention of hurting him,"[62] while *délit* imports intention. This distinction, which seems to have originated with Pothier,[63] is of course wholly foreign to Roman Law.

The French code in two much commented articles declares:—
Art. 1382. Tout fait quelconque de l'homme qui cause à autrui un dommage oblige celui par la faute duquel il est causé de la reparer.

---

[58] (1765) 3 Burr. 1663.

[59] *Law Revision Committee, Sixth Interim Report* (1937) *Cmd.* 5449.

[60] "This name we have borrowed though rather in treatises on law than in actual practice, and applied to a similar but far from identical group." Buckl. & McNair, p. 254.

[61] Maasdorp, *Institutes of Cape Law*, vol. iv, 5th ed., p. 5.

[62] Planiol—Ripert (1947) t. II. § 949.

[63] *Traité des Obligations*, § 116.

Art. 1383. Chacun est responsable du dommage qu'il a causé non seulement part son fait mais encore par sa negligence ou par son imprudence.[64]

This is the principle of the lex Aquilia (la faute Aquilienne, as it has been called) carried to, or beyond, its extreme consequence. The reader will remember that the Roman statute related only to damage to property and by praetorian extension to damage to the person.

The question whether in English Law there is a Law of Tort, or only a law of torts continues to be the subject of academic debate.[65]

---

[64] Art. 1382. Any act by which a person causes damage to another binds the person by whose fault the damage occurred to repair such damage.

Art. 1383. Everyone is liable for the damage which he does, not only by his wilful acts but also by his negligence or imprudence. (Blackwood Wright's translation.)

[65] Winfield, *Textbook of the Law of Tort*, 3rd ed. (1946), p. 13; Pollock, *Law of Torts*, ed. Landon (1939), p. 43; Salmond, *Law of Torts*, 10th ed. (1945), ed. Stallybrass, p. 15.

BOOK V

THE LAW OF ACTIONS

665. "An action," says Justinian, "is nothing other than the right of suing before a judge for what is due to us." The phrase is wide enough to include both the law which defines the nature of the remedy appropriate in any given circumstances and the process by which the remedy may be rendered effective. In other words it includes both the law of actions proper and the law of procedure.[1] But the part of the Institutes which is devoted to the subject of actions (Book IV, Tit. VI to the end) is not confined to these topics. It includes also much that belongs to the substantive law, as, for example, the liability of fathers and masters in respect of the contracts of sons in power or slaves.

4. 6 pr.

666. HISTORY OF ROMAN CIVIL PROCEDURE.—The history of Roman Law from the Twelve Tables to Justinian from the point of view of procedure falls into three periods:—

    I. The period of the legis actiones;
    II. The period of the formulary procedure;
    III. The period of the extraordinary procedure.

We shall consider these in order, and distinguish in each period:—(A) the process by which a defendant is brought before the court; (B) the trial of the action; (C) the execution of the judgment.

I. THE LEGIS ACTIO PROCEDURE

667. Gaius says that the actions in use in early times were called legis actiones (statute actions) either because they were created by statutes or because they were adapted to the language of statutes and were, therefore, held to be as immutable as the statutes themselves.[2] When Gaius speaks of statutes he must be understood to refer in particular to the Law of the Twelve Tables; but it must not be concluded from this that some of the legis actiones had not a remoter origin in customary law. One of the five which he mentions had a later statutory origin.

668. (A) SUMMONS.—In the earliest times it was left to the plaintiff to get his man before the court in any way he could.

---

[1] Buckl. M. p. 363.   [2] G. 4. 11.

The process is prescribed by the Twelve Tables in the terse staccato language characteristic of this enactment:—

> "If he calls him to court, he must go: if he does not go, call witnesses: then seize him: if he evades or flies, lay hand on him: if he is sick or old, give him a vehicle: if he does not choose, need not provide a carriage."

This simple method of procuring attendance—if the plaintiff was strong enough to compel it—was still in theory in use in the latest days of the Republic, as appears from what Horace tells us of his providential escape from the bore who attached himself to him on the Sacred Way.[3] But the practice was for the defendant to give security for his attendance before the court (vadimonium),[4] and there were means of punishing him if he evaded arrest.

669. (B) TRIAL.—The trial of an action was a matter of solemn formality. In this period, as in that which followed, the procedure took the form of a judicial arbitration in which the question to be referred was settled in the presence of a judicial officer, normally the praetor, and was then referred to a single judge (judex) or arbiter, or to a board of judges (recuperatores) or to a standing college of judges (centumviri, decemviri).[5]

669a. PROCEEDINGS IN JURE.—The first stage of the proceedings was said to take place in court (in jure), the second before the judge (the normal case)—apud judicem—in judicio. The preliminary proceedings in jure assumed one of several forms, which gave names to different legis actiones, viz., sacramenti (by wager), per judicis postulationem (by asking for a judge), per condictionem (by giving notice). There were two other legis actiones of which we shall speak later, viz., per manus injectionem (by laying on of hand) and per pignoris capionem (by taking a distress). They were not modes of trial, but regulated methods of self-help.

670. LEGIS ACTIO SACRAMENTI.—This took its name from the money staked as a wager, which was a cardinal feature of the proceedings, and was known as sacramentum. The word evidently has a religious significance. The sum of the wager, forfeited by the party found to be in the wrong, was anciently

---

[3] *Sat.* 1. 9.

[4] Horace again may be cited:—

> "Ille datis vadibus qui rure extractus in urbem est
> Solos felices viventes clamat in urbe."
>
> (*Sat.* 1. 1. 11–12.)

[5] Buckl. *T.* p. 614; *M.* p. 374.

devoted to religious purposes, later went to the public chest. But there is reason to think that at a still earlier period the word sacramentum meant, not a thing staked as a wager on the result of litigation, but an oath by each party as to the justice of his cause, involving a penalty to be paid to the offended deity if the oath was found to be false.[6] Combined with this was a symbolic fight followed by a reference to arbitration. The whole procedure has been characterised by Sir Henry Maine as " a dramatisation of the origin of justice." [7] It brings into close association three distinct methods of redress—the appeal to arms and self-help, the appeal to the divine power, the appeal to civil justice.

G. 4. 13.

671. Unlike the other two modes of trial, the legis actio sacramenti was of general application. It was employed both when the plaintiff's claim was in rem, *i.e.*, to assert ownership (or a servitude) and when it was in personam, *i.e.*, to enforce an obligation, and in the first case whether the thing claimed was movable or immovable.

G. 4. 13.

672. In actions in rem, if the thing claimed was a slave or other movable property, which could be carried or brought into court, the proceedings were as follows: —

G. 4. 16.

(a) The parties, A and B, appear before the praetor (in jure), each armed with a rod (festuca) representing a spear (quiris or hasta), the symbol of quiritary ownership. The thing in dispute, for example, a slave, is present in court.

(b) A, grasping the slave, says: " I say that this man is mine by quiritary title (*stating the cause for which he is claimed*) as I have spoken look you I have laid my rod upon him." [8] Then he touches the slave with his festuca. B says and does the same. This mock fight was called manum conserere—manus consertio.

(c) The praetor says: " Both let the man go." They do so.

(d) A says: " I demand of you, do you say for what cause you have vindicated? " B replies: " I exercised my right as I laid on my rod."

---

[6] Girard, p. 1047.   [7] *Ancient Law*, chap. x.
[8] Hunc ego hominem ex jure Quiritium meum esse aio secundum suam causam sicut dixi ecce tibi vindictam imposui. I have purposely omitted punctuation. The formula admits of different interpretations. Muirhead: " I say that this man is mine in quiritarian right, on the title I have already explained ; behold, I have laid my vindicta upon him." Poste: " This man I claim as mine by due acquisition, by the law of the Quirites. See, as I have said, I have put my spear (vindicta) on him." de Zulueta: " I affirm that this man is mine by Quiritary right according to his proper title. As I have declared, so, look you, I have laid my staff upon him." My translation makes another suggestion.

(e) A says to B: " Since you have vindicated without right I challenge you with a sacramentum of fifty *asses*." B replies in like terms: " And I challenge you." The amount of the sacramentum was five hundred *asses* if the property in question was worth a thousand *asses* or more, otherwise fifty *asses*. This was so provided by the Twelve Tables. But if the question at issue was a man's liberty the amount was always fifty without regard to the value of the alleged slave. This provision was made in favour of freedom.

G. 4. 14.

(f) The parties then proceed to the sacramentum, originally on oath ; later, a deposit by each of the amount of the penalty (to be returned to the innocent party, forfeited by the guilty party (*infra*)) ; later, reciprocal promises by stipulation with a pledge of land by third parties (praedes) to secure performance.[9]

(g) The praetor awards interim possession of the thing in dispute to one or other party. who furnishes a similar security for the restoration of the res and the incidental profits, if he fails to establish his claim (praedes litis et vindiciarum).

(h) The praetor then remits the case to the judex (or otherwise, as the case may be). Anciently the judex was nominated forthwith, but a lex Pinaria of early date provided that the parties should reappear before the praetor on the thirtieth day for the purpose.

G. 4. 15.

(i) The judex having been nominated, each party gives the other notice to appear before him on the third day following. This adjournment was called comperendinatio from comperendinus dies—the third day following, *i.e.*, the day after the morrow.

(j) On the third day each party states his case (causae conjectio) and, if necessary, supports it by argument (causae peroratio) and evidence.

(k) Finally, the judex adjudicates upon the issue submitted to him, which may involve matter of law as well as of fact, and by his sententia decides in favour of one or other litigant. This he does, not directly, but indirectly, by adjudging the sacramentum of one or the other to be injustum. This meant originally that he had taken a false oath ; later, that he had lost his wager and forfeited the penalty.

673. Such was the procedure when the action was in rem and the thing in issue was a slave or other movable. If it was an immovable it was symbolically transported to the court.

---

[9] Buckl. *T*. p. 611.

"If the thing was of such a character that it could not conveniently be carried or brought into court; for example, if it was a column or a ship, or a herd or flock, part of the whole was taken and brought into court, and then vindication was made of the part as if the whole had been present in court; thus a single sheep or goat from the flock was brought into court, or a hair from an animal was taken and brought into court. If the subject of dispute was a ship or a column, some piece was broken off. Similarly, if the controversy related to land or houses or an inheritance, a piece was taken and brought into court, and vindication was made of the part just as if the whole were present in court; for example, a sod was taken from the land or a tile from the house, and similarly if the controversy related to an inheritance, some thing or part of a thing belonging to the inheritance was taken." *G. 4. 17.*

G. 4. 17.

674. This is the account of the procedure given by Gaius. But there was an earlier period when the mock fight took place on the land; and there was an intermediate or alternative procedure, in which the parties present in court made a pretence of leaving the court, fighting on the land, and coming back to have the issue decided by the pacific method encouraged or imposed by the State (ex jure manum conserere). In other respects too it is not to be supposed that the procedure remained unchanged through the centuries. It became stylised and may have been in part unintelligible even to the people who employed it.

675. As remarked above, the legis actio sacramenti was of a general character and available for actions in personam as well as for actions in rem, but an unfortunate lacuna in the Verona palimpsest leaves us uninformed as to the way in which the procedure was adapted to this purpose.

676. LEGIS ACTIO PER JUDICIS POSTULATIONEM.—The same uncertainty and for the same reason existed with regard to the legis actio per judicis postulationem. But unexpected light was thrown upon it by the Gaius fragments discovered in 1933.

The relevant passage runs as follows:—

Lib. IV. 17 (a). "The actio per judicis postulationem was brought if there was a statute commanding this mode of procedure, as the Twelve Tables did in the case of a claim based upon stipulation. The proceedings were more or less as follows:—The plaintiff said: 'I say that by your solemn promise (ex sponsione) you ought to give me ten thousand sesterces. I demand of you, do you admit it or deny it?' The defendant said that he ought not to give. On that the plaintiff said, 'Since you deny, I ask you, praetor, to give a judex or arbiter.' Consequently, in this kind of action a man might deny the plaintiff's claim without incurring a penalty. The same statute directed that proceedings for the division of an inheritance between co-heirs should be conducted in this way; and the lex Licinnia [10] did the same in the case of the actio communi dividundo. So the plaintiff named the cause for which he brought his action, and an arbiter was immediately asked for."

677. LEGIS ACTIO PER CONDICTIONEM.—The gap in the palimpsest extends to part of the passage dealing with the legis actio per condictionem, and this too is usefully supplied from the same source. The relevant text (new and old) runs as follows:—

17 b. Proceedings by condictio were taken in this way:— "I say that you ought to give me ten thousand sesterces"—I ask, "Do you admit or deny?" The defendant said that he ought not to give. The plaintiff said:—"Since you deny, I give you notice for the thirtieth day to have a judge appointed." Then the parties had to be present on the thirtieth day for the appointment of a judge. In the old language condicere means "to give notice"; 18. so this action was properly termed a condictio, because the plaintiff used to give notice to the defendant to appear on the thirtieth day for the appointment of a judge. But nowadays we improperly give the name "condiction" to the action in personam in which we allege that something should be given to us, for there is no notice given in the modern procedure. 19. This action was created by the lex Silia and the lex Calpurnia, by the lex Silia for a certain sum of money, by the lex Calpurnia for every [other] certain thing. 20. Why this action was required when a claim for what ought to be given to us could be brought either by sacramentum or by asking for a judge, is much discussed.

678. PROCEEDINGS APUD JUDICEM.—The solemnities in court being duly concluded, the case was referred to a single judex or other appropriate tribunal. The course of the proceedings is sketchily indicated in some fragments of Table I of the Twelve Tables, which have come down to us. If the parties failed to come to terms, each party was to state his case before noon. The judge was to give his decision in the afternoon. Proceedings were not to be prolonged beyond sunset. No doubt as time went on the proceedings became more elastic and took much the same course, as later under the formulary procedure (§ 712).[11]

679. It is probable that the two legis actiones described in the foregoing sections were, to quote Prof. de Zulueta, "just a rationalisation of the older procedure" in the actio sacramenti in personam. They both had the merit of avoiding the formalities of the sacramental wager and the forfeiture of a

---

[10] There is a reference to this statute of unknown date in Dig. 4. 7. 12.
[11] For further details see Jolowicz, p. 188.

penal sum to the State. But the question mentioned by Gaius which was " much discussed " must have been too intricate to admit of an " obvious explanation." The dates of the lex Silia and the lex Calpurnia are unknown.[12]

680. (C) EXECUTION—LEGIS ACTIO PER MANUS INJECTIONEM. —The judex was powerless to give effect to his sentence, nor did the praetor undertake to do so. This task devolved in the earliest period of civil procedure upon the litigant himself, and took the form of the legis actio per manus injectionem. This was a proceeding which took place in jure, i.e., before the magistrate, and must be distinguished from the extrajudicial arrest above described (§ 668). The process was as follows. The presence of the defendant having been procured by per- suasion or force, the plaintiff said to the defendant : " Inasmuch as you have been adjudged to me for ten thousand sesterces and have not paid, I lay hand upon you for a judgment of ten thousand sesterces." With that he laid hand on some part of his person.   G. 4. 21.

681. The defendant might not resist arrest on his own behalf, since judgment had already been pronounced against him. He must either (a) satisfy the judgment (or furnish security which the plaintiff was willing to accept) ; or (b) find a vindex, prepared in a separate suit to contest the validity of the judgment, who, if he lost, would be cast in double damages with the ultimate menace of manus injectio against himself, the effect of his intervention being to set free the original debtor.[13] If the defendant could do neither of these things the creditor might take him away and keep him in confinement and bonds. This followed (probably) upon a formal addictio by the magistrate which made him not yet a slave, but on the way to become so (adjudicatus).

682. So much and no more we are told by Gaius. For further particulars and the sequel we turn to the Twelve Tables, and to the exposition of its provisions which Aulus Gellius, a man of letters contemporary with Gaius, puts into the mouth of Sextus Caecilius Africanus, an eminent jurist of the time.

> " When a debt is confessed or judgment has duly been pro-
> nounced, thirty days must be allowed. After that let putting
> on of hand take place (post deinde manus injectio esto). Let
> him take him before the court. If he does not satisfy the

---

12 Buckl. *T.* p. 617.
13 Buckl. *T.* p. 621.

judgment, and if no one comes forward as vindex, let him lead him away. Let him bind him with cord or fetters fifteen pound weight, not heavier; if he chooses, lighter. If he chooses, he may live at his own cost. If he does not live at his own cost, the man who shall have him bound, shall give him pounds of corn day by day. If he chooses he may give him more."

683 At this point Aulus Gellius takes up the story [14]: —

"Meanwhile there was the right of coming to terms; if they did not come to terms, they (*i.e.*, the debtors) were kept in chains for sixty days. During these days they were brought before the praetor in the comitium on three successive market days and proclamation was made of the amount of the judgment. On the third market day they were put to death or sold away from Rome across the Tiber."

684. If there were several creditors they were entitled to share in the liquidation of the corpse. The climax is recorded in the language of the statute: —

"On the third market day let them cut the shares. If they have cut too much or too little, be it free from blame." [15]

The last words anticipate and avoid the point made by Portia in *The Merchant of Venice* [16]: —

"Therefore prepare thee to cut off the flesh.
Shed thou no blood; nor cut thou less, nor more,
But just a pound of flesh: if thou tak'st more,
Or less, than just a pound, be it but so much
As makes it light or heavy in the substance,
Or the division of the twentieth part
Of one poor scruple, nay, if the scale do turn
But in the estimation of a hair,
Thou diest and all thy goods are confiscate."

685. As we have seen, the Twelve Tables (so far as they are preserved to us) admit the process of manus injectio in two cases, confession and judgment. Confession may perhaps be taken to include the case of the debtor who offered no defence (indefensus). But manus injectio, as appears from the form G. 4. 21. of words recorded by Gaius (quod tu mihi judicatus sive damnatus es), applied also to the damnatus, a term which may have included the nexal debtor (§ 522), the heir liable to a legatee by the legacy per damnationem (§ 346), and other cases.[17] Gaius tells us that in many cases a manus injectio pro judicato ("as if there had been a judgment") was given by

---

[14] *Noctes Atticae*, 20. 1. 46 ; Jolowicz, p. 396.
[15] Tertiis nundinis partes secanto : si plus minusque secuerunt, se fraude esto.
[16] Act IV, Scene 1—as judicial assessor, not as advocate. **Pollock**, *Essays in the Law*, p. 198.
[17] Girard, p. 511 ; Buckl. *T.* p. 620 ; *M.* p. 377.

special statutes, as by the lex Publilia against a debtor for whom   G. 4. 22.
another person had bound himself as surety by sponsio if he
failed to reimburse him within the six months next ensuing, and
by the lex Furia de sponsu against a creditor who had exacted
from one of several co-sponsors more than a rateable share of
the debt (§ 582).

686. In these cases manus injectio was applied with all its
rigorous consequences. In other cases a modified process was
allowed called manus injectio pura, *i.e.*, non pro judicato, in   G. 4. 23.
which the defendant might, if he chose " throw off the hand "
and defend himself (manum sibi depellere et pro se lege agere).
He was in fact his own vindex. But, if he did not defend the
cause or defended it unsuccessfully, the process of execution
took its normal course. Of this kind were the actions given by
the lex Furia testamentaria against one who, not being an
excepted person under the statute, took more than a thousand
asses as legacy or gift *mortis causa* and by a lex Marcia to
recover usurious interest from moneylenders (§ 355). These
were cases in which the law from motives of public policy
allowed an immediate manus injectio, placing upon the defendant the burden of proving his innocence.[18] A lex Vallia
(between 204 and 169 B.C.) made all manus injectio pura except
in the case of the judicatus and of the principal debtor under the
lex Publilia.   G. 4. 25.

687. Such was the procedure under the Law of the Twelve
Tables. But from the earliest times of which we have any
record it was mitigated. The insolvent debtor was not sold
into slavery or put to death. The creditor might still, if he
pleased, keep him in chains. This method of execution upon
the person continued in force during the whole of the classical
period of Roman Law and even until Justinian, the debtor
being kept a prisoner until he had satisfied the debt, or com-
pensated for it by his labour.

[The procedure above described suits a claim for an ascertained money
debt (supra, § 680). In other personal actions a further process might be
needed to ascertain the defendant's liability in terms of money (arbitrium
litis aestimandae?) If the action was in rem (*i.e.*, against the thing, not
the person), the praetor would allow the successful litigant to keep or take
the res.]

688. LEGIS ACTIO PER PIGNORIS CAPIONEM.—There does not
seem to have been during the legis actio period any method
of execution against the debtor's property. There was, however,

---

[18] Girard, p. 1045.

a fifth legis actio, which, as it did not imply any pre-existing judgment, cannot be described as a mode of execution. This was pignoris capio, or distress. It was given to a limited number of privileged creditors and only in relation to claims of a public or sacral character. This is what Gaius has to say about it: —

> 26. "The legis actio per pignoris capionem rested in certain cases on custom, in certain cases on statute. 27. It was introduced by custom in respect of military matters, for a soldier might levy a distress for his pay on the person whose duty it was to distribute the money, if he failed to do so. Money given to soldiers for their pay was called aes militare. Again, he might levy a distress for the money with which he was to buy his horse. This was called aes equestre. Again, he had the same recourse for the money with which he was to buy barley for his horse. This was called aes hordiarium (hordeum = barley). 28. Pignoris capio was introduced by statute, for example, by the Law of the Twelve Tables against the man who had bought a victim and not paid for it and against one who did not pay the hire of a beast which another person had let to him on hire for the purpose of applying the hire money for the expense of a sacrifice. Again, the regulations of the censors gave a right of distress to farmers of the public revenue of the Roman People against persons who were liable for taxes under any statute. 29. In all these cases the distress was levied with certain formal words, and for this reason it was generally held that this process, too, was a kind of legis actio; but some thought differently: first, because the distress was effected extra jus, that is, not before the praetor, and, usually, in the absence of the debtor, whereas other actions took place before the praetor, the defendant being present; secondly, because a distress might be made even nefasto die, that is on a day on which it was not allowed to conduct statute process."

We are not informed as to the details of this procedure, whether, for example, the debtor had any means of impeaching the legality of the distress, or of recovering his property in the event of his satisfying the debt.

G. 4. 30.
689. The system of the legis actiones, Gaius tells us, became odious owing to its excessive technicality and formalism. He cites the case of a plaintiff who, suing a defendant for cutting his vines, lost his case because he used the word " vines " when he should have said " trees," for the Law of the Twelve Tables, which gave the action, spoke in general terms of " trees " (actio

G. 4. 11.
de arboribus succisis). In consequence, " the statute actions were abolished by the lex Aebutia and the two Julian laws, and it was brought about that we should litigate by written instructions to the judex, that is by formulae." Unhappily, we know little about the lex Aebutia beyond what Gaius tells us. It is thought to have been enacted about B.C. 120. The leges Juliae

were no doubt the leges Juliae judiciariae of Augustus (B.C. 18).
It is not necessary to conclude from what Gaius says that the
formula was not in use before the lex Aebutia. It may be that
the statute was a legislative recognition of a method of procedure which had already found its way into the practice of the
courts.[19]

690. In two cases alone, Gaius tells us, the legis actio
procedure survived the lex Aebutia, namely damnum infectum
(apprehended damage, § 778) and proceedings before the cen-
tumviral court. This was a court consisting of 105 members
(three from each of the thirty-five tribes) which exercised a
concurrent jurisdiction in petitio hereditatis and other civil law
causes, on a reference from the praetor urbanus or peregrinus,
the proceedings in jure being by legis actio sacramenti.[20] The
legis actio procedure in damnum infectum was in practice G. 4. 31.
superseded by the praetorian jurisdiction exercised by means of
missio in possessionem and the cautio damni infecti (§§ 778,
779), a process at once more convenient and more satisfactory.
There was a technical survival of the legis actio in the fictitious
process of manumissio vindicta (§ 77) and in jure cessio (§ 165).

691. Different views have been advanced as to the origin
of the formulary system of litigation. It has been surmised : —
(1) that it arose under the legis actio procedure in connection
with the legis actio per condictionem ; (2) that it was introduced by the praetor peregrinus for the use of foreigners
resorting to his court ; (3) that it was an institution of provincial, particularly Sicilian, origin, and perhaps ultimately
derived from Greece.[21] These views are not mutually inconsistent. It is obvious that, as soon as the issues raised in an
action became at all complicated, they must have been reduced
to writing, to aid the memory of the parties to the litis contestatio (§ 713), whose business it was to inform the judex of
the matter in question between the parties. It is equally obvious
that the praetor's jurisdiction was extensive enough to admit of
considerable adaptation to changing circumstances without the
need of legislative enactment.

692. The formulary procedure retains the fundamental
character of the legis actio procedure of being a reference to

---

[19] Buckl. *M*. p. 382 ; Jolowicz, p. 203.
[20] Girard, p. 1038. Under the Empire the number was increased. The
court continued in existence until about A.D. 200. Girard, p. 1059, n. 4.
It usually sat in three or four divisions.
[21] Girard, p. 1055. There are other theories. Buckl. *T*. p. 629.

arbitration. There is the same division of the proceedings into proceedings in jure and proceedings apud judicem. Only, instead of the terms of reference being rigid and inelastic, expressed in an invariable spoken ritual, they admit of the most various expressions in a written formula (concepta verba) settled by agreement of the parties with the concurrence of the praetor. But the range of choice was not unlimited. It was essential that the praetor should give an action. The actions which he had at his disposal were set forth in his Edict, accompanied by pattern formulae. The character of the formula was determined by the character of the action.

Classification of Actions

693. At this point it will be convenient to consider the various classifications of actions made by the Roman Law. Logically, this should have preceded the topic of procedure, but, as most of them only came into existence, or at all events assumed importance, in the period of the formula, it has seemed best to reserve the subject for treatment in this connection. What follows is in the main based upon Justinian's Title de actionibus (IV. 6), which should receive careful attention.

694. Actions in Rem—Actions in Personam—*i.e.*, brought against a thing or against a person. Actions in rem were brought to assert ownership or to assert or deny a servitude G. 4. 2. (actio confessoria—actio negatoria or negativa).[22] Actions in personam were brought to enforce an obligation—a duty to give, to do, to make good.[23] The scope of the action in rem was wider than appears from the Institutes. It included the action brought by an heir to establish his right to an inheritance (hereditatis petitio) and actions brought to establish status (vindicatio in libertatem—vindicatio in servitutem). In fact, all 4. 6. 13. actions which were not in personam seem to have been in rem. Justinian himself refers to this head praejudicial actions, that is actions brought to establish a question of status as a preliminary to further proceedings, *e.g.*, the question whether such a person is free or slave.[24]

---

22 G. 4. 2 ; Inst. 4. 6. 1–2 ; *supra*, § 274.

23 Dare—facere—praestare.

24 These actions appear to be actions in rem in the modern sense, *viz.*, actions " directly determining the status of property or persons " (Halsbury—Hailsham, vol. 1, § 84). The Roman vindication no less than actions in personam merely tended to a decision *inter partes*.

695. It was characteristic of actions in rem that the defendant was not named in the intentio, only in the condemnatio (§ 727), whereas in personal actions the defendant was named in both. Consequently, personal actions in which (exceptionally) the defendant was not named in the intentio were said to be in rem scriptae [25]—inscribed in rem. Such were the judicia divisoria and the actio metus.

696. CIVIL ACTIONS—PRAETORIAN ACTIONS.—This division is historically important, but does not touch the nature of the claim. Actions descended from the civil law, or created by statute, were civil. Actions introduced by the praetor's Edict were praetorian (honorary). Both classes of action might be either in rem or in personam.

4. 6. 3.

697. The praetorian actions were either adaptations of a civil law action or new actions for which there was no civil law precedent. The adaptation consisted either (1) in the insertion of a fiction in the formula (fictitious action), or (2) in naming one person in the intention, another in the condemnation (transferred action). Actions for which there was no civil law precedent were known as actions in factum (§ 700).

698. FICTITIOUS ACTIONS.—A familiar instance of the use of a fiction is the actio Publiciana in rem given to the bona fide possessor with an instruction to the judex to find for the plaintiff if it appeared that he would have been owner, if the period of usucapion had run its course.[26] Another is the hereditatis petitio possessoria (§ 387), brought by the bonorum possessor with a fictitious allegation of heirship. Yet another is the actio Pauliana in rem, given to recover property alienated in fraud of creditors on the assumption that alienation had not taken place. As instances of the use of a fiction in personal actions may be cited the actio furti and the actio legis Aquiliae brought by or against a peregrinus with a fictitious assumption of citizenship; the action given against the adrogatus as if adrogation had not taken place (§ 111); the action given to or against the purchaser of an insolvent estate (§ 755), with a fictitious assumption of heirship (actio Serviana).

4. 6. 4

G. 4. 34.
4. 6. 6.

G. 4. 37.

G. 3. 84;
4. 38.

G. 4. 35.

699. TRANSFERRED ACTIONS.—The substitution of one name for another in the condemnation served various purposes:—
(a) Representation in litigation. The name of the representative was substituted for the name of the person in whose name the

---

[25] Dig. 4. 2. 9, 8.
[26] See § 177.

action was brought or defended. Thus: "If it appears that
Numerius Negidius ought to give ten thousand sesterces to
Publius Mevius, judge, condemn Numerius Negidius [to pay] ten
thousand sesterces to Lucius Titius: if it does not appear,
absolve him." Here, Lucius Titius represents the plaintiff. If
he represented the defendant the formula would conclude
"condemn Lucius Titius to pay to Publius Mevius," etc.; (b) In
the so-called actiones adjecticiae qualitatis (§ 563) the name of
the agent appeared in the intentio, the name of the principal in
the condemnatio; (c) The same contrivance was employed in the
actio Rutiliana (so called after the praetor Publius Rutilius, who
is credited with inventing the process), in which the purchaser
of an insolvent estate "names the insolvent in the intentio and
substitutes his own name in the condemnatio, requiring the
defendant to restore, or to pay to him, what belonged to or
was owed to the insolvent." This was the appropriate action
if the insolvent was alive; the actio Serviana, if he was dead
(§ 755).

G. 4. 86.

G. 4. 35.

700. PRAETORIAN ACTIONS IN FACTUM.—A civil law action
had a formula which gave expression to a civil law right
(formula in jus concepta), e.g., "If it appears that the thing in
question belongs to plaintiff by quiritary right" (§ 726), or
"if it appears, or whatever appears, that defendant should give
or do" (§§ 730–3). Nor did a civil law action lose its character
as such by being manipulated by the praetor in the ways
described above (§§ 698, 699). Its formula was still in jus
concepta. But a praetorian action which had no civil law
prototype had a formula in factum concepta, that is one which
directed the judge to condemn if he found facts to which the
praetor attached a right of action. It is known in consequence
as an actio in factum.[27] The praetor would at first give the
action in a particular case, and, ultimately, if such cases became
frequent, embody it in his edict, thus making it a "praetorian
action" in the technical sense (§ 696). Not technically, but in
fact actions in factum also may be distinguished as in rem and
in personam,[28] though if the praetor wished to give a new action
in rem he usually adapted a civil law action as in the actio Publiciana. An action in rem of wholly praetorian creation was
the actio Serviana (to be distinguished from the actio Serviana
mentioned above), by which a hypothecary creditor obtained

---

[27] In a larger sense "actio in factum" includes also "actio utilis"
(§ 701). Jolowicz, p. 213, n. 3.
[28] Strictly speaking, civil law actions alone are so classified (§ 694).

possession of the subject of the pledge (§ 261). There were
many personal actions in factum, such as the actio de peculio,   4. 6. 9.
the actio de pecunia constituta, the actio jurisjurandi, and a
great number of penal actions, such as the action given against 4. 6. 11.
a freedman or son who had taken proceedings against his patron
or paterfamilias without the praetor's permission. In the older 4. 6. 12.
law the praetor gave actions in factum against a person who
being duly summoned neither appeared nor found a vindex and
against a person who forcibly rescued a person summoned to   G. 4. 46.
appear.

701. ACTIO DIRECTA—ACTIO UTILIS.—This distinction is
rather descriptive than technical. An actio utilis was an
adaptation or extension of an existing action,[28a] sometimes
contrasted as the actio directa. The basic action might be
civil or praetorian. But the description " actio utilis " is usually
applied to a modification of a civil law formula (§ 698) or to
the application of a civil law formula to a new state of
facts or to persons not primarily entitled to make use of it. In
the course of these pages we have met with many instances: the
utilis actio given to creditors of the adrogatus (§ 111), the utilis
vindicatio of the original owner of a canvas upon which another
person has painted a picture (Inst. 2. 1. 34), the utilis actio given
to and against a fideicommissarius (§ 365), the utilis actio legis
Aquiliae (§ 630), and the utilis actio occasionally allowed to the
cessionary of a right of action (§ 649. See also §§ 133, 570, 571,
643). If something was poured or thrown from a ship (not
from a house) utilis actio lay against the master.[29] This was an
extension of an actio in factum.

702. ACTIONES STRICTI JURIS—BONAE FIDEI.—This is a   4. 6. 28.
classification not of all actions but of personal actions in jus,
" though in many respects the rules of real actions resembled
those of stricta judicia." [30] The principal actio stricti juris was
the condictio, a general term with many applications. It might
be brought for a certain sum of money (condictio certae
pecuniae), or for some other certain thing (condictio triticaria),
or to assert an illiquid claim (condictio incerti) (§§ 729–32). The
various forms of condictio were also distinguished according to
the cause which gave rise to them, as condictio furtiva, condictio
indebiti, and others mentioned above in speaking of obligationes

---

[28a] Buckl. *T.* p. 687; *M.* p. 368. Utilis is variously rendered
" adapted," " modified," " equitable," " analogous," etc. Perhaps it is
best left untranslated.
[29] Dig. 9. 3. 6, 3.
[30] Buckl. *M.* p. 364.

quasi ex contractu (§ 595).[31]   Another stricti juris action was the
actio ex testamento brought to enforce a legacy. The bonae
fidei actions, which were numerous, included actions brought
upon all the real contracts other than mutuum, on the consensual
contracts, on negotiorum gestio, on the judicia divisoria, as well
as the actio tutelae, the actio praescriptis verbis, and some
others.[32]   Justinian, while abolishing the actio rei uxoriae,
anomalously retained its bonae fidei character in the actio ex
stipulatu, by which he replaced it (§ 227).

4. 6. 29.

703. It was characteristic of the bonae fidei actions that the
formula instructed the judex to ascertain what the defendant
ought to do or to give ex bona fide and to condemn accordingly.
This allowed him to take equitable defences into consideration
and made it unnecessary for the defendant to raise them
expressly by way of plea (exceptio), as was necessary in the
stricti juris actions. The most important equitable plea was the
exceptio doli, and accordingly the rule was that in bonae fidei
actions the exceptio doli was implied—bonae fidei judiciis
exceptio doli inest. So was the exceptio pacti conventi.[33]
There were many other distinctions between the two types of
action.

704. ACTIONES REI PERSEQUENDAE GRATIA—POENAE PERSE-
QUENDAE GRATIA.—Actions may be, and most often are, directed
to getting something which belongs to the plaintiff, or to
redressing an unlawful disturbance to his detriment of the
economic balance. In such cases he may be said to be claiming
something which is or ought to be his. The action is brought
for a res. Such actions are reparative, or, as the technical term
is, "rei-persecutory" in character. Other actions, though they
may incidentally compensate the plaintiff and, perhaps, do no
more, are considered to have for their object the punishment of
the defendant; that is, they are penal in character. It is
irrelevant that the penalty may be placed to the credit of the
plaintiff and not of the State. The principal distinction between
the two classes of actions was that actions of the first class were,
with few exceptions, both actively and passively transmissible,
i.e., passed to heirs of plaintiff and of defendant; penal actions,
on the other hand, were, as a rule, actively transmissible, but
not passively, though the heirs might be held liable to the extent

4. 12. 1.

---

[31] Buckl. *T.* 682; *M.* 366.
[32] G. 4. 62; Inst. 4. 6. 28.
[33] Dig. 24. 3. 21; 30. 84. 5; 18. 5. 3.

of their enrichment.[34]   All actions ex delicto were penal, even if, as in the actio doli, they only led to compensation.[35]   But Justinian makes a new distinction.   If the plaintiff was entitled to claim recompense apart from the action ex delicto, as in case of theft, the action was merely penal ; if the action ex delicto included a claim for compensation, as in the case of rapina, the action was mixed.   For the same reason he describes as mixed the action for double damages given in the case of depositum miserabile (§ 436), and the actio legis Aquiliae ; in this last case, not only because the damages were doubled in the case of denial (§ 632), but also because the measure of damages being the highest value in the last year, or thirty days, a plaintiff might in fact recover much more than compensation for his actual loss. But this seems to depart from the original nature of the distinction, which depended rather upon the purpose of the action than on its consequence.

4. 6. 19.

705.   TEMPORAL—PERPETUAL.—Some actions could only be brought within a limited time, others without limit of time. Actions of the first class were termed temporal, actions of the second class perpetual.   Most civil law actions were perpetual. Most praetorian actions were temporal, and, in fact, annual. But there were many exceptions.   Theodosius II imposed a general period of prescription of actions of thirty years (with longer periods in exceptional cases).   After this, a perpetual action meant an action which was so prescribed.

4. 12 pr.

706. The distinction between actions transmissible and not transmissible has been mentioned above (§ 704).

707.   JUDICIA LEGITIMA—IMPERIO CONTINENTIA.—This distinction belongs to the old law.   The first class included cases which came before a single judex in the city of Rome or within the first milestone, the parties being Roman citizens.   All other cases depended upon the jurisdiction of the praetor, which means that they could not be prolonged beyond the year of office of the praetor who gave the action, and ceased to be valid when the year was over.   There were procedural differences into which we need not enter.   The distinction has nothing to do with the nature of the claim, which in either case might be a civil law action in rem or in personam or a praetorian action in factum.[36]

---

[34] The actio injuriarum was neither passively nor actively transmissible ; *supra*, p. 390.
[35] Buckl. *M.* p. 370.
[36] G. 4. 103.

708. Actio Popularis—Actio Privata.—There were cases in which in the public interest any member of the public was allowed to sue for a penalty, which he either kept for himself or divided with the State. Actions of this character were called actiones populares.[37] We have met with instances in the actions given for res dejectae and res suspensae (§§ 635, 636). It was a contrivance to supplement the very inadequate criminal law. If the plaintiff brought his action in his own particular interest the action was private.

709. Mixed Actions.—The term mixed action (actio mixta) is used in a variety of senses:—(1) as above, of an action directed to obtaining both redress and a penalty (§ 704); (2) of the judicia divisoria. Justinian described these as mixed because, as he says, they are both in rem and in personam (Inst. 4. 6. 20). The semblance of truth in this is the fact that they may end either in adjudication, which is a mode of acquisition (§ 182) or in a pecuniary condemnation, or in both. But they were essentially personal actions, at all events under Justinian; (3) Ulpian uses the term in yet another sense.[38] He says that mixed actions are those in which each party is plaintiff, and instances the judicia divisoria and (using the word action in a wide sense) the double interdicts (§ 772).

710. The above description of the different kinds of action and their various classification may serve as an introduction to the second period of Roman civil procedure, the period of the formula, which we shall now consider, distinguishing, as before, the process of procuring attendance, the trial, and the execution of the judgment of the court.

II. The Formulary Procedure

711. (A) Summons.—In principle the old process of in jus vocatio remained in force. But in practice it was usual for the defendant to give by stipulation, with or without sureties, an undertaking to appear. This was called vadimonium.[39] If the defendant kept out of the way to avoid arrest, the praetor gave a missio in possessionem (§ 778) of his goods with ultimate sale, and there were other methods of compulsion.

712. (B) Trial.—The cardinal feature remained a division of the proceedings into the two stages of in jure and apud

---

[37] Buckl. *T.* p. 694; *M.* p. 371. [38] Dig. 44. 7. 37, 1.
[39] Girard, p. 1062.

judicem. The procedure retained the character of a reference to arbitration, which could only run its normal course with the consent and co-operation of both parties.

713. (i) PROCEEDINGS IN JURE.—Both parties being present, or represented, before the praetor, the plaintiff stated the nature of his claim and asked for an action. It lay in the discretion of the praetor to give or to refuse it. If the issue was simple and unquestioned the action was given as of course. But whether an action should be given and what action should be given were questions which might lead to protracted argument and to the production of evidence by both parties to the litigation. If, in the event, the praetor refused any action at all, or any action which the plaintiff was willing to accept, the matter was at an end; though, it seems, the plaintiff, if so advised, might make a fresh attempt before another, or even before the same, praetor. If, on the other hand, subject to the direction and approval of the praetor, the parties agreed upon the issues to be referred, it remained for them to embody their agreement in a formal document which named the judex. This document was the formula. It was probably executed in duplicate, and sealed by the parties and by witnesses. The plaintiff handed one copy to the defendant which the defendant accepted. A document framed in identical terms was issued to the judex by the praetor as his authority to act (nominatio judicis). This ceremonial in which three persons concurred (plaintiff, defendant, praetor) was the litis contestatio.[40] It concluded the proceeding in jure. Normally, the judex was chosen by agreement between the parties. But there might be protracted debate, each party raising objection to the other's candidate. The last resort was to settle the matter by lot. The reference might be not to a single judex, but to a board of recuperatores or to a standing college of judges (§ 669).[41]

714. The effect of litis contestatio was to freeze the plaintiff's right as at that moment. Apart from the extraordinary remedy of restitutio in integrum (§ 777) he could not in any subsequent proceeding revert to the situation as it was before this event. This would be contrary to the principle that the same matter cannot be litigated twice—ne de eadem re bis sit actio. As the

[40] Wenger, p. 130; the phrase litis contestatio ante-dates the formula and recalls a time when there was a solemn appeal to those present to witness what was taking place. Jolowicz, p. 187.

[41] Recuperatores means "recoverers." They were not necessarily drawn from the panel of judices. Buckl. *T.* p. 636; *M.* p. 384.

law is stated by Gaius, litis contestatio in some cases extinguished the pre-existing right *ipso jure*, in others grounded the
exceptio rei in judicium deductae.[42] On the other hand, the
plaintiff's right was defined and fixed as it was at the moment of
litis contestatio. Subsequent events did not affect it. From this
the Proculians drew the conclusion that even satisfaction of the
plaintiff's claim after litis contestatio would not affect his right
to have the defendant condemned if the judex decided that the
right existed when the issue was framed. The Sabinians took
the contrary view expressed in the maxim " All actions admit of
absolution "—omnia judicia absolutoria esse [43]; and this
doctrine prevailed. Another consequence of litis contestatio
was to render transmissible actions otherwise intransmissible,
and there were others besides.

715. All this assumes the presence and co-operation of the
parties. But there are other situations to be considered. The
defendant might :—(1) fail to put in an appearance, or refuse
to go to trial on the action given by the praetor; or (2) admit
the plaintiff's claim in whole or in part. In the first case he
was said to be indefensus, in the second case confessus. Either
event interrupted the normal course of litigation with different,
and, in each case, various consequences.

716. If the plaintiff claims that a thing is his (vindicatio rei)
the defendant need not go to trial. He may just do nothing.
This is because the action is supposed to be brought in rem,
i.e., against the thing not against the person (§ 694), and " no
one is compelled to defend a thing against his will." [44] In
such case the praetor would allow the plaintiff to take possession of the thing if present in court, or give him a personal
action against the possessor for the production of movables—
actio ad exhibendum—or the interdict quem fundum to get
possession of an immovable. Finally (as also in all undefended
personal actions) there was the menace of missio in possessionem and ultimate sale of the goods of the defendant (§ 778).[45]

717. If the defendant in a liquid money claim admitted his
liability the effect was the same as if judgment had been pronounced against him.[46] This goes back to the Twelve Tables in

---

[42] G. 4. 106.
[43] G. 4. 114; Inst. 4. 12. 2.
[44] Invitus nemo rem cogitur defendere, Dig. 50. 17. 156 pr.; Wenger,
p. 104.
[45] Wenger, pp. 104, 225.
[46] Wenger, p. 110.

which aeris confessi are associated with judicati as liable to immediate manus injectio (§ 682) and the later law asserts the principle confessi debitores pro judicatis habentur—" debtors who admit their liability are deemed to have had judgment given against them." [47] But this is not so simple as it seems. If the subject of the litigation was a res or an incertum a reference to a judex might still be necessary to assess the admitted liability.[48]

718. (ii) PROCEEDINGS APUD JUDICEM.—The names of persons qualified by law to act as judges, who must be not less than twenty-five years of age, were placed on a list or panel from which the judge was chosen for the case in hand. Before proceeding to execute his functions he had to swear that he would administer justice truly and with due observance of the laws.[49] The proceedings take the same general course as the proceedings in jure, but with an important difference. Before the praetor, the plaintiff's task was to show that he had a case to go to trial; before the judex he must show that he is entitled to a decision in his favour. Speeches are made by advocates. The parties and their witnesses are heard. The opinions of jurists (responsa prudentium) may be put in, in support of a legal argument. The judex is armed with the necessary authority to exercise an effective control over the proceedings. Like the praetor he has a board of advisers (consilium), selected by himself, whom he is expected to consult. Finally, he pronounces his finding, which must answer the question posed in the formula. This is his sententia—an opinion, not a judgment. It cannot in itself be the basis of a decree in execution. The G. 4. 48. process of execution will be described below. Condemnation was always in a sum of money. Decrees of specific performance were unknown. There was no appeal from the sentence of the judex.[50] Very occasionally the praetor would cancel it by giving restitutio in integrum. If it was formally irregular it was treated as a nullity. If the judex found himself unable to decide the case one way or the other, he might take an oath that the matter was not clear to him (sibi non liquere), and the praetor would release him from his duty. Another judex might be appointed in his place.[51] Aulus Gellius, the author of Noctes

---

[47] Paul. *Sent.* 5. 5a, 2.
[48] Wenger, p. 111.
[49] Cod. 3. 1. 14 pr.
[50] Wenger, p. 201. This seems to have changed under the Empire to some extent. *Ibid.*
[51] Jolowicz, pp. 188, 223.

Atticae (§ 682) has left a most interesting account of his own experience, when, still a young man, he was called upon to act as judex and, being unable to make up his mind, took the oath which procured his discharge.[52]

The Formula

719. We now turn to a description of the formula, which, varying with the circumstances, was determined in each case by the cause of action, and in turn determined the character of the sentence. At the head of the formula stands the nomination of the judex. After this come the " parts " or clauses of the formula: *viz.*, 1, demonstratio ; 2, intentio ; 3, adjudicatio ; 4, condemnatio. All of these may be described as usual, in the sense that they commonly occur. There were, besides, two other clauses, which were only employed in special circumstances, *viz.*, praescriptio and exceptio. These will be explained later. Our knowledge of the structure of the formula is mainly derived from Gaius, with whose aid we are able to piece together some typical formulae. He describes the parts of the formula as follows :—

G. 4. 39.

720. The demonstration is the part of the formula which is placed at the beginning to indicate the matter in issue, as, for example : " Inasmuch as Aulus Agerius has sold a slave to Numerius Negidius "; or " Inasmuch as Aulus Agerius has deposited a slave with Numerius Negidius."

G. 4. 40.

721. The intention is the part of the formula in which the plaintiff embodies his claim; for example : " If it appears that Numerius Negidius ought to give ten thousand sesterces to Aulus Agerius "; or, " Whatever it appears that Numerius Negidius ought to give to or do for Aulus Agerius "; or, " If it appears that the slave belongs to Aulus Agerius by quiritary title."

G. 4. 41.

722. The adjudication is the part of the formula which gives the judex authority to adjudicate a thing to one of the litigants; for example, if proceedings are taken between joint-heirs for the division of the inheritance (actio familiae erciscundae), or between co-owners for the division of property owned in common (actio communi dividundo), or between neighbours for the ascertainment of boundaries (actio finium regundorum). The formula runs : " So much as ought to be adjudicated, do you, judge, adjudicate to Titius."

G. 4. 42.

723. The condemnation is the part of the formula by which the judex receives authority to condemn or absolve; for example : " Judge, condemn Numerius Negidius to Aulus Agerius in ten thousand sesterces, if it does not appear, absolve "; or " Condemn Numerius Negidius to Aulus Agerius in not more than ten thousand

G. 4. 43.

---

[52] Aul. Gell., XIV. 2.

sesterces"; or simply, "Judge, condemn Numerius Negidius to Aulus Agerius," without more.

724. Gaius goes on to say that these clauses do not occur in every kind of formula. Some occur, others not, according to the nature of the action. In a small class of cases the intentio stands alone; namely, in the proceedings which are known as praejudicia, directed to the ascertainment of a preliminary question of fact, *e.g.*, whether such a person is slave or free, or what is the amount of a dos. In such cases the whole formula will be: "Be Titius judge whether this man is free (or slave)"; "Be Titius judge what the dos amounts to." The demonstration is a clause which occurs particularly in personal actions in jus with an intentio incerta, *i.e.*, in two classes of cases, namely, bonae fidei actions and the actio ex stipulatu (§§ 733, 732).[53] It invariably begins with the word quod— "whereas," or "because." The intentio is a normal part of every formula. Except in the praejudicia, it always begins with the words si paret—"If it appears"—or, quicquid paret— "Whatever appears." The adjudicatio is met with only in the so-called judicia divisoria enumerated in the text. The condemnatio is common to all formulae except the praejudicia. It may be certa, in which the judex is instructed, if he condemns, to condemn for a certain amount, or incerta, in which the amount of the condemnation is left to his discretion, or incerta cum taxatione, which leaves him free to condemn up to, but not beyond, a stated limit.[54]

G. 4. 44.

725. We will now give some illustrations of the formulae in the usual classes of action, *viz.*, I. Civil law actions in rem; II. Civil law actions in personam; III. Praetorian actions in factum.

726. I. CIVIL LAW ACTIONS IN REM.—The most typical of these is the vindicatio rei. The formula is as follows:—

> "Titius judex esto: si paret fundum Cornelianum quo de agitur ex jure Quiritium Auli Agerii esse, neque is fundus arbitratu tuo Aulo Agerio restituetur, quanti ea res erit,[55] tantam pecuniam, judex, Numerium Negidium Aulo Agerio condemna, si non paret, absolve."[56]
>
> "Be Titius judge: if it appears that the Cornelian estate, now in question, belongs to Aulus Agerius by Quiritary title, and the said land shall not to your satisfaction be restored to

---

53 And in some other cases. Buckl. *T.* p. 650.
54 G. 4. 49-51.
55 Quanti res est, id est quanti adversarii interfuit; Dig. 6. 1. 68.
56 G. 4. 41, 51.

Aulus Agerius, at what sum soever the amount shall be assessed, in so much money, judge, condemn Numerius Negidius to Aulus Agerius: if it does not appear, absolve."

727. A few details call for remark. First, the intention contains the name of the plaintiff only, not of the defendant. This is a common characteristic of actions in rem. Next, the condemnation· is conditional upon the failure to restore. If the property is restored, condemnation does not follow. Lastly, the condemnation, which for the first time introduces the name of the defendant, leaves the amount of the condemnation to the discretion of the judge. It was the practice for the plaintiff to swear to the value of the property, or to his interest in having it restored (jusjurandum in litem). He would naturally estimate his interest at a high figure, and was encouraged to do so.[57] This was an indirect method of procuring specific performance. But it was always open to the defendant to pay the assessed damages and keep the thing, so that litis aestimatio was in effect a mode of acquiring ownership (§ 183).[58] The words importing "restoration at your discretion" are known as the clausula arbitraria, which is a common feature of real actions.[59]

728. The formula of which we have given a specimen is termed the formula petitoria. In the time of Gaius the plaintiff in a real action had the alternative of suing by a procedural wager initiated by a sponsio in the terms, "if [the thing] in question is mine by Quiritary title do you promise to give twenty-five sesterces? " This was a mere form designed to raise the question of title. The plaintiff was said per sponsionem agere.

G. 4. 91.

729. II. CIVIL LAW ACTIONS IN PERSONAM.—These are stricti juris or bonae fidei. The principal cases of the first class are the condictio certae pecuniae, the condictio triticaria and the actio ex stipulatu. Examples follow.

730. (a) Condictio certae pecuniae.

"Titius judex esto: si paret Numerium Negidium Aulo Agerio sestertium decem milia dare oportere, judex, Numerium Negidium Aulo Agerio sestertium decem milia condemna, si non paret, absolve." [60]

"Be Titius judge: if it appears that Numerius Negidius ought to give to Aulus Agerius ten thousand sesterces, do you, judge, condemn Numerius Negidius to Aulus Agerius in ten thousand sesterces, if it does not appear, absolve."

---

[57] Dig. 12. 3. 11.   [58] Dig. 6. 1. 46.
[59] And of many others, Inst. 4. 6. 31; Buckl. *T.* p. 659; *M.* p. 400.
[60] G. 4. 41, 43.

THE LAW OF ACTIONS

445

This is a simple formula consisting after the nomination of the
judge of two parts only, intention and condemnation. Since
the action is in personam, the name of the defendant appears in
the intention. The words dare oportere indicate the civil law
character of the action. The condemnation is certa. No
mention is made in the intentio of the cause of the action.
Whether this is mutuum, stipulation, or anything else has no
effect on the structure of the formula.

731. (b) Condictio triticaria, *i.e.*, claim for any res certa
other than money (§ 420).[61]

"Titius judex esto: si paret Numerium Negidium Aulo
Agerio tritici Africi optimi modios centum dare oportere, judex,
quanti ea res est, tantam pecuniam Numerium Negidium Aulo
Agerio condemna, si non paret, absolve."

"Be Titius judge: if it appears that Numerius Negidius
ought to give to Aulus Agerius one hundred bushels of best
African wheat, whatever is the amount involved, in so much
money condemn Numerius Negidius to Aulus Agerius, if it does
not appear, absolve."

The condemnation is incerta. It is for the judge to ascertain
the amount. Here again the causa is not stated.

732. (c) Actio ex stipulatu.[62]

"Titius judex esto: quod Aulus Agerius de Numerio Negidio
incertum stipulatus est, quidquid paret ob eam rem Numerium
Negidium Aulo Agerio dare facere oportere, ejus, judex,
Numerium Negidium Aulo Agerio condemna, si non paret,
absolve."[63]

"Be Titius judge: Inasmuch as Aulus Agerius has stipulated from Numerius Negidius for a performance undefined in
amount, whatever it appears that on that account Numerius
Negidius ought to give to or do for Aulus Agerius, thereunto,
judge, condemn Numerius Negidius to Aulus Agerius, if it does
not appear absolve."

Here for the first time we meet with the demonstratio. As in
the last example the condemnatio is incerta.

733. (d) Bonae fidei actio in personam. The actio venditi
or ex venditio may be taken as typical of this group.

"Titius judex esto: quod Aulus Agerius Numerio Negidio
hominem vendidit, quo de agitur, quicquid paret ob eam rem

---

[61] Dig. 13. 3. 1.
[62] The term was limited to stipulations for an incertum, *i.e.*, for something which was neither certa pecunia nor certa res., Dig. 12. 1. 24;
13. 3. 1. (§ 451). But the actio ex stipulatu was not the same as the
condictio incerti, which developed later and lay in cases to which the actio
ex stipulatu was inapplicable. Buckl. *T.* p. 683; *M.* p. 267.
[63] G. 4. 136.

Numerium Negidium Aulo Agerio dare facere oportere ex fide bona, ejus, judex, Numerium Negidium Aulo Agerio condemna, si non paret, absolve."

"Be Titius judge: Inasmuch as Aulus Agerius has sold to Numerius Negidius a slave in respect of whom this action is brought, whatever it appears that Numerius Negidius in good faith ought to give to or do for Aulus Agerius, thereunto, judge, condemn Numerius Negidius to Aulus Agerius, if it does not appear, absolve."

Here again there is a demonstratio, as is usual in bonae fidei actions, and the bonae fidei character of the action is marked by the insertion in the intentio of the words ex fide bona.

734. III. PRAETORIAN ACTIONS.—(a) *Fictitious actions, i.e.,* actions with a fiction in the formula. A typical example is the *actio Publiciana in rem* (§§ 176–7) with the following formula:—

"Titius judex esto: si quem hominem Aulus Agerius bona fide emit et is ei traditus est anno possedisset, tum si paret eum hominem ejus ex jure Quiritium esse oportere, neque is homo arbitratu tuo Aulo Agerio restitutur, quanti ea res erit, tantam pecuniam, judex, Numerium Negidium Aulo Agerio condemna, si non paret absolve."

"Be Titius judge: if it appears that the slave whom Aulus Agerius bought and who was delivered to him should be his by quiritary title if he had possessed him for one year and the said slave shall not to your satisfaction be restored to Aulus Agerius, at what sum soever the amount shall be assessed, in so much money, judge, condemn Numerius Negidius to Aulus Agerius: if it does not appear absolve."

(b) *Transposed actions.* (1) The simplest case is one in which a person represents another in litigation. Thus, a man suing in right of another person frames the *intentio* in the name of his principal but transfers the *condemnatio* into his own name. For example, if L. Titius is suing on behalf of P. Mevius, the *formula* is framed thus:—

G. 4. 86.

"Sextius judex esto: si paret Numerium Negidium Publio Mevio x milia dare oportere, judex, Numerium Negidium Lucio Titio sestertium x milia condemna: so non paret absolve."

"Be Sextius judge: if it appears that N. N. ought to pay to Publius Mevius 10,000 sesterces, do thou, judge, condemn N. N. to Lucius Titius in 10,000 sesterces: if it does not appear, absolve." [64]

If the debt is proved, Titius will get the money. What he will do with it will depend upon his arrangement with Publius Mevius. He may hold it for his account. He may keep it for himself by virtue of a *mandatum in rem suam* (§ 649).

---

[64] de Zulueta's translation.

Another application of this formula is in the actiones adjecticiae qualitatis as in the following case: —

(2) *Actio quod jussu* brought against a father who has instructed a third party to deal with his son in power.

> "Titius judex esto: quod jussu Numerii Negidii Aulus Agerius filio ejus Gaio cum is in potestate Numerii Negidii esset togam vendidit, qua de re agitur, quicquid paret ob eam rem Gaium Aulo Agerio dare facere oportere ex bona fide ejus judex, Numerium Negidium Aulo Agerio condemna: si non paret absolve."

> "Be Titius judge: inasmuch as Aulus Agerius by the instruction of Numerius Negidius sold to Gaius, his son then in his power, a toga, the same being now in question, whatever it appears that in respect of this matter Gaius should give to or do for Aulus Agerius in good faith, therein, judge, condemn Numerius Negidius to Aulus Agerius: if it does not appear, absolve."

If the intermediate debtor were not a son but a slave in power, it would be necessary to have recourse to a fiction condemning the master to pay what his slave Stichus would have had to pay *si liber esset*—"if he had been free," because the slave could not incur a civil law liability. In this case the two praetorian contrivances would meet in the same formula.

G. 4. 35.

(c) *Praetorian actions in factum.* Gaius gives two illustrations, and in each case reproduces the whole formula from beginning to end. The first, which cannot have been of frequent occurrence, is the formula of the action given by the praetor to the patron against whom his freedman has brought an action without previous permission obtained from the praetor.

> "Lucius et Titius et Sempronius recuperatores sunto: Si paret illum patronum ab illo liberto contra edictum [illius] praetoris in jus vocatum esse, recuperatores, illum libertum illi patrono sestertium decem milia condemnate, si non paret, absolvite." [65]

> "Be Lucius and Titius and Sempronius recuperatores [66]: if it appears that such a patron was summoned to court by such a freedman, contrary to the praetor's edict, do you, recuperatores, condemn the freedman to the patron in the sum of ten thousand sesterces, if it does not appear, absolve."

735. Another example of the praetorian actio in factum is the actio depositi. The formula runs: —

> "Titius judex esto: si paret Aulum Agerium apud Numerium Negidium mensam argenteam deposuisse eamque dolo malo Numerii Negidii Aulo Agerio redditam non esse, quanti ea res erit, tantam pecuniam, judex, Numerium Negidium Aulo Agerio condemnato, si non paret, absolvito." [67]

[65] G. 4. 46. [66] Supra, § 713.
[67] G. 4. 47.

" Be Titius judge: If it appears that Aulus Agerius deposited a silver table with Numerius Negidius and the same through the misconduct of Numerius Negidius has not been returned to Aulus Agerius, whatsoever shall be the value thereof, in so much money condemn Numerius Negidius to Aulus Agerius, if it does not appear, absolve."

736. In the case of deposit (as also in the case of commodatum) there was an alternative formula with an intentio in jus concepta, which ran as follows: —

" Titius judex esto: quod Aulus Agerius apud Numerium Negidium mensam argenteam deposuit, qua de re agitur, quidquid ob eam rem Numerium Negidium Aulo Agerio dare facere oportet ex fide bona, ejus, judex, Numerium Negidium Aulo Agerio condemnato, si non paret, absolvito." [68]

" Be Titius judge: Inasmuch as Aulus Agerius has deposited with Numerius Negidius the silver table which is in question, whatsoever in respect thereof Numerius Negidius ought to give to or do for Aulus Agerius in good faith, therein, judge, condemn Numerius Negidius to Aulus Agerius, if it does not appear, absolve."

737. Of these two formulae the first was the older. In process of time, doubtless under the influence of the jurists, deposit, from being merely matter of fact, which the praetor recognised as grounding an action, came to constitute a legal relation between the parties giving rise to a civil law action. There were other relations which went through the same course of development, but in deposit as in commodatum (which was not always the case) the older and the later formulae continued to exist side by side.

738. The difference between the two types of action appears in the structure of the formula. The first consists of two parts only, the intention, embodying the fact, and the condemnation, which follows if the fact is established. Since this action is not one of the small group of actions in factum which contained a direction to the judex to condemn to what shall seem right and just, equitable defences, if any, must be raised by way of exception.[69]

The second type of the actio depositi is in jus concepta. There is a demonstration. The intention contains the words ex fide bona characteristic of a bonae fidei judicium. There is no need to plead equitable exceptions, for they are implied in the instruction to the judex.

---

[68] *Ibid.*

[69] Buckl. *M.* p. 368. In this respect actions in factum resembled actiones stricti juris (§ 703).

739. Reference has been made to two other clauses employed in special circumstances, the praescriptio and the exceptio.

740. The praescriptio was so called, Gaius tells us, because it was inserted before the formula,[70] and therefore, properly speaking, was not part of it. The purpose of the praescriptio was to limit the scope of the action, so that future claims arising out of the same transaction might not be consumed by litis contestatio. For example:—

> " It often happens that out of one and the same obligation there arise both an immediate and a future claim, as when we have stipulated for a certain sum yearly or monthly; at the end of the first year or month the payment in respect of it then becomes due, but there is not yet any claim for the payments applicable to future years [or months], although an obligation for them is held to have been contracted. If therefore we desire to sue for what is now payable, and to submit our claim in respect of it to judicial decision, and at the same time to reserve entire our future claims under the same obligation, we must have a prescription in these terms: ' Be the action limited to claims which have accrued due (ea res agatur cujus rei dies fuit).' " [71]

Gaius gives this as an illustration of a praescriptio introduced for the benefit of the plaintiff (pro actore). There were also cases of praescriptio inserted for the benefit of the defendant (pro reo), in opposition to the plaintiff's claim.[72] But these were superseded by the system of exceptions and need not occupy our attention.

741. The exceptio was a defence to the plaintiff's claim. It did not deny the plaintiff's right, but denied his right to enforce it. It was inserted in the intention as a negative condition of the condemnation:—

> " All exceptions are a contradiction of the plaintiff's affirmation. For example, if the defendant alleges that the plaintiff is doing something fraudulent, as, for instance, if he is suing for money alleged to have been paid, which he did not in fact pay, the exception runs: ' if in this matter Aulus Agerius has not acted or is not acting fraudulently ' [73]; or, suppose the defendant says that the plaintiff is bringing the action in breach of an agreement not to sue, the exception runs: ' if Aulus Agerius and Numerius Negidius did not agree that the money should not be claimed ' [74]; and so in other cases. The exceptio always proceeds from the defendant and is inserted in the

G. 4. 119.

---

[70] G. 4. 132.
[71] G. 4. 131 (mainly Muirhead's translation).
[72] G. 4. 133.
[73] Exceptio doli: " Si in ea re nihil dolo malo Auli Agerii factum sit neque fiat."
[74] Exceptio pacti de non petendo: " Si inter Aulum Agerium et Numerium Negidium non covenit ne ea pecunia peteretur."

formula so as to make the condemnation conditional, that is to say, the judex is not to condemn the defendant unless there has been no fraud on the part of the plaintiff, or unless there has not been an agreement not to sue."

742. Of all exceptions the exceptio doli was the most important. Like the exceptio metus it came into use in the last century of the republic.[75] In its developed form it was available as a defence not merely when a transaction was initially tainted with fraud, but also when the plaintiff acted dishonestly in bringing the action. Thus, it was available to a bona fide possessor who had built on another man's land against an owner seeking to vindicate his land, who refused to compensate him for the price of the materials and the wages of the workmen, and it came to be admitted in substitution for any other exception founded on matter of fact known to the plaintiff : —

2. 1. 30.

> "And in general it must be remarked that all matters of exception founded on the facts give rise to the exceptio doli because a plaintiff acts fraudulently if he advances a claim which can be defeated by any kind of exception; for even if the plaintiff did not act fraudulently to begin with, he does so now in bringing the action, unless his ignorance of the circumstances excludes the imputation of fraud." [76]

743. This passage indicates the very elastic nature of this paramount exception. The commentators distinguish an exception based upon an initial fraud as exceptio doli specialis (or praeteriti), and an exception based upon the fraudulent conduct of the plaintiff in bringing the action as exceptio doli generalis (or praesentis).[77] It must be noticed that by pleading an exception the defendant did not admit the plaintiff's legal right. The exception was a second line of defence, not a confession and avoidance. The defendant might put the plaintiff to the proof of his allegation. He might say, for instance: "I did not enter into the alleged stipulation"—this might be a question of the construction of a cautio—"and if I did, you procured my promise by fraud." The burden of proving the exception naturally fell upon the defendant.

> "The word agere applies also to a defendant who pleads an exception: for as regards an exception the defendant is in the position of a plaintiff." [78]

---

[75] The actio doli was introduced by Aquilius Gallus, praetor together with Cicero in the year 66 B.C. The exceptio, according to Girard (p. 450, n. 2) was introduced soon afterwards.
[76] Dig. 44. 4. 2, 5.
[77] Sohm, ed. Ledlie (3), pp. 279, 280.
[78] Dig. 44. 1. 1.

744. The exceptio might in turn be challenged by a counterplea called replicatio and this again by a duplicatio and this again by a triplicatio, and so forth.[79] Not to carry the pleading to any such unusual degree of complication, it may suffice to indicate a possible case of replicatio—*viz., plaintiff's case*—promise by stipulatio; *exceptio*—pact not to sue; *replicatio*—substituted pact allowing the plaintiff to sue. It will be remembered that in bonae fidei judicia the usual equitable defences and, of course, further pleas of the same character, were implied, so that they need not be expressly pleaded in the formula.

745. The principal exceptions may be properly described as equitable defences. There were other exceptions based upon a lex or a senatusconsultum.[80] At first sight it might be thought that if the defendant set up a statutory prohibition this was a flat denial of the plaintiff's case, which should result *ipso jure* in absolution. But it must be remembered that a statute might prohibit a transaction without penalising or annulling it (lex imperfecta), or might prohibit and penalise without annulling (lex minus quam perfecta). This explains why defences based upon the lex Plaetoria (§ 139) and the lex Cincia (§ 214) were raised by way of exception.[81] It must be remembered, too, that the many important senatusconsulta of the early empire were not technically legislative acts, but instructions to the magistrates. They did not abrogate the right of action at civil law, so in this case also the defence was raised by way of exception. Such were the exceptio senatusconsulti Macedoniani, senatusconsulti Vellaeani, senatusconsulti Trebelliani.[82]

746. What has been said explains the statement of Gaius, repeated by Justinian, that exceptions owe their existence to statutes or to equivalent enactments, or to the jurisdiction of the praetor.[83] It would be more correct to say that all exceptions proceeded from the praetor, though some were given under directions derived from an outside source.[84] In the cases in which the praetor was free to act on his own initiative he pursued the same course as in regard to actions. The circumstances in which an exception would be granted might be stated in the Edict; or the exception might be allowed in view of the

79 G. 4. 126; Inst. 4. 14.
80 G. 4. 118; Inst. 4. 13. 7.
81 Ulp. I. 1.
82 Dig. 36. 1. 28 (27), 7.
83 G. 4. 118; Inst. 4. 7. 7.
84 Girard, p. 1096.

particular circumstances of the case, and either after preliminary inquiry (causa cognita) or of course upon the defendant's presentation of the facts. An instance of an exceptio granted upon a special state of facts was the exceptio given to the defendant in an action brought by his patron or parent. It would be too disrespectful to set up an exceptio doli, and this was not allowed; but the same issues of fact might be raised in a special plea. An instance of an exceptio given after inquiry is the exceptio justi dominii (exception of lawful ownership),[85] given to the owner against a possessor in course of usucapion, who brought an actio Publiciana in rem. Since the formula directed the judex to proceed as if the usucapion were already complete, the owner who said that it was incomplete could only raise the issue by way of exception. This was a very anomalous case in which a defendant with a civil law title could not meet the plaintiff's action with a flat denial of his right.

747. Exceptions are variously classified as:—

      1. peremptory (or perpetual)—dilatory (or temporary).
      2. in rem—in personam—rei cohaerentes—personae cohaerentes.

748. Peremptory exceptions [86] were exceptions which might be pleaded without limit of time; e.g., a pact not to sue at all; dilatory exceptions were exceptions which were available only within a limited time, e.g., a pact not to sue for five years. A dilatory exception might also be founded on an objection not to the time of suing, but to the person of the plaintiff; if, for example, a person was suing by a cognitor, when the Edict forbade him to do so, or had accredited as his cognitor, or, in Justinian's day, procurator, a person who could not act in that capacity (for example, a soldier or a woman).[87] Before Justinian as regards their effect there was no difference between peremptory and dilatory exceptions. If the plaintiff allowed the matter to go to litis contestatio, either of them was fatal to his claim, not only in the present proceedings but for all time; for any renewal of his claim might be met by the exceptio rei in judicium deductae (the exception that the matter had been brought to trial).[88]

---

[85] Dig. 6. 2. 16 & 17; 17. 1. 57.
[86] G. 4. 120; Inst. 4. 13. 8.
[87] G. 4. 124; Inst. 4. 13. 11. For the difference between cognitur and procurator, see G. 4. 83, 84.
[88] G. 4. 123; Inst. 4. 13. 10.

749. Exceptions were further distinguished according to their scope. Some, as we might say, went to the root of the matter (in rem scriptae—rei cohaerentes) and were general in their application; others were available against, or to, specific persons alone (in personam—personae cohaerentes).[89] The exceptio metus might be objected to any person seeking to profit by the transaction in question, even an innocent third party; not so the exceptio doli, which, in general, could be objected only to the author of the fraud. The exceptio cognitoria or procuratoria mentioned in the last section had the same personal character. These were cases of exceptions personal in relation to the plaintiff. Others were personal in relation to the defendant. Of two partners one might be entitled to plead the so-called beneficium competentiae (exceptio quod facere possit),[90] another not. A pactum not to sue (pactum de non petendo) might be construed as a pactum in personam limited to the promisee, or, more often, as a pactum in rem, available also to his sureties.[91] The exception " unless he has made cession of his goods " was naturally not available to sureties.   4. 14. 4.

750. This concludes what we have to say with regard to the mode of trial in the formulary procedure. We pass to the third stage in the proceedings, namely, execution of the judgment.

751. (C) EXECUTION.—This might be directed either against the person, or against the property, of the debtor.

752. (i) EXECUTION AGAINST THE PERSON.—The mitigated system of manus injectio (§ 687) remained in force. But the legis actio was replaced by an action on the judgment (actio judicati). This reproduced in its initial stages the incidents of an ordinary action: summons, appearance, statement of plaintiff's case. As a rule there was no defence. But it might happen that the defendant challenged the formal validity of the judgment or said that it had been satisfied. He was entitled to raise these questions by way of defence in the action on the judgment. But he had to find a surety for the satisfaction of the judgment (cautio judicatum solvi), and if he was defeated in this second action he and by consequence his surety were liable for twice the amount of the judgment. This was a reminiscence   G. 4. 102. of the legis actio. Sometimes he could defend the action without incurring this risk, as for instance when he pleaded a beneficium

---

[89] Dig. 44. 4. 4, 33 ; 44. 1. 7.
[90] Dig. 44. 1. 7 pr.
[91] Dig. 2. 14. 7, 8 ; 21, 5 ; 22 ; 32 ; 44. 1. 19.

competentiae (§ 217) or a set-off in reduction of his liability.[92] If the debtor did not defend the action, because he had no defence to offer, or no confidence in the result, or could not find a surety, the proceedings came to an abrupt end with a magisterial decree authorising the plaintiff to take him away (duci jubet). This meant that he might be kept in confinement and bonds until he had satisfied the debt or liquidated it by his labour.

753. (ii) EXECUTION AGAINST PROPERTY.—This is said to have been introduced by Publius Rutilius, who was praetor not later than 118 B.C. It is thought to have followed the procedure adopted by the quaestors against persons indebted to the State (sectio bonorum).[93] It was in general an alternative (perhaps a cumulative) remedy. But in some cases it was the only available method. Such were:—1, if the debtor evaded arrest, being within the jurisdiction ; 2, if he was absent from the jurisdiction and had not appointed a representative to defend him ; 3, if he had made cessio bonorum under the lex Julia judiciaria ; 4, if the debtor had died insolvent and no one took up the estate as heir or bonorum possessor. The procedure, prescribed in the Edict, in which the praetor said, " I will order the goods to be possessed, advertised and sold " (bona possideri proscribi vendique jubebo), was as follows.[94]

G. 3. 78.

754. Missio in possessionem rei servandae causa.—A certain interval having elapsed after judgment, perhaps thirty days as under the legis actio procedure, a judgment creditor might apply to the praetor to be put in possession of the debtor's estate for the purpose of watching it. This would normally be granted as of course. Its effect was not to give the petitioning creditor juristic possession (§ 267), but merely to put him in possession " to preserve the property," and in particular with the object of preventing alienation in fraud of creditors. The order was made for the protection of the general body of creditors. The person put in possession (missus in possessionem) had a limited power of management. He was protected by interdict against interference in the exercise of his functions. It was his duty to make an inventory and advertise the fact of seizure (proscribere). If the circumstances called for it, the praetor, at the instance of the creditors, would appoint one of their number, or a stranger, to act as caretaker (curator bonorum). This would imply a postponement, perhaps for an indefinite time, of the next step in the procedure, namely, the sale.

755. Venditio bonorum.—In a normal case the possession was not long continued. A short interval was allowed to elapse

---

[92] Wenger, p. 220.   [93] Girard, p. 1110.
[94] Girard, p. 1112.

after the first decree in order to give the debtor an opportunity
of coming to terms with his creditors. After thirty days if the
debtor was alive, fifteen if he was dead, the praetor made a
second order directing the creditors to come together for the
purpose of appointing one of their number manager (magister). G. 3. **79.**
If a living debtor had not by now made cession of his goods he
became infamis. The function of the magister was to publish a
catalogue of the items comprised in the estate and the conditions
of sale (lex venditionis). After a further interval of ten or five
days, according as the debtor was alive or dead, the sale took
place, not in detail but in block, to the bidder who offered to
pay the highest dividend to the creditors. Finally, perhaps after
a further interval, the magister (under praetorian authority)
assigned the universitas bonorum to the purchaser. This gave
him bonitary ownership (§ 152), which in a short time would
ripen into dominium by ususcapio (§ 172). Meanwhile, the G. 3. 80.
purchaser, termed the bonorum emptor, had a possessory interdict (interdictum possessorium) to recover any item of the estate
from third parties, and he might maintain any action which was
competent to the debtor, whether in rem or in personam, in the
form known as the actio Rutiliana if the debtor was alive, and
in the form known as the actio Serviana if he was dead (§ 698).
He could be sued in the same actions by creditors of the estate
to the extent of the agreed dividend. It must be noticed that
the emptio bonorum did not release the debtor from liability.
If he acquired fresh assets they might be the subject of another
sale. For this amongst other reasons, this sale in execution
cannot properly be regarded as a case of universal succession,
though Gaius and Justinian describe it as acquisition per
universitatem, and Gaius speaks of it as a succession, Justinian
as a succession per universitatem.[95] But, as Buckland points
out, what the purchaser acquired was a universitas rerum, a mass
of res, not a universitas juris.[96]

756. The cessio bonorum already mentioned, i.e., a voluntary
surrender of the estate for the benefit of the creditors, culminated in a sale as above described, but it was more
advantageous to the debtor for:—1, it exempted him from
arrest and imprisonment; 2, did not render him infamis; 3, his
after-acquired property was not liable beyond the excess over
what was necessary for the subsistence of himself and his
dependents (beneficium competentiae). 4. 6. 40.

757. We set out to speak of the execution of a judgment.
What we have been describing is the liquidation of an insolvent
estate. In fact they are indistinguishable. Before the time of
Gaius a modification of the procedure had been introduced
particularly in favour of clarae personae (persons of high
rank),[97] whereby, as Girard puts it, the sale en bloc to a specu-
lator who resells in detail is replaced by a sale in detail made
for the benefit of the creditors themselves by a curator. This
process, known as distractio bonorum, superseded the (so-called)

---

[95] G. 2. 97; Inst. 2. 9. 6. G. 3. 77; Inst. 3. 12 pr.
[96] Buckl. *M.* p. 246.   [97] Dig. 27. 10. 5.

universal succession of the old procedure, but it still remained necessary to seize the whole estate in order to realise a single debt or to execute a single judgment.[98] It was merely a modification of the old procedure in insolvency.

758. This brings us to the end of what we have to say about the normal process of litigation per formulas. It is known as the formulary procedure, or the ordinary procedure, because it derived its character from the ordo formularum. Procedure which deviated from it was said to be extra ordinem. Even during the period of the vigorous existence of the formulary system there were departures from it. We have seen that its fundamental characteristic, perpetuated from the period of the legis actiones, was the division of the proceedings into proceedings in jure and proceedings apud judicem. The first took place before the magistrate, the second before a judge or arbiter agreed to by the parties. But many important matters were not submitted to this process. They never left the court of the magistrate, who saw the litigation through from beginning to end. We have seen an example in the " extra-ordinary " aid given to the mandatory (nominally unpaid) to recover an agreed salarium (§ 515). Even in the early days of the Empire whole fields of law were placed in the hands of special praetors, whose procedure was extra ordinem. Such were the praetor tutelaris, who handled questions arising out of guardianship,[99] and the praetor fideicommissarius, who was charged with jurisdiction in questions relating to fideicommissa (§ 361). As time went on the new system more and more prevailed at the expense of the old, first in the provinces and in Italy, ultimately in the capital. The process of disintegration was probably complete by the end of the third century (reign of Diocletian). A rescript of Constantius and Constans of 342, to the effect that—

> " Legal formulae which contain an insidious snare in every syllable are to be radically removed from every person's acts " [1]

has been regarded as marking the final elimination of the formula from legal procedure, but the old distinction between jus and judicium was already a thing of the past.

III. The Extraordinary Procedure

759. We have seen that in the period of the legis actiones legal process took the form of regulated self-help. It was

---

[98] Girard, p. 1114.
[99] *Vat.* 232. Ulpian wrote a monograph *de officio praetoris tutelaris.*
[1] Cod. 2. 57 (58). 1.

left to the plaintiff to procure the attendance of the defendant before the court, and, the parties being present, the trial postulated a reference by consent to a chosen arbitrator. Nor did the formulary procedure effect an essential change, however much the growing power and activity of the State may have asserted themselves in controlling and modifying the traditional procedure. In the third period all this is changed. The attendance of the defendant is procured by an official summons. The trial is conducted in all its stages by a salaried magistrate, subject in a fit case to appeal to a higher court, or to the Emperor. However, it remained open to him to delegate a case to a private person (judex datus) and, it seems, he often did so. The process of execution against property is simpler and more rational. In general, therefore, the procedure in this period is not far removed from that with which we are familiar in modern systems. A summary statement of its character will suffice. As before, we speak of the three stages of Summons, Trial and Execution. We describe the culmination of the system in the law of Justinian, without noticing the intermediate stages through which it passed in the course of its development out of the earlier system.

760. (A) SUMMONS.—At the instance of the plaintiff a competent court issued and through its officer served upon the defendant a summons accompanied by the plaintiff's statement of claim. This was the libellus conventionis. The defendant was required to give security for his appearance and by a named date to lodge in court his answer, known as the libellus contradictionis or responsionis.

761. (B) TRIAL.—This followed the normal course, with evidence and argument. Evidence might be oral or written, but the first was regarded as relatively of little value. The trial culminated in the sentence of the magistrate, which was usually, but no longer necessarily, expressed in terms of a pecuniary condemnation. It might decree specific performance. There was usually a right of appeal to a higher court or to the Emperor.

762. (C) EXECUTION.—If specific performance was ordered the court would employ its officers to give effect to it, or to compel compliance with the order. In the last resort it had at its command the armed force of the State.[2] If the condemnation was pecuniary, execution was levied upon the property of

---

[2] Dig. 6. 1. 68 (interpolated) ; Girard, p. 1088.

the judgment-debtor, which was sold to the amount required to satisfy the claim. This was the pignus ex judicati causa captum, which had been introduced by the Emperor Antoninus Pius in connection with the procedure extra ordinem of his time. Execution against the person with confinement in private prisons continued to exist in spite of repeated attempts to suppress it.[3] If there were several judgment creditors, and in case of insolvency, the debtor's assets were liquidated by distractio bonorum.

THE INSTITUTES

(BOOK IV, Tits. VI, XII–XIV)

TITLE VI

Of actions

It remains to speak of actions. An action is nothing else than the right of prosecuting a claim in a court of law.[4]

§ 694.

1. All actions in which a question is raised before judges or arbitrators fall into one or other of two principal classes; they are either actions in rem, or actions in personam. For a man either brings an action against some one who is liable to him under an obligation from contract or delict, in which case actions are given in personam, whereby the plaintiff alleges that the defendant ought to give him something or do something for him, or makes some other claim; or he brings his action against a person who is not bound to him by any obligation, but raises a question of right with regard to a thing, in which case actions are given in rem. For instance, suppose someone possesses a corporeal thing, which Titius alleges to belong to him, while the possessor on the other hand says that he is owner; if Titius brings an action claiming the thing as his, the action is in rem. 2. So, again, if a man brings an action alleging that he has a right of use and enjoyment (usufruct) of something— of land or a house, for instance—or asserting a servitude of iter, actus, or aquaeductus, the action is in rem; so, too, if the action is brought to establish an urban servitude, such as a servitude of building higher or a right of prospect and the like. There are also contrary actions given in respect of usufruct or of rustic or urban servitudes in which a plaintiff alleges that the defendant has not a right of usufruct, or of rustic or urban servitude. In these cases the actions are in rem, but negative. This kind of action is inapplicable when a corporeal thing is in question, for in such cases the action is brought by the person who is out of possession, and there is no corresponding action in which the person in possession alleges that the thing does not belong to the opposite party. There is, indeed,

---

[3] Cod. The. 9. 11. 1; Cod. 9. 5 (de privatis carceribus inhibendis); Cuq, *Manuel*, p. 906.
[4] Dig. 44. 7. 51 (Celsus)

one case in which the possessor assumes the role of plaintiff as may be seen in the ampler text of the Digest.[5]

§ 696.

3. The above-mentioned actions and others like them are based on statute and the civil law. There are other actions both in rem and in personam which the praetor has introduced by virtue of his jurisdiction, of which we will give some examples. Thus the praetor often gives an action in rem, in which a plaintiff is allowed to say that he is in the same position as if he had usucaped a thing when in fact he has not done so, or, conversely, that a defendant has not usucaped when in fact he has. 4. Thus, if a person has received a thing by tradition for any just cause, such as, gift, dower or legacy, and before he has become owner by usucapion has through some accident lost possession of the thing in question, he has no direct action in rem for its recovery, for no one but the owner can vindicate property in a civil law action. But since it would be harsh to deny him an action, the praetor gives an action in which the person who has lost possession alleges that he has usucaped and so reclaims the thing as his. This action is called the actio Publiciana because it was a praetor Publicius who first propounded it in his edict. 5. Conversely, if a person who was absent on public affairs or in the power of the enemy [6] has usucaped a thing belonging to a person who remained in the city, the latter, when the possessor comes back, may, within a year, bring an action to recover the thing by a rescission of the usucapion, that is to say by alleging that the possessor has not usucaped and that the thing belongs to him (the plaintiff). There are other cases in which the praetor is moved by similar considerations of equity to allow actions of this character, as will be found explained at large in the Digest.

6. Once more, if a person has alienated his property in fraud of creditors who have been put in possession by order of the governor, they are allowed to bring an action cancelling the alienation, that is alleging that the property has not been alienated and therefore remains an item in the debtor's estate.

§ 699.

7. Again, the actio Serviana and the actio quasi-Serviana, also called actio hypothecaria, owe their existence to the praetor's jurisdiction. The actio Serviana is brought by a land-owner to get possession of the movables of an agricultural tenant which are pledged to him to secure the rent. The actio quasi-Serviana is the action by which creditors in general realise a pledge or hypothec. So far as this action is concerned there is no difference between pledge and hypothec, for whenever a creditor and debtor have agreed that a thing is to be bound to secure a debt the transaction may be indifferently described by either term. But in other respects there is a difference; for the word pignus is correctly employed when a thing (particularly a movable thing) is handed over to a creditor; but if a

---

[5] What this case is, nevertheless, remains obscure. It may simply be the case mentioned in the text (Read sane hoc uno casu?). It may be the exceptio justi dominii in the actio Publiciana in rem. Dig. 6. 2. 16. (§ 746).

[6] This would be an exceptional case. It could only arise of a filius or servus acquired a res ex causa peculii. Dig. 4. 6. 23, 3; 41. 3. 43, 7. This section is not up to date, for by a constitution of 531 (Cod. 7. 40. 2) the usucapion could be interrupted by notice to the appropriate authority. Girard, p. 1128, n. 6.

thing is bound by simple agreement without delivery, it is properly
described as a hypothec. 8. There are also actions in personam
which the praetor has propounded by virtue of his jurisdiction, for
example the actio de pecunia constituta, and another action very
like it called the actio recepticia;[7] but our constitution,[7] which
attached to the first of these actions any advantage which belonged
to the second, has rendered the actio recepticia unnecessary and we
have deprived it of authority and declared it to be no longer in force.

§ 565.

Other praetorian actions in personam are the actions which the
praetor allows to be brought in respect of the peculium of a slave or
a son in power and the action to determine whether the plaintiff has
taken a procedural oath, and there are many others. 9. The actio

§ 528.

de pecunia constituta lies against any one who has promised to pay
a debt owed by himself or a third party, that is to say where there
is no stipulation. For one who has promised in answer to a stipulation is bound at civil law. 10. The praetor has given the actio de
peculio against fathers and masters, because though they are not
bound at civil law by the contracts of their sons and slaves it seemed
fair that they should be held liable to the extent of the peculium of
which sons and daughters and slaves may in a way be said to be
owners. 11. Again, if a plaintiff, being challenged thereto by the
defendant, has sworn that the sum which he was claiming was due,
and it is not paid, the praetor most justly allows him an action in
which the question is not whether the money is owed him, but
whether the plaintiff has sworn.[8] 12. There are also a great number
of penal actions which the praetor has introduced by virtue of his
jurisdiction; for instance against any one who has tampered with his
album (§ 12), or summoned to court a patron or parent without pre-

§ 734.

vious permission from the magistrate, or violently released a person
who was being summoned, or wrongfully connived at such a release,
and there are many other cases too numerous to mention. 13. Pre-

§ 724.

judicial actions seem to be in rem. Such are actions brought to
determine questions of status, for example whether a person is a free
man, or whether he is a freedman, or to decide a question of legitimacy. Of these perhaps one only is derived from the civil law,
namely, the action brought to inquire whether a person is a free
man. All the rest are praetorian.

14. Actions being thus discriminated, it is apparent that a
plaintiff cannot claim a thing which belongs to him by using the
words, "if it appears that the defendant ought to give," because,

§ 721.

of course, a thing is understood to be given in order to make it some
one's property, and a thing which already belongs to a plaintiff
cannot be made his any more than it is already. To be sure, to mark
the odious character of theft and to accumulate actions against
thieves, it has come about that in addition to the penal action for
double or quadruple value, there is also an action for the recovery of
the property expressed in the words "if it appears that they ought

§ 610.

to give," though thieves may also (in the alternative) be sued in the
actio in rem in which the owner seeks to recover his property.

---

[7] Cod. 4. 18. 2.
[8] This is the so-called jusjurandum necessarium. See Moyle *ad hunc
loc.*; Buckl. *T.* p. 633 ; *M.* p. 383 ; contrast the jusjurandum voluntarium,
supra, § 528.

15. Actions in rem are termed vindications, actions in personam in which a plaintiff claims that the defendant should give or do are called condictions. The word condicere in the old language means to give notice, but today the word is applied to an action in personam in which the plaintiff claims that something should be given to him, but incorrectly, for no formal notice is given as in the old procedure. § 677.

16. The next division of actions is that some lie for reparation, some for a penalty, some are mixed. 17. All actions in rem are for reparation. Of actions in personam, almost all actions based on contract are for reparation, such as an action for money lent or due under a stipulation, actions on loan for use, deposit, mandate, partnership, purchase and sale, giving and taking on hire. No doubt if an action is brought on a deposit made on the occasion of civil disorder, fire, earthquake or shipwreck, the praetor gives an action for double the loss against the depositee, and against his heir as well if the heir has acted dishonestly. In this case the action is mixed. § 704. § 436.

18. Of actions on delict, some are given to recover a penalty, others lie to recover a penalty and for reparation as well, and are therefore mixed. The actio furti, whether for quadruple damages when the theft is manifest, or for double damages when the theft is non-manifest, is merely penal; for the owner has in addition an action for the recovery of the thing based upon the assertion of ownership, which lies against the person in possession, whether the thief or any one else, and there is also a condictio for the thing against the thief.

19. The action for goods taken by violence (actio vi bonorum raptorum) is mixed, because the quadruple damages recoverable in this action include the value of the thing, and the penalty is for thrice the value. So too the action which lies for damage to property under the lex Aquilia is mixed, not only when the claim is for double damages against a defendant who denies his liability, but also in some cases when the action is brought for single damages; as, for instance, if a man has killed a slave who when he was killed was lame or had lost an eye, but within the year was sound and of great value; for the defendant is condemned (as explained above in speaking of this subject) to pay the highest value in the past year. Again, it is a mixed action which is brought against persons who have been so dilatory in paying a legacy or fideicommissum left to a holy church or to any other sacred place that it has been necessary to take legal proceedings. In such a case they are compelled to give the thing or to pay the money left by the deceased, and as much again by way of penalty, so that the whole condemnation is for double value. 4. 2 pr. § 632. 4. 3. 9.

20. Some actions may be said to be mixed in the sense that they are at the same time actions in rem and actions in personam. To this class belong the actio familiae erciscundae, which lies between co-heirs for the division of the inheritance; the actio communi dividundo, given for the division of property owned in undivided shares; the actio finium regundorum, which is brought between neighbours for the ascertainment of boundaries. In these three actions the judge is empowered to adjudicate property to one of the § 709.

§ 722.

litigants as may be right and just, and if the share assigned to one outweighs the share assigned to another, he is to condemn the person who gets the better share to pay a certain sum of money to the other.

21. All actions lie either for single, double, treble or quadruple damages; beyond this the assessment is never carried.

22. Single damages are claimed in actions brought upon a stipulation, a mutuum, on purchase, sale, letting on hire, taking on hire, mandate, and in a great many other cases.

23. We sue for double damages in the action for non-manifest theft and sometimes in actions for damnum injuria under the lex Aquilia and for deposit and in some other cases, also for corrupting a slave and in the case just mentioned of a legacy to sacred places. The action for corrupting a slave lies against one at whose instigation or advice another man's slave has run away, or become disobedient or dissolute, or, in short, has in any way been made worse. The estimate of damages includes the value of any things which the slave carried off when he ran away. 24. An action lies for triple damages when some one has overstated the value in his writ of summons, with the consequence that the process-server has demanded too large a fee. The person who has sustained this loss will recover from the plaintiff thrice the amount of the expense incurred. A provision to this effect is inserted in our Code,[9] which makes it clear that a condictio can be brought under the statute. 25. The claim is for quadruple damages in the case of manifest theft, in the action metus causa and when money has been given as an inducement to a person to take vexatious proceedings against another or to refrain from doing so. Likewise our constitution allows a statutory condiction for quadruple damages against process-servers who exact from defendants sums in excess of the permitted tariff. 26. The actions for non-manifest theft and for corrupting a slave differ from the others in being always for double damages; but the others, that is the action on the lex Aquilia, and in certain cases the action on deposit, are doubled in case of denial, but lie in simplum against the defendant who admits liability; claims arising out of legacies to sacred places are doubled not only by denial, but also if settlement is delayed until process issues by order of the magistrate, but if the claim is admitted and if payment is made before summons, then nothing is due beyond the simple value.

27. The actio metus causa differs from the others above mentioned, because it contains the tacit condition that the defendant is absolved if he obeys the judge's order to restore the thing in question to the plaintiff. In other actions this is not so, but the defendant is in any event condemned to pay the quadruple value, as for example in the action for manifest theft.

28. Some actions are bonae fidei, others stricti juris. The bonae fidei actions are the actions on purchase, sale, letting on hire, taking on hire, negotiorum gestio, mandate, deposit, partnership, tutelage, loan for use, pledge, familiae erciscundae, communi dividundo, the actio praescriptis verbis, which is given on the transaction called aestimatum, and the action on an exchange. The hereditatis petitio is also bonae fidei. This was formerly uncertain but our constitution

§§ 606, 550.

§ 702.

§ 524.

---

[9] Cod. 3. 10. 2.

has declared it to be so. 29. Formerly there was an action for dower (actio rei uxoriae) which was bonae fidei. But, finding that it was more advantageous to sue on a stipulation, we have abolished the former action and merged it (but with many distinctions), in the action on stipulation, which is given for the recovery of a dos. Having thus effected a desirable reform we thought proper that the action on stipulation should assume the bonae fidei character of the action which it replaced, but only when brought to recover a dos. In addition to this we have given the person entitled a tacit hypothec, and if the wife is the plaintiff, but in no other case, since this provision is intended for her exclusive benefit, a preference over other creditors. 30. In bonae fidei actions the judge is understood to have full power to assess on equitable grounds the amount to which the plaintiff is entitled, and, consequently, when the defendant has a counter-claim against the plaintiff, this should be set off against the claim and the defendant condemned to pay the balance. The Emperor Marcus by rescript allowed the defence of compensation to be raised also in stricti juris actions by pleading the exceptio doli. But our constitution [10] has given a wider application to counter-claims of an evident character by providing that they shall reduce the plaintiff's claim *ipso jure,* whether the action is in rem or in personam or of any other kind, with the one exception of the action on deposit, for in this case we thought it quite wrong to allow a counter-claim to be opposed to the plaintiff's demand and so make it possible for a defendant by pretending a right of set-off fraudulently to prevent a plaintiff from recovering property which he had deposited.[11]

§ 227.

31. Some actions are called arbitrary, because they depend upon the arbitrium of the judge. These are actions in which the defendant is to be condemned unless as directed by the judge he satisfies the plaintiff's claim, as by restoring or exhibiting the thing in question or by payment or by surrender of a slave when the action is noxal. Actions of this kind may be either in rem or in personam. Examples of the first are the actio Publiciana, the actio Serviana brought in regard to the [movable] property of an agricultural tenant, the actio quasi-Serviana, also called the actio hypothecaria. Examples of personal actions with an arbitrium are the actio metus, the actio doli, and the action brought upon a promise which names the place of performance (*infra,* sec. 33c). The actio ad exhibendum also depends upon the arbitrium of the judge. In these and other like actions the judge is directed to decide on equitable principles according to the nature of the case the way in which the defendant is to satisfy the plaintiff's claim.

§ 726.

§ 638.

§ 698.

§ 261.

32. The judge must take care, so far as possible, to give judgment for a determined sum of money or an ascertained thing, even if the claim was for an uncertain amount.

33. Formerly, if a plaintiff claimed more in his intention than he was entitled to, he failed in his action, that is to say, he lost what was due to him, and it was not easy for him to get restitutio in integrum from the praetor, unless he were under twenty-five years of age. For, if he were, the praetor, as in other cases, would relieve

G. 4. 53.

[10] Cod. 4. 31. 14.   [11] Cod. 4. 34. 11.

him from the consequences of youthful error. No doubt, if the circumstances were such that even a thoroughly well-balanced person might reasonably have made a mistake, relief was given even to persons of maturer years; for example, when a man had claimed the whole of a legacy, and afterwards codicils were produced which took away part of the legacy, or gave other legacies, which had the effect that the plaintiff was found to have claimed more than the three-quarters to which legacies are reduced by the lex Falcidia.

G. 4. 53a.

33a. A claim may be excessive in one of four ways, that is, either in substance, time, place or cause (re, tempore, loco, causa). There is over-claim in substance, when for example a person to whom ten aurei are due claims twenty, or to whom part of a thing is due claims the whole or too large a part.

33b. There is over-claim in time if a person claims before the day, or before a condition is satisfied. For, just as a person who pays later than he should, is said to pay too little, so a person who demands before he should is said to demand too much.

33c. There is over-claim in place if a person who has stipulated for performance in a certain place, brings his action elsewhere without mentioning the place of performance; for example if a person has stipulated—" Do you promise to give at Ephesus? "—and then brings his action at Rome without any qualifying words. This is understood to be an over-claim because by making an unqualified demand he deprives the defendant of the advantage which he might have in paying at Ephesus. Consequently in such cases the plaintiff is given an arbitrary action (arbitraria actio) in which the judge is to take account of the advantage which the defendant would have had in paying at the place named in the contract.[12] This advantage is most apparent in matters of commerce, as, for example, in contracts relating to wine, oil or grain, which have different prices in different places, and the rate of interest on money loans is not everywhere the same. But if, in the case put, the plaintiff brings his action at Ephesus, that is in the place of payment named in the stipulation, he may take his claim in unqualified terms, as the praetor points out, because the promisor retains the advantage of paying in the place agreed.

33d. Very similar to overstatement in place is overstatement in cause; for example, if some one has stipulated from you—" Do you promise to give the slave Stichus or ten aurei? " and then sues for one or other of the alternatives. This is an over-claim, because in a stipulation of this kind the promisor has the choice of giving the money or the slave. If, therefore, a plaintiff claims only the slave or only the money he robs the defendant of his election, and improves his own position at his expense. He ought to frame his claim in the alternative, following the words of the stipulation. Similarly, there is an over-claim if the plaintiff. having stipulated in general terms for a slave, or for wine or for purple, sues for this particular slave Stichus, or for wine of Campania, or for Tyrian purple. Even if the thing claimed is worth very little, none the less there is an over-claim, for it is often more convenient for a defendant to give a thing of greater value.

---

[12] This was the actio de eo quod certo loco.

33e. But all this is now disused, and the law is confined within the limits of two constitutions, the first issued by the Emperor Zeno, the second by ourselves.[13]   Zeno's constitution says what must be done where there is an over-claim in respect of time.   In all other cases our constitution condemns the plaintiff to pay to the defendant thrice the amount of the expense which he has incurred in consequence of the over-claim, as mentioned above (sec. 24). 34. If in his statement of claim the plaintiff has demanded less than that to which he was entitled, for instance five instead of ten, or part of the land, when he was entitled to the whole, he runs no risk, because Zeno's constitution directs the judge none the less to condemn the defendant for the balance in the same action. 35. If a person in error claims one thing instead of another he runs no risk, for we allow him, when the truth is ascertained, to correct his mistake in the same proceedings; suppose, for instance, he has claimed the slave Eros when he should have claimed the slave Stichus or has stated that something was due to him under a testament, when in fact it was due upon a stipulation.

36. There are some actions in which we do not always get the whole of what is due to us, but sometimes the whole, sometimes less.   For instance when the action relates to the peculium of a son or a slave, if the amount of the peculium is sufficient to satisfy the demand the father or owner is condemned to pay the whole; if it is insufficient he is condemned to the extent of the peculium. What is meant by peculium is explained in Title VII of this Book (*supra*, p. 361).   37. Again, if a woman sues for the recovery of her dos the rule is that the husband is to be condemned to the extent of his ability, that is so far as his means allow. Conse-§ 226. quently, if his means admit of it, he is condemned to pay the whole amount, but, if not, only to the extent of his ability to pay. Further, the amount which may be claimed as dos is reduced by the husband's right of retention for necessary expenses incurred upon the dotal § 227. property,[14] for these *ipso jure* reduce the dos, as will be found explained more fully in the Digest.

38. If a person brings an action against his parent or patron and in proceedings between partners the plaintiff gets judgment for § 511. what the defendant is able to pay and no more.   The same applies when a donor is sued on his promise to give.   § 217.

39. The right to set off an opposing claim often has the effect that a plaintiff recovers less than the amount due to him. For, as explained above (sec. 30), the judge may make an equitable estimate of what is due from the plaintiff to the defendant in respect of the same set of circumstances and condemn the defendant to pay the balance. 40. If an insolvent has made cession of his goods and subsequently acquires property sufficient to justify such a course, the creditors may take fresh proceedings and recover what

---

13 Cod. 3. 10. 1 & 2.
14 Cod. 5. 13. 1, 7.   Property retained by the wife was called *parapherna* (a Greek word meaning outside the dos).   It was usually managed by the husband as his wife's mandatary. Cod. 5. 14. 8; Dig. 23. 3. 9, 3. For the wife's *paraphernalia* in English Law (a term of very limited application) see Blackstone, *Commentaries*, II, 435.

§ 756.   he is able to pay, for it would be inhuman to condemn without limit a man who is already despoiled of his fortune.

NOTE ON SECS. 30, 39

These sections relate to the subject of compensatio or set-off. In bonae fidei actions the words of the formula—quidquid ex fide bona dare facere oportet (§ 733)—empowered the judge to take account of counter-claims arising ex eadem causa and to give judgment accordingly. The Emperor Marcus, we are told in the text, allowed counter-claims to be asserted also in stricti juris actions by means of the exceptio doli (opposita doli mali exceptione compensatio inducebatur). Since these actions always arose out of a unilateral transaction, the counter-claim was necessarily ex dispari causa. Justinian allowed set-off in every kind of action (except the action of deposit and actions for the recovery of land wrongfully occupied),[15] provided, of course, that claim and counter-claim were of the same kind and nature (money against money—goods of a kind against goods of the same kind, etc.), so that they could be set off one against the other. Further, the counter-claim must be liquid,[16] i.e., ascertained or easily ascertainable. In such cases the compensation is said to take place *ipso jure*. Compensationes ex omnibus actionibus ipso jure fieri sancimus (Cod.)—ut actiones ipso jure minuant (Inst.). This phrase has given endless difficulty. It is now thought to mean merely that the set-off need not be expressed in the pleadings (Buckl. *M.* p. 406). The traditional view was that as soon as claim and counter-claim co-existed, there was *pro tanto* a mutual cancellation as if by a reciprocal payment. There is a text in the Code (4. 31. 4) which lends itself to this interpretation. It has influenced modern Codes, which treat compensation as one of the ways in which an obligation is extinguished. See in particular *C.C.* art. 1290, which says: " La compensation s'opère de plein droit par la seule force de la loi, même à l'insu des débiteurs." But the Roman Law, i.e., the Corpus Juris, always regards compensatio as a question of procedure. For more detailed information Girard and Buckland may be consulted. The text sec. 39 *per incuriam* seems to limit compensatio to claims arising from the same set of circumstances (ex eadem causa), but we have seen that this was not Justinian's law.

G. 4. 61.

G. 4. 66.

TITLE XII

Of actions perpetual and temporal, and what actions may be brought by and against heirs

§ 705.   Formerly, until limits were fixed by imperial constitutions, actions based upon statutes, senatusconsulta or imperial constitutions might be brought without limit of time, but the life of actions derived from the special jurisdiction of the praetor was usually limited to one year, this being the duration of the praetor's authority.

---

[15] Cod. 4. 31. 14, 2.
[16] Cod. 4. 31. 14, 1.

Sometimes, however, they were perpetual, in the sense that they continued within the limits fixed by the constitutions; such are the actions given to the bonorum possessor and to others who are in the place of heirs. The action for manifest theft, although of praetorian origin, is perpetual, because the praetor thought it absurd that it should not last beyond the year. §699.

1. It is not the case that all actions which are competent at civil law or are given by the praetor against a person are equally competent or given against his heir. Thus, it is an established rule of law that penal actions arising from delict, such as the actions of theft, robbery, injuria, and damnum injuria datum, do not lie against heirs. But actions of this kind are competent *to* heirs and the praetor does not refuse them, with the exception of the actio injuriarum and any other of the like kind. It sometimes happens that even an action on contract does not lie against an heir. This happens when the action arises out of fraudulent conduct on the part of a testator, and the heir has derived no advantage from the fraud.[17] If one of the penal actions above mentioned has reached the point of litis contestatio between the parties it is transmitted to and against heirs. §704.

2. In conclusion it must be remarked that if a defendant satisfies the plaintiff's claim before judgment it is the judge's duty to absolve him, though at the time when issue was joined the circumstances were such that the defendant ought to be condemned. This is the meaning of the old maxim that all actions give the power of absolution (omnia judicia absolutoria esse). G. 4. 114.

TITLE XIII

Of exceptions

We must now consider exceptions. These have been introduced for the benefit of defendants; for it often happens that though an action is good in law; it is inequitable in relation to the defendant in question. §741.

1. For instance, suppose that in answer to a stipulation you have made a promise which you would not have made if you had not been coerced by fear, induced by fraud, or misled by error; it is plain that you are legally bound and, if the promisee brings an action against you alleging that you ought to give, his claim is well founded in law, but since it is unfair that you should be condemned, you are allowed to resist the action by pleading the exceptio metus or the exceptio doli mali or an exception based upon the circumstances of the case.

2. The law is the same if on the pretext of making a loan of money a person has stipulated from another for a payment [*i.e.*, repayment of the loan] and in fact the loan has never been made. You can certainly be called upon to pay, because you are bound by the stipulation, but, since it is unfair that you should be condemned,

---

[17] This statement is contradicted by other texts in the Digest. See Moyle *ad loc.*

it is settled that you may raise in your defence the plea that the money was not paid (exceptio non numeratae pecuniae). We have

P. 301.
Inst. 3. 21.

spoken of this defence in an earlier part of this book and mentioned that we have reduced the limit of time within which it is available.

3. Again, if the creditor has promised the debtor not to sue him, the debtor remains liable none the less, because obligations are not in every case extinguished by agreement between the parties; and consequently an action conceived in the form "if it appears that he ought to give" is well founded. But since it would be unfair that he should be condemned contrary to the terms of the pact he may plead the exceptio pacti conventi.

4. Again, if the creditor has challenged the debtor to swear, and the debtor has sworn that nothing is due from him, in law he remains bound, but since it would not be right (in the circumstances) to go into the question of perjury, the defendant, if sued upon his obligation, may plead the exceptio jurisjurandi. In actions in rem, too, exceptions may be needed; for example, if a plaintiff has challenged the possessor to swear, and the possessor has sworn that the property is his, and, in spite of this, the plaintiff proceeds to vindicate it, although his statement of claim alleging that the thing belongs to him may be true, it is nevertheless unfair that the possessor (having sworn at the instance of the plaintiff) should be condemned. 5. Once more, if I have taken proceedings against you in rem or in personam, this does not extinguish my right of action, and so in strict law I can repeat my claim in a subsequent action, but you may call in aid the exceptio rei judicatae.[18] 6. The above cases may suffice to illustrate the nature of an exception. How many and various are the causes which give rise to exceptions may be seen by any one who will consult the Digest, where the matter is more fully treated. 7. Some exceptions are based upon statutes, or enact-

§ 746.

ments having statutory force, others are derived from the jurisdiction of the praetor. 8. Exceptions are distinguished as perpetual or peremptory, and temporary or dilatory. 9. Perpetual or peremptory

§ 748.

exceptions always bar the plaintiff's claim and destroy his cause of action. Such are the exceptio metus, the exceptio doli mali and the exceptio pacti conventi, when there is an unqualified agreement not to sue. 10. Temporary or dilatory exceptions are temporary obstacles, which have the effect of delaying the plaintiff's action; as when there is an agreement not to sue for a certain time, for example, for five years; for nothing prevents the plaintiff from bringing his action when the time has elapsed. Therefore, if people who want to bring an action are confronted with an agreement not to sue for a certain time or anything of the kind, they ought to defer their action and bring it later. This is why these exceptions are termed dilatory. If they bring the action within the time-limit and the defendant pleads the exception, they take nothing by their action in consequence of the exception. Formerly, they could not

G. 4. 123.

bring a fresh action later, because the whole cause of action was consumed and lost by being brought into court. But nowadays the consequences are less serious. The plaintiff who is too precipitate in

[18] The exceptio rei in judicium deductae of Gaius (3. 181) is not mentioned, because litis contestatio no longer consumed the right of action (§ 630).

bringing his action is required to postpone his action for twice the time of the original delay, whether this was voluntarily accorded by the plaintiff himself or implied in the nature of the action, and the other party need not enter a defence until he has been fully indemnified for all the costs of the former action. This is provided by Zeno's constitution on over-claims in point of time (tempore plus petitio).[19]

11. There are exceptions which are dilatory in respect of the person who brings the action. An example of these is the exception which is taken when the plaintiff is represented by a procurator who is not qualified to act as such, for example, a soldier or a woman. Formerly exceptions might be taken on the ground of the infamy of the representative or of the person represented, but since we have found that they were no longer met with in practice we declare them abolished.

TITLE XIV

Of replications

Sometimes it happens that an exception which at first sight seems just is found to be unfairly prejudicial to the plaintiff. In this event the plaintiff must call in aid another allegation, called a replication, because it rebuts and annuls the effect of the exception. For example, if it has been agreed that the plaintiff shall not sue, and afterwards there is a contrary agreement allowing him to do so; then, if he sues, and the defendant pleads that he is to be condemned only if there was no agreement not to sue, the exception is fatal to the plaintiff's case, for there was in fact such an agreement, even though there was a later agreement to the contrary. But since it is inequitable that the plaintiff should be barred, he will be allowed a replication based upon the subsequent pact. § 744.

1. Again, it may happen that a replication which at first sight seems just is unfairly prejudicial to the defendant. When this is the case he may have recourse to another allegation called a duplicatio.

2. And this, in turn, may be met by a triplicatio.

3. All these exceptions may be carried even further than we have indicated, if the diversity of business transactions requires it, as is fully explained in the Digest.

4. The exceptions which may be pleaded by a debtor are usually available to his sureties; and rightly, because what is demanded of sureties is, in effect, demanded of the principal debtor, because he may be required in an actio mandati to reimburse them what they have paid on his account. Consequently, if a creditor has promised not to sue the principal debtor, his sureties may plead the exceptio pacti de non petendo, just as if they had themselves been parties to the agreement.[20] But some exceptions are not available to sureties. For example, if a debtor has made cession of his goods and a creditor sues him, he may plead the exception, " unless he § 576.

---

[19] Cod. 3. 10. 1 ; Inst. 4. 6. 33b.
[20] *i.e.,* in the absence of a contrary intention. Dig. 2. 14. 21. 5 ; 22.

§ 753.

has made cession of his goods," but this exception is not allowed to sureties. This is obvious, because when a man takes sureties for a debt, the thing which he has above everything in view is that, if his debtor becomes insolvent, he may be able to come upon the sureties for payment.

IV. INTERDICTS AND OTHER PRAETORIAN INSTITUTIONS

763. An interdict was an order issued by the praetor requiring the person to whom it was addressed to do or not to do the thing indicated in the order. It might assume one of three forms—*viz.*, (1) an order to produce (exhibeas); (2) an order to restore (restituas); (3) a prohibition (veto). From this results the principal division of interdicts into exhibitory, restitutory and prohibitory. Examples of each will be found in the text.

4. 15. 1.

764. Interdicts might be matter of public law or of private law. Examples of the first are the prohibition to build on sacred ground or to impede the navigation of a public river. Where public interests were in question the interdict was populare, *i.e.*, any member of the public might ask for it. But the infringement of a public right might affect private interests and so give rise to the usual private process,[21] as in English Law an action lies in respect of a public nuisance from which the plaintiff has suffered particular damage beyond that suffered by him in common with other members of the public.

765. There were many interdicts of private law. The possessory interdicts were the most frequent and of outstanding importance. They were directed to acquiring, retaining or regaining possession (adipiscendae vel retinendae vel reciperandae possessionis causa). This is the second division of interdicts, not indeed of all, but within the possessory group. The principal interdict for acquiring possession was the interdict quorum bonorum, given to enforce a praetorian grant of bonorum possessio (§ 387). The interdicts for retaining possession were uti possidetis and utrubi (§ 772). The interdict for regaining possession was unde vi.

4. 15. 2.

4. 15. 6.

766. Interdict procedure, as we shall see, followed the model of an ordinary action. This implies a plaintiff and a defendant. But in the interdicts for retaining possession neither party was plaintiff or defendant more than the other.

---

[21] Dig. 43. 8 (ne quid in loco publico vel itinere fiat) 2. 2.

This introduced into the procedure a complication to be explained below. Interdicts of this kind are termed double. All others are simple. This is the third division of interdicts. 4. 15. 7.

767. All interdicts proceeded from the praetor. Some were given in support of a civil law right. Most were created by himself.

768. It might be supposed that an interdict was issued after inquiry, in the expectation that it would be immediately obeyed. But this was not so. In form absolute, the praetor's order was in intention conditional. He did not say " obey at your peril," but " obey if you ought to." This permitted a reference to a judex or arbiter to determine whether the person to whom the interdict was addressed ought to obey the order to produce or to restore, or had disobeyed the prohibition. The question will be, in other words, whether he comes within the scope of the order. It rests with him to raise the question. If he does not, the interdict takes effect as a mandatory injunction to be enforced by such means as the praetor sees fit. If he does raise the question and it is decided against him, the proceedings culminate not as might be expected in a peremptory order or in the infliction ex officio of a penalty, but as in any ordinary action in a pecuniary condemnation.

769. But there is a complication. In all interdicts the defendant may, and in some cases must, enter into a procedural wager to pay a penal sum of the case goes against him. This is not in substitution for the action for damages, but in addition to it.

770. If the interdict is prohibitory the proceedings are penal. The defendant has no choice. If the interdict is exhibitory or restitutory he may elect to litigate without a penalty, but he must make his decision before leaving the praetor's court by asking for an arbiter.[22] He then gets a formula arbitraria ; so-called, not because it is a reference to an arbiter, but because the arbiter is instructed to condemn, if the defendant does not obey the direction to exhibit or restore—nisi arbitrio tuo exhibeat (vel restituat). By exhibiting or restoring forthwith he escapes the effect of the condemnation, which is conditional upon his failure to do so. How the amount of the condemnation was assessed does not appear. It would probably be fixed arbitrarily by jusjurandum in litem.

771. If the proceedings are penal, because they must be, or because the defendant has not chosen the alternative procedure, the parties are required to make a wager on the result of the litigation. As in all procedural wagers, this consists in a stipulation and a re-stipulation. The plaintiff says to the defendant: " Do you promise to pay me so much, if you have disobeyed the praetor's order? " Answer, " I promise." The

defendant says to the plaintiff: " Do you promise to pay
me so much if I have not disobeyed the praetor's order? "
Answer, " I promise." Then the case goes to trial on claim
and counter-claim for a sum certain—two condictiones certae
pecuniae. The decision of these two actions will decide which
party has won the wager. But this does not formally decide
the main issue whether the defendant has disobeyed the interdict. This, too, must be referred.[23] If the case goes against
the defendant he will have to pay the amounts incurred under
each of the two stipulations and in addition the amount of the
condemnation on the principal issue. This he may escape by
prompt exhibition (or restoration), but he will not escape the
double penalty of the wager. Though this procedure involves
three distinct references to the arbiter, the decision of one is a
decision of the others.

772. The double interdicts—uti possidetis and utrubi—
involved a further complication. These were usually employed
to determine which of the parties was to have the advantageous
position of defendant in an action brought to vindicate the
property, in other words to determine who was entitled to be
maintained in possession. Since both claim to be so, neither
4. 15. 4.   can be regarded as plaintiff or defendant rather than the other ;
and so, as Gaius puts it, the praetor uses the same language to
both,[24] forbidding each to do violence to the kind of possession
which the interdict is designed to protect. What that is appears
from its terms—in uti possidetis: " I forbid any violence being
done to prevent you two continuing to possess as you do now " ;
—in utrubi: " I forbid any violence being done to prevent that
one of you with whom [e.g.] the slave in question has been for
the greater part of this year from taking the said slave away
with him." But it is not any kind of possession that the praetor
will aid with his interdict. It must be not clandestine, or contested or precarious in relation to the other party—nec clam,
nec vi, nec precario ab adversario.[25]

773. Having ordered the parties not to do violence to
possession, the praetor, curiously enough, forthwith requires
them to do so. This is what is called conventional violence—
(vis ex conventu).[26] It was a formal aggression, designed to
clear the ground of unnecessary controversy as to matter of
fact. Then the issue as to the right to be maintained in possession is remitted to the judge on the hypothesis that A has been

---

[23] G. 4. 165.

[24] G. 4. 160.

[25] This condition is embodied in the more complete formula for uti
possidetis preserved in the Digest. Uti [nunc] eas aedes, quibus de agitur
nec vi nec clam nec precario alter ab altero possidetis quo minus ita possi-
deatis vim fieri veto. Dig. 43. 17. 1 pr. The word " nunc " is supplied
from Gaius. For utrubi the formula is reconstructed as follows : utrubi hic
homo quo de agitur majore parte hujusce anni nec vi nec clam nec precario
ab altero fuit quo minus is eum ducat vim fieri veto. Dig. 43. 31. 1 pr. ;
Buckl. T. p. 734 ; M. p. 416. Justinian assimilated utrubi to uti possidetis.
Inst. 4. 15. 4a.

[26] Buckl. T. p. 740 ; M. p. 419.

disturbed in his lawful possession by B and on the hypothesis that B has been disturbed in his lawful possession by A. Each hypothesis calls for a wager, each wager for two stipulations, four in all. The judge must decide the issue of each stipulation, and, further, the principal question, whether the interdict has been disobeyed by A or B, assessing the damage. But this is not all. One of the parties must have interim possession *pendente lite*. The praetor puts it up to auction (fructuum licitatio) and assigns it to the party who makes the higher bid secured by stipulation (stipulatio fructuaria). Here is another question to refer, *viz.,* the right to the interim possession, and lastly, there is the question of the value of the fruits, which is not the same as the right to take them.[26a] This makes seven questions to go to the judex, but substantially there is only one question at issue, the right to be maintained in possession. The party against whom the judge pronounces his decision incurs the double penalty of the two wagers and the condemnation, perhaps in a nominal sum, for having done violence to the other's possession. Further, if he was given interim possession, to which, as the event proves, he was not entitled, he will have to pay to the other party the amount of the fructuary stipulation [27] and the value of the fruits, and the victorious litigant will have a further reference to a judex or arbiter for recovery of possession or damages. This was called the judicium Cascellianum sive secutorium.[28]

774. This, or something like it, so far as can be gathered from the imperfect text of Gaius, was the interdict procedure in his time. Like an ordinary action, it postulates the voluntary co-operation of the parties. But what if one of the parties was recalcitrant—refused to play the game—would not offer the vis ex conventu—would not make the wager, and so forth? The praetor issued a secondary interdict (interdictum secundarium),[29] which it may be supposed was short, sharp and decisive, though the view is also held that here too there was a further reference in which the defendant could assert a third party's right to possess as an answer to plaintiff's claim.[30] Unhappily there is a gap in the text.

775. What has been said relates to interdict procedure in the period of the formula. It seems likely that there was an early and more summary procedure by interdict in the period of the legis actio. But nothing is known. In Justinian's system the interdict procedure above described was wholly disused. 4. 15. 8. There was no difference between interdicts and actions.

[26a] G. 4. 167.
[27] If the fructuary stipulation had been omitted—omissa fructuaria stipulatione—the question of liability for the amount of the bid was the subject of a separate reference based directly upon the result of the licitation. This was called judicium fructuarium. G. 4. 169. There was some difference of procedure.
[28] G. 4. 166 *in fine*; Buckl. *T.* p. 741; *M.* p. 419. It may have derived its name from Aulus Cascellius, a jurist of the age of Augustus. Dig. 1. 2. 2, 45.
[29] G. 4. 170.
[30] Girard, p. 1127.

776. The interdict was not the only praetorian institution which lay outside the main course of the ordinary action. There were besides restitutio in integrum, missio in possessionem and the praetorian stipulations.

777. Restitutio in integrum [31] was a praetorian remedy granted after inquiry [32] into the circumstances to a person who had suffered prejudice from some act or event which had legal consequences, and who on equitable principles was entitled to relief. It was given for various reasons. Paul [33] enumerates fear, fraud, change of status, just error, necessary absence, and minority (there were some others). Most of these explain themselves. Change of status means capitis deminutio minima.[34] We have seen above that the praetor allowed creditors to pursue the property of the adrogatus in the hands of the adrogator— rescissa capitis deminutione (§§ 111, 698). This can be described as restitutio only in a general sense, for it took effect by virtue of the fiction in the formula without previous inquiry and special licence. Absence has reference to the special case of usucapion, when the person against whom time was running, owing to his own or the possessor's absence, was unable to arrest its course, but it was extended to many other cases, for example, failure to put in a timely appearance in legal proceedings. As a rule, the praetor did not actively intervene to restore the status quo, but allowed the person entitled to restitution to use actions and defences which had the same effect. In particular he would give litis restitutio, which cancelled a litis contestatio and put the parties back where they were before (D. 4. 1. 7, 1). The oldest and always the most important grounds of relief were minority and absence. The first,[35] which was a continuation of the policy of the lex Plaetoria (§ 139), was particularly favoured. Restitutio was an unusual remedy, which was not given when there was an adequate remedy at law,[36] but it was preferred to the actio doli because of the infaming character of the latter.[37] In general, it was not accorded unless the party seeking it and the party against whom it was sought could both be restored to their former position. Thus, if a vendor sought relief from a contract of sale, he obtained it only on the terms of restoring the price, or, if he was a minor,

4. 6. 3.

---

[31] Girard, pp. 1129–30; Buckl. T. pp. 719, 723; M. pp. 410, 411.
[32] Dig. 4. 1. 3.
[33] Paul. Sent. 1. 7. 2.
[34] Dig. 4. 5. 2.
[35] Dig. 4. 4. 1, 1.
[36] Dig. 4. 4. 16.
[37] Dig. 4. 1. 7, 1.

his enrichment.[38] As a rule, restitutio was only effectual against parties to the litigation and their civil or praetorian successors. In the case of minors it sometimes operated in rem,[39] even against bona fide third parties, such as a sub-purchaser. It must be claimed, before Justinian within an annus utilis, under Justinian within four anni continui from the cessation of the cause which justified the application. In process of time the development of the system of actions and exceptions confined the restitutio within narrow limits. Apart from the case of minority, its function belongs rather to the field of procedure than to that of substantive law.

778. Missio in possessionem was a process by which a person was placed in possession of another person's property, either of his whole estate (missio in bona) or of some particular thing (missio in rem). Of the first we have seen an instance in the case of insolvency (§ 754). An example of the second is the case of damnum infectum (apprehended damage). If the owner of land or a house, apprehending damage from the ruinous state of a neighbour's building, complained to the praetor, and the neighbour declined the stipulation to be presently mentioned, the praetor would put the complainant in possession as a measure of precaution. This was *de facto* possession, not (so-called) juristic possession, but if the owner remained recalcitrant, a second decree might follow giving juristic possession, which might lead ultimately to acquisition of ownership by usucapion.[40] Unless some measure of precaution was taken as provided by law, and damage actually occurred, the aggrieved proprietor was without remedy. The neighbour could escape liability by abandoning, for example, the tiles from his ruinous house which had caused the damage. The victim had the poor, and only, satisfaction of letting loose his vengeance against the materials,[41] as he might against a wild beast escaped from his neighbour's menagerie.

779. Praetorian stipulations were stipulations into which the praetor required a person to enter as an incident of legal proceedings and in many other cases. Examples of the first kind are the cautio judicatum solvi, the cautio de rato (or ratam rem dominum habiturum). Examples of the second kind were the

4. 11 pr.

3. 18. 4.

---

[38] Dig. 4. 4. 24, 4 ; 27, 1 (*in fine*).
[39] Dig. 4. 4. 13, 1.
[40] Dig. 41. 2. 3, 23. In other cases missio gave a possession, which was usually de facto, sometimes juristic.
[41] Girard, p. 279.

stipulations required of a tutor (rem pupilli salvam fore) or of a usufructuary (§ 247). The cautio de damno infecto was called for in the circumstances above described. The praetor required the neighbour to secure the complainant by stipulation against eventual damage. A somewhat similar case was that of operis novi nuntiatio (denunciation of new work). If my neighbour was carrying out, or about to carry out, operations upon his land, certain or likely to affect adversely my enjoyment of my property, after notice on the spot I could summon him before the praetor.[42] Meanwhile he was obliged to suspend operations.[43] The praetor on proof that the complaint had some foundation would require him to enter into a stipulation, with or without security, either to restore the land to its former condition, or, at the option of the complainant, to make compensation if he was found not to be acting within his rights. He might, for instance, be constructing an embankment which would divert water on to my land in volume or in direction other than its normal flow. It must be kept in mind that the process of nuntiatio only applied to works contemplated or incomplete. If the work had been carried out the interdict quod vi aut clam and other remedies were available.[44] It was said to be vi factum if it was carried out in the face of a prohibition, commonly indicated by the symbolism of throwing a pebble (jactus lapilli). It was said to be clam factum if it was done in the face of a controversy actual or expected.[45]

THE INSTITUTES

BOOK IV (Tits. XV, X, XI, XVI–XVIII)

TITLE XV

Of interdicts

It remains to speak of interdicts or of the actions which have taken their place. Interdicts were formal pronouncements of the praetor ordering something or prohibiting something. The most frequent occasion for an interdict was when parties were contending on a question of possession or quasi-possession.

§ 763.
1. The principal classification of interdicts is that they are prohibitory, or restitutory, or exhibitory. Prohibitory interdicts are those which forbid something to be done, for example, forbid

---

[42] Dig. 39. 1. 5, 2.
[43] Dig. 39. 1. 1 pr.; 8, 4.
[44] Dig. 39. 1. 1, 1; 43. 24.
[45] Dig. 43. 24. 1, 5 & 6; 50. 17. 73, 2.

violence to be offered to a person in clean possession,[46] forbid interference with the exercise of a right of sepulture, forbid building on sacred ground or doing anything in a public river or its bank of a nature to impede navigation. Restitutory interdicts are those which order restoration, for example, order a person who possesses as heir or without pretence of title to yield possession of things belonging to the inheritance to the praetorian successor, or order possession to be given back to a person who has been violently ejected from the possession of land. Exhibitory interdicts are those which order production, for example, of a person whose freedom is in question, or of a freedman, of whom the patron wishes to require services, or production to a parent of children in his power. Some think that the term interdict is properly confined to prohibitory orders because the word interdicere means to notify a person that a thing must not be done and that restitutory and exhibitory orders are properly termed "decrees," but the practice is to call all these orders interdicts because they are interdicta, orders rendered between two persons. § 79.

2. Interdicts [more precisely possessory interdicts] are further classified as interdicts to obtain, to retain, and to recover possession. § 765.

3. An interdict to obtain possession is given to the bonorum possessor. It is called the interdict quorum bonorum, and its effect is that anyone who as heir or without pretence of title is in possession of goods belonging to an estate, is required to yield possession to the person to whom "possession of goods" has been given. A person is said to possess "as heir," if he thinks that he is heir. He possesses "as possessor," if without legal title he is in possession of something which is part of an inheritance, or, of the whole inheritance, knowing that it does not belong to him. This interdict is said to be for the purpose of obtaining the inheritance because it is available only to the person who is trying for the first time to get possession; accordingly, it is not available to a person who has got possession and lost it. Another interdict for obtaining possession is the interdictum Salvianum, which is given to the owner of land, to get possession of the movable property of a tenant-farmer, which he has pledged to secure the rent. 4. For retaining possession we have the interdicts uti possidetis and utrubi, which are used when there is a dispute as to ownership, and the preliminary question is raised which of the litigants should defend, which should bring the action. For until it is ascertained which of the two has possession a petitory action is impossible, for law and reason unite in saying that one person must be in possession and another person must bring the action; and, since it is far more advantageous to be defendant, there is often or almost always a great fight over the question of possession. The advantage of having the possession is that even if the possessor is not owner, yet if the owner cannot prove his title, the possession is left undisturbed, and consequently when it is difficult to say which of the litigants has the right on his side, the practice is to decide the case against the plaintiff. 4a. The interdict uti possidetis relates to the possession of land or a house, the interdict utrubi to the possession of movables. Formerly the effect § 387.

§ 261.

§ 772.

---

[46] Sine vitio possidenti, infra, sec. 4a.

of the two interdicts was very different. In uti possidetis the decision went in favour of the party who was in possession at the time of the interdict, provided that his possession was not obtained by violence, or clandestinely or by permission from the other party (nec vi nec clam nec precario ab adversario), even if he had obtained it by any of these methods from a third party. In utrubi the victory went to the party who was in possession nec vi nec clam nec precario ab adversario for the greater part of the year preceding. But today this distinction is no longer observed and both interdicts as regards possession have the same effect, namely, that the victory goes to the party who at the time that the case is ripe for trial possesses nec vi nec clam nec precario ab adversario.

5. A person is held to possess not only if he possesses in person but also if any other person is in possession on his account. Such person need not be in his power; he may for instance be a tenant of land or of a house, or may have taken the thing by way of deposit or loan for use. This is what is meant by the saying that we retain possession by any one who possesses in our name. Indeed, possession may be retained by the mere intention to possess, for even though a man is not in possession himself, and no one is in possession on his account, still, if he left the property with no intention of abandoning possession but intending to come back, possession is retained. Through whom possession may be acquired has been § 230.   explained in the Second Book (Tit. IX). It is quite clear that possession cannot be acquired by mere intention. 6. An interdict § 765.   for recovering possession is given if a person has been violently ejected from land or from a house. The appropriate interdict is the interdict unde vi, whereby the ejector is compelled to restore possession to the person ejected even though in relation to the ejector the possession was violent, clandestine or precarious. But, as has been stated in an earlier Title, imperial constitutions provide that a person who has taken forcible possession forfeits the thing if it is his; if it belongs to another, he must give it back and in 4. 2. 1.   addition pay its estimated value to the victim of his aggression. One who has dispossessed another by violence is further liable under 4. 18. 8.   the lex Julia de vi, whether the violence is private or public. Violence is private, if it is not effected by armed force; if armed force has been employed, it is public. The term arms includes not only shields and swords and helmets, but also clubs and stones.[47] § 766.   7. The third division of interdicts is into simple and double. Simple interdicts are those in which one person is plaintiff, another defendant. All restitutory and exhibitory interdicts are of this character, for the person who demands exhibition or restitution is

[47] In the earlier law a distinction was drawn between simple violence (called by the commentators vis quotidiana) and armed violence (vis armata). In the first case a plaintiff was required to show dispossession within the year and might be met by the plea that his possession was vitiosa ab adversario (G. 4. 154). In the second case there was no limit of time and the plaintiff was in any event entitled to be replaced in possession (G. 4. 155). This was an anticipation of the medieval actio spolii—spoliatus ante omnia restituendus est. By the time of Justinian this, as appears from the text, was the general rule, the distinction between vis quotidiana and vis armata having disappeared. But now in all cases proceedings must be taken within the year.

the plaintiff and the person from whom it is demanded is the defendant. Prohibitory interdicts may be either simple or double. They are simple when the praetor forbids something being done on sacred soil or in a public river or its bank; the person who demands that the thing should not be done is plaintiff, the person trying to do it is defendant. Uti possidetis and utrubi are double interdicts. They are called double, because either litigant is in the same position as the other, neither of them being plaintiff or defendant any more than the other, so that each one of them appears in both capacities. 8. It is superfluous to speak of the course and consequence of interdicts in the old law; for whenever proceedings are taken extra ordinem, as is always the case at the present day, the issue of an interdict is not necessary, but the matter is decided without an interdict just as if an action had been given in the circumstances in which the praetor used to grant an interdict.

TITLE X

Of representatives in litigation

A man may bring an action in his own name or in the name of another. This last occurs when he sues in the capacity of procurator, tutor or curator, though in former days no representation in litigation was allowed unless the action was brought on behalf of the people,[48] by an assertor of freedom, or by a tutor on behalf of his ward. The lex Hostilia [49] further provided that actions of theft might be brought in the name of persons who were in the power of the enemy, or absent on business of State, and of the wards of such persons. It was, however, very inconvenient that no representation was allowed in bringing or defending an action and the practice grew up of litigating by procurators, for illness, age or necessary absence from home and many other causes often prevented a man attending to his affairs in person. 1. It is not required that a procurator should be appointed by any special form of words or in the presence of the opposite party [50] (indeed, as a rule he does not know anything about it), for any person whom you allow to bring or defend your action is understood to be your procurator for the purpose. 2. How tutors and curators are appointed has been explained in the First Book.

TITLE XI

Of taking security

The old method of taking security was not the same as that now in use. Formerly, if the action was in rem the possessor was required to give security, with the consequence that, if the case went against him and he did not restore the thing in question or pay the amount in which he was

---

[48] *i.e.,* in the public interest for a penalty. Buckl. *T.* p. 694; *M.* p. 371.
[49] Otherwise unknown.
[50] In these respects the procurator differed from the cognitor. G. 4. 83, 84.

condemned, the plaintiff could bring a personal action against him or his sureties. This was called security for satisfaction of the judgment (cautio judicatum solvi). It was so-called because the plaintiff stipulated for payment of the sum adjudged to him. There was still greater reason for this, if the person against whom the action was brought was defending it on another person's behalf. On the other hand, a plaintiff in a real action suing in his own name was not required to give security. If he was suing in a representative capacity, he was ordered to give security that his principal would ratify his acts (cautio ratam rem dominum habiturum), because there was the risk of the principal claiming the same property in another action. The edict required the same security to be given by tutors and curators suing in the name of their wards, but this was sometimes remitted. 1. This then was the law in the case of real actions. If the action was in personam, the rules were the same for the plaintiff as in the case of actions in rem. A defendant intervening on another person's account was always required to give security, for without security no one is considered to be competent to undertake another person's defence. But if he was defending in his own name, he need not give security for the satisfaction of the judgment. 2. But all of this is no longer in use. According to the modern practice, if a person is defending an action, real or personal, in his own name, he is not required to give security for the amount of the judgment, but merely a personal undertaking to submit to the jurisdiction until the case is decided. This varies with the standing of the defendant. It may be a promise accompanied by an oath, the so-called juratoria cautio, or a bare promise or a promise with sureties. 3. If an action is brought or defended in a representative capacity the rules are as follows. The plaintiff, unless his authority to act is entered in the records of the court, or the principal is present in court to confirm it, must give security that the principal will ratify his acts. The same applies if a tutor or curator or any other person who has undertaken to conduct another person's affairs brings an action by a representative. 4. If a defendant appears and is prepared to appoint a procurator, he may come into court and confirm the procurator's authority to represent him by entering into the usual stipulations judicatum solvi, or give security out of court by binding himself as surety for his procurator in respect of all the clauses of the security for satisfaction of a judgment. Further, he must in either event give a hypothec over his property, which can be enforced against his heirs as well as himself, and must furnish a bond or security that he will be present in court when sentence is pronounced, and that, if he fails to appear, his surety will satisfy the judgment unless there is an appeal. 5. If for any reason a defendant does not appear, and some one is willing to undertake his defence, he may do so whether in a real or personal action, giving security judicatum solvi, for, as observed above, it is an old rule that no one is competent to undertake another person's defence without giving security. 6. Acquaintance with the everyday practice of the courts will make all this perfectly clear. 7. These rules are to be followed not only in our capital city, but also in the provinces.

TITLE XVI

Of the penalties incurred by reckless litigation

The law has always been concerned to restrain reckless litigation. It does so today by imposing a pecuniary penalty, by the sanction of an oath, and by the fear of infamy.

1. By our constitution [51] no defendant is allowed to put in his pleading until he has sworn that he has good grounds for defending the action.

---

[51] Cod. 2. 58 (59), 2 pr.

Sometimes a defendant who denies liability runs the risk of being condemned in double damages. This is, for example, the case in the actio damni injuriae and in actions brought on legacies left to holy places. (There are, of course, cases in which from the beginning the action is for a multiple of the damages, as for four-fold in the actio furti manifesti and for double in the actio furti nec manifesti ; in these the action is always for more than the single value whether the defendant admits or denies.) Plaintiffs also are required to swear to their honesty, and, besides, an oath is required of the advocates on both sides. All this has replaced the ancient actio calumniae [52] for one-tenth of the amount in dispute, which has entirely passed out of use. Besides this an unprincipled litigant has to indemnify the other party for his expenses and the costs of litigation. 2. There are some actions in which condemnation involves infamy. Such are the actions on theft, robbery, injuries (actio injuriarum), fraud (actio de dolo) ; guardianship, mandate and deposit (in these last cases when the action is direct, not when it is contrary), and the action on partnership (actio pro socio). which is always direct, so that any partner who is condemned is branded with infamy. In the case of the actions for theft, robbery, injuria or fraud, this consequence follows not only in case of condemnation, but also if the action is compromised ; and rightly so, for there is very much difference between liability on delict and liability on contract.

3. All actions begin with a summons (in jus vocatio) as provided in the praetor's edict. For the first step in the proceedings is to call the defendant in jus, that is before the magistrate. The praetor accords to parents and patrons (and to the children and parents of patrons of either sex) this special respect that their children and freedmen may not begin proceedings against them without applying for and obtaining permission to do so, subject to a penalty of fifty solidi if they disobey this order.[53]

4. 6. 26.

Title XVII

Of the office of the judge

It remains to speak of the office of the judge. In the first place he must be careful to conform his judgment to statutes, imperial constitutions and usage.

1. Accordingly, if he is assigned to a noxal action, he must condemn in the terms :—" I condemn Publius Marcius to Lucius Titius in ten aurei or to surrender the noxa." 2. If the action is in rem and he decides against the plaintiff he must absolve the possessor ; if against the possessor he must order him to restore the thing together with the fruits. If the possessor says that he cannot presently restore and his request for time seems to be made in good faith, it should be granted on the terms of his entering into a bond with a surety to pay the assessed damages if he fails to restore within the time allowed. The rule as to fruits is the same when the plaintiff claims an inheritance as when he claims a particular thing. As regards fruits which the possessor has culpably failed to gather, the rule is much the same in both actions, if the possession was *mala fide*. But in the case of the bona fide possessor no account is taken of fruits consumed or not gathered, that is, until proceedings have been instituted. But after that, fruits which the possessor has culpably failed to gather, or has gathered and consumed, are also taken into account.

§ 638.

§ 201.

3. If an action is brought ad exhibendum, it is not enough merely to produce the thing ; the title to the thing must also be produced. That is to

---

[52] G. 4. 175.
[53] Dig. 2. 4. 25 (interpolated).

say, the plaintiff must get the title to the thing which he would have had if the thing had been produced when proceedings were first taken for its production. Accordingly, if during the course of the litigation the thing has become the property of the possessor by usucapion, he will none the less be condemned. Further, the judge must take account of mesne profits, that is of fruits which have accrued between the beginning of the proceedings and judgment. If the defendant says that he cannot produce immediately and asks for time, and does not seem to have any purpose of evasion, his request should be granted, conditionally upon his giving security for restitution. If he neither produces when ordered to do so by the judge nor gives security to produce at a later time, he must be condemned to the extent of the plaintiff's interest in having the thing produced when proceedings were first taken.   4. In the actio familiae erciscundae

4. 6. 20. particular things must be adjudged to the heirs severally, and if this gives any one heir a disproportionate advantage he must, as explained above, adjust this by a money payment, and he must be condemned to compensate a co-heir, if he has gathered the fruits exclusively, or has damaged or consumed something belonging to the inheritance. This applies whether there are two or more than two co-heirs. 5. The same principles govern the actio communi dividundo, for division of property between owners in common, when it relates to several different things. If it relates to a single thing, as a piece of land which admits of physical partition, portions must be adjudged to the several co-owners with pecuniary adjustment, if necessary. If the thing does not admit of partition, a slave, for instance, or a mule, the whole must be adjudged to one co-owner, and he must compensate the other [or others] by a money payment.

6. In the actio finium regundorum, which is brought for the determination of boundaries, the judge must consider whether adjudication is necessary, as it will be, if it is desirable to have the boundaries more precisely defined than was previously the case. In this case it becomes necessary to adjudge to one owner a portion of the adjoining owner's land and the matter should be adjusted by a money payment. Another ground of condemnation in this action may be some dishonest conduct of one of the proprietors, for example stealthily removing landmarks or cutting down trees on the boundaries. Again, contumacious conduct is a ground of condemnation; for instance if opposition is offered to the judge's order for a survey to be made of the land.

7. In all these actions an order of adjudication of any property vests the ownership forthwith in the party concerned.

TITLE XVIII

Of public proceedings

Public proceedings do not follow the course of a private action and have no resemblance to the proceedings above described.

1. They are called public because they can usually be set in motion by any member of the public.

2. Of public proceedings some are capital, some are not capital. Capital proceedings are those which involve the extreme penalty of the law, interdiction of water and fire, deportation to an island, or condemnation to the mines. Proceedings which involve infamy and a pecuniary penalty are public, but not capital.

3. The following are instances of public proceedings. The lex Julia majestatis is directed against those who have conceived designs against the Emperor or the State. The penalty is death and posthumous infamy.

4. The lex Julia de adulteriis punishes with the sword adultery and sodomy. The same statute attaches the penalty of stuprum to any one who corrupts a virgin or a widow of honourable standing. The penalty

pronounced against offenders, if they are of the better classes, is forfeiture of half their goods; persons of low condition incur corporal punishment and relegation.

5. The lex Cornelia de sicariis [54] punishes with the sword of vengeance those who are guilty of homicide or go about armed with weapons with the design of homicide. The word weapon (telum), as Gaius points out in his commentary on the Twelve Tables, is commonly understood of a weapon of offence discharged from a bow, but it also means any weapon discharged from the hand, such as a stone, a block of wood, a piece of iron. It is derived from the Greek and means " thrown from a distance." The word sicarii comes from s a, meaning an iron knife. The same statute inflicts capital punishment on poisoners, that is men who by odious contrivances, whether by poison or by magical charms, bring about men's death, or sell to the public mischievous drugs.

6. Another statute—the lex Pompeia de parricidiis [55]—inflicts a strange punishment on a terrible crime. It enacts that, if any one has hastened the death of a parent or a son or of any one else to whom the term parricide applies, secretly or openly, or has procured the same, or been privy to such a crime even though unrelated to the victim, he is not to be punished by sword or fire or any other usual method, but is to be sewn up in a sack with a dog, a cock, a viper and a she-ape, and in this horrible prison is to be cast into the sea or into a river, so that living he shall be denied all use of the elements, and while he yet survives the air of heaven, and when he is dead, the boon of earth shall be withheld from him. If any other relative by blood or affinity is killed, the penalty is that prescribed by the lex Cornelia de sicariis.

7. The lex Cornelia de falsis [56] (on forgery), otherwise called the lex Cornelia testamentaria, punishes any one who forges a will or other instrument, or who seals, reads or substitutes any such forgery, or makes, engraves or impresses a false seal with guilty knowledge. The punishment in the case of slaves is death (as also under the statute of de sicariis et veneficis), in the case of freemen, deportation.

8. The lex Julia de vi publica seu privata is directed against those who are guilty of violence armed or without arms. In the case of armed violence the punishment is deportation under the lex Julia de vi publica; if the violence is unarmed it is forfeiture of one-third of the criminal's goods. Rape of a virgin or a widow, whether dedicated to religion or not, entails the death penalty on the perpetrators and on any one who has aided the outrage. Particulars will be found in our constitution.[57]

9. The lex Julia peculatus punishes those who steal money, or any other thing, public, sacred or religious. If judges embezzle public funds during their term of office they incur the death penalty. This applies also to those who aid them in the commission of the crime or with guilty knowledge receive the proceeds. Other persons who offend against this law are punished with deportation.

10. Public proceedings may also be taken based upon the lex Fabia de plagiariis.[58] The penalty is sometimes capital under imperial constitutions, sometimes less severe.

11. Other statutes giving rise to similar proceedings are the lex Julia ambitus, the lex Julia repetundarum, the lex Julia de annona, and the lex Julia de residuis, all of which deal with special offences.[58] They do not involve the penalty of death, but various lesser punishments.

12. We have given this summary account of public prosecutions, which may furnish you with a guide to the subject. You may with Heaven's help acquire a fuller knowledge from the study of the Digest or Pandects.

---

[54] B.C. 81.　　　　　　　　　　　　　　　　　　　　[55] B.C. 52.
[56] B.C. 81.
[57] Cod. 9. 13.
[58] For these statutes, see Moyle, *ad loc.*

(484)

VOCABULARY

6. *pontifex maximus* = chief priest.

7. *rex sacrorum* = king of sacred rites.
   auctoritas patrum = sanction of the fathers, *i.e.*, patrician senators.

9. *senatusconsultum ultimum* = ultimate or final senatusconsultum.

29. *jus respondendi* = right of giving responses, *i.e.*, legal opinions.

44. *de adquirendo rerum dominio* = of the acquisition of the ownership of things.

67. *sui juris—alieni juris* = of one's own right—of another's right, *i.e.*, of independent and dependent status.

77. *libertus orcinus*. Orcus was the abode of the dead. Orcinus is the adjective.

79. *obsequium—operae—bona* = respect—services—property.

114. *adoptio plena—minus plena* = complete adoption—incomplete adoption.

126. *perpetua mulierum tutela* = perpetual tutelage of women.

130. *tutor dativus* = a tutor given or appointed.

136. *accusatio vel crimen, suspecti tutoris* = accusation or charge brought against a suspected tutor.
   satisdatio rem pupili salvam fore = security that the pupil's property shall be safe.

138. *Nemo post haec, etc.* Let no one hereafter ask of us the right of children, for by this law we grant it to all women.

169. *res habilis, titulusque, fides, possessio, tempus* = a thing capable of being owned, title, good faith, possession, lapse of time.

178. *dominium ex jure Quiritium* = ownership by right of the Quirites (Roman citizens).

180. *longissimi temporis praescriptio* = prescription of a very long time.

183. *litis aestimatio* = assessment of the matter in issue.

190. *actio ad exhibendum* = action for production.

194. *per medium filum aquae* = through the middle line of the water.

196. *superficies solo cedit* = the surface goes with the soil.
   actio de tigno injuncto = action about annexed material.

197. *jus tollendi* = the right of removal.

208. *traditio brevi manu—longa manu* = delivery with the short hand—with the long hand.
   constitutum possessorium = agreement to possess (instead of owning).

210. *traditio per cartam* = delivery by deed.

221. *donatio ante nuptias—propter nuptias* = a gift before marriage—on account of marriage.

226. *quod aequius melius est* = what is fairer and better.
   lex Julia de fundo dotali = the Julian statute about dotal land.

227. *actio rei uxoriae* = the action relating to the wife's property.

253. *usus transeundi personae datus* = use of transit given to a person.

PARA.

257. *cujus est solum, etc.* = the owner of the soil owns up to heaven and down to hell.

259. *lex commissoria* = condition of forfeiture.

262. *qui prior est tempore potior est jure* = the person who is first in time is preferred in right.

269. *animus sibi habendi* = intention to have for oneself.

293. *dies certus an—incertus quando* = a date certain whether, uncertain when.

320. *boni viri arbitratus* = the decision of a fair-minded man.

321. *actio ad supplendam legitimam* = action to make up the statutory portion.
petitio hereditatis = suit claiming an inheritance.
bonorum possessio contra tabulas = possession of goods against the will.

329. *bonorum possessio secundum tabulas* = possession of goods according to the will.

338. *jus antiquum* = old law.

393. *nova clausula, etc.* = Julian's new clause about joining with an emancipated son his children.

399. *ecclesia vivit lege Romana* = the Church lives under Roman Law.

406. *impubes* = a child beneath the age of puberty.

444. *reus stipulandi—reus promittendi* = party to a stipulation, to a promise.

464. *lex commissoria* = condition of rescission.

466. *venditio spei—rei speratae* = sale of a hope, of a thing hoped for.

474. *uti optimus maximusque* = as best and biggest.

476. *actio auctoritatis* = action of warranty.

477. *in duplo ejus quod mentitus est* = for double the extent of the deception.

484n. *res perit domino* = the thing perishes for the owner; *i.e.*, is at his risk.

503. *prout quisque habitaverit* = according to his actual occupation.

515. *mandatum credendae pecuniae* = a mandate for lending money.

526. *Nuda pactio, etc.* = A nude pact does not beget an action, but begets an exception.

556. *solutionis gratia adjectus* = added for the purpose of payment.

560. *jus quaesitum tertio* = right acquired for a third person.

595. *condictio ob causam datorum* = reclaim of things given for a purpose which has failed—*causa data causa non secuta* = purpose given, purpose not realised—*condictio ob turpem vel injustam causam* = reclaim on account of an immoral or illegal cause—*sine causa* = for want of cause—*ob causam finitam* = because the cause has ceased to exist—*odio furum* = from hatred of thieves.

632. *adversus infitiantem lis crescit* = the amount in suit is increased against the person who denies.

633. *fraus creditorum* = fraud on creditors.

649. *mandatum in rem suam* = a mandate in his own interest.

651. *res litigiosa* = thing in litigation.
660. *animus novandi* = intention to novate.
674. *ex jure manum conserere* = fighting out of court.
694. *vindicatio in libertatem—in servitutem* = claiming as free—as a slave.
714. *exceptio rei in judicium deductae* = exception that the matter had been brought to trial.
716. *invitus nemo rem cogitur defendere* = no one is compelled to defend a thing unwillingly.
743. *exceptio doli specialis vel praeteriti* = exception of special or past fraud—*generalis vel praesentis* = of general or present fraud.
746. *exceptio justi dominii* = exception of lawful ownership.
749. *beneficium competentiae, etc.* = benefit of competence—exception of what he is able to do.
754. *missus in possessionem* = the person put in possession.
773. *fructuum licitatio* = auctioning of the fruits.
779. *operis novi nuntiatio* = denunciation of new work.

INDEX

[The references are to pages. References to the text of the Institutes are in italics.]

INDEX   495